KURT HAHN

and the United World Colleges with Other Founding Figures

David Sutcliffe

'But the best works are in classic bronze. Notable among these, in a central place of honour, is a study by Mrs. Gladys Baron of "Kurt Hahn, Esq., L.L.D., founder and first headmaster of Gordonstoun School". Built up from the bone structure of the skull, the portrait portrays the inner character of the sitter in addition to being a readily recognizable likeness, with the lurk of a smile in eyes and on lips giving lightness and mobility to the disciplinarian thrust of head and jaw.'

A Preview of the Eighth Annual Exhibition of Portrait Sculptors, Glasgow Herald 18th November 1960

St.Donat's Castle – UWC of the Atlantic

Castello di Duino – UWC of the Adriatic

David Sutcliffe

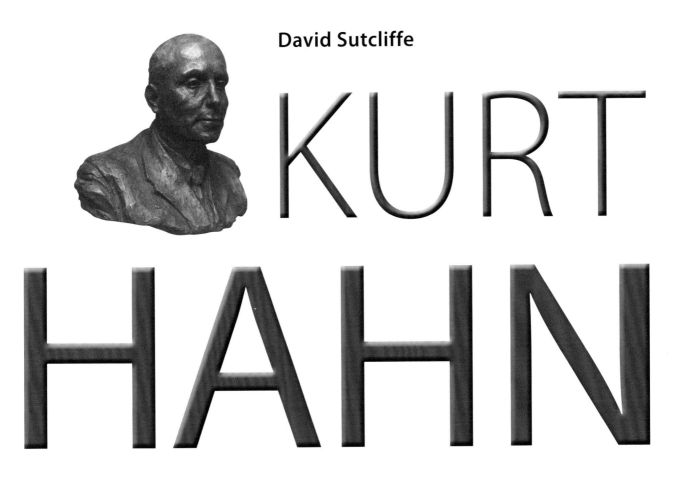

KURT HAHN

and the United World Colleges
with Other Founding Figures

Published by David Sutcliffe
© David Sutcliffe, 2013

Designed by Paul Barrett Book Production, Cambridge. www.pbbp.co.uk
Print production by Wayment Print & Publishing Solutions Ltd. www.waymentprintandpublishing.co.uk
Printed and bound in the UK by Butler Tanner and Dennis Ltd.

ISBN 978-0-9576458-0-6

Picture acknowledgements

Eric Berthoud, The Air Marshal Lawrance Darvall and George Schuster as a young man: National Portrait Gallery, London

KNRM The Netherlands

Mountbatten moving to present the first IB Diplomas: Courtesy of the International Baccalaureate, Geneva, Switzerland

Desmond Hoare crouched over a rescue boat and engine with A C students watching him: Maurice Bloomfield

Photographic Archives of UWC International, UWC Atlantic and UWC Adriatic

Prince Max of Baden walking to the Reichstag in October 1918 (page 58):
Bundesarchiv, Bild 183-R04159 / CC-BY-SA

This book, with certain additional texts in Italian, was first published in September 2012 by the Region of Friuli-Venezia Giulia and the United World College of the Adriatic to commemorate the 50th and 30th anniversaries respectively of the UWC of the Atlantic and the UWC of the Adriatic.

I am very grateful to the Ufficio Stampa Regione FVG for their generous agreement to allow the book to be published now in a second edition.

I am also deeply indebted to six individuals who, with comparable generosity, have underwritten the costs of this second edition. They are Willem de Vogel, Tom Gresvig, Luca Velussi and Philippe von Stauffenberg, all former students of the Atlantic College and Adriaan de Mol, a former student of the Adriatic College; and Detmar Hackman, a former Gordonstoun and Hahn pupil and, briefly, a teacher at two of Hahn's schools, Anavryta in Greece and Salem in Germany.

David Sutcliffe
May 2013

Contents

Introductions

Renzo Tondo

President of the Autonomous Region of Friuli Venezia Giulia

Just 30 years have passed since the foundation of the United World College of the Adriatic, but in this time the geopolitical scenario has changed profoundly. In 1982 none foresaw the fall of the Berlin Wall, there was no talk of globalisation, the Cold War border with Yugoslavia still weighed heavily on the Region of Friuli Venezia Giulia; the echoes were not yet extinguished of the tragedies that had taken place from the rise of Fascism to the Second World War in this tormented part of Italy and of Europe.

Nevertheless there was, at that time, a far-sighted ruling class in Friuli Venezia Giulia, capable of imagining an international role for this Region, of anticipating the enlargement of Europe. In celebrating these 30 years, I would therefore like to recall two figures of that extraordinary time, two leading personalities responsible for the birth and the development of the College: the President of the Autonomous Region Antonio Comelli and Corrado Belci, Member of Parliament for Trieste and later long-time President of the College, both of whom had seized upon and brought to life the intuition of Ambassador Gianfranco Facco Bonetti, then a young diplomat at the Italian Embassy in London.

Friuli Venezia Giulia is the territory where the three great European cultures meet and 'infect' each other: the Latin, the Slavic and the Germanic. And Duino is, in this sense, truly unique: it is the place in which Italians and Slavs live together at the northernmost point of the Adriatic, where the Mediterranean enters the heart of Europe; it is the magical place in which one still senses the presence of the German-speaking poet Rainer Maria Rilke, where he walked the cliffs and wrote his Elegies. And it is here in Duino, in this small fishing village at the feet of an ancient castle, that the values for 50 years at the heart of the great family of the United World Colleges have taken root and grown: the education of the young as a great force uniting peoples, nations and cultures, a great force for building peace and a sustainable future.

The 30 years of the United World College of the Adriatic are being celebrated at an historical moment that is delicate and difficult. There have been the years of hope: the end of totalitarian regimes, the end of a world divided into separate blocs, the creation and enlargement of the European Union, new international relations based on peace and making common cause with the developing world. Today, in a period of deep economic crisis and of recession, we see ghosts re-emerging from the past, those of retreat into nationalism, of ethnical and territorial demands. For this reason we need, more than ever today, the inspired presence of the College of Duino, of its educational model, of its young people destined to take leading responsibilities throughout the world. Because 30 years on we still need those who can look far ahead.

Gianfranco Facco Bonetti

President UWC Adriatic

This book has been written for the many who, over the past five decades, have known or had some contact with the United World Colleges but who are, wholly or in part, unaware of the often adventurous circumstances of their now distant origins.

The book fills a gap in the historical records of a movement of, today, 12 Colleges across the globe. It does so thanks to the direct and personal testimony of one of the principal figures, David Sutcliffe. Indeed, it is difficult to see who other than David, whose relationship with all the personalities portrayed here was one of close cooperation if not also warm friendship, is better placed to bring back to life, with a prose whose liveliness is equalled only by the historical precision that inspires it, the achievements of the founding fathers of the movement, of those who were present and active at the start , and the memories of whom, faded and eroded by the passage of time, deserve to be revived and handed on to future generations.

I, now writing these lines, who had the privilege for some years in the early 1970s of leading the project of the United World College of the Adriatic through its first stages, cannot be anything other than immensely grateful to David for his work which, among other things, restores to us our legitimate pride in recalling that Italy, in what was and remains the epic period in the development of the United World Colleges, was represented by a number of figures of rare distinction, memories of whom must be jealously guarded and passed on intact to all those generations of Italian students who, as the years pass, will succeed their forebears in the halls of the Adriatic College and of the other colleges elsewhere in the world.

I have however to point out that the fascinating pages that David Sutcliffe has given us suffer from one serious shortcoming, perhaps inevitably so given the author's determination not to write about himself, but grave none the less: they fail to give us the biography of one of the key figures in the United World Colleges movement. One seeks in vain references to the person and work of David himself, beyond doubt one of the main actors in the events that are described here through the lives of our founders. We can only hope that this gap will be filled soon in order to secure a fitting and lasting tribute to his role in our movement, now completing its first half-century and, in the academic year 2012–2013, celebrating three important milestones: the 50th anniversary of the Atlantic College and the 30th anniversaries of the Colleges of the Adriatic and the American West.

David undoubtedly played a decisive role in the founding stages of the first two of these colleges and contributed more than anyone else to giving them their distinctive academic and educational profiles. And then, over the past decade, he committed himself with dedication and youthful enthusiasm to the creation from nothing of the United World College in Mostar (Bosnia and Herzegovina). This college is universally recognised as the most incisive and concrete example of peaceful cohabitation and of reconciliation between the ethnic groups of a city that has suffered the agonies of a merciless civil war.

This brief note would not be complete without a warm expression of gratitude to the Autonomous Region of Friuli Venezia Giulia for its understanding and support also at this moment. In particular, I want to thank the President. Without their support our book could hardly have seen the light of day. It is dedicated to one of the most innovative educational experiments of the last 50 years, whose extraordinary success is living proof that the education of young people above and beyond their cultural, social, religious and racial differences, and of situations riven by conflict, even by warfare, is a central principle in the assertion of one of Man's most positive and yet most thwarted aspirations, and which the United World Colleges have made the core of their mission: living in peace with one's fellow human beings, in the awareness that our diversity is a source of irreplaceable spiritual wealth for all mankind.

Arrigo Levi

Counsellor for Foreign Relations to the President of Italy, Life Patron of the United World College of the Adriatic

The challenge of the 21st century can be summed up in a few words. For the first time in the history of humanity, there has come into existence a united world. Alas, not united in government, but in the innumerable links now existing between all nations, which raise unprecedented possibilities for creative cooperation and progress, but also for conflict and war. All this in a nuclear age, mankind having acquired weapons capable of destroying life itself on the face of Earth. This means that we must create those institutions of 'world government' which a great prophet like Immanuel Kant had already described, two centuries ago, as the necessary condition for our very survival. Will nations be capable of achieving such a revolution in their relations? Yes, but only if enough people will come to know and appreciate their neighbours, and acquire a similar basic education. This, and nothing less, is the aim pursued by the United World Colleges: creating such an elite, as numerous as possible, in the largest possible number of countries. To this end, great progress is being made thanks to the United World Colleges. To those who imagined and created UWCs, overcoming great difficulties, we owe the greatest possible gratitude.

Tom Symons

Thomas H.B. Symons, C.C., O.Ont., FRSC, LL.D., D.U., D.Litt., D.Cn.L., FRGS.
Founding President and Vanier Professor Emeritus, Trent University
Chair, the Ontario Heritage Trust
Chairman of the International Board of United World Colleges, 1980–1986

This considerable volume provides what the author calls 'biographical sketches' of some of the key creative figures who played leading roles in the founding of the United World Colleges. He provides, however, much more than sketches. Each of his chapters is a perceptive and illuminating portrait of the individual concerned. One chapter, that on Kurt Hahn, is indeed in itself a full-blown and richly described biography of one of the most interesting and unusual educators of the twentieth century. Another chapter deals with a family, three individuals, Max, Eric and Lola Warburg.

But, beyond this, the book provides, in addition to these substantial biographical pictures, insights and anecdotal glimpses pertaining to a multitude of people involved in the early days of the United World Colleges.

In his Preface the author emphasises the personal nature of his choice about whom to write; he has the advantage of having been involved with the first College from the very outset and therefore knowing and working with many of the key creative figures both then and at later stages of UWC development. Depending upon their own experience and interests, every reader will have their own list of other personalities whom they would like to have seen included or treated more fully. While reading this manuscript, I found many such people coming to mind. The history of the United World Colleges is replete with colourful, dedicated, and often larger-than-life people who have given great service to the organisation. One hopes that as the movement spreads these, too, will find their well-deserved place in later volumes.

Students of history, education and international relations may well each claim that this book belongs in their section of the library. In fact, it belongs in all these bibliographic classifications and several more. It is loaded with information, perspectives, and insights that will enhance knowledge and understanding in a dozen fields. As the story unfolds of the birth and growth of the United World Colleges, the contemporary politics and history of the nations, regions, cultures, and peoples concerned is observed and often discussed and explained. The narrative holds up a mirror for people and societies to see themselves, but it also very frequently takes us behind the mirror to see a closer reality. It is a reality in which the jostling and tensions, the struggles between diverse values and points of view, which mark and mar education, occur. Such rivalries are often heightened when national interests are either involved, or are thought to be involved.

In the Preface and Foreword, Mr. Sutcliffe sets the stage for the action that follows with those about whom he writes. The beginnings of the United World College movement are traced from their earliest origin and followed through in a useful and informative way up to current times. The book records, often in astonishing detail, a saga that is worth the telling. The United World Colleges embody one of the truly great ideas and one of the truly great initiatives in international education.

Mr. Sutcliffe, as a teacher, administrator, planner, College Head, and International Board member, has himself been at the heart of this endeavour through many years. Thus, this volume is, in a sense, an autobiography. In writing about people and events with whom and which he has been so closely associated, the author, without ever seeking to do so, tells us much about himself. His personal dedication and commitment and his determination to serve are as admirable as they are unmistakable.

By providing this thoughtful description and critical analysis of the formative years, David Sutcliffe has made another immense contribution towards the betterment and further development of the United World Colleges in the future. In his forthright Afterword, he offers thoughts about the needs and challenges which lie ahead. There are many. The United World Colleges have addressed, separately and together, many difficult and important issues of educational substance with imagination and success. But large unresolved problems remain of funding, of forward planning, and of governance in so far flung and disparate a family of colleges. Much has been accomplished, but there is clearly much to be done.

Preface

Not long before his death, Desmond Hoare pressed me to write a history of the United World Colleges.

The idea has never appealed to me. The Colleges all have their own individual stories which, if written at all, must be written by people who know them well. As for the movement, an historical account may, I fear, always be hard put to escape the dangers of consensual blandness.

But Desmond's proposal generated a different thought in my mind – to write up in brief monographs my memories of some of the personalities whom I judge to have been critical to the creation of our enterprise. Celebrating as we do the 50th anniversary of the Atlantic College, it seems an appropriate moment to recall a number of outstanding people without whose collective contribution we would not be where we are today.

Of course this is a subjective matter. I have written about the people whom I personally learned to respect and admire. I had also to feel that I knew them well enough to write about them both as individuals and in the context of the United World Colleges. I have sought no advice on my selection.

One key person is missing: Q. W. Lee of Hong Kong. Despite a series of promises of help, I have been quite unable to assemble sufficient background material to include him. I rank him among the first half dozen or so true pioneers of the movement. I regret his omission enormously.

My own UWC experience has been strictly European. This will be clear from my choice of subjects. But I attach special importance (and I hope that my readers will come to share my conviction in this matter) to the inclusion of two personalities from Eastern Europe, Irena Veisaite from Lithuania and Pawel Czartoryski from Poland. For the United World Colleges to have attracted their devotion to our affairs, and the circumstances of their remarkable lives, have added a dimension to our movement of, I maintain, very particular significance.

Looking back at these personalities and at documents associated with them has reminded me of the directness, precision and vision of the language with which our project was launched. Kurt Hahn wrote during the First World War *'Words today are battles: the right words victorious battles, the wrong words lost battles.'* Our founding figures wrote and spoke with a simplicity and directness that was an eloquent expression of vision, clarity of purpose and strong personal engagement. I have for this reason quoted them freely.

I have long felt that the greatest tribute to the United World Colleges lies in the quality of those who, immensely distinguished already in public life, decided that our activities and aspirations merited their devoted attention and, often, personal generosity, over periods of many years. We expect idealism from our students. They and we have no further to look for inspiration than at the lives of those I have written about.

A second 'of course': there are scores of others, many of them unknown to me even by reputation. One Chairman of Atlantic College remarked that the variety of people he met within the UWC reminded him of the richness and variety of Shakespeare's plays. I have mentioned some of them, mostly those associated with the Atlantic College in the early days, in my Foreword. Justice will, I am sure, not have been done. Nor have I presumed to imagine or to portray what it has meant to be a student in one of our colleges – or a teacher. They must speak for themselves.

I have been helped by many people. One of several no longer with us is Michael Schweitzer. It is at least questionable whether, without his contribution as his secretary and amanuensis from 1956 until 1962, Kurt Hahn could have left us so rich a legacy. Michael earns his place in this personal pantheon for the exemplary integrity of his life and because the circumstances of his life are an illustration of so much of what the United World Colleges have been founded to combat.

My final and very sincere thanks go to the Region of Friuli-Venezia Giulia. It was the Regional Government, under the inspiring leadership of President Antonio Comelli, that grasped with immediacy, vision and generosity the challenge of bringing into being the United World College of the Adriatic. In the late 1970s when, as Headmaster of the Atlantic College, I was making occasional advisory visits to Trieste and Duino (two places that I had first visited on my honeymoon), I encountered much scepticism back at home about the viability of this eccentric Italian venture. One day, alone, I went to explore the International Centre of Theoretical Physics in nearby Miramar, set up and funded some years earlier by the Italian Government through the Ministry of Foreign Affairs in cooperation with the Region of Friuli-Venezia Giulia. For me, it was the proof of the sincerity, trustworthiness and ability to fulfil promises on the part of the Region's political leadership.

This never faltered, and the College became an integral part of Friuli-Venezia Giulia's determination to recover its historical vocation across borders and cultures through the creation of so many distinguished cultural and academic institutions that have now achieved world reputations. All of us who were there in the early days recall with pride and enjoyment our relations with such figures as *Sergio Coloni, Alfredo Mizzau, Antonini Canterin, Dario Barnaba, Dario Rinaldi, Adriano Biasutti* and *Franco Richetti*. Now, the Region with this anniversary publication is rightly also celebrating its own role in bringing Italy into the movement of the United World Colleges. The UWC movement is once again indebted to Friuli-Venezia Giulia for exceptional understanding and support.

The Author

A modern languages graduate of St. John's College, Cambridge, David Sutcliffe taught for four years at Salem School in South Germany where he got to know Kurt Hahn well and met his wife Elisabeth. A member of the founding staff of Atlantic College in 1962, he became successively Director of Studies/Deputy Headmaster (1967–1969) and Headmaster (1969–1982). In 1982 he moved to Italy to be the Founder Headmaster (Rettore) of the United World College of the Adriatic. From 1985–1989 he was also Vice-President of the International Baccalaureate Council of Foundation and Deputy Chairman of the IB Executive Committee and from 1994–1999 Executive Director of United World Colleges International. On retirement from the Adriatic College in 2001 he became a co-founder of the United World Colleges-International Baccalaureate Initiative in Bosnia and Herzegovina which set up the United World College in Mostar (2006), and is now the Chairman of the Bosnian Foundation Education in Action. In 1976 he took part in the Observer Single-Handed Transatlantic Race (OSTAR) in his 26-foot yacht, the *Contessa Lady Anne of St. Donat's*. Granta Editions has published his account of the rescue boat that was developed

at Atlantic College in the 1960s (*The RIB: The Rigid-Hulled Inflatable Lifeboat and its Place of Birth – the Atlantic College*) and is now used worldwide. In 2001 he was awarded the Silver Order 'Naim Frasheri' by the President of Albania and appointed Grand'Ufficiale dell'Ordine al Merito della Repubblica Italiana by the President of Italy. He is the official biographer of Kurt Hahn.

Acknowledgements and Thanks

So many have helped in the preparation of these essays that I have begun to wonder what my own part has been.

My former colleagues Andrew Maclehose and Colin Jenkins have, I hope with success, helped to ensure that the Foreword is not simply a nostalgic promenade. Laurence Nodder and Mike Linden were very helpful and precise with information on the early days and founders of Waterford.

Another former colleague, Sergio Cimarosti, has not only been invaluable with his comments and editing of the piece on Corrado Belci; he has provided all the Italian texts for the Italian edition of this book. I am also grateful to Arrigo Levi for reading the piece on Corrado Belci and for saving me from an important historical inaccuracy.

Antonin Besse and his daughter Joy have been extraordinarily patient in helping me to assemble material on the somewhat elusive Besse family history.

Members of his family, some close friends, but above all two former students of the Adriatic College, Bogna Obidzinska and Ola Ossowska, have been vital to the essay on Pawel Czartoryski. Their help over the linguistic problems but also sensitive areas of Polish history has been unstinting, inspired I know by their own love and admiration for 'their professor'. I also owe a special debt to Pawel's cousin, Dr. Zygmunt Tyszkiewicz, for his meticulous guidance in the closing stages.

Lawrance Darvall was an irreplaceable figure in the critical period 1955–1962, radiating confidence, leadership and unshakeable belief in the outcome. It has to be said that he faded fairly rapidly from the scene once the College opened. The consequence has been that his early decisive role is little known. His grandchildren, with all of whom I have corresponded, have expressed some regret that my piece on him ends on a sad note, but I feel that this is the reality and that recognition of this may help the United World Colleges to reassess their debt to him.

Kurt Hahn lived a complex life. He generated reactions of immense loyalty and affection alongside others, happily far fewer in number but of great intensity, of antagonism and dismissal. His political work, which deeply influenced his educational ideas, is little known outside Germany – indeed, little known within it. The most knowledgeable authority on Hahn documentation is undoubtedly Michael Knoll. I think that any serious writing on Hahn, especially on the German side, is impossible without reference to his two publications and especially *Kurt Hahn: Reform mit Augenmass*. To Jocelin Young, another early pupil in both Salem and Gordonstoun, belongs the unique merit of having founded the first class Kurt Hahn archive in Salem which, following his withdrawal from the scene, has been lovingly cared for by his daughter Sophie Weidlich, whose hospitality and untiring help on numerous occasions I warmly acknowledge. The essay in this book is intended to convey something of Hahn's life and personality. A more detailed account, including an attempt at a balanced assessment of both his political and his educational activities, will follow in an imminent full-length biography.

Desmond Hoare has not been easy to write about. Naomi Hoare has shown much understanding. The key, irrefutable fact is that he is one of the quartet, with Kurt Hahn, Lawrance Darvall and George Schuster, without whom the United World Colleges simply would not exist. He has been a major influence on my life.

When Giangiacomo Migone came to our flat in London to talk about his father, I simply switched on my tape-recorder and then transcribed the result, adding a few personal memories.

John Nichol, in the company of Jim Coutts, submitted himself to several hours of recording reminiscences in the course of a memorable two-day excursion to his property, with attendant llamas, on Vancouver Island. I am also grateful to him for having read and suggested improvements to my Afterword.

Many years ago Alec Peterson's widow Corinna lent me, with remarkable confidence and generosity, a private typewritten copy of Alec's frank, intimate memoirs. This essay, originally written for the opening of the Alec Peterson building at the IB examinations centre in Cardiff, is reproduced here by kind permission of IB.

It would have been impossible to write about George Schuster without his autobiography *Private Work and Public Causes*. This autobiography would in turn have been impossible – it came out when George Schuster was 97 and practically blind – had the then Head of History at Atlantic College, Colin Reid, not worked closely with him for four years on assembling the material from his long life and preparing it for publication, an heroic achievement.

I had known Michael Schweitzer since 1956, but it was the family history *The Twelve Grandchildren of Eugen and Algrunde Hollaender Schweitzer: The Impact of Nazi Racial Policies on one Family*, written jointly by him and his brothers, that provided me with all the background information.

It was only after I had known her for several years that a sudden intuition persuaded me that Irena Veisaite of Lithuania might have a remarkable life history. I went to see her daughter in London and rapidly realised, initially through a video she lent me that Irena had recorded for the Holocaust Museum in Washington, that my intuition was well-founded. Irena invited my wife Elisabeth and me to Vilnius where I engaged her in long discussions and also met some of her students and Open Society and other colleagues. We greatly treasure our friendship with her.

The numerous Warburgs feature in many books on both sides of the Atlantic, but the authoritative and impressively comprehensive account of this family dynasty is Ron Chernow's *The Warburgs: A Family Saga*.

Colin Reid has been kind enough to edit my scribbles, a time-consuming but, I hope, not entirely thankless task.

I realise in retrospect how much I have lost by not having been one of his history students. Even more important than his corrections has been his encouragement. I owe him an immense debt. He is one among a veritable host of outstanding UWC colleagues. All errors of fact or judgement are of course mine.

Professor Tom Symons has generously written an introduction. This is a privilege for me. He has, I realise, received inadequate attention in my text, so let me now reiterate and emphasise my gratitude to him for exceptional leadership as Chairman of the UWC International Board from 1980 to 1986. His diplomatic footwork was especially nimble and effective behind the scenes as the Adriatic College was being launched.

Giorgio Pontoni, the first Director of Administration of the Adriatic College who returned to the College in retirement to become once again a decisive influence in helping it to meet formidable financial and related challenges, has also been the irreplaceable figure in seeing the first edition of this book into print under the sponsorship of the Region of Friuli-Venezia Giulia. In all my Italian activities, professional and private, I remain enormously in his debt.

Finally, my thanks to my wife Elisabeth, whose sharp proof-reading eye will have saved Colin Reid much work. Our first 50 years of married life have coincided almost exactly with the first 50 years of the United World Colleges. This has been a double blessing. This book is dedicated to her in gratitude for her contribution to the United World Colleges.

ATLANTIC COLLEGE (UNITED KINGDOM) LIMITED

Minutes of the First Meeting of the Council
of the College held at 9-12 Cheapside, London
E.C. 2 on Tuesday the Eighth day of November, 1960
at 3.p.m.

PRESENT: Sir Lawrence Darvall (In the Chair)
            Dr. Kurt Hahn
            Mr. Richard Hornby

IN ATTENDANCE: The Bishop of Norwich
              General Hare
              Mr. J.H. Thomson
              Mr. J. V. Rutter

1. IT WAS REPORTED that the College had been incorporated on the Twentieth day of October, 1960 and the Certificate of Incorporation was produced to the Meeting.

2. There was produced to the Meeting a copy of the Memorandum and Articles of Association of the College as registered and a Memorandum signed by a majority of the subscribers to the Memorandum of Association appointing the following persons as the first members of the Council:-

    Admiral Sir Michael Maynard Denny
    Sir Lawrance Darvall
    Dr. Kurt Hahn
    Richard Hornby, and
    Rudolf Hahn

3. IT WAS RESOLVED that Sir Lawrance Darvall be and he is hereby appointed Chairman of this Meeting.

4. IT WAS REPORTED that Major-General J.F. Hare had been appointed Secretary of the College and that pursuant to Section 200 of the Companies Act, 1948 particulars of his full name and address had been lodged with the Registrar of Companies.

5. IT WAS RESOLVED that Messrs. Peat, Marwick, Mitchell be invited to accept appointment as Auditors to the College

---

-2-

the terms of such appointment as to remuneration and otherwise to be agreed.

6. IT WAS REPORTED that the Registered Office of the Company had been registered at 9/12 Cheapside, London, E.C.2.

7. IT WAS RESOLVED that Glyn, Mills & Co., Holts Branch, Whitehall be and they are hereby, appointed the Bankers of the College.

That all cheques, bills, and other documents for sums in excess of £50 drawn on, or made payable at Glyn, Mills & Co. be signed by any one member of the Council for the time being, of the College with the counter signature of the Secretary for the time being, and all cheques bills and other documents for £50 or less be signed by one member of the Council for the time being or the Secretary for the time being and that Glyn, Mills & Co. be and are hereby authorised to charge to the account of the College all cheques, bills, and other documents so signed.

That all negotiable instruments payable to the College be endorsed for the College by any one member of the Council or Secretary.

That Glyn, Mills & Co. be furnished with a list of the names and signatures of the members of the Council and the Secretary of the College and be from time to time informed by an Extract from the minutes duly signed by the Chairman of any changes which may take place therein.

8. IT WAS REPORTED that the Secretary had obtained a Minute Book, and Register of Members for the College.

9. IT WAS RESOLVED that the seal, of which an impression appears in the margin hereof, be and the same is hereby adopted as the Common Seal of the College.

10. The members of the Council had given to the Secretary

-3-

of the College formal notice pursuant to Section 199 of the Companies Act, 1948 that they were directors and/or members of the following companies:-

    Admiral Sir Michael Maynard Denny
    Cammel Laird Co. Limited.
    Brown Brothers (Edinburgh) Limited.
    British Steel Corporation Limited.

    Sir Lawrance Darvall
    Gordonstoun School
    Dover College

    Rudolf Hahn
    B.K.L. Alloys Limited.

    Richard Hornby
    Bow Publications Limited.

and were to be regarded as interested in all transactions with those companies.

11. The Chairman reported as follows :-

(1) He had in accordance with the arrangement made at the meeting held on the 13th October 1960 of the subscribers to the Memorandum and Articles of Association of the College, by a contract dated the 18th October last agreed with The National Magazine Company Limited to purchase St. Donats Castle and grounds having an area of 111.342 acres or thereabouts at the price of £65,000.

(2) The contract provided that (a) the College when incorporated should be entitled to the full benefit of the contract (b) part of the purchase price, namely the sum of £42,500 could if desired be paid over a period of twelve months such sum to be secured by a first mortgage of the property in favour of the vendors, which sum would bear interest at £6 per cent per annum and would be payable by two equal instalments of £21, 250 each the first payable on the 17th day of May 1961 and the second on the 17th day of November 1961 and (c) he the Chairman

---

as a party to the contract should have an option until the 17th of November 1961 (subject to prior repayment of the mortgage) as more particularly mentioned in clause 14 of the contract to purchase for the sum of £40,000 certain of the farms and premises (totalling approximately 487 acres) that adjoined or were in the neighbourhood of the Castle which farms were more particularly edged in blue on the plan attached to the aforesaid contract.

(3) The consent of the Ministry of Education had been obtained in respect of the aforesaid mortgage.

The Chairman produced to the meeting the contract dated the 18th October, 1960, also an engrossment of a mortgage made between the College of the one part and The National Magazine Company Limited of the other part to secure the aforesaid sum of £42,500.

The meeting after discussing the aforesaid contract and mortgage resolved unanimously that the College should (a) adopt the aforesaid contract, (b) seal the aforesaid mortgage so that the purchase by the College of St. Donats Castle and grounds could be formally completed on the 17th November 1960 (c) take over the benefit of the option to purchase the adjoining farms and lands, and (d) indemnify and keep indemnified the Chairman from and against all costs claims and liability under or in connection with the contract dated the 18th of October, 1960.

12. There being no further business the meeting then terminated.

L Darvall.

CHAIRMAN.

23.3.61

IL CAPO DELL'ARCHIVIO

481

Rep.n. 116833   Racc.n. 6915

Trieste, 9 ottobre 1981.

ATTO COSTITUTIVO

DEL COLLEGIO ADRIATICO DEL MONDO UNITO

REPUBBLICA ITALIANA

L'anno millenovecentottantuno, addì nove - - - - - -

del mese di ottobre, - - - - in Trieste, nel mio

Ufficio in Via Trenta Ottobre 19.

Avanti a me dottor Vladimiro CLARICH, Notaio in

Trieste, iscritto in questo Collegio,

è comparso il signor

Antonin BESSE, nato a Cavalaire - Sur - Mer il 22

febbraio 1927, residente a Parigi, 14 Avenue de

Verzy,

della cui identità personale io Notaio sono certo,

il quale, previa rinuncia ai testi con il mio

consenso, mi richiede di redigere il presente at-

to, e mi premette:

- di essere Vice Presidente e legale rappresentan-

te della "UNITED WORLD COLLEGES (INTERNATIONAL)

LIMITED" - reg. UK Charity n° 313690 in Gran

Bretagna -, con sede in Londra - London House -

Mecklenburgh Square -, autorizzato a intervenire

nel presente atto giusta delibera di data 24 apri-

le 1981 del Consiglio di Amministrazione, come da

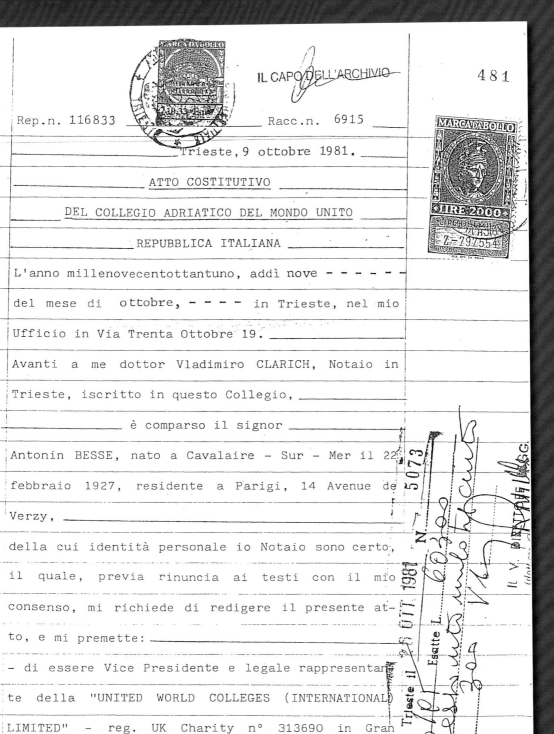

484

attestazione a firma della Segretaria, Mrs. Shena
Garland, autenticata in data 29 aprile 1981 dal
Consolato generale d'Italia in Londra, attestazione che viene allegata al presente atto sub A); -
- che l'"United World Colleges (International)
Limited", prenominato, per il raggiungimento dei
propri fini intende costituire, in base al proprio
Statuto, un'Ente per svolgere la propria attività
anche in Italia, con sede nel Comune di Duino -
Aurisina; -
- che in base allo Statuto dell'ente stesso, il
comparente ha i poteri necessari per quanto sopra,
come risulta pure dall'attestazione allegata sub
A); -
- che l'Ente è stato a ciò autorizzato dallo Stato
italiano in base all'articolo 46 del Decreto Presidente Repubblica 6 marzo 1978, numero 102; -
tutto ciò premesso, il comparente, nella veste di
cui sopra, dichiara di costituire, ad ogni effetto
di legge, il "Collegio Adriatico del Mondo Unito". -
Articolo 1 - La costituzione ha luogo per
determinazione della "United World Colleges
(International) Limited" - reg. UK Charity n°
313690 in Gran Bretagna -, in base al consenso
espresso dallo Stato italiano con l'articolo 46

485

soggetti pubblici e privati, anche mediante lasci-
ti e donazioni. -
Alle spese di gestione si provvede con borse di
studio ed eventuali sovvenzioni, erogate dalle Com-
missioni nazionali per i Collegi del Mondo Unito e
da altri soggetti pubblici e privati. -
Articolo 6 - Il Collegio è retto dallo Statuto,
che viene allegato al presente atto, sub B). -
Articolo 7 - Fino a quando non sarà completata la
prima costituzione degli organi del Collegio, pre-
visti dallo Statuto, lo Statuto stesso potrà essere modificato ed integrato in relazione alle eventuali osservazioni della Commissione nazionale
italiana per i Collegi del Mondo Unito e delle
Pubbliche Autorità, cui le norme statutarie fanno
riferimento per la formazione di tali organi e per
altri adempimenti. -
Le eventuali modifiche ed integrazioni saranno ri-
portate, mediante dichiarazione aggiunta o con nuovo
per atto rogato da Notaio, dalla "United World
Colleges (International) Limited" o da chi la rap-
presenti. -
Nella fase transitoria fino alla completa costituzione degli Organi del Collegio, fermo restando
quanto stabilito nell'articolo 20, primo comma e

---

del Decreto Presidente Repubblica 6 marzo 1978,
numero 102. -
Articolo 2 - Il Collegio è al servizio della
comunità mondiale. -
Fa parte della Organizzazione mondiale dei Collegi
del Mondo Unito, il cui obbiettivo fondamentale è
quello di promuovere la comprensione internazionale attraverso l'educazione e di fare, della educazione, una forza che unisce le nazioni e le razze
umane. -
Articolo 3 - Il Collegio ha sede nel Comune di
Duino - Aurisina. -
La sua definitiva denominazione sarà stabilita dal
Consiglio di amministrazione, con il voto favorevo-
le della maggioranza dei suoi componenti. -
Articolo 4 - Il Collegio accoglie, per i due anni
che precedono gli studi universitari, allievi di
ambo i sessi, senza distinzione di censo, nazionalità, razza, lingua, religione e fede politica. -
Al compimento del biennio di studi, gli allievi
sono ammessi agli esami per il conseguimento del
diploma del baccalaureato internazionale. -
Articolo 5 - Il Collegio non ha scopo di lucro. -
Il suo patrimonio è costituito da beni mobili ed
immobili e da apporti finanziari, conferiti da

IL CAPO DELL'ARCHIVIO 485

nell'articolo 21, secondo comma, dello Statuto, le
attribuzioni del Presidente e del Consiglio di
Amministrazione, compresa quella di cui all'articolo 3 del presente atto costitutivo, sono esercita-
te da un Comitato provvisorio, composto: -
- dal Signor Antonin Besse, in veste di Presidente, -
- dall'Assessore regionale dell'Istruzione e delle
Attività culturali o da un suo delegato, -
- dall'Ambasciatore Dottor Bartolomeo Migone, -
- dal Dottor Gianfranco Bonetti, -
- dall'Avvocato Gaspare Pacia. -
Richiesto io Notaio ho ricevuto il presente atto,
di cui ho dato lettura, assieme agli allegati, al
comparente, che da me interpellato lo approva, e
quindi con me Notaio sottoscrive. -
Scritto da persona di mia fiducia, l'atto occupa
in due fogli, quattro pagine intere e parte della
quinta interamente dattiloscritto con nastro inde-
lebile.

Antonin Bernard Besse

NOTA		
Originale		
Onorario	L	32.000
Cassa Notar.	"	8.000
Tassa arch.	"	4.000
Bolli	"	6.000
Scritturaz.	"	2.500
Repertorio	"	500
Copia - Registro		
Onorario	L	5.000
Bolli	"	14.000
Scritturaz.	"	12.500
Copia - Catasto		
Onorario	L	/
Bolli	"	/
Scritturaz.	"	/
Totale	L	84.500

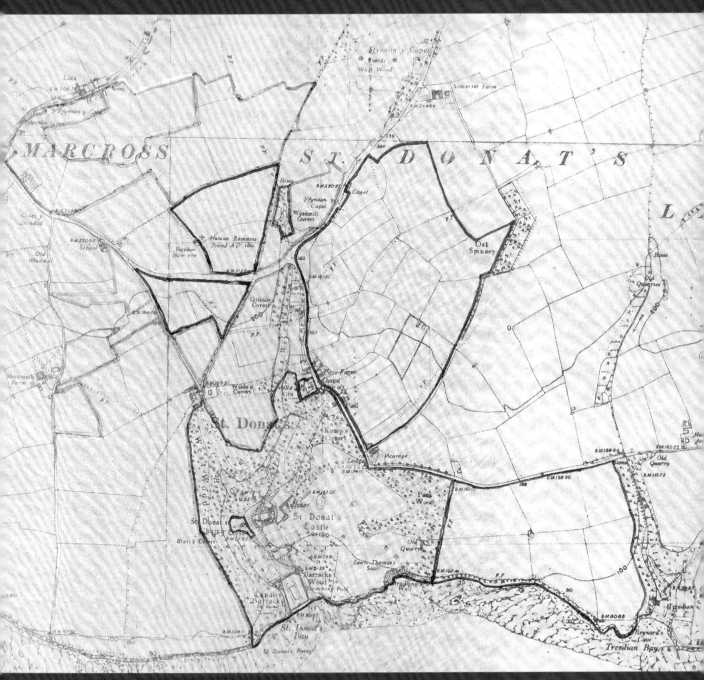

St. Donat's: This map illustrates the farmland that was available in 1960 for an additional £35.000 had the funds been available

Foreword

The Origins and Early Days of the Atlantic College Project

There is no doubt that the starting pistol was fired during Kurt Hahn's lecture visit to the NATO Defense College in Paris in 1955. *'If we can plant the germ of new loyalties in mature men* (he was referring to the success of the NATO College with senior officers from opposing sides in the recent Second World War), *how much deeper are the roots we could sink in the youth of the Atlantic Community if, at their most impressionable period, we could gather them together in residential colleges …'* However, as with any serious athlete, there had been a long period of preparatory training.

Kurt Hahn was increasingly anxious as he grew older to *'bring in the harvest'* of his life's work. His hopes had been centred on *'Greater Gordonstoun'*. Gordonstoun, by example, despite its comparative remoteness in Scotland, had been a forerunner of many important changes in the British Public Schools. *'Greater Gordonstoun'* meant, not the physical completion of rudimentary facilities, many of them still wooden huts, and the consolidation of woefully precarious finances, but the confirmation of the school's role as a launch pad and active laboratory for his wider ideas, the vibrant embodiment of his life's work. Alas, after years of struggle in evacuating Gordonstoun for war reasons from Scotland to Wales in 1940, then moving back again in 1945, helping Salem in Germany on to its feet after 1945, seeking sponsorship for the opening of new like-minded residential schools in Germany, interpreting events within Germany during the war for the British Government and maintaining a ceaseless correspondence, both public and private, on Anglo-German affairs after the war, ensuring funding for the Outward Bound School in Aberdovey that had been opened in Wales during the war and for the subsequent Outward Bound expansion, his health gave way in the autumn of 1952 when he was fundraising in New York. His breakdown was both physical and mental. Retirement from the school was forced upon him.

My 'alas' over Hahn's departure from Gordonstoun is nonetheless misplaced. Once recovered, and his powers of recuperation were always astonishing, he set about the bringing in of the harvest in decisive fashion: new Outward Bound schools in Britain (by the early 1950s some 70 British Local Education Authorities were sponsoring boys on Outward Bound courses), in the USA, Malaysia and Australia; the purchase and commissioning of the two square riggers *Pamir* and *Passat* for sail training for young Germans; a founding role in the Institute of Strategic Studies of whose Council he became a member; an intensive preoccupation with the issues of atomic warfare and graduated deterrence; the setting-up of the Trevelyan Scholarships to Oxford and Cambridge; a growing concern for juvenile delinquents whose prospects he discussed with governors of the Prison Commission and on whose behalf he made applications for funding to the Nuffield Foundation; the *Service by Youth Trust*, intended to provide coordination and direction of his multiplying activities, the wrist to control the fingers; and The Medical Commission on Accident Prevention.

These achievements were beyond the grasp of a working Headmaster and a single school. All, including Gordonstoun, must accept the judgement of a notable Hahn disciple, George Turner, a distinguished former Headmaster of Marlborough College, when he wrote in a paper for the Gordonstoun Governors in March 1955: *'We cannot replace Hahn himself … Hahn was the origin of this great development, and he worked from Gordonstoun. How far can Gordonstoun now continue to be functionally connected with this wider work? … In all this connection I am shy of the accepted term "Greater Gordonstoun"; for the achievement is Hahn's, not Gordonstoun's …'*

It was Hahn's efforts to reinforce the bridges between Salem and Gordonstoun, Germany and Britain, which point most directly towards the Atlantic College. In May 1948, in a fundraising memorandum aimed at donors in the United States, he proposed *'the foundation of "Rhodes Scholarships" at the adolescent stage – that 30 scholarships per annum be given to selected German boys ... to be sent to Gordonstoun for a period of two years as potentially effective transmitters, on their return, of responsible and active citizenship'.* In June of that year he secured €10,000 from the Rockefeller Foundation for German boys for this purpose. Encouraged, he raised his figure to 50 in a supplementary memorandum the following year, hoping to achieve this by 1953, and added the idea of a French branch.

In addition to securing a limited number of scholarships for German boys, especially the sons of members of the German Resistance, to spend terms in Gordonstoun, he engaged in vigorous efforts to enable the German Abitur to be taught and examined in the Scottish school, yet enjoy full recognition for university entry in Germany. Furthermore, he also persuaded Dr. Eugen Löffler, the retired Chairman of the Standing Conference of Ministers of Education in Germany, to prepare a document outlining a possible curriculum that might lead to university entry recognition in both countries. This paper came uncannily close to the framework that eventually composed the Diploma of the International Baccalaureate.

But from 1955 onwards, the year of his lecture visit to the NATO Defense College, he was working on an even broader canvas. His experience of the military officers working together *'on a common task'* had had an electrifying impact on him.

Early Steps

His essential ally in those seven years that led to the opening of the Atlantic College in 1962 was the soon-retired Commandant of the NATO Defense College, Lawrance Darvall. Darvall was captured by the Hahn charisma. He devoted himself full-time for weeks on end to supporting Hahn's dreams and schemes, his involvement embracing Salem and Gordonstoun as well as the embryonic Atlantic College. Hahn shared Goethe's enthusiasm for the cultured military officer, *'den gebildeten Offizier'*. In Lawrance Darvall he came close to his ideal.

Early critics of the College had an easy target in its associations with NATO, but Darvall's personal contacts and friendships went well beyond the military. It was Lawrance Darvall who first drew Lester Pearson into what he and Hahn called *'active operations'* on behalf of the College, and the then Secretary General of NATO, General Ismay, was a figure of formidable political experience. Other distinguished personalities readily accessible to Darvall included Senators William Fulbright and Adlai Stevenson, in addition to numerous European politicians, among them Henri Spaak and Robert Schumann, who had

visited and lectured at the Defence College. The French philosopher Raymond Aron was another remarkable ally whose interventions on behalf of the College in his native land were determined but fruitless.

Kurt Hahn's letter of 22nd September 1955 to Hilda Besse, the widow of his great friend and supporter Antonin Besse, father of Tony, describes *'plans I am submitting to UNESCO – the foundation of a UN College for boys from 15 to 19 ... possibly located in Banff ... UNESCO would be very interested in sponsoring a university entrance examination ...'* On 12th October of the same year: *'I long to tell you about my experiences in Paris. UNESCO is a sterile organisation. They can however give help to limited projects – exchanges, etc. Lord Ismay (Secretary General of NATO) was most sympathetic. At his request I am writing a memorandum setting out in detail the plan for the foundation of a NATO College for adolescents in Britain ... Lord Ismay was really hopeful about gaining the support of the NATO governments. He strongly felt that fear alone would not keep the great alliance together. We must plant a new solidarity in the young of all the NATO nations ...'*

In early 1956 the Salem middle school Spetzgart was briefly considered as a site for a college in Germany. In August came the invitation to Kurt Hahn to address the Bruges Conference at which some 100 leaders from Western Europe, the United States and Canada were gathered to consider the intellectual and cultural issues facing the Atlantic Community. It was here that he met Alec Peterson, with whom he was to make common cause on the issue of broadening the narrowly specialised English A Level Sixth Form system of education. In November 1959 a meeting in Hamburg, attended by Kurt Hahn, Lawrance Darvall, Tony Besse, Eric Warburg and Countess Marion Dönhoff, editor of *Die Zeit*, resolved to place the first college in Britain, with the possibility of a college on Fishers Island in the US in association with Phillips Academy Andover as a solution held in reserve.

In 1960, despite all this activity, the three key issues remained unresolved: site, funding and headmaster.

Early Supporters

Desmond Hoare, a Rear-Admiral in the Royal Navy, had approached Kurt Hahn of his own initiative in his enthusiasm for introducing Outward Bound pursuits into the Navy. I tell his story elsewhere in this book.

The same chapter also describes Desmond Hoare's clear-minded, precisely formulated decision to reject Scotland as a site in favour of St. Donat's in South Wales, an early indication of his ability, rare in the small group of founders, to think independently of Hahn and to stand up to him.

The chapter on the Warburg family outlines the patient, persistent, purposeful pursuit of funds from the United States by Eric Warburg, the brother of Hahn's sister-in-law Lola. It also describes the skilful courting of Tony Besse.

But no-one, not even Tony Besse, would donate unless Britain gave a lead.

The aim of Hahn's Trevelyan Scholarships to Oxford and Cambridge had been to mitigate the increasing concentration on examination performance in three highly specialised subjects through the presentation of a project that would illustrate the applicant's ability to devote himself with passion, thoroughness and perseverance to a theme of personal and, ideally, unusual interest. The historian and Master of Trinity College, Cambridge, George Trevelyan, had given his name, and a foremost supporter was the physicist and Nobel Prize winner Nevill Mott, also of Cambridge. British industrialists were keenly interested, with Sir Walter Benton Jones, Chairman of the United Steel Companies, in the lead. For Hahn it was a natural step to enrol them now in the cause of the Atlantic Colleges, for here was another area in which, with its long experience of residential education, Britain had a leading role to play.

But no project for a school gains credibility for donors until there is a site. Here, benevolent good fortune intervened. Lawrance Darvall spotted an advertisement in the magazine *Country Life* for the Castle and Estate of St. Donat's in South Wales.

The Purchase of St. Donat's Castle: an Act of Faith

St. Donat's was a Norman castle built around 1150 into which an Elizabethan country mansion had later been skilfully incorporated. Now, in the 20th century, it had central heating and 32 marble bathrooms, 150 acres of land including Tudor gardens stretching down to the Bristol Channel foreshore, an historic Tythe Barn, and a 25 metre open-air swimming pool! A dream site and, one might say in retrospect, a dream price: £65,000. But first, there was no money; and secondly, there was competition.

The Welsh businessman Julian Hodge had failed on his first attempt to gain local planning permission to convert the estate into a high class caravan holiday camp. He lodged an appeal with the Secretary of State for Wales, Henry Brooke. How fortunate that Henry Brooke as a young man had been the first journalist to visit Gordonstoun School soon after it opened and had steadfastly supported Hahn in his efforts to draw the attention of the British public to the events unfolding in Dachau and other concentration camps throughout the 1930s! But appeals will sooner or

later be resolved, and the original option that had expired in August had already been extended several times. Thus the College's Sponsoring Committee attended an anxious meeting on Thursday 13th October 1960 in Kurt Hahn's London haunt, Brown's Hotel in Dover Street. Present were Kurt Hahn, his brother Rudo, Admiral Sir Michael Denny, Ronnie Grierson (a Director of S. G. Warburg and Co.), Lawrance Darvall, and General Hare (Director *pro tem* of the Atlantic College Trust).

At this stage Tony Besse had offered £50,000 in one year's time on condition that British donors gave evidence of British commitment by putting up £200,000. He had however assured Eric Warburg in August that he would not be inflexible if £150,000 were to hand. On hand that day were £30,000.

Kurt wrote that same evening to Tony Besse. '*The Sponsoring Committee decided today to purchase St. Donat's Castle on Tuesday, October 18th, provided the £65,000 are guaranteed on that day ... the decision was unanimous ... the people present were, I believe, influenced by ... Sir Michael Denny offering to give a loan without interest of £1,250 ... until such time as the Council is assured that repayment can be effected without impediment to the conduct of the College ... by Admiral Hoare who made the announcement that the only capital he has will be a £4,000 gratuity paid to him when he retires from the Navy but he is so certain of the financial success of the Atlantic College that he would not mind investing it ... Darvall offered another £1,000 ... owing to my brother's lead, the contributions from the Service men are not required. The contract will be signed on Tuesday.*'

By thus narrow a margin, and by such acts of faith, did Atlantic College see the light of day. The contract with the owners, the National Magazine Company, was signed on 18th October and the purchase completed on 17th November.

And on 17th November Kurt Hahn took Tony Besse down to St. Donat's Castle for the first time. The following day Tony wrote to Eric Warburg: '*had I ever had any apprehensions about foregoing the provisos to which I had subjected my contribution, they would have been dispelled by the visit I paid to St. Donat's Castle yesterday in the company of Kurt Hahn ...*'

St. Donat's Castle had already enjoyed a long, romantic history. But the utterly decisive ownership had been that of the American newspaper despot, William Randolph Hearst. For Hearst, regardless of expense, had installed the marble bathrooms, the central heating, added two wings that gave the College an assembly hall, a dining hall and a large library, and the swimming pool; in a word, created a 20th-century home for a modern school within

Kurt Hahn and Desmond Hoare, anxious after the successful purchase of St. Donat's to get started

Desmond Hoare giving a maths tutorial in his Lady Anne study

a medieval and Elizabethan estate of almost matchless beauty and enduring historical as well as almost contemporary associations. John Kennedy had swum in the pool in July 1938 during a five-day visit when his father was the US Ambassador in London; Lloyd George had been a frequent visitor; earlier owners, notably the Stradling family, had been important in Welsh cultural life. There can be no doubt that the castle itself, its impressive gardens, and the backcloth of the mighty Bristol Channel off the foreshore below, endowed the College with a sense of permanence and strength from the very first day. The impact on students, visitors and donors – and on Tony Besse – was an inspiration.

And so the small group of founders now had a magnificent location. It is true that the surveyors' report had described it as *'an excellent site for an antique dealer's shop'*, with the nearby Nash Point fog horn having been known to *'shake the premises'*. But the new tasks remained formidable: funding to adapt the castle for its new purpose, funding to run the College, the release of the headmaster from the Navy on acceptable terms, and the assembling of staff and students. The year 1961 saw active but inadequately focused efforts to raise money, and the only employee was the retired naval Captain John Pearson who, as the future Bursar, moved down to St. Donat's to keep an eye on the place. The College's Founding Committee took the formal decision on 9th January 1962 to open the College in September that same year. Thus Desmond Hoare, released from the Navy under terms that demanded much personal and financial sacrifice on his part, was now able to tackle the challenges single-mindedly and without other professional obligations, but nine months is not long when you are starting from scratch.

Early Days, Early Aspirations and Early Reactions

By April there was a teaching staff of 11, selected from some 400 applicants. By the end of August the interior of the castle had been adapted to provide dormitories, classrooms, the first school language laboratory in Britain, a staff common room, offices, living quarters and an infirmary; one boarding house had been completed; the 25-metre Hearst swimming pool had been modified for school use with a new heating and filtration plant; a gap had been driven through the sea wall to gain access to the sea; and laboratories for the sciences had been set up in an old war-time wooden hut.

The official opening was celebrated on 3rd October, 21 years almost to the day since the boys had arrived at the first Outward School in Aberdovey in North Wales. The founding generation of students numbered some 60 from the following countries: Brazil, Canada, Denmark, England, France, Germany, Greece, Holland, Northern Ireland, Norway, Scotland, Sweden, Switzerland, USA and Wales. More than half had been enrolled with scholarships.

It is perhaps of interest to reflect on some core statements of the College's philosophy as set out by Desmond Hoare in the first prospectus.

The first boys come from the countries of the western community but only because this is a convenient starting point. In time boys will come from a wider range of countries and, it is hoped, from Eastern Europe. But the national groups must be large enough to represent their countries adequately …

The project has a two-fold aim, the first being concerned with the social integration of the western community. The countries of Europe are still divided. Nevertheless there are strong forces tending to draw them together and, for the first time, the energies and many-sided genius of the European nations are being combined in peace instead of being wasted in conflict. Education cannot stand aside from this great creative movement …

A man today, who goes abroad to work from almost any European country and who takes his family with him, cannot educate his children overseas and have much chance of entering them in the universities of his own country. One reason is poor language teaching, especially in Britain. University admission procedures are a still greater problem. It is inconceivable that such barriers will exist at the turn of the century. Nevertheless, we have yet to remove them. Change by political means is uncertain and slow. The force of example is needed and, to be effective in this area of strongly entrenched views and practice, it must be on a scale and of an academic stature to carry conviction. The Atlantic College project is aimed at setting this example. Eventually, it should become practicable for an able boy of any nationality in any Grammar School in Britain, or Lycee, Gymnasium, or Senior High School on the continents of Europe and North America to enter any university in any country. The international agreements achieved within the Atlantic College project should be transferable to state education …

The second aim is more fundamental in nature. The advancing material prosperity of the western world has brought evils in its train. Among these are a decline in the physical fitness of young men, insufficient satisfaction of the youthful instinct for adventure, and that decline of compassion which is reflected in the plain business of individual unhelpfulness one to another. We need to show in a convincing manner that the educational needs of modern society do not have to be met at the expense of more important human characteristics. The heart of the matter is the need to demonstrate that self-discipline, devotion, imagination, courage and response to challenge can be developed in materially prosperous societies …

Our civilisation has many roots. One is that sense of obligation to the community which overrides self-interest when the issue is important. The instinct to helpfulness

is present in every youth; it can either be fostered and flourish or it can be neglected and fade away. It is not enough to preach the virtue. Boys must be encouraged to achieve physical fitness and to learn the necessary techniques which will permit them to work for others and to do this in situations which can also satisfy their instinct for adventure. To this end we have planned our rescue services, beach rescue, canoe life guards, cliff rescue, etc. Nothing convinces as much as does the saving of life that the common humanity of men is more important than race or colour. The recognition of this by youth, through their own shared experience must, we feel, make some contribution to peace …

The College is the first major international boarding school to be founded in Britain. It is also one of the first all sixth-form colleges to be established. It requires and maintains the highest academic standards but resists excessive specialisation as a matter of educational principle. In terms of study and social organisation, it accords as much with a university college as with a grammar or independent boarding school …

During his time at the College each boy undertakes a project of his own based on the requirements of the Trevelyan Scholarships. The realities of a scientific age demand an early exercise of the powers of research such as this scheme demands. There is a common course on the fundamental problems of philosophy, and all boys are introduced to science, including biology …

Later projects introduce a social purpose, such as working in a steel works or coal mine, living with working families, studying juvenile crime, the courts and approved schools; or they may be archaeological, artistic or religious in nature …

Of course the College did not escape critical comment. One educational journal in October 1962, whilst sympathetic to the academic aims, considered '*the non-academic aims … more subtle and, one feels, more suspect …*' and detected '*the tattered baggage of the leadership principle*' (it was, in Hahn's words, one of Hitler's posthumous achievements to have tainted for so long the concept of leadership); and another: '*an outside observer would be surprised to find many of the boys who take kindly to this regime in the ranks of the CND; this is not a place for non-conformists.*'

The Director of Education for Surrey was not surprised by these comments. An early supporter, he wrote in 1965: '*The idea of a separate college for sixth formers as a basis for secondary education was, when it was put forward, regarded as a conception on the further fringes of heresy …;*' and comments from the Heads of some of the great English

Public Schools certainly accorded with his judgement. The Head of Charterhouse, having had the scheme carefully set out for him in 1962, described the proposal as *'a transit camp for teenagers'*; and the Chairman of the prestigious Headmasters' Conference (HMC) was quoted in the *South Wales Echo* as late as 1968 as stating that *'no member of the Conference can see any sense in the idea of sixth form colleges, and if you want to throw children into a jungle, this is the right way to do it.'* [•] The Minister of Education had declined an invitation to speak at the opening ceremony with the explanation that the College was *'educational poppycock'*. Yet more colourful was the comment in the issue of 29th August 1965 of the journal *Time and Tide* which, alarmed by the suggestions arising from the visit to the College of the Queen and the Duke of Edinburgh that Prince Charles might become a student there, described Atlantic College as *'an eccentric institution dedicated to promoting the current poisonous craze for internationalism. Internationalism is the enemy of patriotism, and patriotism is the very essence of the monarchy …'*

The enthusiasm, excitement and sense of purpose that prevailed at the College were more than a match for these and other comparably hostile comments, and *The Times Educational Supplement* was an unfailingly generous and thoughtful advocate. The rapid build-up of active interest and involvement from Europe and North America, expressed through the increasing provision of scholarships, the conclusion of academic agreements with European Ministries of Education over equivalence issues, and the growth and activities of the Atlantic College National Committees, were fully adequate evidence that the College was engaged in important educational work. On 1st September 1962 *The Economist* had published a long article in which it had drawn attention to the speech given by Eisenhower the previous month in London, calling for an international college to promote understanding between nations. This was the task.

[•] It is satisfying, as Atlantic College approaches its 50th anniversary, to note the change in attitude. *'Figures show that the number of 16–18 year olds boarding at independent and state schools has risen by a fifth in the past decade … Richard Harman, the Chairman of the Boarding Schools Association and headmaster of fee-paying Uppingham School in Rutland, said sixth form boarding prepared children for living away from home "but in a structured way with an appropriate level of pastoral support …".' The Daily Telegraph*, 26th December 2011

Progress Educational and Financial

The build-up in numbers was steady. By 1964 the demand already exceeded the number of places. 156 students were enrolled from 21 countries, 90 of them on scholarship. By the fifth academic year there were 235 students from 35 countries, including Czechoslovakia and Poland, the first from the bloc of the Warsaw Pact.

The scholarship element was of capital importance. Entry was to be independent not only of race, religion and politics but also of financial background. Writing in *The Spectator* in June 1965, Alec Peterson reported that, of the 68 British boys in the College, 55 were from local authority schools on local or trade union scholarships and, of the other 21 nations represented, 12 had scholarship schemes and six more were considering them.

All of this required intensive public relations, fundraising and negotiations overseas.

Kurt Hahn had received a very encouraging letter as early as June 1961 from the office of the Federal Chancellor Adenauer in Bonn, and in 1963 the College received its first governmental support – £45,000 from Germany, followed by a second grant in 1965 of £27,000, a total of £72,000. Stirred no doubt by this precedent, the British government followed suit in 1964 with £50,000 with two supplementary grants raising the total to £100,000. A remarkable feature of these grants was that they were approved successively by Conservative and Labour administrations.

British business, banks and foundations, the Dulverton Trust and the Bernard Sunley Charitable Foundation in the lead, added their support to that of many generous individuals. Other highly significant endorsement came from the Ford Foundation which, in 1963, made its grant of $140,000, the first time in its history that it had given money to education below university level in Great Britain or Europe. In 1964 the City of London Drapers Company donated the funds for a new boarding house, celebrating its 600th anniversary with the statement that, in the 1880s, support for universities had been as rare as support was now for sixth form colleges.

One great disappointment was the failure of the College, despite support from the highest levels, to achieve recognition as part of Britain's memorial to the slain American President John Kennedy. Desmond Hoare called it *'the most significant opportunity which has been offered to us since we opened the College, and I am sure that we will have to exert all our energies to pull it off'*. We cannot be sure; it seems that we were very close; but the difference between success and failure in these matters is absolute.

Another very high-level exploration was made in fine, eloquently supportive letters from the government's senior scientific advisor, Sir Solly Zuckerman, in 1964 to university colleagues in the United States, among them Henry Kissinger. This too remained without tangible results.

The Bristol Channel and Coast Rescue

Outside the classroom and mostly on the cliffs or in the waters of the Bristol Channel, the College achieved national recognition for its remarkable accomplishments in coastal rescue. Here, as in other areas, the inspirational rhetoric was Hahn's: *'William James has challenged statesmen and educators to discover the moral equivalent of war. It has been discovered: the passion of rescue releases the highest dynamics of the human soul.'* The practical achievement was Hoare's.

All students underwent training in essential life-saving skills: first aid, swimming, and the rescue of drowning persons, gaining the relevant qualifications of the British Red Cross and St. John's Ambulance Organisations, the Amateur Swimming Association and the Royal Life Saving Society.

The College developed rescue units in inshore lifeboats of the Royal National Lifeboat Institution (RNLI), cliff rescue (HM Coastguard) and beach rescue (Royal Life Saving

XII – one of the most succesful designs

Society (RLSS), and the Surf Life Saving Association of Australia (SLSA). The teams worked closely together on call-out emergencies. These rescue teams were entrusted with official responsibility for the safety of life over a 20-mile stretch of the dangerous Bristol Channel coastline and were the first such coordinated service in Britain.

The cliff rescue, under the direction of its first chief instructor Peter Jolley, who was also the College's senior scientist and, from the second year onwards, Director

[1] *A typical if quiet afternoon, … and the usual assembly of craft afloat*
[2] [3] *College prototype rescue boats under construction*
[4] *An early stage in the development of the rigid-hulled inflatable: directional fins copied from the growingly popular surf boards*
[5] *The final outcome*

The course of the first Round Britain Power Boat Race in 1969

The College-built craft Psychedelic Surfer *during the race*

of Studies, developed and used an ingenious crane that enabled the recovery of casualties either from the rock face or the foot of the cliff without dislodging debris from the crumbling vertical surface that represented a major hazard to all operations on the Channel cliffs.

The sea activities took place all year round on six afternoons a week. This was only possible because of the adoption of the neoprene skin suit. Here too the College was a pioneer. All sea-going students made their own, patterns having been skilfully designed by Desmond Hoare's wife Naomi, who measured each boy and presented him a day or so later with the appropriate parts for gluing together. The winter temperatures of the Bristol Channel were a strong incentive for careful workmanship. The College's Norwegian students, struggling with their English, coined the phrase *'frost-biting'* which passed rapidly into common usage among sea-going enthusiasts in Britain.

The inshore lifeboat unit began with small inflatable dinghies that rapidly proved unable to resist the daily wear and tear and lacked the speed, strength and manoeuvrability to handle the demanding conditions of the Bristol Channel. Several years of intensive developmental work under the leadership of Desmond Hoare led to the creation of the rigid-hulled inflatable lifeboat that was adopted by the RNLI in the early 1970s for stations around Britain's coast and was named, in recognition of the College's role, the B Class Atlantic Lifeboat. These craft are now used worldwide by lifesaving and coastguard organisations, the offshore energy industry, the military, the marine racing world and the leisure market. This was a remarkable technological achievement for a school. Desmond Hoare's gift of the patent rights to the RNLI in recognition of their support, in return for a token cheque for £1 which he never cashed, ruled out any possibility that might have existed of securing a long-term financial benefit for the College's budget. [●]

The breakthrough in the recognition of these boats came in dramatic fashion.

In mid-June 1969, Desmond Hoare took a telephone call from a young man who wanted to enter the first-ever Round Britain Power Boat Race in an inflatable boat. A firm had let him down. Could the College help? The race was in four weeks' time. The RNLI had not yet accepted the concept of the rigid-hulled inflatable. Desmond Hoare saw his chance and said he would build one for the £700 on offer. He designed it that night. Two Dutch students

[●] I have told the full story of these boats in *The RIB: The Rigid-Hulled Inflatable Lifeboat* Granta Editions 2010

and the College carpenter began work the following morning. There were special requirements in equipment not yet encountered by the College, but three weeks later to the day *Psychedelic Surfer* was afloat. Of 52 starters in this tough race, *Psychedelic Surfer* was the smallest, the cheapest, the most quickly built – and nineteenth to finish! RNLI crews right round Britain saw her for themselves and the case was made.

From the outset the College trained members of its third service, the beach rescue unit, in the techniques and for the awards of the Amateur Swimming Association, the Royal Life Saving Society and the Surf Life-Saving Association of Great Britain, determined always to do whatever it could to harmonize the procedures and purposes of these three national organisations. Twice, in 1968 and 1970, the College team won the SLSA of GB national championships, the first and only school or college ever to do so, and were well in line for a high place in 1969, when the last-minute introduction of a visiting team from South Africa led the team by open vote to withdraw on the morning of the final day – a decision of conscience which was controversial and little understood on the beach itself, but which earned the team a standing ovation the next morning from the assembled student body of the College.

Between 1964 and 2008 the College services were credited with 97 lives saved, 103 persons recovered unharmed, and nine persons recovered injured. Until the most recent years in this period the boats were always launched with the crews made up of students alone. Unhelpful health and safety regulations eventually made this impossible. Training standards ensured that no student suffered injuries at any time.

The impact of the sea, the challenge of saving life, come through with special and forceful clarity in a letter from Michael Code, a Canadian who had led the College beach rescue team and been President of the Student Council. [•] He was replying to a paper by Desmond Hoare in April 1970. Beginning with comments on the plans for a College in Western Canada: *'they appear to be having difficulties with a site on Vancouver Island, but I think they have made a bad decision anyway because they've limited all possibilities to an area south of a specific parallel on the island ... the sea in that area is all very calm ... I don't see that there's much point in having a United World College on an ocean unless*

[•] When authorising me to quote from his letter Michael wrote: *'I was a very earnest young 20-year-old man but it was all quite sincere and genuine'.*

that part of the ocean moves a little ... it might as well be on a lake.' And then: *'you have a long passage describing a Students' Council and then a short sentence about second year instruction and responsibility in Rescue Services ... this is a complete reversal of the reality ... the vital areas of student responsibility are in the rescue and social services and the academic programme, in all of which the students are given fairly demanding tasks and left to get on with it by themselves ... and are not watched over like children ... each individual is responsible for his own academic success or failure, for his own rescue service and for his own safety ... in the section on activities it is again mentioned almost casually that "the social services opportunities offered should include some in which there is an element of personal risk" ... this, to me, is perhaps the most vital part of any United World College ... Atlantic College has one or two highly* <u>*practical*</u> *ways of achieving that understanding and by far the most important and effective means is the rescue services with the degree of danger involved ... understanding between nationalities only happens when people can share a common danger (the sea, the cliffs), when they are confronted together with something much greater than themselves ... it was in the rescue services that people came closest to each other without saying anything and without realising it ... just living together is not enough and certainly talking together with each other is not enough ... the only truly effective way of achieving understanding is through some form of communion with an external force which re-introduces a form of spirituality common to everyone ... just by bringing students from all over the world to one school they're not going to solve all their problems.'*

The Advent of Co-education

There was one other major development in this early period.

From the very beginning Desmond Hoare had wanted a co-educational college. There is little doubt that this would have been an innovation too far and, in the atmosphere of the time, fatal to the College's prospects for financial survival. He knew and accepted this, but when he was challenged by a visiting journalist in 1966 to state why he was interested in only one half of humanity, he responded immediately that, if someone would put up £40,000, he would commission girls' accommodation the next day. The money arrived in a London bank 14 days later. The donors, Sonny and Phebe Maresi, were to become the College's largest private donors. Phebe's forebears on her father's side had helped to found Cornell University, the only Ivy League university to have been co-educational from the outset. Phebe herself was a Quaker and very

Phebe and Sonny Maresi, major Atlantic College benefactors, in the ruins of the Cavalry Barracks whose restoration they funded, alongside the new swimming pools and several other projects including parts of the Tythe Barn

strongly committed to equal educational opportunities for women. [●]

There was some delay in bringing the girls in as members of the Governing Body were much upset by this spontaneous initiative about which they rather reasonably felt they might have been consulted. Kurt Hahn expressed his concerns about the kind of co-education *'that breaks out after dark'*. The College, staff and students, was almost unanimously in favour (the one energetic teacher opponent having his case subsequently undermined by the birth of three attractive and outstandingly able daughters), but it was nonetheless necessary for Desmond Hoare to resort to a subterfuge. He was authorised to enroll nine day-girls on a trial basis in September 1967. To enable them to take a full part in College life he was also authorised to accommodate them just outside the College grounds. His case to the Chairman of Governors was convincing: their home was to be the Old Vicarage. It was left unsaid that St. Donat's had had no vicar for 45 years, that the *Old Vicarage* was nothing more than a name. But from 1968 onwards successive generations of girl students joined their male colleagues not only on campus but in co-educational houses. The

Atlantic College took this step ahead of all Oxford and Cambridge Colleges. [●] (It is only fair to add that a number of residential and co-educational schools had been running for many years by this time.) Nor was it long before the number of girl applicants from practically all countries exceeded, often by a large margin, the number of boys.

Desmond Hoare's written submission to his Governors on this matter had the brevity and focus that one perhaps takes for granted from naval engineers. *'To many of our foreign students and parents our failure to mix the sexes is regarded as unnatural in the fullest sense of the word … The philosophy of the Atlantic College is just as applicable to girls as it is to boys, and few parents would question that the mothers of future generations are as important as the fathers in the creation of human attitudes … In almost every aspect other than team games, the Atlantic College is at present a half school … This paper is brief, but there is really nothing more to say on a decision which only in Britain could be regarded as very significant.'*

The Atlantic College magazine provided supportive student editorial comment from Howard Newby, a future Vice-Chancellor of Liverpool University and Chair of Trustees for the National Centre for Social Research, that referred (a little nostalgically, I suspect) to the past *'thrice-termly dances in the <u>deliberate</u> gloom of the dining hall'*, and noted with expectant excitement the press headline *Wanted: Twelve Amazons.*

Some Essential Elements in Support and the Opening of a new Chapter

The 1962–1969 headship of Desmond Hoare was the natural first chapter in the story of the Atlantic College.

By 1969 we had a school of 270 students, a campus with enviable if not yet completed facilities, an outstanding record of university entry success (by 1967 former students were attending 116 institutes of higher education across the world), a co-ordinated coast rescue service with national

[●] This initial contact led to a life-long interest in the United World Colleges by Sonny and Phebe Maresi. Their daughter Beatrice recently wrote to me:
'It would be hard for me to convey how important Atlantic College and United World Colleges were to my parents' daily lives. Not only did they visit many of the schools, Atlantic College, Duino, Lester Pearson, Armand Hammer College of the West, the School in Africa, they discussed the aspects of the different schools constantly. It was almost as if we had a new sibling! I think it is amazing what did come to fruition.'

[●] Soon after the girls arrived, and somewhat boastful of the College's latest pioneering innovation, I asked a much loved and much respected bachelor Classics don at my old Cambridge College, St. John's, when the College (and the university) would follow our example, pointing out that 'co-education' (of the Hahn interpretation) had been flourishing for decades. *'If we have to join the Gadarene swine, that is no reason why we should be in the front rank'*, he replied, and walked off.

recognition, and an embryonic international organisation of national committees which was funding some 100 scholarships each year for new students. But the most important achievement was to have proved that it was possible, against widespread scepticism, to bring 17 and 18-year-olds from so many different countries, systems and languages up to a common standard within two academic years and to enable them to compete successfully for university places. The only students who did not go straight on to university were those who had military national service obligations to carry out first. The most potent factor, overlooked by the sceptics, was the motivation of the students themselves – and this has proved true of every successive generation. All have made a conscious decision to apply for a scholarship place; all have been ready to leave home, examination system, and often language, for the sake of the international ideal. Little wonder that all are so determined to make the best of themselves!

These first seven years also carried a number of vital lessons for the well-being of this international college and future sister-colleges.

Survival and progress were impossible without exceptional support from exceptional individuals and, whilst the key relationship was that between the Head and the Chair of Governors, the Chair had to be of a stature and experience in public life to carry conviction in the highest business, banking, industrial and political circles. The full burden rested on the shoulders of Desmond Hoare for the first 18 months, indeed until the moment when the College Bursar informed him early in 1964 that there no funds left to cover the salaries at the end of the month. Desmond was the first to state that, without Sir George Schuster, the College would have gone down that summer.

Another vital element was the composition of the Governing Body and Council. The representation of local government by Directors of Education, of the Foreign and Commonwealth Office by the Head of Cultural Affairs, and of the British Council by its former Chairman Sir Paul Sinker (for the role of the British Council in advertising the College overseas and overseeing the selection procedures was crucial for many years) expressed the firm endorsement of the College by public life in Britain.

And a third, a recipe practised by all subsequent colleges, was the warmth of the hospitality extended to all visitors in a team effort of Headmaster, staff, wives and students. There was no more powerful site of fundraising in those early years than the elegant, welcoming sitting room of the Lady Anne Tower, with dinner prepared by Naomi Hoare, teachers and students as hosts, the guests already enthused by spontaneous and direct meetings with teachers in the Stradling Hall Common Room over morning coffee, and by their student-guided tours of the College's afternoon activities. There can have been few within the College who did not feel a personal responsibility for contributing to the College's financial survival.

Of course, this intense effort at St. Donat's required a comparable effort overseas. Here the winning formula was the College's reliance above all on two distinguished retired British ambassadors, Robin Hankey and Eric Berthoud, who worked for many years for the College as unpaid volunteers, embracing with enthusiasm this new diplomatic challenge. George Schuster had appealed to the patriotism of the City of London when the College's financial fortunes were at their lowest ebb. These two emissaries were inspired by the same sentiments.

Robin Hankey, who had been Britain's Ambassador in Sweden, became an immediate ally and offered his help on his imminent retirement. His father had been one of Britain's most influential, distinguished civil servants, Secretary to the Cabinet in the First World War, a prominent member of the British Delegation at Versailles in 1919 and advisor to Neville Chamberlain on the formation of the first war cabinet in 1939. A. J. Balfour, Britain's Foreign Secretary from 1916–1919, said of him: *'without Hankey we should have lost the (first world) war'.* [●] Robin came to unwitting early prominence through having been on duty in the British Embassy in Warsaw on the night the Germans invaded Poland in 1939. The then young and inexperienced, later famous war correspondent Clare Hollingworth telephoned at three o'clock in the morning from inside Poland to

Eric Berthoud

[●] Quoted by A. J. P. Taylor *English History 1914–1945* Pelican Books 1970 page 28

report the German invasion. It was Robin who took the call, robustly insisting that there must be a misunderstanding; *'negotiations are still under way.'* Robin Hankey had some engaging eccentricities. Whenever he saw a pebble or some other small object lying on the pavement, he would reverse his umbrella and strike it a mighty blow with the umbrella handle with a pin-point accuracy that never failed; and he had the curious ambition of skiing, if only for 15 minutes, in every country in the world that had snow, and would arrange intervals in his flying schedules that enabled him, still clad in a business suit, to take taxis from airports to the nearest patch of white to notch up another country. Robin returned to Warsaw after 1945 and later became known in the Foreign Office for advocating a policy of aggressive containment towards the Soviet Union. He was extremely uneasy when the Atlantic College was visited by Soviet Embassy representatives and sent urgent warning notes that no students were to be allowed to engage in unsupervised conversation with them. But his work for us in Sweden and later in Canada and Singapore were of very influential importance. His setting up of the UWC Committee in Ontario in 1967 led to 50 applicants for the first Canadian provincial scholarship. He also became a member of the *IB Council of Foundation*.

Eric Berthoud, of Anglo-Swiss origins, had behind him a distinguished career in business, chiefly as a Director of British Petroleum, eventually joining the diplomatic service. Before becoming an ambassador, first to Denmark, then Poland, he had been Joint Chairman of the International Committee which founded the *Organisation of European Economic Cooperation* to distribute Marshall Aid across war-stricken Europe. Reading a profile of Kurt Hahn in *The Observer* newspaper, he wrote to him to enquire whether the Atlantic College project had any serious intention of enrolling Polish boys in due course. Within months of the College opening, he had become its advocate and emissary in Finland, Holland, West Germany, Austria, Italy, Belgium, Switzerland, France, Luxembourg, Spain and Portugal. He is said to have had a fearsome reputation as an ambassador and to have lined up his staff in the mornings to inspect the cleanliness of their shoes and their finger nails. Given this meticulousness, bordering almost on obsession, for protocol in behaviour and written documentation, it was with some bemusement that, after his visits to the *Studienstiftung des deutschen Volkes* in Germany, we read his reports referring to the SS. I never rose to the challenge of questioning this premature instance of the contemporary disease of *'acronymitis'.* In his privately printed memoirs he describes his post-retirement activities: a non-executive directorship of British Petroleum, founding membership

James Whitaker

of the Council of the new University of Essex, Anglo-Polish Round Table conferences which he revived and chaired, the Anglo-German *Königswinter* Conferences, the Essex Prison Board and Board of Visitors of Chelmsford Prison, the Civil Service Selection Board, the Sue Ryder Foundation (on behalf of which his Polish connections were invaluable), the Katherine Low Settlement in Battersea in London, and the Educational Interchange Council. Hardly retirement, one may feel, but we can take some considerable satisfaction that he devotes more pages to the Atlantic and United World Colleges than to any other of these involvements.

The list of College friends is long, all generous with their help and, often, their pockets. The industrialist Eric Weiss who began his spectacular career in metallurgy on the nearby Bridgend trading estate after fleeing Nazi Germany in the 1930s; David Wills, who created the Ditchley Foundation to promote dialogue between Great Britain and the United States, and the Twenty First Century Trust that brings together talented young professionals from across the world – the College had no greater or more generous, indeed more passionate friend in its early days; Bill Shapland, the administrator of the Bernard Sunley Foundation and the family's business interests; Rio-Tinto Zinc who set up a major scholarship endowment in memory of their deceased Chairman Sir Val Duncan and added a memorial garden adjacent to the Tythe Barn; perhaps most humanly impressive of all James Whitaker, who came to the project through his friendship with Lawrance Darvall, and whose unobtrusive common sense and gift for personal loyalties were a golden thread through more than 20 years of the College's existence. None sought less recognition than he, and his repeated comment as he made yet another, usually annual gift was *'use it for something no one else will help you with like the drains'.*

There were equally notable friends overseas.

Hartmut Rahn, Director General of the *Studientiftung* in Germany, was one of our most active and capable supporters. Identifying himself completely with our purposes and aspirations, he set up magnificent selection procedures for us, was a frequent visitor, and organised Studienstiftung summer schools at both the Atlantic College and the Adriatic College in Italy after it opened.

Dagfinn Paust of Norway was another unforgettable figure, generous, humorous, exemplary in his attendance at meetings, with a robust common sense knowledge of human nature that refused to tolerate headmasterly waffle. It was probably a relief for the Danish students that his Danish counterpart, Erik Nyegaard, was not either the Headmaster or a regular visitor since, whenever he came, he refused to tolerate their use of the heated swimming pool for the early morning swim and led them all remorselessly down the slipway into the Bristol Channel for an extended exposure to healthy living. It was rumoured of him that he had once entered a pool on an iceberg and that a polar bear enjoying a dip had fled when he appeared. The impressive thing about the story was that you could imagine that it might just be true.

Lord Mountbatten enters the Scene: The Atlantic College becomes the United World College of the Atlantic

The College was in many respects like a pressure cooker, and the achievements of this formidable team of supporters, many of them distinguished in public life, were to generate, as had been hoped from the outset, enthusiasm for expansion. By 1967, National Committees or informal groups were active in 37 countries, both in raising money for scholarships and in selecting students through increasingly well-publicised and respected selection procedures. In late 1967 Lord Mountbatten accepted the Presidency of the newly-established International Council, and the Atlantic College Project entered a fresh stage. This exciting line of development was further emphasised when Desmond Hoare voluntarily gave up the College Headship in 1969 to lead the drive for new scholarships and new colleges overseas.

The UWC International Council meeting at St. Donat's dedicates a memorial plaque to Kurt Hahn. From the left, Alec Peterson, Ian Gourlay, HRH The Prince of Wales, Robert Blackburn, Lord Mountbatten, Tony Besse; with their backs to the camera Michael and Deirdre Schweitzer

As might readily have been foreseen, this new stage brought its own tensions, for the most part creative. The overriding mission was to share and multiply the experiences of the founder college in Wales. Immediate pressure from Mountbatten led to a new name, the *United World College of the Atlantic*, a change not welcomed by all, and the innovation of a logo that has remained essentially unchanged since 1968.

There can hardly have been a door worldwide that remained closed to Mountbatten, by this time already the President or Patron of some 180 organisations. Despite the reservations of friends who, vociferously at times, felt that he should be devoting his final years and his immense prestige to something more *'elevated'* than a series of secondary schools, however exceptional, he threw himself at the challenges with breathtaking energy and enthusiasm, supported only by his personal secretary and former naval warrant officer, the admirable John Barrett, and a staff of two in the UWC international office in London, Robert Blackburn and Nina Little. Monarchs in Britain, Scandinavia and Holland, Presidents and Prime Ministers in all other European nations and further afield, two successive Presidents of the European Commission, Francois-Xavier Ortoli and Roy Jenkins, other Commissioners of the then European Economic Community from whom he extracted a series of scholarships for students from the developing countries of the Lomé Convention, two Presidents of the United States (Nixon and Ford), national leaders across South East Asia, individuals ranging from the Secretary General of the UN U Thant to Senators Hubert Humphrey and Edward Kennedy, the UN High Commissioner for

Refugees Sadruddin Aga Khan, Lester Pearson, the Indian Prime Ministers Indira Gandhi and Morarji Desai, the Shah of Persia (from whom Alec Peterson was able, thanks to his Mountbatten introduction, to secure $100,000 in 1974 for the IB), President Saragat of Italy with whom he founded the Italian National Committee in 1969, the British Minister of Education Shirley Williams whom he persuaded to host the Second IB Inter-Governmental Conference in London in 1978 – all were subjected to his drive to support 'his' United World Colleges and, with them, the International Baccalaureate.

Entirely characteristic of the exuberant Mountbatten style was the Night of Nights on 16th November 1970 in the London Festival Hall that raised £220,000, said to have been at the time the largest sum ever raised in one evening in London. Bob Hope and Frank Sinatra, compèred by Grace Kelly, filled the hall twice for consecutive performances on the same evening. The showmanship was not confined to the performing artists.

It is true that things did not always go to plan, even for this last Viceroy of India. At the outset of one International Council meeting he invited the delegates to endorse him formally as their 'Chairman'. The charming but rather determined lady representative from Iran invited Mountbatten 'in these times and at an international meeting' to call himself 'Chairperson'. Mountbatten was, at best, half amused, but she stood her ground. The meeting, amid growing embarrassment, was unable to move forward for several minutes. Suddenly Mountbatten cut through the whispered comments of would-be helpful colleagues by answering that he would be happy to become 'Chair-Persian' for the day, and 'surely you will be happy with that'. Amid the general merriment she really had no choice. Another occasion ended rather less successfully. Mountbatten had secured an interview at short notice with the Prime Minister of Sweden and was rattling away in his high-flying English about the International Baccalaureate and the UWC, and how beneficial it would be for Sweden to increase its grants to both organisations. Unfortunately the Prime Minister did not understand English, which Lord Mountbatten only realised in the final stages of the interview. He then remembered that the Premier came from the Agrarian Party, so he began 'I am also a farmer, I have a place called Broadlands with so many cows, so many sheep…' Understanding dawned with the Prime Minister. 'So that makes you a peasant too.' Lord Mountbatten was, said Dagfinn Paust, rather quiet about the outcome of this meeting.

It became nonetheless an almost decisive tragedy for the United World Colleges that the Mountbatten-Hoare relationship that had been so strong in their naval days did not survive the perhaps foreseeable and perhaps inescapable tensions of these fast-moving developments. Outsiders, dazzled by the Mountbatten profile, started to attribute many achievements, including the moves to set up new colleges, to Mountbatten, when the actual work and much of the background thinking had been accomplished by Desmond Hoare. UWC graduates too were now being taken far more seriously. Mountbatten knew how important they were for future success and cultivated their company and their counsels on all his foreign travels; but they had all been Hoare pupils who, Desmond Hoare could not help but feel, owed their first loyalty to him.

Mountbatten was not, of course, a man to be crossed. Burma had not hitherto been represented at the College, and when Mountbatten of Burma sent a Burmese girl down to the College for interview, he was something less than pleased when she was turned down. There was also the memorable occasion when he gave a talk to the assembled students on the Second World War, afterwards known as 'How I won the war with a little help from Winston Churchill'. It had not gone well; he knew it, and he was hurt. His reaction was to request a second invitation. He came down again and held the students spellbound with his account of the last days of the British Empire in India. It was difficult not to be moved by his relief and delight over his recovery.

He never failed to give his heart to the task in hand. John Nichol, the founding Chairman of Pearson College, recalls how he would enter a crowded room and offer his audience of potential sponsors the chance to make a real difference. Most of them took it. He did not, he said, want a third, nuclear world war, for the fourth would be fought 'with bows and arrows'. Leading the British delegation to the Soviet Union in 1975 to celebrate the end of the Second World War, he persuaded Kosygin and his Minister of Education to allow the first ever Russian student and a Russian teacher to join the College the following September. He had persuaded the Chinese ambassador in 1973 to send his cultural attaché down to St. Donat's to explore the idea of sending Chinese students. A fortnight after this visit, the Headmaster received a telephone call from the Embassy announcing the intention to send 12 students in three weeks' time. It was already mid-April, the academic year almost over, but the opportunity was too important to be missed. Present students were moved from their accommodation to some happily vacant staff accommodation; the new Chinese students, who all arrived in Mao uniforms and clutching, literally, the little Red Books as they climbed down from the bus, were immediately made to share rooms with students from across the College's nationalities. They were most of them remarkable personalities. Many had been Red Guards in the Cultural Revolution. From that year on, there were Chinese students in every new entry. Not the least remarkable feature of the whole enterprise was that not a single letter was written in either direction, nor did the embassy ever default on its payments. These were the first Chinese students to enter a non-Chinese school anywhere in the world after the Cultural Revolution.

But we should not perhaps have been surprised that the Chairman of one European National Committee wrote to the College Chairman of Governors to express his disbelief that the College Headmaster should have taken such risks over the exposure of doctrinally ill-prepared western students to the dangers of communist ideology. The thoroughness of their training could not be surprising *'for a government which does not allow any subject to leave the country without permission, and shoots those who try to escape … the *** National Committee hopes that those who took this decision will try at least to get rid of this national tutor as soon as possible and in addition will instruct the Headmaster to present a frank report.'* George Schuster did not falter: *'I can assure you that, before agreeing to take these students, we ascertained that this move had the complete approval as a matter of policy by the British Foreign Office.'* He might equally well have expressed confidence in the intellectual robustness of the rest of the student community

Mountbatten had no doubt that these were the bridges that had to be crossed. He took the first possible opportunity of coming down to the College to meet the Russian and the Chinese students, the Russian teacher especially intrigued to meet a man who had spent part of his childhood playing in family rooms in the Kremlin. Another nationality – the Japanese – caused him greater heartache. As Allied Supreme Commander in South East Asia in the closing months of the war, he owed a special debt of loyalty and remembrance to all those service-men who had suffered so atrociously in the Japanese camps. He had therefore declined to attend the banquet at Buckingham Palace during the State Visit of the Emperor in 1971. Rather courageously confronted by Desmond Hoare on this as an issue of principle, he relented, seeking and of course gaining a personal interview. Tony Besse saw much of him on UWC business and travels when he was serving under Mountbatten as the first Chairman of the UWC Board. He recalls his extraordinary sense of duty, his readiness to take advice, even hostile advice, from people he trusted, and his meticulous attention to the

protocols of courtesy, on one occasion insisting on signing personally some 50 letters of thanks, typed up overnight by the ever-present John Barrett on a manual typewriter, before boarding a cargo aircraft in the United States and sleeping on an improvised bunk bed in order to be on time for an appointment the following day in England. [●] But Tony also remembers the occasion when a Mountbatten suitcase containing only shoes was lost after a flight to Jeddah; British Ambassadors throughout the Middle East were alerted as a matter of urgency to recover the missing footwear.

It is undeniable that Mountbatten gave the project an international profile beyond that achievable by any other person. A long-serving UWC Director General, Ian Gourlay, has committed to paper his conviction that the UWC *'would do well to ensure that someone of global stature, like Mountbatten, was always in place as its leader'.*

Desmond and Naomi Hoare open up South East Asia for the Movement and explore the Claims of the Developing World

Desmond Hoare was meanwhile deeply engaged, with Naomi as his travelling companion and personal wit-ness of the St. Donat's success story, in extending the movement's horizons above all to South East Asia. He, like Mountbatten, was impatient for action and results. His vigorous efforts to set up a two-year college on the Atlantic model in Singapore, Malaysia and Indonesia, the students to spend one third of their course in each loca-tion (this was a time of recent 'confrontation' between these three increasingly powerful countries) failed. He thereupon embraced with pioneering enthusiasm the concept of an all-age international school in Singapore with a scholarship entry to the sixth form. In this manner, the British Chamber of Commerce School of St. John's in Singapore, originally established by the British Ministry of Defence for the children of service families, became by stages the United World College of South East Asia. Mountbatten's immediate, unhesitating support gave some

[●] Gianfranco Facco Bonetti of Italy, who first conceived the idea of an Italian College and who for several years acted as project manager, treasures to this day the memory of a letter from Mountbatten which thanks him for *'the miracle of Sistiana',* Sistiana having been the first fully developed College proposal. It is sadly a memory only as the letter was stolen along with other possessions many years ago.

the impression that it was he, Mountbatten, who was the instigator and founder. The founder, of course with allies based in Singapore, was Desmond Hoare.

The Hoares' repeated, tiring journeys to South East Asia led among other things to the first moves for a college in India, already in 1970. Desmond negotiated the first scholarships in Japan with the legendary founder of Sony, Akia Morita; and he greatly strengthened the commitment of the somewhat half-hearted National Committee in Hong Kong. Much of this work was done with the support of the eloquent and influential George Thompson from Singapore, whose belief in South East Asia as a future financial and political power base in the 21st century persuaded Desmond Hoare to abandon thinking in purely European and North American terms. But his heart came to lie increasingly in the concept of what he christened 'bamboo colleges', colleges adapted to the modest and harsh conditions and the needs of the developing world. The project he followed up the most closely and actively was a school for apprentices in Thailand, developed in cooperation with an innovative Thai Headmaster who had earlier visited St. Donat's. This was not just idealism; his advocacy included clear warnings about the threat to the future of the United World Colleges arising from unsustainable costs if the scholarship principle were to be maintained, even if only partially. He did not carry his case in London, but the vocational agricultural college set up in Venezuela in 1988 carried his unmistakable imprint. The Prince of Wales, by that time President of the UWC International Council in succession to Mountbatten, was the key figure in securing the support of the President of Venezuela, but the Prince's enthusiasm for the concept went back to a conversation on the top lawn of St. Donat's with Atlantic College students on the fringe of a Board meeting in the nearby Bradenstoke Hall, students who had already been well briefed and well indoctrinated by Desmond Hoare.

Canada

Whilst Desmond Hoare was concentrating on South East Asia, the Canadians had been active. After an abortive attempt at a College at Lake Louise in Banff, led by Senator Donald Cameron, the death of Lester Pearson in 1972 galvanised this distinguished statesman's political friends and allies, notably John Nichol and Jim Coutts, to establish a Canadian College in his memory. Pearson College opened in 1974.

One of many conversations that led eventually to the opening of Pearson College: Bob Houston, then head of the Canadian UWC National Committee, Lord Mountbatten, Lester B. Pearson, and George Schuster

Lester Pearson had been to Atlantic College twice. I have a vivid memory of his first visit. He arrived exhausted. When however he finally retired after dinner, he took with him the College year book. By 8 a.m. the next morning he had not only walked the campus but had sufficiently memorised the year book to recognise without hesitation and without introduction our Canadian teacher and all our 12 or so Canadian students – and to their delight he also knew all the latest Canadian ice hockey scores. His second visit was made to introduce his wife to the UWC concept, and I remember the long discussion late one evening during which he listened attentively as the Polish chairman of our Students' Council explained how significant it would be if the socialist countries of Eastern Europe could have their own United World College.

The continuing insistence of Pearson College that all students should attend on full scholarships, without parental contributions, though immensely difficult to sustain, has greatly stiffened and encouraged the resolve of the movement as a whole to insist on entry by merit alone. The village atmosphere of the beautiful Pearson College site on the southern tip of Vancouver Island, and the warm, informal relationships established there between all members of the College community under the inspiring leadership of the founder Head, Jack Matthews, have been very important contributions to the evolution of the UWC educational style.

There was action too, a little later, in Africa.

Africa

Waterford School in Swaziland had been set up in 1963, a few months after Atlantic College, by idealists who wanted an alternative to the apartheid-driven schools of South Africa. Their premises could not have been more different from those of Atlantic College – two indigenous buildings, *rondavels*, on high ground overlooking Mbabane, the capital. I recall Desmond Hoare's irritation when he discovered that some members of the Atlantic College Council were also involved in the Waterford venture but had kept this to themselves. Deon Glover, Deputy Head of Waterford, joined the Atlantic staff in 1974 to teach geography. Sitting together in his kitchen soon after his arrival, he and I wondered why the two schools could not have at least a partnership. Events moved swiftly from that moment onwards. The Director General of the UWC International Office, Ian Gourlay, and I made a first reconnaissance visit. Others followed. There were thoroughly understandable reservations on the Waterford side. Would the school lose its crucial African identity? Would its regional role be lost

in a more amorphous international context? But greater familiarity brought in this case mutual respect, and the school was welcomed into the UWC movement by acclamation at the last meeting of the International Council chaired by Lord Mountbatten in 1981.

Waterford has a very distinguished record. Nelson Mandela had children and grandchildren attend the school. Bishop Tutu's grandchildren were pupils. So too was the son of the writer Nadine Gordimer. It was a focal point for the most outspoken opponents of apartheid as for like-minded but lesser-known families. Its founding personalities were exceptional people.

On the 10th October 1954, the London *Observer* newspaper published an article by an Anglican priest and monk working in Johannesburg, Father Trevor Huddleston, *The Church Sleeps On*, an indictment of the failure of white South African Christians to oppose or even to recognise the intrinsic evil of apartheid and a passionate call to Christians to act. Michael Stern, the 32-year-old Deputy Head of an Approved School for boys in England, wrote the same day to Huddleston, asking what he could do to help. [●] Huddleston replied by return: *'St. Peter's, the historic school for black boys in Rosettenville, Johannesburg, needs a headmaster … your letter reached me an hour or two ago … I believe it is a direct answer to prayer … We need you very much indeed and just as soon as you can come … I really am asking you to make an act of faith, resign your present job and get here as soon as you can!'*

The Anglican Diocese of Johannesburg had already decided to close St. Peter's as a school for black boys and re-open it as a school for whites. Michael built up the school in facilities and numbers to 253 pupils by 1961, always confident in the expectation that, before long, black pupils would be able to join the white – in retrospect, a naïve illusion. And naïve illusions were unmistakably dispelled when his decision to allow the black domestic staff to use the swimming pool while the white pupils were doing their homework became a national scandal.

By this time the liberal Bishop Ambrose Reeves had been deported from South Africa and succeeded by the cautious, compromising Bishop Leslie Stradling, rather sadly a descendant of the Stradlings who had owned St. Donat's castle from 1298 to 1736. When, after the school had been chosen as the venue for an annual diocesan retreat and Michael had secured the agreement of his Council to allow black clergy to sleep in the school dormitories,

[●] Approved Schools were residential institutions to which young offenders could be sent by a court.

Bishop Stradling reacted with the statement that *'I did not think that a furore about black boys in white water had so far advanced the Kingdom of God that I now wanted another furore about black men in white sheets.'* Michael Stern wrote later: *'Finding we could be neither liberal nor even Christian (racially speaking) in the Republic of South Africa, we moved across the border in 1962/63 to start a new school in Swaziland, the first in that part of the world completely open to all races.'*

Those close to the history of the College will have their own additional names, but the personality who for all of us in the UWC movement stands out as the critical, creative partner was Christopher Newton Thompson.

Christopher Newton Thompson came from one of the oldest and most influential English-speaking South African families, attended perhaps the most famous of South African private schools, and ascribed his entry to Cambridge to connections rather than intellectual performance. Volunteering for the Guards Armoured Division in 1939, playing rugby for England in 1940, and hoping desperately that his call-up would come before the exams which he knew he had no chance of passing, he fought in the North African and Italian campaigns, being seriously wounded in the latter and earning a Military Cross. After the war, to his relief, Cambridge awarded him his degree without requiring him to sit the examinations. After a brief business and political career in England he returned to Africa, crucially having married Philippa. There they came to personify the white active liberal conscience, allied with an immense circle of influential friends, an enviable social life, a gift for generous, warm and informal hospitality, an unashamed enjoyment of the good things of life (frequent returns to England for Wimbledon and a cricket Test Match at Lords), membership of the Progressive Party, and a deep friendship with Helen Suzman, for 13 years the sole representative of the party in the South African Parliament and for six years the only woman, in which weekly bridge sessions were as important as politics. [•]

[•] In early 1995, Christopher and I were taken to meet Nelson Mandela by the Atlantic College graduate Ghaleb Cachalia. Ghaleb's parents Yusef and Amina had been leading Indian activists against apartheid and were intimate friends of Mandela. The ground having been prepared by them beforehand, we had gone to ask Mandela to accept the Presidency of the United World Colleges. Christopher introduced himself by referring to his weekly bridge parties with Helen. Mandela smiled conspiratorially and confided that, if he ever conducted an illicit affair, Helen would be his chosen partner. Helen Suzman, as is well known, was the only white politician to visit Nelson Mandela during his imprisonment on Robben Island.

On my first visit to the Newton Thompsons' home in Johannesburg with Ian Gourlay and my first exposure to Africa and apartheid, Christopher and Philippa invited to lunch the black Headmaster, Wilkinson 'Wilkie' Kambule of Orlando High School in Soweto. Wilkie's pupils had gone on strike in 1976 and refused to attend classes in protest against the *Afrikaans Medium Decree* of 1974 that forced all black schools to use Afrikaans (in the words of Desmond Tutu *'the language of the oppressor'*) and English in a 50-50 mix as languages of instruction. The protest had spread rapidly to other schools, leading eventually to a mass rally on 16th June 1976 and, on the following day, violent police repression which resulted in still hotly-contested estimates of fatality numbers ranging from 200–600. Philippa Newton Thompson became legendary for her work over more than 40 years in setting up crèches and infants' schools in Soweto. It is impossible to recapture in words the warmth and trust with which she was received and embraced by children and adults alike; unforgettable too the occasion when she conducted, with my wife Elisabeth and me, Diana Mosley around the township, the widow of the British Fascist leader Oswald Mosley as irreproachably charming with her black hosts as she was elegantly aristocratic. Christopher, whose admiration for his wife's morally and physically courageous work in Soweto drove him forwards, dissembled his ruthless fundraising for Waterford and, later, the similarly non-racial school Maru-a-Pula in Botswana, behind the façade of a genial sports- and club-loving exterior. He said of himself that he was the only man who could empty the bar of the Johannesburg Country Club simply by walking in. Waterford was utterly dependent for its founding, its funding and its survival on this extraordinary, dedicated and passionate partnership between Michael Stern and Christopher and Philippa Newton Thompson.

The Prince of Wales

Mountbatten was succeeded as UWC International President by the Prince of Wales. Prince Charles devoted himself to the movement for 15 years. He visited all Colleges, established a fine rapport with students, and achieved the critical breakthrough that enabled the founding of the Simon Bolivar College in Agricultural Management in Venezuela, the UWC's first and hitherto only venture into post-secondary and vocational education. He also attracted the (for some) controversial support of the oil magnate Armand Hammer that led with astonishing speed to the purchase of the old castle and estate in Montezuma, New Mexico, bringing the United States into the movement with their own college in 1982, in the same year and month in which the Adriatic College opened in Italy. But his own thoughts and interests were leading him in different directions, and at the UWC International Council meeting held in Italy in March 1990 he spoke his mind: *'what we now need, in my view, is to plan for new smaller colleges in the critical areas of the developing world, based on the model of the Simon Bolivar College … with an emphasis on training those young people who are technically rather than academically gifted … it is essential to respond to the practical needs of mankind … if we could aim for a series of colleges, basic, simple colleges in developing countries in Africa, South East Asia, or South America, the effect that we could have on local communities in these countries could be substantial … I realise that there are no easy answers to these questions, but after all, taking the initiative while others hesitated was always one of the principles underlying Dr. Hahn's educational philosophy'.* A determined local effort to create a second Simon Bolívar-style College in South Africa in the

1990s failed. The Simon Bolivar College itself continued to struggle with seemingly endless funding problems much accentuated by growing political indifference that has now culminated in overt hostility. Desmond Hoare and the Prince of Wales would surely be at one in their disappointment and disapproval.

The transition between the Presidencies of Lord Mountbatten and the Prince of Wales was also a step-change in the movement's international governance. The Mountbatten era might be compared with running a high-performance motor (Mountbatten loved high-performance cars) on high octane fuel. A tiny international office (Robert Blackburn and Nina Little), a devoted 'all-hours' private secretary John Barrett, and an impatient former Viceroy of India who allowed nothing to hold him up; Prince Charles feeling his way, royal obligations bearing down on him with pressures of time and protocol that Mountbatten could ignore except when they worked to his advantage, but supported by an international office

HRH The Prince of Wales as UWC International President-Elect

that set important precedents for the future. Professor Tom Symons of Canada [●] chaired the UWC International Board for six decisive years. His quiet, meticulously planned meetings were based on scrupulous attention to the balance between detail and broad principle. Above all they relied on intimate contact with the leading UWC personalities, frequent direct consultation with them, deep insight into the nature of both academic life itself and the special world of academic administration, and a clear acceptance of the distinctive roles of leadership and administration. Or was it all due to the always steaming pot of tea without which he refused to open any Board meeting, and the frequency of replenishment that was more important than the maintenance of detailed Minutes? This was the era too of Ian Gourlay as Director General – Ian a former Commandant of the Royal Marines, personal choice of Mountbatten to lead the UWC International Office under Charles' Presidency, and a pillar of integrity and loyalty for all within the movement worldwide. If the metaphor high-octane fuel was appropriate for Mountbatten, then perhaps it is legitimate to talk of high grade oil for the sense of ease and competence with which Tom Symons and Ian Gourlay endowed UWC affairs and handled many an occasion that required exceptional courtesy and diplomatic skills alongside a clear sense of direction.

Back to Atlantic College: Academic Life and the new International Baccalaureate

The first prospectus had made explicit the College's intention of working towards an international school-leaving examination.

The significant figure was to be Alec Peterson, the Director of the Department of Education at Oxford University. His eloquent 1960 report to the Gulbenkian Foundation, *Arts and Science Sides in the Sixth Form*, had, it was clear, fallen on deaf ears, although its findings were not seriously disputed in the educational press. Aided

[●] Professor Tom Symons is the Founding President of Trent University, Founding Vice-President of the Social Sciences and Humanities Research Council of Canada, and past Chairman of the Commission on Canadian Studies. He was also Chairman of the Association of Commonwealth Universities in the academic year 1971–1972. He is a Fellow of the Royal Society of Canada, an Officer of the Order of Canada (1976), and holder of the Queen's Silver Jubilee Medal and of the Canadian Centennial medal and other honours.

by Sir John Cockcroft of Cambridge University on the science side, Alec Peterson recommended to the College a programme based on the English Advanced Levels but sufficiently broadened to meet the ideals of the College and to reassure the Europeans. The result was a stop-gap, since the College's self-generated subsidiary courses could not lead to any recognised qualification, but there were two important consequences. First, the College marked up a number of notable successes in bi-lateral agreements with foreign ministries of education, thereby enabling students from many countries to qualify for university entry at home. Secondly, the scene was set for the development and adoption of the International Baccalaureate.

Already in October 1962 the Director of Studies, Robert Blackburn, had become Chairman of the UK section of the European Association of Teachers. From there it was a short step to a close working alliance with colleagues of the International School of Geneva. In 1962, these teachers had stimulated the International Schools Association (ISA) into holding a conference on history in international schools. In 1963, the UNESCO General Conference had passed a resolution inviting the ISA to investigate standards and curricula in international schools. In 1964, the International Schools Examinations Syndicate was established in Geneva to pursue these matters at the secondary level, the primary schools' curricula being left to the ISA; and in October 1965 30 experts from Europe, Asia and North American met to examine the broad principles of the proposed examinations in modern languages for the new Baccalaureate.

In 1966, Alec Peterson took a year's sabbatical leave from Oxford to become the first Director General of the newly-named International Baccalaureate Office. A major conference in Paris in 1967, with delegates from 11 countries, observers from UNESCO and the Council of Europe, and the directors of three important national examining boards (the French Baccalaureate, the London University GCE and the Advanced Placement Programme of the American College Entrance Examination Board), gave the whole project credibility and confidence. Trial examinations were prepared and written. For a while Atlantic College attempted a promising comparability study by requiring all its students to write the A Levels, the American Scholastic Aptitude and Achievement Tests, and the trial IB papers. Colleagues were frequently absent at 'important study meetings in Geneva'. One had the conviction of being in the forefront of something really important, and the aim of using the College as a field laboratory for experimental work in international education was transparently being achieved. The students, who were being asked to carry the burden of the staff enthusiasm, did not complain – indeed, they seemed to share the sense of excitement, albeit with less rhetoric!

The pace of development was intense. Given the very small number of schools involved at that stage, the College was represented on almost every subject panel set up to establish the original IB syllabuses. In many cases results had to be achieved within 48 hours. It was taken for granted that the participating schools covered the expenses of attendance – what was the alternative?

In September 1971 the College dropped the GCE Advanced Level examinations, the final session of A Level examinations taking place in the summer of 1972. The Atlantic College thereby became the first school in the world to abandon for all its pupils a national in favour of an international curriculum and examination. Honesty compels one to admit that the majority of parents, unfamiliar with both the English language and the English educational system, had little understanding of what was taking place, but their instinctive confidence in the College was not misplaced. The College staff nonetheless carried a heavy burden immediately following this change, since the International Baccalaureate Diploma enjoyed little recognition either in Britain or elsewhere in those early days. In close cooperation with the IB schools liaison officer, College staff engaged in intensive advocacy of the IB's merits through conferences and seminars held at the College and constant visits to university admissions officers. The lead given by the London School of Economics, the first UK university to commit itself to a formula for IB equivalence with the English system of A Levels, was invaluable. It is probably fair to claim that the confident and convincing lead and practical example given by the College were essential to the survival of the Diploma in Britain, arguably further afield as well.

The College may also take some satisfaction from its role in saving the IB infant in 1976. Alec Peterson as Director General sent a letter to IB Heads in May of that year, asking them to inform their Governing Bodies that the IB would be closing down for lack of funds; the last examination session would take place in 1977. A meeting of College Heads of Departments, the Bursar in attendance, flatly refused to accept this decision. The Bursar himself proposed that the College set an example by offering emergency stop-gap funding. Alec Peterson was urged by the College to call a meeting forthwith. This meeting took place in the first week of June; the IB Heads present guaranteed the necessary emergency funding from their school budgets; and it was decided on the spot to establish the Conference of IB Heads under the Chairmanship of the Director General

of the International School of Geneva, in order to enable the schools to become active partners in helping to avoid similar emergencies arising in the future. [●]

By the early 1970s, the Atlantic College numbered over 300 students and thereby offered for many years the largest single group of IB examination candidates. This fact gave the College an influential voice in IB developments. An early significant example was the introduction, following the suggestion of the College's Director of Studies, Andrew Maclehose, of the compulsory extended research essay for all diploma candidates in replacement of the long essay required as part of the examination requirement in a small number of subjects only, an arrangement that had exposed some students to a double long essay requirement, the majority to none. The combination of the extended essay requirement and the availability of the termly project weeks for individual or group research led to the introduction of the College *Science Project Journal*, guest edited by Professor Brian Brinkworth of Cardiff University.

This combination of extended essay and project week led to many significant pieces of work by students who went on to distinguished careers in science and medicine. Among them were Mary Jo Greenan, whose work on the identification of bacteria by bioluminescent techniques led to requests from 400 scientists around the world for her paper; Pedro Alonso, whose extended essay in biology was the first academic step towards his founding of the Manhica Health Research Centre in Mozambique where his current research into anti-malaria vaccines, supported by the Gates Foundation, has, experts say, the potential to save millions of lives; Patrik Brundin, his interest in Parkinson's disease stimulated by his father's illness, whose essay led on in a straight line to his professorship in neuroscience at Lund University in Sweden, the publication of over 300 scientific papers and the award of the European Research Council's Advanced Grant for 2010; and Tunde Morakinyo's essay on Welsh lichens which was recognised as a standard reference work and lodged in the National Museum of Wales.

High recognition for these activities was achieved with the decision of the Nobel Committee to invite the

[●] There were two further United World College interventions on behalf of IB finances, once (already mentioned) when Mountbatten as President of the UWC enabled Alec Peterson to secure the support of the Shah of Persia, and once when the Prince of Wales, also as President of the UWC, persuaded Armand Hammer to step in at a critical moment.

authors of the two best essays each year to attend the Nobel Ceremonies in Stockholm.

Another of the pioneering features of the International Baccalaureate, and still unique in pre-university education, was the course in the Theory of Knowledge. This study of the nature of knowledge, how it is acquired, retained and put to use in diverse areas of intellectual and practical activity, was a brilliantly skilful response to unwavering French insistence on the presence of philosophy in the curriculum. From the start it was compulsory for all Diploma candidates. For IB teachers at the College and elsewhere, it offered groundbreaking scope for bringing subject teachers together in a common syllabus that compelled real reflection on themes that gave their work both unifying and distinctive elements. The College staff was especially active in the development of this course, hosting conferences, drafting and testing a number of curriculum and assessment initiatives, and organising numerous summer schools. The College involvement was led principally by Andrew Maclehose, whose salary for a number of years was paid for this purpose by an industrialist anxious to promote innovative thinking skills in schools. Andrew was known for this time as the Comino Fellow in the Theory of Knowledge.

The College also had fine opportunities for developing its own internal school-based courses that, once accepted by the IB authorities, formed an integral part of the final diploma qualification. A syllabus that attempted to answer criticisms that the College (and the IB) gave too little attention to spiritual matters was entitled *The Religious Experience of Man*; it had a hard time achieving acceptance against the strong secular leanings of the French elements in the IB administration. The College's *Peace Studies* syllabus, enthusiastically promoted by the Peace Studies Department of the University of Bradford and supported by the Leverhulme Trust, became one of the activities in this field that was subjected to an unfriendly review in a publication *Peace Studies: A Critical Survey*, issued by the Institute for European Defence and Strategic Studies that clearly feared left-wing pacifist infiltration – *'the politicisation of education … the lowering of intellectual standards, and the assumption of foregone political conclusions'* – into British education. And their comment on the Atlantic College objectives: *'to condense a great amount of sentimental eyewash into a pinch of salt; the student should grow up.'* In subsequent correspondence the College Head, Andrew Stuart, suggested that it might have made sense if the two authors had visited the College to find out how the course was taught before attacking it. It is hard to envisage the United World Colleges fighting shy of issues

of this kind; even harder to imagine the students allowing themselves to become the victims of indoctrination from any direction. Most students on the course took part in joint study and community service visits to Belfast. The support of the Leverhulme Trust was achieved largely thanks to a strongly supportive letter from Mountbatten, who at the time was much involved in the work of SIPRI, the Swedish International Peace Research Institute. The course has meanwhile remained strong enough to attract participation by other schools.

The same teaching department, in those days called 'Study of Man', offered alongside a core syllabus of 20th-century global themes a range of options in 19th and 20th-century European, American, African and East Asian history at the IB Higher Level, leading to the setting of examinations in the last three areas for the first time. The head of the languages department, a specialist in German and Russian, introduced Chinese around this time, learning the language himself a few stages ahead of his classes and doing so, happily but by chance, shortly before the first Chinese students arrived. These academic developments encouraged the Kleinwort Benson Bank to sponsor a teacher and the setting up of a China-Japan Resource Centre at the College which worked up an IB Subsidiary Level course in Chinese Studies, ran a series of workshops for teachers from other schools, and offered lessons in East Asian studies to a number of local Welsh schools.

Political Thought and *Photographic Science* were further examples of successful staff innovation, as was too the very first new course set up by College staff: *Marine Science*, a natural development of the College's activities on the Bristol Channel. This course, with the addition of sub-aqua diving as a College activity, was to become a leading feature of College life.

A major achievement arising directly from marine science was the College's critical role in the setting up of Britain's first underwater marine reserve around the island of Lundy in the mouth of the Bristol Channel. A 33-foot enlarged version of the rigid inflatable was the transport vessel between the College and Lundy, and college students, trained in sub-aqua techniques, completed the plotting of the underwater geological formation known as the Knoll Pins, acknowledged by the Lundy Field Society as *'a brilliant contribution to increasing our knowledge of the richest area in the marine nature reserve … accurately and very competently executed …'* The Lundy involvement had followed a major scientific project on behalf of a governmental committee investigating the feasibility of a barrage across the River Severn for the generation of electricity. This year-long research project, intended to contribute to biological productivity in the Severn Sea, required the division of the coastal areas of the Channel into 1 kilometre squares and the collection of seaweed for later analysis along carefully laid transects at 10 metre intervals from the high watermark down to the lowest underwater depth at which it continued to exist before the lack of light prevented growth. A fascinating sideline of all this sub-aqua activity was the College training of deaf and dumb persons who, underwater and able to communicate readily and rapidly by sign language, found themselves for the first time in their lives at a clear advantage over their fellows. Several of them took part in the College's research activities on Lundy, and College students who learned the deaf and dumb language as a requirement for their involvement suddenly found it a useful means of communication across a crowded and noisy dining hall. The Marine Science course and its associated activities were made possible by a grant of £100,000 from British Petroleum.

This marriage of the sea, the boats, the diving, project weeks, extended essays and academic life in general helped to stimulate the later development of an IB course *Environmental Education*. It also provided the basis for the UNESCO Intergovernmental Oceanographic Publication on Marine Education.

BP also sponsored a research teacher for the development of *Maths Studies*, a course that helped to answer the problems posed by the IB insistence on mathematics as an examinable subject for all diploma students. Over a period of several years a new syllabus with accompanying pamphlets and teaching notes was worked up and made available, with guidance, for other IB schools.

In all these undertakings, the enthusiasm of the teaching staff was constantly refreshed by the stimulus of students from so many diverse academic and linguistic backgrounds and by the constant flow of international visitors, including two national ministers of education and numerous official delegations from ministries in other countries who came to be briefed on the IB, sat in on lessons and talked with staff and students.

The immense importance the College had given to its programmes of physical, cultural and service activities, all closely aligned with the Hahnian ethic as well as representing the wholehearted convictions of Desmond Hoare and all his staff, had an undeniable impact on the development of similar programmes in IB schools. Indeed, the IB Diploma was to be the first ever university entry qualification to require a proven participation in activities of this nature for all examination candidates. The explosion in community services in educational establishments

around the world owes much to this example. It is right, however, in this context to ally the name of Alec Dickson of Voluntary Service Overseas (VSO) and Community Service Volunteers with that of Kurt Hahn. His inspirational leadership in this matter, at Atlantic College, in other IB schools, in education generally across the world, runs the danger of becoming forgotten as service by young people approaches the status of a routine feature of schools and universities. Alec had a very distinct, strongly-accented diction that was extremely effective in public utterances but somewhat off-putting in private social conversation. Kurt told him on a visit to Salem in 1958 that, if he were ever appointed to the House of Lords, he must take the title *The Marquis of Emphasis*. He shared with Kurt Hahn a mastery of improvisation when the means to apply his idea were not readily available and, again to quote George Turner on Hahn, an acceptance of *'muddle ... derived from the accretive process of vigorous pioneering.'* He kept all the VSO files under his kitchen table!

One other initiative, based substantially on Atlantic College experience, was the proposal, formulated in comprehensive detail in 1998, for a Welsh Baccalaureate that would reflect the principal lessons of the IB in broadening the traditional A Levels curriculum with the intriguing addition of vocational options. The chief drafters were Colin Jenkins, the then Principal of the College, and John David, former Housemaster and Deputy Head at Atlantic College, later Head of Radyr Comprehensive School, with the close assistance and cooperation of the Institute of Welsh Affairs. At a late stage in the debate, this proposal was superseded by a more conservative scheme adopted by the Welsh Assembly government.

Extra-Mural Programmes, Music and the Arts Centre

The College's extra-mural activities were first launched in the summer of 1963 and were focused very intensely on the concept of coastal rescue by teenagers, a cause that Desmond Hoare had seized upon as the most significant contribution that Atlantic College could make to British national life.

As early as April 1964, the College had felt ready to hold a conference on Coast Rescue Services in the County of Glamorgan. Attended by representatives of the RNLI, HM Coastguard, RAF Mountain Rescue, the British Canoe Union, the St. John Ambulance Brigade, the Central Council of Physical Recreation, many local councils and the Chief Constable of the Glamorgan County Police, this meeting concluded that *'upwards of one thousand teenagers*

– boys and girls – could be fully committed to Coast Rescue in Glamorgan. This suggests at least twenty-five times that number for Britain as a whole, the engagement of twenty-five thousand young people to save the lives of some five hundred a year; each of these twenty-five thousand would have acquired First Aid and Life Saving skills which they could also use in the home, in industry and on the roads, where so many accidents occur. As parents, they would be likely in later life to encourage their children to acquire similar qualifications.'

And of course Desmond Hoare pressed the College case: *'the College is the only place in Britain presenting a fully coordinated Coast Rescue Service manned entirely by teenagers and safeguarding ten miles of coast'.* A few weeks later, he wrote to the Minister at the Department of Education and Science: *'As we see it, there is a real need for a focal point in Britain for teenage coast rescue development, and the Atlantic College fits this need … there is a virtually unlimited demand for training of young teachers, youth leaders, police cadets, etc., and our training facilities are only part used … there are some who are surprised that an all-sixth form international school, preparing boys for universities, should regard this development as one in which to play a part. Others see that our high academic intent is exactly the reason why we should seek, not just a part, but a leading part in a development affecting the human attitudes of youth at large. It is right that the brightest boys should be those most deeply committed in human affairs and that in their education they should share some of the resources given to them …'*

By 1968, the Extra-Mural Department had set up seven local lifeguard clubs and 29 lives had been saved; the numbers coming to college courses each summer had continued to rise. A Lifeguard Federation Committee was established under the Chairmanship of the Head of the City of London Police, Sir Arthur Young, which brought together the Surf Life Saving Association, the Royal Life Saving Society, the Royal National Lifeboat Institution, the British Canoe Union and HM Coastguard. At the same time the decision was taken to open the National Coast Rescue Training Centre at Aberavon, near Port Talbot, where exceptional facilities were already in place. For the first time there was to be a training centre available to all the relevant life-saving organisations for training, the study of methods and techniques and the development of equipment. The Director of this new Centre was Charles Thomson, who had been Director of Activities at the College from the beginning and was now to become a major figure in the world of life-saving in Britain.

This transfer of activity elsewhere challenged the College to re-think the nature of its extra-mural responsibilities.

Artur Rubinstein visiting the College with Polish students before giving his recital in the Bradenstoke Hall on the Steinway grand piano donated by Sonny and Phebe Maresi

A cautious start was made with the assumption of extra-mural development by a Housemaster, Jeremy Rowe. His work rapidly made clear that there was a high demand both for the facilities and the expertise that the College could offer to an enormous range of young people with, in time, a special emphasis on the disabled, the socially deprived and those who had acquired delinquent records with the police.

It was the College's first Director of Music, the distinguished composer John Metcalf, who recognised the opportunity of securing initial funding for the renovation, first of the Tythe Barn, later of the Cavalry Barracks at the sea front, through governmental funding for the training 'on the job' of young unemployed people. This opening was then fully exploited by the College Bursar Ron Cornelius in the complete renovation and redevelopment of the entire sea area, including the building of the new swimming pools, thanks also to really substantial new funding by Sonny and Phebe Maresi.

No doubt partly as a consequence of the introduction of co-education, social service – work with the physically and mentally diaabled, the elderly and the socially deprived – added an important new dimension to the College's hitherto physical coast rescue expression of community service. On the environmental side, the creation of a small College farm gave an outlet for those with horticultural and livestock interests. And John Metcalf dreamed up and brought into being not only the Annual (and still flourishing) Vale of Glamorgan Festival of Modern Music, but also the St. Donat's Arts Centre in the centuries-old, now restored Tythe Barn. Artur Rubinstein gave a recital for the College in the Bradenstoke Hall on 4th October 1974, commenting afterwards that he had never played to an audience *'with more pleasure and sense of communication'*. He became a Patron of the Arts Centre, to be joined shortly afterwards by the French playwright Eugene Ionesco.

John Metcalf brought new standards and sophistication to the College's musical life, but the first choir under John Lello (membership compulsory for all and, in good Welsh tradition, 'all male'), had been an impressive and above all enjoyable start. And at least the vigour of the students' musical endeavours (post-Lello) comes through in the published review of the South Wales music critic A. J. Sicluna: *'Verdi, Bach, Britten and Brahms – the College choir waded into every piece with utter assurance … I have no doubt that choruses by Verdi from Rigoletto and the Force of Destiny would have sounded completely different had they simply been sung in tune.'*

The renovated Cavalry Barracks has provided the perfect site for a permanent hostel and accommodation for staff. In 1979, the year in which the restored Cavalry Barracks became available, the renamed Extra-Mural Centre provided 14 residential courses for Local Education Authorities for disadvantaged children, three courses in probation and after-care, and a total of 57 other courses for charitable organisations from Belfast, Birmingham, Bridgend, Lewisham, London, Oxford and Wales. The clearly emerging priority and need was work for youngsters at risk, of which the so-called Intermediate Treatment and Aftercare Services were the principal feature.

With this work the Extra-Mural Centre became one of the most distinctive features of the College, possibly an example for other residential schools to emulate.

Some Personal Memories of Guest Speakers

Thanks often to the influence and personal contacts of distinguished Governors, the Atlantic College students benefited from an extraordinarily rich flow of visitors. It is almost a truism that great leaders of advanced years draw immense strength from a supportive interaction with young people. Even a Mountbatten, as we have seen above, was critically affected by the nature of his relationship with them. Many distinguished men and women were quite ready to make the long journey down to St. Donat's, responding to the proclaimed ideals and curious to encounter the reality.

I found few occasions more rewarding that sitting quietly in the background as College students engaged guest lecturers in informal discussion after the main event. My two most memorable encounters in this context were the visits of Father Trevor Huddleston and the war hero, holder of the Victoria Cross and founder of the Cheshire Homes, Leonard Cheshire.

I have seen no more expressive face than that of Trevor Huddleston, deeply lined, sunk in absent repose until the question was out; then shining eyes, a total absorption in the questioner and his concerns, to fall again into complete repose until the next question was put. This meeting was marked by long periods of deeply reflective silence. Leonard Cheshire had been the British observer aboard an accompanying aircraft when the atom bomb was dropped on Hiroshima. The students confidently expected a condemnation of the dropping of the bomb and its successor

Leonard Cheshire visits the College

on Nagasaki. They were confronted by a detailed exposé on the dilemma facing US President Truman and the almost unimaginable cost in American lives, had the Allied Forces been compelled to conquer the Japanese forces island by island. [•] And when they engaged him in discussion on the severely sick and handicapped people for whom his homes provided care, he again took them aback by stating with firmness that the greatest tragedy was that of a young and fit person who, through an accident such as diving into shallow water, was in a split second condemned to a lifetime of paralysis. Prince Sadruddin Aga Khan when UN High Commissioner for Refugees spent three days at the College as a Visiting Fellow and moved the students with his frank confession of deep disappointment when he failed to achieve election as UN Secretary General, his life's ambition. Thor Heyerdahl accompanied Mountbatten to the College, assured the surprised students that he far preferred his rafts to their swift rigid hulled inflatable lifeboats, and subsequently invited two Atlantic graduates to join his crew for his final raft voyage, that of the *Tigris* in 1978, for his 6,800-kilo-metre voyage down Shatt-el-Arab in Iraq to the Persian Gulf, out into the Indian Ocean, then via Muscat in Oman to the Indus Valley in Pakistan, before finally leaving Asia and crossing the Indian Ocean to Africa.

But what are we trying to do anyway?

I borrow, with his permission, this heading from a paper written in October 1990 by Ted Lockwood, the Founder President (Head) of what was then called the Armand Hammer United World College of the American West.

[•] Leonard Cheshire has in fact given a clear and balanced summary of his views in *The Spectator* in August 1965: 'to those who dropped the atom bomb, only two questions mattered. Would the bomb end the war? Would it cost fewer lives than the alternative, an all-out invasion of Japan? Undeniably the answer to both questions was yes; and, therefore, undeniably the bomb was right. Today the emphasis has shifted. It is the dead of Hiroshima and Nagasaki, not the suffering that the world was spared … who have become the one lasting reality … which of these two views, one may ask, is right? … In my opinion, neither … the honour of the cause for which we were fighting demanded that we should give the enemy at least one chance to think twice – by dropping the bomb offshore, or something of the sort. Because we did not give them that chance, both our own honour and the justice of our cause have been degraded in the eyes of the world.'

Peter Jolley, a senior member of the Atlantic College staff in 1962 who was later to lead the UWC of South East Asia in Singapore, was very strongly committed to the concept of comprehensive, all-ability schooling in Britain. He was clear about his expectations of the United World Colleges. *'I have always envisaged the Central Organisation of United World Colleges not as the guardian of a fixed model but as a powerhouse of ideas, a kind of resources centre for those who want to venture into interna-tional education …'*

Desmond Hoare's record in his Provost role after giving up the Atlantic headship illustrates how powerfully and rapidly his restless mind moved to new priorities. One had the sense when he returned from his long journeys to Asia that he was discovering the world anew. Jeremy Rowe, an Atlantic College housemaster with years of African experience, once said of him that he understood very little about the third world countries but *'by goodness, could he enthuse students about their problems!'* No one will now quarrel with Desmond's efforts to realign the movement away from its previous European/North American/Atlantic Alliance axis. *'The situation is now entirely different and the main cockpit of the world is the Pacific basin in which the four great powers (of today) USA, Russia, China and Japan confront each other with India not far away. Yet UWC policy seems to me to be largely stuck in old thinking with the first priority being given to setting up schools in Europe and North America. Some of the practical consequences seem absurd. We plan now to set up a school in the USA where the running costs will be highest of any country in the world; we plan to build one in Canada where building and running costs will also be at peak level. In Europe we choose the most expensive country (Germany) we could find in that continent. Are we perhaps thinking more in terms of the interests of our elderly generation rather than in the interests of the young generations to come?'*

And in his attempts to win over the UWC hierarchy to the cause of the world's suffering and hungry populations in Asia and Latin America, he invoked the spirit of Kurt Hahn in an essay written shortly after Hahn died in 1974: *'if his strength had lasted another ten years he would, I am sure, be pushing the Atlantic College project into the problems of 1980, especially the problem of hunger in the Third World. His passion for rescue as an educational force could not have led him elsewhere.'*

A good Irish friend and admirer of his who also did a teaching spell at Pearson College, Tom McGelligott, echoed some of Desmond's worries some years later, in August 1984, in the journal *Education*: *'The existing colleges are almost all extravagantly impressive and this in itself may discourage the building of new ones.* [●] ... *Where to site the new ones may be less of a problem than to what standards they should be built ... excellent as it (IB) undoubtedly is as an examination, it does pose the question whether the study of a limited number of subjects is the ideal preparation for the kind of flexibility needed for living in the contemporary world ... have the colleges settled for a safe academic approach and are they in danger of becoming colleges for the middle and upper classes in which middle class values will predominate and middle class power be preserved?'*

In his efforts to put his own personal mark on the movement Prince Charles, as we have seen, went down the environmental road, but it has not been followed. Ted Lockwood was forthright in identifying the fault lines. *'Have the original aims'*, he asked in 1989, *'lost their pertinence, piquancy, eloquence and purchase on world issues? ... The most pressing of the environmental issues concerning energy, pollution and resources remind us promptly that anyone interested in longer term solutions must appreciate the political factors ... the United World Colleges ... cultivate an awareness of complexity; they foster the concept of service on behalf of the less fortunate; and they insist on the freedom to probe for solutions to the critical issues before us ...'*

And a year later he returned in even stronger terms to the political potential of the UWC task: the constructive use of power, awareness of the world political situation, the understanding of complexity, honing of the mind, an international perspective, a rigorous academic programme, freedom of enquiry, cultural interaction, personal growth, a commitment to action. *'What distinguishes these goals? First, they do not prescribe necessarily what physical and mental skills are desirable; they do not automatically establish a curriculum; and they are limited by neither time nor location. They are aspirations and they are attitudes. To some they are distant hopes; to others they define the goals as much by what they emphasise as by what they preclude, like vocational training.'*

And Ted concludes with some points that may well merit some reflection today.

> *'Physical well-being: singularly neglected, outside the infirmary, both as a goal and as a practice.*

[●] Atlantic College students of the time may not agree. The overriding physical impact was, it is true, that of the historic castle buildings and the dramatic site. The teaching accommodation was much as would be found in a British state school. Student accommodation, mostly four to a room with old army beds, was basic. A key element was the provision of family accommodation for almost all the teaching staff on site.

> *Personal traits of honesty, integrity, etc. ... we assume that the virtues will be absorbed but never confronted firmly. Moral education is too far down the list ...*
> *Quality of life* (here a respectful nod in the direction of Desmond Hoare): *as these are expensive colleges offering a distinguished programme, they should be special communities, not reflecting society but offering a model to inspire society ... there may well be a structural fault in the design in this regard. More self-help? Fewer amenities?'*

Has there, I wonder today, been a slackening in the pace and vigour of policy debate? And if so, is this because it is fully clear where we are going? For my own part, I find it much easier now to make observations, much more difficult to draw conclusions. When we started at Atlantic College 50 years ago, I could not really see what was happening, or why, but I was sure I knew where we were going.

Additional International Development and Concluding Reflections

The 1990s saw several projects come to fruition under the Board Chairmanship of Mark Hoffman: 1992 the Li Po Chun College of Hong Kong, 1995 the Red Cross United World College in Norway, 1997 the Mahindra United World College of India. 1995 was the year when Nelson Mandela accepted the Presidency of the International Council, HM Queen Noor the Presidency of the UWC Movement. Vigorous but unsuccessful efforts were made to launch a College project in Jordan for the Middle East, the Israeli UWC National Committee having agreed that the lead should be taken by their neighbours. More College founding activity took place in the 2000s, with the United World Colleges in Mostar (Bosnia and Herzegovina) and of Costa Rica opening within days of each other in 2006. The UWC of Maastricht in The Netherlands followed in 2009.

The 50th Anniversary of Atlantic College in 2012 thus witnesses a dramatic story of growth, not least because most colleges also run their own summer and extra-mural programmes, and because certain National Committees, in addition to selecting and in some cases funding students to attend colleges, also organise short courses, often for those who have narrowly missed college selection. Others are determined to found colleges in their own countries. It has become an inescapable consequence that the issues of international governance and above all of scholarship funding have simultaneously grown immensely in complexity. Colleges struggle to maintain their scholarship base. The worldwide impact of globalisation has endorsed

Javier Pérez de Cuéllar, UN Secretary General, on a College visit, with the Principal Andrew Stuart and UWC Director General Ian Gourlay

in dramatic degree the early initiatives. What are the new challenges? The task of maintaining a front line position in international education is severe.

Fifty years is also a time for reflection in addition to celebration. These years have brought magnificent life opportunities for our students but also confronted them with painful dilemmas. None of those who were present at the College debate in the old, not yet restored Tythe Barn on the morality of political assassination will forget the long silence that followed the challenge to the College's one black student: *'Would you have wielded the knife that killed the South African Premier Verwoerd?'* or the almost inaudible sincerity of his quietly spoken, affirmative response.

Our Argentinian student Jorge Born wrote to me in 1982, just as we were moving from Wales to Italy and Margaret Thatcher was readying her Task Force to retake the Falklands: *'during this last week, I've been receiving very distressing news from my country. All young men born in 1962 have been called into the army. Most of my friends are under arms. As you may see, I'm forced to choose – either defend my country if need be or follow my deeply entrenched principle of internationalism. As an ex-student of Atlantic College the latter should be the option, but as a national of Argentina the former path seems more appropriate. During this week's turmoil, my Atlantic College experience has been dominant. I will never be able to put up a finger against UK, which received me and kept me so well whilst I was a student at AC. My doubt is, how strong can my feelings be for international understanding, if war is declared and my friends and relatives are ordered to fight. This is followed by a second doubt, namely how practical is it, in the short term, to think about the ideals so cherished by the UWC organisation? In the long term, I have no doubt, they will succeed, but what sort of sacrifices are we expected to make so that these ideals become realities?'* A letter many years later in *The Times* of 16th November 1998 may have given him some comfort: *'I fully concur with the feelings expressed by Sir Ian (Gourlay), his remembrance of the dead on both sides in a futile war and with his emphasis*

on the Argentine and British flags flying together over the college's ancient walls ...' It was signed by Carlos Menem, the President of the Argentine Republic.

Timothy Knatchbull, who attended the College a year or so later than Jorge, was the surviving grandson of Lord Mountbatten whose twin brother Nick died in the bomb blast that also killed Mountbatten and others in the summer of 1979, the victims of the Irish Republican Army. In his moving account of the attack, and of his long, painful efforts to come to terms with the loss above all of his brother, Timothy recalls the College in which *'peace was given an extra chance through the helping hand of an international approach to education ... critics lampooned it as at best impractical, at worst a dangerous piece of elitism ...'* but for him it was *'a place of dazzling diversity and giddy idealism.'* [●] He recalls especially a lecture on Ireland in which the speaker, James Hawthorne, Head of the BBC in Northern Ireland, had said that *'peace in Ireland would ultimately come from a marriage of the Catholic and Protestant communities. There could be no marriage until there was an engagement; before that a courtship was needed; and prior to that a friendship. First, he said that they had to get to know each other.'* Ireland has a special and a tragic significance for Timothy, but these words are not a bad description of the task of the Atlantic College.

The rigid-hulled inflatable lifeboats developed at Atlantic College so successfully in the 1960s are now used the world over, for all to see. The educational accomplishments are in the nature of things less tangible, more open to debate and to the diversity of human judgement, their success however to some extent measurable by the growth from one to 12 colleges and the existence of some 130 national and selection committees across the globe. This brief, anecdotal account of the early years has omitted many personalities and many events, and it has made no attempt to assess the impact of the College experience on the students and their later lives. An authoritative, comprehensive review with appropriate documentation and statistical detail must await a more official historian. As to the later colleges, it will be for others who know and who love them to tell their stories. But the one common thread that for me clearly united those early pioneers is that they were all fighters – and, to borrow a word from Robert Louis Stevenson's *Kidnapped*, 'bonny' fighters – for causes. It is our good fortune that one of the causes they chose and treasured most highly was that of the United World Colleges.

[●] Timothy Knatchbull: *From a Clear Blue Sky* Arrow Books 2010

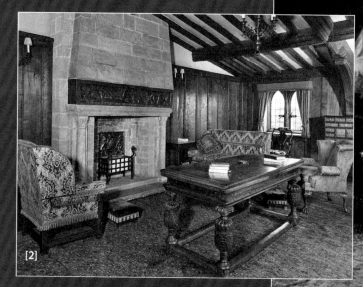

[1] *A bird's eye view of the entrance and inner courtyard*

[2] *A Hearst sitting room, later the College history department*

[3] *The Hearst games room, later part of the College library*

[4] *The historic Great Hall, later the admirable staff common room*

[5] *The Hearst Banqueting Hall, later the College dining hall*

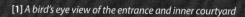

[4]

[5]

Kurt Hahn

'Build up the imagination of the boy of decision and the willpower of the dreamer, so that in future wise men will have the nerve to lead and men of action will have the vision to imagine the consequences of their actions.'
Kurt Hahn

The Founding Achievement

Often in the past, and until I began preparing this memoir, I have had a glib statement ready when asked about the relationship between the Atlantic College and Kurt Hahn. It ran: *'Without him we would not have been born; with him we could not have survived'*. I was influenced by Desmond Hoare who in his final years told me: *'He was once my guru'*; and by our early need to distinguish ourselves clearly from Gordonstoun School and from Outward Bound. Even within the past few weeks I have been asked by Cambridge University contemporaries whether 'my' Atlantic College Outward Bound School still exists.

My glibness has, I believe, a sufficient kernel of truth with which to launch this memoir, but the College's 50th anniversary is a good moment to reflect on both the nature of the founding achievement and elements in Hahn's educational principles that we may, at some cost to ourselves, now be ignoring.

The Atlantic College project, as it was known in its early days, was a natural progression in Hahn's educational vision, even if it had to shed some of the Hahnian baggage. In their efforts to draw together the threads in Hahn's ideas, to underline the common themes, well-intentioned admirers fail, I think, to recognize that he had many different groups of young people in mind. I can remember telling him that there was a restaurant in Cambridge (I think my imagination was running away with me) with a central kitchen and two

dining areas in close but different streets, the one serving Indian, the other Chinese food. *'Wonderful'*, he said in those unforgettable guttural tones. *'Just like my schools.'*

The headlong expansion of international schools in the past two decades has, for many, pushed to one side the historical interest of nations in defining and protecting their identity and culture through education. The acquisition of 'international competencies' has become the aim; and the market-driven nature of the vast majority of international schools, fee-paying and serving large business and diplomatic communities 'on the spot', is pushing towards convergence in outlook and practice in a manner comparable with the equally market-driven pressures in the learning of English – who is not familiar with the HSBC advertisement that more people are learning English in China than live in England?

Let us therefore place Hahn in his time and context and try to understand his national with his political background, the conclusions he drew, and their implications for us today.

But first: *'Without him we would not have been born.'*

The First Steps 1955–1962

In 1955, two years after a painful and humiliating separation from Gordonstoun, Hahn was intensely immersed in the expansion of Outward Bound, the launch of the Duke of Edinburgh's Award Scheme, and the Trevelyan Scholarships for entry to Oxford and Cambridge. His hopes for a European, initially Anglo-German Department at Gordonstoun, had by now faded into oblivion. The lightning bolt, the electrifying inspiration, which hit him on a lecture visit to the NATO Defense College, turned him, not back to Gordonstoun, but towards a true innovation in education: a staff college for teenagers. The NATO Defense College, modelled on British staff college experience, brought together senior NATO officers for a period of intensive, cooperative learning with fellow-officers from other countries and different armed forces, many of them having been opponents in the recent war. If the courses were academic (in the military sense), the lessons learned were in human relations and human attitudes. The British Sixth Form with its distinctive two-year duration provided the perfect formula for the transfer of the concept into pre-university education. And it is this staff college concept that explains why our Atlantic College education precedes university, for it is at the Sixth Form stage and the age of 16 to 19 that adolescents are at their most open, curious, formative, yes idealistic, for it is now that they are entering adulthood and, not yet committed to a particular course of studies or career, are open-mindedly seeking their way forward in life.

If the timing was politically right – the growing intensity of the Cold War, the accelerating awareness that two incompatible ways of life must resolve their differences peacefully if the world were not to disappear in a nuclear holocaust, the critical importance of maintaining morale in the western world – it was also the right time in Hahn's life. He was at the height of his powers. He had shed administrative responsibilities. His authority, stemming from his achievements since the Second World War, had secured him, not an uncritical mass audience but individual admirers of passion and influence. In Britain these were above all the allies he had made in Oxford, Cambridge and British industry on behalf of Outward Bound and the Trevelyan Scholarships; and in the United States, supporters of Outward Bound and the members of the American-British Foundation for European Education, set up by him to fund new boarding schools, Outward Bound schools and sail training vessels in post-war Germany.

Hahn's fundraising skills were much practised and finely honed. *'A good retriever must go into many thickets'.* *'Sponsors can only be influenced by the seductive sound of a bandwagon. We must not build on good will alone; we have to rely on supporting lesser motives. Recognition is vital.'* And he also knew the importance of patience: *'The response at the luncheon in New York exceeded our expectations but this was a sowing, not a harvesting operation.'*

But if there is one lesson to be learned here, it is that courage, persistence and total confidence in the outcome are inseparable from successful fundraising, and especially for a concept that is new, unproven, and a challenge to existing practice. The small informal team that carried the Atlantic College message from 1956 until 1962 – Eric Warburg, Lawrance Darvall, Desmond Hoare, Alexander Fleck of ICI, Walter Benton Jones of United Steel, the Chairman of Outward Bound Spencer Summers – all turned to Hahn at every single stage for guidance and encouragement. It is inconceivable that, either singly or together, they could have accomplished the task without him.

Fifty years on it is perhaps natural, looking back, to assume some all-embracing Hahn doctrine that the Atlantic College could achieve much to overcome religious, cultural and racial misunderstanding if young people from all over the world could be brought together at this impressionable age. In reality, he was far more sharply focused; and I strongly doubt whether so generalised an aspiration could have either motivated him or secured him the necessary support.

Kurt Hahn's Family Life in Berlin

Kurt Hahn was born into a prosperous Jewish family in Berlin in 1886. On his father's side his people were successful self-made merchants and businessmen from eastern Germany, his grandfather and father strong anglophiles. The Hahns' home and receptions were a dazzling focal point of Berlin society. Younger relatives have recalled them with nostalgic admiration: *'Well-known scholars, politicians and artists … from this circle flowed human warmth … a wide view of the world … like the intellectual atmosphere of the Berlin of the days before the First World*

Kurt the schoolboy, his long, fine hands already a distinguishing feature

Father Oscar Hahn with the brothers Franz (left) and Kurt

Kurt's mother, Charlotte Hahn

Growing older, but still a sailor

War, the atmosphere of the parental home was at once German and cosmopolitan.' [1]

His mother, with her elegance, beauty, charm and musical talent, was a magnet for all. *'She read philosophical books seriously and played the piano perfectly. The nature of her influence on others was an art in itself; the magic of allurement towards the good.'* [2] Artur Rubinstein, then a poor young boy struggling to make his way, had his first introduction to Brahms from her. *'Lotte Hahn loved chamber music. She opened the world for me to Brahms by playing his quartets in A major and C minor one afternoon with a good ensemble. I cannot describe the enthusiasm with which I listened to this music. She noticed my rapt attention, made me stay on when the others left, and played other Brahms' piano pieces to me which only increased my love and understanding for him.'* [3] She was, he wrote in his memoirs, *'a radiant lady in her mid-thirties, a pianist of notable talent who would without doubt have achieved much – without her riches, her husband and her children.'* [4] The great pianists Artur Schnabel and Edwin Fischer were also frequent house guests and performers.

Rubinstein also remembered Kurt for the reading circle he led: *'This circle was run in a professional manner, following the example of the Comédie Francaise as an independent association. The roles were decided by voting that could not be challenged; protests were not allowed … over time we became lively and vivid role players.'* [5] *'Kurt,* (of course, one feels) *always played the noble hero. It was not possible for him to be anything else.'* [6]

But Kurt Hahn's father was to die young, at 49, an elder brother at 11. Kurt, one might say, entered education early, for he felt himself wholly responsible for the healthy development of his fatherless younger brother Rudo. *'Renne schneller als Du kannst'* – run faster than you can – remains his most quoted advice to Rudo. He adored and admired his mother, the closeness of this relationship providing later psychologists with quotable material for controversial interpretations of his emotional life. *'Die Mutter',* he once said to me at a difficult moment, *'muss man ehren'.* *'One must honour one's mother.'* One of his early essays on education carries this handwritten inscription: *'To my best friend, my conscience and my guardian, my beloved mother, who is always present in me whenever I do or think the right thing.'* [7]

His was unquestionably a happy, high-spirited childhood, with explorations of the countryside around the Wannsee Lake, hunting, rowing, theatre performances with original Hahn and family scripts, and practical jokes. An English friend wrote to him in 1919: *'Do you remember the evening when you rowed across to us in your little boat through the mist and rain?'* And Katia Mann, the wife of Thomas Mann, wrote to him much later, in 1955: *'You are quite certainly no stranger for me. I have such lively memories still of our childhood days together on the Wannsee – you were several years younger than I – I can see you still as the wonderfully handsome boy you were in those days … and then came the years when we shared the anxieties over Golo.'* [8]

School was another matter. It was the formal, sternly-disciplined Kaiser Wilhelm Gymnasium, and its contrast with the high-spirited spontaneity and enthusiasm of life outside school, that inspired Kurt Hahn with his life-long antagonism to education based on academic activity alone. He later gave expression to his feelings in a novel *Frau Elses Verheissung* (*Frau Elsa's Promise*), which achieved a favourable review from the writer Herman Hesse, who commented that it had been written by an author who had not forgotten what childhood was about.

The Illness that Changed his Life

'*I will,*' he confided to private papers, '*never forget 4th July 1904.*'

The day before, he had played the fairy prince in a play written for him and had declaimed with a conviction that struck all: '*The girl with the voice that can sing the song will be my wife or I shall never marry.*' [9] Now, at a sports gathering and as he crossed the line as the victor in the 100 metre sprint, he sought the girl with the voice and won a rejoicing, encouraging smile in response. '*I was 18 years old and was tasting for the first time a great passion and felt with all the high spirits and strength of youth the promise of a victorious life.*' [10]

Four days later he rowed across the Havel on what, it was later reported, was the hottest day for 100 years. Throwing himself exhausted on the river bank, he awoke after half an hour with strong pains in the back of his head but managed to row back home. Sternly warned by his uncle, a Berlin doctor, to remain indoors for several days, he ignored this instruction and set out the following afternoon in the family dog cart to keep an appointment with his fairy princess. After four kilometres, pain forced him home. From then until October he was unable to go out in the day, tormented by sharp pain and sudden awakenings at night. He had become an invalid.

There now began his ten-year, unsuccessful struggle to achieve a university degree.

The Hahns' summer home on the Wannsee, his father's creation, was almost a piece of England – extensive lawns, a rose garden, tennis courts and a croquet green, stables and orchards. It was a given that Kurt should study in Oxford although not, as many have subsequently assumed, as a Rhodes Scholar.

The first winter term at Christ Church College passed off well enough in the hesitant English sun, but the return to Berlin brought yet worse nightly pain. His symptoms were dismissed by the family as psychological. There was however no respite. In the spring of 1906 he was forced to abandon his written examinations in Oxford in growing despair at an inability to concentrate, harassed by mental bewilderment, even the inability to articulate his words clearly. His features, he wrote, became slack and drawn, and Oxford friends took to imitating 'Hahn after having been in the sun'. He made spasmodic efforts to study from home on dull days at the University of Berlin. Four specialists, including his two medical uncles, the surgeon Professor Leopold Landau, who was President of the Berlin Medizinische Gesellschaft, and the hygienist Martin Hahn, now declared him to be suffering from neurasthenia, or mental debility. It was a diagnosis that was to pursue him mercilessly throughout his life. Most bitter of all was his mother's refusal to accept that her beloved son could be anything other than vigorous, healthy, and above all psychologically irreproachable. She sent him out into the sun time and again. The consequences were disastrous.

Kurt Hahn as the Prince, Lili du Bois-Reymond as the good witch in Lili's fairy play The Bartered Princess. *This must have been the last occasion when Kurt took part in family theatre before his illness.*

We have a pitiful insight into his condition around this time. He was being dispatched by an increasingly desperate, bewildered family to the mountains for bracing physical rest cures and to psychiatrists for mental treatment. One such treatment assigned him to a stay in the renowned clinic of the legendary Dr. Oskar Kohnstamm in Konigstein on the Taunus, thought by some recent inventive literati to have provided the real-life personalities for the cast of Thomas Mann's *Der Zauberberg*. Dr. Kohnstamm, Hahn recalls, *'… was a man of unusual powers of suggestion. It was easy for him to persuade me, as he did all his other patients, to direct the emphasis of our attention to the psychical elements of our complaints. He was a particularly spirited advocate of the theory that all functions of the body are decisively influenced by the psyche, and so it was natural for him not to take the physical basis of symptoms of illness seriously until the treatment of the soul had failed. I was at the time only too ready to place those gifts for autosuggestion that were available to me at the disposal of his theories, that is to say, my readiness to do so lasted only until the undeniable consequences of the sun stroke set in again in their usual crescendo. This coming to my senses was eased for me by the knowledge that a lady patient in the sanatorium died of cancer who, until very shortly before her demise, had been treated by psychotherapy.'* [11]

Dr. Kohnstamm's son Peter, paying a return visit to his childhood home in 1985, has described suddenly halting at door number 31.0.7 on one of the lower floors. *'The room behind is used today as a store for cleaning materials. It has no window. This is where the patient Hahn was accommodated. He was suffering from a heavy psychosis against light. The only source of light he accepted was a candle. His food was brought to his door. Dr. Kohnstamm strictly forbade me to open the door to visit Herr Hahn, something we did with other patients, often with playmates from the street.'* [12]

This and subsequent exposure to psychiatric treatment involving the use of multi-coloured lamps, a large revolving magnet and electrical currents, treatment, he noted, that was also applied to morphine addicts and drunkards, must have done much to determine Kurt Hahn's life-long distrust of psychotherapy in education. He was left to return to what his family saw as his *'stubborn infatuation with my illness'*. [13]

No appreciation of Hahn's personality, life or work is complete without an awareness of the implications of these early experiences. He was never able to free himself entirely from suggestions of mentally indulging his inability to withstand sunshine or heat. His precautions – his enormous hats, his sun topee in which he would join hockey games in Salem, his throwing open of windows to admit fresh air whatever the temperature, the drapery with which he

surrounded his face and shoulders when travelling by car and aeroplane in his late years, the darkness of the rooms in which he worked – suggested to lazy observers and superficial commentators a somewhat sinister presence. He suffered from these misunderstandings all his life, as he had suffered from his mother's inability to accept that her son was anything other than robustly healthy. But they were to cast the mould of his personality, to give him deep insights into human strength and weakness, and to nurture qualities of self-discipline whose severity were to strike some as almost unnatural. They were also to make him an essentially lonely man.

Loneliness! As late as 1950 he was writing to Minna Specht, the Head of the Odenwald school in Germany whom he greatly respected although he had little time for the principles and practices of the school: *'Both harmonies, to echo Plato, ought to find their rightful place in the life of the young: the Doric and the Phrygian … you will perhaps be surprised when I tell you that the Phrygian harmony has played the greater role on my life, especially in that fruitful period of my development, when a serious illness forced me to avoid the daylight for several months and I was left with no alternative but to submit myself to self-examination. I believe that certain truths about human nature were thereby revealed to me …;'* [14] and to another: *'I owe the stronger part of my nature not only to the compelling circumstances of illness and misfortune, but to the misunderstandings I encountered from people I loved.'* It became of high importance to him to accustom his pupils to 'aloneness'. They must try to understand that, if they were lonely in their own company, they were spiritually impoverished.

Not long before his father's death, a new consultant, an expert on tropical diseases and with extensive experience in the colonies, was to conduct a lumbar puncture and to give Kurt Hahn the first solid evidence that his condition had a physical cause, that there was an organic reason for his troubles. It was the first encouragement he received to resist the family's growingly hostile scepticism and to develop a style of life that took open account of his problems. He began rowing long hours by night on the Havel, discovered that sweating after physical exertion relieved the pressure in his head, developed the ability to cat-nap that he retained throughout his life and from which he drew disproportionate refreshment, and forewent meat in favour of fruit and vegetables. The many, colleagues and pupils, who found themselves in later years accompanying Kurt Hahn on evening runs through shaded woodlands, or playing tennis with him after sunset, or longing in vain for some good red meat at his table, often took a self-conscious pride in sharing briefly these apparent eccentricities. They were for him the essential conditions for his ability to live and work.

The Inspiration to Heal

There was one more life-transforming experience in these early years. In 1909 he was following classical studies at the University of Göttingen. His cousin, the Göttingen Mathematics Professor Martin Landau, was married to the daughter of the Nobel Laureate and immunologist Paul Ehrlich. Kurt Hahn revered this eminent scientist for qualities that he was to idealise and to covet for himself. His description of the discoverer of Salvarsan, the first treatment effective against syphilis, is self-revealing: *'I had listened to him with hero-worship and excited participation as he, half lost in thought, gave news of the victorious progress of his research … I felt his fears and his hopes for suffering mankind … the rapt absorption which could become complete absence of mind … the dull, colourless eyes, which would suddenly light up in a sacred will to save, as the certainty grew in him that his intuition had reached its target …'* [15] Kurt Hahn even maintains that he was one of the first to hear, from Ehrlich, the word *Zauberkugel*, the "silver bullet", that became so important a contribution to modern chemotherapy. Shortly before Christmas that year, Ehrlich's 4-year-old grandson died of diphtheria. Hahn was in the home of the parents, helping where he could. Ehrlich himself was inconsolable, sunken almost into unconsciousness. Hahn was watching over him, unable to elicit any response, when the postman arrived with a postcard for the stricken grandfather. Glancing hopelessly at it, Ehrlich sprang up: *'Kurt, I have conquered syphilis. Read this!'* His colleague Iversen, the Director of the Obuchow Hospital in St. Petersburg, had achieved complete success in 70 of 90 cases with injections of the compound 606, arsphenamine, or Salvarsan. *'Ehrlich was restored again. The blessing of healing had renewed his will to live.'* [16]

From this moment on, Ehrlich took a fatherly interest in his studies and his health, engagingly reciting his own failures and successes in his medical researches, and insisted that Kurt accompany him to a celebratory dinner in Berlin offered by his senior medical colleagues. And as they descended from their carriage after the dinner at which Ehrlich had given a major address, they were approached in the dark by an elderly bearded man who, unable to find words, embraced Ehrlich in tears – it was his former teacher of anatomy. These were powerful experiences for a young man whose vocation, fatefully threatened by ill-health, was to educate. For Hahn, to educate is to heal. He wanted his schools to be centres of healing in their neighbourhoods.

Plato

Hahn was a university student from 1904 until 1914. His recurrent ill health not only prevented him from ever entering an examination hall; he moved constantly, as was and to an extent remains German practice, from one university to another: Oxford, Göttingen, Berlin, Freiburg, Heidelberg. But the theme of his studies remained consistent: classical languages, art history and philosophy. And it was from these studies that he derived his early ideas on education. For the rest of his life he quoted Plato as his master, with wisdom selectively.

One robust commentator on Plato [●], pointing out that the *Republic 'has been … the trusted companion of educators and reformers, and men with their finger firmly on the pulse of government and current affairs'*, adds that *'its apparent political implications are mainly disagreeable, and often appalling … in so far as Plato has a legacy in politics, it includes theocracy or rule by priests, militarism, nationalism, hierarchy, illiberalism, totalitarianism, and the complete disdain of the economic structures of society'*; further, *'Plato's high summer, in England at least, lay in the golden glow of the late Victorian and Edwardian age – the vaguely homoerotic, vaguely religious, emotionally arrested, leisured, class-conscious world of playing fields, expensive schools and lazy universities …'* Dangerous ground!

I suppose that no educator concerned with the moral rather than the purely academic, and wishing to have an impact on society, can escape the dilemma: how does one define and educate for leadership?

'Is it not the case … when each of these three classes – the one that works for a living, the auxiliaries, and the guardians – performs its proper function and does its own job in the community, then this is morality and makes the community a moral one?' (Book IV)

Hahn used Plato's word, the Guardian, for his head of school in both Salem and Gordonstoun.

Communities require government. The welfare of the community lies in the hands of the élite. The Guardians must treat their friends and neighbours with kindliness, their enemies with ferocity, for Plato assumes the presence, or at least the threat, of enemies. The Guardians need martial virtues, manly courage. Self-discipline, mastery over emotions, total dedication to the collective: extreme

[●] Simon Blackburn's *Plato's Republic* (Atlantic Books London 2006) should, I think, be obligatory reading for any educator who declares a loyalty to the teachings of the Republic. I draw on it heavily at this point.

critics, foremost among them Karl Popper in his *The Open Society and its Enemies*, have, writes Blackburn, seen Plato's authoritarianism in these matters as a precursor of Nazism and Stalinism.

And there is another difficulty.

'Go, soar with Plato to th'empyreal sphere.' [●]

Plato's belief in order and rationality, a world in which knowledge achieves fulfilment independent of the seductive and bewildering influence of the senses, imposes moral expectations that in turn have deep implications for the education of the élitist leaders. Beauty, goodness and truth are the vital guides. It is a rarefied equation, with overtones of moral superiority and estrangement from the real challenges of life. *'Until philosophers are kings, or the kings and princes of this world have the spirit and power of philosophy … cities will never have rest from their evils.'*

But Plato was a young man when Athens was defeated by Sparta. He had confidence in neither the integrity of the rich nor the abilities of the masses to save the state. Further, *'access to power must be confined to men who are not in love with it.'* [○] Better to turn one's back on politics! But the Greek word for a man who stands aside and remains a private person, who does not engage in public affairs, is *idiotes*. Plato engaged himself by writing his *Republic*. I am surprised that Hahn never praised his decision.

Oxford

Kurt Hahn's College, Christ Church, has always had a good opinion of itself. In his biography of the historian Hugh Trevor Roper, Adam Sisman recalls John Betjeman's remark that Christ Church men *'always seemed to give the impression that they were just dropping in at Oxford on their way to a seat in the House of Lords'.* [■]

At the end of his first term, Hahn wrote to his friend and former member of his reading circle in Berlin, Leonard Nelson. His reading of Horace had opened his eyes to the dangers of enveloping himself exclusively in intellectual affairs. For his interests were hitherto all literary – his reading circle had been a very serious matter for him – but now *'I have seen that it is my duty to throw myself into the world's dirt, to help and to rescue, to the limits of my strength, that*

my morals were pure aesthetics and not much more … this recognition brought healing.' [17] His future was becoming clear. *'My aesthetic gifts will serve me only as a means of achieving the profession in life that my moral outlook prescribes for me … the one-time art historian now wishes to become a teacher …an educator and purveyor of knowledge.'* [18]

Hahn gives the credit for his new self-awareness to Leonard Nelson and to certain English friends who had brought the English progressive school Abbotsholme to his attention. [●] His long letter to Nelson reads somewhat pretentiously to English ears, and it is perhaps not surprising that an Oxford acquaintance, a gifted young artist who was killed in the First World War, Brian Hatton, had this to say about him in November 1905: *'he is German and very nice but frightfully aesthetic or whatever you call it. Goes into rhapsodies over Burne Jones's life by his wife – scarcely healthy in his mind, I should say. He's too young to talk such drivel about Burne Jones and Watts, though very good drivel of its sort, accompanied by plenty of action. He indulges in walks and hockey in the afternoons, so I expect to have the pleasure of a walk with him some time! If he jaws much about the scenery I shall go mad …'* Strangely, another contemporary, the famous conductor Adrian Boult, describes him also in 1905 as having been *'an absolute hermit'.*

But Hahn's letter to Leonard Nelson had also made a reference to *'the old, gray castles and the healthy figures who throw themselves around in youthful exuberance on the lawns …'* [19] He had entered the more extrovert English world. His life's work was to span the period of greatest tension and hostility between the two nations Germany and England. He would become one of the most perceptive and often courageous interpreters of the one to the other.

Many, many years later he was to write to a Salem pupil about to go up to Oxford: *'There is no place in the world where one can be so lazy with a good conscience as in Oxford; but in the end only those get on who decide to become their own severe taskmasters …'*

Collegiate life at the university was a revelation for him: the tutorials, the sport, the social relationships – and, as he wrote to Leonard Nelson, *'one can learn*

[●] Alexander Pope

[○] *The Republic* Book VII page 520

[■] Adam Sisman adds that Christ Church as late as 1964 had the largest proportion of Public School boys of any Oxford college and the largest proportion of undergraduates failing their final examinations.

[●] Commentators on Hahn's debt to Abbotsholme often overlook the fact that this school owed its founding inspiration to German thinking in progressive education. There was much two-way influence between German and British progressive educators. Reddie at Abbotsholme consciously adopted ideas picked up at Jena while Hermann Lietz took the Abbotsholme model back to Germany. Later, A. S. Neill spent formative years teaching in Dresden.

The university student

Greek here magnificently, and if one chooses a particular course of studies, must work very hard even in one's first year …' [20]

Insights into Hahn's Oxford career are fragmentary. A note from the College librarian states that, whilst having matriculated in 1904, he did not come into residence until 1909. Another manuscript note from the Steward's Office records a total of eight terms, one in 1904, three in 1905, one in 1906, two in 1911 and one in 1912. Neither appears reliable. But they confirmed that he sat no examinations. Hahn himself always maintained that he had returned to Oxford in 1911 to *'draw from the past impulses for shaping the present'.* His active, fruitful period came in his later Oxford years.

Between 1900 and 1911 200 Germans studied in Oxford, and a further 100 were to become undergraduates before the outbreak of war. Prominent among them were the German Rhodes Scholars, whose selection was under the direct guidance of the Kaiser, and most others were from notable families both socially and economically. Anglo-German activities (Hahn called them Anglo-Germanities) were a leading feature of university life. 1908 saw the creation of the Anglo-German Society, 1909 of the German Literary Society, 1911 of the Hanover Club, so named (aristocratic allusions were casually taken for granted) to record the dynastic connections between the two countries which had also helped to ensure a peaceable relationship over 200 years.

It was however the Union, the university's prestigious debating society, around which political life revolved. Rated consistently in the leading group of Union speakers, Hahn was deeply impressed that eminent national figures were willing to debate with 'mere undergraduates'. Donald McLachlan, in his biography of Hahn's Oxford contemporary Robert Barrington Ward, refers to the Union as *'a paddock for inspecting likely Tory and Liberal politicians',* and it was here that ambitious undergraduates had access to the friendship and advice of influential men.

This was the nursery for democracy of the kind that Hahn so missed at home, a magnificent showcase for education in active democratic citizenship. On 7th March 1912 he had spoken against the motion: *'This House is of the opinion that in view of the existing European situation a rapprochement between England and Germany is an unrealisable ideal.'* The motion was defeated by 82 to 64 votes. Hahn was generally thought to have made the decisive speech. On another occasion, in a *'highly-welcomed speech, Hahn yearned for a parliamentary system in Germany'.* His main point of criticism concerning the current state of affairs in his country was that *'the government was elected by the Emperor and not by the people'* and that *'no Liberal (was) allowed into office'.* As a result, educated people withdrew into a critical attitude and abstained from taking an active part in politics. At a Club meeting three weeks later Hahn was *'tragic and melodramatic'* when speaking of the defunct liberal party in Germany.

The impact of Hahn's personality comes through vividly in the memories of certain contemporaries, and Hahn colleagues will recognise the descriptions of him: *'Hahn stalks about when he speaks, like a caged lion … he can't sit down. He gets very excited.'* They will not be surprised that he was *'a tremendous personality in Oxford',* or that he was *'very popular indeed with all the Oxford political people, and very deservedly so'.*

One letter dated 4th February 1912, most probably from a good friend who was also to die early in the War, reads: *'Last night I had an extraordinary time … the German*

A photograph taken in boisterous Oxford company suggests a melancholy and withdrawn Kurt Hahn (fourth from left in the second row)

Kempner came to me in a great hurry to ask me to go at once with him to the American Club … about 100 people there … Baron von Dalwig, a German Conservative, read a long paper on German school and university education … Hahn made a terrific attack on von Dalwig, Hahn being a Liberal (German) and von Dalwig one of the old Conservatives … we got back to 'the House' (Christ Church) at about 12.15, and then went to Hahn's rooms. Hahn never wakes up till about that hour. He then did an extraordinary feat, by taking a standing jump right over the back of a high arm-chair in his room (the letter has a sketch) … the arm-chair had an exceptionally high back too … Kempner told me how Hahn, when he was a fresher, climbed down the wall of Meadow Buildings and over the roof of the Porters' Lodge into the meadows at night and was caught by the Gate Porter …certain members of Eton think they are athletic and active, but they are not comparable in physical activity with Hahn … .' Another, probably his best friend in Oxford, wrote rather gushingly: 'he is inspiring, and a marvellous man for ideals; and a greater command of the English language than any Englishman I have ever met and a better speaker than anyone. He is also a very good athlete … he is so refreshing, and vivacious; it is a tonic to be with him. He is also frightfully strong and muscular, and a tower of strength in character too. I have never known anyone with so much moral courage, and physical courage too. He is quite unique.'

Decidedly Hahn had entered England by the front door, not the tradesman's entrance.

… and the Public Schools

Perhaps the most significant discovery he made at Oxford was the British Public Schools, whose former pupils and ethos dominated the life of the university. A senior German civil servant, having observed Hahn at work during the First World War, wrote this about him: *'He wanted always to go directly to the important men himself and, if that was not possible, to those who exercised a decisive influence over them. Who is the most influential advisor of Minister X, he would then ask. Around every important personality there are friends and advisors who will always be admitted and listened to. He asked about them and then set off for his goal.'* [21][•]

[•] Arnold Brecht: *Aus nächster Nähe.* Deutsche Verlagsanstalt 1966

In Oxford, Hahn absorbed for life his awareness of the decisive importance of contacts with and between influential personalities; furthermore, how much this all arose from the British nation's educational system. It is sufficient to cite one example: Henry Montague Butler was the Headmaster of the famous Public School Harrow from 1859 to 1885. His pupils during his Headship and others with whom he had close relationships included one Prime Minister, one Archbishop of Canterbury, John Galsworthy the author of *The Forsyte Saga*, ten bishops, 17 judges, four Viceroys, 12 colonial governors, 12 ambassadors, 33 Privy Councillors, and 64 generals. [●]

But whilst he saw so much to admire and to envy in the Public Schools, above all their ability to inspire their pupils with a deep, active sense of responsibility for their school's reputation and welfare, he experienced at Oxford too their tendency to arrogance, their over-worship of sport, their assumption and use of privilege (in the language of our time, their sense of entitlement). We return to Plato.

'Well, your guardian must be brave if he is to fight well … and is he likely to be brave who has no spirit … did you never observe how the presence of spirit makes the soul of any creature absolutely fearless and invincible … But then, Glaucon, these spirited natures are apt to be furious with one another, and with everybody else … whereas I said, they ought to be gentle to their friends, and dangerous to their enemies; or, instead of their enemies destroying them, they will destroy themselves … how shall we find a gentle nature which has also a great spirit, for they seem to be inconsistent with one another … and yet he will not be a good guardian who is wanting in either of these two qualities … may we not say confidently of man also, that he who is likely to be gentle to his friends and acquaintances, must by nature be a lover of wisdom and knowledge? … then he who is to be a really good and noble guardian of the State will require to unite in himself philosophy and spirit and swiftness and strength … Then we have found the desired natures; and now that we have found them, how are they to be reared and educated?' [○]

And so we read later in Hahn, who applies lessons learned in the German country boarding schools of Hermann Lietz ('*Landerziehungsheime*'), that *'the honour of the school will be upheld with enthusiasm and tenacity not only on the sports field but also in the workshops. Rough*

[●] Wikipedia suggests that these were all Harrow pupils, but the school archivist was unable to confirm this without undertaking extensive and time-consuming research.

[○] *The Republic* Book II, pages 375 and 376

ground will be tilled. Experiments will take place in the laboratories. Research projects will be carried out in the countryside. Plays will be performed. There will be music and painting. Huts will be built, swimming pools constructed, observatories and collections set up. The vitality of the children, constantly refreshed by sporting activities, will benefit not sport alone as in Eton, Harrow, etc., but more important activities in preparation for life.' [22]

The Foundations of Personality

But by 1909 he had developed one more line of thought that was to determine his educational philosophy more distinctly than any other. The voice of reason, says Kant, is audible to all. No, says Hahn, the power of a man's emotions can make him incapable of listening honestly. These emotions can be so strong that a man can even deceive himself into believing that it becomes his duty to follow them rather than his conscience. *'There are feelings in man that, when they achieve a certain strength, so work upon the will that the will succumbs. It is the task of education so to weaken these feelings that respect for the (moral) law may overcome them.'* [23]

Integrity, says Hahn, is self-knowledge and self-discipline. How are the emotions so to be trained and mastered that man is enabled to follow the moral law? By the influence of memories that come to one's support in times of crisis. How can memories be given this decisive power? Only if – and here Hahn takes his lead from the American philosopher William James – noble emotions at the time they are aroused are transmuted through action into a life-long heritage. For *'if a man does not translate his fine feelings into practical action; if, as the American psychologist William James says, he does not accustom himself to discharging these feelings into motor activity, then the temptation becomes overpowering forcibly to prolong this condition; and he eventually finds himself no longer seized by the beauty of the world around him and by the fate of his fellow men, but instead by his own absorption with himself; that is, he takes aesthetic enjoyment in his own feelings and, in so doing, he destroys his innate sense of dedication, his own sensitivity which he had wished to enjoy.'* [24]

It is a small move from here to Hahn's *Erlebnistherapie*. But here there is a problem of translation, for Hahn's education is generally described as *experiential* education. (Not once did he use this unattractive word, which was scarcely in use at the time of his death in 1974.) *Experiential* omits the healing function that was central to Hahn's thinking, the *therapy*. He has often been criticized for laying artificial emphasis on the ills of modern civilisation, as though without them his principles might have no validity. Let us each judge for ourselves these ills as he first formulated them in Salem soon after the school's foundation and reflect on their continuing, perhaps increased relevance in the years since his death:

> The decline of fitness due to modern methods of locomotion
> The decline of initiative and enterprise due to the widespread disease of 'spectatoritis'
> The decline of memory and imagination due to the confused restlessness of modern life
> The decline of skill and care due to the weakened tradition of craftsmanship
> The decline of self-discipline due to the ever-present availability of stimulants and tranquilisers, and
> The worst decline of all, the decline of compassion due to the unseemly haste with which modern life is conducted

It is time to return to Hahn's life. Before doing so, and having quoted Blackburn in his critical assessments of Plato, let us also understand, through two additional quotes from the same author, the precise and ennobling nature of the challenge accepted through Plato by Kurt Hahn.

'It is the extraordinary purity of Plato's aim that is overwhelming, his power to pursue one question – how we are to live our lives – through thick and thin, through arguments that might seem fanciful, myths that might seem purely distracting, comparisons that may or may not seem helpful, to circle again and again back to that question ...'. And

'Plato insists on the supremacy of education over law.'

Scotland, Continuing Illness and Operations

Kurt Hahn had made Scottish friends at Oxford. Their friendship and his need to escape the sun and heat took him north. The landscape and the character of the people became a dominant influence in his life.

In January 1906 he visited a primary school in Logie, attended some classes, gave a talk on Frederick the Great, and then, true to his future principles, went out into the school yard to play with the children. 'Mr. Hahn is a very tall and civil man ... when we were out playing he came out and played with us and ran exceedingly fast'. 'Mr. Hahn is very tall and strongly built and speaks English very fluently.'

In April 1909 he immersed himself in the Scottish countryside by riding a horse alone from Glasgow over the Highlands to Morayshire, recovering confidence in his

A face changed by illness

physical stamina and proud to have come successfully through a violent snow storm.

It was also in Scotland that he found and took away with him a document that listed the qualities in school pupils on which the teachers were required to comment. I have little doubt that the extensive Leavers Report that featured so strongly in Salem and Gordonstoun has its origins in this rather remarkable paper. Here is a selection of the required topics for comment: power of observation, intensity of application to mental tasks, capacity for sustained application (spontaneous and by virtue of effort of will), natural or spontaneous interests, memory, power of logical inference or reasoning, confidence in observation and judgement, liability to anger, fear, curiosity, joyousness, courage and resolution, altruism, egoism, conscientiousness, sensitivity to the opinions of others, sociability, initiative, masterfulness, suggestibility, competitive or emulative spirit, aesthetic feelings, energy bodily and mental.

One close friend, Alastair Cumming, was the son of Sir Mansfield Cumming who created the British Intelligence Service in the First World War and was the first 'C' of MI6. Alastair was to lose his life in a car accident during the war when driving with his father. Lady Cumming was and remained until her death an intense admirer and patron of her son's friend Kurt. It was through this family that Hahn came to know of the Gordonstoun estate.

But he was still an invalid.

At Christmas 1911 Paul Ehrlich referred him to the eminent London surgeon Sir Victor Horsley. At the end of an hour's consultation Horsley was convinced of the need for an operation. *'I will go in if you are willing.'* He proposed an intervention to relieve the pressure on the brain by creating an escape channel into the lymph system. The operation had been carried through only twice previously. Horsley operated in March 1912. Hahn was sent to a sanatorium on the Isle of Wight to recuperate. He claims he lived for six weeks on milk alone. *'The brutes have put me to bed here, feed me on milk, forbid me to write letters, so my temper is not of the best, but I am looking forward to a brighter future.'* Most of his letters during these spells of ill-health were handwritten by others and only signed by him.

Hahn returned to Oxford but the symptoms continued. The sudden awakenings at night became more frequent and more violent. Horsley was from the start unhappy about the first operation and wanted a second to enlarge the drainage by the removal of some bone. This took place in June 1913. A respite! But in the winter 1913–1914 the symptoms worsened yet again, even to the extent of his once more having difficulties in expressing himself. By May 1914, even in Scotland, he was unable to leave his darkened room in the daytime. He was now, in agreement with Horsley, taking medication. He was summoned back to Oxford by the doctors at the end of the month. Increased drugs and a further, if minor, operation were proposed. And here his family intervened. His uncle, Dr. Martin Hahn, was the emissary. The family and especially his mother were worried beyond further endurance by all this experimentation. His uncle Martin told Kurt: *'There are illnesses to which the patient must learn to resign himself with dignity … you had interesting and wide-ranging plans for the founding of a school … nothing can ever come of all that now, but you can maintain contact with the young by settling permanently in northern Scotland with its climate that suits you, leading a quiet and withdrawn life, and letting the village children come to you on Sundays and reading to them about beautiful things.'* [25] Horsley was unwilling to insist in the face of this family front.

There followed a dramatic intervention of the kind that characterised Hahn's life. He cherished such moments, cultivated their significance, and sought to introduce them into the lives of others whenever opportunity offered. They were frequently effective but also gave his sceptical critics some helpful material.

At two o'clock in the morning, Hahn heard loud whispering and disturbance on the corridor outside his room in the nursing home. Sir Mansfield broke in. *'I have bowled Sir Victor over at 10 pm tonight. He is going to do this little operation this Saturday. All is fixed now. May* (Lady Cumming) *is downstairs and sends her love. Good luck to you.'* He had driven from London to Oxford, naturally in an open car, and of course the weather had been terrible! These dramatic details inescapably set the scene, but the intervention was successful. Horsley later sent written instructions to Germany for the continuing medical treatment which included life-long drugs. Hahn concludes this personal account with the comment that, throughout the war, he worked for between 14 and 18 hours a day and is unable to resist the temptation to add that, when working in the Reichskanzlei in October 1918, he set the European record for the European standing high jump, although he prudently adds that it was not officially recognised.

In August war broke out. Hahn, assisted by the Cummings, left Scotland through Scandinavia for Germany.

Hahn and the First World War

This essay cannot attempt a detailed account and critique of Hahn's war-time activities which must await the full biography. They were often secretive, conspiratorial, frustratingly elusive, but always immersed in the central, controversial issues of the time. A bare-bones outline of his accomplishment is nonetheless clear. In 1914 he was a young man unfit for military service who, fluent in English, was drafted into a department of the Ministry of Foreign Affairs, the *Zentralstelle fur Auslandsdienst*, to read the British press and to provide summaries and interpretations

Prince Max of Baden (in the light overcoat), accompanied by Erhard Eduard Deutelmoser, Head of the News Department of the Ministry of Foreign Affairs (left) and Wilhelm Freiherr von Radewitz (right), Head of the Imperial Chancellery, walks to the Reichstag in October 1918

of British policies and morale for the government. By 1918 he was the personal secretary and confidant of the last German Imperial Chancellor, Prince Max of Baden, whose appointment to that position had been skilfully manipulated by Hahn himself. He was a member, as a modest secretary it is true, of the German delegation to the Peace Conference in Versailles, but was intimately involved in the preparation of the German resistance to the terms eventually imposed on Germany, and he drafted the main parts of the contentious speech delivered by the German Minister of Foreign Affairs, Graf Brockdorff-Rantzau, in response to the terms laid down by the Entente powers.

He began on the wrong foot, but this error is significant in highlighting the dramatic development in his beliefs.

The German Nationalist Background

In March 1913 Hahn had contributed an essay to *The Blue Book, the Oxford Undergraduate Review*, on Anglo-German Relations. *'I cannot deny that there is an attitude of suspicion and distrust towards England in my own country … we were once popular in England, when our map showed so many pretty colours; when we were producing poets and thinkers by the dozen and quarrelling among ourselves with such a delightfully German waste of energy. Then came Bismarck and the German Empire … Germany had good reasons for being jealous, came too late into the world and found the best part of it 'engaged' … it is a great illusion to believe that the martial ideals of the two nations have grown feeble. Our intellect may despise them, but our blood still warms to them … I believe in the danger of the whole of this century being turned into an anachronism by an Anglo-German war … we know and like English human nature … we feel that you have developed possibilities for our common race and creed which we have neglected … we do not take our national character as a "fait accompli" but as a living organism which can be well or badly nurtured. Much of the nurture we most need can only come from England … but I dare to ask for a little more curiosity about Germany.'*

In January 1915 the *Oxford Review* published a letter from Kurt Hahn addressed to his friend Lord Sandon. *'My Dear Sandon! I hesitate to write to you, knowing that all confidence between our two nations has been destroyed, and that the love of your country is the ruling passion of your life. But I cannot forget my Oxford days …'* It was too strong – an attack on the integrity of Sir Edward Grey, the uncompromising (and false) assertion that Belgium's neutrality was violated first by France, not Germany: *'Belgian men, women and children have murdered German soldiers peacefully sleeping*

in their houses … the town and population of Louvain was not touched until the German garrison was fired on by the whole civilian population …' The editorial comment was damning: *'one of the most pathetic documents we have seen since the outbreak of war'.*

We must look at the background.

His chief in the *Zentralstelle fur Auslandsdienst* was a noted political author and publicist, Paul Rohrbach, who in 1912 had written a book which, his translator claimed in 1915, had probably inspired more Germans than any other book since 1871. [•] *'We start very conscientiously from the conviction that we have been placed in the arena of the world in order to work out moral perfection, not only for ourselves but for all mankind … the Anglo-Saxons have spread over such vast expanses that they seem to be on the point of assuming the cultural control of the world, thanks to their large numbers, their resources and their inborn strength … if a nation wishes to maintain itself as an independent entity by the side of such a gigantic power and culture as the English, and take part in the shaping of the culture of the world, it is obliged to prove by its deeds that it has a right to such a claim. … we shall be able to maintain our power only if we continue to spread the German idea … we are like the tree rooted in the cleft rock. We may press the rock asunder, or the resistance is so great that we are stunted for lack of food … the strengthening of our world position as the Greater Germany of the future … is a good and happy thought only on the one and definite condition, that not only the political and economic Germany must become greater, but equally that the sum of the moral duties of the German nation grows accordingly.'* [26] Indigestible material for the Entente powers and the Anglo-Saxon world, but the fact of having Russia on the opposing side gave Germany, not for the first time and not for the last, the added moral pretence of defending European civilisation.

Thomas Mann was another notable personality whose eloquent writings at the time expressed similar ideas, with a yet greater emphasis on Germany's cultural mission – and led to the bitter feud with his brother Heinrich.

And even closer to Hahn, in October 1914, 97 university professors, artists and writers, the "literary patriots", representative of the strangely nationalistic loyalties of the intelligentsia, had signed the notorious *Manifest of the 97*, an aggressive rejection of allegations of German war crimes in Belgium and a declaration of Germany's

[•] *German World Policies/Der deutsche Gedanke in der Welt,* translated by Dr. Edmund von Mach, the Macmillan Company New York 1915

sacred cultural destiny, its style intentionally drawn from Luther's 95 Theses of 1517. Hahn had adopted some of its content and some of its style into his letter to Lord Sandon. We must not be surprised, for among the signatories were Paul Ehrlich, his admired university teacher Ulrich von Wilamowitz-Moellendorff, and the intellectual and liberal mayor of Berlin Georg Reicke, a frequent visitor to his mother's Berlin home. [●]

This was all to change for, as the war proceeded, Kurt Hahn worked tirelessly for the passions aroused to be brought under political control. This, however, required the morally courageous intervention of enlightened statesmanship. Only thereby could the latent forces for peace in the opposing camps wrest the control of public opinion from the chauvinistic politicians and newspapers, could the 'jingoes' (a frequent word in his war-time notes) be isolated from genuine patriots and men of good will, could an irrational war be concluded on honourable terms.

It remains important to note that Kurt Hahn also had strong convictions on the civilising cultural mission of Germany, that Germany had noble humane and military traditions, and was emphatically not alone guilty of the outbreak of war; that the best hope for tolerance and prosperity in the contested areas of Prussia and further east depended on Germany exercising there the role of a benevolent colonial power, an idea given some intellectual and political validity in Naumann's articulation in his *Blaubuch* of the concept of *Mitteleuropa*; that Alsace-Lorraine must never be surrendered; that Germany should emerge from the war at least as strong as she was at the outset, her colonies restored to her. And he was emphatically not a pacifist: *'I do think war is not the greatest of evils, even not the most terrible war. I know one greater evil; and that is triumphant wrong confident of impunity, gloating over the war-weariness and pacifism of the right-minded … I think it is a sign of decay when one is afraid of rousing the passions of moral indignation for fear that they could get out of control …'*

The brilliance of Hahn's work in the Zentralstelle, his eloquent analyses of political developments in Britain, and his tireless pursuit of foreign journalists and influential contacts in foreign embassies, notably that of the United States, rapidly secured him a reputation based entirely on the quality of his personal achievements. But he was not an analyst alone. Despite all the confused emotions

of patriotism and chauvinism, he pressed ceaselessly for imaginative, statesmanlike solutions.

One wonders how physically he stood the strain. A few days ahead of delivering a major address in 1916, he confessed in a letter to a colleague in The Hague: *'… I have now come to the conclusion that I must really convalesce before I can present myself. I am already getting better. I have had two completely pain-free days, I am living very quietly …'* [27] The young son of his secretary Lina Richter has described how Hahn would take him rowing on the Havel at all hours of the night by way of rest and recuperation.

Hahn's Concepts of Psychological Warfare and Statesmanship

The context of his rapidly-developing attitudes had been well delineated by the contrasting views of two of his countrymen, Field Marshal Moltke and Chancellor Bismarck. Politics first enters the scene *'when the armed conflict has been resolved and the enemy has been defeated'* (Moltke), and *'the government of a nation at war has also to look in other directions … not only towards the battle field'*. (Bismarck) [28] [●]

The fatal fault line in Germany, the allegiance that was to be broken only by military defeat, was the army's direct accountability to the Kaiser, Wilhelm II; and it was the Kaiser too who appointed the Chancellor. During the turbulent reign of this erratic monarch, politicians in the Reichstag and successive Chancellors had through skill and subterfuge achieved increasing if unsteady influence over home affairs and social policies, but the Kaiser proved able to find dangerous expression for his unflagging personal ambition with his growing role in foreign affairs which, with the outbreak of war, moved naturally into the sphere of military command. *'In all Central and Eastern Europe the soldiers were in the saddle and rode mankind.'* [○] Nowhere was this more true than in Germany.

Armed with the social confidence he had acquired both from home and Oxford, and massively assisted by his complete fluency in English, Hahn from the outset sought the company of prominent politicians, professors, publicists and diplomats. He was active in the influential *Deutsche Gesellschaft von 1914*. He inserted himself into a series of missions to neutral countries, building up a network of contacts that no German journalist or diplomat was able

---

[●] … and grandfather of Michael Schweitzer, private secretary to Kurt Hahn 1956–1962 and subsequently Bursar of Atlantic College

[●] Cited in Lothar Albertin: *Liberalismus und Demokratie am Anfang der Weimarer Republik* page 203

[○] George Trevelyan: *Grey of Fallodon* page 248

to rival. In April 1915 he attended a peace conference in The Hague in the company of notable public personalities from Germany where he met advocates on the British side of a negotiated settlement, members of the Union of Democratic Control. This conference was an attempt by intellectuals, diplomats, academics and economists to bridge the gap between the failed national political systems and the 'new diplomacy' which, they believed, represented the only hopeful way forward. Hahn claimed consistently for the rest of his life that the meeting had the covert approval of both Sir Edward Grey and the German Chancellor Bethmann-Hollweg, and that *'if both statesmen would have had the courage of their convictions on receiving our reports, an honourable peace would have been concluded before the summer of that year'.* [●] This was the forerunner of many optimistic assumptions that the sincerity of the would-be peacemakers could overcome the forces that had been unleashed.

Where Hahn merits our attention is in the scope and style of his memoranda which, one commentator wrote, sweep the reader along with the pace of a filmed news reel. The reader must at this point be patient and accept extensive quotation; Hahn's views are more eloquently expressed in his words than mine.

First, the importance of studying the psychology of the enemy and his morale! This was best and accurately achieved by searching for information, indiscretions and even deliberate governmental leaks in the enemy's press. *'The British press shows the attentive observer, as with flares, the vulnerable spots in the British home front.'*

'The Ministry of Foreign Affairs has a clerk's concept of its own importance in war. The reasons for this lie deep in a mistaken understanding of human nature. The gentlemen do not know that the outcome of war depends on the peoples' morale. There is no sensitivity to movements in public opinion; the invaluable diagnostic materials of the enemy's press are not adequately analysed, in contrast with which the importance of agents and "confidential contacts" is exaggerated. The more secretive the news, the better!' [29] [o]

[●] Kurt Hahn in a letter of 12th May 1949 to an American friend

[o] A sentiment expressed in more colourful language by Stuart Hampshire in the Second World War: that British Intelligence valued information in proportion to its secrecy, not its accuracy; they would prefer some nonsense *'smuggled out of Sofia in the fly-buttons of a vagabond Rumanian pimp'* to what they could learn *'from a prudent reading of the foreign press'* (*Spectator* Book Review 17th–24th December 2011)

And

'Words today are battles: the right words victorious battles, the wrong words lost battles. If we want to achieve victory behind the English front in preparation for victory on the battlefield, we must choose those words that make it possible for the patriotic party of peace in England to step forward to the people and to say: if you follow us, the way forward to negotiations is open, the honour and security of England are safe …' [30] [●]

On 12th December 1916 the Reichskanzler Bethmann-Hollweg, encouraged by the German conquest of Romania and at the same time worried by increasing American war preparedness, made proposals for peace negotiations. To the Entente powers they were at once suspect, undermined among other things by his simultaneous statement to the military High Command that peace was dependent on a German victory. Hahn's comment:

'One does indeed do well to remember Bethmann's words. From the very beginning it has been clear that, as the outcome of this world war, three great aims of humanity must be achieved, and that victory will go to that country that first has the courage to inscribe those aims on its flag:

1) *The guarantee of the independence of the small nations*
2) *The freedom of the seas with everything that flows from that. The security of non-combatants on sea and land, their life, their livelihood*
3) *Development of the work of The Hague towards the prevention of future wars.* [o]

Bethmann has repeatedly made moves towards elevating these three conditions to the status of a national demand. We almost had from him an unequivocal declaration on Belgium. He almost demanded the freedom of the foreign populations in Russia in the name of Germany. He almost made the case for German U-boat warfare to world opinion as a weapon in the service of the freedom of the seas. He almost accepted the concept of the League of Nations in a form that would have disarmed the enemy. But the final decisive words he never uttered. History will not make the technical obstacles that he faced responsible, but the political will, which was not strong enough to overcome them … he would have been counted

[●] An analysis unwittingly confirmed by Field Marshal Hindenburg: *'I had the feeling that the business of diplomacy made unfamiliar demands on us Germans'* (quoted in Wheeler-Bennett: *Hindenburg – The Wooden Titan* page 83)

[o] A reference to earlier conferences in The Hague in 1899 and 1907 on disarmament

among the great statesmen if he had had the strength to lead the way in the direction he had pointed ...' [31]

Hahn's comment reflects well the enigmatic impression left by Bethmann-Hollweg. References are often made to the British Foreign Minister Grey's apparent willingness at this time to lend his authority to a negotiated settlement, but the German Chancellor's unskilful speech had omitted all reference to Belgium and included his wish that Germany should head the proposed League of Nations, thereby thoroughly undermining Grey's position. Hahn's insistence on greater boldness and political courage emerges clearly.

On 19th July 1917 the Reichstag, at last transforming its restlessness into action, the first time it had shown some political independence on war issues, adopted the equally ill-fated Friedensresolution, the Peace Resolution. The tired Bethmann Hollweg – *'I am considered weak because I seek to end the war'* – was replaced by the army's politically feeble nominee Michaelis, the Reichstag being completely ignored by the Kaiser in the matter. Michaelis did not believe in the Friedensresolution and, perhaps unintentionally, wholly undermined it for both home and foreign observers by accepting it in his Reichstag speech with his notorious *'as I understand it'*. He took the Reichstag itself no more seriously. *'I do not consider a body like the German Reichstag a fit one to decide about peace and war on its own initiative during the war.'* [•]

Hahn was under no illusions. Influence at the negotiating table would depend on military strength. *'Whether we obtain a good or a bad peace will be decided, not by the personality of the negotiator, but by the military power that stands behind our demands. Everything will depend on when the negotiations begin. A Germany from whom the world can expect another Hindenburg offensive could push through what it needs at the conference table. But if Germany enters the negotiations tired, with exhausted reserves, under the pressure of a demoralised home front, without the strength to say no, or to be able to strike militarily again, then the enemy will achieve its demands ...'* (May 1917) [32]

But on 19th May 1917, as the issue of the relative powers of the Reichstag and the Military High Command was coming slowly to the boil, he was equally clear about the issue of democratic accountability.

'It is of the greatest importance for our entire political development at home that peace should be achieved on the basis of a reduction in the military sphere. If our own people are to continue to accept their army, it must never be said

that a diplomatic situation that held the promise of peace was allowed to pass by because the soldiers were determined first to play all their aces. Even the most brilliant field marshal, even Moltke, needed the counterbalance of political restraint. Today we have no Bismarck as counterbalance ...'* [33]

All this may be straightforward orthodoxy today. In the Germany of 1917 it was radical, with transparent implications for the position of the Kaiser.

In August of the same year he was expressing his concerns about the success of the Entente powers in creating divisions between Germany and her allies, precisely the technique that he advocated for his own government: *'their objective is to deepen the division between the German government and the German people and between Germany and her allies Austria, Bulgaria ... unnoticed, the suggestion is gaining ground that the German government carries the responsibility for prolonging the war ...'* [34]

At the beginning of 1918 Germany's military position appeared stronger than it had ever been, but here Hahn was prophetic. *'Germany is in the greatest danger since the war began, despite our magnificent military situation ... the national barriers are still in place, but they are fragile, and one fine day, under the pressures of a general world depression and world poverty, these instincts will break out and conclude a peace that will leave Germany in ruins ...'* [35]

In March 1918 he summarised his principles.

'There are three approaches for politically liquidating the war ...

First: the diplomatic approach ... to meet somewhere with an agent of the enemy in order, in a friendly conversation, to find a solution for ending the world war ... vieux jeu.

Second: The democratic approach ... representatives of international social democracy meet and try to found a new world ... on the basis of principles in which they believe but have not yet tested.

Third: the approach of healing statesmanship – negotiations are prepared through a public dialogue which not only finds the basis for an understanding but makes it so clear to the peoples that public opinion everywhere insists on attempts to bridge the remaining differences through diplomatic discussions ...' [36]

His implicit abandonment of the second method, unsuccessfully attempted in 1915 in The Hague, in favour of clear, enlightened, healing leadership, is inseparable from his campaign to place the leadership and the destiny of Germany in the hands of Prince Max of Baden.

Fine principles! What about the practice?

[•] Quoted in Wheeler-Bennett *Hindenburg: The Wooden Titan* page 108

Hahn's Practical Achievements

Hahn's participation in The Hague conference of May 1915 had given him personal introductions to notable personalities in both the British and the neutral camps. Carefully cultivated friendships with US diplomats and journalists opened lines of personal communication that, with his fluent English and Oxford background, rapidly made him an influential point of reference, especially for those who placed their hopes in the emergence of German liberalism despite the crushing domination of the Military High Command and the Kaiser. By the war's end he had become the principal intermediary between the German government on the one hand, neutral and even enemy opinion on the other.

In a series of memoranda Hahn foresaw in 1914 that England would eventually introduce military conscription; in 1915 that Lloyd George would, with the help of the obsessively anti-German newspaper owner Northcliffe, form a coalition government, taking over from Asquith; and that by the end of the year Russia would be *hors-de-combat*. In 1916 Ludendorff requested copies of his reports and complimented him personally on having forecast British battle plans on the basis of British press indiscretions.

His lecture in 1916 to the prestigious *Deutsche Gesellschaft, The English Will for War in the Light of the English Press*, brought him to the centre of political attention.

Also in 1916, again on the basis of his knowledge of the English press, he had assisted with the drafting of Bethmann-Hollweg's speech of 12th December to the Reichstag, providing arguments on the Russian mobilisation of July 1914 that were designed to provoke a reply from Lord Grey. Grey duly responded in the House of Lords: *'I would like nothing better than to see these statements – that the Russian mobilisation was an aggressive and not a defensive measure, and that any other power than Germany had trafficked in the neutrality of Belgium, or planned to attack through Belgium, – I would like to see those statements investigated before an independent and impartial tribunal.'*

Hahn was tireless in placing Belgium at the centre of debate. Bethmann-Hollweg's comment to the departing British Ambassador in 1914 – how could Britain go to war for the sake of a scrap of paper (The Treaty of London of 1839 that guaranteed Belgian neutrality) – crystallised Britain's dominating moral justification for refusing to negotiate or compromise.

Equally fateful was the decision of 1st February 1917 for unrestricted U-boat warfare. This had been proposed jointly by the army and navy authorities to the Kaiser on 8th January 1917. *'(The Kaiser) voiced the very curious viewpoint,'* Georg von Muller, head of the naval cabinet, noted in his diary, *'that the U-boat war was a purely naval affair which did not concern the Chancellor in any way'.* [●] By this time Hahn was in intimate discussion with the US diplomats Bill Bullitt and Christian Herter. He was among other tasks engaged in drafting a reply for the German government to the Note from the United States on the U-Boat issue. He was utterly clear, in a sharply-worded memorandum of February 1917, that this decision could only lead to the entry of America into the war. He wrote: *'The British government not only prayed that the German decision might be what it was, but has worked for it with all their resources of publicity and diplomacy …'* [○]

Hahn's memorandum led to his dismissal from the Foreign Ministry (the Zentralstelle was also wound up), and to his transfer to the Military High Command's Foreign Affairs Department (OHL Auslandsabteilung) under Colonel von Haeften, who was Ludendorff's political advisor in Berlin. In effect Hahn thereby became political advisor to Ludendorff himself at one remove. He was able nonetheless to insist that he be allowed sufficient liberty to retain his role in coordinating moderate liberal opinion and transmitting it through personal channels to his like-minded allies in both England and on the other side of the Atlantic.

The dilemma had become even more acute: how was this war to be brought under political control? What prospect survived for an honourable peace?

Prince Max of Baden – a Leader of Moral Authority: 'Max = Pax'

Overriding all his other concerns, and arising directly from his morally-driven concepts of peace-making, Hahn realised that, if Germany was to make an impact on the

[●] Hew Strachan *The First World War* Simon and Schuster UK Ltd, Pocket Books page 219

[○] *Finis Germaniae*, Valentini, Chief Secretary to the Kaiser, wrote in his diary (Wheeler Bennett page 92). Winston Churchill later went into greater detail: *'If the Germans had waited to declare unrestricted U-boat warfare until the summer, there would have been no unlimited U-boat war and consequently no intervention of the United States. If the Allies had been left to face the collapse of Russia without being sustained by the intervention of the United States, it seems certain that France could not have survived the year, and the war would have ended in a peace by negotiation, or, in other words, a German victory. Had Russia lasted two months less, had Germany refrained for two months more, the whole course of events would have been revolutionised. Either Russian endurance or German impatience was required to secure the intervention of the United States.'*

Entente powers and the United States, she needed a statesman of irreproachable credentials, a personality not compromised by associations with the previous political direction of the war.

It is not known exactly when Hahn first met Prince Max of Baden. Lina Richter, Hahn's secretary, has stated that, with her own and Max's leading involvement in the Red Cross, it was she who introduced them early in the war. Another distinct possibility is the time in 1916 when Max was in close touch with the Dutch Embassy in Berlin where a Dutch businessman, Jakob Noeggerath, was a close confidant and ally of Hahn's. What is certain beyond any doubt is that, from 1917 onwards, Hahn was providing Max with regular, detailed briefings on all issues affecting the conduct of the war, encouraged in this by his chief von Haeften, and was also beginning to draft papers for his personal use as Max slowly allowed himself to become involved in the growing political crisis. All this took place in close consultation with a tight-knit, small group of allies that included the Reichstag Deputies Conrad Haussmann and Edward David, Wilhelm Solf (Minister for the Colonies from 1911 until 1918), Walter Simons (a senior official in the Ministry of Foreign Affairs), the diplomat Wolf Metternich, and the Hamburg banker Max Warburg. It is not seriously disputed that it was Hahn, conspiring tirelessly, who persuaded this group that Prince Max was the one man who could offer the leadership required. Arnold Brecht, quoted earlier, is clear on this in his memoirs: *'Hahn was the first who in July 1917 had proposed Prince Max as a possible Chancellor to a number of influential politicians such as Haussmann and David and who, after two failures (the nominations of Michaelis and Graf Hertling) finally got his way in October 1918 with his recommendation.'* [37] [●]

A noble man in both outlook and by birth, Prince Max was not only related to all the royal families of Europe, including that of the Tsar; he had devoted himself with conspicuous success and sincerity to the cause of prisoners of war, foreign prisoners in German captivity and German prisoners in other countries. Slowly, almost gently at first, he had entered the political arena, expressing already in 1914 his unease over the occupation of Belgium, later his opposition to U-boat warfare, and above all the move toward unrestricted U-boat activity. Hahn, the now 31-year-old, set himself the seemingly impossible challenge of persuading Max to offer himself as the future leader of

Germany, and to persuade politicians to contemplate this extraordinary scenario.

It was in the intense cauldron of politicking in Berlin in these years that Hahn perfected the skills of drawing others into privileged intimate consultation, of investing every move with a degree of conspiratorial plotting, of adopting what he later, much later, confessed to as his 'M' (Max) technique – marking memoranda as *Strictly Confidential*, or *10 Copies Only*, or *For Private Circulation Only*, a fiction to ensure that they engaged the reader's full attention. How many of us later allied ourselves to his causes with our own ego, stimulated by this technique, as our point of departure? [●]

A Hahn paper, sent to the Reichstag Deputy Conrad Haussmann with an accompanying letter on 17th August 1917, sets out his case for Max.

'The terrible phrase of the Englishman, the "Moratorium on the Sermon on the Mount", [○] *applies to all countries, also to Germany … the nation that first lifts this moratorium will with one blow have won the moral leadership. And this leadership role would also have its influence on the peace negotiations …'* [38]

'It is necessary that the leading personality … should be seen by other peoples in a positive light, thanks to his record … the world must be informed already about the new man … let us assume that Germany resolves to give the healing signal, and that the new government is completed with this humane personality as its leader … the new Chancellor would have no need to speak of peace. His attitudes and his achievements are known in the enemy's camp. He must only speak clearly about Belgium … he who does not sit in a glasshouse is entitled to throw stones …' [39]

[●] Hahn wrote later: *'My Report must always remain a strictly confidential document. I ought to have explained before that my decision to print it resulted from certain campaigning experiences which I made under the guidance of Prince Max. We discovered that typescript failed again and again to carry conviction because the key men to be influenced had acquired, through the enormous amount of typewritten material presented to them, the bad habit of slapdash perusal. So we printed confidential documents, at times only in five copies, and reported that only five had been printed. Such an announcement enhanced the interest taken in the document, sharpening the curiosity, because the reader – the specially selected reader – felt it a privilege to be admitted to the intimacy of internal communication – just as a whisper makes the listener keener to absorb everything, anxious not to lose a word.'*

[○] Sir William Byles had used this phrase in a debate in the House of Commons on 26th May 1916

[●] Arnold Brecht: *Aus nächster Nähe*. Deutsche Verlagsanstalt 1966 page 203

Golo Mann's portrayal of Prince Max, above all in his introduction to the second publication of the Prince's memoirs in 1968, which he co-edited, alerts us to his gentle character, his loyalty to friends, his interest in the arts and music. Despite being an officer in the Prussian Guards, he had withdrawn early from a military career. It seemed natural that he should have directed his humane instincts, combined with his family connections, to the Red Cross and prisoners of war. He had the qualities, foremost the aristocratic, which made him, the irreproachable German counterpart of the English gentleman, so attractive to Hahn. [●]

Letters addressed to Hahn by Prince Max in 1917 and 1918 are almost movingly revealing. Max was not physically robust. *'I am not able today to write to you in detail. I have been struck down by a most unfortunate condition of nervous exhaustion which I felt coming on but sought as hard as I could to suppress. Now I really need some time to rest … if possible, spare me from communications for 8–10 days. I am really not well.'* (27th August 1917). [40] Nor did he conceal from himself or from Hahn his sense of inadequacy for what might come. *'We need a personality of Bismarck's strength of will to master the enormous challenge … I confess, the more I look at this task, the less does its solution seem possible. It would mean fruitless exhaustion and self-annihilation* (14th October 1917) … *I fear you greatly overestimate my abilities and underestimate the difficulties of decisions in matters that I am not familiar with … if one wishes to act publicly, one must be able to speak and to be rapid in response. I lack both gifts …'* [41] Prophetic words! And on 28th October, in words that also sprang from his artistic nature: *'What you say about the matter honours me more than I can say … you hint at what Wordsworth so beautifully expresses in one of his most profound poems: "a great distress has humanised my soul" … I fear I exasperate you, in that I play the role of spectator … if I hear the call, then I shall have to come, and then it will all be all right. This is how it has always been with me, and I believe that I have understood you enough to know that you understand me and would not wish to have me otherwise. To be chosen, not to choose, that says roughly what I feel'.* [42]

It had, it is clear, rapidly become a remarkable and remarkably close relationship between the 50-year-old Prince and the younger man of 31 years. One senses even at this distance the mutual sympathy between the two, both constrained by physical weakness, the future educator investing his trust in his doubting older pupil, the pupil already seeking to live up to his teacher's confidence in him.

In October 1917 Chancellor Michaelis fell, to be succeeded by Georg Hertling. Hertling was once again the choice of the military and therefore readily acceptable to the Kaiser. The case for Max had not yet achieved critical momentum, nor were the conditions yet quite grave enough to justify a radical solution. But, as the historian Hew Strachan comments, Hertling had to govern *'with the administrative structures of a small nineteenth-century state that had'* (a telling detail, this, for us, in our study of Hahn) *'never collected its various propaganda agencies into a ministry of information.'*

Max of Baden's reactions were those of a man who had not yet accepted his destiny. As it became clear that the days of Michaelis were numbered, *'I do not wish to lift a finger in the matter. If it does not come of its own from necessity, it is of evil …'* [43], and after Hertling's nomination: *'A great weight has been lifted from my heart. For with the thought of taking his place I would have had only the feeling of sacrificing myself if the Fatherland needed it and no-one was there who could seek to unite all our forces …'* [44]

But the pace quickened.

On 29th November 1917 Lord Lansdowne had published his famous letter in *The Daily Telegraph*, calling (not for the first time) for a negotiated settlement. It followed his memorandum of the previous year to the British Cabinet. *'Surely it cannot be our intention … to declare … that the word peace is sacrilege.'* The episode is emblematic. Hahn seized on the letter to underline his conviction that British morale was low, that a negotiated peace had a chance. Lansdowne was after all a very distinguished figure in British public life: Governor-General of Canada, Viceroy of India, Secretary of State for War, Foreign Secretary, Leader of the Conservative and Unionist Peers, a member of Asquith's war-time coalition. Golo Mann, among others, has expressed his belief that powerful political personalities were ready in support on condition that Germany gave a clear signal of its intention to abandon all aggressive aims including the unconditional evacuation of Belgium. [●] But

[●] A contemporary German historian takes an altogether different and ideologically hostile view of Max's personality and character (Lothar Machtan: *Die Abdankung* Propylaen 2nd Edition 2008 and other writings). His comments on Prince Max as Chancellor are unremittingly critical.

[●] And A. J. P. Taylor was typically forthright in his *English History 1914–1945*, page 83: *'The British people were clear why they had gone to war: it was for the sake of Belgium. Liberation of Belgium, and full reparation, remained always their primary aim, and the Germans would have caused great turmoil in British opinion if they had offered it – which, fortunately for national unity, they never did'*

Lansdowne had a well-established record for stepping out of line, Germany gave none of the desired signals, Rudyard Kipling called him *an old imbecile – some woman must have worked on him'*, [●] and as recently as June 2011 Paul Johnson in *The Spectator* was able, uncontested, to refer to him as *'the moth-eaten old Lansdowne, a former foreign secretary (who) spoke up for peace and was promptly shouted down.'* Grey called the outcry *'absurd … it was a wise discussion of the possibilities in an uncertain situation.'* Max of Baden's interventions in Germany were however no more successful than those of his fellow nobleman on the other side the Channel. That the issues were elsewhere more evenly balanced is perhaps illustrated by the fact that, in the month of Lansdowne's letter, the French government of Alexandre Ribot fell because of the split between those in favour of war and those in favour of peace. The election of Clemenceau decided the issue irrevocably for war.

In a much later letter of 12th March 1968 Kurt Hahn has described how Lansdowne's letter stimulated and encouraged both him and Max in the preparation of the decisive Karlsruhe speech that was to follow. *'Under the war façade there are doubts and misgivings both in enemy countries and at home: is it really inevitable that we go on fighting and suffering?'* he asked.

On 15th February 1918 Prince Max gave a public interview, aimed at Lansdowne without naming him, challenging the Entente powers to negotiate before the expected bloody German spring offensive. But nothing, he and Hahn recognised, could equal an unequivocal advocacy of negotiations by the Chancellor, Hertling. Prince Max secured a meeting but the Chancellor, supported by the Vice-Chancellor Payer and the Foreign Secretary Kuhlmann, was indifferent. Max made one further attempt, travelling to the military headquarters to press Ludendorff into making a clear declaration on Belgium. The moral responsibility for the coming bloodshed would, he argued, lie with the side that rejected the offer of negotiation. Max's meeting with Ludendorff had been preceded by the arrival of a memorandum drafted by Hahn and Alfred Weber, the brother of Max Weber, signed by among others the industrialist Robert Bosch, Friedrich Naumann, trade union leaders and the Swiss historian Stegerwald, underlining the unique and probably final opportunity of launching a political offensive ahead of a military campaign. The memorandum again concentrated on the vital importance of a clear renunciation of German claims to Belgium. The inclusion of the trade unions was not symbolic, for unrest in the German working population was growing. When on 4th March Lansdowne once again, and again through *The Daily Telegraph*, challenged Hertling to respond on Belgium, he too had increasing unrest in the British trade unions behind him. Prince Max and Kurt Hahn were in The Hague when Lansdowne's second letter appeared. Max travelled at once to Hertling to renew his pleading for a Belgian declaration. But Hertling was now wholly committed to the belief in military victory. On 17th May Hahn sent his friend, the American Lithgow Osborne in the US Embassy in Copenhagen, a long memorandum that, discovered years later in the Lansdowne archives, had successfully reached its intended recipient, Lansdowne himself. Hahn never changed his mind: *'if there had been one man in the German government in 1917 who at this moment would have stood up to Ludendorff and insisted on the Belgian declaration, on the supremacy of political over military power, peace could have been negotiated before the offensive of March 1918'.* [●]

On December 12th 1917 Max, in his office as President of the Badische Erste Kammer, delivered the speech in Karlsruhe that in October 1918 enabled his supporters – too late for any hope of saving Germany – finally to secure his nomination as the last Imperial Chancellor of Germany. Max dictated the first draft. In a letter to Hahn he apologises for *'the stupidity of the mistakes … the absolute absence of punctuation … my trust in your intelligence is however so great that I leave the solution of even these problems to you with confidence …'* [45] He gave key indications of the concepts he wished to underline. *'For the first time in my life I have more to say than I ought to say.'* [46] And he knew what was at stake. *'In the practical questions of peace I must emerge from this speech without any obligations. That would be different were I to speak as Chancellor. So – simply, the squaring of the circle! But I am supposed to be the solution of this problem, as you once said to me.'* [47] And *'I regard this*

[●] The Lansdowne affair has an interesting journalistic footnote in an article in *The New York Times* of 16th February 1968, in which C. L. Sulzberger called for a modern Lansdowne letter in an effort to bring the Vietnam War to an end. *'The (original) letter was viciously attacked by contemporary allied "hawks" and, as later history disclosed, efforts by sensible Germans to use it in search of peace got lost amid concentration on one last grand military offensive.'* But *'the evident fact that Hanoi, which controls Vietcong military and political operations in the South, continue to use the hint of readiness for diplomatic solution as a useful weapon of political propaganda, makes it more essential than ever that our own views should be effectively presented.'*

[●] Quoted in Adam Hochschild *To End all Wars: How the First World War Divided Britain* Macmillan 2011 pages 302–303

youngest child of my mind with a certain lack of confidence ... I shall accept every comment from your side with grateful trust in your judgment' [48] [●]

Hahn took his chance. Golo Mann says that in this speech above all one traces Hahn's style. This is not enough. It is also the most forthright, most eloquent and, in its consequences, the most important statement of the principles that governed his work throughout the war.

It is, first and emotionally, a defiant reaffirmation of German pride. How dare the English and the French continue to uphold the myth that they were the victims of unprovoked aggression in 1914! How dare the President of the United States now proclaim a crusade against the German nation! *'I put the question: does the President of the United States have the right to step forward as the world's judge?'* [49]

There follows outspoken, bitter criticism of America's support of the oppressive old regime in Russia under which thousands of German prisoners-of-war were allowed to suffer and to die (noteworthy that, notwithstanding his commitment to the prisoners-of-war, Prince Max felt able to express such formidable criticism of the regime of his Tsarist relatives). *'Thus the message of democracy has become an enormous lie in the mouth of the western powers. "Vox populi vox Dei", the western demagogues proclaim, and they blaspheme thereby against their God and the people. They are like the priests who dare to deceive their idols because in reality they do not believe in them.'* [50]

But then he turned to Germany, the absence of active citizenship, the willingness of many Germans who *'... remain passive towards the authorities, without any desire for shared responsibility in the cause of the Fatherland ... many of the best held back from political involvement because the weapons of the fight did not appeal to them. The German people need however the sacrifice of the best for the common cause in peace as in war.'* [51]

But the war has brought us alive: *'The war has come as a great awakening.'* [52] Great reformers in German history wait to see whether we shall fulfil our destiny. *'This will be decided alone by the character of our people ... institutions by themselves cannot guarantee the freedom of a people. There is only one real guarantee; that is the character of the people itself.'* [53]

And, finally, the international message, the reaching out to the enemy in the name of humanity. *'Everywhere today the forces for healing are listening out for one another; everywhere people tire of the moratorium on the Sermon on the Mount. Humanity longs for its lifting even before the war ends ... for a Christian soldier the spirit of the Red Cross belongs as much to the army as the spirit of aggression ... similar voices come today from England that tell us that English priests have learned respect for the enemy from the fighting troops which the dictatorship of the inflammatory press at home does not tolerate ... to love your enemy is the sign of those who remain loyal to the Lord even in times of war.'* [54]

That same evening Max wrote to Hahn:

'My dear colleague

Now the die has been cast. I felt strange during the speech. I was completely calm ... I noticed from my tone, from my voice, that I was not speaking at all for them but for unseen faces ...' [55]

Indeed, the unseen faces! Hahn noted at once the self-confidence that the Prince had now won in himself and in his approaching destiny. Just before his nomination as Chancellor in October 1918, the *Frankfurter Zeitung (Abendzeitung)* wrote *'the political public knows of this President of the Baden First Chamber really nothing apart from the three speeches he has delivered in December 1917 and in February and August 1918 ... these speeches had in one move made of the hitherto barely known person, who in the same breath was described as a "worthy representative of German idealism", a political personality'.* [56] [●] And the Karlsruhe speech was read attentively across the Atlantic. William Bullitt, a Hahn ally in the US Embassy in Berlin until the United States entered the war, wrote to him in 1919: *'The moment the Prince Max government came into power I felt sure that you were very close to the heart of it and it seems to me that I heard a good many echoes of your voice in his one great address – do you remember your old simile of the German people possessing a violin but not having learned to play on it? At that time I was handling our policy towards Germany in the Department of State.'*

The German Military Situation in the Spring of 1918 'Brilliant and Hopeless'

On 8th January President Wilson launched his Fourteen Points. The American State Department immediately sought an informal German reaction through Kurt Hahn,

---

[●] Quotes from letters in the private Prince Max Archive in Salem and in Golo Mann's introduction to his edition of Prince Max's memoirs of 1968

[●] Cited in *Die Regierung des Prinzen Max von Baden* by Erich Matthias and Rudolf Morsey, page XXVI

acknowledged by Bullitt himself and other US colleagues as the voice of German liberalism in which lay the best future hope for honourable negotiations. '(Hahn) *offers us an opportunity to knit together the minds and efforts of the liberals of Germany and the United States … Are we going to let this opportunity slip?'* [●] The public utterances of the German Chancellor Hertling gave them little encouragement, and a fatal blow came with the Treaty of Brest Litovsk of March, signed on 3rd March. *The Forgotten Peace*, it was christened by the British historian Wheeler-Bennett. Its consequences were fateful and far-reaching. Whilst its military significance lay in the large number of German troops that could now be redeployed on the Western Front, its political significance was likewise unmistakable. Ethnic Germans, especially the Balts, could now be brought into the greater German Empire, and the Russian Empire would be reduced progressively and rapidly to a series of partitioned states that would become dependant on Germany for their economic and political protection. European Russia was effectively dismantled. Reparations were set at 6,000,000,000 marks, and Russia lost 34% of her population, 32% of her agricultural land, 54% of her industrial base and 89% of her coal mines. [○]

The terms dismayed Liberals everywhere, even within Germany. *'One sees from the Russian peace how little healing power oppression possesses.'* [57] [■] Now the world knew what to expect, were Germany victorious. Gone was the opportunity of presenting Germany as the liberator and the protector of western civilisation against the Bolsheviks, or of fighting a defensive war against encirclement. The Treaty had become a powerful confirmation of German war aims, German imperialism and German militarism. Would-be peace-makers within the camp of the Entente countries had the ground swept from beneath their feet.

Kurt Hahn knew and had worked with the most eloquent, most active proponent of Mitteleuropa, Friedrich Naumann of the Catholic Central Party, whose writings and speeches on the theme had a dangerous plausibility. But as the historian Headlam-Morley wrote in his memoir of the Peace Conference, *'the new continental union of Mitteleuropa, though nominally free, would in fact be dominated by a German army, a German administration, a German agricultural and industrial organisation'.*

These developments gave the British historian Robert Skidelsky a stick with which to beat Hahn in an exchange of letters in 1967, so it is important to underline Hahn's ideas and ideals as expressed most fully, if in many respects naïvely and controversially, in his memorandum *Der ethische Imperialismus* of 20th March 1918, and his dismay over the gulf between them and the terms of this Treaty. One senses Hahn longing here more than ever for the friendship and support of his Oxford contemporaries, for the incorporation of British ideals and traditions into the German scene.

'Such enormous power of the kind we have developed in this war must justify itself ethically if it is to be tolerated … we must make clear that we wish to act honestly as the protector of all peoples on our borders … a Belgium in German hands would disqualify us for our task of liberation in the East … Clarity in the Belgian question is also here a decisive step…' [58] And there follows an ambitious attempt, fuelled by a beguiling combination of nationalism, admiration and envy, to propose a role for Germany as a world imperial power of the future. *'Before the war the world had been disposed of … England had a better name in the world than us. It stood everywhere in our path.'* [59] The secret of England's success: her power *'stands in the service of right and freedom. Only for this reason could the world tolerate, even favour, the fact that an island people of 45 millions brought the best parts of the world under its domination … England needed and possessed a large number of administrators whose character and daily conduct of business embodied the principle: England absorbs the happiness and the rights of other peoples into its national mission … between us and the right there stands only the Belgian question …'* [60]

Of Germany's military dominance at this point there was little doubt.

In Switzerland the military historian Hermann Stegemann had been following events closely. His memoirs describe a visit by a member of the diplomatic section of the German military high command. Their conversation moved swiftly from the strategic to the political plane *'in which my visitor was clearly at home'.* [61] He does not name his visitor, but his reference to him as a confidant of Prince Max identifies him for us clearly enough. Stegemann's message to Hahn could not have been more direct.

'Germany's military situation is brilliant – and hopeless … a declaration on the abandonment of Belgium would be no renunciation but the recognition of a situation that through the withdrawal of Russia and the opening of the borders in the East has been defined anew … but now the best

[●] From the *Memoirs of William Bullitt* in the House Collection, Yale University

[○] These observations and figures are taken from Professor John Steinberg's presentation to the seminar *The Fischer Controversy 50 years on* at the German Historical Institute in London 13th–15th October 2011

[■] Conrad Haussmann

psychological moment has passed … this was the moment when the army advanced and the strategical threat weighed in untold measure on the enemy. When the first orders to attack were given, this moment was lost. The Germans should have acted politically … if this political offensive had failed, one would have been able to say to the German people, we have made an open offer of peace, of a free Belgium, and have been turned down; then your military offensive would have been carried through with a moral élan that would have multiplied its effect a hundred times … tell the people the truth as long as you are poised to attack and act before it is too late.' [62] [●]

And he concluded that there was only one man who could bring the necessary moral authority to the task of leading Germany: Prince Max of Baden.

Germany's military strength at this moment alarmed the Entente powers, had led to the change of government in France, and consolidated Ludendorff's position as the true ruler of the country. *'Ludendorff … intervenes decisively in the East question, in the issue of autonomy for Alsace-Lorraine, and blocks a clear position over Belgium.'* [63][○]

Ludendorff's answer to the Hahn and Weber memorandum had been clear. *'One cannot choose between war and peace, but only between waiting and taking action.'* [64]

His answer to the government was even less equivocal. *'Attack has always been the fighting tradition of the Germans.'* [65]

The Beginning of the End

Germany's political paralysis is strikingly illustrated during these critical months by the cessation of all activity from July until the autumn of the Reichstag and of the Inter-Party Committee (Interfraktionelle Ausschuss).

On 24th September came the news from the Military High Command, paraphrased in the subsequent report of one Parliamentarian: *'There is no reason for despair, the western front is unshakable.'* [66]

On 28th September Ludendorff suffered a physical collapse. Military realities had exerted their price. He had also only recently been confronted with the body of his fallen airman stepson.

On 29th September, in the presence of the Kaiser, he demanded an immediate armistice on the basis of

[●] Hermann Stegemann: *Erinnerungen aus meinem Leben und aus meiner Zeit.* Deutsche Verlagsanstalt 1930 page 438

[○] Conrad Haussmann

Wilson's Fourteen Points. The Chancellor Hertling joined the meeting too late to offer a judgement and resigned. It was now that Prince Max was called to become Germany's last Imperial Chancellor. He took up office on 1st October.

The Chancellorship of Prince Max of Baden

Max arrived in Berlin with a list of ministers drawn up by Hahn with accompanying notes. It was hardly surprising that the emotionally aroused politicians viewed them with scepticism, in one or two cases with derision. As noted by the historians Matthias and Morsey, Max was now more critically dependent on his existing allies, first and foremost Colonel von Haeften and Kurt Hahn, than ever. This had already been clear, to cite one example, to the German-American businessman Noeggerath, with whom Hahn maintained constant communication throughout the war years, when he wrote to Hahn in 1917: *'Prince Max is the right man, even if he shows little initiative of his own; this must come from others in his surroundings …'* [67]

The problems were formidable.

The Western Front was reported about to break.
The Secretary of State for Foreign Affairs had the previous evening informed the Austro-Hungarians, the Turks and the Bulgarians of Germany's intention to seek an armistice through President Wilson on the basis of his Fourteen Points.
Thousands of deserters were wandering out of control behind the lines.
Spanish flu was creeping its way from the military front into home territory.

Max had arrived in Berlin with a clear policy: no offer of peace but a willingness to enter into negotiations for a peace of understanding (*Ein Verständigungsfrieden*); a clear declaration of Germany's war aims; the readiness to guarantee Belgium's freedom and independence; or a fight to the death.

But this was a policy for March 1918, not October. The most recent Note from Wilson required an urgent answer. Max fought for three days to respond on his (and Hahn's) terms and using Hahn's draft. On 2nd October Hindenburg, briefed by Ludendorff and, even in Ludendorff's absence, dominated by his subordinate, insisted in a meeting with Prince Max and the Kaiser on an immediate truce. The Kaiser, combining his habitual inconsistency with his equally habitual deference to the military, dismissed his new Chancellor's arguments. Hindenburg confirmed his judgement the following day in writing: *'The Supreme Command adheres to its demand, made on Sunday September 29th, for the immediate dispatch of the peace offer to our enemies … it is imperative to stop fighting in order to spare the German people and its allies further useless sacrifices. Every day lost costs thousands of brave solders' lives.'* So much for the *'Dolchstosslegende'*, the myth of the stab in the back! A separate report to the political party leaders along the same lines, that shocked its unprepared audience almost beyond human belief, left Max with no further room for manoeuvre or delay. The Cabinet, gripped by the military panic, defeated him. *'Hahn fought like a lion.'* Wilson was told early on 4th October that Germany was ready to negotiate, for all practical purposes, unconditionally. On the 5th Prince Max addressed the Reichstag. Simons and Hahn had drafted a speech that interpreted Wilson's Fourteen Points favourably for Germany. Von Haeften and the Cabinet raised violent objections. Max gave way. His Reichstag address effectively confirmed the acceptance of defeat.

Max's memoirs make emphatically clear how deeply he came to regret his weakness under the combined pressures of Hindenburg and Ludendorff at this point. The man who became the Deputy Chief of the General Staff on Ludendorff's subsequent resignation, Wilhelm Groener, summarised Max's political destiny in one sentence in his own memoirs: *'By allowing Ludendorff's demand for an armistice to be forced upon him, he pulled the carpet for political action from under his own feet.'* [68] [●]

Historians have understandably portrayed Germany's increasingly desperate struggles now to tie all the warring parties firmly into the obligations expressed in Wilson's 14 Points of January 1918 as the dishonourable wriggling of a defeated nation. It was the mortifying destiny of Prince Max to take on to his politically lightweight shoulders the reality of Germany's military defeat in circumstances that were to leave no room for any salvation of German honour.

Too late! This was Kurt Hahn's constant refrain for the rest of his life. If only Max had succeeded to the Chancellorship instead of Hertling in October 1917; instead of Michaelis in July. But in the confusion of October 1918 the Entente powers were asking: who is in charge in Germany – the Army, the Kaiser, or the politicians? It was the liberals who had been unable to make their voices heard who had now to settle the accounts. It was, in the end, a failure in democracy. In Golo Mann's expressive epithet: *'Those who*

were ignorant gave the orders, those who understood fell in line.'* [69] As for the German people, the increasingly public dichotomy between the determination to fight and the willingness to negotiate was sapping both military and civilian morale and would make a major contribution to the social unrest and revolution after the armistice.

And there were two further profound humiliations.

As the implications of the German concessions expressed in Max's first reply to Wilson sank in, the German High Command, with Ludendorff still in post, recovered its confidence and strongly, publicly opposed the policies into which they had forced the government by their own earlier collapse of morale. Tensions with the politicians were heightened by Hindenburg's and Ludendorff's continuing access to the Commander-in-Chief, the Kaiser. The notorious *Dolchstosslegende*, the stab in the back legend, was the thoroughly unjust fall-out of this double-dealing behaviour of the High Command. Max and Hahn were to be maliciously saddled with major responsibility for this evil deceit.

The second humiliation was personal.

Kaiser Wilhelm II, in whose hands lay the appointment of the Chancellor, had been openly uncomfortable with a 'member of the family' achieving this political power. The Kaiser's identification with the military was clear to all in the increasingly socialist and increasingly anxious, increasingly mutinous nation. Now he became a critical obstacle to the achievement of peace, for the moral crusader President Wilson was making it clear that terms could only be agreed with a Germany that was irrevocably committed to a more democratic future. Away with the war lords and away with the nobility!

Although it is not, I believe, recorded elsewhere, Simons and Hahn were commissioned in late October to find out discreetly whether, if the Kaiser abdicated and a number of generals resigned, the Front would hold.

The Kaiser was himself well aware throughout October, not least from the public press, that his continuing presence was controversial and that abdication was a lively possibility. Max, too, was compelled to accept this as increasingly inevitable, although his belief in the monarchy led him to hope that Wilhelm II might be replaced, not by his unpopular son the Crown Prince, but by his grandson. The wholesale disappearance of the German nobility across Germany after the military defeat happened with little drama except for the individuals and families who, for the most part, had to abandon their palaces and, in all instances, residual constitutional responsibilities. The drama was focused on the Kaiser. It requires a conscious act of imagination now to envisage *'the strange sense of awe,*

[●] Wilhelm Groener *Lebenserinnerungen* page 378

almost of superstition, in respect of the sovereign' (Wheeler Bennett) that rendered the abdication issue the one that imprisoned and paralyzed Max's powers of decision and physical and mental well-being. On the one hand, as a fellow noble and member of the family, he had the authority to speak openly; on the other, the shared bonds of nobility rendered personal disloyalty even more unthinkable. He tried to persuade the Grand Duke of Hesse, at one moment to be accompanied by Prince Charles Frederick of Hesse, to be his spokesman. They were unconvinced. The dilemma achieved physical expression with the Kaiser's withdrawal, vehemently opposed by Max, from Berlin to the military headquarters in Belgium on 30th October. His place, said the Kaiser, was with the army; but in reality he was fleeing the pressures on him in Berlin to abandon the throne.

Max Weber wrote dryly later of the *'dynastic sentimentality'* that had lamed the will power of the Chancellor, but the Prince's insistence that the abdication must be voluntary also made political sense – it would otherwise lose all credibility with the military; and it would represent an undignified submission, even for the Socialists, to foreign interference in German affairs. But, with the military mutinies and the revolution already well under way, Max now submitted his own resignation to the Kaiser. He drew attention in his written communication of 7th November to the danger of military dictatorship, the civil war that would follow, the *'dissolution of the whole organism of the German nation in Bolshevism'*, the impossibility for the Kaiser of forming a new government without the Socialists. The Kaiser's own withdrawal from the scene was the only way of reserving to the Crown some measure of dignity and initiative whilst making it possible for the Social Democrats to remain in government. The Kaiser requested him the following morning to remain in office until the armistice had been signed. The press was informed.

This exchange was followed by a telephone conversation between the two men. It was apparently minuted by the Prince's adjutant. This record is strongly characterised by Hahnian language and concepts: *'your abdication has become necessary … to fulfil your mission as the Peacemaking Emperor … the abdication might produce a decisive turn in the course of the peace negotiations and take the wind out of the Entente's Jingoes' sails … it would be hailed as a liberating and healing act … your name will be blessed by future generations …'*

On 9th November, believing that he had the Kaiser's agreement, Prince Max issued a statement to the press on the abdication of Wilhelm II as both Kaiser of the Empire and as King of Prussia, and on his intention of proposing the appointment of the socialist leader Ebert as Chancellor. He left Berlin that evening.

Max had been in power for 40 days. Ebert took over immediately. The war had been brought to a close; the supremacy of the politicians over the military had been established; Germany was no longer a monarchy but a fledgling parliamentary democracy. But Versailles lay ahead, and among its victims were the reputations of Prince Max and his amanuensis Kurt Hahn.

It was reported by contemporaries that Kurt Hahn was shattered by the failure of the Max Chancellorship. Would the Prince have achieved greater success if he had been appointed earlier? Hahn's subsequent life was decisively shaped by his unwavering personal loyalty to Prince Max. The ideals they shared were absorbed into his schools and into his writings. It becomes difficult to distinguish between the concepts and aspirations of the two men. Hahn repeatedly emphasised that his educational work had its roots in his political experiences in the First World War. He continued throughout his life to ascribe many of his beliefs and his practices to his wartime 'Chief'.

Hahn during the Chancellorship of Prince Max

Kurt Hahn had flourished in the informal atmosphere of confidential meetings, exchanges of memoranda and political debate that had ultimately brought Prince Max to power. But just as Max was himself unequipped to manage the politics of a democracy struggling under the desperate tensions of military defeat and the shedding of an imperial military dictatorship, so too Kurt Hahn had neither experience nor, in those decisive final weeks, an official position from which to exercise accountable influence. The judgements on him from the time illustrate his dilemma: *'a young man of pacifist outlook, with political knowledge and stylistic gifts, but without experience and not in possession of the nerves required for such situations, unknown to all of us and difficult to assess, therefore viewed with considerable mistrust and from the administrative point of view often with antipathy'* – thus the Vice-Chancellor Payer. [70] He was placed under the direction of Dr. Walter Simons, Head of Cabinet (Ministerialrat) in the Reich Chancellery. Simons commissioned a colleague, the aforementioned Arnold Brecht, to *'bureaucratize'* Hahn. The politicians with whom Max was struggling with an increasing sense of loneliness resented Hahn's unofficial but influential role, and Max Warburg, later the father-in-law of his brother Rudo, also reacted harshly to his increasing emotionalism as the strain took hold: *'Above all Hahn's hectic behaviour was irritating:*

I have today written to our cock-a-doodle-doo friend. He must remain calm, for this raving in corridors and halls and streets does not go unnoticed; this kind of agitation transfers itself, without anyone realizing it, to others.' [71]

The hostile personal tone of these judgements must be set against the achievements.

Hahn's influence over Max and von Heaften over the negotiations with President Wilson in holding the line against the military High Command, precipitately defeatist, then aggressive, is the key element in assessing his contribution at this critical moment. Matters broke into the open in the days 18th–19th October. An answer was required with urgency to Wilson's latest Note. Simons and Hahn were commissioned by Max to prepare the draft. There was surprise and disapproval that it was once again this 'Herr Hahn' who was wielding the pen. The central issue was whether to abandon U-Boat warfare. But the first Note sent out by the Prince Max government in the first week of October had amounted, against the new Chancellor's (and Hahn's) wishes, to surrender. Negotiations could no longer be conducted on this matter, for the maintenance of U-Boat warfare could be nothing other than a provocation for Wilson. Two ambassadors who were present from Copenhagen and The Hague and the former ambassador to London confirmed this judgement. The decision to abandon the U-Boat warfare was approved, but the following day naval intervention persuaded the Kaiser not to endorse this *'military, not political'* decision. Prince Max succeeded in getting the Kaiser to meet him. The Kaiser gave way and the German Note was dispatched. On 21st in the afternoon the Kaiser was coerced into receiving a parliamentary delegation.

On 24th the crisis intensified with the arrival of the American answer, for President Wilson was clearly ready to negotiate on otherwise acceptable terms with a parliamentary government, but with the implication that the Kaiser must go. When Ludendorff learned this through von Haeften, Hindenburg independently issued a general order: *'negotiations have been broken off, the fighting will continue'*. The order was issued on the basis of incomplete and unconfirmed information and without higher authority. The Cabinet wondered whether President Wilson was bluffing over the abdication issue in order to satisfy his sceptical critics at home, recognised the growing inevitability of abdication, but resented this interference in domestic affairs by a foreign power. In this moment of extreme tension between the political and the military authorities Prince Max, who was ill, summoned Hahn and commissioned him to tell von Haeften to instruct Hindenburg and Ludendorff, who were on their way from

their headquarters to meet the Kaiser, to refrain from all political involvement. Von Haeften flatly refused to follow these instructions. Then, said Hahn, this is Ludendorff's last journey. He knew his master's mind – and had helped to form it. That same evening Prince Max addressed a letter to the Kaiser, warning him that a failure to signal beyond all doubt to Wilson that, through the dismissal of Ludendorff, power in Germany had passed from the military to the politicians, could lead only to the loss of the throne. Should Ludendorff remain, Max must request to be relieved of all his responsibilities. Ludendorff, alerted by von Haeften to the turn of events, offered his resignation the following morning. It was accepted immediately. Max is known to have written this decisively important letter without consultation with the Secretaries of State or with any other Cabinet colleagues. It remains a matter of intriguing speculation whether it could have been written without Kurt Hahn.

It was now too that Hahn's cultivation of his American contacts once again became critical to the further developments.

In January 1918 Hahn had, as we have seen, responded to a confidential request from the State Department for a commentary on Wilson's 14 Points. The Americans had been especially struck by his response that, with this speech, Wilson had secured the leadership for the United States in the search for an honourable end to the conflict. Indeed (rather ambitiously and unrealistically), he had even suggested that the British and French rejection of Chancellor Hertling's measured response in his address to the Reichstag on 24th January raised the possibility that this leadership might be shared between the United States and Germany. How serious was Wilson's insistence now on the abdication of the Kaiser? Max sent Hahn to Copenhagen in late October, ostensibly to consult the German Ambassador there, in reality to confer with his American friend Lithgow Osborne in the US embassy.

'A last straw attempt' is how the German historian Klaus Schwabe describes this journey, for Lithgow Osborne, whatever his German sympathies, could not know the inner mind of President Wilson. [●] But a disregard (so argued Hahn to Osborne) of the German people's readiness now to accept a peace on the lines of Wilson's Fourteen Points, and the imposition of a humiliating defeat that allowed no freedom of action to work towards a more

[●] Klaus Schwabe: *Deutschland Revolution und Wilson-Friede.* Droste 1971 page 209 democratic future, free of the dictates of foreign powers, would discredit any future peace treaty and create long-lasting bitterness in the German population. *'Prophetic words'* is Schwabe's concluding comment.

Hahn's report to Max expressed his intensely personal understanding of the dilemma that faced him in his relationship with his kinsman the Kaiser, but *'the Hohenzollern dynasty can only be saved if the abdication of the Kaiser, which must come as a law of nature, takes place as early and in such a form as to render the people grateful to the Kaiser for it'.* [72]

And in one further respect was Hahn's position throughout the Max Chancellorship made both more difficult and more central. The Head of the Reichskanzlei, Arnold Wahnschaffe, was to write a report later in which he stated that Prince Max had spent roughly half of the six weeks bedridden. It is well known that, suffering from flu and insomnia, Max had been prescribed an ostensibly light sleeping draught by the doctor summoned by Hahn that had rendered him unconscious for 36 hours in the period 2nd–3rd November. The records show that he attended only one Cabinet meeting between 23rd October and 4th November. Hahn, the person closest to him in personal terms, was the gatekeeper. It is unsurprising that his role was distrusted by many. *'Who advises the Chancellor? Hahn? … I regret that we cannot gain access to the Chancellor … one sees Hahn the whole day in the building.'* [73] [●]

But we do not have to rely on German judgements alone. *'The first democratic Chancellor of Germany (was) too much of a 'border-line man' (in another reference: 'that transient, embarrassed phantom'), and during the six weeks of his Chancellorship he alternated between a policy of war-like cunning and a child-like belief in humanity … the new Chancellor's mainstay and support throughout those troubled weeks was … his private secretary and alter ego, Kurt Hahn, to whom must be given the credit for such constructive moves as were made by the Prince … .'* [○]

It is accepted wisdom to state that, whatever Hahn's success as an educator, he had no success as a politician. Few figures, however, emerge from the First World War political scene in Germany with more credit.

[●] The Social Democrat Deputy Philipp, cited *inter alia* in Matthias and Morsey: *Die Regierung des Prinzen Max von Baden* page 388

[○] J. Wheeler-Bennett *Hindenburg: The Wooden Titan* Macmillan 1936 page 164

Between the Armistice and Versailles

In early December Hahn received a telegram from the US State Department signed by Secretary of State Lansing. *'Come to Berne as quickly as you can. We have important matters to discuss with you.'*

This remarkable confidence in the figure of Hahn suggests that, despite his informal and emphatically personal status, he was in certain US eyes an essential representative and negotiator in efforts to accelerate the conclusion of peace following the Armistice. He now found himself endeavouring to present the emerging democracy in Germany in the best possible light (not a task that he found easy) and, above all, to get American foodstuffs into starving Germany. Before travelling to Berne he went to Copenhagen to see Lithgow Osborne again on the same errand. It is a notable feature of Hahn's reputation that, despite the personal antagonisms and distrust that he had aroused during the six-week chancellorship, he continued to act as a government emissary in the weeks following the end of hostilities and Max von Baden's complete withdrawal from the political scene.

Kurt Hahn had first met Christian Herter in Berlin in 1916. Herter had been a close colleague of the American Herbert Hoover in the latter's efforts to combat the famine in Belgium that had so impressed Max Warburg. Hahn now travelled to Berne, taking with him his medically qualified uncle Martin Hahn, to negotiate with Hoover's representatives Taylor and Kellog. In the course of the negotiations Christian Herter took Hahn aside into a neighbouring room, and Hahn recalls this incident in a letter to Marion Grafin Dönhoff on 31st December 1956:

'I can still today give you a word-by-word account of what he said then.'

'Ch. H: Do you believe that Wilson will keep faith? KH: I am certain this is his intention, but he will be powerless at the Peace Conference. The allies will present peace conditions which will violate the treaty of the 14 Points and Wilson will most reluctantly endorse these conditions. The only hope for the 14 points as the basis for peace would have been Germany's ability to say no to these conditions. Ch. H. (putting his hand on my shoulder): for God's sake don't say this. If Wilson breaks faith he will not only break faith with you but with us. I have lost my only brother in the war, and if Wilson betrays the cause for which he died, I do not want to live any more.'

The memories, of course, of a much older man! But the issue of the continuing hunger blockade (food supplies in Germany were estimated to run out at the end of February) still being used as a weapon of war by the European Entente powers Britain and France, and the moral scruples on the American side, foreshadowed many of the conflicts within the Entente delegations during the Versailles negotiations.

Hahn had instinctively understood why the Americans had called him to Berne. They wanted a report on the latest political developments inside Germany. In particular they wanted to see brought forward the date of the German elections, and as a result of these discussions and Hahn's subsequent report to Berlin, they were in fact brought forward from March to February. But Hahn was at pains – and it was indeed painful – to stress that food aid should be focused on those areas in Germany that were *'in good order'*, that is to say, quite specifically not areas that were under the control of the right wing Spartakus movement (Hahn referred to them as criminals), or to Munich and those parts of Bavaria that were under the communist revolutionary Eisner. But above all President Wilson must regain the moral leadership (easing of the blockade, easing of armistice conditions, and guarantee of a just peace). *'But if the weight of victory is too heavy for the President, if he is not in a position to remain true to his ideals … then give us for God's sake no fine words … if there can be no negotiated peace but only a dictated peace, then dictate it in the name of glorious France and the cruel, well-fed and yet ever hungry bulldog England, and not in the name of humanity and the League of Nations. Those are noble and holy concepts. They should continue to live, even if our generation is too mean and incapable of acting in accordance with them …'* [74] [●]

The Berne report, including sections of Hahn's written account, was passed directly to President Wilson.

One of the US negotiators recorded his impressions of Hahn at this time. They ring true: *'a personality of strong emotions, filled with a deep love for his country and a typically "Teutonic" inclination to adopt a philosophical position, at pains to be objective and honest, and yet highly sensitive when the conversation turned to the currently so humiliating condition of his country …'*

The continuing blockade of foodstuffs leading to widespread hunger and deaths in defeated Germany was to prove an emotional issue in Versailles. The Germans, and here Hahn was a leading exponent, bitterly reproached the Entente powers with prosecuting the war by other, inhuman means. France and England for their part suspected the Germans, accurately enough, of seeking to bypass them in direct negotiations with the Americans. Kurt Hahn had no scruples in the matter – he was acting *'in the name of humanity'*.

Versailles

Kurt Hahn attended the conference in rather typically backstage style as the private secretary to Carl Melchior, a senior Board member of the Warburg Bank in Hamburg and financial advisor to the delegation, but rapidly became a key contributor to the German efforts to resist the direction the negotiations were taking under the angry pressures of the French and the British.

We must be content here with a couple of personal highlights: Hahn, in the words of Max Warburg, striding up and down his bathroom whilst simultaneously dictating and chewing his long-suffering handkerchief; Hahn jogging in his pyjamas in the early morning around the perimeter of the park to which the German delegation was confined. Why the pyjamas? Because then the guards could not possibly suspect that he might be trying to escape.

Hahn's Oxford contemporary and friend Robert Barrington Ward, in the 1940s to be Editor of *The Times* newspaper, wrote to him in October 1921: *'No sane person here thinks that the world has really been cast in the mould of Versailles or doubts but that the Treaty will be revised … peace is not a matter of reparation but of reconstruction.'* George Kennan's verdict has also been much quoted and was taken as the dedicatory quote and title of Paul Rohrbach's memoirs: *'The Peace of Versailles was a peace in which the tragedies of the future were so inscribed as if it had been written by the hand of the devil.'* [75] [●]

Recent historians have in the main defended the work done at Versailles. The Great War of 1914–1918 and the Treaty that followed it are stories that, in the language of the theatre, will run and run. It also seems extraordinarily difficult to separate the issues from the personalities. Margaret Macmillan's presentation of the German Foreign Minister Brockdorff-Rantzau in her *Peacemakers* is not atypical: *'… witty, cruel and capricious, and most people were afraid of him. He loved champagne and brandy, some said to excess. The Head of the British military commission believed that he took drugs.'* More importantly and more convincingly, she writes critically of his speech in response

[●] Schwabe pages 242–243

[●] Paul Rohrbach: *Um des Teufels Handschrift* Verlag Dulk, Hamburg 1953

to the handing over to the Germans on 7th May 1919 of the peace terms. The ceremony, General Smuts wrote to his friend Margaret Gillett, had been prepared by the French *'more in a spirit of making war than of making peace'.* But Brockdorff-Rantzau, to quote Margaret Macmillan again, *'had decided to pursue a particular strategy that was to have dangerous consequences'.* He had entered the Trianon Palace Hotel nervous, well aware of the hostility he would encounter, under few illusions over the conditions to be imposed, and with two draft speeches in his pocket. He delivered the longer, prouder one. His behaviour (he remained seated), his manner interpreted as arrogance, his harsh voice, no doubt the impact of the German language itself, generated intensely hostile reactions that can be summarised in the one sentence of the Englishman Philip Kerr, private secretary to Lloyd George, later Lord Lothian: *'at the start everyone felt a little sympathy with the Hun, but by the time Brockdorff-Rantzau had finished, most people were almost anxious to recommence the war …'*

The importance of all this for us is that the principal drafter of this speech was Kurt Hahn, and the speech is especially remembered by history for the two challenges it threw out to the hostile audience:

'It is expected of us that we should acknowledge that we are alone to bear the guilt for the outbreak of war. This confession in my mouth would be a lie.' [76]

And

'There are crimes in war for which there is no excuse, but they occur in the midst of a terrible struggle for victory, when the passions of the battle and the worries about the survival of the nation numb the peoples' consciences. The more than 100,000 non-combatants who died after 11th November from the blockade were killed with cold calculation, after the victory had been won and guaranteed. Think of this when you talk of guilt and atonement.' [77]

There are also sentences in Hahn's draft that did not find their way into the final text but are important for us.

'He who is a patriot can only be an administrator in the national cause, not a judge. Clarity in the controversial relationships and motives of the tragic 12 days can only be achieved through a neutral commission of enquiry before which all the leading participants should give evidence and to which all archives are opened. Only in this manner can it be established where ill will was at work and where, despite good will, incapable and weak men failed.' [78]

'The German people expect a hard and stern peace. But it must be a peace of justice … a peace of force which cannot be upheld before the German people in the name of justice will rouse everywhere both secret and open opposition against its implementation.' [79]

The reference to the 100,000 who died of malnutrition reflects clearly Hahn's vain attempts in Berne to break the blockade and to import American food. The discomfort produced by this remark was not confined to the American liberals. [●] The controversy over war guilt continues to this day, much influenced in recent years by the research of the German historian Fritz Fischer whose book *Deutschlands Griff nach der Weltmacht*, published in 1961, [○] and later associated writings, generated such intense controversy in Germany when it appeared because for the first time a German historian attributed the principal culpability to Germany. There is no record of Hahn's reactions to his findings, but a confrontation between the two would have generated a memorable and passionate debate.

It is an easy matter to identify and to name prominent personalities on the allied side who were profoundly disturbed by the manner in which the Treaty had been drawn up, its terms and its implications. Few now dispute that the bad conscience it generated in liberal circles lamed the world's response to the rise of Nazism in the 1930s. The English historian Headlam Morley had been a regular and authoritative commentator during the war whose expertise had also been called upon by the Foreign Office. *'Neither Headlam nor any of this colleagues doubt that, apart from the specified exceptions, we were legally and morally bound by the President's statements. They had been voluntarily accepted by the Allies and must be given a just and impartial interpretation. The obligation was all the stronger since, as a result of the change in circumstances, including the disorganisation in Germany, a breach of the agreement on our part could not be resisted by force. It might well have been in our interest to impose unconditional surrender. This had not been done. The whole honour and reputation of the Allies and of this country in particular is involved in our carrying out in the strictest manner the undertakings which we have made;'* [■] and General Smuts, whom Hahn met at Versailles and on a number of later occasions, wrote to the British Prime Minister Lloyd George: *'… the punishment clauses could not honourably be accepted by any government … the*

[●] See for example the comment of Wheeler Bennett: *'… if Bolshevism had triumphed in Germany in the winter of 1918, the blindness and stupidity of the diplomacy of the Entente Powers would have been very largely to blame …' Hindenburg: The Wooden Titan* page 211

[○] *Germany's Aims in the First World War*

[■] From *A Memoir of the Paris Peace Conference 1919* (1972) edited by Agnes Headlam-Morley, Russell Bryant and Anna Cienciala

terms of peace … will either not be accepted or, if accepted, they will not be carried out. They will leave a trail of anarchy, ruin and bitterness in their wake for another generation …' [●] Headlam Morley's argument that the obligations on the Entente were all the stronger, given Germany's inability to resist, will have made a strong appeal to Hahn's ethical thinking, and in fact Headlam Morley spent several days in Salem after the war reviewing the course of events to assist the writing of Prince Max's memoirs.

It is light years beyond the competence of this essay to have pretentions to an authoritative judgement on Versailles, but a doubtless naïve comparison with the running of a school suggests that one should never try to impose rules that have few prospects of being either promoted or obeyed. Grey's comments were succinct: *'I am glad I am not there. They are out for loot'* and *'he thought the refusal to allow the Germans to be heard an outrage without precedent'.* [o]

The harsh terms gave the German right wing and the militarists all the ammunition they could wish for in the 1920s and 1930s. But it was also the attempts, after all the ruthless brutalities of war, to settle the German issues by Wilsonian moral criteria that created yet more misunderstanding and bitterness. The German historian Schwabe, reflecting naturally enough a German view, considered it was the moral imperatives generated by Wilson that made the success of the Treaty impossible. Germany for its part, exploiting Wilson's early commitments to moral criteria, tried to cling to a literal and idealistic interpretation of Wilson's Fourteen Points of January 1918 as its basis for having accepted the Armistice, but she was a defeated nation whose internal reforms – the subordination of the military to the Reichstag and the abdication of the Kaiser – had taken place at the last minute under unyielding pressure from the United States. Indeed, the constitutional changes rushed through in October to transform the German Reich into a parliamentary democracy were compared by Golo Mann with the emergency baptism of a weakly infant. But it is also an undeniable fact that the

[●] I suppose I should add that Headlam Morley had a greater insight into the German side through having a German wife, and that, *a la Paul Johnson* on Lansdowne, the English historian A. J. P. Taylor (the 'contrarian', to use Margaret Macmillan's word), had this disparaging comment on Smuts in the Second World War: '… *contributing the loud-sounding nothings of which he was a master* …' (not a widely shared judgement).

[o] Quoted in George Trevelyan's biography *Grey of Fallodon* pages 350 and 351

support of the French and the British for the Wilsonian ideals was for them a military necessity whilst Germany remained undefeated. After victory, their national interests took precedence.

The temptation to link the rise of Nazism with the alleged failures of Versailles is strong but increasingly resisted by historians on the grounds that it was the abandonment of the Treaty, rather than its inherent weaknesses, that allowed Hitler to seize power. But if nothing can excuse and little can explain Hitler's evil, it does not thereby become justifiable to grant Versailles some form of *cordon sanitaire* from the events that followed. Kurt Hahn fought hard for a peaceful revision of the treaty. The traction given Hitler by its terms took him far. A. J. P. Taylor wrote about the Labour Party in the 1930s, *'the moral arguments seemed to favour Germany … they felt, with a puzzled embarrassment, that Germany's demands were just, even though Hitler was not entitled to make them … Guilty conscience was undoubtedly the strongest factor.'* He was reflecting a widely held view.

Kurt Hahn remained convinced throughout his life that, had Prince Max von Baden come to power in time, history would have played both Germany and Europe a different hand. This *"if only"* of history can be given a more direct and personal reinforcement by another. *"If only"* Prince Max rather than Count Brockdorff-Rantzau had spoken in the Trianon Palace! Conrad Haussmann notes in his reflections that he had asked the new President of Germany, Ebert, on 21st November 1918 ' … *not to reject a possible approach on the part of the new government to Prince Max that he should represent Germany in the peace negotiations …'* [80] Whatever Ebert's reply, Max would never have accepted.

Post-War Work

The political and social tensions that now dominated Germany found their counterpart in an astonishing outburst of intellectual activity focused above all on disputing Germany's sole responsibility for the outbreak of war in 1914.

The personal burden for Prince Max of having led the government that paved the way to the enforced abdication of the Kaiser and the armistice weighed heavily on his health and morale. But he now gave his name and his energies to the setting up of the Heidelberger Vereinigung, a group with a distinguished membership including Max Weber, substantially funded by the industrialist Robert Bosch, whose initial task was to provide the German delegation in Versailles with convincing material to dispute what became the war guilt clause. Once again the principal driving force and drafter of memoranda was Hahn. A study of the correspondence of the fluctuating membership quickly reveals a lack of unity in pursuing the stated aims, some disagreement about procedures and methods of consultation, reluctance by Bosch to continue his support, and the acceptance by Max himself that the body was not carrying conviction. There were too many others in the field, and one also gains the slightly distasteful impression that some were as anxious to prove their intellectual and patriotic credentials as to further the national case. But the group provided a number of eloquent, closely argued statements on the main issue, and the verdict of the American historian Alma Luckau merits quotation: *'This much seems to be certain, however: this group, started by some of the most influential intellectual leaders of Germany, was far more important than is generally known.'* She also felt that, whilst the Vereinigung had been ineffective in awakening German opinion to the immediate effects of Versailles, their researches became the starting point for more effective efforts in later years.

If it is arguable that the Heidelberger Vereinigung was too tightly focused on the war guilt issue, Hahn was able to write to his friend Professor Eberlein on 28th December 1922: *'In the meantime the Institute for Foreign Affairs has been founded in Hamburg.'* [81]

In the wake of the Versailles conference, delegates from both Britain and the United States, disturbed by the conduct of the conference and the emotions it had failed to discipline, resolved to found an institute that would provide for the well informed and dispassionate study of international affairs with the aim of preventing future wars. The outcome was the setting up in 1920 of the British Institute of International Affairs that, with the granting of a royal charter in 1926, became the Royal Institute of International Affairs, or Chatham House. In the United States, related efforts gave birth to the Council on Foreign Relations. Kurt Hahn was well aware of these plans through personal discussion in Versailles with individual British and American representatives, notably Christian Herter. The Institut fur Auswartige Angelegenheiten was the German parallel response. After rapidly achieving a distinguished reputation, it was progressively taken over by the Nazi Party from 1933 onwards but was revived in the post-war years in cooperation between the City and the University of Hamburg. It is again characteristic of Hahn's backstage style, not only that his letter, quoted in the preceding paragraph, knowledgeably anticipated the public launch of the institute by several weeks (the foundation that established the institute was set up on 31st January 1923), but that his name has effectively vanished from the public records of the preparatory activities, to be found today only in the private Warburg archive in Hamburg. He and the banker Max Warburg, with Prince Max, had been the moving spirits.

It is entirely plausible to argue that the German (and Hahn) cultivation of the war guilt complex proved an impediment to German recovery long before Hitler seized on its propaganda value. Hahn, for example, opposed Germany's entry into the League of Nations because the war guilt issue had not become the subject of neutral adjudication. Thus he found himself rebuked by the Cambridge historian J. R. M. Butler, brother of the Neville Butler whom he had successfully extracted from the Ruhleben internment camp in 1915 (and son of the Harrow headmaster), in a letter of 14th November 1924. The League of Nations, *pace* Butler, was the one great constructive contribution of the age; Germany must either join the League or seek a deeper rapprochement with Russia (a course that, to Hahn's deep dismay, Germany had already embarked upon with the Treaty of Rapallo in April 1922); Germany may have signed the Treaty of Versailles under duress, but why reject the one part that might prove beneficial to her; furthermore, the covering letter delivered to Brockdorff-Rantzau by the Entente partners had pointed out that they had created the machinery for the peaceful adjustment of all international problems by discussion and consent, whereby the settlement of 1919 itself could be modified from time to time to suit new facts and new conditions as they arose.

The two alternative approaches to the Versailles terms have been called the policy of fulfilment and the policy of obstinate resistance. Hahn, despite his undeniable nationalism, did not allow himself to be drawn uncompromisingly into the latter camp, but nor did he now support the socialists who, in the 1920s under Ebert and Stresemann, made major advances in restoring Germany's good name.

In 1927 the Tannenberg Memorial was dedicated with Hindenburg the principal figure and speaker. With Republican and Jewish ex-servicemen excluded from the ceremony, this great patriotic occasion was themed explicitly to repudiate German war guilt. Wheeler Bennett comments in his account of this event that *'whether the accusation had been justified or not, Germany would have been better advised to allow it to lapse by tacit consent than to demand the impossibility of its public withdrawal'.* Two years later Prince Max died. On his death bed (note again the Hahnian drama), he sent a letter to the British Prime Minister Ramsay MacDonald: *'I am certain that we must wait many years, and I want to address my last words to my fellow countrymen: do not lose patience. But I regard it as my duty in this letter openly to express the warning: unless the hope of an eventual revision of the Versailles Treaty can be kept alive, Germany will not expect its salvation by peaceful means.'* [82] Revision of the Treaty in the eyes of both Max and Hahn concerned the moral issue of the war guilt and Germany's eastern frontier. Over both, Brest-Litovsk cast too long a shadow.

There remained one more First World War task for Hahn.

The Memoirs of Prince Max

It is a challenging, a sobering thought that, in the very years in which he created and built up the school of Salem against all the odds of Germany's political and economic chaos, Hahn was able to conduct research of extraordinary thoroughness and to draft these memoirs. Figures who had been active participants in the Max von Baden Chancellorship took part in carefully minuted seminars in Salem, Hahn's war-time secretary Lina Richter playing a key role. Max was often present, always consulted when absent over the conclusions. It is true that Hahn was also telling his own story, but his role in the memoir text parallels exactly his role in the war-time years – a background figure, his style of thought and expression ever present, the pace of the narrative never slackening, his interpretations of the role of human character and human personality always decisively in the foreground.

These memoirs, which appeared in 1927, two years before Max died, achieved his rehabilitation in German public life. Their impact was as decisive in restoring his reputation as his Karlsruhe speech in 1917 had been in propelling him towards the Chancellorship ten months later. The roles of the two protagonists were the same. The memoirs were Prince Max's permanent memorial.

This leaves us with the question much asked at the time. *What could Max have achieved without Hahn?* Yet more damaging was the journalistically sweeping, mocking review of the Memoirs by the eloquent left-wing, pacifist Veit Valentin! *'This German prince is a decent, benevolent man – an exception therefore even among princes. And this is why he was discovered by Hahn … Kurt Hahn ruled Germany for four weeks – say many today. If only he had! It is rather the case that he ruled Prince Max for years, and also "co"-authored this thick book – they are for a good part Kurt Hahn's collected works; it is just that during the Chancellorship of the Prince he was separated from him, or at least not given full access to him, and in what he wanted to achieve, overruled.'* [83]

The socialist Philipp Scheidemann's comment in an inter-party meeting on 7th November 1918 had fed such impressions: *'The Chancellor is not a very decisive figure. There are already various men swarming around him who*

Prince Max of Baden

have no official position and yet are involving themselves in all sorts of things, among them Kurt Hahn, for example …' [84]

Golo Mann would have none of this. Probably closer in temperament to the old German nobility and their contributions to the Länder over which they ruled, he had gone out of his way when editing and re-publishing the Memoirs in 1968 explicitly to bring the Prince's personality more clearly into the foreground: his artistic temperament, his learning, his clear understanding, arising from his international family relationships, of the movement of public opinion in other countries and of their significance for Germany. The Markgraf's private archive in Salem contains numerous, mostly handwritten letters from Max to Hahn, expressing reactions, wishes and clear guidelines for the emerging text. Underlining, as he saw things, Hahn's greater educational than political gifts, Golo brings the talents and humanitarian beliefs that Hahn recognised in the Prince into harmony with Hahn's achievement in strengthening the Prince's own confidence in these very talents and making them available for the highest public service – and personal sacrifice.

This sympathetic interpretation has however not survived well the test of posterity. Even Golo Mann acknowledges that, when Max came into power, he was dependent first and foremost on von Haeften and Kurt Hahn, only after them on Conrad Haussmann, Max Warburg, the Minister for the Colonies Solf and Walter Simons. But we gain little by seeking to dramatise disparities between the two men. Theirs was nothing if not a symbiotic relationship. We can state baldly that, without Hahn's skilful manoeuvring over months and without the Karlsruhe speech of December 1917, Prince Max von Baden would never have become Chancellor of Germany, stepping thereby, however briefly, on to the world's stage. Without the Memoirs, his reputation would probably have remained in the desolate wasteland of bitterness and calumny in which it lay from 1918 until 1927. Without the Prince, Kurt Hahn could not have achieved the political if largely hidden prominence that was his in the concluding weeks of the war; nor could he have embarked so rapidly and so convincingly on his life's dream, that of founding a pioneering school. Given, however, Hahn's conviction that his educational work owed much of its direction to his political experiences between 1914 and 1918, we cannot escape one further reflection.

'In democratic times the statesman must also be a politician.' [85] [●] This was a problem for Hahn too.

To borrow loosely from Kant, liberalism is essential but is it possible? It is arguably easier to achieve if a public-spirited and independently-minded aristocracy is on hand to assert liberal values without having to seek the endorsement of the ballot box.

'Aristocracy is the salt wherewith democracy should be salted.'

This favoured sentiment, repeatedly quoted by Hahn, readily interpreted by him and accepted by friends and colleagues as meaning the aristocracy of merit and public service rather than the exercise of inherited privilege, comes rather unfortunately from the Swedish writer and politician Gustav Steffen who was expelled in 1915 from the Swedish socialist party for outspoken support of German imperialism. Hahn had an admirable example of aristocracy in the shyly talented gentleman from the quiet Cistercian monastery in the countryside of Lake Constance. Modern life was however not to be kind to a liberalism that was dependent on such privileged circumstances. And Hahn, believer though he was in the voice of the people, attached little value to the legitimacy of the ballot box. This was to be his Achilles heel as the Nazi Party moved towards power.

[●] *Prinz Max von Baden Erinnerungen und Dokumente* edited by Golo Mann and Andreas Burckhardt 1969 page 56

Before the memoirs were published, they were read aloud chapter by chapter in Salem by Kurt Hahn in the autumn of 1926 before the Prince and his wife, their son Berthold, their daughter Marie Alexandra and son-in-law Prince Wolfgang of Hesse, and a small number of others. Hahn's style, his sense and appreciation and exploitation of the dramatic, the pace of his narrative, his emphasis on human personality and human relationships, the warmth of his loyalty (and one must add, too, of his gratitude) to the nominal author and protagonist of the story, the feudal surroundings, endow the complex political narrative with an almost romantic overtone of majestic if flawed achievement against impossible odds. It was fortunate as well as prudent that the true author, the self-avowed ghost-writer of the early 20th century, had taken such scrupulous care to document his researches and his memories. But one episode is revealing. The memoirs relate how Max, before leaving Berlin, had a final meeting with his successor, Ebert. *'At the door I turned back once more: Herr Ebert, I entrust the German Empire to your heart. He answered: I have given two sons to the Empire.'* [86] As a small party crossed the courtyard after the final reading, the former Prussian Minister of War General Scheuch turned to Hahn and said: *'But, Herr Hahn, the end of the book is not right at all. Prince Max did not see President Ebert again,'* [87] to which Hahn responded: *'but for God's sake, General, do not alter this sentence, I beg you, for if you do, you pluck the most beautiful feathers from my bird of paradise'.* [88]

This episode is recited in the privately printed memoirs of Prince Wolfgang of Hesse, whose father Friedrich Karl had reasons for unhappiness over the firm implication in the memoirs that, had he accepted the task of intervening with the Kaiser on behalf of Max for abdication, whatever the outcome, Max would have been absolved of weakness in pursuing this essential aim.

Kurt Hahn's passport of 1920 identified his profession as that of *Schriftsteller* (author). He always had a persuasive pen. Perhaps his far later judgement on Prince Max was the most honest, and it does him credit. Reflecting after 1945 on the nature of moral resistance, he described his patron and wartime chief in the following words: *'He was not a great leader, but the wisest and noblest of guides.'*

Hindenburg's confidential letter of 24th June 1927, thanking Max for a copy of the memoirs, brings together in one paragraph a widely accepted summary of the Prince's character with its strengths and weaknesses, the equally widely shared resentment over the activities of the Prince's advisors, and an unreserved acceptance of his integrity over the issue of the abdication. This last must have been especially consoling for Max, the Prince of Baden.

'Although I am not in agreement with the decisions taken by Your Royal Highness, I see the reason for this solely in the fact that Your Highness had too sensitive a nature for the cruel realities of those difficult times and in the false counsel that you were repeatedly given. In no sense, however, did Your Royal Highness, with the premature announcement of the abdication of His Majesty the Kaiser and King on 9th November, wish to serve ignoble ends. Your Highness, himself heir to a crown, and following unclear news from Spa, believed that only in the manner in which the events took place could you make possible the salvation of the monarchy.' [89]

Salem

There is a music hall story from Berlin in which an old man gives his young grandson a button and tells him to go and sew an overcoat onto it. Prince Max wanted schooling for his son Berthold and Hahn created Salem.

It is a remarkable story and has been told in admirable detail by Salem in several publications in recent years. Let us just note certain features of this achievement.

The school was conceived by both Hahn and Max as an educational response towards the restoration of Germany's name and place in Europe and to the lack of courageous and independently-minded leadership that had so dismayed Hahn among the politicians during the war.

Almost without a break, both its formal founder Max and Hahn himself were subjected to vindictive public attacks arising from their perceived role in Germany's defeat and humiliation, Hahn's Jewish background giving the aggressors added ammunition. These attacks included physical threats and a clumsy attempt at kidnap or assassination. As his close colleague Marina Ewald told the story, and only of Hahn could such an account be credible, Hahn was sheltering one day in the autumn of 1923 from a thunderstorm in a barn and entered into a long conversation with a young man sharing his refuge about the dire political situation in Germany. Eventually the young man confided that he was scouting out the countryside since he was preparing the capture of *'that Jew Hahn, dead or alive'*. Then, said Hahn, I am your man, and persuaded his new acquaintance to abandon his plan and give himself up to the police. The outcome was a trial in Constance in which prison sentences were imposed on three men for conspiring to kidnap Hahn, the murder charges not being upheld. A fourth, Hahn's friend from the barn, was found work in the United States by Eric Warburg, son of Max Warburg.

Hahn's educational ideas now began to be formulated in simpler, briefer and more accessible ways. The so-called Salem Laws are well worth quoting here.

Give the children opportunities for self-discovery
Make the children meet with triumph and defeat
Give the children the opportunity of self-effacement in the common cause
Provide periods of silence
Train the imagination
Make games important but not pre-dominant
Free the sons of the wealthy and powerful from the enervating sense of privilege

The school had outstanding, nationally recognised directors of studies in these early years. An Englishman, Claude Sutton, who went on to become a don at Oxford, has confirmed in writing that the academic standards were entirely satisfactory, although Hahn was not then and never became a respecter of academic timetables if he saw an immediate opportunity for some character-challenging enterprise. But Golo Mann, an early pupil, has made it clear that Hahn was a riveting teacher.

Another Salem pupil (1922–1928), Alice von Platen, later Alice Ricciardi, [•] a contemporary and close friend of Golo Mann, told me in conversation that Hahn *'was not a real German … we never came back to Goethe and Schiller and classical Weimar. It was all Greece and England.'* The pupils, she said, were always conscious that theirs was a *'different'* school, perhaps too happy an island, composed of many social levels, and that Hahn, often mysterious, was an extraordinary personality. It was, she also said, *'an excellent political school'*. There were debates when Hahn spoke politically. She remembers especially one remarkable evening when Golo Man spoke for and Hahn against pacifism. Neither she nor Golo liked certain sides of Hahn, and here *'he showed his worst side, encouraging as many boys as possible to join the army'*. He was, she said, *'Deutschnational'*, in the way that so many assimilated Jews were. We are taken back to that speech in Karlsruhe when he praised the military virtues: *'But the war has come as a great awakening. Everywhere the hidden powers of the people have been stirred into life … the armed nation will return with the strength of steel…'* [90] and to his paper on Ethical Imperialism: *'In this war a new Germany has been born … everywhere there is the will to contribute to the common cause … the fortunes of war have done us the service of making this new German bearing known across the world …'* [91]

[•] Alice Ricciardi became an early pioneer in group psychiatry and spent seven and a half months studying testimony at the Nuremberg medical trials.

It was not until much later that Hahn carried his praise for the military virtues over into the training and discipline required for rescue, citing his old master William James, who *'has challenged statesmen and educators to discover the moral equivalent of war. It has been discovered: the passion of rescue releases the highest dynamics of the human soul.'* I am utterly convinced that in no school has this message been more faithfully and more effectively expressed than in the early years of the Atlantic College. At the same time I have always regretted that Hahn never made reference to other parts of William James' famous *Remarks at the Peace Banquet in Boston* in 1904: *'All the qualities of a man acquire dignity when he knows that the service of the collectivity that owns him needs him. If proud of the collectivity, his own pride rises in proportion.'* James writes then of the inequalities of the burdens carried by men owing to mere accidents of birth and opportunity. But a conscription of the whole youthful population, with challenging tasks in the global fight against the harsh forces of nature (how easy it would be to transform this into environmental and social tasks) *'would preserve in the midst of a pacific civilisation the many virtues which the military party is so afraid of seeing disappear in peace'.*

It is extraordinary, looking back over the documents, to realise the outspokenness with which the Salem school was linked with the struggle to re-assert the spirit of Germany. There is no more powerful example than the speech delivered by Prince Max at a patriotic ceremony (*'eine vaterländische Feier'*) of the school on 7th February 1923. The ceremony began with the singing of the Dutch hymn *Wir treten zum Beten vor Gott den Gerechten*, originally written and composed to mark the victory of the Dutch over the Spaniards in 1597, enthusiastically adopted by Kaiser Wilhelm II on behalf of the German Reich, later much used and therefore compromised by the Nazi Party on mass occasions. (This same hymn was to be used with an English text in Gordonstoun and again in Salem after the Second World War.) Less than one month earlier, France had occupied the Ruhr. *'There are dark years in the history of a nation … all men of conscience long for the great call … on us Germans depends whether we survive or perish as a nation … it is right that at this moment especially German youth should listen, hold its breath and seek to understand this historical hour …'* [92] Max continued with words that found an audience far beyond Salem: *'The German people had lost their respect for their own history. The morals of the Balkans have infected not only our cities; they have infected our politics, until in this last year our deceived youth believed that in Germany one can be a murderer without becoming an outcast. A heavy responsibility is borne by those educated*

people who have uttered sympathetic and even encouraging words about murder. In Germany there was no public conscience …' [93]

There follow strong words against France, against England, against the United States, against the attitude *'but they are only Germans'.* And his final sentence echoes Schiller. *'I hear the warning: the way forward is hopeless. That may be. But millions in the German people will then reply: rather death than life in slavery.'* [94]

The ceremony ended with a performance of the Rutli scene from Schiller's *Wilhelm Tell* in which the three representatives of the cantons of Uri, Schwyz and Unterwalden meet to swear an oath for unity and freedom

Wir wollen sein ein einzig Volk von Brüdern, in keiner Not uns trennen und Gefahr.	We shall be a single People of brethren, Never to part in danger nor distress.
Wir wollen frei sein, wie die Väter waren, eher den Tod, als in der Knechtschaft leben.	We shall be free, just as our fathers were, And rather die than live in slavery.
Wir wollen trauen auf den höchsten Gott und uns nicht fürchten vor der Macht der Menschen.	We shall trust in the one highest God And never be afraid of human power.

As the 1920s progressed, Salem, in common with many other organisations, engaged increasingly in activities that had a ring of military training: rifle shooting, the building of gliders, games across large tracts of countryside that involved opposing groups seeking by rapid movement and skill to outwit the other party. A similar philosophy of youth training was also making its appearance that had the following aims:

'The army – the irreplaceable school – the army educated for idealism and devotion to the fatherland and its glory – schools in a nation of the people must devote vastly more time to physical education … our intellectual leadership has always achieved brilliant successes, whereas our education of the will has been beyond contempt … loyalty, readiness for sacrifice, trustworthiness, are virtues that a great nation requires …' [95] [●]

It is all so easy looking at these matters in retrospect. G. K. Chesterton warns us: *'It is the fact that falsehood is*

[●] Adolf Hitler; *Mein Kampf*

never so false as when it is very nearly true.' The moment came when Hahn had to make the differences clear. He was already a marked man after openly challenging Hitler over his telegram to the five young Nazi thugs who had trampled a young communist to death in August 1932 in Potempa in Upper Silesia in front of his mother. Hitler sent the men, imprisoned and under death sentences, a public message of solidarity. The death sentences were commuted soon afterwards. The men were released from prison and publicly celebrated when Hitler came to power.

In February and March 1933, Hitler now in power, Kurt Hahn spoke out in Hamburg, Göttingen and Berlin. An educator could, he said, continue his work in accordance with his own ideas, quietly, without worrying what was going on all around him, taking the wind as it came, waiting until it turned, and holding the young entrusted to him distant from all political events and debate. But an educator with this idea in mind would, he said, be entirely unfit to educate citizens for today's Germany. If, he continued, one looked at the programme of the Balilla, the Italian fascist Youth Organisation, one could imagine that one had the headings of the entire Salem Final Report before one's eyes, among them

> *Public Spirit*
> *The Ability to face and to overcome Discomfort,*
> *Hardship and Danger*
> *Physical Exercise (Fighting Spirit and Endurance)*
> *Presence of Mind in the Face of the Unexpected*

One heading only would be missing and had to be missing:
> *The ability to carry through what one believes in one's conscience to be right*

There could, he said, be *'… sacro egoismo, sacred egoism. There is also sacred lying, sacred murdering, sacred perjury, the sacred breaking of promises …'*

It is worth quoting one letter he received at this time. *'Unfortunately we were not able to speak with you again after your lecture and to shake you by the hand for the courageous words you spoke in this difficult situation in which the nation finds itself … here there spoke a man who is fully and deeply conscious of his task as an educator in the sense of a national 'humanitas' and a humane national consciousness … let us hope that our people in its national movement does not forget the eternal human and German values … may it not be forgotten what you, especially you, have done and continue to strive for with your clear, pure sense of national feeling…'* [96]

Within weeks he was in prison.

The Rise of Nazism, Imprisonment, and Flight to England

Salem School had achieved an astonishing reputation in Britain and even across the Atlantic. Hahn's arrest led to immediate protests from well-placed English friends. A letter from the British Prime Minister Ramsay MacDonald, skilfully drafted and advocated by his private secretary Neville Butler whom Hahn, with prescient networking skill, had befriended and rescued from internment in Berlin during the war, was sent to the Minister of Foreign Affairs Baron von Neurath. By the time it arrived, Hahn had been released but was then banished from Baden and forbidden all future access to the school.

Kurt Hahn's efforts to exercise influence over the political developments in the late 1920s and early 1930s require a more detailed examination than this memoir can accommodate. The key practical problem was that he had no 'Max card' to play. In his letters and memoranda from 1930 onwards and the first electoral successes of the Nazis, there is a strengthening note of desperation combined with a clear forecast of the dangers to come. *'The national socialist youth includes first rate human material. I know these young people who sing their warlike songs in secret and reckon with the sacrifice of their lives as something they do not fear. The expression on their faces often recalls the volunteers for war in 1914. What is the real source of strength of the National Socialists? … It is the disgust at the corruption of the German parliamentarianism.'* [97]

And there we have the problem. The Social Democrats were all too easily confused with the Communists and the Bolsheviks, and by the Nazis deliberately so. The nation required strong leadership that would undermine the attractions of Nazism by pressing with no further hesitation or inhibitions for the peaceful revision of the Versailles Treaty, the re-ordering of the eastern frontier, and the setting up by Chancellor Bruning (September 1930) of a new government whose ministers would be men of integrity and stature, not parliamentarians. Above all, the President of the Republic Hindenburg must guarantee the future of the nation. *'But one thing is clear: if Hitler comes, Hindenburg must go. Whoever advises Hindenburg to work with Hitler as Chancellor … assumes of Hindenburg that he will be unfaithful to his character and his convictions … Hindenburg should launch the slogan for the election: "no to the power of the parties, yes to the sovereignty of the people, no to parliamentarianism, yes to the President chosen by the people".'*

Prince Max, Max Weber and Kurt Hahn had all been of one mind. Their position is perfectly captured in a statement by Weber that Hahn had used in his speeches in February and March 1933, referring to the time when Weber had been consulted over the drafting of the Weimar Constitution. *'So, now I have won a great victory over the German corruption that will follow. We shall experience the worst kinds of cronyism, above all party patronage, the most evil form of corruption. But the President elected by the people can heal the corrupt state.'* [98] In moments of crisis, Hahn declared, the nation's President could call on the people to rise up against the Parliament. [99]

Herein lay of course the attractions of Hitler as the Fuhrer set about dismantling the Versailles Treaty and rebuilding national morale. Like others, Hahn was briefly tempted to imagine that, if Hitler's eyes could only be opened to the brutalities that were being committed in his name, all could be well, even giving a major hostage to fortune by speculating, in 1933, that Hitler had *a warm, even a soft heart'*. [●] This credulity is, we now know, a common enough phenomenon under dictatorships. In his *Stalin: The Court of the Red Tsar*, Simon Sebag Montefiore tells us how, once the grand massacre of 1937 had got underway, directed mainly by Yezkov, the Head of the NKVD, with an estimated 700,000 executed, *'the writer Ilya Ehrenburg met Pasternak in the street: he waved his arms around as he stood between the snowdrifts. "If only someone would tell Stalin about it."'* So it is good to recall a letter that Hahn had sent his English friend Charles Trevelyan back in June of 1920: *'… a new democracy has sprung up at Weimar, ungainly and tarnished by personal and party ambitions, but still a democracy … the German people are in the same plight as the Jews are, when taunted by their oppressors. Remember the saying of an old Rabbi addressed to an anti-Semite: you hit us till we are lame, now don't reproach us if we limp.'*

A few more weeks in Berlin and northern Germany, and a clear warning from a former Salem pupil with access to Nazi intentions, led to his departure by train from Berlin to London in July 1933. He returned to Berlin at least once more, in 1934, almost certainly to see his ailing mother, but all communications to him had now to be sent from Switzerland to escape censorship. News from Salem reached him regularly, and he was exchanging occasional letters almost up to September 1939 with Heinrich Blendinger who, as headmaster, carried Salem

[●] It is simple enough, in retrospect, to identify (and disapprove of) the many optimistically tolerant assessments of Hitler. John Wheeler-Bennett, who spent much time in Germany between 1927 and 1934, described Hitler in the May 1933 issue of the journal *International Affairs* as *'the most moderate member of his party'*.

through the Second World War years with unblemished courage and integrity.

Scotland Again

By the autumn of 1933 Kurt Hahn had opened a small school in Rothiemurchus in Scotland. 1934 was the year in which he founded Gordonstoun. Influential friends and their vast family connections made it all possible. His Salem reputation convinced many but not all. *"Listening to sermons by mystical Germans who preach from ten to four"* had already been identified by Gilbert and Sullivan's Mikado as a curious pastime typical of Central Europeans (but not of Britons). He wrote, lectured and broadcast. Just one example is the series of lectures he gave at the London Institute of Education in 1934, the closing one under the Chairmanship of the Headmaster of Eton, Claude Elliott. Salem, he confidently stated, would survive *'the transitional period – only desertion could destroy it'*. Not all were convinced, but Gordonstoun which, like Salem, has told its own story well on many occasions, carried the Hahn message confidently forward.

The Approach of War

With his arrival in Britain, Kurt Hahn found himself quite literally on the other side. The Nazis kept a close eye on him, reports being sent to Berlin on his activities by the German consul in Glasgow. When he passed through a Swiss airport, the fact was reported to the Nazi authorities. An unsigned postcard from Switzerland warned him not to risk setting foot again in Germany as he was listed for immediate arrest. Well aware of the increasing brutalities in the concentration camps, for an English friend had gained surprising access to Dachau, and accounts also came to him from other sources, he tried, repeatedly and unsuccessfully, to alert influential Englishmen to the realities of life under the Nazis. He succeeded in June 1934 in putting together a small group, led by Sir Wyndham Deedes, which travelled to Berlin with a memorandum drafted by Hahn and co-signed by, among others, the Archbishop of York William Temple, Lord Allen of Hurtwood, the historians George Trevelyan and G. P. Gooch, Maynard Keynes, Gilbert Murray and the actress Sybil Thorndike, in a vain attempt to press Hitler to acknowledge and to bring under control the brutalities of the concentration camps. The delegation was brushed aside, the memorandum was brought back home, and Geoffrey Winthrop Young as a member of the group included in a long report the comment on Hitler that *'there is one characteristic of his about which there is almost complete unanimity of opinion and that is that he will never throw over his friends and that even if he himself is convinced that a "purge" is desirable, he will lack the courage'.* The Roehm Putsch followed within six weeks, one of its many victims the former General von Schleicher with whom Hahn had briefly conspired, in joint efforts with General von Hammerstein, to persuade President Hindenburg to reject the thought of Hitler as Chancellor.

Hahn took a special, indeed a passionate interest in the fate of a lawyer, Hans Litten, whom the Nazis had arrested without legal justification of any kind on the night of the Reichstag fire, and who following brutal treatment and torture finally took his own life in Dachau. Litten had subpoenaed Hitler in a court case in 1931. Hahn's own public protest again the Nazi thugs' murder of the young man in Potempa in August 1932 was on exactly the same issue: criminal brutality sanctioned by the Party leadership. Hahn got the mother across to England, looked after her financially, encouraged her to write up her crusade to save her son, saw to its translation into English and subsequent publication, [●] and arranged that the BBC employ her for broadcasts to Germany. With satisfaction he noted after the war had started that the American edition of the book was sold out within one week, eliciting from Mrs. Roosevelt the comment that she was proud to belong to the human race which had produced Mrs. Litten and her son. But all this had to be done without endangering his industrialist brother Rudo in Berlin, or his wife Lola and their two children. Nor should the Nazis be given any grounds for increased pressures on Salem, which was holding its own with difficulties but made a fine name for itself by winning three times the Public Schools athletics competition at the White City; the successful athletes not allowed to greet Kurt Hahn but taken twice to Windsor Castle where they were given tea by the Dean and also presented to King Edward VII. The school's success was of course fine propaganda for Germany and strengthened its credibility with the country's rulers and prospects for survival.

As the 1930s progressed and appeasement took its hold of British public opinion, Hahn's ability to generate memoranda and to ensure their purposeful distribution to personalities such as Malcolm Macdonald in the Colonial Office and Lord Halifax and Alexander Cadogan in the Foreign Office accelerated with the quickening pace of events. There were anxious negotiations with

Archbishop William Temple of York and Bishop George Bell of Chichester, principally on the sabotage of the existing Christian Churches in Germany brought about by the creation of the German Evangelical Church *(Deutsche Evangelische Kirche)* that was declared compatible with National Socialism. There were meetings too with his old friend William Bullitt, now US Ambassador in Paris, Sir Robert Vansittart, the leader of the Liberal Party Archibald Sinclair, and his Oxford contemporary Robin Barrington Ward, now Deputy Editor of *The Times.*

Hahn's friendship with Barrington Ward came under especially severe strain.

In March 1939 Henry Brooke, a journalist and Member of Parliament, had had a series of articles on the concentration camps, documented with evidence obtained for him by Hahn from eye-witnesses and survivors, rejected by *The Times.* *'I think we shall weaken our power if our Press merely becomes a sort of Bradshaw of atrocities, minor and major, from day to day,'* Barrington Ward wrote to Hahn on 7th March by way of explanation. Hahn did not spare him in a reply on 24th March 1939: *'murder and massacre by order are not purely domestic concerns of either the Russian or the German governments. The best informed man I know in England told me in January that, according to his information, the conditions in concentration camps, while still cruel and rough, had virtually improved. This at a time when tortures were no longer the acts of cruel individuals but efficiently and bureaucratically organised into a system! Sufferers and witnesses were in this country but they could not obtain a hearing. The name of my friend is RBW, late of Balliol … Throughout this dark year the commandants of Buchenwald and Dachau operated, confident that public opinion in England is well-controlled …'* Robin Barrington Ward responded with dignity. *'… I do not believe that we really disagree on the fundamentals … what was and is all-important to us, compromised as we have been by the Treaty of Versailles, is the issue on which we should take our final and unequivocal stand, with all that it means for the lives of millions … our only hope is to rally Germany against the Nazis … That also must help to define the issue … Further, our idealism must also have material as well as moral strength or it will be empty … fortunately our strength is rising fast.'*

Hahn was dismayed. *'In the present situation I derive my only hope from the words of my old master Hans Delbruck: The English have a gentleman's agreement with Providence that they come to their senses five minutes before twelve. It is two minutes to twelve now.'*

[●] Irmgard Litten, *Beyond Tears,* Alliance Book Corporation, New York (1940) and Irmgard Litten, *Die Hölle sieht dich an,* Ed. Nouvelles Internat., Paris (1940)

On the Other Side

Kurt Hahn was, it is true, just one of thousands of often highly gifted Jews compelled to leave Hitler's Germany, whose loyalties must in differing measures have been divided as the war progressed – Hahn the Headmaster who now had former pupils fighting and losing their lives on opposing sides, those from Salem and her sister schools misused and compromised in a cause of undisputed wickedness; Hahn the Oxford graduate who in his heart had envied England in the First World War, now an exile, *'sorrowing for his erring homeland'*. In this new conflict he was to play, albeit in a minor key, the role he had played from 1914–1918: interpreting policies and morale in the enemy camp. Once again however, and even more emphatically, he had no M card to play.

In 1938 he had put forward proposals for the resolution of the Czech crisis, his position made the more authoritative by his opposition from the outset to the Versailles incorporation of the three million-strong German minority in the Republic of Czechoslovakia: a *'way out which is honourable and could be made acceptable to Czechoslovakia: no plebiscite in fever heat and the atmosphere of a Civil War, but a plebiscite to be held after a year when there has been appeasement. The alternative – cession to Germany or autonomy within Czechoslovakia … the area to be governed in the meantime by an international commission, supported by international police, to be composed of, say, Dutch, Swiss and Swedish units … one could point out to the Czechs that in a year's time the Sudeten area would have tasted the peace of honourable democracy … many waverers might be less attracted by the restlessness of the Dictatorship … Hitler would probably remonstrate, but opinion in Germany will consider the proposed settlement just, or at least one which does not justify war … should Hitler say no, he will in the eyes of Germany bear the responsibility for the coming war …'* Barrington Ward's diary records a meeting with Hahn on the day of Chamberlain's first journey to meet Hitler. *'(Hahn) … is fearful of a peaceful success for Hitler's method which would make him the Prince of Peace in Berlin and a victorious gangster'* – characteristic and penetrating Hahn phrases.

The outbreak of war intensified yet further his writing activities, much of it, following his First World War practice, for the signatures of others.

The Archbishop of York, William Temple, made a broadcast address on 2nd October 1939; on 9th October Lord Clydesdale wrote to *The Times*; Sir Arthur Salter published articles in *The Picture Post* and *The Spectator* (27th October); on 4th December William Temple wrote to *The Daily Telegraph*, generating a long follow-up correspondence;

on 15th December *The Spectator* published an anonymous article on the *Christian Peace Procedure*. All included information and substantial drafting provided by Hahn. The anonymous *Spectator* article was his, the editor however being especially careful to emphasise that the views expressed were not those of the journal. William Temple broadcast again in January 1940, recalling Lord Lansdowne's letter of 1917, called for a clear statement of the conditions on which Britain would be prepared to negotiate with Germany, assumed that these conditions would not be accepted by the present German government but that very many Germans might silently in their own hearts answer Yes; the most vital point was the acceptance of the principle of 'third party judgement'. This alone was a true substitution of reason for force as the supreme arbiter. *'It is of course a surrender of complete national sovereignty; but many of us believe that this surrender, painful as it must be to national pride and costly as it may be in other ways, is the essential condition of lasting peace.'* Hahn had woken his pupil and nephew Oscar from his bed to take dictation in the middle of the night, and assembled the school at the appropriate time to listen to Temple. Only then did Oscar realise for whom he had been writing.

Certain friends of Hahn, notably Arthur Salter, tried hard from October 1939 until May 1940 to persuade the Foreign Office to use Hahn's knowledge of the German scene in an unofficial capacity, but without success. But in May 1940, Rab Butler, at this stage an Under-Secretary of State in the Foreign Office, wrote to him after they had met: *'I am now considering your generous offer of services … I think it would be valuable if you could meet Sir Walter Monckton at an early date.'* Walter Monckton was another Oxford contemporary and friend with whom Hahn had kept up in the intervening years and was now in the Ministry of Information. Hahn was 'loosely' attached to the department until February 1941 and given access to German newspapers.

On 27th June 1941 Brigadier Brooks from the Political Intelligence Department of the Foreign Office was in touch: *'I wonder if you would care to send me an assessment of the Russian situation. It would be most illuminating to have your views of the effect on the German people of a) The Russo-German war; b) Hitler's proclamation and the subsequent propaganda campaign and c) of the large scale appeasement drive, should Hitler succeed in destroying in a relatively short time any organised resistance by the Red Army.'*

His first two reports of 7th and 8th July were passed to the Prime Minister, now Winston Churchill, but caused resentment and criticism and the supply of newspapers to him was cancelled. But he had established a good personal and working relationship with Brigadier Brooks and delivered eleven further reports between February and July of 1941. He was however by now, even by his absentee standards, neglecting his headmasterly duties, and was forced to abandon these reporting commitments. There is also a record of a spell in a nursing home in July. In May 1942 he was approached again with a request for an interpretation of a major speech by Hitler, to which he replied that he could not guarantee *'the quality of his workmanship'* for lack of access to the papers. Informed once more that his services were no longer required, he met Richard Crossman, the later Cabinet Minister and diarist in Harold Wilson's Labour government, now working in the Political Warfare Department of the Foreign Office, who eagerly solicited his views and wrote to him on 18th November 1942: *'I hope you will feel yourself able, without any sense of frustration, to send us your suggestions, and will feel confident that they will receive every attention.'* A special radio and access to German newspapers in Crossman's office enabled him once again to prepare his commentaries.

Hahn's reports reveal the intriguing blend of strategic insight and moral pedagogy that had placed his First World War documents elusively beyond the imagination and reach of hard-pressed political and military leaders. His underlying message was unfailingly recognizable: *'No peace with the murderers. A Germany that has cleansed and liberated itself has nothing to fear from the West.'* The good conscience of Germany must be roused and strengthened against Hitler by clear statements of Britain's integrity of purpose. Of this he had been convinced by Churchill's and Roosevelt's Atlantic Charter of 1941, which he compared to Wilson's Fourteen Points. *'It is too late to adopt the policy: "No promises". Solemn pledges have been given not to the German people but to humanity: The Atlantic Charter and unconditional surrender. I do not regard them as contradictory, just the reverse, they are supplementary, and taken together and properly implemented, they would form an admirable spearhead of a political offensive which can hasten the military debacle of Germany …'*

And once again it was from the Press that one could and must read the enemy's mind, *'flares lighting up the home front'.* As early as June 1941 he wrote to the Cabinet Office: *'there has been no important strategical move on the German side which was not foreshadowed in the German press in time for us to act …,'* citing the Rommel offensive of 1941 in North Africa which he claimed to have foreseen through indiscretions in the 1940/1941 New Year speech of the Head of the German Army Walther von Brauchitsch, through similar indiscretions in the *Frankfurter Generalanzeiger* newspaper issues of 8th and 9th March, and above all through a Hitler speech in which the Fuhrer revealed clear intentions in Africa with references to the transfer of the Allied offensive to other areas and his intention of pursuing them and hitting them *'where the blow will be most crushing for them'.* And one should also learn from the highly skilled propaganda skills of the Germans, who did not hesitate to exploit British headlines to stiffen their people's morale. Duff Cooper [●] was quoted: *'after the war there must no longer be a German nation';* the *Daily Express: 'if Germany were a Libyan desert a smile would dawn on every British face'.* And what had the Deputy Prime Minister Attlee, in a major speech, promised his countrymen after the war? Sufficient nutrition for everybody, abolition of the lazy rich and unemployed poor, a just distribution of wealth, and educational opportunities for all the people – self-confessed evidence of the deplorable condition of the nation the Germans were fighting. And *'a week ago* (January 1941), *the German wireless announced with relief that the distinction made at the beginning of the war between Nazis and Germans was finally dropped'.*

On 8th July 1940 to Walter Monckton: *'I repeat what I said to Ogilvie* [o] *during the September crisis in 1938: it is frivolous not to install the wireless in the House of Commons. Just imagine if America had listened in to Churchill's last speech …'*

There was always the moral imperative. *'The German soldier regards Hitler as master of his conscience; otherwise the fiendish practices in Poland would have been impossible.'* But what of British practices? On night bombing: *'supposing a joint note were addressed to Hitler and Churchill by the Pope or a Swiss/Swedish combination, or Mr. Roosevelt, this note asking both belligerents to stop night bombing; and supposing Hitler would say No and Churchill would say Yes, we should have won three vital battles in this war for morale'.*

On Russia he had no illusions.

'I may be accused of Russo-phobia. I love and admire the Russians; they are in deadly earnest about their ideals … to be a true Russian is to be a missionary with a zeal embracing also the destiny of other nations. Stalin wants to establish a Europe that is safe for workers; he has decided to tolerate on Russian borders only states which maintain a system of social defence; that means safety for men of the right creed and extermination for the dissenters. Let us drop the Western illusion that mass murder and idealism are incompatible. For Stalin the two are inseparable, as they were for the Church militants … Who will restrain Stalin once he is victoriously

[●] Minister of Information in the first year of the war

[o] Director General of the BBC

established in Middle Europe? I am told he will restrain himself. It is an insult to the man to suspect him of leanings to democracy, tolerance and Christianity. He is true to his own creed …'

His reactions to Hitler's invasion of the Soviet Union were characteristically psychological in nature. Stalin and Churchill arm in arm – what an embarrassment for Roosevelt! The Vatican will be tempted to support the onslaught on Bolshevism. England, in quotes again from the British press, absolves Stalin from past crimes, does not believe that Soviet Russia subjugates alien nations. Christian England has abandoned Europe. The German war effort now gains a renewed moral purpose. The German armies will be greeted by millions as liberators; men are held in readiness to form national governments in Lithuania, Estonia, Latvia, Georgia, Ukraine … He foresaw this clearly, as the nationalist, anti-Russian and anti-Communist movements allied themselves with the German forces, tragically also allowing themselves to become all-too-active participants in the persecution and slaughter of the Jews. Even here Hahn allowed himself few illusions. *'He (Hitler) might well impose new pogroms on a gigantic scale. But that will not do him much harm abroad. I am afraid that by now world opinion is getting almost angry with the Jews when new miseries are inflicted on them. In Russia pogroms will be a help and not a hindrance for whatever new order Hitler wants to impose.'*

It was natural that Hahn should have tirelessly sought evidence for active, effective resistance inside Nazi Germany. *'My own conviction is that every revolution is doomed to failure, however well planned, until our armies have won a crushing victory on the Continent.'* But, with his fine ear for the human story, he noted in April 1943 that bishops were now speaking more freely, that the military obituary notices in the *Deutsche Allgemeine Zeitung* were referring in increasing numbers to those who died *'faithful to their Redeemer'* rather than faithful to the Fuhrer, and picked out in particular one old lady of the nobility who *'will live with us as an example, as an upright character <u>maintaining her convictions against everybody'</u>,* her death mourned by the local Catholic and Protestant communities alike.

Hahn's report of 9th October 1943 was headed *'The Coming Crisis in Germany'. 'The Nazis are getting ready to forestall an attempt to overthrow the regime … executions are more frequent than is indicated in the German press, but they have not yet reached the wholesale scale … victims are carefully picked from the various centres of opposition, but key men are not exterminated so as to avoid provocation* [*] *…'* Perhaps unfortunately, he could not resist the moral overlay. *'I am all in favour of Unconditional Surrender – on one condition: that British statesmanship gives a pledge, not to Germany specifically, but to the whole world, that this time victory will not be defiled.'*

When the news of the 20th July 1944 assassination plot came through, he could not entirely conceal his relieved satisfaction. *'No more generalisations about Germany. May it be left to Vansittart to talk about Germans as Hitler talks about Jews! Vansittart would have been invented by Hitler if he did not exist. Admit the existence of an honourable Germany but taunt it with its helpless impotence throughout the years of "crime triumphant". Make it clear that a cleansed and liberated Germany has nothing to fear from this country.'* Five months earlier, on 17th February, he had underlined all his concerns about the dangers of Soviet domination, with England *'the liberator, leaving a Europe in ruins to the mercies of Stalin'. 'Our political strategy should be aimed at breaking the German resistance against the West before the Russians gain a decisive victory and chaos engulfs Germany.'* But despite this proof of *'another Germany'*, the overriding aim must remain *'humiliating defeat on the battlefield and unconditional surrender, such warning memories we must for the sake of Europe indelibly implant into German history …'* [●]

Hahn and Crossman were kindred spirits. On 28th August 1944 Crossman wrote from the Psychological Warfare Division of the Supreme Headquarters of the Allied Expeditionary Force to which he had been transferred: *'it is certainly most remarkable how your prophecies of last October have been borne out … those enormously stimulating*

[*] It is intriguing to compare this 1943 assessment with the statement of Noel Annan who, as a member of the British Joint Intelligence Staff, was at the heart of intelligence operations throughout the war:
Once Overlord was launched, the Joint Intelligence Staff could only sit back and watch. It was for the intelligence staffs in the field to analyse and act upon the mass of decrypts that revealed how the German army reacted to the Allied assault. But in the summer we were suddenly called to interpret an event that we had believed was improbable: a plot to kill Hitler.
Noel Annan: *Changing Enemies*, Harper Collins 1996 page 107

[●] I can never put out of my mind the story I heard soon after first meeting him that, the day the failed attempt of 20th July became known, he had mislaid a list of the plotters and, panic-stricken, rushed down from his room in Brown's Hotel in London to his waiting taxi and literally picked up the diminutive hall porter by the shoulders and shaken him in the belief that the list would fall out of his clothes. By the time these matters became of serious interest to me the hall porter had long passed away, but the story rings true. Hahn always crystallized his thinking through his pen. It is entirely predictable that he will have made a list, and it will have been an accurate one.

evenings …'; and Hahn replied on 5th September: *'there are millions of patriots inside Germany today who would accept total defeat and total occupation, but who will go on fighting against dismemberment and against indiscriminate and vindictive punishment such as the Russians administer and such as Vansittart recommends'.* But Hahn lost heart. His letter to Crossman of 13th November explains why. *'May I ask you to give instructions that the German papers be no longer sent to me … foreign policy must control propaganda; our foreign policy today has a two-fold platform: dismember Germany; throw her to the avengers … It is vital to write indelibly into history: 1. that Germany has suffered defeat, overwhelming and inescapable 2. And that Britain does not trifle with her pledged word, in contrast to our enemies.'*

For the explanation we must return briefly to 1939.

Soon after the outbreak of war, his friend and ally Sir Arthur Salter, Gladstone Professor of Political Theory and Institutions, a Fellow of All Souls and a Member of Parliament, with others, tried to secure him a meeting with Winston Churchill. One later note suggests that Salter got him as far as the waiting room in No. 10 Downing Street, but personal access to Winston Churchill was blocked, it was said, by Churchill's friend and, later, Minister for Information Brendan Bracken, who was worried that Hahn's message could weaken the unanimity and strength of British purpose at this critical time. But he persisted. By July 1940 his views had reached Churchill. Churchill's private secretary, John Colville, records in his *The Fringes of Power; Downing Street Diaries 1939–1955,* his view that *'now, I think, is the psychological moment to define our own war aims and state our terms. They would be such that Hitler must refuse them, but in so doing he would lose credit in the eyes of the outside world and also in those of his own people … Mr. Kurt Hahn has produced an interesting note on this subject which Tony Bevir has obtained and passed on to the PM … it is important that the odium of saying "No" to peace terms should be laid on Hitler and not on ourselves'.* [●]

And on 9th December 1940, in a continuing effort, Hahn wrote to Brendan Bracken, by now Churchill's Minister of Information: *'I am sending you as you suggested an attempt to condense our conversation into two pages … I am not recommending a road to compromise but to victory … diagnosis and propaganda become matters of vital military relevance …'* There is no acknowledgement in Hahn's papers. The pressures on Downing Street were clearly intense. A

contemporary comment suggests with some justification that Hahn's memoranda did not always put the case in the way that an Englishman would find persuasive. His style may have fallen a victim to these pressures.

Kurt Hahn admired Churchill. Churchill had transcended politics and become a statesman. Hahn trusted his integrity, the nobility of his war aims, his dismissal of vengeance. The Atlantic Charter was a pledge, not to Germany alone but to humanity. If it was respected, even unconditional surrender was a legitimate war aim. But now, with his statement in the House of Commons on 25th May 1944, *'the Atlantic Charter in no way binds us about the future of Germany nor is it a bargain or contract with our enemies',* Churchill had broken faith. His rough dismissal of the German officers who had risen against Hitler on 20th July was additional confirmation, for Hahn, that Churchill was abandoning the ideals that had inspired both him and the nation in 1940.

One other topic emerges from Hahn's wartime reports of much interest for his educational work in Britain. In early 1941 he had noted the *'sensational revelation'* in a turnover article in the *Kölnische Zeitung* of 23rd January that the German Olympic Games secretary Diem, the pioneer of the national athletic movement before Hitler and the inventor of the German Sports Badge in 1919, had been travelling for three months from village to village in Bulgaria, organising pre-military training on the German model, whilst respecting the characteristics of Bulgarian national life. A newly created voluntary organisation *Brannik* (Defenders) – open to boys and unmarried men up to 30 – had received a special charter of privileges in a Bill that had now become law. The Bulgarian youth were, the newspaper claimed, being invigorated to 'steel' them for their coming tasks.

Hahn commented in the same report that the Nazi Deputy Leader Rudolf Hess had recently addressed an athletics meeting in Garmisch Partenkirchen, attended by boys from many European countries including Denmark. Hess' message was simple: the importance of peaceful competition which really ought to constitute the normal impact between nations such as would have taken place had it not been for England. Hahn went on to draw attention to the 14-day training courses for youth leaders of some 90–100 at a time, commenting that in England the training of the adolescent had not been taken seriously as if it were of no importance whether in 1940 it would take six or two months to turn a citizen into a soldier. *'Since the outbreak of war the young have been waiting in vain for a call that will summon them to training and service. It is not too late yet; we will also face a moral crisis and will be grateful then*

[●] pages 198–199

for the tonic effect a trained eager youth always has on the middle-aged.' [●]

It is certain that Hahn drew his inspiration for his late 1930s Moray County Badge Scheme from Diem's German Sports Badge; furthermore, that Outward Bound, which he launched successfully in 1941, grew from the same origins. His passionately conducted campaign during the war to train Britain's adolescents in the national cause found its practical expression in these two schemes, but his efforts to transform the Moray Badge into a National Badge generated some strong anxieties that he was trying to set up the kind of state youth movement that was typical of the Communist and Nazi regimes. An article in the *Sunday Express* explicitly identified Hahn as a follower of Hitler with his Badge project. Baden-Powell, a supporter in 1936, wrote from his war-time home Kenya to warn against contaminating youth movements in Britain with state-sponsored schemes. Outward Bound survived these reservations with ease – the founding links with Lawrence Holt and his Blue Funnel Line in Liverpool, and with the merchant navy sea-training vessel and school *HMS Conway* in North Wales, safeguarded its credentials, but the badge scheme did not achieve national status until the Duke of Edinburgh supported his former headmaster in 1956 with his name, active interest and personal leadership in the launch of the Duke of Edinburgh's Award Scheme.

One dramatic wartime affair in particular crystallised Hahn's involvement and attitudes.

The Hess Affair of May 1941

Hahn had difficulty in controlling his emotions when the news came through that the Deputy Fuhrer Rudolf Hess, ejecting himself from the Messerschmitt fighter plane in which he flown himself solo from Augsburg in Southern Germany, had landed by parachute in northern Scotland on 10th May, his alleged mission to seek peace with England. Hahn wrote immediately to Brigadier Brooks: *'the flight of Hess is an event ranking in importance with a major battle …*

[●] Or was it already too late? The American journalist and historian William Shirer wrote in his *The Rise and Fall of the Third Reich* of his memories of the May days of 1940, when *'along the road between Aachen and Brussels one saw the contrast between the German soldiers, bronzed and clean-cut from a youth spent in the sunshine on an adequate diet, and the first British war prisoners, with their hollow chests, round shoulders, pasty complexions and bad teeth – tragic examples of the youth that England had neglected so irresponsibly in the years between the wars'.* Pan Books page 319

might even become the starting point of a campaign yielding decisive results … a daily reference to the Hess drama of a factual kind … a report on Hess' sanity by a <u>neutral</u> commission of specialists … a parliamentary commission presided over by the Archbishop of York, set up to investigate the truth about German atrocities both in concentration camps and Poland … it is in our power to make the name of Nazi stink in the nostrils of millions of Germans'. The report he wrote on the affair achieved some notoriety, chiefly through having been kept, together with most other Hess papers, in confidential files for many years. (Some documents have still not been released.)

A complex, endlessly recounted episode, it begins for us in 1933.

Kurt Hahn's mother had suffered a breakdown at the end of 1933. Kurt was in Scotland. His sister-in-law, Lola Hahn, sought the help of a well-known psychiatrist. This man, at the time an anti-Nazi, recounted how over a long period he had been treating Hess for a split personality, describing him as full of repressions, frank in his comments and ever ready to make confessions about past misdeeds. All very unprofessional, no doubt, but who could resist Lola? Lola was subsequently encouraged to visit Frau Hess and spent one hour with her: *'… an extremely nice, simple, unambitious peasant type, very sympathetic to all the things I told her … promised she would inform her husband … no sign of anti-Jewish feeling towards myself …'* All of this Lola reported to the British Foreign Office in a letter of 14th May 1941.

Rudolf Hess became in fact protective of Salem. He even made it possible for a Salem pupil, Wolfram Gunther, who was a half-Jew, deposed as school Guardian for this reason and compelled to move out into the neighbouring village as a day pupil, coincidentally a nephew of Hahn's, to study in Aachen, an experience that, so Wolfram told me, he found desperately unnerving because he was not allowed to mix with others and remained wholly isolated and lonely. He was later, of course not as an officer, to fight on the Eastern Front whence he escaped at war's end despite being told when troops were being evacuated from a surrounded pocket that he should remain; his sort were not required for the final defence of the Fatherland. Hess' help came because Wolfram was the close friend of a boy well known to the Hess family.

Rudolf Hess as a young man and student had become a personal friend of the Munich university professor Karl Haushofer who developed the concept of geopolitics, giving Hitler much intellectual endorsement for his Lebensraum ideas. Karl Haushofer visited both Hess and Hitler in the Landsberg prison after the failed Putsch of

1923, having previously concealed the fugitive Hess from the authorities for three weeks.

One Haushofer son, Albrecht, a fluent English-speaker, also an advocate, albeit an increasingly hesitant one, of his father's geopolitical ideas, had met Lord Clydesdale, later the Duke of Hamilton, on the latter's visit to Berlin for the Olympic Games in 1936, and maintained the personal connection. Rather remarkable evidence for this lies in the long manuscript letter of 16th July 1939 written *'cruising the coast of Western Norway'* (shades of the Kaiser doing exactly the same as the Sarajevo assassination crisis developed in the summer of 1914) and addressed by Albrecht to his 'dear Douglo'. This intriguing letter has survived despite the writer having requested that it be destroyed *'most carefully … or freedom for your own discretion to show this letter personally to Lord Halifax or to his Under-Secretary – under one condition: that no notes should be taken, my name never to be mentioned, and the letter be destroyed immediately afterwards'.*

By now Albrecht Haushofer was acting as advisor to Hess on foreign affairs. His letter gains some additional weight in this light. *'… I want to send you a word of warning. To the best of my knowledge, there is not yet a definite timetable for the actual explosion – but any date after the middle of August may prove to be the fatal one … the most dangerous thing is that he (Hitler) is racing against time … economic difficulties are growing, and his own feeling (a very curious and remarkable one) that he has not a very long term of life ahead of him, is a most important factor … on the merits of their present government the Germans are less united than at any date since 1934. But if war breaks out on the Corridor question, they will be more solidly behind their present leader than over any case that might have led to war in these last years. The territorial solutions in the East Corridor and Upper Silesia have never been accepted by the German nation … a war against Poland would not be unpopular … war against Poland would – for the first weeks at least – unite, not disintegrate the German nation … people in England mostly do not know that there are some 600,000 Germans scattered through the inner (formerly Russian) parts of Poland … your people would be wise not to forget that they refused a 'plebiscitarian' solution in the Corridor (and that subsequently the Poles drove some 900,000 Germans out of their former German provinces).'*

Defenders of the Versailles Treaty may not take kindly to lectures from a friend and advisor of Hess, but the resentments it generated had a long and poisonous life.

Even after war broke out, Albrecht Haushofer tried to maintain this personal friendship. In a letter dated 23rd September 1939 from Berlin, he sought a meeting with Douglo, *'somewhere on the outskirts of Europe, perhaps Portugal. I could reach Lisbon any time (and without any kind of difficulties) within a few days of receiving news from you.'* The letter, intercepted by the censor, finished with instructions for his reply through an address in Lisbon.

On 15th September 1940 Albrecht Haushofer is known to have had a two-hour meeting with Hess on the attractions of peace with England. His memorandum following the meeting ends with the mention of his friend Clydesdale.

Lord Clydesdale, Douglas (Douglo) Douglas-Hamilton who in 1940 became the Duke of Hamilton, and his three brothers were close friends and supporters of Kurt Hahn. They were all active in supporting the experimental courses in the Scottish Highlands that led eventually to Outward Bound. David, the youngest brother, knew Germany well.

In the light of all these circumstances it is not surprising, when Hess landed and asked to be taken to the Duke of Hamilton, that Hamilton should have alerted Kurt Hahn, or that Hahn, with all his background knowledge, should have immediately attributed the motivation behind the flight to Haushofer. Hahn did not of course meet Hess, but Haushofer visiting cards were found in the pockets of the Deputy Leader of the Nazi Party. [●]

Told of Hess' arrival, Churchill decided to watch a Marx Brothers' film before considering the matter. The government's eventual decision was to say nothing at all, leaving the Germans to worry intensely about what Hess might have revealed. But Hess must not be allowed to become either a hero or a martyr. This calculated passivity upset Hahn, and not only Hahn.

On 20th May Hahn wrote his 15-page memorandum *The Flight of Hess: an Attempt at Reconstruction.* It circulated in government circles, especially the Ministry of Information.

[●] Albrecht Haushofer associated himself with increasing decisiveness with the resistance movement from 1940 onwards. After the failed 20th July plot of 1944 he fled into the Bavarian mountains but was later imprisoned by the Nazis. Kept alive until almost the end of the war, reportedly as a possible bargaining counter with the Allies, he was taken from his cell on the night of 22nd April 1945 and shot. His body was found in the street on 12th May by his brother. On him were the 80 sonnets, the *Moabiter Sonette*, he had composed in prison. *'Schuldig bin ich/ Anders als Ihr denkt/Ich mußte früher meine Pflicht erkennen/ … Ich habe gewarnt/Aber nicht genug und klar/Und heute weiß ich, was ich schuldig war.'* 'But I am guilty, not though as you think/my duty I should long have recognised … I did warn, but my voice was faint and low/ and what I should have done, today I know.'

One account speculates that Douglas Hamilton took it to the King. [●] This is extremely likely.

In the text we find perhaps Hahn's most explicit and detailed exposition of what he now called 'the dual policy'. Indeed, it is more a personal statement than a cool analysis of Hess' motives. But he was able to use the knowledge of Hess' character that he had gained from his sister-in-law Lola.

'Hess is not a war lord. This war is eclipsing his importance … we can imagine how they (these hideous memories) haunt this "humanitarian Hess", as Hitler contemptuously calls him now … as a family the Haushofers were not popular but the son is said to have charm …

… the Germans are always inclined to exaggerate the importance of their English friends … even so it must seem strange that the Douglas Hamiltons should have been singled out as the spearhead of a British peace movement … I believe this is the explanation … Haushofer had obviously been employed in reading the British press very carefully … Lord Clydesdale's letter to The Times *of 9th October could not have escaped his notice; it contained the word Lebensraum and suggested at a given moment a "meeting of honourable men" … the Clydesdale letter expressed the dual policy which four days before was powerfully stated by the Archbishop of Canterbury in his broadcast …'*

Hahn's access to the German press enabled him to contrast Hitler's first reactions – *'Hess is sick and insane'* – with later responses: the calling together of the Reichsleiter and Gauleiter to issue a joint expression of faith in victory (*'surely a sign of weakness and anxiety brought about by a crisis'*); the restoration of Hess' good name; and an implicit endorsement of the presumed aim of the Hess mission – to offer peace terms from a *'reasonable Hitler'* to an *'unreasonable British leadership'*, thereby leading to a closing of the ranks on the German side and a hoped-for opening of divisions on the British. The classic Hahn doctrine is given additional lively expression with the proposal that David Douglas Hamilton, a near-fluent German speaker, should broadcast *'what I told Hess'* along the following lines:

I understand certain German grievances.

I admire certain German social achievements: the care of the adolescent, no malnutrition among the working classes, the de-urbanisation (a typical Hahn touch, this) *of the young.*

My shock over Nazi methods and my hope that honourable Germans might rally round you, Hess, and win the day.

[●] Picknett, Prince and Prior: *Double Standards – The Story of Rudof Hess* Time Warner Books 2001

My deep suspicion that Hitler loves his own power more than his country and will stop at nothing, not even a world war, to save himself.

But, convinced though I am of your passionate sincerity for peace, where was your conscience on 28th February when the Reichstag was set on fire, on 30th June 1934 when at least 700 Germans were murdered in cold blood in the Roehm Putsch, on 25th July when Dollfuss was murdered and a memorial was set up in honour of the murderers, on 3rd March 1938 when Pastor Niemöller was acquitted by the law courts and at once re-imprisoned in a concentration camp where he remains today, and on 1st September 1939 when the lie was told to the German people that Britain and Poland had rejected the compromise of the 16 points which had never been submitted to them?

Hahn ended with some skilful acknowledgement of Churchill's moral leadership (*'he has the courage of his convictions, even when they make him unpopular … in 1918 he urged the immediate raising of the blockade by seizing German ships and sending them back with grain … the unwritten laws of our race are safe in his keeping even though the passions of anger and hatred are surging around us'*). But, as his secretary John Colville revealed after the war, Churchill was convinced that the propagandists would get it all wrong and refused to authorise PR exploitation of the Hess landing. And other events – the bombing of the House of Commons, the invasion of Crete, the loss of *HMS Hood* and the sinking of the *Bismarck* – rapidly removed Hess from the headlines. During the First World War, Hahn had constantly preached *'make your own war a people's war and turn your enemy's war into a Government war'*. Now, despite all the hesitations and the pressures for peace-making and compromise by senior political colleagues, Churchill had achieved the overwhelming loyalty of the British nation. It was left to Richard Crossman in the Ministry of Information bitterly to regret the lost propaganda opportunity of dividing the German people and of demonstrating that theirs was a governmental, not a people's war.

Gordonstoun in the War Years and the Birth of Outward Bound

Gordonstoun School in Morayshire in Scotland was within a short walking distance of the coast. Two military aerodromes were nearby. There were several German masters and a number of German boys, mostly Jewish. Local rumour and local disquiet grew when war broke out. The masters were not accepted into the Home Guard. Five masters and eleven boys were interned. Hahn had taken British nationality in 1938 and been formally deprived by the Nazis of his German nationality shortly thereafter. Nonetheless, great pressure was exerted by one senior official, with much local support, to have him interned, an initiative honourably and firmly resisted by the Home Office. But the school had to move. A dramatic meeting, now a firm part of the Hahn mythology, conducted aboard a train travelling south from Inverness, with his car following at high speed to pick him up from whichever station marked the successful completion of the negotiation, enabled Hahn to transfer the entire school from Scotland to the home and estate of Lord Davies of Llandinam in mid-Wales. And so the setting up of a school began yet again.

Hahn's achievements during this new war give yet another picture of his feverish energy and drive to achieve results. The sea had become a really important part of Gordonstoun life: *'My best schoolmaster is the Moray Firth.'* He had developed enormous respect for the character of the Moray fishing communities. The school had a sea-going sailing vessel that made adventurous voyages to Scandinavian waters (Hahn's contribution to sail training in sea-going vessels in both Britain and Germany during the post-war years almost merits a book on its own). Now, in war-time, she made her way with a schoolboy crew down to Cardigan Bay in Wales. Near the Welsh site was the merchant navy training school *HMS Conway*. One of his Gordonstoun parents was Laurence Holt, the head of the Blue Funnel Shipping Line of Liverpool. Many lives were being lost at sea following torpedoing because the sailors, above all the younger ones, lacked physical stamina and morale. The meeting of minds between Hahn and Holt led to the launch of the first Outward Bound School at Aberdovey in 1941. Hahn had recognised that lack of fitness in British youth that had been so clearly identified by William Shirer in 1940. In Scotland he had begun work on the Moray County Badge. Now he began the task of making it national. He was called upon to advise the War Office on the training of young recruits to the army. He engaged in similar consultations at the Admiralty with Lord Mountbatten, whom he already knew from the time that he had successfully persuaded him that the young Prince Philip, a Gordonstoun pupil, could find his own way into the Dartmouth Naval Training College without the help of a friendly nepotistic nudge.

But it was not easy. His *Times* friend Barrington Ward lunched on 3rd January 1941 with another Hahn adherent, Sir Neill Malcolm, who had been the Chief of the British Military Mission to Berlin from 1919 to 1921. His diary entry for that day reads: *'N. anxious that KH should give up his political work and stick to his county badge and other schemes for youth, which he will otherwise compromise. Already ill-natured people are saying that Hahn is a dangerous ex-German, preaching forgiveness for Germany, wanting to let her down lightly. All nonsense of course!'* And another close Hahn friend, J. H. Oldham, Editor of the *Christian News Letter*, urged him in October 1942 to hide his name if his projects were to be successful – his *'Germanness'* and overzealousness were deterring supporters.

Return to Scotland and a Continuing Political Involvement

1945 brought victory and unconditional surrender, a conclusion that Hahn accepted, indeed welcomed, but also a dramatic mental breakdown that was sympathetically but precisely documented in a confidential note by his Gordonstoun deputy Henry Brereton. Merciless sleeplessness, a persecution mania, break-outs at night seeking help, the conviction that he was being pursued by assassins, were the price he paid for the strains of these years. But it was the suffering in his country of origin, Germany, which restored him to action. Refused papers by the Foreign Office to travel, he decamped to Paris where his sister-in-law Lola's brother, Eric Warburg, now with the US army, arranged transport for him to motor to Salem, which was occupied by the French army. Within weeks he had secured their evacuation, and Salem re-opened in circumstances of immense difficulty in November 1945. Unhesitatingly, despite the hostility of many Germans at this time towards the resistance movement, he arranged for the children of resistance figures to join the school. He had found his way to Berlin in August 1945 and has left us this oft-quoted memory: *'I was staying with an American who will live in the history of the times as a Good Samaritan. This man said: "I want you to go to the Lehrter Station to see the refugees (from East Germany) arriving." We drove there and a young sergeant sat in front, a kindly-looking man, and while we were passing through scenes of misery and death which will haunt me all my life, he was continually listening to jazz on the wireless until my host, the Good Samaritan, leaned forward and touched him on the shoulder and said: "for God's sake, stop". What had happened to this young man? He had a dispersed soul which he could not assemble even before the majesty of death.'* His companion in the car, Giro von Gaevernitz, wrote to him on his 80th birthday: *'unforgettable remains for me our experience together after* the war's end in Berlin. At that time you represented for me and for many others hope for a better future.' [100] Back in Britain, he at once tried to set up a small committee to enquire into conditions among the German populations of East and Central Europe but was unable to gain any support. As Bishop Bell, once again his ally, commented, there was little public attention available just then for the deportations.

Another episode is less well-known. The two sons of his First World War chief General von Haeften, Hans Bernd and Werner, had been executed by the Nazis for their role in the plot against Hitler. Hans Bernd's widow Barbara had borne her fifth child a few weeks before the assassination attempt. Now she was alone, 90 miles north of Berlin, under Russian occupation. One morning in September 1945 an unknown woman entered her kitchen. She had come from Berlin with a message from an unnamed Englishman. She should come at once to Berlin. Barbara wrote in her brief memoirs of her immediate realisation that this could only be Hahn. Leaving her five children with a neighbour, she made her way to Berlin the following morning and found Hahn in the cellar of a ruined house. His first words to her were that he had just converted to Christianity, for he had recognised that men such as her husband were capable of their actions only through the power of the Christian faith. He arranged for her sons to come to Salem and for the family to move to Lake Constance.

It was Hahn who gained the first access to the German manuscript of the account of the resistance, *Offiziere gegen Hitler*, written by one of the survivors, Fabian von Schlabrendorff, and who insisted on its immediate translation into English and publication. It was the first record of the German resistance to appear.

A Gordonstoun governor, Tom Bedwell, has left an account of how Hahn returned from his first experience of post-war Germany shattered and on the verge of another breakdown, keeping him up all night and talking wildly in German.

Gordonstoun had now returned home to Scotland, but to buildings that had been left uninhabitable by the military. The wearisome, seemingly impossible task of starting all over again had to be faced. Yet he spent almost as much time in Germany as in Scotland, seeking better nourishment for the Salem pupils, teaching, producing Shakespeare plays, restoring morale.

In April 1946 he circulated his *State of the Young in Germany*. A journey had taken him through the Rhineland and Westphalia, via Hanover to Berlin, and from there through Göttingen to Salem in the French zone. Characteristically, one may say, he sought out those

who 'sorrowed for their country in the midst of other private miseries'. He spoke with different groups: the active young officers for whom everything had been better than defeat, and 'to this fallacy they had sacrificed their conscience', but who had also declared 'We shall not allow the memories of the front to be taken away from us;' [101] members of the resistance movement; the age group 15–18 'which had experienced in their childhood men and women around them, aglow with faith in the destiny of their nation'. To whom now were they to look for inspiration? How was the battle for the soul of the young to be won? There must be open sources of truth, the setting up of an Historic Commission of men of proven character. 'I hear the argument, "why duplicate Nuremberg?" Nuremberg is a polluted source of truth. The Allies missed a unique opportunity of chiselling the Nazi crimes on to the pillars of history so that neither time nor legend could wash them away. All that was required was to set up an International Court composed of impartial judges … in Nuremberg the aggressor of Finland, Lithuania, Estonia, Latvia and Poland – I am mentioning countries taken by storm, not by sap – sits in judgment on the Nazi crimes of aggression. In Nuremberg the murder of 8,000 Polish officers at Katyn is laid at the door of Germany by a representative of the Government responsible for this very murder … the mass murder of the Polish officers happens to have been discovered by a member of the German opposition, no less a man than Schlabrendorff, who brought about the exhumation of the corpses at Katyn. He offered twice to give evidence in Nuremberg. His offer was refused. The fact of this refusal has not been kept secret, but is freely discussed in Germany.' And now, for his Germany 'that could recover from a defeat but never from a victory', he proposed the foundation of short term boarding schools, at least 100 of them, holding 11 courses a year for some 100 young people, each to be led by a Christian activist who had suffered under Hitler, with vocational training in mining, forestry, sea-fishing, agriculture, engineering, plumbing, mountain rescue, fire fighting.

Hahn and Salem have both encountered the criticism: how many of your pupils were themselves active members of the resistance? Hans Ulrich Von Oertzen, at the centre of the movement in Berlin, who committed suicide the day after the assassination attempt rather than face interrogation by the Gestapo, was one. A second was Edward Waetjen, who was the liaison person between the resistance in Berlin and the head of the American espionage in Berne, Allen Dulles (another Hahn contact and friend from Versailles). [•] It may be true, as Robert Skidelsky states, citing Golo Mann, that 'an unusually large proportion of Salem's Old Boys withdrew into that particular outlet for innocence and chivalry, the Wehrmacht' [○] (an 'unusually large proportion' not, however, being placed in any kind of context); but it also remains true that, when confronted by this hostile charge, Hahn put himself immediately into the place of the individual with the gentle implication *'and what would you have done?'* He can never have met Friedrich Reck-Malleczewen, murdered by a bullet in the neck in Dachau in February 1945, but he understood his state of mind: *'You judge us and find us wanting, and we, here, suffer in loneliness and dread. You point at us and at our lack of resistance … the night lies black over our heads, and we suffer, we suffer as you shall never suffer, no, not on your deathbed. Beware, the man who would make light of our suffering!'* [■]

> *'The sufferer calls out, the echo is silent*
> *The neighbour pretends to be deaf; the world remains*
>   *unmoved*
> *The evil star has appeared in the heavens*
>   *And the hearts of all beat more weakly'* [102] [◻]

Salem and Gordonstoun – A Brief Comparison

To have founded two major schools, with associated educational initiatives, in two different countries, was by itself a remarkable achievement. To have done so as a Jew in 1920s Germany and as a German in 1930s Britain compels distinctive admiration. The nature of the achievement is inseparable from Hahn's personality.

When does a group of pupils become a school? The informal improvisation of Salem's beginnings is picturesquely illustrated by the differing accounts of the early numbers: the son of Prince Max, Berthold, and a handful of local boys (Max had set up in the neighbourhood in 1906 a school for apprentices and in 1919 an agricultural school

and wanted his son to grow up with his local contemporaries); 20 pupils, boys and girls, eight of them boarders and the rest living locally; 28, of whom 20 lived locally; and a printed list numbering 49. Hahn himself has stated *'we only had three boys and one girl at the beginning'.* What is certain is that growth was rapid. After a period of intense anxiety and faltering enrolment in the inflation of 1922 and 1923, recovery was dramatic. By 1933 there were over 380 pupils and, even more striking, they came not only from all parts of Germany but from ten other nations as well: Austria, Czechoslovakia, Estonia, Finland, Great Britain, Holland, Hungary, Italy, Romania and the United States. There were also five stateless pupils. And the one school in Salem had grown to five schools, three of them junior schools for Salem, one a new senior school in Spetzgart, almost directly on the banks of Lake Constance, and the fifth Birklehof in the Black Forest, some 3,000 feet above sea level and intended for children in delicate health – it was later to become independent of Salem. By the early 1930s Hahn, through Salem's former pupils, was endeavouring to create a network of university students from all the German country boarding schools who would commit themselves to observe strict training conditions (athletics training with no smoking or drinking) for four weeks in the year, to engage in adventurous pursuits, and to carry out social work in areas of social deprivation. He had plans for a hostel in the University of Heidelberg that would in some way emulate the Oxbridge colleges (and provide an alternative to the notoriously powerful German student fraternities); and he was making his first attempts to recruit state schools in cities to adopt some of his ideas in programmes that would last the entire day, extending the school's responsibilities well beyond the academic. Politics in the form of the Nazis intervened.

Education with explicitly political objectives is a dangerous concept, and it is fortunate that Salem was founded in a former Cistercian monastery whose ideals were embodied in the school's purpose. *'Who can awaken in the morning in the shadow of our Minster and become a man without honour or culture?'* Work in the local fields and learning from the local craftsmen were written into the weekly programme. But if the political aims can be roughly aligned with the classical 19th-century role of the British Public Schools in assuring the nation of incorrupt and self-confident leadership, Salem's political destiny was pre-determined by the reputations of the two founders, Prince Max and Kurt Hahn, inseparable as they were from the outcome of the war and of Versailles. And, as we have seen, Salem soon began to develop activities that included rifle shooting, the building of gliders, and formal drill, leading to

[●] SEE PAGE 94 I have constantly been puzzled and disappointed that on no occasion I can trace did Hahn ever mention that truly heroic small group of young resisters called the White Rose, although a Salem pupil, George Wittenstein, was actively on the fringe of their activities. It is just possible that he was inhibited from doing so because another former Salem pupil had shared lodgings with Sophie Scholl in Munich and had given circumstantial evidence against her.

[○] Membership of the army did not require party membership

[■] Friedrich Reck-Malleczewen: *Diary of a Man in Despair*

[◻] Max Hermann-Neisse, *Apokalypse 1933*

The famous sun topee, now in the Hahn archive in Salem

participation in the camps organised by the Stahlhelm for military sports. It all offered good pickings for later critics in spite of, for example, the longstanding existence of Officers' Training Corps in British schools.

A demoralised refugee in 1933, Kurt Hahn was persuaded by friends to start all over again in exile in Britain. His friends were a powerful family network, linked with him both through joint efforts at reconciliation during the First World War and by their admiration for Salem's achievements in the 1920s. This network made the new start possible. Charles Trevelyan, appointed Secretary to the Board of Education under Prime Minister Asquith, who had resigned from the government on the outbreak of war in 1914, was a regular visitor to Salem in the 1920s. His brother was the historian George Trevelyan. The mountaineer and educator Geoffrey Winthrop Young was another fervent Hahn admirer. The Arnold Forster family, directly descended from Thomas Arnold of Rugby fame, were also disciples – Ka Arnold Forster had also taught in Salem and been the person who intervened with Ramsay MacDonald's secretary Neville Butler to persuade the Prime Minister to write his letter seeking Hahn's release from the Nazi imprisonment. Through them and their further contacts, Hahn was able to call on formidable allies and support. Nowhere is this more powerfully illustrated than in the list of Gordonstoun Governors of 1937, which included, among others of notable individual distinction, the Archbishop of York, the former Governor-General of Canada, the Deputy Editor of *The Times*, the Senior Tutor of Trinity College Cambridge, the Professor of Greek at Edinburgh University, the Headmaster of Eton, the Vice-Chancellor of

the University of Aberdeen, the Principal of the University of the South West (later Exeter), the Professor of Education at the University of London, the Director General of the BBC, the Secretary of the International Missionary Council, the Master of Downing College Cambridge, the Regius Professor of Modern History at the University of Cambridge, and the Master (Headmaster) of Marlborough College.

But the start in September 1933 was modest although impressively prompt: Hahn and two boys from Salem, Jocelin Winthrop Young and Mark Arnold Forster, in a large house Doune in Rothiemurchus, Morayshire, where they were joined by two further boys in November and moved to Duffus House on the edge of the Gordonstoun Estate that same month. As in Salem, growth was rapid: 36 (boys only) in May 1934 had become 66 by September and 98 by September 1936. In 1937 a preparatory school was opened nearby with 18 pupils, and by 1939 the total in Gordonstoun alone, excluding the preparatory school, was 135. Scotland had been Hahn's haven for his physical well-being since his Oxford days. It was now to restore his educational health too.

In this new environment Hahn had no political mission to fulfil, although the increasing numbers of Germans, mostly Jewish boys and masters and mostly fellow-exiles from Salem, were to stimulate unease in the local community as war approached. But his new school had to make its way against the well-established position of the British Public Schools. What boys would be entrusted to this far-off, ill-equipped establishment unless they had been rejected or even expelled by the better-known places? Kurt Hahn of course welcomed the challenge of educating the late developers, the rebels and the misfits, but Henry Brereton, his Director of Studies and Deputy, was frank in acknowledging that the school's success with *'boys academically backward or of poor health or of difficult character gave it a deserved but dangerous reputation'*.

The Moray Firth and the coastal fishing communities led to the most striking new dimension in the Hahn philosophy after Salem – training through the sea as an integral part of secondary education. The challenges of deep water sailing and the personalities of the local fishermen made a profound impression on Hahn, to whom the Scottish marine and mountain surroundings offered opportunities on the doorstep that the gentle countryside and placid waters of Lake Constance could not rival. It was not long before a succession of sailing craft were taking the Gordonstoun boys on ambitious voyages: in 1936 around Orkney and Shetland, in 1937 to Norway, in 1938 round Cape Wrath and through the Caledonian Canal to the Clyde 1939, all now part of the school's mythology; and before a pioneering schoolboy unit of HM Coastguard was set up on the nearby cliffs. It was indeed surprising that it took a German to exploit British maritime traditions in this way. Seriously under-recognised by all commentators on Hahn's accomplishments in this area has been the influence on him of the naval historian and Master of Downing College Cambridge, Admiral Sir Herbert Richmond, and of his book *Naval Training*, which reads almost as a primer for Gordonstoun and Hahn enthusiasts. The old cliché of British yachtsmen has long been that the three most undesirable things afloat are an engine, a cow and a naval officer. Richmond's answer was straightforward: all naval personnel must be trained in the handling of small sailing craft. The enrolment into Gordonstoun of the *HMS Conway* boys led not only to Outward Bound but also to the setting up of Gordonstoun's vocational nautical training department which flourished for a number of years after the war. Scholarships offered by the Blue Funnel Line, the Marine Society, the Honourable Company of Master Mariners, Shell Tankers Ltd., the Pacific Steam Navigation Company, the Blue Star Line and Scottish Local Education Authorities enabled a whole new range of boys to enter the school.

What then did the two schools have in common, apart from a Headmaster who, often absent, was always straining at the leash to launch new schemes?

Both schools were hierarchical, and both were governed by a formalised system of trust that, although abandoned in both places after Hahn's time, was respected and treasured in retrospect by the overwhelming majority of Hahn pupils. An individual training plan required the entry every evening of + and – signs that indicated whether the owner had respected or failed to respect certain simple daily obligations: physical exercises, hygiene (washing and teeth cleaning), punctuality, and items of personal choice and relevance. The right to wear the school's more formal evening uniform usually came a few weeks after arrival, followed by the award of the white stripe. Subsequent promotions enabled some to become colour bearer candidates and others, fewer in number, actual colour bearers, from whom Hahn selected his Guardian or Head Boy. Although the colour bearers elected their fellow colour bearers, it was hardly democratic. Punishments too in Hahn's time were matters of honour and consisted of having to walk prescribed routes alone before breakfast. Colour bearers were required to undertake a weekly walk alone to encourage reflection, to experience the stimulus and enrichment of 'aloneness'. Recited in this manner, these practices invite disbelief, perhaps especially in Anglo-Saxon audiences. It is clear that, under Hahn, they worked. They have, however, not survived.

Kurt Hahn as Gordonstoun boys will remember him

Sport limited to two afternoons a week, opportunities for handicrafts, work on the school grounds, music, visiting lecturers, expeditions into the surrounding countryside, an emphatic emphasis on individual projects – all these were shared as well. Common to both schools under Hahn were the theatrical performances directed by him, usually Shakespeare, but the drama was provided not only by the playwright since Hahn's choice of pupils to play noble characters had to be earned (or, at least, not forfeited by dishonourable behaviour). Common too, in reflection of Hahn's determination to enable the admission of pupils from modest homes, was the expectation that parents would assess their own abilities to meet the fees and, where possible, contribute more than required in order to fund scholarships. Henry Brereton, writing in 1966, claims that for the school's entire history up to that date, between one quarter and one fifth of Gordonstoun parents had voluntarily paid more than they must so that others could pay less.

There was one further bond between Salem and Gordonstoun. Both had to confront hard times that threatened their very survival, and in both cases these hard times had their origins in the 12-year life of the Third Reich.

The Gordonstoun story is the more straightforward and briefer to tell.

With the outbreak of war in 1939 the Gordonstoun community had become suspect. Eleven German pupils and five members of staff were interned. It was hardly surprising that the enforced move to West Wales, where the boys on arrival spent their first nights sleeping in tents and washing in the river, led to a fall in numbers to below 90 by 1942, a situation salvaged only by the recruitment of the *HMS Conway* boys. Financial survival over the war years was a miracle. In their absence, the army had virtually destroyed Gordonstoun through neglect and the outbreak of a major fire. On return, old army huts were purchased and erected and some compensation was eventually secured from the military authorities. And then, in 1947, the College's bankers were taken over. Their successors withdrew the agreed credit facilities at the very time that the Trust that had offered the funds for the purchase of the Gordonstoun Estate, hitherto rented, withdrew its offer. Miraculously, the school enrolment had grown to 190 in Wales and by 1951 had reached 400. But Antonin Besse came on the scene just in time with his support of £65,000.

The Salem story is inevitably more complex and is not recoverable in all its details. For the events between Hahn's enforced departure in May 1933 and his return visit in July 1945 we are almost entirely dependent on two accounts, one by a teacher Hildegard Disch, the other by a pupil who joined the school in 1939, Joachim Jung. [●] Human nature being, as Hahn often said, quoting Tom Jones, Deputy Secretary to the Cabinets of four Prime Ministers, whom he had got to know during Gordonstoun's Welsh exile, *'very prevalent'*, the reports on Nazi incursions into the life and spirit of the school are recognised as *'facts of life'* but remain impressionistic, elusive, and not fully absorbed into the mainstream of the institutional memory. Compromises

were necessary – how else could the school have survived? The Jewish families withdrew their children very soon after Hahn's departure. Jews could no longer be accepted into the school, and even those of mixed parentage found themselves under direct threat. The board of governors ultimately placed the school's survival above loyalty to its Jewish inheritance. One has little right to judge but is left regretting that, 60 years later, so little is apparently known about the fate of Salem's Jewish pupils. They have achieved infinitely less attention in the school's annals than the many who died for the Fatherland in the armed forces. There is ground here to be made up.

Hahn's imprisonment and banishment were nonetheless followed by acts of great courage. The Markgraf Berthold, who had been Hahn's first pupil and Guardian, posted the following notice on the school notice board on 13th May:

> 'The new government in Baden has ordered that there should be no school tomorrow and that national school celebrations should be held.
>
> To mark the day, Herr Baumann will in both Salem and Spetzgart, after a reference to the significance of the day, read out two speeches delivered by the founder of the school, Prince Max of Baden, the one he gave on the opening of the school, and the one given at the time of the (French) march into the Ruhr …
>
> Flags are not to be raised as the school is in mourning as long as Herr Hahn remains in prison.' [103]

Berthold also travelled to Berlin to confront Hitler in person over Hahn's imprisonment, to be angrily repulsed by the Fuhrer in a face-to-face meeting.

The origins and nature of the protests against Hahn's imprisonment throw a problematical light on his and Salem's position now after the advent of full Nazi power. Markgraf Berthold had printed, also in 1933, a substantial collection of papers that documented his father's, Hahn's and the school's dedication to the national cause. They included memoranda against the signing of the Versailles Treaty, Germany's moral campaign for justice including his father's letter of 1st December 1919 to the Archbishop of Canterbury, the case for revision of the German-Polish border, and the 1932 introduction of military games into Salem's programme. His introduction read: *'We are resolved to serve that Germany of which these papers give testimony, and believe that we have a just claim to recognition and protection by the national movement.'* [104] It cannot therefore surprise us that one strong letter addressed to Hitler on Hahn's behalf came from the man who was later to become Commander-in-Chief of the German Army

---

[●] Hildegard Disch *Die Schule Schloß Salem in den Jahren 1933–1945* (Salem Sonderheft N. 28 April 1949) and Joachim F. Jung *Das Leitende und das Tragende; Erinnerungen 1928–1960*

in the early years of the war, Walther Brauchitsch – he had one son in Salem; his other son was ADC to Goering in 1945 and negotiated his chief's surrender to the US army. Another came from the hero of the 20th July 1944 failed assassination plot against Hitler, Claus Schenk von Stauffenberg: '… *that this taking into custody may be based on a misunderstanding, perhaps following an unchecked denunciation. To cast doubts on the national loyalties of Herr Hahn seems to me to be as unimaginable as if one were to doubt my own, when I as a member of the Stahlhelm stand four square behind the present government, which I see as the last bulwark, the ultima ratio, against the international threat of Bolshevism.'* [●] [105] Alas, neither had understood Hahn. Stauffenberg was to celebrate the Roehm Putsch publicly in the streets as the necessary cleansing of the army before his later convictions and experiences led him to the leadership of the July plot and martyrdom.

In the months of confusion immediately after Hahn's banishment, there were Nazi attempts to install their own director, and several teachers were suspended. Erich Meissner, Hahn's senior colleague, was able briefly to take control and delivered an address of astounding frankness and cold-blooded courage to his colleagues but, soon after, alerted during a drunken Nazi celebration in Salem itself by a former Salem pupil and Party member that he was in imminent danger, fled that same night over the border into Switzerland to rejoin Hahn in Scotland. Salvation came through the appointment in October 1934 of Heinrich Blendinger, already a Hahn admirer, whose first address to the assembled Salemers established his truly extraordinary relationship with teachers and pupils until his enforced withdrawal in the spring of 1943 owing to ill health. '*Show me the real Salem as you understand it and I will help you to keep it.*' [106]

Joachim Jung's recollections may not be typical, but they bring these school years alive for us. His best friend who disliked the regime but enrolled in the army earlier than required and lost his life within days of arriving on the Eastern Front – why had they not engaged in deeper personal discussion whilst they had the time? The sight of the nearby Swiss mountains and their unspoken encouragement to listen to foreign broadcasts (the BBC and the jazz trumpeter Teddy Staufer) which carried the death penalty; the '*Giftschrank*', the '*poison cupboard*' in the teachers' library which held the books of Jewish authors under lock and key; the wild evening of jazz and dancing in the spring of 1940 – King Oliver's Hot Swing Risen Band – which Blendinger had agreed on condition that the noise was kept under control (jazz was forbidden under Nazi rules) during which the floor shook and only Blendinger's arrival brought to a close; the sister of a fellow pupil, a member of the Rote Kapelle communist resistance group, who was executed by guillotine on 5th August 1943; the visit of the diplomat, father of two pupils, who gave a completely frank description of the unannounced German bombing raid on Belgrade – not even the German embassy had been forewarned, and the ethical implications were clear to all; the transport and rapid hanging and re-hanging of the few available Hitler photographs ahead of the route through the classrooms of the visiting Nazi Minister Rust; the failed recruitment visit in the summer of 1942 of the SS, not one pupil stepping forward for enrolment.

It is undeniable that Salem's connections with England were influential in the pre-war years, Salem's three successive victories in the Public Schools athletics championships in the White City in London bringing the Nazi regime unintended prestige. It is equally undeniable that Salem exercised a clear fascination on senior Nazi leaders. When in 1934 the Markgraf as Chairman of the Governors was contemplating closure in preference to the sacrifice of ideals, the official in Karlsruhe who had been given the responsibility for the school's supervision, Ministerialrat Kraft, reacted vehemently, so keen was he to see the school more closely allied with the Party. In time he appears to have developed a genuine appreciation of the school's aspiration and inner life. When in 1938 Blendinger's dismissal had been decided upon by the Party, Kraft defended him forcefully, stating that guidelines had already been set up on 21st October 1935 for the exclusion of Jews – the two remaining Jews would leave Salem in Easter 1938, and '*did colleagues realise that a nephew of Hess was an enthusiastic pupil*'.

After Blendinger's ill-health removed him in 1943 there followed increasing confusion and a severe lack of unity and common purpose. In December 1944 the school was finally taken over and turned into a Napola, a Nazi elite training school for future political and military leaders. It had survived all but the remaining five months of the war.

Hildegard Disch summarised the school's choice with realism. '*We did it (i.e. compromised) with a heavy heart, recognising that it was better through keeping Salem in existence to maintain a position that was against national socialism and for a better future than to become martyrs.*' [107]

This is an incomplete and assuredly not objective account, but three further observations are relevant.

[●] Letter to Baron Hornstein in Salem of March 1933, cited in Rupert Poensgen – *Die Schule Schloß Salem im Dritten Reich*

Salem's survival was inconceivable without Blendinger. The finest insight into his personality is given us today through the inspiring nature of his correspondence with his former pupils 'in the field'.

As the war advanced and turned against Germany, Salem's male pupils became ever more aware of their limited mortality, a phenomenon of course by no means unique to Salem. The temptation to relax morals and to enjoy what remained of life grew ever stronger. It was Blendinger's spiritual leadership that enabled so many of his Salem pupils to maintain personal standards of integrity and self-respect.

For many, the training plan provided a daily refuge for reflection and self-discipline.

Kurt Hahn knew how much he owed Blendinger. *'As an educator he went his own ways which I today feel to have been a healing correction of the style of my headship. His work was a renunciation of the dramatic tempo of the pioneer phase, which can be attributed not only to the stormy events of the time but also to the debit side of my often restless temperament.'* [108]

Breakdown and Dismissal from Gordonstoun

Who can be surprised that, after the war and the strain of the immediate post-war years, Hahn's health again gave way under the strain?

The explanation that has achieved almost official status is that Hahn was stricken during a fundraising visit to the United States in October 1952, but there had been unmistakable warning signs. His assistant secretary at the time gave her parents regular accounts from the autumn term of 1951 onwards: *'Hahn is always giving orders and then cancelling them, drawing up schemes and then abandoning them … he is always setting people time limits. One minute to find Brereton. Three minutes to have lunch. Nine seconds to make a précis of the Leader in* The Times.' A master turned up for interview and found that Hahn had forgotten all about him and was away (but the housekeeper ushered him into Hahn's room and promptly forget about him herself. When she reappeared three and a half hours later he greeted her with a beaming smile: *'Well, I've got your little trick. It was an endurance test, wasn't it?'* He was not amused by her apologetic explanation).

Strangely in the light of subsequent events, Hahn had received his clearest warning in a curiously sympathetic and prescient letter from the wife of his Deputy, Peggy Brereton, already on 11th January 1952: *'… at this stage you should and ought to assume a dignified aloofness, if you attach any value to your work and good name … the threat, if any, comes from that dangerous old bear, HLB* (her husband), *who was once told he was to look after a baby* (the school) *when the time came. He is under the impression that the time has come, and rather than drop the baby, he will fight to the death … the question is: Do you love the baby well enough to leave it to him, while you look after the world you have created … or would you rather nurse the baby (it's growing teeth, and can almost stand) and give your conscientious old bear a kick in the pants … I grieve to think it should come to this …'*

One of Hahn's most faithful disciples, Roy McComish, later a co-founder of the Round Square Conference of Hahn-minded schools, wrote: *'There were two schools really – the school when Hahn was away, the school when he was there – one could almost feel the barometric pressure rise when his car turned up the driveway.'* Now, on his return from the United States, the pace became even more frenetic. In Henry Brereton's words *'…he gives the most incoherent orders and is generally incomprehensible … one of the symptoms of his disease is an increased and feverish activity. He gave three successive breakfasts this morning and then embarked on a major row involving about 16 boys. The row dragged on till lunch time … the trouble is that he does not go to bed but sees more and more people and has more and more meals. All last week he had three breakfasts to which about 25 people came, two lunches to which about 18 people came, two teas and two suppers with often a party at Burnside afterwards so that he can meet everyone all over again.'*

The abundant crossfire of letters, typescript and hand-written, memoranda, notes and references to telephone conversations and informal meetings that followed for months leaves us, inescapably, a very confused picture, but the figure at the centre of the storm was Hahn's long-serving, personally devoted deputy, Henry Brereton, whose confused loyalties at this point have resulted in a controversial legacy. In a letter on 20th September 1951 he had written to Hahn, disclaiming any wish to become headmaster on Hahn's retirement, or suitability for the post (it appears possible that these sentiments had been generated by some dissatisfaction that Hahn had recently expressed about his performance as Director of Studies); he had written, he explained, because Hahn had raised the matter after the school's successful return to Scotland from Wales. On other occasions, however, it is quite clear that he regarded himself as the chosen successor. By this time Hahn was 68.

Hahn's behaviour on return from the United States led Brereton to record confidentially on 30th October his conviction that Hahn must be regarded as sick; furthermore, that he was *'like a clock without a governor … switching from subject to subject with bewildering inconsequence'*, that Hahn was himself anxiously aware that he was not well. On 31st October he addressed a clear and impressively fair personal letter to Hahn which, he claims, Hahn refused to open, in which he offered to take over for the rest of the term. At this point Hahn prepared to leave on another of his regular journeys south.

Alarmed by the news, his brother Rudo travelled up to Gordonstoun. His subsequent handwritten letter to *'the only one of his medical advisors in whom he has complete trust'* made no bones about the seriousness of it all. *'He has been ill for a year, he has suffered great disappointments, his friends have deserted him, he trembles, he has constantly to show off to make other people believe that he is normal, at times he shows awareness of his condition and of its dangers for the school; his greatest fear is to be considered abnormal; mention of a psychiatrist or mental doctor produces violent resistance and strongest mistrust.'* Then, importantly given later developments: *'finally, I have to tell you that Gordonstoun is not able to accept my brother as active headmaster in his present state. There is no doubt if he remains up here there is the greatest danger that he will destroy his life's work.'* But the brief postscript was in retrospect no less significant: *'his power of recuperation and capability of regaining a normal state of mind are most astonishing'*.

Rudo and his family removed Hahn from Gordonstoun, sought medical treatment for him in Oxford, supported the decision to confine him for a period of seven weeks to a mental home in Northampton (the signature on the documents was that of his sister-in-law Lola whose act remained a wound on her conscience for the rest of her life – his handwritten notes to her from the home, pleading for a review of his case and a reassessment of his legal rights which, he claimed in irreproachably clear language, had not been respected, have been preserved); but there remained no doubt in the minds of the Gordonstoun authorities that his headship was over. But now, the leadership of the governing body failed.

The Chairman of Governors, Sir William Hamilton Fyfe, a former headmaster of Christ's Hospital School, later Principal and Vice-Chancellor of the University of Aberdeen, with whom Hahn enjoyed exchanging epithets in Greek, was old, almost blind, lived in the south, and visited the school rarely (one account claims he had not been there for the past five years), now gave Rudo Hahn a handwritten account of a board meeting in December. Six of the eight governors present had agreed unanimously that Hahn should not return to Gordonstoun as headmaster, but *'the decision was not minuted because we all hope that Kurt will himself proffer his retirement on the grounds that he has*

passed the normal age … we have made Henry Brereton Acting (instead of Deputy) Head for the rest of the year … I need hardly add that we all most earnestly hope that Kurt will remain at Gordonstoun under some style or title to be later agreed upon so as to give his continual inspiration to the school he created … if Kurt should worry about the choice of his successor, will you tell him my confident opinion that we should appoint HB for a period of years to be agreed upon between him and the Directors. This hasn't been decided, but I give you the information – as "Top Secret" – in case it would comfort Kurt to know that …' This well-intentioned, embarrassed confusion was exacerbated by Henry Brereton's contemporary suggestion to the governors, confirmed by him in a later memorandum of December 1953, that the minimum period for the interim headship should be five years, this being a part of the unminuted decision that was however not communicated to Rudo Hahn.

Kurt Hahn had meanwhile withdrawn to his German home Hermannsberg, near Salem, accompanied by the admirable Miss Wicken, his secretary, who wrote to Lola in January 1953 in cheerful mood: *'The only sign that he is not himself is that he is very punctual and very tidy but no doubt he will recover from this too in the course of time.'* To his great nephew Michael Gunther he distracted himself (Michael's words) by dictating his memoirs in alternating periods of intense passion and long pauses of silence. He also found the time and the resolution to write to Hamilton Fyfe: *'In order to camouflage the dismissal as it should be camouflaged in the interests of Gordonstoun, I enclose a letter of resignation. You will note that it is undated, so that you may fill the date in at a convenient stage of the present crisis …'* And then, despite all the pressures to restrain him, he returned to Gordonstoun.

There followed unhappy months. *'There is no doubt that the restoration of the patient has created an embarrassing situation.'* Hahn's own words were not inappropriate. He was not ready to give up. Hamilton Fyfe was sufficiently impressed to contemplate Hahn's return as headmaster after May and to give Brereton a sabbatical term. Brereton refused categorically to serve again under Hahn and all positions hardened. *'I should be given the chance of bringing about an orderly and dignified transition … I have had evidence that I am still needed; humanity is not an extra – it is the mainspring'* (Hahn to Hamilton Fyfe on 11th July). At the beginning of the month he had spoken in the near-by Duffus Church. *'His address … last Sunday was magnificent and delivered more clearly than I have ever known him do it'* (Miss Wicken on 14th July). He spoke to the staff on 18th July and the Colour Bearers (senior boys) on 19th. He pleaded for one further year, with a new headmaster to be appointed as an observer for these 12 months. In a series of memoranda he undertook however to withdraw on certain conditions: the appointment of a Director of Activities to ensure safety, an overall Principal for Gordonstoun and the nearby sister school Altyre, a new Chairman, and protection against personal rumour. It required the intervention of one of Hahn's oldest friends, Geoffrey Winthrop Young, who was President of the Gordonstoun Association, to force the issue, and Hahn informed the governing body on 25th July not only of his definitive resignation but also of his unwillingness to take up the suggestion of becoming the non-executive Principal of the two schools. Hamilton Fyfe's successor, Brigadier Houldsworth, whom Hahn trusted, undertook a search in 1954 for this position, and it was characteristic of Hahn to have pressed the candidatures of two military figures, John Hunt, the leader of the Everest expedition, later Founder Director of the Duke of Edinburgh's Award Scheme (he refused to be considered), and Desmond Hoare, later Founder Head of Atlantic College (ruled out because he was a Roman Catholic); and the sequence of events played out in a natural way and, with hindsight, as might have been predicted: Brereton served his five years as headmaster; Hahn's Salem colleague Erich Meissner continued for these five years as Warden (a Hahn idiosyncrasy copied from the concept of Eton's Provost and intended to protect the inner conscience of the school with the right *'to be consulted, advise and warn'*); when Gordonstoun and Altyre were compelled to amalgamate in 1958 the Altyre headmaster Robert Chew took over the headship of the unified schools; and Brereton assumed the Wardenship on Meissner's retirement until his own.

These events left a scar for years, for never again did Kurt Hahn address either staff or pupils or enter the school save on exceptional occasions such as visits of the Royal family. Perhaps this exile was in part self-imposed. He wrote to Lola late in 1953 that *'bitterness seeks entry every day. I resist, but it knocks again and again'.* [109] The hurt of wounded pride that he so often reproached in others had come to him, although years later he was able to acknowledge the insistent temptation to give way to feelings of martyrdom. His fear of mental instability and of psychiatrists that he had learned in the Konigstein clinic undoubtedly cast its long shadow. And at the heart of it all was the broken, never to be restored personal relationship with Henry Brereton, for it was Henry to whom he had entrusted intimate thoughts and anxieties at the time of his earlier breakdown in 1945 which Brereton had so carefully and frankly recorded in confidential notes. Some time after these events, his Old Boys collected money with which to commission a bust by Jacob Epstein. I remember his

getting me to accompany him on a visit to Cardiff in 1960 to examine Epstein's Christ in Majesty in Llandaff Cathedral. He turned down the offer of the bust.

So dominant had Hahn been in the creation and survival of Gordonstoun, so committed were he and his mostly admiring colleagues to the mission that he encapsulated in the phrase Greater Gordonstoun, so completely had he personally selected and appointed his governing body, that resistance to him was inconceivable as a unanimous and combined operation. As Hahn continued his personal campaigning, it was again the wisdom of the former Headmaster of Marlborough and Charterhouse, Hahn friend and admirer George Turner, that merits recollection: *'... of course all powerful action such as your own creates reaction; it is our responsibility to see that it is not a damaging reaction, but a creative one',* he wrote to Hahn in April 1955.

Two postscripts are also worth recalling. Geoffrey Winthrop Young it was who compelled Hahn to entrust *'his life's work'* to others; and no one, not even Brereton, came close to rivaling Erich Meissner in outspoken, often bitterly expressed opposition to Hahn's return. Kurt Hahn was the last person outside the family to bid farewell to Geoffrey on his death bed. *'I regard Geoffrey's friendship as one of the blessings of my life – what does it matter, if we read the events of June differently?'* he wrote to his widow. And when Eric Meissner in retirement in London was quite simply failing to make ends meet, Hahn moved him into a small house which he provided near his home Hermannsberg in southern Germany and comforted the now fearful and demoralized earlier colleague and friend in his last days.

Life and Work after Gordonstoun

„Friede Deinem Alter", sagt Goethe zu Lotte in Thomas Manns Roman, als sie von ihm Abschied nimmt …' ('Peace in your old age' Goethe says to Lotte in Thomas Mann's novel when she takes her leave of him). So wrote Meissner to Hahn on 25th August 1955 in yet another attempt to keep him away from Gordonstoun. Nothing could have been further from Hahn's mind. And the proof found expression on a page of *The News Chronicle* on 23rd February 1956. This page featured a long article by Hahn, *Horse Sense and the H-Bomb,* an editorial leader commending his views, a second leader reporting the move of Sir John Hunt from the Camberley Staff College to take over the recently launched Duke of Edinburgh's Award Scheme, and a lady reader's letter complaining very critically that this scheme was for boys only.

The Award Scheme

No achievement in Hahn's life is more illustrative than the Award Scheme of his essential characteristics: his poaching of an existing idea, his skilled recruitment of public personalities leading to the creation of a band-wagon of enthusiasts, and his utter refusal, embedded in conspiratorial plotting, ever to give up.

The German Sports Medal (*Sportabzeichen*) that had its origins in Sweden gave him the initial framework. He had been deeply impressed by the calibre of the local people living around Gordonstoun. He became determined to open the school in ways he had not attempted in Salem. *'The time is past when one can with a easy mind segregate boys and girls in beautiful houses and cut them off from the outside world.'* His determination to extend Gordonstoun's influence led to the creation already in 1936 of the Moray Badge that combined tests, not for the trained athlete but for the 'average boy' and those not gifted for games, in athletics, expeditions, first aid and life-saving. An open letter to *The Times* advocating the scheme drew only one response – from the founder of the scout movement, Baden-Powell. But in 1938, the Regional Committee of the National Fitness Council ran three courses of a fortnight each, based on the Moray Badge principles.

The war sharpened his conviction that British youth were quite simply unfit. Gordonstoun's move to Wales proved no impediment. In the summer of 1940 Gordonstoun in Wales ran a three-week residential course for boys from the Public Schools, from state secondary schools, the Merchant Navy and some 20 young soldiers sent by the War Office. In all these developments the growing relationship between the school and *HMS Conway* was a key factor. By the autumn of 1940 he had secured the support of the War Office (and the hostility of the Board of Education) for experimental courses and wrote enthusiastically (and optimistically) on 15th October of plans for ten courses with 100 participants each.

His advocacy, direct and through others, was formi-dable. A collection of papers from 1939–1940 on the County Badge Scheme contains five major articles and 15 letters from *The Times*, other essays and reports including a long exposé by Hahn's colleague Dr. Zimmermann on 'open country games' that highlighted at length the new sport of orienteering, and even a report from the Deputy Governor of the Province of El Fasher in Darfur: *'the town Koranic schools have cooperated with the Government School in the practices and tests – such boys include young offenders who are in confinement or under probation, who are allowed to mix on equal terms with other boys – I consider this a most*

promising line for the treatment of these young offenders that might easily be worked into the Criminal Justice Bill (at present shelved)'. This was the first intimation of the future contribution of the Duke of Edinburgh's Award Scheme to the educational recovery of juvenile delinquents.

And the bandwagon? In December 1940 the County Badge Experimental Committee was set up under the Chairmanship of the Master of Balliol College, Oxford, A. D. Lindsay; and the Committee included among others the then Headmasters of Charterhouse and St. Pauls, London, the philosopher Julian Huxley and the Chairman of the University Grants Committee. Signatories of a joint letter to *The Times* included the Master of Downing College Cambridge, the Archbishop of Canterbury and the Chairman of the British Alpine Club. Not only the Dollar Academy in Elgin but also the Public Schools Charterhouse, Felsted and Malvern were participants. Organisations wishing to become involved even at this early stage included the County Councils of Middlesex, Kent, Oxfordshire, Glamorgan, Hertfordshire, East Sussex and Dorset, the Home Guard, the Air Ministry, the National Federation of Women's Institutes, the National Association of Organisers of Physical Education, the Welsh League of Youth (Cwmni Urdd Gobaith Cymru) and even the Colonial Service in Kenya. The whole story of how the Country Badge Scheme and Outward Bound emerged from these activities is told in absorbing human detail by the secretary appointed to implement their ambitions, Jim Hogan, in his *Impelled into Experiences.* [●]

Perhaps the most decisive personality to influence the practical implementation in later years, John Hunt had sent a memorandum to Geoffrey Winthrop Young, the President of the Alpine Club, in 1940, in which he described the value of mountain terrain in preparing troops and above all commandos for war, and its wider relevance to the education of youth in general, calling also on his previous experience with young Bengali schoolboys. This was the Brigadier John Hunt who led the first successful Mount Everest expedition in 1953. Winthrop Young sent the note on to his friend Kurt Hahn. In his memoirs John Hunt recalls how he *'invited him* (Hahn) *two years later (1942) … to watch some battle drills … on the slopes of Beguildy Beacon above the Teme valley, not far from the wartime home of Gordonstoun … the essence of his creed was that each boy needed a challenge personal to and attainable by himself, rather than being assessed in competition and comparison*

[●] J. M. Hogan: *Impelled into Experiences – The Story of the Outward Bound Schools* Educational Productions Ltd. 1968

with the performance of others ...' Noteworthy in Hunt's memoirs is his emphasis at this point on *'the working boy'* and across all classes; and he was influenced too by his own lack of success and recognition on his school's playing fields. He goes on: *'Later, Hahn was to offer me the post of Provost of Gordonstoun and its preparatory establishment, but I declined. I felt that it would be restricting to remain in a supervisory role in the school which had been the nursery for Hahn's ideas when the time was ripe for spreading them more widely'* – convincing evidence of the unintended blessing of Hahn's enforced removal from the constraints of Greater Gordonstoun.

Of course there was opposition, and not only from the Board of Education that clearly resented an intrusion, even if supported by the War Office, into an age group that was its responsibility. The *Sunday Express* identified Hahn as a follower of Hitler in his advocacy of the Badge methods. At a more thoughtful level, concerns and hostility were expressed towards the apparent introduction of a national youth training scheme with a political inspiration. Compulsory state movements were, it was claimed also by Baden-Powell, repressive, lacking a spiritual heart, and designed solely to achieve mass cohesion at the expense of individual character. One may contrast this view with the judgement of the historian Tony Judt that, by 1945, *'a broad consensus that the physical and moral condition of the citizenry was a matter of common interest and therefore part of the responsibility of the state'.* [●] Hahn was clear that his proposals were in the national interest and a national responsibility.

By 1954 the issue was settled. *'It would never have started but for Hahn, certainly not. He suggested I ought to do it, and I fought against it for quite a long time.'* Thus the Duke of Edinburgh as recorded by one of Hahn's most fervent admirers, the American Josh Miner. Prince Philip transferred a planned committee meeting from the King's Jubilee Trust on 15th October 1954 to Buckingham Palace and took the Chair. In 1957 the scheme was introduced into the Borstal Schools that accommodated and attempted to re-educate convicted juvenile delinquents. By 1970 it was operating in 28 counties. In 1980 it was established in the United States as the Congressional Award and is now used the world over under varying names. That its aspirations were not confined to the purely physical is underlined in a letter from Kurt Hahn to Judge Adrian

Curlewis of Australia on 4th June 1959. *'As you know, it is of the utmost importance to me that within the fourfold achievement demanded in the Duke of Edinburgh's Scheme, the balance is not disturbed in favour of the purely or mainly physical performances. That is why I rejoice to hear that you are likely to introduce the scheme in Australia ... .'* What was he defending above all? The requirement for a project that required sustained commitment over a period of time and a properly documented conclusion rather than an open-ended pursuit or hobby! This was a theme that was to form the core of the Trevelyan Scholarships to Oxford and Cambridge. It is reflected too in the extended essays of the International Baccalaureate.

Did and does the Award Scheme reach enough 'street corner loiterers'? This pointed question is a useful reminder that the scheme was aimed at young people in the youth club world of the big cities, at those who do not have the supportive framework of well-endowed, well-equipped and well-staffed schools, and at their leaders who most need the encouragement of a structure and system of rewards for those they are leading. Over the now nearly 60 years of its work, its most striking success has been its contribution to the training programmes for young convicted criminals.

The Trevelyan Scholarships to Oxford and Cambridge [●]

Kurt Hahn was ruthless in pressing the claims of his pupils to places in Oxford and Cambridge, especially Oxford. John Masterman, one of the English internees in the camp of Ruhleben whom Hahn had befriended in the First World War and who was to become Vice-Chancellor of Oxford University, remembered his old friend Kurt Hahn *'bombarding me with harrowing tales of good men but late developers, kept out of colleges because of insufficient examination and paper qualifications ... his ace instance a Belgian on whom the school reported that it strongly advised against his attempting the entrance examination ... he was ignorant of this report, went to a university and ended as a Nobel Prize man'.* So it was perhaps natural that he described the Trevelyan Scholarships as *'an experiment that stirred my interest more than any other'.*

Rab Butler's Education Act of 1944 had opened up university places to many new applicants, encouraged

[●] Tony Judt *Postwar: A History of Europe since 1945* Vintage Books London page 72

[●] This account relies heavily on *Trevelyan Scholarships* by Roland Peddie, Roundwood Press 1975 as well as on Hahn's papers

by state scholarships and means-tested grants from the Local Education Authorities. The immense increase in the number of applicants and the resulting problems of selection led inescapably to an increased emphasis on academic performance, measured by specialised and examinable knowledge. Many (not all) schools were unhappy with this strengthened specialisation in the sixth form, and the state grammar schools were especially hard pressed to keep up. There was unhappiness too within the universities and above all Oxford and Cambridge who had fond memories of the broad outlook and active attitudes of the traditional outstanding *all-rounder*. The change was made even more distinct for them when they recalled the extraordinary human calibre of the men who had come up to university after war-time experience. Industry too was unhappy with the lack of *'character'* they were now recruiting among graduates. One leading industrialist expressed the matter in the following words: *'What we need … is for the scholar to share with the responsible industrialist his method of attack on problems and in so doing to ask searching questions … the industrialist will pose his own questions in return … we need a new relationship to be established between the universities and industry …'* And the Vice-Chancellor of Bristol University, Sir Philip Morris, made a public statement that *'revision of the sixth form curriculum will have to be accepted as soon as we have a prophet and a group of people with the will to show us how it ought to be done'.*

Fertile ground indeed for Kurt Hahn, and he was typically keen to take action!

He opened the campaign very soon after leaving Gordonstoun with a long letter dated 10th February 1953 to the Master of Trinity College, Cambridge, the historian George Trevelyan, asking him *'with great diffidence'* to read a boy's project on Anglo-American Relations during the War of Secession which had been disregarded by Clare College as a contribution to the boy's entry qualifications. Hahn's letter included some rather imprecise references to past practice by some ten Oxbridge Colleges in accepting Gordonstoun projects as relevant when assessing applicants, together with flattering allusion to this boy's careful study of Trevelyan's own *Nineteenth Century History of England*. This was however but a preliminary skirmish. The real follow-up came in 1956.

Through his industrialist brother Rudo, Kurt secured an introduction to the Managing Director of the United Steel Companies Gerald Steele and his successor Sir Walter Benton Jones. The decisive planning meeting took place between these two, Hahn and others on 21st March 1956. It was decided to concentrate on Oxford and Cambridge in the belief that their potential influence was the greatest.

Hahn's emphasis on personal development independent of straightforward athletic achievement, coupled with individual initiative and active service to the community, was attractive to the industrialists. Hahn was nonetheless well aware of disquiet within schools, and of opposition from members of the influential Headmasters' Conference of the Public Schools, and he had to work hard to ensure support from within the two universities. His most important conquest was the Nobel physicist Sir Neville Mott, whom he first addressed in a letter in March 1956. Mott had confided his concerns about the lack of able science students to *The Cambridge Review,* and associated the low academic standards he was encountering with narrow human attitudes. A dinner at Claridges Hotel in London in July, hosted by United Steel, saw Mott and Harry Ree, the admired Head of Watford Grammar School, commissioned to draft a statement for the two universities; and by December the scheme was ready for launching, the first scholarships to be advertised in September 1957 for entry to the universities in 1958. By this time, and thanks in large measure to Mott's endorsement, Hahn had secured the support in Oxford of seven Heads of Colleges (one of them Rhodes House), and four professors in the natural sciences; and in more sceptical Cambridge of three Heads of Colleges, two professors and five other senior academics. It was, he always maintained, the calibre of support, not consensus, that counted, and this was good enough. And George Trevelyan had consented to allow the scholarships to carry his name.

Hostility to specialisation in the sixth form was readily assumed to imply lower standards. Hahn and his allies had repeatedly to emphasise that the awards were not designed for boys of an intellectual calibre inferior to that of college entrance scholars. Premature specialisation, they argued, tended to narrow intellectual interests and to enfeeble initiative. It was the methods employed for diagnosing academic promise that would be different; evidence would be sought as to the presence of character likely to help in the fulfilment of that promise. The central requirement was the presentation of a project of exploration and investigation *'carried to a well-defined end'* and reflecting *'enterprise, originality and character'.* The reader today will be astonished to learn that Hahn was advocating, against Mott's reservations, that this project could act in support of one GCE Advanced Level qualification only, although it must be recalled that two so-called A Levels were normally sufficient for university entry. The complementary supporting evidence would be provided through the Headmaster's confidential report and a personal interview.

A letter in *The Times* and a press conference in December 1958 (the launch had been delayed) generated a disappointingly weak impact, but there could be no turning back now. Over the eight years of the scheme's life, £291,000 was paid out in scholarships, the entire administration being paid for by United Steel. Nineteen awards were made in the first year, rising to between 23 and 27 in subsequent years. The number of First Class degrees achieved by Trevelyan scholars was two-thirds higher than the average. Unsurprisingly, the greater expertise of the Public Schools in these matters gave them the edge: of the total of 1,420 applications received, 868 (61%) came from the Public Schools, 552 (39%) from the grammar schools. Public School boys took 136 awards, grammar school boys 50.

The short life of the scheme suggests failure, but Peddie's report stresses that it had been conceived as an experiment and a demonstration, and that there was no pressure among the instigators for a transfer to permanence. It is nonetheless easy, looking back on it all now, to identify weaknesses. The universities worried that the generous awards on offer, which were not means-tested, would divert applicants from their own Open Scholarship arrangements. Not only the Public Schools but also middle class parents were the first and most able to seize the opportunities. At no stage were girls ever mentioned. The scholarships were in practice only within the reach of the academically gifted because the applicant had to be reasonably assured already of an Oxbridge place before deciding to devote energy and time to a demanding project (and many projects were completed by applicants who had already secured their university admission). It is thus impossible to maintain that many entered Oxbridge who would not otherwise have done so. And whilst an impressive total of 1,420 projects were carried out in schools, they had no broadening effect on the curriculum because they were not part of what was taught. But the decisive disappointment was that very few Trevelyan scholars entered industry, not one taking up employment with any of the scheme's sponsors.

These scholarships offer us nonetheless yet another example of Hahn's extraordinary tenacity in challenging current practice and in assembling distinguished personalities – and money – in achieving his aims. Quixotic it may have been, but it was a small bandwagon that was in tune with later times, for Alec Peterson among others was stirred also by the Trevelyan Scholarship scheme to press for curricular reform in English upper secondary education. The termly project weeks of Atlantic College were created explicitly to enable the students to carry out Trevelyan-style projects of exploration and research; and the extended essays of the International Baccalaureate owe

their origins in part to the Trevelyan Scholarships. There may even today be some lessons that IB schools could learn from the Trevelyan scheme. One of the criteria circulated to school heads in 1957 stated that *'preference will be given to projects which involve contacts with others or which involve enterprising travel as compared with projects carried out in isolation'*. On one occasion Trevelyan Awards were made to two applicants jointly who had worked together on the same scientific project. Does the IB allow team extended essays? Does the IB go out of its way to encourage the human qualities of courage, enterprise, imagination and exploration in the preparation of these enterprises, or has it allowed them to become too drily academic and too subordinate to teacher guidance?

Thanks to the Trevelyan Scholarships, Hahn had been introduced to Sir Walter Benton Jones, the Head of United Steel. It was Sir Walter, now an enthusiastic Hahn disciple, who stimulated and led by example the early industrial support of the nascent Atlantic College.

Fighting the Cold War

It is not easy now to recall or to evoke the intensity of the fear that almost numbed ability to confront the issues of nuclear deterrence in a rational manner.

True to past form, Kurt Hahn was anxious to make his voice heard. On 10th April 1954 he addressed a long letter to *The Times*. It followed the recent test of the new hydrogen bomb. *'Fear and doubt are spreading throughout Christendom. Dies irae; Man does not deserve his might. He has mocked God.'* But until there was agreement at the highest level, accompanied by valid powers of inspection and enforcement, Britain had no alternative but to develop these hideous weapons. Speaking at the World Scientists Conference in London in August 1955, he stated *'I am alarmed at his (Bertrand Russell's) statement that the use of atomic weapons is inevitable in any war …'*

Hahn's principal discussion partner during these years was Rear-Admiral Anthony Buzzard, the youngest man ever to have been appointed Director of Naval Intelligence and, after retirement, a founder member of both the Institute of Strategic Studies and the Council of Christian Approaches to Defence and Disarmament. It was above all he who developed the concept of graduated deterrence. No pacifist, and therefore no unilateralist either, Hahn was nonetheless also in constant contact with his wartime ally Bishop Bell of Chichester and with the Bishop of London, attending both public and private meetings of the Council of Christian Approaches. At the World Scientists Conference in 1955 he spoke against the fateful reliance on the stark alternatives of absolute deterrence and pacifism. He attended annual meetings of the World Association of Parliamentarians for World Government and in June 1956 was one of two opening speakers alongside Bertrand Russell on *'How can the world authority be prevented from becoming a tyranny? What checks, balances, political and judicial controls are needed?'*

Unwaveringly critical of the Allied use of the atomic bombs over Japan, Kurt Hahn was also able to quote and call on the support of world figures in physics whom he knew: Max Born, whose daughter had attended Salem, whose son he had helped when he was being bullied in a school in Edinburgh, and whose New Year message in the *Physikalische Blätter* he cited frequently: *'when I came to Cambridge in 1933 I found Fritz Haber there. He was sick and broken in spirit after his expulsion from his country. I tried to bring him together with Rutherford but Rutherford refused to shake hands with the originator of chemical warfare … how would Rutherford act today? Perhaps he might have succeeded, thanks to his powerful personality, in preventing the unconditional surrender of the new means of destruction to politicians and military men …'*; Niels Bohr: *'may the great scientists pursue public affairs and politics with equal zeal as their own scientific targets! I have thought this ever since I had the privilege of talking with Niels Bohr on Hiroshima, which had thrown a shadow over his life'*; [●] James Franck of the 1945 Franck Report addressed to President Roosevelt: *'the nation capable of suddenly releasing this new indiscriminate weapon might not be trusted by mankind, should it proclaim its desire to see such weapons abolished by international agreement;'* (in 1933 Kurt Hahn had helped to draft a letter signed by Franck that appeared in the *Frankfurter Allgemeine Zeitung* protesting against Nazi anti-Semitic policies and his letter of resignation from the University of Göttingen; Hahn saw Franck again in Germany a year before he died for a discussion on western defence policies); and Sir Nevill Mott, his Cambridge ally in the Trevelyan Scholarship scheme.

In the immediate post-war years the West had unassailable supremacy. By the 1950s the USSR was rapidly achieving parity (and had been the first to detonate a hydrogen 'device'). Could the West, through NATO, employ tactical nuclear weapons in response to Soviet aggression without succumbing rapidly to all-out strategic war? Henry Kissinger was arguing that the only and acceptable alternative to mutual destruction in total

war was the employment of tactical nuclear weapons in 'limited' war, but *'we should make every effort to limit their effect … we would not use more than 500 kilotons explosive power* (25 times that at Hiroshima) *unless the enemy used them first'*. [●] The West, which had rapidly demobilised after the war, the Soviet Union having maintained massive numbers under arms, now relied entirely on the nuclear deterrent. But *'total war as an instrument of policy paralyses the will on any occasion but the least likely one (that of total aggression) and plays into the hands of an enemy commanding more flexible military power, thereby opening up to the Soviet Union numerous possibilities of using forces locally to advance their interests without approaching the point where the West would react by threatening total war'*. [○] The writer, Patrick Blackett, draws the conclusion that the West would never initiate the employment of tactical nuclear weapons and quotes the precedents of Korea, Indo-China and Suez where stalemate, partial defeat and complete withdrawal were accepted by the nuclear powers without nuclear weapons being used.

For Kurt Hahn (of course not him alone), this dilemma highlighted the uncertain western commitment to conventional forces, manpower and morale. Only by the proper training of adequate armies, he argued, could flexibility and credibility be maintained in facing down the Soviet Union. Another commentator Osgood pointedly drew attention to the comparative populations of the NATO countries (430 million) and the Soviet Union with all her satellite states (280 million). The issue became the more acute with the publication of the British White Paper on defence in 1957 which for political and economic reasons committed the nation to an absolute reliance on the total nuclear option.

Hahn's thinking owed much to Patrick Blackett, whose paper *Thoughts on British Defence Policy* perfectly crystallised the issue most naturally foremost in his mind: the moral issue. *'Parallel with the acceptance of the policy of preparation and training for atomic attack on enemy civilian populations went inevitably a transformation of moral standards. If the Strategic Air Command had been set in motion to carry out the plan for which every man had been trained to the limit, then the six million victims of Hitler's gas chambers would be hardly remembered; the humane and civilised West*

[●] By 1959 Kissinger had changed his opinion in favour of the greater importance of conventional weapons (*Observer* newspaper 7th June 1959)

[○] The Nobel physicist Patrick Blackett in his paper *Thoughts on British Defence Policy*

[●] Kurt Hahn to Sir Edward Appleton 25th May 1954

would have sunk to the level of Ghengis Khan ... till recently there has been a surprising lack of protest from the moral leaders of the western countries ... it was not the invention of the atomic bomb but the loss of its monopoly by the West that sent the Churchmen back to Grotius' formulation three hundred years ago of the "Principles of the Just War".' There followed a letter to *The Guardian* in August 1961, signed by Hahn, Buzzard and Nott among others, with clear signs of substantial Hahn drafting, advocating a *'conventional defence policy'*: *'We should have taken a step toward laying the curse of Hiroshima, brought into the world by a West which then had a nuclear monopoly such as unilateralists would now like to entrust to Russia – we should have made a start in regaining the faith of mankind by proving that we are in earnest about the rule of law which we defended in two world wars.'*

George Kennan's BBC Reith Lectures of 1957 gave him much additional encouragement that the Cold War was a matter to be resolved not by weapons but by morale, for Kennan drew attention to the relationship between the regime and the people in Soviet Russia, to the restlessness of the Soviet intelligentsia and the student youth, increasingly determined to do their thinking for themselves. Hahn himself pointed out that Khrushchev had not dared to imprison or silence Pasternak. The danger, writes Kennan, was intimately associated with the weakness in western civilisation itself. *'The true end of political action is, after all, to affect the deeper convictions of men. This the atomic bomb cannot do ... the fortunes of the Cold War will begin to turn in our direction as and when we learn to apply ourselves resolutely to many things that, superficially viewed, have nothing to do with the Cold War ...'*

In 1959 Hahn put his thoughts down in a series of memoranda that were distributed with his customary 'M' technique: For Private Circulation, with numbered copies. In June: *'Khrushchev has persuaded the West that he is Russia – his greatest propaganda triumph. Yet there is within Russia a hidden opinion – there are signs that he fears it.'* And he goes on to suggest that the West should offer to withdraw from Berlin on the condition that the whole of Berlin be re-established as a united city under a UN police force. *'To this proposal Khrushchev is bound to say no, for if he were to accept there would be heard all over the Eastern Sector the "sound of fetters breaking". He hates that sound as if it were the death knell of his power ... there would then take place in Russia a trial of strength whose outcome is unpredictable.'*

In July: we have a triple task – to restore morale on our home fronts and to strengthen the solidarity of the NATO nations, to repair the neglected part of our defence, and to establish before world opinion and before the hidden opinion inside Russia that our intentions are peaceful and just. *'What took place in the Algiers torture chambers and in the police prison of Paris has given our enemies great occasion to gloat. "I could never be valiant where I was not honest": so spoke the Duke of Albany in* King Lear *when he defended Britain in a tainted cause. Even the policy of the graduated deterrent fails to respect the Geneva Convention in its prohibitions "binding alike the conscience and practices of Nations" ("the words make us blush").'*

By 1961 he was convinced that Khrushchev did not want war but continued to need a series of triumphs to underscore the advance of communism and the waning power of the western democracies. The confrontations of that year and building of the Berlin Wall offered, Hahn maintained, new opportunities for winning the battle of morale. In October he proposed that the entire Soviet Zone, Eastern Germany, be transformed into a second German state on condition that the inhabitants choose their own government. Again, Khrushchev would refuse, but the relief in the Soviet Union after his historic admission in 1956 that massacre and torture were part of the system he served was a condition that *'lasts only while one rejoices over sufferings past; the moment comes when the present is compared less with the past from which one has escaped than with a future as one hopes to shape it ... the West underestimates Khrushchev's passionate eagerness to win the world's confidence ... Nevertheless, I believe that today he would say no ... world opinion would say yes, as would a secret Russia, which is weary of continued threats to peace.'*

The following month he was again in correspondence with his First World War colleague and friend Christian Herter, now US Secretary of State for Foreign Affairs. He sent him his memorandum on Berlin with a covering letter in which he set out the background to his thinking.

Russia's fears of Western Germany are legitimate although unfounded. They are an emotional necessity.

Khrushchev is susceptible to pressure from world opinion and from opinion inside Russia.

Both these opinions should be influenced by Western statecraft.

The offer should be made to recognize *de jure* a separate German state, disarmed and guaranteed in its neutrality by a four-power guarantee with Berlin as its capital, on condition that the inhabitants choose their own government.

At this stage the offer would be turned down by Khrushchev, although the Stalinist Ulbricht was a liability to Russia's mission in the world and particularly also in Africa where self-determination has become the battle-cry of Russian propaganda.

- For all that, Khrushchev will go on saying No to such an offer as long as he has no hope of closing the hole in the Iron Curtain by a coup liquidating Berlin.

- He can maintain this hope as long as Western defence policy is based on threats which he is tempted to disbelieve.

Kurt Hahn had felt encouraged to write to Herter because Herter had made it clear in a Senate hearing in 1959 that the United States would in his view not be justified in resorting to all-out nuclear weapons in the initial stages even if Russia committed an overt act of war in the Berlin air corridor. Herter responded promptly, inviting Hahn to meet him in Paris in January and assuring him that his paper had been passed on to those *now working officially on this problem'*.

As we now know many years later, the downfall of Communism began under the faltering political and economic leadership of its elderly dictators across Central and Eastern Europe. The historian Tony Judt comments: *'the Communist system might corrode indefinitely at the periphery; but the initiative for its final collapse could only come from the centre'.* [•] It was time for Gorbachev. The 1987 Intermediate Range Nuclear Forces Treaty, signed and ratified the following year, represented Soviet acceptance that a nuclear war in Europe was unwinnable.

Kurt Hahn liked to assert that his educational achievements were rooted in his political ideas. The link between them – his insistence on morality in politics, the decisive role of morale, and the constant efforts to persuade the politicians and statesmen, though imaginative initiatives, to seize the higher ground – ran never more closely than in these years when he was preparing the launch of the Atlantic College. The rhetoric may now seem overblown to us. Hahn could never be accused of under-statement. *'Many of them* (Atlantic College boys) *will go out into the world … having learned that resolute humanity is the true bond of free people and should be the spiritual basis of the Western Alliance … there is spiritual unrest among the youth of Russia … many young people look westward with hope and with distrust and ask us a question which will make us*

blush: *are you in earnest about the ideals you profess? Who shall give an answer? Young men and women who render hard and willing service to their fellow men, in danger and in need.'* It was the language that, at the time, successfully launched the first United World College.

This quotation is taken from a lecture he gave in April 1965 at the University College of Swansea during the Annual Meetings of the General Assembly of Unitarian and Free Christian Churches, not many miles from St. Donat's and less than three years after the Atlantic College opened. Any doubt over the driving force in Hahn's mind in the founding of the College is surely resolved by the title he gave this lecture: *The Young and the Outcome of War.*

Why the Atlantic College could not have survived with him

My answer is best started with a simple story. Hellmut Becker, a former Salem pupil, a faithful Hahn disciple, the young lawyer who had led the defence in Nuremberg on behalf of the former head of the German Foreign Office Ernst von Weizsäcker, now the legal consultant for German boarding schools, later the Founding Director of the Max Planck Institut für Bildungsforschung/Institute for Human Development in Berlin, came to visit in the first year. Desmond Hoare sat him down with a group of students in the sitting room of the Lady Anne Tower with a crate of beer between them and left them to it. Hellmut Becker, accustomed to Hahnian austerity in these matters, was first astonished, then completely won over.

A residential college composed of only two generations of students, with its rapid turnover, its absence of younger pupils over whom the older pupils could exercise responsibility, was an innovation with its own dynamics, still to be explored. Hahn, the life-long admirer of British Public Schools, and Hoare, the engineering admiral, were out of step on these and other essential points.

Desmond Hoare's life in the Navy, his responsibilities for engineering apprentices from walks of life that Kurt Hahn was not familiar with, and his subsequent youth work with the tough teen-aged gangs of Notting Hill in London, combined with his deep scepticism about the privileged and enclosed lives of the Public Schools, had endowed him with a relationship with adolescents that escaped the boundaries of Kurt Hahn's direct personal experience. A carefully-staged hierarchy of duties and privileges that governed the classical boarding schools, possibly reinforced by the trust system that Hahn had operated in both Salem and Gordonstoun, was not going to carry credibility with able, questioning, highly motivated

[•] Tony Judt *Postwar – A History of Europe since 1945* Vintage Books page 584 and impatient international sixth-formers. The discipline that would work was the discipline of the situation, and the situation was an intense two-year course in (for most) the foreign language of English that would determine their university entry, social relationships across major diversities in cultural background among young people who were away from home for the first time in their lives, and the natural environment, the Bristol Channel cliffs and tides, against which the large majority were to match their College training to emerge as fully qualified members of the major British lifesaving organisations. These were the expectations, and staff and students became a strongly-motivated team to meet them.

The brevity and pace of the two-year course and the scholarship nature of entry to the College also imposed challenges that were not 'Hahnian'. There was no room for the late developer except through inspired intuition by a national selection committee that saw clearly and confidently beyond the formal academic record at the age of 16. Character and personality were by common agreement more important than knowledge and intelligence, but the UWC education takes place within the firm context of ambitious and realisable intellectual achievement. Hahn's practices had not previously been exposed to this degree of academic scrutiny. Bertrand Russell has told us that the problem with Thomas Arnold and his Rugby School tradition is that it sacrificed intellect to virtue (and Goebbels that intellectual activity is a danger to the building of character!). But as late as the mid-1970s a dinner gathering of leading Public School Headmasters was astonished to be told by the Headmaster of the Atlantic College that all Atlantic College students went on to university. Perhaps the final word on this issue lies with a member of the early College founding group, the Nobel Laureate Sir Nevill Mott, who commented in the context of the Trevelyan Scholarships: *'we recognised that intellect developed best in an environment where other qualities can grow too …'*

So it was not surprising that tensions emerged as Kurt Hahn recognised that the Atlantic College was not and did not intend to be a loyal, internationalised development of Gordonstoun but a different institution standing on its own feet and its own principles. I suspect that Desmond Hoare was to some extent influenced in these matters by the visit in 1967 of Frank Bowles of the Ford Foundation. Bowles, Desmond Hoare reported to George Schuster, wanted, not a European/American but a European school, with top rate students and top rate academic results. He had little interest in humanitarian service or idealistic efforts to involve Britain's adolescents in coast rescue duties, argued for a thorough sociological research project into the

school's aims and practices, and viewed the approaching International Baccalaureate as a new form of international straightjacket to replace a national one. It was certainly from this moment onwards that Desmond Hoare demonstrated a growing fascination with the American approach to the automated use of aptitude tests for deciding university admissions in preference to the costly, cumbersome and slow-moving European methods.

The papers of George Schuster, the Chairman of Atlantic College, make clear the extent to which his ability to lead the College out of its financial emergencies relied on his friendship and shared vision with Kurt Hahn. But he too was clear that the College was a new concept that must find its own way on its own merits and that its educational significance lay in its independent stance. He felt unable to respond actively to Hahn's long letter to him of 23rd January 1970, written after Hahn was recovering from having been struck by a car outside the Hahn home Burnside near Gordonstoun and the subsequent period of severe depression. The letter gives evidence not only of Hahn's renewed vigour and old determination, but of the continuing broad sweep of his ambitions and of his reliance on Atlantic College for their realisation. To give a *staccato* taste: *'St. Donat's the laboratory of his (Desmond's) inventiveness … Aberavon* (the National Coast Rescue Training Centre) *to grow into a training centre for the nation … beach rescue … mountain rescue … 12 other rescue and relief organisations … helping the blind, the deaf, the old, the cripples, approved schools, nature conservancy, technical emergency services, fire service, coastguard, cave rescue, traffic police, Red Cross … an appeal to schools … an appeal to rescue and relief organisations … an appeal to the young of the free world and even beyond … the key-note of the appeal "We need your help" … the Atlantic College would grow into the fountain head of a movement.'*

It is regrettable and sad that Kurt Hahn remained at odds with Desmond Hoare over the social-disciplinary framework that Desmond had established at the College: the lack of hierarchy, the personal freedom (by comparison with Public Schools) given to the students individually and collectively, the controlled access to alcohol and tobacco, the relative lack of formal emphasis on matters of daily routine and control. But Desmond Hoare was right.

Bernhard Bueb, the long-serving headmaster of Salem who so successfully guided the school into the post-Hahn era, has traced, in the context of Salem's 75th anniversary in 1995, the difficulties faced by his predecessors. Confronted by both the physical presence of Hahn himself in the post-war years and by the pressures, implicit and explicit, to recreate the Salem of the 1920s, their loyalties were in conflict – with the legendary founder whose energies and ambitions remained untiring, and in confronting society's challenges that were to change so dramatically with the advance of the German *Wirtschaftswunder*, the economic miracle, and the crises of 1968. Bueb took up the Salem headship only a few months before Hahn's death in 1974, and Bueb was able then to make his own way on his own terms, although Salemers know that he faced bitter attacks as he moved forwards that at times threatened the survival of the school. We must remember that Hahn's attachment to Salem was that of a parent toward the first born. One must understand him. But those who led the Hahn projects also needed their independence from him. The international development of Outward Bound and of the Award Scheme has prospered beyond all possible expectation under leadership inspired by him but not constrained by him. Desmond Hoare was clear-sighted and courageous in these matters, but it was not always easy.

Kurt Hahn the Man

In early 1919 the American diplomat William Bullitt wrote to his Dutch war-time friend and colleague Jacob Noeggerath: *'… and particularly ask Hahn to write to me. I am more curious to talk with him than with any living being'.*

And Desmond Hoare: *'I remember most of all his entertainment value … all over the world one meets for the first time new people who knew him … does one discuss his addiction to Plato or his concern for the perils of puberty? Very rarely, but much more his disregard of trivial conventions, his enrichment value and his extraordinary ability to move people to do better than they knew …'*

After completing the memoirs of Prince Max, Kurt Hahn liked to refer to himself as the world's first ghost writer; he had richly earned this title already by the unceasing succession of memoranda that he generated during the war for the signatures of others. His jogging in the park at Versailles was followed by frequent nightly outings in Green Park, 100 metres from his office and entertainment base in London, Brown's Hotel. He was once arrested by a distrustful London copper, but this activity also earned him a mention in *The Spectator*: *'Ever since I discovered that Kurt Hahn went running in St. James at the age of 72, I have taken to pounding round the block (now and again) before breakfast, just to show I can do it.'* [●] Was Hahn also the world's first jogger? He liked to think so.

[●] Miles Howard in *A Doctor's Journal* in *The Spectator* 30th January 1959

Tall, stooping slightly, a big man with a fine head and steady, piercing eyes, rather fleshy hands with long, sensitive but technically clumsy fingers, he was a courtly, enigmatic and theatrical figure, the drama heightened by the large hats he wore whenever out of doors. As his pupils discovered, he had a remarkable memory for people, recalling with a quick movement of his hand the names, not only of the pupils themselves but of their brothers, sisters and other relatives. His surviving papers include an impressive series of address books. Today we would call him a 'networker'. Whilst in Gordonstoun he is said to have had the largest telephone bill in Scotland and maintained that the inventor of the telephone, Alexander Graham, had known in advance that he was coming. *'Oh yes, that Hahn, that's right, he had "telephonitis"'* [110] – a comment in a German letter! He cultivated his eccentricities, climbing into a London taxi and giving his Scottish telephone number, *'Hopeman 244'*; being stopped in his car as he was leaving the school by a boy who waved him down and told him he was due for his history lesson – the boy was told to climb into the back seat, the fellow passenger (the Chairman of Governors), was moved next to the driver, and Hahn taught history all the way from Elgin to Aberdeen; and, characteristically, the granddaughter of the same Chairman of Governors who at the age of four rode her tricycle alone and along the main road to her grandmother's without asking her parents' permission. Hahn was so impressed by her courage and enterprise that he insisted that she was always invited for tea. Another attractive story has it that a local laird brought his son for interview. Hahn said the son should go to Eton, but he would take the chauffeur's son.

His German colleague from both Salem and Gordonstoun, Erich Meissner, a remarkable educator in his own right, an intellectual, a writer and a painter, who had worked with Hermann Lietz before joining Hahn, described him as a man very much of his age, *'a late Victorian with the manners and courtesy of an Edwardian'*. In Wales he apparently used to walk about the town with two hats on his head and raise both of them politely to passers-by, much to their astonishment. He was always very concerned to help old people and see to their comforts and needs. It is related that on one occasion, having lunch with an old lady, he seized the plate and began cutting up the meat into small pieces for her benefit. But a few minutes later, still talking and conversing in an animated fashion, he began to eat the meat himself, leaving the old lady with nothing. In his later years he would often pick up strangers in the nearby town Uberlingen and bring them home for a meal, anxious to hear their life's stories. On his long solitary walks through the local woods he would engage all he met in conversation, often sending them afterwards presents and money. Once, hearing from a man in a ticket office in London that his wife was seriously ill, he invited the couple out to Germany for a restful holiday. His driver, Manfred Vorbiller, told me of Hahn's unhappiness in his last years, how he would spend an entire day without talking, stand still for an hour in indecision on a walk, how one afternoon when having tea in Vorbiller's home (Vorbiller had married the daughter of his housekeeper), he sat silent at the table until the small son crawled under the table and tried to tie his forever loose shoe laces, at which a slow smile spread across his face. I remembered then that Alice Ricciardi had told me of her conviction back in the 1920s that Hahn longed for a family of his own; and how, soon after the opening of Atlantic College, he had intently and for several minutes watched our small son Michael, then, turning to me, commented rather sadly: *'My schools are my sons.'*

His secretary Michael Schweitzer was not alone in saying that he was a fine judge of character in young people, a bad judge of adults. This must be understood in the context of his incurable optimism about human nature, but especially human nature in the young, for the young were still being formed. *'Plus est en vous.'* This motto, now used in commercial advertising in its country of origin Belgium, he took over for Gordonstoun from the Besse family with the agreement of Anton Besse's widow Hilda days after her husband's death in Gordonstoun. Anton Besse had discovered it on the memorial to Lodewijk van Gruuthuse in Bruges when he married his first wife, Marguerite Godefroy from Brussels. This gesture served above all to bind the Besse family more closely to the school at a time when the relationship had yet to develop strong roots. Hahn never quoted it himself, but its remorselessly frequent use by those who describe his work and his schools assumes the best possible interpretation of human nature. It is a reworking of the words of Pindar, used by the German country schools before Salem as well as by Salem itself: *Werde der du bist.* – grow into what you are. Or, one assumes, of Pindar's meaning when he expresses himself in his third Pythian Ode: *'I will work out the divinity that is within my mind'*. The promising and cheerful, innocent youth who becomes a Nazi storm trooper is not foreseen in this equation. Faith and optimism are the criteria that are followed with almost messianic conviction.

Hahn can never have been easy to work for. He would change course without hesitation and without telling people. His frequent, often long absences from the school threw a burden on senior colleagues that could not have been made lighter by his frenetic activity when he returned. Wayland Young, the nephew of Geoffrey Winthrop Young, wrote in the *Sunday Times* of 10th January 1971: *'The immensely high tone of Hahn's moral principles was accompanied by that dash of naïveté which is so often found in men of passionate conviction.'* He allowed nothing to stand in his way, and the loyalty of colleagues was inseparable from great patience.

Kurt Hahn the Writer and Speaker

Kurt Hahn constantly emphasised how much of his educational thinking he owed to his experiences of weak human leadership in the First World War, but his writings before 1914 offer more insights. They have remained largely inaccessible to English readers, partly for straightforward linguistic reasons, but they also do not translate well. And so it becomes important to look at him through both German and English eyes, and it is not too surprising that what is seen differs. Robert Skidelsky, with whom he had an outspoken exchange of views around the publication of Skidelsky's book *English Progressive Schools* in 1969, complained that, whenever he brought forward an argument, Hahn replied with an anecdote or an aphorism. If this comment refers to their exchange on this occasion it does not withstand scrutiny, for Hahn answered him with chapter and verse. But he has a point, for anecdotes were the tools with which Hahn gently warmed up his audiences, identified his listeners with his arguments, kept them amused and attentive, before challenging them with the moral issues that his educational principles were designed to confront.

If it is true that, stripped to the bone, there are just three reasons for communicating – to inform, to entertain and to persuade – Hahn was a strict disciple. It is vital to understand that every memorandum, every speech, indeed almost every conversation, had a precise objective, which was to win over the audience, to gain support and, more often than is comfortable to remember, to raise money. From Salem onwards but especially following the 1933 move from Germany to Britain, his language became less abstract, more concise, more *Anglo-Saxon*. As with his personality, there were those who disliked it, found it contrived, others who were captivated. On both sides of his move to England he was fond of praising the British Public Schools that *'teach the young to argue without quarrelling, to quarrel without suspecting and to suspect without slandering'*. A distinguished British and international headmaster thought this a meaningless cliché. *The Observer* newspaper included it in *Sayings of the Week* on 19th January 1961; and we find the biochemist and Nobel Laureate Hans Krebs, who also left Germany in 1933, acknowledging his debt and that of fellow Jewish refugees to England when he recalled how refreshing he found it that people would *'argue without quarrelling, quarrel without suspecting, suspect without abusing, criticize without vilifying or ridiculing, and praise without flattering … these are some of the characteristics of this country …'* [●] Not without interest in this context is the difficulty experienced before the First World War over the translation of Cecil Rhodes' will into German, especially in finding phrases to convey the ideal of *'gentle manly virtues'.* [○] Hahn had himself written in 1954: *'it is well to remember that "gentleman" is still the word of highest praise to be heard on the Continent. There is no translation except in ancient Greek.'*

Hahn was a compelling, indeed almost hypnotic speaker, with personality, to borrow the words of one critical commentator, *'pouring off him in waves'.* [■] But it remained true to the end that there was a degree of artificiality in his communication in English, and it was enough to hear him on the telephone in German to recognise that he thought better and more naturally in German. And because he always had a precise objective in mind, a target to be achieved, he talked at and not with his audience, even when his audience was a single person. With the young, however, it was different – he listened, and with great sensitivity. In 1954 he wrote to his Cambridge friend and Versailles critic, the historian Jim Butler: *'Emotional reticence is a form of chastity as characteristic of the normal German boy as it is of the normal English boy. I have always discouraged what a friend of mine called "a noisy inner life" … to have a purpose does not mean to profess it.'*

His letters show the same precise focus, the recipient engaged, flattered, almost ensnared in the sequence. *'As you are able to hear the fleas cough, you will feel the hopes and anxieties, the bitterness and the thanksgiving, and all sorts of other moods which lie behind this report',* he wrote

[●] Address on 8th November 1965 in the Livery Hall of the Saddlers Company on behalf of the Association of Jewish Refugees in Britain. On this occasion, as a gesture of gratitude to Britain, the Association presented the British Academy with £90,000 'for the furtherance of scholarship'.

[○] I owe this reference to Colin Reid and his discussions with his friend Richard Sheppard who wrote the chapter on the German Rhodes Scholars in the centennial history of the Rhodes Trust.

[■] Jonathan Gathorne Hardy in *The Public School Phenomenon* Penguin Books 1977

to an ally, another 'brother-in-arms', in April 1952. But, the irrepressible ghost-writer himself, he was possessive of his language and would not allow others to speak or write for him. *'Forgive a frank letter. I like your style very much; in fact I regard your original MS as a masterpiece. But your style is not my style and I cannot bring myself to sign anything unless the grain of the wood is visible',* he told a devoted American colleague in joint fundraising operations in the US in 1953.

Hahn the Christian Educator?

For several months in the late 1950s I followed Hahn's weekly classes with a group of senior Salem pupils. The subject was *Gemeinschaftskunde,* Civic Education. The context was almost always the First World War. Every pupil was required to prepare a long research essay. The phrase that has remained with me is *'the spiritual realities'.*

Hahn's religious life is inseparable from that of all those other German Jews who, following the Enlightenment, found their intellectual talents and cultural aspirations increasingly satisfied and increasingly rewarded in the Germany of the late 19th century. His mother's own salon in Berlin was one of the many whose role in the gradual loss of Jewish culture and Jewish identity led inexorably to abandonment of the Jewish faith in favour of conversion to Christianity. Proud he certainly was of his Jewish heritage, and Jo Nold caught his essence when he addressed the Conference of Round Square Schools in 1980: *'… the Jewish patriarch, the Biblical prophet, demanding in his friendship, firm in his judgments, and restlessly moral in his pronouncements.'* But Hahn's personal papers include scores of sheets covered in his often illegible handwriting as he struggled with, as he saw things, the conflicts between the Old Testament and the New. He is said to have been specially influenced by the Gospel of St. Matthew whilst at school. He is on written record as having contemplated conversion in the 1930s but felt that this was not the moment to abandon his fellow Jews. He was finally admitted into the Anglican Church in July 1945 by Bishop Bell of Chichester. Years later, on 14th August 1972, he was baptised in his German home Hermannsberg by Bishop Lancelot Fleming who wrote of this occasion: *'he was troubled in mind because, although Bishop Bell had confirmed him, he said he had never been baptised (it may well be that he was confused about this) … he had only four times been to a synagogue and, since the 1930s, had identified himself with the Church of England, the Episcopal Church of Scotland and had close links with the Presbyterian Kirk …'.*

In these acts he was aware of hurting the two persons closest to him, his brother Rudo and his sister-in-law Lola.

He informed them of his conversion with a brief note after the event.

It is not difficult to identify at least some of the human examples that led to his decision. One was undoubtedly Bishop Bell, who had led a morally exemplary fight throughout the war years 1939–1945 against assumptions that all Germans were Nazis, that unconditional surrender was the only valid war aim, that the carpet bombing of German cities was a legitimate act of war, and who forfeited thereby the Archbishopric of Canterbury on the death of William Temple. Another that moved him profoundly was the Christian example of the son of his First World War chief von Haeften, Hans Bernd, who as a boy had refused to come to Salem because he was engaged in looking after a frightened Jewish boy in his school class, and whose letters from prison before his execution in August 1944 as a member of the July 20th 1944 plot against Hitler are among the most moving of Christian testaments to emerge from the war anywhere.

Even after conversion Kurt Hahn was not a churchgoer, nor did he preach sermons in the Thomas Arnold tradition. But there are two Hahn sermons that must engage our attention, both delivered in Liverpool Cathedral in war time. It cannot be a common occurrence for a Jew to preach in an Anglican cathedral. The first was on 22nd December 1940. His beliefs, with which we are now familiar, are set firmly within a Christian context.

'We cannot deny the watchman's virtues are demanded also by Hitler. They are neither heathen nor Christian: they may be used for good or evil but it is vital that Christians should not lack them … the attackers of Christian Civilisation are hardy, fit, disciplined, self-sacrificing, slaves who bear all things, believe all things, hope all things and endure all things … Hitler's slaves are moved, it is true, by great passion. What is this passion? They certainly love their country, but their love is feeble compared with their hatred. Their hatred is their magical spring. It is not only inspired by sermons and songs of hatred, it is trained and stimulated through early action … let us learn from the enemy. We must nourish love by early action … "how did you know of your father's suffering?" is Kent's question to Edgar? His answer is: "by nursing him" … Let us shake ourselves free from the heresy that love can be sustained by words alone … in the parable of the Good Samaritan I am sure that the priest who went by made himself believe that his help would come too late for the man who fell among thieves, or he thought that the problem of thieving was altogether too complicated and needed a lot more careful discussion … neither the love of man nor the love of God can take root in a child that does not know aloneness … habits of prayer are vital … what is the difference between Cruelty and Callousness? The one torments, the other neglects. They both challenge Christianity to intervene on behalf of their victims … these findings put a clear choice before us: neglect and console or heal and train. On this issue there is no room for honourable neutrality.'

The sub-text of Hahn's second Quinquagesima sermon in 1943 was clear. *'There is another Germany.'* By this time the Soviet Union was the great, the life-saving ally, and Stalin was Uncle Jo.

'Compassion seems a great impediment in war … we have all heard of the oath of the Russian guerrilla fighters: "I promise to avenge always mercilessly and without pity. Blood shall be avenged by blood and death by death." There is a fierce grandeur about this oath. It is born of an agony we have not experienced; we have no right to sit in judgment, but for all that no Christian can make this view of vengeance his own … when Nazi jargon insidiously corrupts our language, and we gloat about the suffering of the innocent among the enemy, then a blight falls on the faith of the best … The Christians in this country are longing for a sign to rally … we are only united on one issue – the need for victory; victory complete and overwhelming … we are deeply divided on the spiritual issues of the war, and of the peace to come. Christian statesmanship cannot speak out without challenging the anti-Christ in our midst … for this challenge, all Christian England and Christian Europe are waiting. I include Christian Germany and Christian Russia … they are anxiously hoping for a promise that discriminating and stern justice will be done by a victorious England from which a cleansed and liberated Germany has nothing to fear … will Christian England prevail? … Conscience is ever again held in emotional bondage. Compassion alone can liberate it.'

The Cathedral authorities, having published the first sermon, refused to publish the second. His criticism of the Soviet ally was too strong.

To George Schuster he wrote in July 1966: *'I agree with your diagnosis of the attitude characteristic of "vast numbers who are groping for some support to which they can hold," but I fear most of them will not find it in the Christian message unless they engage in labours of love and through that discover God's purpose in their inner life …'*

And from the same conviction came his adherence to William Temple's declaration: *'Samaritan service is a source of the revelation.'* His words and thoughts also recall the message of a fellow German educator whom he had much admired when he was setting up Salem, Georg Kerchensteiner: *'Good actions are the real evidence of spiritual values.'*

Did he pray? We cannot know. But he reflected constantly. He found counsel in his intimate friend Reverend

Alec Frazer who had been the founding Head of Achimoto College in Ghana. In a letter of 3rd June 1953 he wrote to him: '*I have just finished another reading of St. Matthew and I am more deeply impressed than ever, on the one hand with the ruthlessness against hypocrisy, and on the other hand with the belief in transforming experience*'; and on 3rd June: '*My daily readings continue. I am still puzzled that only Luke seems to do justice to Mary. To my layman's mind there is a gap in the Gospels. I am certain that James was a devoted son though I can quite see that there must have been years of estrangement owing to the refusal of his home to recognise his purpose and his mission.*'

Reflection did not bring certainty. On 12th December 1955 he confessed in a letter to a Fraulein Schneider: '*Escape from the world or a lay vocation? That is the question that inescapably every Christian who is honest about his beliefs must face. For the one the decision, taken conscientiously, can turn out quite differently from that of another. But how should the individual know where his duty lies? The call of providence does not always sound with unassailable clarity; but sometimes it does, namely where healing powers are at work in a particular situation and the extinction of these powers would have tragic consequences …*' [111]

Observing once again the emphasis on healing, we can turn to a note he wrote on 27th October 1934. '*I believe that Professor J. is right because hatred is the driving force behind lies and love behind truth: the one untiring and never giving way, the other easily thwarted. I believe the reason is this. The great Christian Churches put faith first and love second. I do not think that this order will be righted (Corinthians XIII) until the Jews come home to Christ …*'

And here we come to that old problem, lucidly described by the Jewish historian L. B. Namier in his book *Conflicts*. '*Nineteen centuries ago our people divided: one branch, the Hebrew Nazarenes, carried into the world our national faith coupled with their new tidings, the other, as a closed community, preserved the old tradition … those who went into the ways of the Gentiles have permeated and trans-formed the heritage of other nations …*' For Namier, both remained part of one nation, although his widow in her biography of him concluded that '*his friends had missed his intended implication – that baptism into Christ was the proper development for a Jew aware of his people's history in its worldwide significance ….*'.

For me, this issue brings to mind the more direct words of H. V. Morton in his *In the Steps of St. Paul*. '*Paul's fury is the anger of a great man who sees the supremacy of Christ threatened. The question at issue is none other than the survival or disappearance of the Gentile Church. Is this fine, true thing that he is trying to create for the whole world to be bent down and narrowed into the porch of a synagogue? Who comes first, Christ or Moses?*' and, words put in the mouth of St. Paul: '*Christ lives in me … I do not annul God's grace; but if righteousness comes by way of the Law, then indeed Christ's death was useless.*'

Alice Ricciardi, whom we met earlier in the context of Hahn's nationalism, speculated in our conversation that Hahn who, she claimed, had followed much of the Benedictine Rule for years before his 1945 conversion, (indeed he quoted it often and insisted early in our acquaintance on giving me a copy), had been deeply influenced by the example of the saint who, she thought, must have descended from the Jewish community of some ten thousand who had been brought to Rome by Titus to form his triumphal procession after the destruction of The Temple around AD 70; they were subsequently resettled in Nursia, in Umbria, Saint Benedict's homeland, by Titus' wife.

But we need not rely on speculation. In August 1922, shortly after the assassination of the Jew Rathenau, Foreign Minister of Germany, and against the background of intensive debate on anti-Semitism, Hahn highlighted the following extract from the Swiss newspaper, the *Neue Zurcher Zeitung*, of 2nd August: '*it can for us as Catholic Christians be subject to no doubt that the religion of the Old Testament, the Mosaic (Jewish) religion, has indeed been supplanted by the New Testament … the bloody crucifixion on Golgotha signifies the final repeal of the old covenant …*' [112]

And in notes he prepared for his courageous speeches in February and March 1933, speeches about which he was warned in letters from friends to be cautious in the light of the political circumstances, we read: '*Just as the individual only achieves clarity over his own life in certain visionary moments, so a people only has clarity over its destiny through certain experiences. Just as the Jews in 30 AD failed irrevocably and beyond redemption to recognise their true mission, to bear the news of their own prophecies … so for the Germans Luther is the most German of experiences. This must also be recognized by the Catholics. The individual, of whatever faith, carries his head higher when he has the conviction: I am the master of my conscience, and my conscience is master of my fate …*' [113]

The reference here to Luther is important. It reminds us of Hahn's German roots and loyalties.

Before conversion, Hahn consulted Dr. Leo Baeck, the Rabbi who survived Theresienstadt and had only just arrived in England. Baeck's blessing of his decision was important for him. Hahn's letter of thanks is worth quoting in full.

'My dear Dr. Baeck

If anything could have shaken the certainty of my decision, it was the encounter with your wonderful spirit and your great heart.

On the one side I hear ever stronger the call to bear witness for Christ and against the anti-Christ who today both openly and secretly seeks dominance. I am more proud than I can express about my Jewish being. Whatever I have been able to achieve in my life I owe to the drop of the blood of the prophets that I feel within me.

My being is directed towards action.

The Anglican Church is today not conscious of her strength; she is helpless so long as she feels dependent on others. But William Temple has shown that the Church is the one voice that can make itself heard in Europe. I can help a little that the tongues are loosened and that the leaders of the Church intervene

Against the spirit of revenge that contaminates the victory today

Against the lack of pity with which innocent people are made to suffer for the sins of their government

Against the lack of compassion for the victims of persecution

Against the lies of the agitators who falsify the realities of the European condition and against the passivity of those who are informed and support the lies with their silence.

I enclose a copy of my letter to the Archbishop of Canterbury. I can only warn and admonish if I cease to stand on the outside.' [114]

And he adds in manuscript the words of Luther: *'So help me God. I can do no other.'* [115] The postscript is revealing of Hahn's continuing sense of German identity.

It may seem bold of Hahn to presume to influence over the lords of the Church. We must bear in mind that he was the principal informant on German affairs and drafted speeches for both William Temple and George Bell.

One of Hahn's Gordonstoun pupils, in his analysis of Hahn's moments when he showed evidence of his inner life, and drawing his conclusions *'out of the context of sensitive memories'*, wrote to me that *'when he felt it appropriate, Hahn gave people real love.'* *'He, coming from the Talmud or Old Testament traditions where God is to be feared as a wrathful and vengeful force, may have seen more clearly the revolution that Christ brought in revealing God as a creative force of only and entirely love … seen darkly through the clouds of fear-based heritage that partly obscure the purity of*

the message even in the New Testament. He would mention Christ and Plato in the same breath.'

Axel von dem Bussche, who after a spell as Headmaster of Salem went on to work for the World Council of Churches, reacted very vigorously against the Hahn *'manipulation'* of Christianity and criticised him forcefully for Pelagianism, the denial of the doctrine of original sin and the substitution of the human will for the gift of Grace. We may be on complex theological terrain here, but Hahn could draw support from the *Ethics* of his friend and Hitler martyr Dietrich Bonhoeffer, who taught that it is how we confront evil when it really matters, that it is action, that determines how Christian we are.

Of her first husband Peter Rodd in her *In Pursuit of Love* and of his work for refugees of the Spanish Civil War, Nancy Mitford wrote that he was *'… really only interested in mass wretchedness, and never much cared for individual cases.'* Kurt Hahn was in this respect his exact antithesis. At the beginning and end of every term in both Salem and Gordonstoun there took place the reading of the parable of the Good Samaritan. We do not gain the full import of Hahn's insistence without being aware of the traditional hatred that existed between the Samaritan tribes and the Jews to whom Jesus was addressing his message. This was compassion and moral courage hand-in-hand.

But it was all not without consequences, and we should not underestimate the burden of this decision for conversion. Hitler's persecution in the 1930s compelled his solidarity with his fellow Jews; his decision to leave the Jewish faith in 1945, at the very time when the full horrors of the Holocaust were becoming apparent, imposed conflicts of a related but different kind that were to become dramatically intensified by events in Palestine. In November 1953, invited to address a church dinner, he replied to the Lord Bishop of Middleton: *'I am not qualified to become a bridge-builder. I am since 1945 a Communicant of the Anglican Church and while I am proud of my pure Jewish race, I find myself in bitter opposition against the Zionist revival of a fierce Old Testament tradition and against all those European Jews who have condoned Bernadotte's murder.* [•] *Moreover, there is great bitterness among a number of important Jews against race fellows who have become converted to Christianity. So you will forgive me if I decline your Council's invitation.'*

[•] Count Bernadotte was assassinated in Jerusalem in 1948 by a militant Zionist group while pursuing his official duties as the UN Representative charged with negotiating an Arab-Israeli understanding

Hahn would, I think, have liked and approved Trollope's comment: *'The Apostle of Christianity and the infidel can meet without the chance of a quarrel; but it is never safe to bring together two men who differ about a saint or a surplice.'* Despite his apparent moral certainties, he remained even late in life a seeker, and a Hahn pupil in religious matters had to find his own way. One of Hahn's governors, Dr. Joseph Oldham, [●] the Secretary of the International Missionary Council, had this to say in 1945: *'how is this programme related to specifically Christian aims? Mr. Hahn's answer is clear and emphatic and, for that reason, a stimulus to clear thinking. The educational programme is neutral in regard to religion. This is not to say that it is indifferent to religion. The Christian inspiration of the whole enterprise is freely acknowledged. But the educational programme as such is concerned with the development of aptitudes and qualities which belong to the natural and human sphere. It remains deliberately in the ante-chamber of religion and does not act as an educational programme to enter the sanctuary. Its service to religion is to prepare the ground by the removal of obstacles …'*

The convention of a religion enabled Hahn to become a member of a community, but the community was one that he chose freely. *'His keen awareness of the forceful power of Platonic love between human beings'* (to quote again the former Gordonstoun pupil) reminds us of the life-long influence on him of his studies of the Greek world, and Donald McLachlan's comment *'I am always curious about the Christian roots of much of his teaching, some of which is curiously pagan or Platonic and yet achieves much the same end as Christian educationalists work for'* remains intriguing. [○] An ethical, not a spiritual Christian? Let us close this section with another phrase of Hahn's, *'but here I find myself in the realm of dogma where discussion should end'*, and allow his optimism about human nature to stand for the source of those spiritual realities.

[●] Coincidentally also a member of the Hilton Young Commission of 1928 on the British East and Central African colonies on which George Schuster played so major a part.

[○] Donald McLachlan was asked by Robert Barrington Ward when Editor of *The Times* to look after Hahn as otherwise he, BW, would not be able to get any work done. McLachlan later more or less appointed himself to become Hahn's biographer but was killed in a motor accident when undertaking research for the book in Scotland

Kurt Hahn the Moral Politician

He was, Golo Mann is careful to point out, not a politician; but *'whoever briefs or informs … is already participating in power, irrespective of whether he is a responsible counter-signing minister.'* [●]

Kurt Hahn moved steadily toward the centre of decision-taking throughout late 1917 and 1918. It is understandable to question the level of his political success, but the question cannot fairly be put without also asking: which politician (I am tempted to add 'of any great power') emerged in 1918 or 1919 with a reputation safe for posterity?

Kurt Hahn once electrified a history class at Atlantic College with the casual remark *'the last time I saw Bismarck'*, but he was not an admirer. The liberalism he dreamed of for his native Germany, made the more desirable by his Oxford experience, had long been stifled by the Bismarckian order, lately reinforced by the increasingly aggressive emotions of imperialism and nationalism.

For Hahn, the failure of Max von Baden as Chancellor was a shattering personal blow, and his subsequent attitudes and activities cannot be divorced from his sensitivity to the extent of both the national and the personal humiliation. The reproof that neither had the political experience to foresee the full weight of the task is hard to hold against them. Enlightened, morally aware circles in Berlin were practically non-existent. A critical mass of individuals combining clear foresight with political clout was simply not available. But the naïveté on the part of Conrad Haussmann and Kurt Hahn that, by installing the moral figurehead, the liberal and international Prince Max, a negotiated peace was within reach, was a fateful under-recognition of the forces that were dictating the pace of events on both sides of the German borders. The only alternative against the background of the Wilson Notes was that advocated by Walther Rathenau – a *levee en masse* and a fight to the death. It would have been an ugly alternative for all.

Was Germany responsible for the First World War? With passion, Kurt Hahn denied her exclusive responsibility and, perhaps motivated by British practice in such matters, called for an independent international enquiry to reach well-documented, neutral conclusions. Recent historical research, provoked above all by the explosive work of Fritz Fischer whose *Germany's Aims in the First World War* of

[●] C. Schmitt: *Der Zugang zum Machthaber: Ein zentrales verfassungsrechtliches Problem*, quoted in Christopher Clark *Kaiser Wilhelm II* Penguin Edition 2009 page 59

1961 [●] and subsequent writings postulated a continuity between the 'war lords' of 1914 and Hitler in the 1930s, has thrown an unfriendly light on Hahn's convictions; and his idealistic concept of the civilising mission of Germany in the East – his *'ethical imperialism'* that drew much of its inspiration from an idealised view of the British Empire – could not and cannot survive the brutal realities of the terms imposed by the German government on the Russian Bolsheviks in the Treaty of Brest-Litovsk. Given the acknowledged brutalities of past Tsarist regimes in the region (and Hahn's feelings were indisputably strengthened by both his Polish family antecedents and his Jewish loyalties to the victims of the Tsarist pogroms), this was a fatal and historic error. Germany's defeat shortly thereafter and the resurgence of Polish nationalism, with its victory under Pilsudski over the invading Bolshevik armies, put paid to further German ambitions in this matter.

Hahn's ideas of political leadership are also too strongly linked with the aristocratic ideal to enjoy contemporary relevance, for today men (and women) must, as Golo Mann underlined, be politicians before they are statesmen. For Hahn, the intrigues of party politics undermined the legitimacy of the ballot box. Independence of judgement and the readiness to oppose mainstream opinion were easier options for the liberal and often independently wealthy leaders of the 19th century than for the democratic leaders of the 20th. It was Hahn's destiny to be politically active as powers passed from the Kaiser and the German aristocracy to socialism, from Prince Max of Baden to Friedrich Ebert. The pressures of war had accelerated changes of this nature in the political order across Europe.

And his ideas were not without their dangers. Just as he had regretted the extent to which Prince Max had found his plans on becoming Chancellor thwarted by the need to carry his cabinet with him, so in the early 1920s he found himself unable to ally himself with the socialists whose leaders were powerless without democratic endorsement. And with some of his declarations he gave notable hostages to fortune. *'This undignified coquetry with the Fascists and the Bolsheviks has done us immeasurable harm. Even Ebert is not free of guilt … we need the constitutional dictatorship, as foreseen by the people's choice of the President, not one that has been illegally installed …'* [116]

His courage as Hitler approached and then took power is unquestionable. His flirtation with the possibility that Hitler might, just might, cleanse the party, having become

Chancellor, was the outcome of his longing for strong leadership combined with his antagonism towards the all-encompassing legacy of Versailles on which entire generations of Germans had been raised, and not least those in Salem.

On his arrival in England in 1933 Kurt Hahn set out his interpretation of the roots of the Nazi movement. His paper that summer has exposed him, with some justification, to criticism, even a touch of ridicule. Versailles, unemployment and parliamentary misgovernment are the three underlying causes. But *'Hitler has a warm, even a soft heart, which makes him over-sensitive to suggestions that he is not hard enough … I do not want to defend but I should like to explain … this is his mission: cure the hereditary curse of Germany – discord; sweep class war away, and make Germany respected again in the world, as an equal among equals … Hitler is not in the hands of vested interests. Millions of workmen trust him to act for the nation against selfish capitalists, as he has acted for the nation against class-bound labour …'*

If Hahn's optimistic and wishful thinking about Hitler was the naïve attitude of an educator, it was neither dishonourable nor unusual. Whilst expressing unrealistic hopes about the imagined power struggle between the genuinely patriotic and the thuggishly evil elements in the Party, Hahn was explicit about the murders and other atrocities that were now commonplace. Unlike the many who, also for honourable motives, placed their own hopes in understanding and appeasement, he had no illusions from June 1934 onwards, the time of the Roehm putsch. In his words: *'I thought … that Hitler was only the condoner of cruelties. I now know that he is the instigator'.* Hitler's evil was a profoundly hurtful blow to his conviction that every person has good in him if only it can be stimulated and released. The courageous 'twin policy' that he advocated throughout the Second World War – no mercy for the murderers, a cleansed Germany has nothing to fear from the victorious Allies – was in part an increasingly desperate longing to discover evidence of Christian civilisation in Germany that would carry conviction among enemies. Robert Skidelsky's jibe (it is difficult to use another word although, judging by the tribute he published in the *Encounter* journal on Hahn's death, I think he now regrets it) that if Hahn had not been a Jew he would not have left Germany in 1933, fails to acknowledge Hahn's efforts to make the truth known in Britain about Nazi atrocities. It also demeans the courage of those non-Jews who, not chased out of Germany, found their way into the opposition. (Skidelsky acknowledges that Hahn was likely to have followed a similar path.) And we must value Hahn's humane decision, despite all, to return to Germany at the

[●] Fritz Fischer: *Griff nach der Weltmacht* 1961

earliest possible opportunity in 1945 to bring help and encouragement. How many, for all too understandable reasons, would have turned and did turn their backs!

Hahn was in correspondence with Robert Birley, then Headmaster of Charterhouse, in late 1940. Birley wrote him a long manuscript letter on 1st December. *'I was very interested in your memorandum. I am afraid I agree with it … In recent years I have admired (Churchill) more because, in contrast to men like Baldwin and Chamberlain, he has been ready to tell people uncomfortable things and because he has shown romantic qualities which this country needs … Liberty, Equality and Fraternity spring from the teaching of Christ. But the message needs restating and re-feeling or it will be lost. This seems to me to be the supreme task for this country … If I were in charge of British propaganda I should first ask myself these questions:*

1. *Why did the Nazis come into power?*
2. *How have they stayed in power?*
3. *What good have they done?*

They have stayed in power by the use of force and the power of fear – by a readiness to accept responsibility – they have made men think there are possibilities in the future – freed them from the dominance of the present– they have spoken in terms that the workers understand because their idea of an aristocracy is an aristocracy which the workers can enter – they have denied the supremacy of material prosperity – the very, very old truth that men will respond in the end more readily to an appeal to sacrifice themselves than to a promise that life will be easy –

Terms of peace:
1. *no annexations, no indemnity, no dividing up of Germany*
2. *after the war, economic collapse of Germany a disaster for us*
3. *You are living in an atmosphere of continual personal fear.*
   You can escape from this by your own efforts, if you will
4. *I should speak continually of the world after the war as a time when great tasks await the nations, claim the cooperation of Germany, and glory in the fact that these tasks will be difficult*

There is for me one great difficulty. I feel the Germans are a people who … do not accept responsibility easily – are they really prepared, can they be made prepared, to get rid of a man and his party who accepted responsibility for them? This is the crucial question, and it is a sign of Hitler's greatness that it is the crucial question.'

It is perhaps no surprise that it was two educators who were largely in agreement. In 1947, Birley became Educational Advisor to the Control Commission in the British Zone in Germany, where he led the rewriting of Nazi history textbooks and was important in founding the Free University of Berlin.

It is said, and I think it is true, that Hahn was a man passionately interested in politics but rejected by the politicians, passionately interested in ideas but rejected by the intellectuals.

His early advice to his brother Rudo, *'renne schneller als Du kannst'*, is a tease and an excitement for children, a challenge for adolescents who are not yet conscious of their boundaries. Its provocation for adults is less easily bearable. Politics with morality, intellectualism with action!

His 1918 paper *Ethical Imperialism* expressed his ideal. *'The tremendous strength that we have displayed in this war must find moral justification in the eyes of the world, if it is to be tolerated. We must therefore make aims common to humanity a part of our national purpose.'* This important, controversial paper has been subjected to much critical commentary, but its final sentence is pure Hahn: *'For this, it is only the creative act of statesmanship that is required.'* [117]

Reviewing a biography of Bismarck, [●] Henry Kissinger has a useful comment on the relationship between ideals and politics. *'By the same token, ideals must be brought, at some point, into relationship with the circumstances the leader is seeking to affect. Ignoring that balance threatens policy with either veering toward belligerence from the advocates of power or toward crusades by the idealists.'*

But Hahn was emphatic about the responsibilities and the powers of the individual. In 1916 he had written: *'the decision whether there was to be peace or war was arrived at in Britain after the sharpest political struggle; and where there is a struggle, human strength decides.'* [118] It is man who must decide his destiny, not fate and forces out of human control.

Hahn drew often in his early writing on the 19th-century German prophet of nationalism, Johann Gottlieb Fichte, whose 1808 *Reden an die deutsche Nation* (*Addresses to the German Nation*) sought to rally Germany under the humiliations of French occupation through *'the consuming flame of higher patriotism which conceives the nation as the embodiment of the Eternal'*. Fichte was a dangerous (and

[●] Jonathan Steinberg: *Bismarck: A Life*. Oxford University Press 2011

anti-Semitic) master, however superficially attractive for an educator who was seeking to rally Germany after the humiliations of 1918 and Versailles. But this link reminds us that Hahn was and remained a German patriot. The 20th Century has driven from view the mutual admiration that characterised Anglo-German relations in the 19th. Thomas Arnold of Rugby drew some of his inspiration for his *'muscular Christianity'* from the work of the German gymnastics educator and nationalist Friedrich Ludwig Jahn. *'Prussia … the mountain of the Lord, the City of God upon a Hill whose light cannot be hid,'* he wrote to the German scientist Bunsen. *'We are the last reserve of the world; its fate is in our hands …'.* He even proposed an Anglo-Prussian bishopric in Jerusalem.

Not once did Kurt Hahn seek to distance himself from his loyalties to his country of birth, combining this loyalty with a fierce determination to heal where he could. The history of the 20th century placed a very heavy burden on his patriotism. If, as one hopes, the coming decades see a true reconciliation between the two nations of his life, his contribution to the new understanding will achieve renewed recognition and understanding. One realises, reflecting on these matters, why he turned again and again to the memory of his meeting with Smuts and the words Smuts left with him: *'Young man, I can console you, this pest will be wiped off the face of the earth … I know the spiritual history of Germany; there is throughout a sense of responsibility for the human destiny. What the Nazis are doing is the most un-German thing that could happen.'*

Tracing the Educational Legacy

At least three attempts have been made to create umbrella organisations symbolising and embodying Hahn's philosophy: his own *'Greater Gordonstoun'* that effectively dissolved with his departure from the school in 1953; the short-lived Service by Youth Trust promoted by the Chairman of Outward Bound, Spencer Summers, in the late 1950s; and the Conference of Round Square Schools set up by Jocelin Winthrop Young and close colleagues and, typically, met with some disavowal and dismay by Hahn himself.

The underlying difficulty is that of finding any principle of systematisation save in the personality of Hahn himself. His achievement lies not in his schools but in his personality, his inspiration, the untiring cunning and conviction with which he reached his objectives. This is why so little of the secret of his accomplishment can be found in books and theses, and why the two most personal accounts of him are essential reading: *Kurt Hahn – An Appreciation of his Life and*

'A courtly, enigmatic and theatrical figure'

Work, edited by David Byatt, published by Gordonstoun School, and Jim Hogan's *Impelled into Experiences*.

How many of the ideas are his?

Anyone with the least familiarity with Hahn knows that he ascribed all his ideas to others – to Plato, to Hermann Lietz, to Max of Baden, to the Cistercians, the Benedictines, to Baden-Powell and the Scout Movement. *'Education is like medicine. One must harvest the wisdom of a thousand years; if ever you have appendicitis and the surgeon offers to cut out your appendix in the most original manner I would advise you to go to another surgeon.'*

Allan Massie, writing in *The Daily Telegraph* newspaper of 26th October 2011 in protest against *'foolish snobs who don't believe in Shakespeare',* maintained that Shakespeare, *'like a Hollywood hack'*, was always reworking others' material, *'improving on it certainly, but still reworking'*. He is, says Massie, *'better thought of as a hack of genius, working in collaboration with other members of his company'*. This assessment gives us a useful insight into Hahn's achievement. Hahn was entirely serious when he described himself as *'a maker of bandwagons'*. His other self-description had him as a midwife, bringing on the schemes of others, then departing the scene.

'One must speak with caution of the philosophical principles of a man who never really expressed his aims theoretically.' [119] [●]

'Again, Hahn is not essentially a thinker. He has a few key ideas, deeply felt, but never elaborated into more than a lecture, let alone a book. Moreover, ideas for Hahn were always a map for action …' [○]

His friend and critical colleague Erich Meissner was worried lest the practical achievements of Hahn be obscured by a philosophy which does not stand up to close examination. Evidence of success in moral, educational and spiritual problems was provided by convenient anecdotes. *'Hahn must step down from some of his more extravagant claims.'*

Kurt Hahn has paid a price for his literary abstinence. This price has been higher in his native Germany than in English-speaking countries, for Germans have a greater taste and a greater need to sink their teeth into some solid theorising. The Anglo-Saxons are happier to look at the practical outcomes, are less worried by the question allegedly put by the Irish Prime Minister Garret Fitzgerald: *'It sounds great in practice, but how will it work in theory?'*

He lived less than a quarter of his life in Britain. It may therefore seem paradoxical that he is better known and has achieved more in the Anglo-Saxon world than in Germany. It is however not surprising.

Private schools and privately initiated educational schemes have long enjoyed greater acceptance in the Anglo-Saxon world than in Germany.

Hahn's record in Germany is represented most of all by a small group of boarding schools and, to a far lesser extent and far less well known, by Outward Bound and the international interpretation of the Duke of Edinburgh's Award Scheme. The Round Square Conference also numbers few German member schools. The contrary is the case in the Anglo-Saxon world.

Physical education, whether as team games (so vital to the classical Public School tradition) or in the outdoor pursuits that were so ably exploited by Baden-Powell when setting up the scout movement, gave Hahn an immediately supportive background for his extremely effective *hacking* developments. And Britain, unlike Germany an island with rich sea and coastal diversity, also has low mountains that, to quote Geoffrey Winthrop Young, are *'rugged enough to be rich in difficulty, and wind and weather change; but they are also arranged conveniently for selection and approach and for unobtrusive supervision. The degree of risk and of uncertainty in their attempting can be governed, so as to suit diminishing inexperience, even novices.'* In the United States the explosion of Outward Bound grew from the opportunities it offered of exposing the young once again to American frontier traditions. And perhaps it all had something in Britain to do too with finding favour in a nation *'that was notoriously both suspicious of abstraction and convinced of the wholesomeness of outdoor activities of all kinds'.* [●]

The absence of serious academic commentary on Hahn is, we can therefore say, his own fault. He has left behind no autobiography despite the Thyssen Foundation having pressured him to write one and offered him the funding to do so. He wrote a brief, incomplete and unsatisfying *Paedagogisches Testament*. Why this apparent vanishing trick? His cousin Charlotte Bergengruen, wife of the novelist Werner Bergengruen and who wrote a perceptive, not uncritical essay on him, considered him incapable of long and sustained intellectual effort. Did he, she wondered, ever read a book right through? Jocelin Winthrop Young, who knew him well, wondered the same, although Michael Schweitzer often mentioned his ability, not to read but to 'gut' a book of its essentials with breathtaking speed. More prosaically, the intensity of the work necessary to launch the Atlantic College in 1962, the Medical Commission on Accident Prevention shortly thereafter, had left neither time nor energy for writing – and he had always preferred to be judged by actions, not words.

It may also have been in part a matter of uncertainty. The passionate conviction with which he expressed his ideas and brought forward his bandwagons 'for sale' could impress his audiences with his feelings of moral confidence, albeit lightened by carefully focused humorous anecdotes. But there was a depressive side to his personality that took over briefly from time to time but

[●] Golo Mann: *Kurt Hahn als Politiker in Bildung als Wagnis und Bewährung*, ed. Hermann Röhrs, Quelle und Meyer Heidelberg

[○] D. Bolam in *Comparative Education Oxford No 2* 1965

[●] Kitty Hauser writing about the field archaeologist Osbert Guy Stanhope Crawford in *Granta 99*

was to predominate for several months after he had been knocked down by a motor vehicle in Scotland in 1968. Isolated, cared for only by his sister-in-law, the widowed Lola Hahn, in her flat in London, he refused all company and visits. 'Unclean', unworthy even to be touched physically by others, his life's work misguided and dangerous! And one recalls sadly his comment to his sister-in-law Lola shortly before he died: *'the difference between you and me is, you always have faith and hope. I wish I had the same'.* I remember vividly one of his rare visits to Atlantic College. He learned that I was returning an essay to my class of German students on the relationship between genius and mental instability. He dropped his other engagements and sat, silent and attentive, in the back row, and left without a word. I was unaware of the issues I had opened, but it is clear to me now. Healing had been the theme of his life. His missionary approach to all he undertook, his commitment to action, his admiration of the Good Samaritan, was also conscious healing of self. An understanding of his life and his achievements must place this inner victory in its central place.

The life-long bachelor who treasured family life but never had a family of his own, the educator who was judged by many to have no understanding of the role of sexual relationships or of the importance of the education of women, who was either intensely admired or deeply resented by the wives of his headmaster-disciples, who mocked and dismissed the kind of co-education *'that breaks out after supper'*, has nonetheless thoughts that will find an echo in today's society. *'Suppression is not the only danger. There is the danger of prematurely intensifying an amorous atmosphere. This intensification is the smaller evil compared with suppression, but it should not be ignored. Intense emotions must not be confused with deep passions which are the basis of tragedy but also of true happiness. I believe that even under modern conditions, a late maturity can come about quite naturally, and that it is the better maturity. The Grand Passions of research and exploration, music and painting, adventure and of rescue ... do not suppress sex, but they prevent the early monopoly of sex in the emotional life of the young.'*

And he also knew what he looked for in headmasters, expressing himself in the following words in 1953: *'Respect is not enough; affection is not necessary and comes by Grace. What is wanted is trust; trust that a boy will be heard in patience by an unoccupied man, that he will be understood if he does not say much, that nothing he says will be misused ... you want a man who is, or was, in close contact with public life. He must be alive to the needs of the country and be able to present them to the senior boys in accordance with their gifts of heart and head. He must be vigilant in observing their behaviour at work, intellectual and practical; in games and expeditions, during training and achievement; discover their bent; stir and direct their ambition ...'* And he was clear about the sometimes hard responsibilities, writing to a headmaster in the United States in the following words: *'Never let a committee expel a boy. A committee has no conscience. Use it to investigate and advise, but you must make the decision. That boy will carry his expulsion through life. There must likewise be someone who will always carry the decision on his conscience – someone who can think back and ask himself if the right thing was done.'*

Leadership and the Elite

Elitism is readily suspect everywhere unless carefully defined. Leadership is, it seems, welcome almost everywhere except in Germany. The Hitler legacy is difficult to combat.

'It was from him that I heard for the first time the regular use of a word that was later to play an evil role in German history: the Fuhrer, the Fuhrer principle. He wanted to educate men to be leaders. Day and night they should be conscious of what it meant to lead, to be a leader ... Germany should be ruled by the principle of the Fuhrer ... the responsible assumption of political and intellectual leadership, which is based on genuine authority and through the personality of the leader radiates and is effective not only downwards but outwards on all sides ...' [120] [●]

These words, with others on the same page, written from the safety of the post-Hitler period, reveal almost all one wishes to know about German inhibitions over the connotations of leadership. One encounters similar hesitations in the remarks of a past Headmaster of Salem: *'(Hahn) openly admitted that Salem's foundation, and that of all his other schools, was intended for the purpose of educating leadership elites'.* [o] The telling word here is *'admitted'.* Hahn did not admit. He stated. He had no bad conscience in the matter. Those who believe in democracy must surely

[●] Arnold Brecht. Nor have matters changed much in the interim. We find the UK correspondent Thomas Kielinger of the German newspaper *Die Welt* writing in the *Daily Telegraph* of 13th November 2011 *'Don't talk to me as a German about leadership. If there is one word that is total anathema in the political parlance of my country, it's the L-word.'* All a shade ironical, given the undisputed calibre of an impressive series of German Chancellors since the war including two praised explicitly in Kielinger's article!

[o] Bernhard Bueb: Round Square Conference 2002

grapple openly with the challenges of providing leadership – the preparation, the skills, the importance and the limitations of seeking consensus, integrity towards the electorate, issues of purpose and vision, the exercise of authority once won, the quality that his biographer Alan Bullock so admired in the British Foreign Secretary Ernest Bevin: *'imagination in the exercise of power'*.

'Hahn believed that success by a strong leadership implied that those who were being led were willing to obey. He expected and received obedience in Salem too.' [●]

Hahn was of course no fan of indiscipline, when *'an order becomes a basis for discussion'*, but the emphasis here is all wrong. In his schools Salem and Gordonstoun, participation in responsibility for the school's well-being was taken down to much younger ages than in other roughly comparable schools through the progressive awards of the right to wear the school uniform, fill in the Training Plan, carry the White Stripe, leading eventually, of course in a minority of cases, to the status of Colour Bearer and Guardian. An examination of school records suggests strongly that correction and punishment were most common for failure to honour the commitments one had accepted at the relevant stage in one's school career. The issue is that of integrity in the possession and exercise of authority, authority over oneself being the point of departure. One searches in vain in all Hahn's writings for any praise of obedience. On the contrary: *'My worst enemy is not bureaucracy but the docility of the state-tamed young who do not know the difference between the laws of man and the laws of God ... In my Oxford days, I would have said if you scratch an English undergraduate or Public Schoolboy, you will find a rebel. Today I say that if you scratch them you will find a civil servant ... .'* *'Contrary to the Prussians, we regard obedience as a virtue only of the 17th order.'*

So much of this lies in the choice of words. Leadership is not suspect in the Anglo-Saxon world and is widely used, for example, in management training. Elitism may be. The moment one begins, however, to define the nature of the leadership or the leader – the leader of fashion, of culture, even the civic or the political leader – the moment the context of the leadership emerges, the anxieties fall away. And at that moment one begins to look for integrity, imagination, reliability, ability, commitment, and success.

As far as Hahn is concerned, one must surely bear in mind that his residential schools now form a small and proportionately diminishing part of his educational legacy. His most widespread impact lies elsewhere. Some 25,000

young people are currently taking part in Outward Bound courses each year in Britain, 80% of them from schools and the remainder either individuals or groups of apprentices from industry; roughly 13,000 of them receive financial support to do so. Worldwide there are now 40 Outward Bound Schools in more than 30 countries, the leaders being Britain, the United States and Singapore, where the activities are financed by the government. The Duke of Edinburgh's Award Scheme attracts 275,000 participants in Britain alone, and the International Award Scheme, set up in 1988, now has 62 sister organisations working under its umbrella.

And despite their influence on his work, Hahn was a consistent critic and would-be reformer of the British Public Schools. *'A residential community transmits self-confidence which is a source of power. The composition of the Public School clientele makes one feel: self-confidence is often placed where it is not deserved'*; and in the emotional language that at times cost him allies: *'I believe the Public Schools are doomed not in their existence but in their historical mission unless they extend their services so as to benefit the unprivileged boys, whose needs cry out. They must be brought to regard their isolation as a curse and not as a blessing.'* He shared more common ground here with Desmond Hoare than perhaps either was ready to acknowledge, as his address of 26th May 1949 to the Annual General Meeting of the Parents' National Educational Union illustrates. *'I advocate that the gulf be bridged between opposing systems of education, the Public School and the Day School systems ... first, may a community life, stretching and testing character, be introduced into a number of our day schools. This can only be done by establishing self-government, by the school assuming responsibility for leisure activities, by creating proper and dignified facilities for study and recreation and feeding for both boys and girls, all of them to be day boarders who would not go home until after their last meal ... may the Public Schools open their gates to the underprivileged class. Scholarships for selected boys given for the purpose of absorbing them into the privileged class, or even the grading of fees, are not enough. I propose that vocational courses for working boys, lasting for several years, be instituted ... at Gordonstoun we contemplate training builder's apprentices for three years ... we have a hopeful precedent in our Nautical Department which trains boys for service at sea. One of our nautical boys, a fisherman's son, rose to be head of school and succeeded as a classical scholar ... may the Public Schools go even further and make themselves responsible for running Short Term Schools on the model of the Outward Bound ... a hundred boys should attend each of these courses, to be held ten times a year ...'*

[●] Ibid

Kurt Hahn in the Eyes of Others

Visionaries are powerful people when they combine unyielding determination with shrewd insight into human nature in pursuit of their dreams. It matters a great deal that their dreams should be benign and welcome to contemporaries.

British critics of Hahn have reacted against his moral systems, his training plan which required all pupils to enter daily on a private list their successes or failures in respecting a list of daily duties (teeth cleaning, cold showers, the completion of routine tasks for the school community), his *Germanic* formalisation of personal relations through hierarchies extending throughout the school. And some [●] have mocked his claims that a grand passion – painting, music, an absorbing hobby – can protect the young against sexual pressures in the years of puberty. It is a revealing paradox that only Hahn himself has been able, through his personality, to run his schools with his training plan and 'trust system', with Heinrich Blendinger in the Nazi period in Salem his one real partner in this area. In Britain all this was of course confined to Gordonstoun, where it has long been abandoned. Desmond Hoare would have none of it at the Atlantic College, leading Robert Skidelsky in his *English Progressive Schools* to comment 'with Atlantic College we are back once more to solid, English common sense'. Other Anglo-Saxon countries, none of which have schools ever headed by Hahn in person, have not had to resolve the Trust System dilemma.

Hahn's most penetrating critic was his colleague Erich Meissner, whose hostility did so much to weaken Hahn's position at the distressing time of Hahn's departure from Gordonstoun. Meissner acknowledged frankly that, as with any educator concerned to develop character and himself having so strong a character, there were bound to be casualties along the way. Even at the moment of maximum strain in 1953, Meissner put his finger on the central importance to Hahn's achievement of his move to Great Britain in 1933: '*You have added to and improved your achievement in this country and have escaped the danger of a one-man show.*' [121] But he also expressed an acute assessment of the constraints that Hahn had allowed to define his political ideas. '*Your concept of history is in my opinion far too one-sidedly formed by the 19th century … as a young man you were engaged in the service of German war propaganda. This was followed immediately afterwards and without the possibility for reflection by the fight against Versailles, which became for you the central focus of your political attitudes. The documentary battle, full of cunning, that then ensued, has to my mind nothing in common with unprejudiced research. The coming to its senses of the nation (on which also depended the recovery) was made thereby the more difficult, if not impossible … it is from this murky spring that you as a politician have constantly drawn. This led to your misjudgment of National Socialists. You idealized impulses to which the Party owed its success …*' [122]

When Hahn left Gordonstoun in 1953, another public school reformer, Coade of Bryanston, did not hesitate to express his recognition: '*… there can be few men (if any) who have done more to bring people to realize the shortcomings and possibilities of public school education … I hope you realize how much your achievements have signified to those who are trying to do something along your lines, and what a lasting influence you have exercised …*' [●] '*Far more than any other man you have stimulated me to reflect upon the essentials of a schoolmaster's work and responsibilities*', George Turner wrote to him at the same time.

'*One cannot walk past Hahn, even if one does not accept all his educational goals.*' [123] The Nobel Laureate Nevill Mott, his Trevelyan Scholarships ally, writes in his autobiography: '*I want to say that, of men I have known at some period of my life rather well, Kurt Hahn, Philip Morris and Niels Bohr have impressed me most as having that indefinable quality of greatness …*' [o] Hahn was a master cultivator and exploiter of the influential contact. The range of personalities whom he recruited for his causes was astonishing. Recognising clearly the nature of his '*noble guile*', they were carried along by his devotion to '*the common causes*' which they also allowed him to identify and to define. Some felt that he was driven by a fear of not having long to live because of his physical disabilities and forgave him his impatience. No one who met him remained indifferent or forgot him.

'*He really lived in a dream, and in this dream he let others take part and placed them in his service. That was always only possible because he thereby forgot himself. In his presence no*

[●] Especially Jonathan Gathorne-Hardy in *The Public School Phenomenon* Penguin Books 1977 but also Henry Brereton as Warden when Gordonstoun was coming to grips with the introduction of girls into the school. Contemporary opinion has been re-awakened to the dangers of the premature stimulus of sex in the lives of young people.

[●] Letter Coade to Hahn 30th August 1953
[o] Nevill Mott: *A Life in Science* page 106

one could think of himself, for Kurt did not think of himself either.' [124]

Jo Nold, one of the most thoughtful practitioners of Outward Bound in the United States, grasps the Hahn personality with a precision and insight equalled for me by few other commentators. [●] His introduction of himself as the well-qualified recruit to the Gordonstoun teaching staff, with its humorous and ironical self-deprecation, illuminates the kind of personality to capture Hahn's attention: '… canoed in Canada, sailed in the Caribbean, climbed in the Alps, read Wordsworth in Tintern Abbey and visited the Parthenon by moonlight.' For him, Hahn was 'the classical alienated man, a wanderer, a Jew, a political refugee … he evokes at once a fierce loyalty and an unsettling ambivalence …' The four Hahn declines of 'fitness, craft, reflection and compassion' tellingly reflect 'man alienated from his work, from his body, from his inner self, from Nature and from God'. Hahn's personal life, he concludes, as well as his educational practice, 'was modelled on a realisation of self and the fulfilment of moral responsibility through action'.

Kurt Hahn and the United World Colleges

Within a few years of the opening of Atlantic College, Hahn's health had begun to fail. Furthermore, as we have seen, he had serious differences of opinion with Desmond Hoare over policy. The Atlantic College was therefore the first school he had founded over which he had little subsequent influence. He had no role at all in the setting up of the next two colleges, the United World College of South East Asia in Singapore and Pearson College in Canada.

Are the United World Colleges truly Hahn schools beyond the indisputable fact that the first of them would not have come into being without him, the most fundamental achievement of all and the one we most take for granted?

The 16–19 age range of the two-year colleges has from the very beginning led to a social-disciplinary framework that could not follow the criteria of the classical Hahn education as shaped by him in Salem and Gordonstoun.

The imperative need for academic success within the two years has imposed 'non-Hahnian' criteria on the selection of students. Late developers, among whom Hahn could point to impressive successes from his two Headships, have been excluded.

[●] Address to the Conference of Round Square Schools in 1980

On the other side the Colleges have, at least to date, exceeded by far his ambitions on entry by merit, independent of social and financial background. This is in addition to the range and wealth of national and cultural diversity that were not within the aspirations of his earlier schools. And, especially in recent years and with the Norwegian College in the lead, the United World Colleges have some remarkable stories to tell of their accomplishments with physically handicapped students. 'Special concessions', Hahn wrote, 'should be made to the physically handicapped – they often have developed a remarkable power to overcome through the very challenge they have accepted in their daily lives: the challenge of their disability.' Memorable for me is the nearly blind Spanish student in the Mostar College who had always to be guided to his place in the various musical performances at his final closing ceremonies. In his two years he had become a much-loved, much admired figure in the city on both sides of the Croat/ Bosniak divide with his regular guitar playing in bars and cafes. Little wonder that his mother was in tears of pride throughout the ceremony! Many colleges will have their own comparable stories.

The early concept of national groups, each accompanied by a national tutor and with national rooms set up to reflect national traditions, never got very far, but one wonders whether the current fragmentation into very small national groups, often reduced to individuals, (Desmond Hoare called this 'the stamp album approach') has not led to a loss of politically significant impact and to a retreat into satisfaction with understanding achieved purely between individuals.

A rapid scan of other Hahn principles leads me now to wonder whether, in our determination to stand on our own feet, we have not, to our disadvantage, ignored other good objectives. What attention have we paid, with consistency, to individual physical fitness, tackling 'physical illiteracy' (a favourite Hahn phrase), challenging our students to set themselves new standards that they have assumed to be beyond their reach? Do we make of tobacco and alcohol issues of imposed discipline or matters of personal honour and self-improvement? Do we, in so far as we practise outdoor education, offer our students the challenges of designing, preparing and carrying through demanding expeditions of the kind required by the Duke of Edinburgh's Award Scheme and Outward Bound? Have we ever explored seriously the benefits of the 'solo', the period of one or two days spent by a student entirely on his or her own, ideally in challenging countryside? What time and space in our surroundings and our timetables do we offer for reflection and 'aloneness', for spiritual growth?

Do we guarantee that all students leaving our colleges are well qualified in the latest methods of first aid *'lest they find themselves helpless spectators when a tragedy unfolds itself'*? Do we respect and allow time for the opportunities and challenges of craftsmanship, for making clear the distinction between the manual and the menial? Have our extended essays driven out in their academic pretensions the possibilities for *'grand passions'* and projects of a more emotional or artistic nature? Is there a danger that our commitment to service, now so successfully embedded in IB and university testimonial routines, is driven as much (or more) by the need to compete and to qualify as by the preparation for compassionate citizenship? Is there in our pursuit of IB grades and university scholarships even a danger (to move from Kurt Hahn to Josef Albers), of forgetting that *'schools should allow a lot to be learned, which is to say that they should teach less?'* Can the Round Square schools teach us some lessons about the value of long-term service projects in the developing world to which successive generations of UWC students could make their contributions in inter-college cooperation?

Richard van de Lagemaat taught Economics and the Theory of Knowledge at both the Atlantic and the Adriatic Colleges. He made a study of Hahn and the United World Colleges and developed his five Cs which have always impressed me as a convincing re-statement of objectives for us.

> Criticism: educating the intellect. *Developing understanding and problem solving skills, together with the virtues of sound judgement and constructive criticism.*
> Creativity: educating the imagination. *Developing the ability to make connections and to experience the world in new ways.*
> Challenge: educating the will. *Developing mental and physical courage and the ability to overcome one's fears and limitations.*
> Compassion: educating the emotions. *Developing the ability to identify with other people and the willingness to take action in order to help them.*
> Contemplation: educating the spirit. *Developing the capacity for wonder and the sense that one is part of something greater than oneself.*

Let us also remember that Hahn wanted the rebel, not the conformist. His public image – physical fitness, the outdoors, yes, cold showers – has distorted, even obliterated, his essential aim: the nurturing of the moral conscience and the training of the spirit of body and mind to follow

its commands. Moral health and martial vigour! The citizen has the duty to speak out. He praised and quoted often Churchill's phrase *'the angry growl of democracy'*. He himself was ever unable to remain silent. Some examples:

When the corpses of thousands of Polish officers were uncovered in mass graves in the woods of Katyn in 1943, he immediately protested against the refusal of the British Government to acknowledge publicly the truth – that they had been murdered by the Soviet, not the German army. *'The Germans have committed much more horrible crimes; but there is one thing they are not capable of doing: they cannot murder men in 1941 who were already dead in 1940.'* This was the key moment when it became clear that Poland, the country for which Britain and France had entered the war in 1939, was being abandoned.

He protested immediately over the use of the atomic bomb against civilians: *'… war necessity or war convenience?'*, quoting the Franck Report written by the German Jewish physicist who had himself been involved in the development of this weapon, whom he knew, and on whose behalf he had drafted a published protest against Hitler in Germany in the 1930s.

A supporter of the policy of unconditional surrender, he nonetheless protested against incompatibilities between it and the terms of the Atlantic Charter agreed previously between Churchill and Roosevelt.

After the war, an especially courageous move for a German Jew who had fled Germany in 1933 and spent the war in Britain, he questioned publicly the justice and legality of procedures under which certain German generals were being tried and condemned.

George Steiner, an inspiring visitor and lecturer at the Adriatic College in the 1990s, has written of *'active indifference'*, of *'collaboratively unknowing'*. This is precisely the failure of character and of citizenship against which Hahn was seeking to arm his pupils. Who better to form world citizens in the highest interpretations of Hahn's education than the United World Colleges, but perhaps the ambition must become explicit, not entrusted alone to implicit expectation! How do we know what we know? Our Colleges, taking their students directly from their national backgrounds, not through the filter of international diplomatic and business communities, bring first hand experience of the world's conflicts and sufferings into our communities. Not the newspapers, nor the television, but the lives of fellow-students create the realities. How active is our response? The integration of thought and action, the testing (once more to echo Jo Nold) of one's commitment and will, may be strengthened by a sense of destiny. We are the stewards of a vision.

Some Final Remarks

'He whom the gods love is still young if he dies at eighty.' [125] Again Kurt Hahn.

We may regret the absence of an autobiography and of comprehensive statements of principle to which we can turn for authoritative guidance and informed debate. We must admire and be grateful for the example, despite illness and mental depression, of the untiring active dedication into old age of our founder.

In 1968 Hahn again visited the United States at the age of 82. This was, as we know, a time of great social turmoil. Once again he wrote a long report. The recent riots in London and in cities across Britain have persuaded me to include here a long extract. They express all the Hahn messages, but the important thing is the context into which they are placed. He had a long meeting with Ted Watkins, a labour leader in the Watts area of Los Angeles that had been torn apart by the riots that first broke out in 1965. No aristocratic elitism here!

'I am told that riots are generally triggered off by teenagers. Could they help to prevent riots?

I am reminded of what happened in Germany in 1932. Hitler rose to power in an emotional climate in which murder became respectable, mainly through the condoning silence of intellectuals. Many of them loathed what was said and done by the Nazis but they failed to defend their faith …

Moral indignation constitutes the sorest of all temptations …

Millions of young people have grown up suffering from the '"misery of unimportance"' – the demonstrators experience a feeling of release from this kind of misery – they feel important, they feel superior, ruthlessness takes over, they feel licensed to commit the very iniquities against which they had revolted, swindling themselves into believing that they were still serving the cause which originally fired them …

The problems of urban decay are being tackled with wisdom and with a will. Hope is being lit in the ghettoes to the dismay of the Black Power agitators.

The Street Academies are doing splendid work … the Phillips Brooks House volunteers are helping in hospitals, in mental homes, with handicapped children, with old and lonely people … I saw young "Nightingales" at work in

Valley hospital … the programme "happiness" operated by Scarborough School. It takes place every Saturday morning. Twenty senior girls and boys sacrifice their precious free morning, bringing Negro children from a near-by slum and occupying them in the school gym for 3 hours, giving them great joy. What impressed me particularly was the absence of adult supervision …

I had a two and a half hour talk with Ted Watkins, the Negro labour leader who cleaned up Watts after the riots in 1965 … Ted Watkins touched upon what had been done to alleviate the physical causes of misery:
> Degrading housing conditions
> Unemployment – sub-employment
> Inadequate transport

And then he spoke at length of his work for the neglected adolescents – he thought this as important as his campaign for the hospital.

Many of the youngsters were fatherless – "welfare pushes the father out of the home".

He began by inducing them to paint the telegraph poles which they are now prepared to defend against vandals. He then enlisted them to build a chicken farm. They now keep pets there – in public housing projects they are not allowed to keep pets. They had been cruel to animals. Now they are the reverse. He used ruined and derelict areas to create "vest pocket parks" – they are beautiful and have become the joy of thousands of mothers and children. He, with the teenagers, ploughed up unused lands outside the town, which will grow vegetables for the hospital. He thought it important for his young people to have an experience right away from Watts. So he applied to the Army for permission during the summer to occupy Camp Roberts. The Army said no. He intimated that he would go anyhow. Then the Army said yes.

So he went with 2,000 boys and girls and some volunteer helpers. They stayed for two and a half weeks, repaired recreational grounds and built a bird sanctuary.

Ted Watkins spoke modestly of the transformation which had taken place in the outlook of his young people. Formerly, so he said, their heroes were the ringleaders in the riots and gangsters. That was no longer so – and then he spoke words of wisdom.

Every youngster should be called upon to make a "sweat investment". Every youngster needs something he can protect – "my young people no longer fight with each other". I learned a great deal from Ted Watkins. I would like to sum it up like this: it is of vital importance for young people to experience
> The pride of belonging
> The pride of achievement

> *The pride of gaining deserved recognition*
> *The pride of having earned gratitude'*

No understatement either! But these lines bring to my mind what Robert Birley once had to say about him despite occasional disagreement: *'I cannot recollect that I have ever had a conversation with him after which I have not found some idea or point of view or even a phrase left stirring in my mind.'*

An Atlantic College housemaster remembers Hahn telling him that every boy could do something well and that it was the task of the schoolmaster to find out what that was. This, said the housemaster, Andrew Maclehose, has governed my work ever since. It is incidents of this nature that help to illustrate Hahn's achievement. *'You look for faults'*, he often said. *'I look for pure gold and I usually find it.'* And at too many schools *'boys learn politeness, but not the courtesy of the heart'.*

As for Atlantic College, we must be grateful for his utter refusal ever to have been daunted. He once wrote of a would-be colleague and ally: *'His circumspection is quite outstanding but, alas, his vision is feeble.'*

'This gift of overlooking difficulties seems often to be a part of leadership', the Swedish bishop Brilioth wrote about Hahn's hero William Temple. Good words for Hahn too!

We hear next to nothing from him in his final years but then, moved by the tragedies of road accidents, he emerges from increasing debility with a short letter urging that the issue of driving licences should at once be made conditional on the possession or the gaining of a certificate in first aid. It seems hard to deny this simple, common sense wisdom.

'We have, it is true, only spoken once or twice, in the Centralverein in Berlin in those unhappy months of the year 1933, but allow me nonetheless to tell you how greatly I have rejoiced at the objective reports in The Times *and* The Manchester Guardian *about you and the lasting success of your life's work. Irresistibly, the words of praise for the teacher (in the highest sense) arose before my eyes … the fire that burns in you, and that has lit so many lights, will despite retirement continue to burn and to be active. This I allow myself to wish you … with warm regards …'* [126] These words came from Alfred Wiener, the Founder of the Wiener Library in London.

'How would Kurt Hahn have reacted?' This is the question which, as I have heard so frequently, is the almost involuntary reaction of pupils of his from Salem and from Gordonstoun as new events hit the headlines.

'For HAHN is a word that neither in earnest nor in jest can be replaced by another. I believe that no true Salemer of the Hahn time can hear it even in his innermost thoughts without for the rest of his life remaining moved by the strength that radiates from it. HAHN was never a comfortable word, never one that could be carried around in one's mouth like a piece of chewing gum, for it was then and remains for us today a call of exhortation that summons the good spirits and banishes the evil ones …' [127] [●]

Let the final words be Hahn's, written on 30th June 1935 from Scotland to a founder colleague of Salem who had written him a self-pitying letter in justification of his decision to leave the school.

'We will then be able to talk in peace about the service to one's own soul. To realize oneself means to forget oneself. What we understand dies. I stand with the carpenter who was called to the Chinese Emperor to give an explanation why the table he had made for the Emperor had turned out so well. "First I forgot the fame that would be mine if the table was a good one; then I forgot the mockery that would strike me if it was a failure; then I forgot my body and finally my soul." My table was Salem.' [128]

[●] The former Salem pupil Heiner Ackermann on Hahn's 70th birthday

German Language Quotations

[1] ‚Namhafte Gelehrte, Politiker und Künstler … von diesem Kreise strömte menschliche Wärme … eine weite Weltsicht … wie die geistige Luft des damaligen Berlins vor dem ersten Weltkrieg war die Atmosphäre des Elternhauses deutsch und kosmopolitisch zugleich.'

[2] ‚Sie studierte ernsthaft philosophische Bücher und spielte vollendet Klavier. Ihre Art auf Menschen zu wirken war Kunst; der Zauber der Verführung zum Guten.'

[3] ‚Lotte Hahn schätzte Kammermusik. Sie eröffnete mir den Zugang zu Brahms, indem sie eines Nachmittags mit einem guten Ensemble das Quartett in A-Dur und das in c-Moll spielte. Ich kann nicht beschreiben, mit welcher Begeisterung ich diese Musik anhörte. Sie bemerkte meine Ergriffenheit, hielt mich zurück, als die anderen gingen, und spielte mir einige Klavierstücke von Brahms vor, die meine Liebe und mein Verständnis noch steigerten.'

[4] ‚eine strahlende Mittedreißigerin, eine Pianistin mit guten Anlagen, die es gewiß weit gebracht hätte – ohne ihren Reichtum, ihren Mann und ihre Kinder.'

[5] ‚Unser kleiner Kreis war ganz professionell aufgezogen, nach dem Vorbild der Comédie Française eine autonome Körperschaft. Die Rollen wurden durch unanfechtbare Abstimmung vergeben, Reklamationen waren nicht erlaubt … Mit der Zeit entwickelten wir uns zu ausgeprägten Charakterdarstellern.'

[6] ‚Kurt spielte immer den edlen Helden, etwas anderes konnte er gar nicht sein.'

[7] ‚Meiner besten Freundin, meinem Gewissen und meinem Schutz, meiner geliebten Mutter, die mir immer gegenwärtig ist, sowie ich etwas Rechtes tue oder denke.'

[8] ‚Ein Fremdgewordener sind Sie mir doch gewiß nicht. So lebhaft erinnere ich mich noch an unsere gemeinsamen Kindertage in Wannsee – Sie waren mehrere Jahre jünger als ich – und sehe ich Sie noch als den bildhübschen Jungen, der Sie damals waren … und dann kamen die Jahre, in denen wir uns die Sorge um Golo teilten'

[9] ‚Das Mädchen mit der Stimme, die das Lied singen kann, wird meine Frau oder ich heirate nie.'

[10] ‚Ich war 18 Jahre alt und kostete zum ersten Mal eine große Leidenschaft und spürte in Übermut und Jugendkraft die Verheißung eines siegreichen Lebens.'

[11] ‚… war ein Mann von ungewöhnlicher Suggestivkraft. Er hatte es leicht, mich wie all seine Patienten dazu zu überreden, das Schwergewicht unserer Aufmerksamkeit auf die psychische Komponente der Beschwerden zu legen. Er sprach u.a. von einer Enterospsyche und nannte das Closet das enteropsychologische Institut. Er war ein äußerst geistvoller Verfechter der Theorie, daß alle Funktionen des Körpers entscheidend durch die Psyche beeinflusst würden, und so wurde es natürlich für ihn, die organische Grundlage krankhafter Erscheinungen erst ernst zu nehmen, wenn die Seelenbehandlung versagt hatte. Ich war damals nur zu bereit, die mir zur Verfügung stehende Gabe der Autosuggestion in die Dienste seiner Theorie zu stellen, d.h. diese Bereitschaft dauerte nur so lange, bis unleugbare Folgen der Sonnenbestrahlung sich in dem üblichen Crescendo einstellten. Die Besinnung wurde mir dadurch erleichtert, daß eine Patientin des Sanatoriums an Krebs starb, die bis kurz vor dem Exitus psychotherapeutisch behandelt worden war.'

[12] ‚Die Kammer dahinter dient heute als Abstellkammer für Reinigungssachen. Es gibt dort kein Fenster. Hier war der Patient Herr Hahn untergebracht. Er litt unter einer schweren Psychose gegen Licht. Als einzige Lichtquelle akzeptierte er eine Kerze. Das Essen wurde an seine Tür gebracht. Dr. Kohnstamm verbot seinen Kindern strengstens, diese Tür zu öffnen, um Herrn Hahn zu besuchen, wie sie es bei anderen Patienten oft noch mit Spielkameraden von der Straße taten.'

[13] ‚eigensinnige Verliebtheit in meine Erkrankung.'

[14] ‚Beide Harmonien, um mit Plato zu reden, sollten im Leben der Jugend zu ihrem Recht kommen: die dorische und die phrygische Harmonie … . Sie werden vielleicht staunen, wenn ich Ihnen mitteile, daß die phrygische Harmonie in meinem Leben eine größere Rolle gespielt hat, besonders in der fruchtbaren Periode meiner Entwicklung, da eine schwere Krankheit mich dazu zwang, viele Monate das Tageslicht zu meiden, und mir nichts anderes übrig blieb als Gerichtstag über mich selber zu halten. Ich glaube, daß mir dabei bestimmte Wahrheiten über die menschliche Natur aufgeleuchtet sind …'

[15] ‚… ich hatte ihm … in Heldenverehrung und spannender Anteilnahme gelauscht, wenn er so halbsinnend Kunde gab von dem siegreichen Fortschreiten seiner Forschungen … ich spürte sein Bangen und sein Hoffen um die leidende Menschheit … die Versunkenheit, die sich bis zur totalen Geistesabwesenheit steigerte … die erloschenen farblosen Augen, die plötzlich aufleuchteten in heiligem Retterwillen, sowie die Gewißheit in ihm aufsprang, daß seine Kombinationsgabe ins Schwarze getroffen hatte … .'

[16] ‚Ehrlich war wieder hergestellt. Die Seligkeit des Heilens hatte seine Lebenskraft erneuert.'

[17] ‚habe ich gesehen, daß es meine Pflicht ist, mich mitten in den Erdenschmutz hineinzustürzen, zu retten und zu helfen, bis meine Kräfte erlahmen, daß meine Moral Ästhetik war und nicht viel mehr … die Erkenntnis brachte Gesundung.'

[18] ‚Meine ästhetischen Neigungen werden mir nur als Mittel dienen, um zu dem Beruf zu gelangen, den meine moralische Gesinnung mir vorzeichnet … der einstige Kunsthistoriker will Lehrer werden … Erzieher und Unterrichter.'

[19] ‚die altersgrauen Klosterschlösser und die gesunden Gestalten, die sich jugendfrisch auf dem Rasen tummeln …'

[20] ‚daß man hier prachtvoll Griechisch lernen kann und, wenn man einen bestimmten Studiengang einschlägt, in seinem ersten Jahr sogar sehr viel arbeiten muß.'

[21] ‚Er wollte immer direkt an die maßgebenden Männer persönlich herangehen und, wenn das nicht ging, dann an solche Personen, die auf sie entscheidenden Einfluß ausübten. „Wer ist der einflußreichste Berater von Minister X?", fragte er dann. Um jede wichtige Persönlichkeit gibt es einige Freunde und Berater, die immer Zutritt haben und Gehör finden. Nach denen erkundigte er sich und ging dann auf sein Ziel los.'

[22] ‚… wird mit Feuer und Zähigkeit zur Ehre der Schule nicht nur auf den Sportplätzen gekämpft, sondern in den Werkstätten gearbeitet, Neuland urbar gemacht, in den Laboratorien experimentiert, in der Natur geforscht; es werden Theaterstücke aufgeführt, es wird musiziert und gemalt, es werden Hütten gebaut und Schwimmteiche ausgehoben, Sternwarten und Sammlungen eingerichtet. Die Vitalität der Kinder, ständig erfrischt durch den Sport, kommt nicht wie in Eton, Harrow usw. nur dem Sport zugute, sondern wichtigeren Lebensbetätigungen.'

[23] ‚Es gibt Neigungen im Menschen, die bei einer gewissen Stärke den guten Willen so feindlich affizieren, daß er unterliegen muß. Es ist die Aufgabe der Pädagogik, diese Neigungen so zu schwächen, daß die Achtung vor dem Gesetz sie überwinden kann.'

[24] ‚Wenn (der Mensch) seine schönen Gefühle nicht in Taten umsetzt, wenn er, wie der amerikanische Psychologe William James sagt, sich nicht daran gewöhnt, die Gefühle motorisch zu entladen, so wird für einen solchen Menschen die Versuchung übermächtig, diesen leidenden Zustand gewaltsam auszudehnen; und der Mensch kommt schließlich dazu, sich eigentlich nicht mehr von der Schönheit der ihn umgebenden Welt und dem Schicksal seiner Mitmenschen ergreifen zu lassen, sondern sich von seiner eigenen Ergriffenheit ergreifen zu lassen, d. h. seine eigene Empfänglichkeit ästhetisch zu genießen; und indem er dieses tut, zerstört er die unbewußte Hingabe, zerstört er seine eigene Empfänglichkeit, die er genießen wollte.'

[25] ‚Es gibt Krankheiten, bei denen Patienten lernen müssen, mit Anstand zu resignieren … Du hattest interessante und weittragende Pläne für die Gründung einer Schule … daraus kann nie etwas werden, aber Du kannst Kontakt mit der Jugend dadurch behalten, daß Du Dich dauernd in Nordschottland mit einem für Dich heilsamen Klima niederläßt, ein ruhiges und zurückgezogenes Leben führst und dann am Sonntag die Dorfkinder zu Dir kommen läßt und ihnen etwas Schönes vorliest.'

[26] ‚die Erweiterung unserer Weltstellung als das Größere Deutschland der Zukunft … ist ein solch gutes und glückliches Wort nur unter der einen und bestimmten Voraussetzung, daß nicht nur das politische und wirtschaftliche Deutschland größer werden muß, sondern daß ebenso auch die Summe der moralischen Pflichten der deutschen Nation sich entsprechend vergrößert.'

[27] ‚… ich bin jetzt zu der Überzeugung gekommen, daß ich mich wirklich erholen muß, ehe ich mich präsentieren kann. Mir geht es schon besser. Ich habe schon zwei absolut schmerzfreie Tage gehabt, ich lebe sehr ruhig …,

[28] ‚wenn der Waffengang gesichert und der Feind geschlagen ist' (Moltke) and ‚die Regierung eines kriegführenden Staates (hat) auch nach anderen Richtungen zu sehen … als nach dem Kriegsschauplatz (Bismarck).'

[29] ‚Das Auswärtige Amt hat eine subalterne Auffassung von seiner eigenen Bedeutung im Kriege. Die Gründe liegen tief in einer Verkennung der menschlichen Natur. Die Herren wissen nicht, daß von der ‚Moral' der Völker der Ausgang des Krieges abhängt. Es fehlt das Feingefühl für die öffentlichen Strömungen, das unschätzbare diagnostische Material der feindlichen Presse wird nicht genügend gewertet, dagegen die Bedeutung von Agenten und ‚Vertrauensmännern' überschätzt. Je geheimnisvoller ihre Nachrichten, umso besser!'

[30] ‚Worte sind heute Schlachten: Richtige Worte gewonnene Schlachten, falsche Worte verlorene Schlachten. Wollen wir den Sieg hinter der englischen Front zur Vorbereitung des Sieges auf dem Schlachtfelde, so müssen wir solche Worte wählen, die es der patriotischen Friedenspartei in England möglich macht, vor das Volk hinzutreten und zu sagen: Wenn ihr uns folgt, ist der Weg zu Verhandlungen frei, Ehre und Sicherheit Englands sind gewährleistet …'

[31] ‚Man tut überhaupt gut, sich Bethmann'scher Worte zu erinnern. Von Anfang an ist es klar gewesen, daß sich als Ergebnis dieses Weltkrieges drei große Menschheitsziele verwirklichen mußten und daß demjenigen Lande der Sieg zufallen würde, das zuerst den Mut faßte, die drei Ziele aufrichtig auf seine Fahne zu schreiben:
1. Die Sicherstellung des Eigendaseins der kleinen Nationalstaaten.
2. Die Freiheit der Meere mit allem, was aus ihr folge. Sicherstellung der Nichtkämpfenden zu Wasser und zu Lande, ihres Lebens, ihres Unterhalts usw.

3. Ausbau des Haager Werks zu einer wirksamen Erschwerung kommender Kriege.

[31] Bethmann hat wiederholt dazu angesetzt, diese drei Gedanken zur nationalen Förderung zu erheben. Beinahe hätten wir von ihm eine unzweideutige Erklärung über Belgien bekommen. Beinahe hätte er die Freiheit der russischen Fremdvölker im Namen Deutschlands verlangt. Beinahe hätte er den deutschen U-Bootkrieg vor der Meinung der Welt als ein Kampfmittel im Dienst der Freiheit der Meere gerechtfertigt. Beinahe hätte er den Gedanken der Liga der Nationen in einer solchen Form akzeptiert, daß der Feind entwaffnet würde. Die letzten entscheidenden Worte aber hat er niemals gesprochen. Die Geschichte wird nicht die technischen Hindernisse verantwortlich machen, die ihm entgegenstanden, sondern den politischen Willen, der nicht stark genug war, sie zu überwinden … er hätte unter die großen Staatsmänner gezählt, wenn er die Kraft gehabt hätte, den Weg zu führen, den er gewiesen hat …'

[32] ‚Ob wir einen guten oder schlechten Frieden bekommen, darüber entscheidet nicht die Person des Vermittlers, sondern die militärische Kraft, die hinter unseren Forderungen steht. Alles kommt darauf an, wann die Verhandlungen beginnen. Ein Deutschland, dem die Welt eine neue Hindenburg-Offensive zutraute, könnte am Konferenztisch was es brauchte durchsetzen. Tritt aber Deutschland in die Verhandlungen ein, müde, mit aufgebrauchten Reserven, von einer enttäuschten Heimatfront gedrängt, ohne die Kraft, nein zu sagen und dann noch einmal zuzuschlagen, so setzen die Feinde ihre Forderungen durch.'

[33] ‚Es ist von der größten Bedeutung für unsere gesamte innenpolitische Entwicklung, daß der Friede zustande kommt auf Grund einer Mäßigung unseres Militärs. Soll unser Volk militärfreudig bleiben, so darf niemals gesagt werden, daß eine diplomatische für den Frieden reife Situation vorüber ging, weil die Militärs erst restlos alle ihre Trümpfe ausspielen wollten. Auch der genialste Feldherr, auch Moltke, brauchte das Gegengewicht des politischen Maßhaltens. Heute haben wir keinen Bismarck als Gegengewicht …'

[34] ‚Ihr Zweck ist, die Spaltung zwischen der deutschen Regierung und dem deutschen Volk und zwischen Deutschland und dessen Verbündeten Österreich, Bulgarien zu vertiefen … unmerklich frißt die Suggestion weiter, die deutsche Regierung trägt die Verantwortung für die Fortsetzung des Krieges …'

[35] ‚Deutschland ist in der größten Gefahr seit Kriegsbeginn, trotz unserer glänzenden militärischen Lage … noch sind nationale Schranken vorhanden, aber sie sind dünn, und eines schönen Tages, unter dem Druck einer allgemeinen Weltdepression und einer Weltknappheit, brechen diese Instinkte los und schließen einen Frieden, der Deutschland in Trümmern schlagen wird …'

[36] ‚Es gibt drei Methoden, den Weltkrieg politisch zu liquidieren.

Erstens: Die diplomatische Methode … sich irgendwo mit einem feindlichen Unterhändler … zu treffen, um in einer freundschaftlichen Aussprache die Lösung des Weltkriegs zu finden … vieux jeu.

Zweitens: Die demokratische Methode … frühere Vertreter der internationalen Sozialdemokratie treffen sich und versuchen, eine neue Welt zu gründen … auf Grund von Prinzipien, an die sie glauben, aber die sie noch nicht erprobt haben …

Drittens: Die Methode der heilenden Staatskunst – Verhandlungen werden vorbereitet durch einen öffentlichen Dialog, der die Basis der Verständigung nicht nur findet, sondern den Völkern so deutlich macht, daß die öffentliche Meinung überall auf den Versuch hindrängt, die noch bestehenden Differenzen durch diplomatische Besprechungen zu überbrücken …'

[37] ‚Es war Hahn, der im Juli 1917 als erster einigen einflußreichen Politikern, wie Haussmann und David, Prinz Max als mögliches Reichskanzler empfohlen hatte und nach zwei Fehlschlägen (nämlich den Ernennungen von Michaelis und Graf Hertling) mit dieser Empfehlung im Oktober 1918 schließlich auch durchdrang.

[38] ‚Das furchtbare Wort des Engländers „Moratorium der Bergpredigt" gilt für alle Länder, auch für Deutschland … das Land, das zuerst das Moratorium der Bergpredigt aufhebt, hätte mit einem Schlag die moralische Führung wieder an sich gebracht. Und diese Führerrolle würde auch den Gang der Friedensverhandlungen beeinflussen …'

[39] ‚Es ist nötig, daß die führende Persönlichkeit … rein durch ihre Vergangenheit eine suggestive Kraft auf die Völker ausübt … die Welt muß über den neuen Mann bereits Bescheid wissen … nehmen wir einmal an, Deutschland faßte den Entschluß, das Signal zur Heilung zu geben, und es würde die Neubildung vollzogen mit der humanen Persönlichkeit an der Spitze … der neue Kanzler bräuchte kein Wort von Frieden zu reden. Man kennt seine Gesinnung und seine Handlungen im Feindesland. Er braucht nur klar über Belgien zu sprechen … wer nicht im Glashaus sitzt darf mit Steinen werfen …'

[40] ‚Ich bin heute außerstand, Ihnen ausführlich zu schreiben. Es hat sich bei mir ein recht unerfreulicher Zustand nervöser Erschöpfung eingestellt, den ich kommen fühlte, aber gewaltsam zu unterdrücken suchte. Nun brauche ich unbedingt einige Zeit der Ruhe … wenn möglich, schonen Sie mich mit Mitteilungen noch 8–10 Tage. Ich bin wirklich leidend.'

[41] ‚Wir brauchen einen Charakter von Bismarck'scher Willenskraft, die ungeheure Aufgabe zu lösen … ich gestehe, je mehr ich diese Aufgabe betrachte, um so weniger erscheint mir ihre Lösung durchführbar. Es bedeutete fruchtlose Erschöpfung und Selbstvernichtung.'

[42] ‚Was Sie über die Sache sagen, ehrt mich mehr als ich es sagen kann … Sie deuten auf das, was Wordsworth so wundervoll ausspricht in einem seiner tiefsten Gedichte: „a great distress has humanised my soul" … I fear I exasperate you, indem ich die Rolle eines Zuschauers spiele … if I hear the call, dann werde ich kommen müssen und dann wird's gehen. So ging es bei mir bis jetzt immer, und ich glaube Sie genügend erkannt zu haben, um zu wissen, daß Sie mich verstehen, and that you would not wish to have me otherwise. To be chosen, not to choose, das sagt ungefähr, was ich empfinde …'

[43] ‚Ich will keinen Finger rühren in dieser Sache. Kommt sie nicht von selbst aus der Not geboren, so ist sie von Übel …'

[44] ‚Mir ist eine schwere Last vom Herzen genommen. Denn bei dem Gedanken, seine Stellung einzunehmen, hatte ich nur das Gefühl des Mich-opferns, wenn das Vaterland es verlange und keiner da wäre, der die Einigung aller Kräfte erzielen könnte …'

[45] ‚Blödheit der Fehler … den absoluten Mangel an Interpunktion … Mein Vertrauen in Ihre Intelligenz ist aber so groß, daß ich Ihnen sogar die Lösung dieser Rätsel zutraue …'

[46] ‚Zum ersten Mal in meinem Leben habe ich mehr zu sagen als ich sagen sollte.'

[47] ‚In den praktischen Friedenszeiten muß ich absolut ungebunden aus dieser Ansprache hervorgehen. Das ist etwas anderes, als wenn ich als Kanzler redete. Also einfach die Quadratur des Zirkels. Aber ich soll ja die Lösung dieses Problems sein, wie Sie mir einmal sagten.'

[48] ‚Ich betrachte dieses jüngste Kind meines Geistes mit einer gewissen Unsicherheit … nehme aber jedes Urteil von Ihrer Seite mit dankbarem Vertrauen entgegen.'

[49] ‚Ich stelle die Frage: hat der Präsident der Vereinigten Staaten ein Recht, als Weltenrichter anzutreten?'

[50] ‚So ist die demokratische Parole im Munde der Westmächte zu einer ungeheuren Lüge geworden. „Vox Populi vox Dei" sagen die westlichen Demagogen, und sie lästern dabei ihren Gott und ihr Volk. Sie sind wie die Priester, die ihren Götzen zu betrügen wagen, weil sie in Wirklichkeit nicht an ihn glauben.'

[51] ‚den Autoritäten indolent gegenüberzustehen, ohne Sehnsucht nach eigener Verantwortung für die Sache des Vaterlandes … Viele der besten hielten sich vom politischen Leben fern, weil ihnen die Mittel des Kampfes nicht gefielen. Das deutsche Volk aber braucht das Opfer der Besten für die gemeinsame Sache im Frieden wie im Kriege.'

[52] ‚Der Krieg ist gekommen als ein großer Erwecker.'

[53] ‚Darüber wird allein der Charakter unseres Volkes entscheiden … Nicht Institutionen allein können die Freiheit eines Volkes verbürgen. Es gibt nur eine reale Garantie, das ist der Charakter des Volkes selbst.'

[54] ‚Überall horchen heute die heilenden Kräfte auf einander hin, überall wird man des Moratoriums der Bergpredigt müde. Die Menschheit sehnt sich nach seiner Kündigung noch ehe der Krieg endet … für einen christlichen Soldaten gehört der Geist des Roten Kreuzes zum Heere gerade wie der Offensivgeist … ähnliche Stimmen kommen heute aus England, die uns berichten, daß englische Geistliche von der kämpfenden Truppe die Achtung vor dem Feind gelernt haben, welche die Diktatur der Hetzpresse in der Heimat nicht duldet …auch im Kriege ist die Feindesliebe das Zeichen derer, die dem Herrn die Treue halten. Ich möchte gern dieses Wort dahin ergänzen: Es ist auch das Zeichen derer, die Deutschland die Treue halten.‘

[55] ‚Mein freundlicher Mitarbeiter
Nun ist der Wurf getan … es ging mir eigen beim Vortrag. Ich war absolut ruhig … ich merkte es an meinem Ton, meiner Stimme, daß ich gar nicht für sie, sondern für unsichtbare Gesichter sprach.‘

[56] ‚Die politische Öffentlichkeit kennt von diesem Präsidenten der Badischen Ersten Kammer eigentlich nichts als die drei Reden, die er im Dezember 1917, im Februar und August 1918 gehalten hat … diese Reden hatten den „bis dahin kaum Gekannten", der im gleichen Atemzug als „würdiger Repräsentant des deutschen Idealismus" bezeichnet wurde, mit einem Schlag zu einer „politischen Persönlichkeit" gestempelt.‘

[57] ‚Man sieht jetzt am russischen Frieden wie wenig Heilkraft die Niederzwingungsform besitzt.‘

[58] ‚Eine so ungeheure Kraft, wie wir sie in diesem Krieg entfaltet haben, muß sich vor der Welt ethisch begründen, will sie ertragen werden … wir müssen deutlich machen, daß wir ehrlich als Rechtsschützer an allen Randvölkern handeln wollen … ein Belgien in deutscher Hand würde uns für unsere Befreiungsaufgabe im Osten disqualifizieren … Klarheit in der belgischen Frage ist auch hier ein entscheidender Schritt …‘

[59] ‚Vor dem Kriege war die Welt vergeben … England hatte einen besseren Namen in der Welt als wir. Es stand uns überall im Weg.‘

[60] ‚stehe im Dienst des Rechts und der Freiheit. Nur so konnte die Welt dulden, ja begünstigen, daß ein Inselvolk von 45 Millionen die besten Teile der Welt unter seine Herrschaft brachte … England brauchte und besaß eine große Anzahl von Administratoren, deren Charakter und tägliche Geschäftsführung den Grundsatz verkörperten: England nimmt das Glück und das Recht anderer Völker in seinen nationalen Willen auf … zwischen uns und dem Recht steht nur die belgische Frage …‘

[61] ‚wo mein Besucher offensichtlich zu Hause war.‘

[62] ‚Deutschlands militärische Lage ist glänzend – und hoffnungslos … eine Erklärung über die Freigabe Belgiens war kein Verzicht, sondern die Anerkennung eines Zustandes, der durch das Ausscheiden Russlands und die Öffnung der Grenzen im Osten neu bestimmt worden ist … nun ist der schönste psychologische Augenblick verpaßt … er war gegeben, als die Armee aufmarschierte und die strategische Drohung noch unausgewertet auf dem Gegner lastete. Als der erste Angriffsbefehl hinausging, war dieser Augenblick verstrichen. Die Deutschen … mußten politisch handeln … wäre diese politische Offensive gescheitert, so hätte man dem deutschen Volk sagen können, wir haben offen den allgemeinen Frieden angeboten, Belgien freigegeben, und sind abgewiesen worden, dann wäre ihre militärische Offensive von einem moralischen Schwung getragen worden, der ihre Wirkung verhundertfacht hätte … Sagen Sie dem Volk die Wahrheit, solange Sie noch im Angriffe stehen, und handeln Sie, ehe es zu spät ist.‘

[63] ‚Ludendorff … redet entscheidend in der Ostfrage, in der Autonomiefrage von Elsaß-Lothringen und verhindert eine klare Stellung in Belgien.‘

[64] ‚Man kann nicht zwischen Krieg und Frieden, sondern nur zwischen Abwarten und Handeln wählen.‘

[65] ‚Der Angriff ist noch immer die Fechtweise der Deutschen gewesen.‘

[66] ‚Es ist kein Grund zum Verzagen; die Westfront ist unerschütterlich.‘

[67] ‚Prince Max ist geeignet, auch wenn er persönlich wenig Initiative entwickeln kann; die müssen dann andere aus seiner Umgebung kommen lassen …‘

[68] ‚Er hat sich dadurch, daß er sich die Ludendorff'sche Waffenstillstandsforderung aufzwingen ließ, selbst den Boden für sein politisches Wirken entzogen.‘

[69] ‚Die Unwissenden befahlen, die Wissenden fügten sich.‘

[70] ‚ein junger Herr von pazifistischem Einschlag, mit politischen Kenntnissen und stilistischer Veranlagung, aber ohne Erfahrung und nicht in Besitz der für solche Situationen erforderlichen Nerven, uns allen unbekannt und undurchsichtig, deshalb auch mit ziemlichem Mißtrauen und vom bürokratischen Standpunkt aus vielfach mit Abneigung angesehen.‘

[71] ‚Vor allem störte die Hektik Hahns: ich habe heute nochmals an unseren Kikeriki-Freund geschrieben. Er muß sich ruhig halten, denn dieses Toben auf Vorplätzen, Hallen und Straßen bleibt ja nicht ungemerkt; solche Unruhe überträgt sich, ohne daß man es glaubt, auf andere.‘

[72] ‚Die Hohenzollern-Dynastie kann nur gerettet werden, wenn die Abdankung des Kaisers, die mit Naturnotwendigkeit kommen muß, so früh und in solcher Form erfolgt, daß das Volk dem Kaiser dafür dankbar ist.‘

[73] ‚Wer berät den Reichskanzler? Hahn? … Ich bedaure, daß wir nicht an den Reichskanzler kommen … man sieht den ganzen Tag Herrn Hahn im Haus.‘

[74] ‚Ist aber das Gewicht des Sieges zu schwer für den Präsidenten, ist er nicht imstande, seinen Idealen treu zu bleiben … dann gebt uns um Gottes Willen keine schönen Worte … wenn es keinen Verhandlungs-, sondern nur einen diktierten Frieden geben wird, dann diktiert ihn im Namen des ruhmreichen Frankreichs und der grausamen, gut genährten und doch immer hungrigen Bulldogge England, doch nicht im Namen der Menschlichkeit und des Völkerbundes. Das sind erhabene und heilige Begriffe. Sie sollen weiter leben, selbst wenn unsere Generation zu klein und unfähig ist, nach ihnen zu handeln …‘

[75] ‚Der Friede von Versailles war ein Friede, in den die Tragödien der Zukunft so eingeschrieben waren, als wäre es von des Teufels Hand selbst geschehen.‘

[76] ‚Es wird von uns erwartet, daß wir uns als die allein Schuldigen am Kriege bekennen sollen. Dieses Bekenntnis wäre in meinem Munde eine Lüge …‘

[77] ‚Es gibt Verbrechen im Kriege, für die es keine Entschuldigung gibt, aber sie geschahen inmitten eines furchtbaren Ringens um den Sieg, als die Leidenschaften des Kampfes und die Sorgen um die nationale Existenz das Gewissen der Völker stumpf machten. Die mehr als 100,000 Nichtkombattanten, die seit dem 11. November an der Blockade starben, wurden mit kalter Überlegung getötet, nachdem der Sieg errungen und verbürgt war, daran denken Sie, wenn Sie von Schuld und Sühne sprechen.‘

[78] ‚Wer Patriot ist, kann in eigener nationaler Sache nur Sachverwalter, nicht Richter sein. Klarheit in die umstrittenen Zusammenhänge und Motive der tragischen 12 Tage vermag nur eine unparteiische Untersuchungskommission zu bringen, vor der alle beteiligten Hauptpersonen zu Worte kommen und der alle Archive geöffnet werden. Nur so kann festgestellt werden, wo böser Wille am Werk war und wo bei gutem Willen unfähige und schwache Menschen versagt haben.‘

[79] ‚Das deutsche Volk erwartet einen harten und unerbittlichen Frieden. Es muß aber ein Friede des Rechts sein … Ein Friede der Gewalt aber, der im Namen des Rechts vor dem deutschen Volk nicht verteidigt werden kann, wird alle heimlichen und offenen Widerstände gegen seine Durchführung aufrufen.‘

[80] ‚einen etwaigen Antrag der neuen Regierung an ihn (Prinzen Max), Deutschland bei den Friedensverhandlungen zu vertreten, nicht abzulehnen …‘

[81] ‚Inzwischen ist das Institut für Auswärtige Angelegenheiten in Hamburg gegründet.‘

[82] ‚Ich bin sicher, wir müssen noch viele Jahre warten, und ich will als mein letztes Wort meinen Landsleuten zurufen: Verliert die Geduld nicht. Aber ich halte es für meine Pflicht, in diesem Brief die Warnung offen auszusprechen: Ohne daß die Hoffnung auf die einmal kommende Revision

des Versailler Vertrages aufleuchtet, wird Deutschland seine Rettung nicht vom Pazifismus erwarten.'

[83] ‚Dieser deutsche Prinz ist ein anständiger, wohlwollender Mensch – eine Ausnahme also, auch unter Prinzen. Und so wurde er von Kurt Hahn entdeckt … Kurt Hahn hat vier Wochen Deutschland regiert – sagen heute noch manche. Hätte er es doch getan! Vielmehr hat er jahrelang den Prinzen Max regiert, hat auch dieses dicke Buch „mit"geschrieben – es sind zum guten Teil Kurt Hahns gesammelte Werke; nur gerade während der Reichskanzlerschaft des Prinzen wurde er von ihm getrennt, jedenfalls nicht ganz herangelassen, und in dem, was er wollte, überstimmt.'

[84] ‚Der jetzige Reichskanzler ist ein verhältnismäßig unselbständiger Mann. Um ihn schnurren jetzt schon verschiedene Männer herum, die kein Amt haben und doch alles mögliche mitmachen, z. B. Kurt Hahn …'

[85] In demokratischen Zeiten muß der Staatsmann auch Politiker sein.'

[86] ‚An der Tür wandte ich mich noch einmal zurück: „Herr Ebert, ich lege Ihnen das deutsche Reich ans Herz." Er antwortete: „Ich habe zwei Söhne für dieses Reich verloren."'

[87] ‚Aber Herr Hahn, der Schluß des Buches stimmt doch gar nicht. Prinz Max … hat den Reichspräsidenten Ebert gar nicht mehr gesehen … '

[88] ‚Aber um Gottes willen, Herr General, ändern Sie diesen Satz bitte nicht, denn Sie reißen sonst meinem Paradiesvogel die schönsten Federn aus.'

[89] ‚Wenn ich mit den Handlungen Eurer Großherzoglichen Hoheit nicht übereinstimme, so erblicke ich den Grund hierfür nunmehr lediglich darin, daß Höchstdieselben für die rauhe Wirklichkeit der damaligen schweren Zeit zu fein besaitet waren und in dieser wiederholt falsch beraten worden sind. Keinesfalls haben aber Eure Großherzogliche Hoheit am 9. November durch die verfrühte Veröffentlichung der Abdankung Seiner Majestät des Kaisers und Königs unlauteren Zwecken dienen wollen. Höchstdieselben haben vielmehr, selbst Erbe einer Krone, in Folge unklarer Nachrichten aus Spa geglaubt, nur noch so, wie geschehen, die Rettung der Monarchie ermöglichen zu können.'

[90] ‚Aber der Krieg ist gekommen als ein großer Erwecker. Überall haben sich die verborgenen Volkskräfte geregt … das Volk in Waffen kehrt dereinst zurück mit gestählter Kraft.'

[91] ‚Es ist in diesem Krieg ein neuer deutscher Mensch geworden … überall regt sich die Lust, an der gemeinsamen Sache teilzunehmen … das Kriegsglück hat uns den Dienst erzeigt, diese neue deutsche Art weltbekannt zu machen …'.

[92] ‚Es gibt dunkle Jahre in der Geschichte einer Nation … alle Menschen von Gewissen sehnen sich nach dem großen Weckruf … von uns Deutschen hängt es ab, ob wir als Nation leben oder sterben … es ist recht, daß in diesem Augenblick besonders die deutsche Jugend aufhorcht, den Atem anhält und die geschichtliche Stunde verstehen will.'

[93] ‚Das deutsche Volk hatte die Ehrfurcht vor seiner eigenen Geschichte verloren. Balkanmoral verseuchte nicht nur unsere Städte, sie verseuchte unsere Politik, bis schließlich im letzten Jahre unsere betörte Jugend glaubte: Man kann in Deutschland ein Mörder sein und braucht kein Ausgestoßener zu werden. Schwere Schuld daran tragen alle die Gebildeten, die über den Mord duldsame oder gar ermutigende Worte gesprochen haben. Es gab kein öffentliches Gewissen in Deutschland …'.

[94] ‚Ich höre die Warnung: Der Weg ist hoffnungslos! Das mag sein. Aber Millionen im deutschen Volk werden dann antworten: Lieber den Tod, als in der Knechtschaft leben.'

[95] ‚Das Heer – die unersetzliche Schule … das Heer erzog zum Idealismus und zur Hingabe an das Vaterland und seine Größe … die Schule als solche muß in einem völkischen Staat unendlich mehr Zeit freimachen für die körperliche Ertüchtigung … unsere geistige Führung hat immer Blendendes geleistet, während unsere willensmäßige meist unter aller Kritik blieb …Treue, Opferwilligkeit, Verschwiegenheit sind Tugenden, die ein großes Volk nötig braucht …'.

[96] ‚Leider konnten wir Sie nach Ihrem Vortrag nicht mehr sprechen und Ihnen die Hand drücken für die mutigen Worte, die Sie in dieser schweren Lage der Nation gesprochen haben … Hier sprach ein Mensch, der sich

seiner Aufgabe als Erzieher im Sinne einer nationalen Humanitas oder eines humanen Vaterlandsgefühls voll und tief bewußt ist …. Hoffen wir, daß unser Volk in seiner nationalen Bewegung nicht die ewigen menschlichen und deutschen Werte vergißt … Und möge dabei nicht vergessen werden, was Sie, gerade Sie, in Ihrem lauteren Vaterlandsgefühl getan haben und noch erstreben …'.

[97] ‚Die nationalsozialistische Jugend umschließt bestes Menschenmaterial. Ich kenne diese jungen Leute, die heimlich ihre kriegerischen Lieder singen und mit dem Opfertod rechnen, wie mit etwas, was sie nicht schreckt. Ihr Gesichtsausdruck mahnt häufig an die Kriegsfreiwilligen des Jahres 1914. Was ist die wirkliche Kraftquelle der Nationalsozialisten? … es ist der Ekel über die Korruption des deutschen Parlamentarismus.'

[98] ‚So, jetzt habe ich einen großen Sieg über die deutsche Korruption errungen, die kommen wird. Wir werden die schlimmste Gevatterles-Wirtschaft erleben, vor allem die Parteipatronage, die böseste Form der Korruption. Aber der volksgewählte Präsident kann den korrupten Staat heilen.'

[99] ‚… die Machtbefugnis des Präsidenten, im gegebenen Augenblick das Volk gegen das Parlament aufzurufen …'.

[100] ‚Unvergeßlich wird unser gemeinsames Erlebnis kurz nach Kriegsende bleiben.'

[101] ‚Wir lassen uns das Fronterlebnis nicht nehmen.'

[102] ‚Es schreit der Leidende, das Echo schweigt, der Nachbar stellt sich taub; die Welt bleibt träge. Der Unstern hat am Himmel sich gezeigt und schwächer werden aller Herzen Schläge.'

[103] ‚Die neue badische Regierung hat angeordnet, daß der morgige Tag schulfrei sein und nationale Schulfeiern abgehalten werden sollen. Zur Feier dieses Tages wird Herr Baumann in Salem und in Spetzgart nach einem Hinweis auf die Bedeutung des Tages zwei Reden des Gründers der Schule, des Prinzen Max von Baden, verlesen, und zwar die, welche bei der Eröffnung der Schule, und die, welche beim Ruhreinbruch gehalten worden ist … Flaggen können nicht gehißt werden, da die Schule sich in Trauer befindet, so lange Herr Hahn noch in Haft ist.'

[104] ‚Wir sind entschlossen, dem Deutschland zu dienen, für das in diesen Blättern Zeugnis abgelegt wird, und glauben, Anspruch zu haben auf Anerkennung und Schutz durch die nationale Bewegung.'

[105] ‚daß es sich bei der In-Schutzhaftaufnahme um ein Mißverständnis, vielleicht auf Grund einer nicht nachgeprüften Denunziation handeln kann. An der nationalen Gesinnung des Herrn Hahn zu zweifeln, scheint mir ebenso unvorstellbar, als wenn man zum Beispiel an der meinen zweifeln würde, der ich ja als Stahlhelmer voll und ganz auf dem Boden der heutigen Regierung stehe, die ich als letztes Bollwerk, als ultima ratio gegen den Internationalismus des Bolschewismus ansehe.'

[106] ‚Zeigt mir das wirkliche Salem, wie es gedacht ist, dann will ich Euch helfen, es zu erhalten'

[107] ‚Wir taten es schweren Herzens in der Erkenntnis, daß es besser sei, mit dem Fortbestehen Salems eine Position gegen den Nationalsozialismus und für eine bessere Zukunft zu halten, als zum Märtyrer zu werden …'.

[108] ‚Dabei ging er als Pädagoge eigene Wege, die ich heute als heilsame Korrektur meiner Amtsführung empfinde. Sein Tagewerk war eine Absage an das dramatische Tempo der Aufbauzeit, das nicht nur den stürmischen Zeitereignissen zuzuschreiben war, sondern auch auf das Schuldkonto meines oft beunruhigenden Temperaments gebucht werden muß.'

[109] ‚Die Bitternis begehrt täglich Einlaß, ich erwehre mich ihrer, aber sie klopft immer wieder an.'

[110] ‚Ach so, ja, der Hahn, richtig, der hatte doch Telefonitis.'

[111] ‚Weltflucht oder Laienmission? Das ist die Frage, die sich unwillkürlich jeder Christ, der es ehrlich meint, vorlegt. Für den einen kann die Entscheidung pflichtgemäß ganz anders ausfallen als für den anderen. Wie aber soll der Mensch wissen, was seine Pflicht ist? Der Ruf der Vorsehung erklingt nicht immer mit nicht zu bezweifelnder Deutlichkeit, manchmal

aber doch, nämlich dort wo Heilkräfte am Werke sind in einer bestimmten Situation und das Auslöschen dieser Heilkräfte tragisch wäre … '.

[112] ‚Es kann für uns als katholische Christen keinem Zweifel unterliegen, daß die Religion des Alten Testaments, die mosaische (jüdische) Religion, durch das neue Testament tatsächlich aufgehoben ist. … das blutige Kreuzopfer auf Golgatha bedeutet die endgültige Aufhebung des Alten Bundes …'.

[113] ‚Wie der einzelne Mensch nur in bestimmten Visionen Klarheit über sein Leben gewinnt, so hat ein Volk auch nur in bestimmten Erlebnissen Klarheit über seine Bestimmung. Wie die Juden im Jahre 30 nach Chr. ihre wahre Mission verkannt haben, unwiderruflich und unrettbar die Mittler ihrer eigenen Prophetie zu sein … so ist eben für die Deutschen Luther das deutscheste Erlebnis. Das muß auch der Katholizismus anerkennen. Der einzelne Mensch, mag er eines Bekenntnisses sein, was er will, trägt dennoch sein Haupt höher, weil er das Vertrauen hat: ich bin der Herr meines Gewissens, und mein Gewissen ist Herr meines Schicksals …'.

[114] ‚Mein lieber Doctor Baeck
Wenn etwas meinen Entschluß hätte wankend machen können, so war es die Berührung mit Ihrem wunderbaren Geist und Ihrem großen Herzen. Auf der einen Seite höre ich stärker denn je den Ruf, Zeugnis abzulegen für Christus und gegen den Antichrist, der heute offen und heimlich nach der Herrschaft greift. Ich bin stolzer als ich sagen kann auf meine jüdische Art. Was ich in meinem Leben ausrichten konnte, verdanke ich dem Tropfen Prophetenblut, den ich in mir spüre.
Mein Sinn ist auf Taten gerichtet.
Die anglikanische Kirche ist sich heute ihrer Kraft nicht bewußt, sie ist hilflos, solange sie sich abhängig fühlt, aber William Temple hat bewiesen, daß die Kirche sich über den Staat erheben kann. Die Kirche Englands ist heute ‚the one voice in Europe that can speak'. Ich kann ein wenig helfen, daß die Zungen sich lösen und Kirchenfürsten eingreifen:

> Gegen die Rachsucht, die heute den Sieg
  verunreinigt
> Gegen die Erbarmungslosigkeit, die Unschuldige
  büßen läßt für die Sünden ihrer Regierung
> Gegen die Herzenskälte gegenüber den Opfern
  der Verfolgung
> Gegen die Lügen der Hetzer, die den europäischen
  Tatbestand fälschen und gegen die Gleichgültigkeit
  der Wissenden, die diese Lügen durch ihr
  Schweigen stützen

Ich lege meinen Brief an den Erzbischof von Canterbury bei. So kann ich nur mahnen and warnen, wenn ich aufhöre, ein Außenstehender zu sein.'

[115] ‚Gott helfe mir. Ich kann nicht anders.'

[116] ‚Dieses würdelose Kokettieren mit den Faschisten und Bolschewisten hat uns namenlos geschadet. Auch Ebert ist hier nicht frei von Schuld … wir brauchen die verfassungsmäßige Diktatur, wie sie die Volkswahl des Präsidenten vorsieht, nicht die illegal eingesetzte …'.

[117] ‚Hierzu bedarf es nur der schöpferischen staatsmännischen Tat.'

[118] ‚Die Entscheidung über Krieg und Frieden ist in England im schärfsten politischen Kampf entschieden worden und, wo gekämpft wird, da entscheidet Menschenkraft.'

[119] ‚Über die philosophischen Grundbegriffe eines Mannes, der sich theoretisch nie eigentlich expliziert hat, wird man mit Vorsicht sprechen.'

[120] ‚Von ihm hörte ich zum ersten Mal den ständigen Gebrauch einer Vokabel, die später eine unheilvolle Rolle in der deutschen Geschichte spielen sollte: der „Führer", das „Führerprinzip". Er wollte Menschen zu Führern erziehen. Tag und Nacht sollte ihnen bewußt sein, was es hieß, zu führen, ein Führer zu sein … Deutschland sollte unter dem Führerprinzip regiert werden … die verantwortliche Übernahme politischer und geistiger Führung, die sich auf echte Autorität stützt und durch die Persönlichkeit des Führers nicht nur nach unten, sondern nach allen Seiten ausstrahlt und wirkt.'

[121] ‚Sie haben in diesem Land Ihr Werk ergänzt und verbessert und sind der Gefahr einer One – Man – Show ausgewichen.'

[122] ‚Ihr Geschichtsbild ist meiner Meinung nach viel zu einseitig am 19. Jahrhundert orientiert … Als junger Mann standen Sie im Dienst der deutschen Kriegspropaganda. Daran schloß sich ohne Übergang und ohne die Möglichkeit der Besinnung der Kampf gegen Versailles, der für Sie zum Mittelpunkt Ihrer politischen Ansichten wurde. Die listenreiche Dokumentenschlacht, welche nun entbrannte, hat in meinen Augen mit unvoreingenommener Forschung nichts gemein. Die Selbstbesinnung der Nation (von welcher auch damals die Genesung abhing), wurde dadurch erschwert, wenn nicht unmöglich gemacht … aus dieser trüben Quelle haben Sie als Politiker dauernd geschöpft. Dies führte zu Ihrer Verkennung der Nationalsozialisten. Sie idealisierten die Impulse, welchen die Partei ihren Erfolg verdankte …'.

[123] ‚Man kann nicht an Hahn vorbeigehen, auch wenn man sein erzieherisches Wollen nicht in allem bejaht …'.

[124] ‚Er lebte eigentlich in einem Traum, und an dem ließ er die anderen teilnehmen und stellte sie in seinen Dienst. Das war immer nur möglich, weil er sich selbst dabei vergaß. In seiner Gegenwart konnte keiner an sich selbst denken, denn Kurt tat es auch nicht.'

[125] ‚Wen die Götter lieben, der ist noch ganz jung, wenn er mit achtzig stirbt.'

[126] ‚Wir haben uns zwar nur im Zentralverein in Berlin in den Unglücksmonaten des Jahres 1933 ein-oder zweimal gesprochen, aber erlauben Sie mir doch, Ihnen zu sagen, wie mich die sachlichen Berichte der Times und des Manchester Guardian über Sie und den bleibenden Erfolg Ihrer Lebensarbeit gefreut haben. Unwillkürlich traten mir all die lobenden Worte für den Lehrer (im höheren Sinne) vor Augen … Das Feuer, das in Ihnen brennt, und so viele Lichter angezündet hat, wird trotz des Ruhestandes weiter brennen und wirken. Das erlaube ich mir, wahrhaftig zu wünschen … Mit ergebensten Empfehlungen …'.

[127] ‚Denn HAHN ist ein Wort, das weder im Ernst noch im Spaß durch ein anderes zu ersetzen ist. Ich glaube, kein rechter Salemer der Hahn'schen Ära kann es auch nur in Gedanken hören, ohne Zeit seines Lebens von der Kraft, die davon ausgeht, unberührt zu bleiben. Hahn, das war nie ein gemütliches Wort, keins, das man wie ein Kaugummi ständig im Munde führen konnte, sondern es ist eins, das trug und trägt, und für viele von uns noch heute eine Beschwörungsformel, die gute Geister ruft und die bösen bannt …'.

[128] ‚Wir werden dann in Ruhe sprechen können über den Dienst an der eigenen Seele. Sich verwirklichen heißt, sich vergessen. Was wir verstehen, stirbt. Ich halte es mit dem Schreiner, der zum chinesischen Kaiser gerufen wird um Auskunft zu geben, warum sein für den Kaiser gemachter Tisch so gut geraten ist. „Ich habe erst den Ruhm vergessen, der mir werden würde, wenn der Tisch gut würde; dann habe ich den Hohn vergessen, der mich treffen würde, wenn er mißriete; dann habe ich meinen Körper vergessen, und schließlich meine Seele". Mein Tisch war Salem.'

Kurt Hahn The Practical Child and the Bookworm Broadcast November 1934, reprinted in *The Listener* 28th November 1934

Let me turn to any of my hearers. Do you know among your acquaintances men and women of great promise which will for ever remain unfulfilled owing to many timidities and hesitations acquired in childhood? And I am sure that you will suspect many more of harbouring a promise which is doomed never to be discovered.

Now let us pause and sit in judgment over these numerous cases. Some of these children have come into their own, but they have done so through accidents, and that in spite of their educators; or they have failed to do so, and they have failed through their educators, who with the best of intentions were misled as to their true selves by the early manifestations of this or that propensity or aversion.

Now the Spartan answers. Your Spartan headmaster will lead you through his day or public school and point out to you in not inconsiderable numbers two victorious and radiant types of boys; the one the scholar, the other the athlete. They stand out from the mass of their rather inky and slouchy contemporaries who, to judge from their looks and gestures, do not seem to have discovered their right of existence.

Now, let us come to grips with our Spartan headmaster. 'What are you doing for the many? He will answer. I am not much interested in them; you see, I am a national institution, and care more for the needs of my country than for those of the individual. I have two filters, the one exams, the other games. Who passes both, has he not the makings of a real leader of men? Do we not single him out in justice to himself and in justice to his country?

Our answer is: 'what passes your filters is good, but what does not pass may be better but may never know it, nor will you ever know it. Take the case of a tenacious dreamer, who cannot learn until rather late how to switch off his mind from one subject to be mastered, to another to be equally well mastered, for his Common Entrance or early scholarship exam. He is, moreover, a slow developer and, if you hustle him, you would wound him, but there is the age limit and you must hustle him.

Or take the case of the practical boy, whose passion for all he can see and finger and pull to pieces and rebuild makes him abhor books of all kinds, perhaps until one day he finds out that even his passion cannot be sustained without books, and he will then learn to master them, but not until he is too old for gaining distinction in his school.

Now, the Spartan headmaster will say, we are doing a lot for boys and girls who want to go off the usual beat – look at the number of hobbies we allow or even encourage. We have a film society, we keep rabbits, we collect butterflies, we run a school magazine, we have a hiking and a railway club; and they may sit alone in the Chapel when they have leisure, and they can build aeroplanes. My retort is: what time and nervous strength have these children to spare for their hobbies? And I further ask: do these hobbies occupy a place of importance and dignity in your community life? Does not the word hobby really preclude this? Your builder and your explorer, your actor and musician, your painter and all the rest, in order not to feel that they not only have the right to exist but that there is a purpose in their existence, must sense a public assent, and this assent is like a good wind behind a weary runner, helping him over periods of self-distrust and fatigue.

I remember a boy once told me that when he was small he always lay awake in the evenings quite a long time dreaming of how one day his grateful parents would come and bring him flowers. I am confident that many a proud and lone lance, many a despiser of the profane crowd, many a sceptic and cynic are longing for just such flowers … to protect and sustain the vitality and self-confidence of our children, we must demand that the boys feel it is as important for the purpose of the school to build for it, to paint for it, to sing for it, to organise for it, to economise for it, as it is to win a Balliol scholarship for the school or to play at Lords.

… Take the case of three youngsters. Number 1 is always unnerved by seeing the wounded. Number 2 asks to be excused from his first battle. Number 3 tried twice to commit suicide. Have you room in your school for this type of boy? The answer is in the negative. And then we say: your school is no treasure house for the nation. Number 1 was Hindenburg. Number 2 was Frederick the Great. Number 3 was Lord Clive of India. Only after the pistol had misfired twice did Clive feel that God meant him to do something in this world.

To give the child this feeing of faith in his or her destiny is our business, and above all our business to give it to the easily wounded boy … .

The Atlantic College Library – Jean-Etienne Lepetit from France and Helge Petersen from Germany

Corrado Belci

A First College on the Continent of Europe

By the late 1960s the Atlantic College was on its feet, the founding headmaster Desmond Hoare was now the Provost with a special responsibility for international expansion, the National Committees were working with enthusiasm and increasing effectiveness, Mountbatten had become the first President of the International Council, insisting on the new name of United World Colleges and action, Desmond Hoare's exploratory journeys to South East Asia were leading to a surge of interest in this rapidly developing part of the world, the Canadians had long been keen on setting up their own college, and the thought occurred to several at the same time: What about a second college in Europe? A project for a German College in Cuxhaven foundered on the inability, for financial reasons, to respond rapidly enough to the city's offer of a site, and a proposal for a Franco-German College was given short shrift, principally by Kurt Hahn, who continued to press for a college on his native soil.

This was a time of keen debate, more intense than I can recall from any other time before or since, about the future of the organisation: Colleges only for 16-19 year-old students, Colleges embracing all ages, vocational colleges, colleges in the developing world, 'bamboo' colleges to be built by the students themselves under the supervision of trained manual workers whose children would be guaranteed an education in them as a reward for their contribution? At this time of impressive ferment the students of Atlantic College asked me to invite embassy representatives from London to lecture at the College on their countries' foreign policies. This invitation brought to Wales a young Italian diplomat, Gianfranco Facco Bonetti. He stayed one night and shared a railway compartment the next day on his return journey to London with Desmond Hoare. This was the moment of conception of the Adriatic College.

It is, I think, fair to say that the Italian proposal for a college was not taken too seriously. The Italians! Whoever thought that they should be next in Europe? Within weeks, however, they brought to an international meeting in St. Donat's detailed architectural plans for a College campus overlooking the Bay of Sistiana, north of Trieste. The Canadians, anxious that this upstart Italian project might threaten their own funding (*'nihil sub sole novi!'*) presented Pearson College builders' helmets to Lord Mountbatten and Sir George Schuster as evidence of practical activity. The Italians were impressive not only on paper but brought with them the detailed architectural model of a complete college campus. Their credibility however suffered a serious blow when it emerged (or so we understood) that the chosen site was owned by some 50 different individuals, most of whom had long since emigrated, and that the legal complications were beyond human grasp. This story seemed too good to be sacrificed to the demands of veracity, but the more mundane explanation, which emerged two years later, was that the site was owned by a company that had gone bankrupt. The likely duration of the legal procedures persuaded the founding team to look elsewhere. Then, in the summer of 1974, a few weeks before Pearson College opened, Gianfranco Facco Bonetti, aided by his boyhood friend and regional employee Giorgio Pontoni, arranged a conference in the Castle of Duino for UWC teachers, students and ex-students, that generated the most practical, helpful and inspiring conference report I have ever experienced. We realised: these people are serious.

Their reasons were serious too.

Friuli-Venezia Giulia and its History

North-eastern Italy, the area north of Trieste, had been Italy's abattoir in the First World War. Reading the histories and walking the villages and battlefields, one has the feeling that every building is stained with blood. The Treaty of Versailles transferred Trieste from the dismembered Austro-Hungarian Empire to Italian sovereignty, but the deep

Italo-Slovene animosities were only further embittered in the 1930s by Italian fascist oppression and cruelty. After 1945, following 45 days of occupation of Trieste by Tito's partisans, further slaughter and inexpressibly terrifying brutalities, almost the whole of the Istrian peninsula was lost to Italy, passing to Yugoslavia, and the Iron Curtain gained its southernmost point within the administrative area of Trieste itself. The surviving post-war animosities were brought vividly alive for me one evening over dinner in a local restaurant when one of those at the table, a Duino 'Italian' albeit with a Slovene name, lent across and said to me quietly: *'Members of the family of that man over there took my sister into the woods in 1945 and cut her throat.'*

Friuli-Venezia Giulia: the meeting place of the Germanic, the Latin and the Slav cultures! By entering this arena of ethnic and historical complexity, the United World Colleges would be embracing an educational role of highly-charged political meaning. They would also be stepping into a world of extraordinary cultural diversity and splendour. In welcoming them, the regional and national authorities were confiding in the United World Colleges an expression of trust and confidence that was to prove irresistible. But as always, nothing was straightforward.

Early Moves and Early Difficulties

Lord Mountbatten had met the owner of Duino Castle, Prince Raimondo della Torre e Tasso, at a conference in Stockholm. Raimondo, despite diminishing means, had long followed his family's tradition of patronizing local initiatives and, encouraged by Mountbatten, began to develop a certain sense of ownership of the College proposal. He visited both St. Donat's and Mountbatten's home Broadlands in southern England. He left Mountbatten with the impression that he was ready to place his castle at the disposal of the College founders. Mountbatten was an emphatically unhappy man when told that he had assumed too much, but the College had by now established more reliable roots. First, Mountbatten had himself, on a visit to President of the Republic Saragat in October 1969, established a National Committee which rapidly acquired prestigious and influential membership; this committee was already sending Italian students of high quality to the Atlantic College. Secondly, a consortium under the chairmanship of the Region's senior lawyer, Avvocato Gaspare Pacia, funded in its early stages by the bank, the *Cassa di Risparmio di Trieste*, was representing the College initiative officially on behalf of the Region in its relationship with the United World Colleges. And thirdly, Gianfranco Facco Bonetti was by now in effect working full time as the project manager. Gianfranco had left his post in London in January 1974 to devote himself to the proposed College, acting against the advice of his chiefs in Rome who warned him that he was endangering his professional career and who acted subsequently to make their words come true. It is a matter of relief as well as satisfaction to note that his final posting abroad was Italy's Ambassadorship in Moscow.

In May and September 1976 there occurred a massive double earthquake in Friuli. 950 people were killed, 2,500 badly injured, 12,000 homes were totally destroyed and another 25,000 severely damaged. 191 villages were razed to the ground. The costs of reconstruction were massive. In London and in Wales it was taken for granted that the College proposal was dead. But it was the earthquake that gave delayed birth to the College.

In 1978 a special law [•] was drafted to authorise national funds for the rebuilding of the region. The Friuli people were quick to seize the opportunity of achieving a long-held dream – a university in Udine to stand alongside the University of Trieste. A parliamentary deputy for Trieste, the Hon. Corrado Belci, took up his pen and added two articles that committed the Region and the government in Rome to the creation of the College. Furthermore, the College's leaving diploma was to be recognised for the purposes of university entry in Italy. The Adriatic College students thus came to enjoy a privileged position in Italy, a privilege subsequently extended to students from the other United World Colleges, before the IB became recognised in its own right in 1986. This final parliamentary recognition was achieved largely thanks to pressures exerted by the College on behalf of IB schools and pupils worldwide.

So strong had been governmental confidence in Gianfranco Facco Bonetti that he had been appointed diplomatic counsellor to the Commissario del Governo in the Region with the responsibility for negotiating and administering all funds donated from abroad. Nonetheless, he had been compelled to make his choice between the UWC leadership in Italy and his professional career as a diplomat, for the period between the 1974 conference and the 1978 decree had been long. His great merit and singular achievement was not only to have envisaged a United World College in northern Italy in the first place; it was to have created the political momentum in Trieste and in Rome that recognised the College's potential.

[•] *Decreto del Presidente della Repubblica* (DPR) n. 102 of 6th March 1978 Articles 46 and 47

The Start despite UWC Reservations

Trieste had once been the great Mediterranean port of the Hapsburg Empire. With major reconstruction Maria Theresa had given the city its Austro-Hapsburghian imprint, but now the hinterland was gone. Trieste had to rediscover itself. Under Allied control from 1945, it was, amid scenes of great relief and jubilation, finally returned to Italy in 1954. It thereupon became imperative that Rome invest enormous political capital in its future survival and success. A new scientific community was created: the International Centre for Theoretical Physics under the Nobel Prize Winner Abdus Salam, the International School of Advanced Studies, the AREA Science Park, the Third World Academy of Science, the Synchrotron and the Centre for Molecular Biology. The Region's border with neighbouring Yugoslavia also gave it a natural frontier role in Italy's important international relations with Central and Eastern Europe.

With Desmond Hoare's withdrawal to Ireland in 1974 and Mountbatten's death by assassination in 1979, the Adriatic College lost powerful advocates at the centre of UWC affairs. Their role for Italy was taken up by Antonin Besse, who brought his loyalties to Kurt Hahn, his attachment to Mountbatten and his familiarity with the Latin temperament to the task of maintaining the links and the momentum. For the Italian politicians he became the essential reference point and UWC authority.

To understand and to sympathise with developing UWC concerns it is necessary to understand what was happening in Italy in the 1970s, for these were the 'years of lead'. The terrorist bloodshed of those years is all too easily forgotten, even in Italy: in 1974, 428 attempted assassinations; in 1977, 2,128; in the first 9 months of 1978, 1,668; in a single incident at the Bologna railway station in 1980, 85 dead and 200 wounded. The official statistics would eventually record 364 deaths at the hands of the Red Brigade between 19th November 1969 and 2nd March 2003. And inflation was running at 20%. Which families from other countries would entrust their children to so dangerous an environment?

And there was an internal reservation too. The oil tycoon Armand Hammer with his immense financial resources was rushing ahead with the setting up of a college in the United States. Was it wise to envisage the opening of two colleges at the same time? The ever-present, ever-valid worry emerged more strongly than ever before: are we asking too much of our national committees? How shall we maintain our scholarship ambitions? A letter of 27th March, a little over one year before the opening of the

college, from James Whitaker, Deputy Chairman of the Atlantic College, to George Schuster, gives the flavour of the concerns better than any other contemporary document: '… *I am sure you know that we are in total agreement on this whole situation. I am dining with Sir John Partridge the night before the International Board meeting to co-ordinate our arguments to try and kill the whole idea … I therefore think that, as you and I have agreed previously, the real priorities remain very much India and the USA, and that we should not be diverted by alternative very doubtful projects. This is not easy, but John and I are having a private meeting with (the UWC Chairman) Tom Symons before the Board meeting, and will do our best.'* He knew his letter would have a sympathetic reception, for George Schuster, still keenly interested at the age of 100, was to address a letter to me in May 1981: '*I personally deplore this decision (of the International Board to go ahead with the proposal for a UWC in Italy north of Trieste) because I do not believe that a UWC in Italy can be a success. My main reason for this is that I cannot believe that parents … will be willing to send their children to a College in Italy in its present political conditions.'* It became clear to me only in retrospect how much we owed to the quiet, committed, professional and diplomatic Chairmanship of the International Board at that time of Professor Tom Symons from Canada.

By the early spring of 1982 firm preparations were under way for opening in September. Giorgio Pontoni as the future Director of Administration set up a small office in February, initially financed out of his own pocket, to begin the detailed planning, and the teaching staff was advertised for, interviewed and appointed. The concept underlying the College was becoming clear. In response to repeated comments from Atlantic College students about the relative isolation of the self-contained Welsh campus, it was decided to aim at a village campus in which the College would become an organic part of the Italo-Slovene village of Duino, the physical layout ensuring that the students would walk the village streets as they moved from one college facility to another. A high priority was assigned to the avoidance of a staff dominated by Anglo-Saxons, also with respect to positions of responsibility; and it was decided to sidestep altogether the traditional hierarchy of the typical Anglo-Saxon residential school by entrusting the pastoral responsibilities to all teachers equally, with the residence tutors (not housemasters) playing a subordinate role. Later familiarity with Italian antipathy to the concept of a 'college' suggested that these were wise moves. Bold plans, or so they seemed at the time, and we attended an important meeting of the Italian National Committee in Rome in March 1982 in confident, optimistic mood. The pace was brisk. The buildings cannot be ready by September, we were told by the Regional representatives. It is too late for postponement, the teachers have been recruited, let us start in a hotel; agreed. We have no money for 75% of the student places, we must take fee-payers; no, we must begin as we intend to go on, early fee-payers will send the wrong message, scholarship students only; agreed. Now we must move to the Quirinale to meet President of the Republic Pertini. An intoxicating baptism!

Early in his international presidency, Mountbatten had stated his conviction that the UWC movement must set up six colleges, after which governments should take over. This never became an agreed policy, but the Italian college was an important step in this direction. For the first time a college was being created at the express initiative of government, regional (Friuli-Venezia Giulia) and national. The College was to possess no property, all buildings to be owned and maintained by the regional authorities. The major part of the running costs was to be provided by the region and by the national government in Rome. This situation had fundamental implications for the College governance, for the College was essentially spending Italian tax-payers' money. This immediately required more formal, more complex, more detailed and publicly acceptable, publicly transparent lines of accountability. Avvocato Pacia with immense skill drew up comprehensive statutes that have admirably withstood the test of time, although they have on occasion baffled UWC colleagues accustomed to a more direct, more Anglo-Saxon approach.

It was inevitable and right that the College President, the leader of the College Council of Administration, should be a regional government appointment following consultation with UWC London; that the College Council should by statute include official representatives of major public bodies, among them three members nominated by the Regional Council, the Director General of Cultural Relations in the Ministry of Foreign Affairs, a representative of the national Ministry of Education, Universities and Research, the Rectors of the Universities of Trieste and Udine, the President of the Province of Trieste, and the Mayor of Duino-Aurisina; that the Chair of the Auditors' Committee should also be a regional appointment with one fellow-auditor nominated by the Ministry of Foreign Affairs; and that the College Director of Administration should be an appointment of the College Council with the legal obligation to report on the College's financial affairs to the committee of auditors which in turn had the duty of reporting independently to the Region and to the courts in Trieste if the College was running a deficit that threatened the closure of the College. Pacias's proposal, embodied in

Giorgio Pontoni, the College's founding Director of Administration, in the College's first year with a cheerful audience including Elisabeth Sutcliffe

his Statutes, that the Chair of the UWC International Board should assume the formal responsibility for the nomination of the College Head (*Rettore*), following consultation with the College President, was not only a thoughtful gesture to balance the criteria guiding the nomination of the College President but also a move, dictated by experience, to isolate this appointment from possible political pressures. And within the College, it was at once clear, indeed clear before the College opened, that the selection of the senior administrative and fundraising personnel must be in the hands of the College President and Director of Administration in consultation with the *Rettore*, irrespective of who signed the formal papers. Attempts to abrogate these responsibilities to the *Rettore*, perhaps in line again with more familiar Anglo-Saxon experience, serve only to suggest misunderstanding of the principles underlying the foundation of this unusual college.

Anticipating last-minute problems, the start date was delayed until the very end of September 1982. The College was allocated two floors of a local tourist hotel little used in the winter months and which had the unusual advantage of a residential catering school. We ate well. But it was not until December of the second year that we entered classrooms and laboratories for the first time in the College's long-term home, Duino. For the first year, small hotel rooms were the classrooms and the students wrote on boards across their knees, squatting in chairs borrowed from a local primary school.

But, as late as the summer of 1982, the College had no President to head the Council of Administration, or Governing Body.

An Inspired Appointment

Corrado Belci had been among a number of Italians visiting the Atlantic College in the 1970s. I could not recall him. My first personal meeting with him took place on a

Saturday afternoon in an upper room in the famed Dama Bianca restaurant on the Duino sea-front. He was clearly in a hurry, doing the rushed interviews that face any politician on home ground during the weekend. He spoke no English and I spoke no Italian. Even in the fairly dark room he was wearing those Italian sunglasses that prevent eye contact. I was left with a feeling of unease, mitigated by the certainty that he would play no significant role in our affairs. So much for first impressions and their reputed reliability!

As I came to know Corrado, I was increasingly struck by the parallels with the founder of Pearson College, John Nichol. Here was a journalist, initially a sports writer, a national politician who never forgot his local roots, a man whose influence was far greater than his public image or modest personal behaviour could suggest, an internationalist who found in his UWC task new sources of inspiration that we ourselves had not seen before, who was able to articulate our hopes and beliefs with a conviction and eloquence that made our own efforts seem puny, and who conveyed that sense of comfort and security embodied by those whose refuge, when all the chips are down, lies with their families.

Corrado wrote a number of books about his political colleagues. They reveal the old truth that, in writing biographies, one also writes one's own story. If Corrado's books have a recurring theme, it is that of *'coerenza'* – indeed, one of his biographical studies is sub-titled *'I Sentieri della Coerenza',* the paths of *'coherence'.* The Italian word has moral connotations that far surpass the almost purely linguistic concept of coherence in English. *'Coerenza'* not only implies but means consistency, transparency, reliability, faithfulness to principle, trustworthiness. *'Coerenza'* was the light by which Corrado lived his life.

Corrado's childhood is told in the small volume he wrote late in life about his grandmother, Nona Marieta. It is also the story of the small village community of Dignano in Italian Istria – sentimental, full of humour and aphorisms, with numerous anecdotes and phrases in the local Veneto dialect, but written with the explicit awareness that this was a life of the past, now lost for ever.

No bath at home, so *'papa took me to the public baths once a week and immersed me in the tub, lathering me with soap from head to toe. My eyes would smart, I would complain, and found the water too hot. Papa tried it with his elbow, then said: "go on, go on. Move around and it won't hurt".'* [1] Family legends that assumed truth through repetition: his father's uncle had been a coachman; droughts were frequent and water scarce; in the worst years this uncle would wash down his coach with white wine which was more easily available

than water. [●] Going to watch the trains at the little local station Cerreto on the shoulders of his grandfather, where the diminutive station master announced the brevity of the train's halt with the loud cry: *'Cerreto – five minutes: time for a pee but not for a …. '.* [2] And one catches glimpses too of his instinctive emerging grasp of what mattered. Writing of his grandfather, a carpenter (*'but a very good carpenter!'*): *'Instruction is one thing. Intelligence is another. You can have a man of intelligence without education and an educated imbecile.'* [3]

And we find too his youthful introductions to democracy and to war, both of them inseparable from his early enthusiasms basketball and football, for he was a notable sportsman. Gathered together on 26th July 1943 for basketball training, they learn of the downfall of Mussolini. How were they now to reconcile their earlier feelings of compassion for other nations not blessed with their own *Duce* with their reactions to this catastrophe? Confused discussions, *'words without a compass'!* It is left to their trainer, *'a friend, an elder brother',* to explain that, in other countries, it is the people who decide who governs. At intervals, there is an election. Then, as in basketball, the team with the most points wins. And it is only when the government has been elected that it acquires authority, and even then it must follow clear rules and answer to something called a Parliament. It was, Belci wrote, the first time we had heard of such things. And in February 1944, playing football, he had been bruised on the shin by an opponent, his football hero, a man destined in other circumstances for the Italian national team. Three days later, his bruise still sore and visible, American Flying Fortresses raided Pula overnight and caused extensive damage. Racing with friends down to the home of his soccer hero Aldo, he found him dead in the ruins, the foot that had injured him lying severed in the rubble.

The Allied troops arrived. His first rather treasured memory was the smell of fried eggs and bacon in his

[●] James Whitaker, a supporter of Atlantic College from the earliest days and later Chairman of Governors, once told me that his family money came from Sicilian Marsala wine. A British ship's captain, he said, had required ballast before leaving Sicily for home and had asked for water. He was given wine, more available and cheaper, and on arriving home had sold it and subsequent 'ballast consignments' at a large profit. I never believed this fanciful story. His son Jack has however now told me that the Sicilian Whitakers supplied Nelson's fleet with Marsala (against scurvy). The family also fortuitously backed Garibaldi, whose legendary red shirts were subsequently copied by the Whitakers' nearby football club in England, Nottingham Forest.

school as British soldiers who were billeted there cooked their breakfast. But the next few months set the pattern for the remainder of his life – journalism and politics. During the aerial bombardments, often sheltering in the church of Sant'Antonio, he and a friend, the brother of the later Bishop Santin of Trieste, had planned the setting-up of the Christian Democratic party of Pola. The church, he wrote, is a natural refuge when you are afraid, but the venue was more than symbolic. He was stirred by the use of the word Christian, a word with which he was after all familiar, in the name of the new, post-Mussolini Christian Democratic government. And in his Christmas 1944 broadcast address Pope Pio XII had spoken of the importance of the personal opinion of each individual, of the right to express one's own opinion on the duties and the sacrifices expected of each individual, of the right not to be compelled to obey without having been consulted – the two rights every citizen enjoys in a democracy. [4]

A few weeks after the Allied troops there arrived in Pola an unknown priest, Don Marzari, a remarkable man who, on being released after torture from a Nazi prison in Trieste for his role in the Italian resistance, had within two hours ordered the church bells to be rung to signal the launch of the uprising against the German occupiers. We shall touch again on the intriguing issue of the involvement of the Catholic Church and Catholic clergy in both the active resistance and in politics. Now in Pola, in the space of three days, Don Marzari created all the essential mechanisms for the establishment of the new party. The motivating ideals were liberty, patriotism, democracy and public service, expressed with a moral and spiritual authority that left no doubt of their religious origin.

Politics is also communication, and Corrado Belci became a journalist on leaving school. On 10th February 1947 he was entrusted with the editorship of the newspaper *L'Arena di Pola*. This was the day of the signing of the Peace Treaty between Italy and the Allies; the day too when the British general De Winton was assassinated in the streets of Pola, a protest against the failure of the Allies to guarantee the future of Istria within Italy. Corrado was just twenty years and three months old, still legally a minor, but no one appears to have noticed the probable illegality of his appointment.

The Italians leave Istria

The Italian exodus from Istria was by now already well under way. The peninsula was left in the hands of Tito's Yugoslav partisans. Corrado Belci's family had already left for Trieste. Corrado and a young colleague responsible for the type-setting lived and slept in the newspaper offices, Corrado with a pistol under his pillow which '*I did not know how to use*'. On one occasion a Yugoslav mob, angered by the continuing appearance of this Italian-language newspaper, prepared to break in by force. Corrado's colleague escaped by a side door, Corrado over the roofs. But it was a matter of honour to continue to publish until the last possible moment. The final issue appeared on 14th May 1947. '*Addio povera nostra Pola!*'

There was one further trait that casts a light of distinction on Belci's early years – the passion of his convictions that gave him the courage to seek out personally the men of influence. He shared the desperation of all his fellow-Italians at the prospect of exile from Pola and Istria, and this desperation was to take him on personal missions to Rome. He was determined to seek the help of Don Sturzo, the founder of the *Partito Popolare Italiano* and vehement opponent of Fascism who had been forced into exile in 1924. One has almost the impression of a small boy on a first big adventure as Belci describes how, in Rome in October 1946, he telephoned the nun who managed Don Sturzo's office and pleaded for a meeting. Without any official accreditation or even informal introduction, he was nonetheless admitted the following day to the studio of this world figure, the priest who had created and led the Catholic resistance to Mussolini and Fascism in the 1920s and 1930s. Then, when the exodus was already well advanced, one of those recurrent *crisi di governo* in Rome suggested that the vessels carrying refugees between Pola and Trieste might be withdrawn, and Corrado again found himself in Rome, commissioned to express the anxieties of his remaining fellow-citizens in the highest quarters. Knowing that the Party leaders were due to meet, he ran to their headquarters and seated himself on the steps outside. As De Gasperi and his colleagues approached, Corrado stood in their way. '*President, I need to speak with you urgently on behalf of the Italian community in Pola.*' [5] De Gasperi, after one question, gives him the assurance he seeks, offers his hand, then places it in a fatherly gesture on his shoulder. Belci has fulfilled his mission.

Istria was a lost cause. Corrado Belci knew this and acknowledged it too. '*The government represents a nation that had declared war and lost. Its international weight is below zero.*' [6] He followed his family to Trieste. There, he had to earn his living. '*I shall never become "dottore" because I shall abandon university studies to master the business of being a journalist.*' [7] His father had shown a similar acceptance of fate with his final gesture as he left his Pola home, pouring cement down the lavatory. '*Before they shit in my house they'll have to clear the drain. That's all …*' [8]

The young journalist and politician

Corrado Belci speaks at the founding ceremony of the UWC of the Adriatic in October 1982

Corrado married Laura Gasparo in 1950. They went on to have six children. Their early life was hard. He worked double shifts as a sports journalist to earn his living, and they had their first three children whilst still living in a single room in his parents' home. He became editor first of the daily newspaper *Le Ultimissime*, then of the *Ultime*, the evening edition of the principal Trieste journal *Il Piccolo*, and finally editorial chief of the *Gazzettino*. But his political commitment never faltered.

The often bewildering, always bewitching frontier city of Trieste owes much of her elusive, magical identity to the affections and contributions of those who have come from elsewhere to help shape her destiny. Her historical debt to these outsiders is immeasurable, and the post-war survival of Trieste as an Italian city is inseparable from Corrado Belci's political achievements.

Corrado Belci the Regional and National Politician

Provincial Secretary of the Christian Democratic Party of Trieste from 1957 to 1962, Corrado Belci was a Member of Parliament for four legislatures from 1963 to 1979. A member of both the National Council and of the Central Executive Committee of the Christian Democratic Party, he was Under-Secretary of State for Commerce in the Ministry of Foreign Affairs in the three governments of Rumor, Colombo and Andreotti between 1970 and 1972. This position took him on numerous visits to Austria, Yugoslavia, Czechoslovakia, Hungary and Bulgaria as well as to many countries in the Third World. But his foremost loyalties remained with the city of which he was now a citizen. The opening sentence in his biography of his political mentor and friend Benigno Zaccagnini runs: '*He was never one of those who, once arrived in Rome, allowed himself to be absorbed by the capital.*' [9]

The immense expansion and modernisation of the port facilities, the laying of the oil pipeline directly from the quay at which tankers moored over the Karst right through to Munich, the *autostrada* highway that bypasses the city to enable heavy traffic to proceed from the port in the direction of Austria and Germany, the environmental law for the protection of the valuable Karst countryside (the first legislative intervention on behalf of the environment in Italy), the creation of the special *Fondo Trieste* that provided major funding for new capital projects with money from Rome, the promotion of the chain of international scientific institutions that has created a unique position for Trieste in Italy and abroad, indeed the setting up of the Autonomous Region of Friuli-Venezia Giulia itself, all stem from Corrado Belci's imaginative local leadership and untiring advocacy in Rome. I remember the excitement and privilege of being present as he made the case to the Minister of Science and Research for the Elettra Synchrotron Light Laboratory in the Science Park on the outskirts of Trieste. Again, it would not have happened without him.

The Historical and the Current Relationship with Yugoslavia and the Slovenes

Disarmingly disclaiming the presumption of historical research in favour of casual journalistic recollection, Corrado Belci identifies [●] the three histories of Trieste: the period of mercantile prosperity as the port of the Austro-Hungarian Empire; the period after the First World War when Trieste, handed to Italy by the Versailles Treaty, was the emblem of vibrant Italian nationalism (but also economic decline); and the third period after the Second World War when Trieste was neither prosperous nor safely anchored within the Italian Republic. Oscillating between enthusiasm and disappointment the city, as already noted the southernmost point of the Iron Curtain, was to be tormented for decades by the drama of the abandonment to Yugoslavia of Istria by the Allies, whose interest in cooperation with Tito after Tito's 1948 break with Stalin far outweighed any sympathy for the defeated former Axis power. It was inevitable that the emotional bitterness of the inhabitants should find its expression in the schism between the Italian and the Slovene populations. Little wonder that the iconoclastic British historian A. J. P. Taylor was an unwelcome figure in Trieste circles, for it was he who wrote that Trieste was the only city in Europe not to take its nationality from that of the surrounding countryside, indeed that *we can be more confident of the future of the Anglo-Soviet Alliance when we have learned to think of Trieste as Trst!'* [○] This was, it must be conceded, an argument that could be applied with equal force to the Italian towns in Istria – already in 1919 the Italian Prime Minister Vittorio Orlando had pressed

Woodrow Wilson at Versailles for a plebiscite in Fiume, confident of an Italian majority for unification with Italy, to be told by Wilson that the plebiscite must cover the entire region. This he would have lost.

Trieste, struggling under the conflicting burdens of the physical, cultural, and ethnic influences of its Friuli, Slav, Istrian and Dalmatian history, now had to emerge from a period of intense Italian nationalism, the inescapable reaction to the loss of Istria, to find its place in contemporary Italy. Corrado Belci put the question, the challenge, but as a politician also recognised the practical consequences: *'can we not become capable of making of the richness of our local differences, not barriers of incurable separation but diverse contributions to institutional unity? ... It is necessary to be strong enough to reject the prophecies of catastrophe ... and to work our way towards a solution that, if it is to be balanced, cannot at the same time satisfy everyone ...'* [●] [10]

In 1960 elections were due in the district of Duino-Aurisina, the future home of the Adriatic College. Here by long tradition the political masters were the Slovenes. But the Slovenes were themselves divided between the communists and the Catholics. Belci proposed to the provincial committee of his own party an approach to the Slovene Catholics for an alliance of party across the ethnic divide. It was, he argued, the responsibility of the Christian Democrats to accept the honours and the burdens (*'onori e oneri'*) of opening up in Trieste horizons based on a new future rather than on fear of the past. It would then be up to the Slovenes to accept the democratic challenge of the election on these terms. [11] He was given the authority to make this approach in absolute confidence and secrecy. He was met a few days later by the courteous but firm refusal of the Slovene Catholic leader to take part. Such a move, an alliance with an Italian political party, would, he was told, hand all Slovene electoral support to the communists. This was the mirror image of the arguments that Belci had faced within his own party. The election, following Belci's predictions, was won again by the Slovenes, the votes once again cast on ethnic lines.

Belci was forced back to his earlier recognition that the essential improvement in relations between Italians and Slovenes lay in the gradual, step-by-step overcoming of the opposing fears rooted in history. But his Duino

---

[●] For example (but not only here) in his *Trieste: Memorie di Trent'Anni*

[○] *New Statesman and Nation* December 1944, cited by Adam Sisman in his biography of A. J. P. Taylor

[●] It is difficult to give Corrado Belci's elegant Italian a comparable elegance in translation, and in this and other renderings in English I have taken some liberties with the original. Bilingual readers will be able to appreciate his language in the endnotes to this chapter

'initiative' led the subsequent Christian Democrat National Congress to adopt a report that formally accepted the need to recognise and to resolve the problems of the Slovene minority. This in turn led to parliamentary legislation that provided for the proper funding and recognition of Slovene language schools in the region; furthermore, also to eventual electoral reform that resulted in close and successful Italo-Slovene cooperation in the Duino-Aurisina constituency.

The report of the Christian Democratic Party on their new approach to the Slovene minority did not hesitate to place their policy in a Christian context. One assumes Belci authorship. The policy, it stated, was intended to demonstrate the ability of Christian doctrine and democratic principles to resolve the conflicts between different linguistic and ethnic groups through solutions that were humane and Christian in inspiration. [12]

Five years later, in 1965, at a time of enormous stress between the Italian and the Slovene communities in Trieste, a Slovene was nominated for membership of the City Council. Opponents assembled 52,000 signatures in protest. Even the Bishop of Trieste, the famed Bishop Santin of Istrian origin, contributed anonymous but easily identifiable articles to the local press. Belci's response: he went secretly to the home of the Slovene nominee, a certain Dusan Hreschak, and achieved an immediate human relationship.

Christianity in Politics

Belci, I heard one Trieste businessman say, was the only Christian and the only democrat in the Christian Democratic Party. This casual, categorical statement may be an injustice towards many, but it illustrates Belci's impregnable reputation for integrity. In his 20 years as parliamentary representative for Trieste he did not enter private homes other than those of family and personal friends to preclude in advance any suggestion of secretive influence or corruption. (When President of the College and driving between Duino and Trieste he would for related reasons never pick up a girl student hitchhiking on her own.) His moral principles were unshakeable. But those unaccustomed to the religious element in active politics will nonetheless find his views clear but undogmatic, tolerant and illuminating.

It was probably not by chance that the two defeated and clearly guilty war nations, Germany and Italy, embarked on post-war politics with Christian Democratic Parties. Conscience and spiritual revival were key necessities in the rehabilitation of these two countries. The former President of the German Federal Republic, Richard von Weizsäcker,

has described in his memoirs the attractions for him of the socialist ethic, of the 19th-century achievements of the Liberals in favour of the democratic ideal, and his difficulties over the 'C' in the Christian Democratic Union (CDU). *'Christ did not proclaim a political programme. He did not say: "that is the truth". He said: "I am the truth".'* [●] But he became a Christian Democrat. As he writes, the 'C', abused by some, was a stimulus for some and an irritation for others. It remained a thorn in the flesh, and therein lay its most important legitimacy.

It was the priest Don Sturzo who engaged the Italian Catholic Church in politics after the Vatican in 1919 reversed its opposition to overt Catholic political involvement. Don Sturzo's People's Party (*Partito Popolare Italiano, PPI*) was critical to the formation of all governments between 1919 and 1924 and profoundly hostile to the Fascists. Under pressure from Mussolini, Don Sturzo was forced into exile in 1924. With his departure, the Vatican gave its support to the creation of the *Unione Nazionale,* a pro-Fascist Catholic political party, which opened the way for right-wing Catholics to join the Fascists. The fateful culmination of this process was the Lateran Treaty of 1929 under which the Vatican became a state independent of the Italian monarchy. Catholicism was recognised as the Italian state religion. This persuaded these same right-wing Catholics, the so-called *Clerici Fascisti,* of Mussolini's legitimacy. Mussolini's persecution of the Left, and his underestimated criminality, gave Catholics of a more spiritual persuasion no alternative but to make explicit their opposition. Thus we have not only a divided country but also a divided Church. The transition of many priests into the war-time resistance against both their countrymen Fascists and the Nazi occupiers was a natural progression, however perplexing for those who view the Church and political action, especially if associated with violence, as things apart. But in the Italian Resistance the divisions persisted as well. It was bitterly fragmented within itself, above all between the Catholics and the Communists, and above all in the eastern areas of Friuli bordering Yugoslavia, where Tito's Slovene partisans were fighting, not for Allied victory but for a Yugoslav and communist post-war takeover.

As in the German Federal Republic under Adenauer, so in Italy under Alcide de Gasperi: the country allied itself with the Western Alliance and NATO. The strength of the

[●] *,Christus selbst verkündet kein politisches Program. Er sagt nicht: Das ist die Wahrheit. Vielmehr sagt er: Ich bin die Wahrheit.'* Richard von Weizsäcker: *Vier Zeiten* page 147 Pantheon-Ausgabe March 2010

Italian communist challenge to this policy is a matter of history. Less well known and less appreciated was the determination of the Christian Democratic Party to regard their left-wing opponents first and foremost as Italians and as fellow citizens, to win them over for the democratic process. They therefore worked patiently and persistently to develop the distinction between the Italian communists and Stalinists. In his *1978: Moro, la DC, Il Terrorismo*, Corrado Belci describes the private dinner that he and his colleague Bodrato attended with the then US Ambassador, Richard Gardner, in 1976. This was the critical moment when it seemed possible that, in the next election, the Communist Party might actually overtake the Christian Democrats in votes cast, the prospect summarised in the lapidary phrase *il sorpasso*.

'*Do you not think*', Ambassador Gardner asks, '*that it would be better to have the communists perhaps a little more Stalinist but reduced to 27%, rather than have Berlinguer's communists at 34%?*' Bodrato replied courteously but firmly: '*but look, Ambassador, we must remember that this 34% of communists is not made up of Soviet divisions but of Italian citizens. And we have to understand why they vote communist and promote their democratic development.*' [13]

When Benigno Zaccagnini, a man intensely admired by Belci, left for Rome for the first time as a newly elected Deputy, he was told by his bishop: '*Benigno, a Christian does not go to Montecitorio* (the Italian parliamentary building) *to do politics but to live the teachings of Christ.*'. [14] And Belci again quotes with unconditional approval the appreciation of another DC colleague in a memorial address: '*he understood politics to be public service, a direct corollary of the commitment accepted by those who dared to apply the adjective Christian to their political activities …*' [15]

He had set his own course from the very start, as we have already seen in his Pola days. And it was that same priest, Don Marzari, who articulated the relationship between Church and State that was to remain his moral and political compass. '*The state has as its objective the secular culture of society's earthly wellbeing. The Church's objective is sanctity (in the sense of eternal salvation), (again in society – "in hoc mundo"). Secular culture therefore and sanctity – these are the two terms: sacred and profane. Distinct but not separable (as the laity would have it), if there is not to be mutual harm: a civilisation insensitive to religious feeling, a sanctity closed to the anxieties of life on earth. The responsibility of both is therefore a striving for mutual openness, of correction that must however, if it is to be healthy, lasting and magnanimous, be achieved as self-correction.*' [16]

Indeed, it is my conviction that the post-war years of the 1950s, the 1960s and the 1970s in Italian politics, the patient struggle to bring the large communist party into responsible parliamentary activity on condition that it abandoned Stalinism, the courageous fight to establish the roots of true democracy ('*la democrazia compiuta*', to echo the phrase so often used by Belci), in a society that had previously seen much of even its Catholic faith absorbed by Fascist ambition, may rightly be called years of moral, even spiritual struggle. Democratic survival of the terrorism of the 1970s, the '*years of lead*', would not have been possible without the steady preparation of the earlier period. And to appreciate the challenges, it is enough to recall that as late as 1960, 62 of the 64 Prefects of the Republic had been functionaries under fascism, and that this was also true of <u>all</u> 135 police chiefs. [●]

Evidence in support comes, significantly, from the communist side, for the Communist Leader Berlinguer, whose wife, we may note, attended Mass daily, had this to say at a communist rally in Bologna in 1977: '*Another task awaits the communists: to achieve communism in the highest spheres of capitalism, to create a "revolution in the West", demonstrating that socialism can and must be indissolubly linked with all civil, cultural and religious liberties.*' [17] And, also in 1977, he responded to a request from the Catholic Church that he should seek from the Soviet communists an attitude of greater openness and tolerance towards religious belief with the following words: '*There exists and is active within the PCI (Partito Comunista Italiano) the wish not only to build up and make alive a lay and democratic party … which does not in fact seek to combat Christian values*' but even '*has the intention of working together with others to create a society that, without being Christian, is organised in such a way as to be always open and welcoming to Christian values …*' [18]

For politicians who, with Belci, acted '*not in the name of faith, no; but inspired by faith, yes…*', [19] the decline in support for Catholic values in the 1960s and 1970s was remorseless. Furthermore, as even the most casual observer will have noted, politics in Rome in the past 20 years have no longer turned on these values, and the spiritual struggles that underpinned the political debate have long passed away, the victims not of communism but of the more debilitating temptations of corruption, materialism, the manipulation of the media and the exercise of power for the sake of power. To Belci and his like-minded colleagues,

[●] The historian Tony Judt gives these figures in his epilogue *The Past is another Country* page 302 of *The Politics of Retribution in Europe: World War II and its Aftermath*, edited by István Deák, Jan T. Gross, and Tony Judt. Princeton University Press 2000

all this must have seemed akin to blasphemy. But before he closed his parliamentary career in 1980, he faced the two major challenges of his political life.

The Treaty of Osimo

Firmness on the part of Churchill and the Allies had successfully expelled Tito's partisans from Trieste in 1945 after 45 days of terror, but the major part of the Istrian peninsula had remained in Yugoslav hands, the so-called Zone B, pending a final settlement.

It is an intriguing footnote to the history of the area to know the background to this final settlement. In 1973 Tito instructed Boris Snuderl, the President of the Federal Committee for Foreign Economic Relations, to set up a confidential line of communication with the Italian government. Snuderl turned to Eugenio Carboni, the Director General of the Ministry of Industry. This led to a private conversation between Carboni and Tito. Tito's line of argument has been recorded in writing.

Italy, he realised, had decided to postpone a settlement *ad infinitum*. He understood the reasons – the resentments of the *Istriani*, and the power of the right wing in Italian politics. These were ideological sentiments that would not go away. But international politics face tight deadlines. One was his death. Italians might assume that, after his death, they would face a disintegrating Yugoslavia. Perhaps! But in that case they would be confronted by weakened nationalistic republics, and weakened parties will not give an inch. Italy had its problems. So had Yugoslavia – Bulgarian ambitions in Macedonia and other pressures both national and international. *'Italy must reflect and choose the time for an agreement; before my death or after, measuring all the unknowns. Before will be easier, after more difficult'* [●] [20]

Inevitably, the negotiations were conducted in secret and lasted two years. When they became known, the sense of betrayal was inescapable. Public tension in Italy and especially in Trieste leading up to parliamentary ratification of the resulting Treaty of Osimo that assigned Istria to Yugoslavia is all too easily imaginable, even at this distance in time.

Suggestions were made that the role of *relatore*, the person responsible for piloting the bill through Parliament, might be taken by a Christian Democrat from Sicily, not by accident the furthermost point from Trieste. Corrado

Belci was clear that this was his direct, indeed his inescapable responsibility. *'I understood that, as the Member of Parliament elected for Trieste, I had no alternative. To have remained silent would have been craven; to have opposed it would have meant going against my carefully reasoned convictions; to speak out in favour (as I did) meant restraining, subduing emotions and moving in the direction opposed to the state of mind of the people.'* [●] [21]

Corrado Belci's speech to the Italian Parliament on the Treaty had little prospect of an understanding audience in Trieste but a fellow deputy nonetheless had this to say: *'I do not share your point of view, but I compliment you nonetheless. I acknowledge the historical context in which you have placed the matter. You made a serious and dignified speech.'* [22]

This meant also the end of his political career, for re-election by the angry electorate in Trieste was impossible. He did not hesitate, dismissing tributes to his courage and integrity with light-hearted comment that he had already exceeded the time he had promised his wife he would spend in politics. For him the Treaty was *'a necessary humiliation to turn the page of history … to begin again to exist, to live as a nation'*. [23] But just as when he had spoken up on behalf of the Slovene schools and the Slovene theatre in Trieste, so again now his children were subjected to insults and abuse not only from their fellow pupils but also from their teachers, and for a time police protection was necessary. On the political front, Osimo led to the creation in Trieste of the right-wing nationalistic Melone Party, the emblem of the melon taken from a carving in the city cathedral of San Giusto. It was also the end of years of almost undisputed Christian Democratic rule in the City and the Region.

Corrado Belci later wrote an admirably calibrated, sensitive account of the history of the border between Italy and her eastern neighbours from the time of President Wilson's proposals in 1919 up to 1945. He has written too about the Osimo Treaty and the Schengen Agreements, although his later ill-health prevented him from bringing this work to the point of publication. But the relationship is clear: without Osimo, there can have been no Schengen. Osimo is the Italian counterpart of the recognition by the government of Willy Brandt of the Oder-Neisse Line between Germany and Poland. The German formerly communist writer Manes Sperber has this chilling reflection in his memoirs: *'in the cemetery of things past the dead do not lie under the gravestones; they crouch and cower on top*

[●] This account from Corrado Belci: Trieste – *Memorie di Trent'Anni 1945–1975* page 183

[●] *Trieste – Memorie di Trent'Anni* page 189.

of them, the oppressors alongside their victims'. [●] It was Corrado Belci's rare accomplishment to have enabled, in time, so many of these unhappy creatures to withdraw more peacefully into their final resting place.

The Kidnap and Assassination of Aldo Moro

The constant, patient attempts by the Christian Democrats, led in this endeavour above all by Aldo Moro, to enroll the Italian communists in a responsible way in the democratic and parliamentary processes, provoked fierce mistrust in right-wing circles and also, significantly, among Catholics who feared the communist influence. It is well known that the Americans, intensely focused on the reliability of NATO, of which Italy with its Mediterranean ports was an important but not entirely transparent partner, shared these anxieties. But the internal social tensions are perhaps best illustrated by the attitudes of a number of prominent intellectuals, expressed for example in this 1971 statement published by, among others, Umberto Eco and Natalia Ginzburg: '... *when they (the extremists) shout "class war, let us arm the masses", we shout with them, and when they commit themselves to "take up arms against the state to achieve freedom from the bosses and from exploitation", we commit ourselves with them.'* [○] [24]

The Osimo Treaty was another flashpoint. Some even called for the prosecution of certain Ministers under Article 241 of the Italian Criminal Code which mandates a life sentence for those found guilty of aiding and abetting a foreign power to exert its sovereignty over the national territory.

The Red Brigade of the 1970s, paralleled by similar movements in other countries, notably Western Germany, was thus not without troublesome social and intellectual support.

When Aldo Moro, then the President of the Christian Democratic Party after having previously been Prime Minister for five years, was kidnapped on March 16th 1978, the five members of his escort shot dead on the spot, Corrado Belci on the central executive of the Party was one of four or five responsible for leading the government

and the country through those dark days. Aldo Moro had been not only a political colleague but a close personal friend. I have a vivid picture of Corrado Belci during those 55 days of Moro's captivity, wearing bullet-proof protection, spending each night on police advice in a different location, telephoning his wife Laura every hour to reassure her that he was still alive. The dilemma is all too easily recalled in cool analytical terms over 30 years on: does the government negotiate with terrorists, or does it maintain the authority of the democratic state?

The noted political journalist Arrigo Levi, subsequently Diplomatic Counsellor to two successive Italian Presidents in the Quirinale, remembers his first brief meeting with Corrado at the height of the crisis '... *in those horrific days for Italian history, when the life of Aldo Moro was at stake and nothing could be done to save him if one cared for the survival of democracy in Italy ...'* [25]

After it was all over, Moro's bullet-ridden corpse recovered from the boot of a car, the Minister of the Interior Rognoni, whilst expressing his absolute endorsement of the government's stern refusal to compromise the principles of democracy, reminded the assembled members of Parliament on 24th October: *'There is also Moro the prisoner, Moro the victim, and we cannot move ourselves away from him, silently take our distance, leave him to his fate without an effort of true understanding ...'* [26] When, to quote Belci again from a different context, must the intransigence of principle prevail, when give way to the flexibility of realism?

Corrado Belci lost many friends and colleagues at the hands of the terrorist Red Brigade in the 1970s. He often spoke too of his friend Pietro Mattarella, President of the Region of Sicily, with whom he had a long telephone conversation on the Sunday morning of 6th January 1978; when he returned from Mass two hours later Mattarella was dead, shot down in this instance not by the Red Brigade but by the Mafia. [●]

But, looking back, Belci was clear. The propaganda success of the Red Brigade had been to make it appear as if the life of Moro lay in the hands of the government. In reality it was the terrorists who had the power to decide his fate. *'For the most seriously-minded students, contestation*

[●] *'Im Friedhof des Vergangenen liegen die Toten nicht unter den Grabsteinen, sie kauern auf ihnen; die Verfolger neben ihren Opfern.'* Manes Sperber: *Bis man mir Scherben auf die Augen legt.*

[○] Cited by Belci and Bodrato *Moro, la DC, il Terrorismo, 1987* page 137.

[●] We are sometimes scornful of Italian courage, and we do well to note that, in the crowded cathedral of the funeral service, his younger brother Sergio rose and announced to the congregation that he was henceforth assuming his brother's political role – he was later as Minister of Public Instruction to take the recognition of the International Baccalaureate through the Italian Parliament.

was a "problem for discussion", for the extremists it was "a solution"...' [27] But the underlying issue was not in doubt. 'The truth is that The Red Brigade sought one thing only: political recognition, that is to say, recognition of their killings as acts of was against an arbitrary state that must be destroyed ...' [28] And as to those who allowed themselves dogmatic judgements: 'What a difference in humanity, of truly wounded humanity, between his immense suffering ... in the endless hours of those atrocious days, and the contrasting, as shameless as it was false, of a policy of no compromise with a policy of negotiation, both based more on abstract political concepts than on the reality of the facts and human behaviour ...' [29]

In his book on the Moro tragedy, Corrado Belci with characteristic openness cites the American historian George Mosse, co-incidentally an early Kurt Hahn pupil in Salem. Mosse questions the validity and durability of a political philosophy so dependent on one or two personalities. 'What foundation could an agreement have which rested on a base as fragile as the life and will of one man? And what foundation could a political concept have that rested on the relationship between two men, even two as influential as Berlinguer and Moro?' [30]

Belci replies robustly that the political concepts advanced by Moro would live on. However, the proposals for compromise and cooperation between the then ruling Christian Democratic Party and the Italian Communist Party, to the evident relief of NATO allies and above all the United States, disappeared from the scene, but the days of the Christian Democratic Party in power were also numbered.

The DC congress of February 1980 marked the sea change. Moro, Mattarella and other major figures were missing – assassinated. Belci spoke briefly. Moro's message was forgotten. The Party closed in on itself, intent only on remaining in power – power without a democratic mandate. The growing secularisation and the social transformation – the Christian Democrats had for example lost referendums on divorce and abortion – had led to a lack of party unity and of a clear mission. 'The concept of politics descended into the sole aim of retaining power – to be parcelled out differently, yes, but never abandoned – and thus were born the conditions leading to a "logical" alliance between economic and political interests or, as would be said later in the face of the devastating consequences of "tangentopoli", [●] between business and politics.' [31]

[●] Shorthand for all the scandals that erupted in Italy in the early 1990s

It is Belci's last public appearance on the national scene. His final effort had been to propose the resignation of the entire Central Committee of the Party. As he explained to his local newspaper Il Piccolo on 31st July 1981: '... the outlook of the party must no longer be focussed on the sole exercise of power. We are a party of government, but we must also become a party that knows how to struggle, that knows how to interpret the needs of society. We cannot remain exclusively concerned with power.' [32] And he quotes the private comment to him of Nile Lotti, a prominent, highly respected member of the Communist Party: 'The conclusions of your Party congress were a great lost opportunity for Italian democracy.' [33]

Corrado Belci's leave-taking of active national politics coincided with the end of the post-war era in which Italian politics were fought over moral and ideological issues, inspired on his side by the Catholic faith. Perhaps this timing was not entirely coincidental. But he did not retreat into inner cynicism or despair, although the books he now wrote, and the articles that he contributed to the press, made no bones about his disdain for the immorality of the new politics. Rather he welcomed the analysis of the priest Mons. Clemente Riva who wrote about an irreversible process with 'its negative aspects, that are perhaps underestimated, but also with certain positive elements, because (this change) finally marks the transition from a faith that was for the most part sociological to a more personal faith ... challenging the Church to dedicate itself to a pastoral mission that is more patient and more laborious than before, and ultimately to a faith that is more demanding and more difficult ...' [34]

The College Presidency

Corrado Belci was in the Ministry of Foreign Trade when Facco Bonetti's first report on the Atlantic College arrived in Rome. He was therefore in at the very beginning. Freed from parliamentary duties in 1980 he was, it seemed, the natural choice to lead the College. President Comelli of the Region of Friuli-Venezia Giulia was however anxious to secure his appointment by a unanimous vote in the Regional Government and refused, with impeccable wisdom, to be rushed. Belci was, after all, the man who had seen the Osimo Treaty through the national Parliament, and who had withdrawn from politics in anticipation of electoral defeat for his party in Trieste. Thus it was that the nomination of the College's President preceded the arrival of the first students by very few weeks. It was well worth the wait.

Corrado Belci's continuing national profile was key to the survival and success of the College. Having been

A happy and fruitful partnership! Tony Besse and Corrado Belci

the editor of the Party daily, *Il Popolo*, in Rome from 1976 until 1980, he had also become, in 1980 (for two years) the editor of the party weekly, *La Discussione*. He remained a member of the central committee of the Party which, with its 30 members, reviewed the candidates for ministerial posts when his Party was in power. Little wonder therefore that he could secure audiences, responses, the attention of the leading politicians, or that in the late afternoon, by custom a dead time in Rome when Ministers are signing their papers, he could interrupt them freely. And despite Osimo, he was most carefully listened to in the Region, for his continuing national influence was recognised, and he was after all a father of both the Region itself and of the substantial *Fondo Trieste* that was critical to numerous regional capital investment programmes, yet itself remained dependent on continuing funding from the central government.

It was his experience of 30 years of confronting the political and ethnic problems of Trieste and the Region that enabled him to place the College at the centre of Italian cultural foreign policy, for from the start the College's central focus was the divide between Western and Eastern Europe. The Ministry of Foreign Affairs was able to associate its funding of the College with scholarships for students from Central and Eastern Europe who soon comprised some 60 or more in a total enrolment of 200. The Region too, with its special 'autonomous' statute granted by Rome in recognition of its geographical and political position, was awarded special funding from Rome and supported the College in turn for this very same purpose. Governmental funding also provided scholarships for students from the small surviving Italian community in Istria, for students from developing countries, and for the sons and daughters of Italian émigré communities in Europe, mainly Germany, Latin America and Australia. Teachers, usually three at a time, were seconded by the Italian Ministry of Public Instruction.

This may all sound dry and formal. But the overriding memory of working with Corrado Belci is one of straight-forward enjoyment. He was in his office in the College every morning that he was not absent in Rome or elsewhere. He was a master of the telephone. Whenever he asked a secretary to make a connection for him he would insist on being ready on the line to ensure that the person being called would find himself in immediate contact with him. Every meeting – they were daily – included coffee and laughter. I remember him arriving one morning in our third year, gesturing silently for coffee, then leaning back in his chair with a contented smile: Now, he said, they must take us seriously, our deficit is so large – and he explained that status in Italy is defined first and foremost by the size of your debts. [35] (I remember our meeting with the Mayor of Quebec, who was telling us that he might be able to allocate us some scholarship funds from his expected surplus that year. Corrado made me translate three times – he was unable to believe that I had understood or translated correctly.) But after smiling about the deficit, he stated his problem in very simple terms. He was usually given 30 minutes with potential sponsors. He needed 25 minutes to explain the College and was left with only five to ask for the money. These figures, he said, had to be reversed. And he then commissioned a two-month-long public relations campaign in all the major Italian newspapers and journals, carefully coordinated to ensure that the College appeared somewhere in the press every single day throughout this period, at a cost of about £80,000. It was the best early investment we made and marked the first turning point in the College's finances. And he was always very carefully focused – he refused to move anywhere to make an approach that was aimed at less than a full two-year scholarship.

He understood what 'sold'. It was not long before the Region found itself adding scholarships for students from areas in conflict – they funded our first Palestinian and Israeli students, for example. The College's programme of mother tongue languages – at one stage we were providing mother tongue tuition by some 30 native speaking tutors, a programme unmatched by any other IB school and a powerful tool in pastoral care, almost more important than the linguistic benefit – sounds like an imaginative educational initiative. It was his idea, for this, he said, would convince all observers that we were serious about international understanding; and again he was right. He took the traditional Opening of the Academic Year ceremonies of the Italian universities and turned them into memorable Opening Ceremonies of our own – in the cities of the Region, in Milan, Florence, Turin, Rome; and abroad in Ljubljana, Vienna, Budapest, Stuttgart, Strasbourg and Geneva. The visits to Slovenia and Hungary preceded the fall of the Iron Curtain and of the Berlin Wall. All of this, of

Romani Prodi, the Italian Prime Minister, names the College's science laboratories after the Nobel Prize laureate Rita Levi-Montalcini

course, was presented to the regional authorities as first-rate publicity for them, as indeed it was, and the Region paid many of the costs.

He did not hesitate to find the money to fund the then IB Journal *Contact* from within the College, nor to provide the premises and many associated costs when for a period of some years it was found necessary to site the work of the UWC International Secretariat in Duino.

Travelling in Australia with a delegation from the Region to celebrate an important anniversary of 'Giuliani' living there, he met the famed Trio of Trieste chamber music trio: the pianist Dario De Rosa, the violinist Renato Zanettovich and the 'cellist Amedeo Baldovino who, with one exception, had played together since they were boys in shorts – early photographs bear witness to their precocious talents. He was dismayed that the City had not given them the recognition their achievements world-wide merited. On his return, he secured the necessary funding and established the Trio of Trieste International School of Chamber Music within the College, with the addition of specialist teaching facilities. In addition to their master classes for young professional musicians, the three *Maestri* taught the small number of college students whose musical backgrounds qualified them for this privileged tuition. Later, for a few years, the College provided scholarships for musically gifted students selected on the basis of their talents through the UWC national committees. It is instructive to note some of the countries that, against initial expectations, won the most awards under this sadly short-lived programme: Albania, Argentina, Belarus, Colombia, Croatia, Hong Kong (China), Kazakhstan, Lithuania, Malta, Malaysia, Mongolia, Poland, Vietnam and Zimbabwe. Many of these musical scholars were in their later training to bring the College to the lively attention of the leading music academies in London and Boston, greatly enhancing our reputation.

Corrado Belci was contagiously enthusiastic about the College's potential for encouraging other schools across

Central and Eastern Europe to adopt the International Baccalaureate and took a direct role, also without the slightest hesitation, in seeking the funds to create a major travelling exhibition on the IB. At his insistence the Region and the Ministry in Rome sponsored the Third Inter-Governmental Meeting of the IB Council of Foundation, hosted in Trieste and presided over by the Italian Minister of Public Instruction; likewise a meeting of the UWC International Council in Duino under the Chairmanship of HRH The Prince of Wales, with no costs to delegates beyond their personal travel. And all successive Presidents of the Italian Republic either received the College in the Quirinal Palace in Rome or visited the College personally.

It all sounds so easy, but Belci revealed the nature of the burden when, having after 15 years announced his retirement from active College affairs, he gave an interview to the local newspaper: '… *intense work, to be undertaken full time.*' [36] The accompanying photograph of his tired face is almost more evocative than his words, and there were indeed hard moments, none more so than in 1993.

The College on the Verge of Closure

At this point the College, with its 200 students all on full scholarship (a tiny minority of National Committees insisted on family contribution to the fees, but at no stage in the College's history up to this moment had the total of family contributions ever exceeded 1% of the overall budget), received scholarship income under the following headings:

1.4 billion Lire	Students from Developing Countries
1 million Lire	Students from Italian émigré families abroad
300 million Lire	Students from Friuli-Venezia Giulia
c. 300 million Lire	Students from other Italian regions (Piemonte, Veneto, Emilia Romagna, Trentino Alto Adige, Sardegna and Lazio)
1 billion Lire	Students from areas bordering Italy (Law no. 19 of 1991)
c. 2 billion Lire	UWC National Committees, Italian banks and industry

These contributions covered the then College budget that amounted to a total of some six billion Lire or three million Euros. In the early autumn of 1993, a series of scandals led the Ministry of Foreign Affairs to cancel at a stroke its entire budget for developing countries.

The Law no. 19 of 1991 was due to expire in 1994.

Financial crises led to the cancellation of almost all regional scholarships outside Friuli-Venezia Giulia and of a large part of the sponsorship from industry, business and the banks.

Within the space of some four weeks almost two-thirds of the College's budget had disappeared. The closure of the College appeared inevitable. The crisis persisted into the spring of 1994, and I well recall the meeting in my office at which it was decided, with somewhat question-able legality, to postpone notification of our dilemma to the relevant court authorities in Trieste. But for the time being the engagement of staff and the acceptance of new students for September 1994 were frozen.

Corrado Belci now achieved a series of *tours de force*.

The first was to have inserted a one-off 'extraordinary' contribution of one billion Lire (€500,000) into the budget of the organisation The Central European Initiative which, again thanks to Belci's influence, had its headquarters in Trieste. This was achieved with the Law 556 of December 1993.

There was now no other way forward than a law dedi-cated exclusively to the College. But to draft and to guide a law through Parliament without the prior certainty that funds would be available for its implementation would have been a straightforward, costly waste of time. The situation was gravely aggravated by the imminent end of the current legislative period. It was therefore essential to secure the endorsement of the Ministry of the Treasury before contemplating the drafting of legislation.

There then occurred one of those miracles that are said to favour the brave. Corrado Belci sought a meeting with the governmental Auditor General in Rome, dott. Andrea Monorchio. He did not know Monorchio, but when he ente-red his room, he was met with '*You do not need to explain the College to me. I know all about it.*' Monorchio summoned a member of his staff, the situation was explained; Belci took the flight back home and found a draft law awaiting him on his facsimile machine on his arrival. This first attempt failed. The draft Law to which the College's needs were to be attached had, it rapidly became clear, no prospect of parliamentary approval. So the College's needs were included in another draft law. Giorgio Pontoni, the Director of Administration, was sent down to Rome with a revised text. When he arrived he found that a document had already been finalised and sent to the Prime Minister's office by motor cyclist for signature as the deadline was that very same evening. It has only to be added that an Italian *Decreto Legge*, of which this was one, requires formal renewal every 60 days until definitively approved by Parliament.

This 'Decree/Law', controversial because, like the typical family suitcase, it had something in it for everybody and was therefore highly irregular, was originally dated 29th April 1994. It was reconfirmed on 27th June 1994, 27th August 1994, 28th October 1994, 28th December 1994, 25th February 1995, 29th April 1995 and 28th June 1995. This last was the final extension, but the College had achieved its breathing space, however precarious. And it led to a longer-lasting although not permanent solution, for in a new law [•] concerning foreign affairs and defence, the College was included through an annual subvention of four billion Lire (€2 million).

Legislative approval of this law now required intensive lobbying at both the regional and the national level. Describing these events afterwards, Corrado Belci cited above all the composition of the College student body as the decisive argument: in round figures, one quarter from developing countries, one quarter from the industrialised world, one quarter from Italy, one quarter (this latter quarter the most influential factor) from Central and Eastern Europe. The campaign was supported wholeheartedly by all local politicians irrespective of Party.

Corrado Belci's Personal Impact

Corrado Belci left the College Presidency in the summer of 1997. He had always written whilst active in politics as a journalist and as editor of the two major journals of his Party. In retirement he became the historian and biographer that could so easily have been his professional calling had he not responded with such dedication to the challenges of active citizenship. He is as wonderfully eloquent on paper as orally. He had little English, but his rather puzzling weakness in this and other foreign languages, not uncommon in Italians of his generation, was intriguingly compensated for by a quality expressed in one simple word that he used often: *'intuisco'*. He seemed to absorb the messages of others by personal osmosis, by an intuitive understanding of circumstances and motives. And the process operated also in reverse, for his ability to communicate his sentiments and his convictions – and his human sympathies – to others never faltered. I think this was the secret of his relationship with College teachers and College students, with whom he had few direct conversations (there were of course notable exceptions), but all of whom had the equally instinctive reassurance that

[•] Law No. 295 of 13th July 1995 Article 1

Corrado never missed, or failed to enjoy, a college occasion when not away from Trieste

he understood them and their needs and was looking after them.

I suspect this is a common human experience; the older one becomes, the more one looks back to the influence of one's parents and grandparents. Corrado Belci, it seems to me, drew much inner inspiration and guidance from his grandmother, Nona Marieta. He describes her daily, early morning visits to the church. Who knows where she prayed, whether she prayed, whether she took communion, because she was always alone on her silent pilgrimage to meet the great Maria after whom she was named. *'A meeting of silence, of course. But, in this kind of dialogue, silence is a channel of communication that is far more effective than many words, that can hide a richness of content and of exchanges that no sound, not even music, can express.'* [37] It is her modesty, her humility, which he recalls above all. *'… the two Marias, in their daily conversations, will have certainly accumulated, between capital and interest, a heritage of humility sufficient to exceed with a positive balance the excessive and flashy dose of arrogance generated daily by humanity, at least that of Dignano* (her little home town) *…'* [38]

Little of which could be said about politicians! Interviewed by the local newspaper, he had this to say about headline-seeking politicians: *'The country is not a stage but a difficult community of men and history. Mussolini performed better than Don Sturzo, than De Gasperi, Vanoni and Moro. I prefer those who perform less well. If I want entertainment I go to the theatre. If I must do politics, I know I am in for a difficult time.'* [39]

On history: *'History is easy to read because it is written in the past; living it in the present is a good deal more difficult.'* [40]

On nationalism and patriotism: *'Nationalism is the intensification of love of country to the point of absolute worship of race and nationality, denying the positions of others; whilst the awareness of nationality is the fruit of the exaltation of the human personality with its duties and its rights, among them that of loving one's country whilst respecting the national loyalties of others …'* [41] He wrote these lines for *L'Arena di Pola* at the age of 20.

On Italy's role when seeking additional concessions in Versailles in 1919: *'the concessions to Italy in the Treaty of London (of 1915) included all the objectives that had been among the aims of the Risorgimento but then went much further, because elements were added to them that clearly exceeded those objectives and belonged to the sphere of power politics, all under the label of the needs of security*

… the people were fascinated by the prospect of "national grandeur" as a cure for internal problems …' [42]

And the consequences for Italy in 1945: *'The frontier that after the First World War had been considered by Italy an insult and a mutilation was invoked after the second as a last hope … some said that we should bang our fists on the negotiating table, but to this table we were not even admitted …'* [43]

On his acceptance of the need for time, patience and tolerance in resolving historical problems: *'there exists neither the day nor the month nor the year; there is neither a partial nor a complete law that can mark the final solution of a problem that will remain for generations with those who live on national boundaries, the solution of which must be entrusted to the recognition of diversity as enrichment rather than as a cause for conflict. A long and difficult journey, strewn with stops and stumbles …'* [44]

On his recognition of the need for clear and courageous leadership: *'… unity on a given line, not unanimity in confusion …'* accompanied by constant self-questioning: *'… as is wise on all complex issues, to insert "at the foot of truth" a touch of doubt …'* [45]

His best-selling book, to his own amusement and satisfaction, was his *Il Libro della Bora*, a richly illustrated history of this legendary fierce, bitterly cold easterly wind that

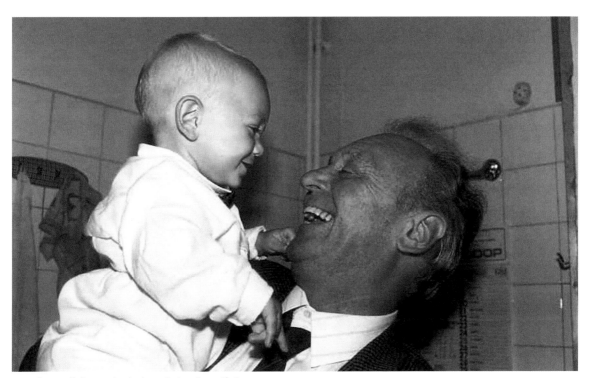

… and, most of all, an enthusiastic and beloved grandfather

Corrado Belci leaves the editorship of the Christian Democrat Party Journal La Discussione

forms part of the culture and history of Trieste. How often he told us of his delight on discovering that the foremost world expert on the Trieste *bora* was a professor in Japan!

But the words that his United World College of the Adriatic will treasure most are those on peacemaking: *'peace is not a comfortable process … it is that little fragment that the young students of the United World College put together … it is the courageous creating of peace between former enemies without waiting for the other to begin, it is that continuous process of giving without receiving in return, above all without knowing whether and when the process will ever achieve completion.'* [46]

Corrado Belci died on Tuesday 3rd May 2011 after prolonged illness. Characteristically, he had asked that there be no formal tributes at the funeral Mass. He had written his own epitaph when recalling his grandfather in Dignano: *'… to speak with the language of St. Paul, he had completed his course when he had exhausted his batteries, and had returned his mandate to its origins. He had fulfilled it in the paths of righteousness'.* [47]

On the first anniversary of his death, family, friends and former political colleagues gathered in an evening of commemoration. We may all treasure the words of Guido Bodrato: *'the greatest act of love for Trieste by Hon. Belci was his creation of the United World College of the Adriatic'.* [48]

Italian Language Quotations

[1] *"Prima di avere il bagno in casa, papà mi accompagnava al bagno comunale una volta alla settimana e mi immergeva nella vasca insaponandomi dai capelli in giù. Gli occhi bruciavano un po', io me ne lamentavo, e trovavo troppo calda l'acqua nella vasca. Papà la toccava con il gomito, poi diceva: "Va dentro, va dentro, movite, che no' scota".*

[2] *"Cerreto: cinque minuti speto. Pisar sí, cagar no."*

[3] *"Una cosa è l'istruzione, un'altra l'intelligenza, ci può essere l'intelligente non instruito e l'istruito imbecille…".*

[4] *"… avere la propria opinione personale, esprimerla e farla valere in una maniera confacente al bene comune … esprimere il proprio parere sui doveri e i sacrifici, che gli vengono imposti; non essere costretto ad ubbidire senza essere ascoltato – ecco due diritti del cittadino, che trovano nella democrazia, come indica il suo nome stesso, la loro espressione …".*

[5] *"Presidente, ho bisogno di parlare urgentemente con Lei a nome della comunità italiana di Pola".*

[6] *"Il governo rappresenta una nazione che ha dichiarato la guerra ed ha perso, il suo peso internazionale è sotto lo zero".*

[7] *"Non sarò mai dottore perché interromperò gli studi universitari per conquistare il mestiere di giornalista …".*

[8] *"Prima de cagar a casa mia dovarè doprar le mine. Nient'altro …".*

[9] *"Non è mai diventato uno di quelli che, una volta andati a Roma, si sono lasciati assimilare dalla capitale."*

[10] *"Come non essere capaci di fare delle diversità locali anziché barriere di insanabile separazione, utili varietà di una istituzione unitaria? … bisognava essere capaci di respingere i catastrofismi … e avviarsi con convinzione verso una soluzione che, se era equilibrata, non poteva veder contento nessuno …".*

[11] *"onori o oneri di aprire a Trieste una prospettiva fondata su un nuovo futuro piuttosto che sulla paura del passato. Sarebbe poi stata la volta degli Sloveni democratici di misurarsi e dire di sí o di no".*

[12] *"… la DC doveva porre il problema dei rapporti tra i due gruppi etnici in una luce nuova "che testimoni la capacità della dottrina cristiana e del metodo democratico di dare al rapporto di convivenza, anche tra gruppi di lingue diverse, una soluzione umana e profondamente cristiana …".*

[13] *"Ma vede, ambasciatore, dobbiamo ricordare che quel 34 per cento di comunisti non è fatto di divisioni sovietiche, ma da cittadini italiani. E noi dobbiamo capire perché votano comunista e favorire la loro evoluzione democratica".*

[14] *"Benigno, un cristiano non va a Montecitorio a far politica, ma a portar anche là il Vangelo".*

[15] *"una interpretazione della politica come servizio che lui deduceva immediatamente come corollario di impegno da parte di chi aveva osato evocare l'aggettivo cristiano per la testimonianza politica".*

[16] *"Lo stato ha per fine la cultura profana del benessere temporale nella società. La Chiesa ha per fine la santità (senso della salvezza eterna) (sempre nella società, in hoc mundo). Cultura dunque e santità: ecco i due termini; sacro e profano. Distinti ma non separabili (come vuole il laicismo) senza danno reciproco: una civiltà insensibile alla religiosità, una santità chiusa alle ansie della vita terrena. Compito quindi delle due organizzazioni uno sforzo di apertura reciproca, di 'raddrizzamento' che però deve strutturarsi per essere sano, durevole e umano come autoraddrizzamento".*

[17] *"Spetta soprattutto (ai comunisti) un altro compito: quello di realizzare il socialismo nei punti più alti del capitalismo, di fare la "rivoluzione in Occidente", dimostrando che il socialismo può e deve essere indissolubilmente legato con tutte le libertà civili, culturali e religiose".*

[18] *"Esiste e opera (nel PCI) la volonta non solo di costruire e far vivere un partito laico e democratico … che non intende affatto combattere i valori cristiani" ma anzi "ha l'intenzione di concorrere a realizzare una societa che senza essere cristiana, sia organizzata in modo tale da essere sempre piu aperta e accogliente verso i valori cristiani …"*

[19] *"non in nome della fede, questo no; ma a causa della fede, questo sì …",*

[20] *"In conclusione l'Italia deve pensare e scegliere il tempo dell'accordo: prima della mia morte o dopo, misurando tutte le incognite. Prima sarà più facile, dopo molto più difficile"*

[21] *"Capii che, come parlamentare eletto a Trieste, non avevo via di scampo. Tacere sarebbe stato vile, opporsi significava andare contro una mia*

ragionevole convinzione, parlare a favore (come feci) voleva dire frenare, piegare i sentimenti e andare in direzione opposta allo stato d'animo della gente"

[22] *"Non condivido la scelta della tua parte, ma ti faccio i miei complimenti. Ti do atto dell'impostazione storica entro cui l'hai collocato, è stato un discorso serio e dignitoso".*

[23] *"... un'umiliazione necessaria per voltare la pagina della storia ... per ricominciare a esistere, a vivere come nazione...".*

[24] *"Quando essi (gli estremisti) gridano 'lotta di classe, armiamo le masse' noi lo gridiamo con loro e quando essi si impegnano a 'combattere un giorno con le armi in pugno contro lo Stato fino alla liberazione dai padroni e dallo sfruttamento' noi ci impegniamo con loro ..."*

[25] *"in giornate tremende per la storia italiana, quando era in gioco la vita di Aldo Moro, e nulla si poteva fare per salvarlo, se si avesse cara la sopravvivenza della democrazia in Italia".*

[26] *"C'è anche il Moro prigioniero, il Moro vittima, e noi non possiamo scostarci da lui, prendere silenziosamente le distanze, lasciarlo al suo destino senza un tentativo di autentica comprensione".*

[27] *"Per gli studenti più seri la contestazione è 'un problema', per gli estremisti invece 'una soluzione' ".*

[28] *"La verità è che le Brigate Rosse chiedevano sempre una sola cosa: il loro riconoscimento politico, cioè il riconoscimento delle loro uccisioni come atti di guerra contro uno Stato arbitrario che va abbattuto ..."*

[29] *'What a difference in humanity, of truly wounded humanity, between his immense suffering ... in the endless hours of those atrocious days, and the contrasting, as shameless as it was false, of a policy of no compromise with a policy of negotiation, both based more on abstract political concepts than on the reality of the facts and human behaviour ...'*

[30] *"Quale fondamento avesse un accordo che poggiava su una base tanto fragile, come la vita o la volontà di un uomo? E che fondamento potesse avere una prospettiva politica fondata sul rapporto tra due uomini, sia pure influenti come erano Berlinguer e Moro".*

[31] *"Si saldava insieme la concezione della politica come puro esercizio del potere – che si può 'spartire' ma perdere mai – e si ponevano le premesse per una 'coerente' congiunzione tra poteri economici e politica o, come si dirà più tardi di fronte agli effetti devastanti di 'tangentopoli', tra affari e politica".*

[32] *"... la dimensione del partito non deve più essere quella di sola proiezione del potere. Siamo un partito di governo ma dobbiamo anche diventare un partito che sa lottare, che sa interpretare le esigenze della società. Non si può rimanere nel solo ambito di potere".*

[33] *"Ah, la conclusione di quel vostro congresso è stata la causa di una grande occasione mancata per la democrazia italiana".*

[34] *"con i suoi aspetti negativi, forse sottovalutati, ma anche con qualche lato positivo, perché in definitiva (questo passaggio) segna il passaggio da una fede prevalmente sociologica ad una fede più personale ... stimolando la Chiesa 'ad una missione pastorale più paziente e più faticosa di prima, e, in definitiva, ad una fede più esigente e più difficile ...".*

[35] *"Ora devono prenderci sul serio, il nostro deficit è così grande ...",*

[36] *"... un lavoro intenso, da fare a tempo pieno".*

[37] *"Un incontro, fatto di silenzio naturalmente. Ma, in questo tipo di dialoghi, il silenzio è un canale di comunicazione assai più efficace di tante parole, può nascondere una ricchezza di contenuti e di scambi che nessun suono, neanche la musica, riesce ad esprimere ...".*

[38] *"... le due Marie, nel loro scambio quotidiano, avranno cumulato certamente, tra capitale e interessi, un patrimonio di umiltà tale da bilanciare utilmente la sovrabbondanza e vistosa dose di superbia quotidianamente prodotta dall'umanità, almeno di Dignano ...".*

[39] *"Il paese non è un palcoscenico, ma una difficile comunità di uomini e di storia. Mussolini recitava meglio di Don Sturzo, di De Gasperi, di Vanoni e di Moro. Preferisco chi recita meno. Se devo divertirmi vado a teatro. Se devo far politica, so di far fatica".*

[40] *"La storia si legge bene perché è scritta al passato, viverla al presente è assai più difficile ..."*

[41] *"Il nazionalismo è un'esasperazione dell'amor patrio che porta all'esaltazione assoluta della razza e della nazionalità, negando le posizioni altrui; mentre la coscienza nazionale era frutto di una esaltazione della personalità umana con i suoi doveri e i suoi diritti, tra i quali quello di amare la patria, ma rispettando la posizione nazionale degli altri ...".*

[42] *"Le concessioni del Trattato di Londra all'Italia comprendevano, dunque, tutti gli obiettivi propri dell'unificazione risorgimentale, ma andavano poi ben oltre, perché ad essi si aggiungevano elementi che superavano palesemente quegli obiettivi e si iscrivevano nella logica della politica di potenza, sotto il segno delle esigenze di sicurezza ... la gente era affascinata dalla prospettiva della 'grandezza nazionale' come terapia dei problemi interni ...".*

[43] *"... la linea di confine che nel primo dopoguerra era stata ritenuta dall'Italia un'offesa e una mutilazione, nel secondo venne invocata come un'ancora di salvezza ... Qualcuno diceva che sarebbe stato necessario battere il pugno sul tavolo; ma al tavolo non eravamo ammessi ...".*

[44] *"Non esiste né il giorno, né il mese, né l'anno; non c'è né una legge parziale, né una legge globale, che possa segnare la 'soluzione definitiva' di un problema che accompagnerà le genti di confine per generazioni e si affiderà al riconoscimento della diversità come ricchezza, anziché come ragione di antagonismo. Un cammino lungo e difficile, costellato di arresti e di cadute ...".*

[45] *"... una unità su una linea, non un unanimismo su una confusione (...) come è consigliabile per tutte le questioni complesse, di mettere in ogni cosa 'a pie' del vero il dubbio' ".*

[46] *"La pace non è comoda ... è quel pezzetto che i giovani del mondo unito mettono insieme ... è la coraggiosa pacificazione tra ex-nemici senza aspettare che cominci l'altro, è questa continua donazione senza contropartita, soprattutto senza sapere se e quando mai l'opera sarà compiuta".*

[47] *"No, Zanetto, per dirla con linguaggio paolino, aveva terminato la sua corsa ... quando aveva consumato le sue batterie, e aveva riconsegnato alle origini il mandato ricevuto. Lo aveva assolto sulle vie del bene ...".*

[48] *"Il più grande atto di amore per Trieste dell'on. Belci è stata la costituzione del College del Mondo Unito dell'Adriatico."*

Tony Besse

Beiti Beitak *[My House is Your House]*

As visitors make their way through St. Donat's Castle, they come across a plaque with this inscription.

Had Tony Besse not made his donation in October 1960, the castle would have passed into other, commercial hands. No one can say whether the Atlantic College project would have survived this setback, or the United World Colleges have come into being.

This is a story that should be carried in the hearts of every member of the United World Colleges.

It is also the story of a family.

On 3rd September 1948, when Kurt Hahn was fighting to re-establish his Gordonstoun School in its original Scottish home after wartime exile in Wales, and the financial situation was desperate, he received the following mutilated but unmistakeably urgent telegram from a long-standing friend and member of his school council:

> *Discussing future development with one who … education on vast scale and who might completely solve Gordonstoun future financial problems would therefore urge dispatch of as complete a documentation as possible regardless expense must reach me by September 10 acknowledge Kurt Hahn or representative Gordonstoun … please send airmail Gordonstoun literature and all Hahn lectures or pamphlets bearing upon underlying aims of Gordonstoun and Salem special reference to international aspects stop acknowledge receipt telegraphically and state Hahns movements next three weeks Chris Arnold Forster.*

The Arnold Forsters had been friends and admirers of Kurt Hahn since the 1920s. Chris had been a prominent member of the Union for Democratic Control, a body that in England had worked for a negotiated settlement of the First World War. Mrs Ka Arnold Forster had taught at Salem. It was she who, sitting at lunch in the Hotel Continental in Geneva in 1933 during Hahn's brief imprisonment by the Nazis, saw the British Prime Minister Ramsay MacDonald at a neighbouring table with his private secretary Neville Butler. A note quickly passed to Neville Butler led to Ramsay MacDonald's letter to the German National Socialist Government seeking the release of Kurt Hahn, then in so-called 'protective custody' – he had been arrested in the early hours of 11th March. By the time the German Minister of Foreign Affairs, Baron von Neurath, answered the letter, Hahn had been released but forbidden all further contact with Salem and expelled from Baden.

Neville Butler had himself been freed from German custody in the camp of Ruhleben, outside Berlin, in 1915, where as an undergraduate he had been studying in Germany and caught by the outbreak of war. He went on to spend several weeks in the Hahn household in Berlin. How strange to envisage an Englishman being allowed to live with a German family in wartime, subject to only minor restrictions! It was all thanks to Hahn's powers of persuasion – he had visited the camp to enquire after Oxbridge graduates in internment there. We must be very thankful, for Neville Butler later provided us with one of the few intimate and truly evocative insights into Hahn's early family life – and at an especially fascinating time.

The Arnold Forsters' son Mark was one of the eight small boys who were enrolled in Hahn's first school in Scotland, Rothiemurchus, opened only weeks after his flight to Britain in July 1933 and the precursor to Gordonstoun which was launched in September of the following year.

The *Macenas*, the *Deus ex Machina* behind the telegram, embodied all the romance, mystery and optimism implied by this dramatic message, although the road was to be longer and more uphill than Chris Arnold Forster foresaw.

It was his neighbour in the south of France, Anton Besse of Aden, the father of our own Antonin (Tony) Besse, the donor of St. Donat's Castle and estate.

Anton Besse of Aden

Anton Besse was born in 1877, lost his father at the age of seven, experienced vividly the sufferings of his mother as she tried to keep up middle class appearances with no money, failed his baccalaureate, joined the army at 18 to become, so he later claimed, France's youngest corporal, and responded in 1899, at 22, to an advertisement from a French firm established in Aden and in Hodeidah, a port in Yemen. It is claimed – the Besse mythology began early and has rarely faltered – that, asked to state his qualifications, he replied: *'I have none; I know nothing'*, and was engaged immediately. The conditions of employment were tough: duration of the contract three years, remuneration 150 Frs. (£6) a month, after three years a holiday of four to six months; *'whether or not the employee is entitled to remuneration while on leave to be decided later'; 'misbehaviour, disobedience or inefficiency on the employee's part automatically cancels the contract and the employee must leave Aden by the next boat at his own expense'*. But by 1900 he was writing that he was getting up at half-past four and working right through until six in the evening: *'One must always be taking the initiative, no time to stop and think, one must work as it were by instinct … big deals and little deals are settled by one word … the whole time one has to take one's courage in one's hands and always, always press forward …'*.

Before long, and despite a clause in his contract that forbade him from setting up his own business in the Aden area for five years after leaving the firm, he had started up on his own.

Two accomplished writers have left us portraits of him. Evelyn Waugh invested him with a degree of immortality in his novel *Scoop* in the character Le Blanc, [●] but his diary (6th December 1930) gives us a more direct impression of the man's energy and way of life, for Waugh partly alarming, partly delectable, above all memorable:

'… after lunch we went for what Mr. B. called a little walk in the hills … luckily I had rubber-soled shoes, otherwise climb absolutely impossible … Besse gave a little skip and swarmed straight up a perpendicular cliff. Later loose stones … "it is better to press with the feet than pull with the hands!" … we were bare to waist and very much scratched and bruised … crossed crater, climbed another cliff, walked along edge, and then came down over red-hot rocks … then long walk on loose cinders to

sea, where servants were awaiting us with towels and tea … bathed in a warm, shark-infested sea … drove back at great speed … Besse had change of clothes … came in full of having fallen in love with a Papist lady doctor … dined Besse and his mistress and clerks … excellent dinner and wine … bed early, slept well …'

Freya Stark gives us the more intimate, romantic picture, for she saw him with a woman's eye, and he was a woman's man:

'M. Besse … is more than charming: he is a Merchant, in the style of the Arabian Nights or the Renaissance: all day long telegrams come to him from India, America, China, Yemen, Africa, Europe … his agents are everywhere … he is a real Epicurean in the good sense of the word; and has made himself here a world of his own – not belonging even to the British club, but knowing everyone worth knowing, and having immense power all over the country … a wonderful person who lets life play upon him as if he were an instrument responsive to all its variations … he has made several fortunes and does not care for money a bit … he sits

[●] Evelyn Waugh's *Scoop* is treasured for its satirical, hugely entertaining debunking of journalism. The background, as he himself readily acknowledged in his *Waugh in Abyssinia* (1936), was infinitely more sinister: *'Fascist empire came first to Ethiopia, following the Italian invasion late in 1935. The fighting itself was conducted with unprecedented brutality by the Italians, who were desperate for a quick victory: gas and chemical warfare, as well as saturation bombing, killed enormous numbers, as did the detention and concentration camps that the Italians brought with them from the pacification campaigns of a few years earlier against the nomadic Senussi. Around 3,000 Italians died compared with tens and perhaps hundreds of thousands of Ethiopians. Neither later nor at the time did this kind of bloodshed occasion much criticism; inside Italy, victory marked the high point of Mussolini's reign, a "golden age" of fascist Empire.'*

'The peace that followed was equally enlightening. Following an assassination attempt on Viceroy Graziani, notorious for his brutality, Fascist squads went on the rampage in Addis Ababa, killing over a thousand people in cold blood. Others were executed in mass reprisals, including several hundred monks. All this offered a foretaste of what Europe – and Italy – would experience a few years later at the hands of the Germans. Meanwhile, Ciano addressed the General Assembly of the League of Nations, and referred to the "sacred mission of civilisation" which Italy was heeding, declaring that his country would "consider it an honour to inform the League of the progress achieved in its work of civilising Ethiopia"'. Mark Mazower *Dark Continent* Penguin Edition pages 72–73.

at his desk across the room and settles huge enterprises in a quiet way – where his ships are to go, whether or not to buy up all the incense of his coast, to send tar and petrol to Abyssinia. The office … an arcaded room with lots of compartments with desks, each with some huge business of its own, a Parsi, an Arab, French, German, Englishman, Russian, running them … it is fascinating to see so huge and varied an affair and one brain the centre of it all …' [●]

In truth, he was not modest. What was his aim in life? To organise all the Red Sea, Arabia, Abyssinia, the Sudan, the Somali lands, British and German East Africa; acquire ships to bring out to these countries all that the local population could need; convey back to Europe and America all that these countries could produce; and establish agencies in London, Paris, Marseilles, Barcelona, New York and Hamburg for this purpose.

In 1914, presenting himself for military duties, he was asked: *'What are you in civilian life?' 'A millionaire'.*

In 1923 he took on the business of Royal Shell. At the time Shell business amounted to 700 tons annually, or some 180,000 gallons. Despite debts, he quickly built three ships and was soon able to report that he had secured 72% of the entire Red Sea trade in oil. In 1936 he installed the first diesel engines in Arab dhows, building up a fleet of 14 craft that could operate in all weathers and seasons – these craft were to carry mutton safely from Berbera to Aden and to supply the fuel for all the British RAF stations on the south side of the Arabian Peninsula. He operated four other trading vessels, some 30 lighters and five tugs, and built a floating dock for their maintenance. He introduced air-conditioning to Aden, electricity, modern plumbing with the first piped water, refrigerators and deep free-zers, washing machines, and the first steel fishing vessel.

His agencies included Austin, Lancia, Renault, Jaguar, Holden & Dodge cars, for all of which he also provided the necessary servicing facilities. Besse & Co. were agents for the Liverpool & London & Globe Insurance Company. Ltd and the Prudential Assurance Company Ltd. and for air and sea travel bookings. His associate company, *The Halal Shipping Company Ltd.*, represented many shipping lines. Shortly after the Second World War he established a fleet of 104 large Italian Lancia lorries, both tanker and goods vehicles, for moving products between Assab, Dessie and Addis Ababa. So rough were the roads that each round journey consumed one set of tyres. It was he who then pioneered the system, now common-place, of raising one pair of tyres when loads were lighter. And he devised cleaning procedures that enabled him to load his tanker lorries with coffee on their return journeys.

But by far his most important if always difficult trading relationship was with the Royal Shell oil company. In 1947 Besse bought two abandoned Italian oil tanks at Assab, then embarked on the building of a jetty made out of a floating dock of oil drums. Shell were reluctant to expose their tankers to so primitive an enterprise. Besse's written response was characteristic. *'I invariably see (a scheme) from the point of view of its potentialities when fully developed. I am so conscious of all the advantages of Assab that if you do not agree I will myself buy a tanker to keep the port supplied.'* Six months later: *'… we are in a position to supply entirely the eastern and northern parts of Ethiopia. Pumps have been erected at all the vital points, and our organization there is growing at such a pace that before the end of the year, when Assab is in working order and able to receive tankers carrying white oil, I hope to be able to turn to you and say: Gentlemen, Ethiopia is yours.'*

One unsuccessful venture was Arabian Airways. In the 1930s steamships capable of carrying passengers were rare. The alternative, dhows, were unreliable, uncomfort-able and slow. The British RAF had simple airstrips across South West Arabia, but charts, ground maintenance, fuel supplies and navigational aids were primitive if available at all. Besse calculated that the creation of a mail service in cooperation with Imperial Airways in Khartoum would generate a useful profit. He jumped too soon. The neces-sary authorisations were not forthcoming, and he sold up in 1939 at a loss. Precisely ten years later he turned down the invitation to become Chairman of Aden Airways, a highly profitable subsidiary of BOAC. But this was one venture among scores. He had been toughened early on by setbacks. In 1921 he had arrived in London to find that a senior business colleague, himself now penniless, had run up debts for the company amounting to £550,000.

[●] The eventual range of his business is well illustrated by his letter heading in the 1950s: A. Besse and Co. (Aden) Ltd. Agents for Anglo-Saxon Petroleum Co. Ltd., Associated British Oil Engines (Export) Ltd., Austin Motor Export Corporation Ltd., Bayer Products Ltd., Candles (Overseas) Ltd. Carrier Corporation, Chloride Batteries Ltd., Chrysler Corporation, CIBA Laboratories Ltd., Citrus Board (South Africa), J. V. Drake and Co., Ercole Marelli and Co., Export Bottlers Ltd., Francolor, Franke and Heidecke, Gilbeys Ltd., Goodyear Tyre and Rubber Export Co., Heineken's Bierbrouwerij Maatschappij N. V., Imperial Chemical Industries Ltd., International Marine Radio Co. Ltd., International Paints Ltd., Kodak Ltd., Nash Kelvinator Corporation, National Carbon (Eastern) Ltd., N. V. Philips, H. A. Riedl Ltd., The Shell Co. Ltd., Societe Anonyme L'air Liquide, Sunbeam Cycles Ltd., Tissot & Fils S. A. (Swiss Watches), Underwood Corporation, Willys Overland Export Corporation

Besse was effectively bankrupt. He was utterly frank with the Scottish manager in London of the National Bank of India, the one bank operating in Aden: *'I will pay back everything, but I shall need your help'.* He then, people said, *'pledged his trousers to the bank'.* At the half-way stage of repayment, the manager called in all his senior staff and told them that Besse must be given all the help he asked for, now and in the future. Anton Besse was influenced for life by this expression of trust.

He had also encountered problems of a more political nature. As the Abyssinian conflict came closer in the mid-1930s, he was carrying through a rapid expansion of all his activities in the country, provoking an order from Mussolini himself forbidding him from trading there. Then he was accused of smuggling, gun-running and trading in drugs, all of which he vigorously contested in a letter to the French newspaper, *Le Journal*, which had published these accusations. More significantly, in the early months of 1935 he had noticed in the trade returns provided by his agent in Asmara a sharp increase in oil fuel supplies ordered from Shell, especially aviation fuel. Knowing that Mussolini had to rely on Shell supplies until able to organise transportation from Italian ports, he suspected military developments in the area. He at once sought an interview with the Emperor, Haile Selassi, who understood the implications immediately but placed his trust in the League of Nations. Besse's efforts to get him to make a direct approach to London were entirely unsuccessful. Shortly after, when the Italians started using mustard gas against the local people, he cut off their fuel supplies completely. He was placed on the Fascist black list. Later, travelling from Beirut to Paris, his plane was held back by headwinds and forced to land for refuelling in Brindisi. The Italians learned that he was on board, took him off the plane and imprisoned him. Pressure from Paris and London secured his release only after some 48 hours.

Writing her memoirs some 20 years after the Second World War, Freya Stark, who during the war had returned to Aden – *'set in remoteness, independent of time'* – remembered *'Hilda Besse and Anton sparkling with gaiety and malice … he enjoyed his enemies with unfailing gusto … he was distressed at this time (1941) because he could not help making money during the war; it piled up "malgré moi"'.*

Illness, Education and St. Antony's College, Oxford

In 1948 Anton Besse suffered a stroke. Other thoughts entered his mind. The business had become *'gigantic'*. *'Where is the man who can take over my burden?'* He had

already opened and financed an apprentice training school in Aden; also a dispensary which within its first 12 months treated almost 2,000 minor surgical and another 2,000 medical cases. He had invested in education for women and in the University of Addis Ababa. There are, it seems, no records that confirm the number and extent of his donations. He had once told Freya Stark that her charity was like the Morse code: *'only dots and dashes'.* His was consistently anonymous and consistently undocumented. But now he had bigger ideas.

Around this time he set out his ideas on education. He had always impressed friends and visitors with his knowledge of literature and love of poetry and the range of his musical interests, and he was especially proud of all this in the light of his lack of education after the age of 18. Looking at extracts from an essay of his on education, one readily comprehends the immediate rapport that was to arise between him and Kurt Hahn:

> *'Yet instead of the Divine, as interpreted by the teachings of traditional and progressive morality, and the Human, as represented by Science, merging and flowing together in one great stream, these two currents have, up to the present, pursued two different courses. Perhaps this is the cause of the ever-hardening division between Education and Instruction, since the latter tends to consider only facts, unrelated to morality … the great savants are not unaware of the force of sentiment; they know that nothing great or strong can be created without it … given teachers who are also converts, and lecturers chosen from the élite of all countries, men known for their international breadth of outlook … the development and strengthening of character can proceed hand in hand with the acquisition of knowledge, by special methods which would include tests of physical endurance and a sense of responsibility …'*

Initiative and independence of judgement and of action were the qualities he was after. In 1947 he went to the Ministry of Education in Paris to offer funding for a French college that would promote these qualities. What rapidly became christened Le College des Rebelles found no friends. It was to be another 50 years before Ferdinand Mayor, the Director General of UNESCO, was to declare that *'the history of our time compels us to affirm that rebellion is one of the basic aspects of being human … Non-violent rebellion, creative disobedience, or the insubordination of those who refuse the unacceptable is the best way to ensure that humankind successfully makes the transition from the logic of force, which still prevails today, to the logic of reason … this idea of peaceful and creative rebellion is essential in order to open us the paths to the future …'.* [●] But France had no need of new institutions! And no private institution could issue diplomas that would enjoy official recognition.

Besse turned to Britain. He had admired the British colonial administration and the British wartime achievements, but now (as he was to write later),

> *'for all too long it has seemed to me that the order of the day in England has been 'Conformity', the training for which begins at school … where British youth is concerned the craze for conformity to a pattern and the failure to exhort boys to set themselves and strive towards a higher ideal, both individually and collectively, has resulted in a standard of mediocrity which is painful to behold in a country I have always loved and admired … the present levelling down of humanity and the widely adopted principle of Safety First represent the very antithesis of my ideal …'*

His purple views were, it must be said, based substantially on his failure to recruit British young men of the calibre to serve him on his terms in the Middle East.

In short, he turned to Oxford. He wanted more Frenchmen to study there. He offered to set up a college for the purpose. Anyone who knows Oxford knows that things there take time. He was in a hurry. Here was Oxford behaving just like those short-sighted Shell executives. His offer was £1.5 million. What was this problem about obtaining a charter? To bring matters forward, he offered £250,000 to be shared between the eight poorest colleges on condition that they favoured applicants of French nationality, and the offer was accepted. Besse was then angered by the university's assumption that he was adding these £250,000 to his original gift rather than redeploying some of it for more rapid results. The Vice-Chancellor Stallybrass had understood Besse and secured his confidence but died after a fall from a London-Oxford train in October 1948. The Oxford working committee was strengthened by the addition of J. C. Masterman, the Provost of Worcester College, by curious coincidence another of those British students who had been interned in Ruhleben in 1914 and befriended by Hahn. [○]

[●] Ferdinand Mayor: Paris July 1998 – *Education at the Dawn of the Third Millennium*

[○] He was later a member of the Atlantic College Governing Council but resigned as a matter of principle when girls were admitted in 1967

The University had realised that looking a gift horse in the mouth for too long was a hazardous enterprise. The Council was convened in the Long Vacation of 1948, and the offer was officially accepted by the whole university in Congregation on 15th September, noting the following: *'Our benefactor (who was insisting once again on anonymity) wishes men of all nationalities, and in particular of his own France, to have the benefit of such an education. For he believes that the future prospects for Europe and the world depend upon international understanding and upon international rather than national action. He has provided, therefore, that admission to the College shall be subject to no test of a religious, political or racial character.'*

Thus was born St. Antony's College, Oxford, but it had been a close-run thing. For in October 1947 Besse was writing to Masterman: *'our mutual friend Arnold Forster has sent me your memo … whereas I was prepared to put my heart and soul into its realisation, I have only one desire today, and that is to forget all about it. The very large sum of money I donated seems to have been rendered useless'.*

And now Gordonstoun

It was just a few days before the formal meeting of the Oxford University Congregation that Gordonstoun received the telegram quoted at the outset. Hahn, despite being an Oxford man, was not to repeat Oxford's mistakes – indeed, he went almost to the other extreme. But it was now Hilda Besse who became the key personality.

Many years earlier, in 1908, Anton Besse had met and married Marguerite Godefroy, a member of a wealthy and aristocratic Belgian family, their anything but leisurely honeymoon taking them to Antwerp, London, Hamburg, Frankfurt, Munich, Vienna, Trieste, Venice, Milan, Lyons, Paris, Havre and Brussels. She both invested her money in the firm and supervised the books. It must have been a good partnership, at least business-wise, for turnover increased by 750% in the first year and by 2,500% by the outbreak of the First World War. But divorce followed, and in 1922 Anton married a rather remarkable Scots lady, Hilda Crowther, initially his secretary, to whom he is said to have dictated letters almost non-stop during the honeymoon, with whom however he had five children, Ariane, Joy, Peter, Tony and Monna.

In June 1949 Besse and his wife visited Gordonstoun. Arnold Forster wrote to Hahn a few days later: *'the visit (has been) a complete success … you completely won his heart … he wants to spend a lot more time with you … he told me last night that his visit would prove "very fruitful" for Gordonstoun'.*

And then the dilemma that faces all fundraisers: *'I could of course press him for an immediate donation … if on the other hand we make no such SOS signal now, our chances of getting a real foundation on a very much bigger scale would in my view be greatly enhanced … but it is no use playing a waiting game if the ship is going to sink in the meanwhile …'*

Kurt Hahn's younger brother Rudo was the enthusiastic hunter and fisherman in the family, but Kurt was no mean angler either. He knew exactly how to play a big fish. [●] *'My faith in <u>our</u> mission'*, he wrote immediately to Besse, *'is strong but vulnerable. It is ever in need of confirmation from independent sources. What you have done in your life, what you have thought and dreamt, could not be realised by me from hearsay only or from the written word; it needed a meeting.'* And a few days later, allowing himself to comment on the difficulties that Besse was still facing over the status of his college in Oxford: *'Oxford always had the saving grace of inconsistency … I believe that with the Vice-Chancellor's loyal support Oxford, already dimly conscious of its failure, will give St. Antony's a fair chance … I have hopes that before long we shall be able to say: "La révolution est en marche".'*

And then he was given his opening by a letter from Hilda Besse in which *'I shall try to express the feelings of happiness and gratitude which our meeting with you engendered. We came away from you with a glow in our hearts which I feel nothing can ever extinguish'*, followed a few days later by *'I regard the short visit to you as the most luminous experience of my life'*.

But Chris Arnold Forster, who was handling some of Besse's financial investments in Britain, had difficulty in pinning him down. Yes, it was his firm intention to see that the school should not be hampered by lack of money, but for the moment he could not contemplate anything approaching the Oxford grant. Long letters exchanged between Arnold Forster and Hahn brought no concrete conclusions, although they included some thoughts from Hahn about withdrawal from Gordonstoun (and 'Greater Gordonstoun'), leaving Gordonstoun to become *'an enlightened Public School with a bit of sea-manship thrown in'*.

As so often, it is difficult to know whether this was sincere sentiment or another tactical ploy, but Hahn went back on the offensive a month later, urging on Arnold Forster

Anton and Hilde Besse, parents of Tony

the impact that would be made on American sponsors by a school *'in Britain, saved by a Frenchman and presided over by a German. What an impressive guarantee of our worthiness to serve Europe!'* Arnold Forster had to reply that his two most recent letters from Besse were *'rather disturbing and very confusing … he is fairly sick in body and mind'*.

All was to be well, albeit not as 'well' as both had hoped, but the saviour now became Hilda Besse, who entered independently into correspondence with Chris Arnold Forster, explaining to him in detail how her husband's innate wish to give had literally bolted in the past year or so. The Oxford donation had become known; he had been besieged by supplicants; he had allowed himself to be taken out of his depth and wanted to feel his feet on the solid sea-bottom again. Nonetheless, in a letter in which he told Arnold Forster that he wanted to make it unnecessary to continue a correspondence *'which must, I am sure, be distasteful to you'*, Besse confirmed the provision of £13,000 a year for five years. The school was able to breathe more easily. Hahn felt like a man *'who has been released from prison and had forgotten what it was like to be free'*.

By January 1950 full cordiality between Besse and Hahn had been restored. Hahn, *'my dear friend'*, visited the Besse home in the south of France in April. Letters of reciprocal admiration flowed between them. *'Since meeting you* (Besse to Hahn), *I have drawn further inspiration from your personality, and the impulse to stretch out my hand to you, to share, if only in a minute degree, the great work you have devoted your life to, became irresistible'*; Hahn to Besse: *'In coming to Le Paradou* (the Besse home) *I was doing what I longed to do ever since I heard Chris Arnold Forster speak of your home – his face alive with blissful memories. But my*

[●] *'How is your French fishery expedition progressing? Is the fish on the hook or still nibbling strongly?'* Eric Warburg to Kurt Hahn on 13th October 1949

special reason was to render account to the man who has given new strength to my purpose in life…' [●] In seeking to draw Besse closer into the actual management of Gordonstoun affairs, he reported on the new financial discipline reigning there, for *'if you had not translated your belief into action, we would not have survived 1950…'* A new Executive Committee and a Controller had been appointed to supervise the budgetary affairs in replacement of a Bursar who, a meticulous accountant, *'only reported on economic happenings which he should have shaped'.*

In June 1951 the Besses responded to repeated entreaties from Hahn to visit the school again. Anton Besse had not been well. He and his wife travelled to Scotland almost immediately after he had received an Honorary Degree from Oxford University on 12th June. Hahn of course wanted to show him everything and set an exhausting pace. Besse felt unwell and was taken to the school sanatorium, where he died on the following day.

At the safe distance of many years later, Hahn was to refer to this irreverently as *'his greatest fundraising mistake',* but he did not put a foot wrong at the time. The body was flown from the nearby RAF and Fleet Air Arm station Lossiemouth via London to the south of France, seen off in formal style by an RAF Guard of Honour, all stage-managed by Hahn. Hahn delivered a memorable address in the school's Michael Kirk. Sixty years later, Tony Besse the son continued to recall his and his mother's gratitude for Hahn's devoted attention to their needs and the dignity with which he surrounded this leave-taking. It is all too easy to be cynical of the sincerity of human relations between donors and recipients in the world of fundraising, but Hilda Besse's letter to Kurt Hahn is surely unambiguous: *'From Anton's desk, in the room he loves, I write you these lines, my dear and noble friend, to try and tell you once again what you have meant to me during those eight days at Gordonstoun. To have reached you … to have had that last talk with you before life was extinguished, almost as suddenly as a flame in the wind … those days will cast*

[●] But what one would not give for sight of the letter from Kurt Hahn after this visit, understandably absent from the files, which Arnold Forster answered in the following words! *Your "very personal" letter amused me vastly. I do not think that anything could so vividly recall my own days at Le Paradou as your description of the Sultan dominating his harem. It is, of course, quite true that for many years past he has assumed the right to command everybody and be commanded by none. There have been moments when I thought that his gallant lady would rebel and box his ears, but she has great patience and very deep affection for him. Chris.'*

their light and blessing far, far beyond the power of our eyes to see … You and Gordonstoun have kindled a spark in our beloved son, Tony, which will become the fire we all need to cleanse and purify the dross within us …'. [●]

There were important practical consequences.

The family resolved that the five-year financial commitment to Gordonstoun, rendered doubtful by Anton's death, would be fully respected, even to the extent of being freed of any possible death duty implications.

Through his first wife, Anton Besse had discovered the motto *Plus est en vous* of the van Gruuthuuse family which remains engraved to this day on the fine renaissance palace, the Grathaus, in Bruges, and adopted it as his own. Hahn now wrote, seeking Hilda's permission to adopt it for Gordonstoun. *'I only dare ask because it is no accident that he and I when we first met felt so strongly moved, as if we had been brothers-in-arms for years unknown to each other.'* Pindar's *'Grow into what you are',* much used by the founders of the German Country Boarding Schools (*Landerziehungsheime*) even before Salem was opened, was thus given more explicit expression.

Hilda Besse became a member of the Gordonstoun Governing Body.

Tony Besse met Kurt Hahn.

The Besse Inheritance

The surviving personal correspondence illustrates the degree to which Kurt Hahn now became an intimate family counsellor, for Anton Besse, as happens so often with men of action, had died intestate, and there was no clear provision for the succession in the leadership of A. Besse and Co. (Aden) Ltd. It was not a simple matter, and we find Hahn holding Hilda's hand: *'Never doubt how much they all need you, even though at times they transfer what was once their rebellion against the paternal authority into a resistance against guidance by their mother. These are passing moods. Victorian patience will carry the day.'*

Would his children be lone wolves like their father, or would they just be sheep? In retrospect there seems to have been little doubt that it was Tony, of the five children, who would take over, but little in the Besse family history was uneventful.

[●] Only a few months later Kurt Hahn's admirable, long-serving secretary Miss Wicken announced her plan that *'Hahn should marry Madame Besse, thus solving all Gordonstoun's financial difficulties in one deft stroke. The lady is willing; Hahn is the only stumbling block.'*

Tony's Youth

In 1940, when it suddenly became clear that France would be occupied by the Germans, Anton Besse, who was in France recovering from back injuries caused by a flying accident, sent a telegram to Aden stating that all the assets of the firm were to be placed at the disposal of the British Government *'as long as Britain remained at war'*. In February 1941 he and Hilda, determined to escape the Vichy regime, left France for Spain with an exit visa secured for them by an American couple who were anxious to purchase their property. They found their way back to Aden by May 1941 via the United States and India. But the children were left behind in the French home, Le Paradou.

This decision would have been impossible without that uniquely British contribution to international child welfare, the nanny. Tony later made the distinction between his biological and his 'real' mother, Miss Ogilvie (she was later to care for the two children of his sister Joy who died painfully in childbirth in 1952). The consequence was that Tony entered adolescence under German occupation and without parental control.

As an independent, physically active and adventurous youngster he was soon running errands for the French resistance, assuming the right not to attend school regularly. One day he stood up in the assembly and shouted at the Headmaster, a Vichy supporter, and was expelled. He became specialized in stealing from the Germans – guns, grenades and binoculars. His home was visited by German officers, accompanied by a Frenchman. His sister sat on one of the pistols he had stolen and left lying around. A German dirk was hanging on the wall. The Frenchman told him to remove it. It transpired later that this Frenchman was a double agent. Tony remembers cold nights awaiting drops of supplies. It was always 'dicey'. No fires; the planes came in low and released the packages without parachutes that had to be collected rapidly before the Germans arrived, alerted by the noise. Eventually Tony and a friend from school who had insisted on accompanying him were picked up by a German patrol and handed over to the Italians who were administering the port of Toulon and the surrounding area. He was confronted by a distinguished and elegant officer who had been in Somalia and knew of his father. *'You have your life in front of you. Run!'* He ran. He moved to Bordeaux, where they engaged in difficult cooperation with Spanish communists who were specialists in resistance activities from their Civil War: *'One man above you, two below.'* It is difficult to get Tony to talk about these events. The loss of life of several young friends weighs heavily on him today.

Essentially, it was all 'fun', the outcome of youthful boredom, no parents to say no, the combination of delinquency and courage that, to take another example, was also typical of the Polish resistance. The thing was to be *'débrouillard'*. After the war he was awarded a resistance medal but decided not to attend the ceremony.

Thus Anton and Hilda Besse found a hardened and independent son at war's end. For Tony, his parents *'had not mattered very much'*. His mother was *'distant'* and always chose her husband over her children. Later, he was remorseful over this judgement, and recognised in her *'a very courageous woman'*.

Just as important, his parents now found themselves back in France without connections or friends, but it was a France on her knees, divided, settling scores (Tony remembers women *'collaboratrices'*, thought to have been involved with the retreating German officers, being thrown over the bridges in Bordeaux, then shot as their bodies bobbed up and down in the water). They observed Tony working the black market, selling silk stockings, putting the money straight into his back pocket as if it were the most natural thing. Tony took them on their first return visit to Paris, finding accommodation for them in the only hotel in the city that had heating, and arranging meetings with Ministers – it was his Resistance connections that made all this possible. His parents, shocked and unsettled, could not wait to move Tony to the more familiar, more trustworthy atmosphere of Aden.

But Tony's efforts to make his way in Aden in the family business were unhappy and unsuccessful, marked by many a dispute with his father and with colleagues more senior, more experienced and above all older than him. After his war-time experiences, he had no taste for life on an office high chair. He was bored and discontented. There was, people said, much of the old man in Tony. There came the day when, in violent argument, he threw in his hand, marched out of the offices, packed a bag, and went immediately to the harbour to see whether any company ships were on the point of departure. *'Yes,'* said the captain, *'for New York'. 'Will there be any stops?' 'I don't know. I haven't had my full instructions yet. What can I do for you?' 'Give me a cabin.'*

Self-Banishment and Return

In New York Tony earned his living as a taxi driver without a licence, parked cars on a series of small parking lots, earning more from tips than wages (this must have led to his dramatically generous tipping of all porters and waiters in later life), and secured two six-month visas before being told by a charmed lady official that, if he wanted a third one, he should go 'up-state' and pretend that he was asking for his first.

When her husband fell ill, Hilda wrote to Tony, asking him urgently to return. Tony was as proud as his father. His father must make the request. Anton wrote. *'No one has ever laid down conditions on me – but please come back.'* This was the moment when Tony abandoned his plans for US citizenship and, confident that he was the one son who could accept the responsibilities, remained close to his father after the latter's stroke and, with his mother's full support, assumed the leadership on his father's death.

Tony Besse thus found himself at the age of 24, without either university or any other form of training, in charge of the Besse empire or, as Tony preferred to describe it, a *'vast series of private shops'.* The immensity of the task was completely unclear to him at the outset. But he recalls with strong feeling and a retrospective sense of pride that all his father's children from both marriages signed a document on the morning after the funeral that divided the inheritance equally between them all, with separate provision for Hilda for the rest of her life. It was his task now to turn the series of private shops into properly constituted companies with statutes, auditors and shareholders, a formidable challenge given the informal, personal nature of his father's management style and the vast distances of the remote and primitive parts of the Besse enterprise. It was not until 19th June 1966, 15 years after his father's death, that *The Sunday Telegraph* could report that Tony had retained control of all operations in Aden together with the shareholdings of one of his sisters, whilst his other brothers and sisters had taken over all the interests in Ethiopia and Somaliland, the value of the divided assets totalling well over £10 million. Tony described his own share as the locomotive and one third of the coaches, but the tumultuous political events in the region now left little long-term scope for survival and prosperity.

Without experience or qualifications, Tony had only his father's example to follow. Be a hard taskmaster but fair to all. Most important: treat locals and expatriates equally. He picked up an oral knowledge of Arabic without much difficulty – bi-lingual in English and French, he has an ear for languages and acquired them with no formal training. It cannot however be surprising that efforts to track his business fortunes end in colourful accounts of individual episodes. Given the then unexplored state of the Middle East and its subsequent rapid enrichment through oil, one cannot help wondering what his tough and experienced father, Shell's major representative and partner in the region, might have made of the opportunities.

Yemen and Ethiopia in the 1950s and 1960s

Yemen had been known to the Romans as *Arabia Felix,* and Aden had been a British Crown Colony since 1838, but the interior remained mercilessly if picturesquely primitive. It is reported in a recent book [●] that, when the British Consul in the country's second city Taiz wanted to go for a walk, he had first to secure the local Iman's permission which could take up to two weeks to arrive; that he then walked with an open umbrella to ensure that he was treated with respect; and that the local people would spontaneously roll up the trousers of visiting white men to find out if they were white all over.

At no time did Tony have more money, power, assets of every kind, prestige and responsibility than when he took over his father's businesses. The Besses enjoyed a privileged position. But from 1950 onwards he was struggling to keep the firm alive. The arrival in the Middle East of the Soviet and Chinese communist missions radically influenced political developments and made life increasingly difficult. The Besse family eventually left Aden in June 1969 and the Besse companies were nationalized in November, 'nationalization' a euphemism for confiscation, for they lost all company assets and personal belongings – the house and its contents, pictures, papers, the children's toys, everything. And after the British authorities abandoned Yemen in November 1967, the People's Democratic Republic of Yemen was to become the source and supporter of insurgency in other parts of the region.

The Yemeni experience was mirrored in his other major trading country, Ethiopia. Again he started from a strong position that reflected his father's relationship with the Emperor, Haile Selassi. For when the Emperor returned in 1941 from war-time exile, he had no money and sent his son-in-law to seek help from Besse senior. Anton Besse knew how to play his cards. After enquiring delicately what the Emperor needed, he replied: *'I do not think that will be enough. I will give you double, but please do not come back for more.'* The Emperor never forgot this gesture, and the Besse companies under his reign were never refused anything.

[●] *The War That Never Was* by Duff Hart-Davids, Century 2011

Tony remembers the Emperor with respect: few roads, famine, people dying of hunger, but all areas had churches and mosques side by side and there was no discrimination. A small man, dressed in a tweed jacket and grey slacks, the Emperor met his visitors in a small side room, more a private saloon, spoke halting French but always wished to lead the conversation, concluding interviews courteously but firmly after 45 minutes.

Haile Selassie was deposed in 1974, his kingdom succeeded by the one-party communist state, the People's Republic of Ethiopia. There followed in the 1980s the notorious famines that affected in total some eight million and left at least one million dead.

From Lebanon, Tony attempted for ten years to control his increasingly fragmented, heavily threatened business interests. It was an intensely unhappy time. Having opened an office in Beirut and taken a suite in the St. George's Hotel, uprooted and, he says, idle, he and his wife Christiane travelled in Syria and Turkey whilst he made spasmodic attempts to revive his business in Aden. The only possibility for travel there was the unreliable fortnightly flight from Damascus in an old Russian aeroplane, for which he spent many days and nights waiting in sleazy Damascus hotels. Why, he asks himself still today, this continuing obsession with Yemen, rather than contemplating a move to one of the Gulf States? Loyalty to his former staff? The home of the 'House of Besse'? The birthplace of their children? A betrayed sense of belonging? Pride?

Much later, over 24 years later, during which he heard nothing from Aden about compensation for the nationalized assets, the reunification of northern with southern Yemen took place after the Soviet withdrawal under Gorbachev. Tony went to the Prime Minister whom he liked and trusted. The Prime Minister compelled the southerners to meet him and eventually to agree compensation for the confiscated business assets amounting to some 5% of their original value. Subsequently the Prime Minister consulted him in strict confidence over borrowing facilities for the repayment of a crippling debt to the Soviet Union. It transpired that the corrupt President was planning to pledge state assets to cover the proposed loan from the World Bank without World Bank authority, a procedure severely prohibited under Bank rules. Tony Besse was able to intervene privately behind the scenes and to save both the country and the Bank misappropriated funds to the tune of some US$486 million.

Memories of the Middle East – Some Sobering

Fortunately hardened by his experiences with the French resistance, Tony was to see at first hand the rough side of life and the regional brutalities: *'the Middle Ages in the 20th century – faithful friendship was jostled by the blackest treachery, and the crude facts of a semi-barbaric life were encountered at every turn.'* Public hangings on the site of the crime were commonplace. He recalls a bitter commercial dispute with Phillips who had started selling radio sets behind his back despite a clear contractual agreement to use the Besse agency. The visiting Dutch manager was so shaken by the hanging bodies lining his route in to the office from the airport that he acquiesced meekly and left as quickly as he could. Tony was compelled to witness one wretch being beheaded. He remembers the uprising in July 1967 in Aden against the lingering British rule. Ten British soldiers were burned alive in their armoured car. The following morning 'Mad Mitch' Mitchell, the Commanding Officer, marched his tough Glaswegian men in ceremonial formation, he and the bagpipes in the lead, into the revolutionary Crater area of Aden and cleansed it of all rebels.

There were more personal episodes too.

Inadequate facilities in the port of Hodeidah were leading to delays of up to six months. Queue jumping and corruption were making trading impossible, and cargoes were being diverted to Djibouti. Tony was well aware that a nearby second harbour, Salif, despite a narrow and shallow entrance, had a quay that his waiting ship could use because, as it normally carried cattle and had large doors on the sides, it could off-load lying alongside without cranes or other equipment. He boarded the ship himself and the off-loading was completed in half a day, the engines holding the ship against the quay. News arrived that the government objected because no authorisation had been given. When he reached the bottom of the gangway Tony was informed that the local Governor required a case of whisky. This was quickly drawn from the ship's stores, but as he reached the bottom of the gangway for the second time he was arrested by two colonels and driven off to Hodeidah where he was told he must spend the night in prison. He retained enough authority to decline this unwelcome hospitality and withdrew to a nearby hotel. The following morning the Prime Minister ordered his release – the previous evening the country's President had without consultation made a major speech welcoming the opening of a second national harbour. Within two days the local Governor had been dismissed, within seven the manager of the main harbour.

But he did not always escape prison and saw them on at least two occasions from the inside. On one he recognised a fellow-prisoner as having been until the previous day the governor of the National Bank, imprisoned on suspicion of having arranged credit facilities for a major debtor. On another, he found himself alongside a sailor whose wrists were bleeding badly from severely tightened ratchet handcuffs for which the warders had lost the key. Taking the revolver off the nearest warder, and recalling lessons learned from the wartime French underground, he shot the handcuffs off and became the hero of the prison. Local justice was pretty merciless. Historical Ethiopian tradition dictated that the punishment for two men in dispute was to handcuff them together and imprison them until they had sorted out their differences.

Memories of the Middle East – Some Happier

The legendary Maria Theresa Thaler had been the currency in Ethiopia from roughly 1730 inwards. At one stage in the reign of Haile Selassi, the emperor decided that large quantities must be taken out of the country. Tony Besse and his company were given the task.

The true Maria Theresa Thalers were 97% pure silver. It was the habit during the rainy season to bury them in kerosene tins. Now they were packed in small cases that could be passed through the manholes into the interior of the Besse trucks. The first convoy from Addis Ababa to the port of Assam, with a military escort, carried 250 tons. In Assam an illiterate Amharic Customs official rejected the documentation he could not read and wanted all coins counted one by one. Tony flew down to Assam, insisted then on an immediate meeting with the Emperor, had the documentation transformed into an order, and all was well. Successive convoys, each of ten vehicles and ten trailers, had no further difficulties.

And there were the Arab dhows.

Tony's father had been quick to exploit their qualities. Tony followed up.

These craft, sailing under the Besse flag, were remarkable for the personalities of their captains. These men were independent merchants. They provided the food and wages for their crews. They took on additional cargo if space allowed, on commission. Successful trading depended on bagged shipments that could easily be offloaded in primitive harbours and carried to their destinations in small consignments by camels or on smaller boats. Thus the quality of the bags was all-important. But the regularity of the local winds, which blow for five months steadily in one

Tony Besse

direction, then five months in the other, discouraged any more sophisticated development of these craft. Engines were not successful because their construction could not resist the vibrations.

The company made regular use of one remarkable marine architect. He was illiterate and thus used neither pencil nor paper. He simply asked which ports would be entered for loading and off-loading, how many crew would be carried, what the cargoes would consist of, and the dhow would emerge weeks later from his yard. Tony Besse was to commission an illustrated publication on Arab dhows and to lecture to the Society for Arabian Studies of Exeter University on these craft that are now almost entirely lost to history. [●]

That Tony Besse was a major figure in the region, both as his father's son and in his own right, was clear to all visitors, and the contacts he made in this way often ripened into long-term friendships. One of these was with the last British High Commissioner, Sir Humphrey Trevelyan. In the closing tense months of British rule, wives were repatriated

[●] MARES, the Marine Ethnography of the Arabian and Persian Gulf and the Red Sea project was launched at the University of Exeter in the UK in 2008

on account of the dangers, and Sir Humphrey became a frequent house guest. Tony recalls the dignified British withdrawal, the deliberate ceremony of the final day, the eloquent lowering of the flag, but also the complete abandonment of all the British houses that lay open to intruders the following morning. Tony himself went to rescue the visitors' book from the official residence which had been forgotten in the rush of events. The Besses and the Trevelyans remained close friends for many years.

Another prominent guest was Sir Hartley Shawcross, who had come to the world's attention as the very young British Prosecutor at the Nuremberg Trials. He had first come out to Aden to represent the interests of the Anglo-Iranian oil company, a subsidiary of Shell, after an Italian vessel, curiously named the *Mary Rose,* had been taken into custody by the Royal Navy after having allegedly broken the embargo placed on non-British ships in the area shortly after Mossadeq had nationalised all oil companies operating in Iran. On his second visit, and already alerted by experience to the indifferent quality of the Shell guest accommodation, Shawcross stayed with the Besses and subsequently invited them to stay with him at his East Sussex home in Friston. They discovered common interests, above all sailing, went on to own jointly some fine yachts, until the day when Shawcross entrusted Tony Besse through power of attorney with the administration of all his estate for the ten years preceding and two years after his death, a formidable task in difficult domestic circumstances that, so Tony felt in retrospect, seemed to absorb almost half of this time and energies.

Other Active Interests

In the unforeseeable way in which contacts are made during wartime, Tony Besse came across Jacques Cousteau. This was when Cousteau was cutting up the inner tubes of motor tyres to make underwater masks. Cousteau, thanks to the influence of his first wife, had been able to persuade the French company Air Liquide and one of their engineers, Gagnan, to develop a self-regulating valve that controlled the pressure of compressed air inhaled by divers irrespective of depth. This was the birth of sub-aqua. The dangers of this new activity were made all too clear when four divers, all known to Tony, died exploring a complex cave system in the Rhone part of France; their air had been poisoned with the exhaust fumes of the local garage compressor normally used for motor tyres. Tony himself got into difficulties when diving with Cousteau. He had no depth gauge, and when the classical depth dizziness began to overcome him, he discovered from Cousteau's

The skipper of Ocean Joy

gauge that they were at 72 metres. By this time he had too little air for the essential decompression stops and found himself with immediate shoulder pains placed in a decompression chamber. But diving with Cousteau at the Farsan Islands off the coast of Saudi Arabia among the 'unbelievable' marine life including friendly sharks that behaved like inquisitive, companionable dogs, and dozens of later diving excursions off the Turkish coast, searching for Greek and Roman treasures before this was prohibited, made this one of the passions of his life.

Tony once spent two months on Cousteau's boat *La Calypso,* which he had helped to finance, and had memorable experiences with Louis Malle, the noted film maker and director of Cousteau's *The Silent World*. Voyages of underwater exploration took them to the Farsan Islands, the Seychelles and the Amirantes. One especially lively memory concerns their joint visit to the Sultan of Abu Dhabi, Sheikh Shakhbout; the annual income of Abu Dhabi at the time was the equivalent of £7,500. Later, in 1954, the *La Calypso's* bow bubble, created to enable underwater filming, collapsed and required major reconstruction. This was done at Tony's expense in the Besse shipyard in Aden. Following this repair, *La Calypso* became the first vessel to engage in offshore survey work off the coast of Abu Dhabi. A large bell was lowered to the sea floor;

shots were fired down; and measurements of the vibration readings as well as core samples were sent to laboratories in Texas for detailed analysis. This truly pioneering work was done on behalf of the energy firms BP and Totale and the engineering company Schlumberger.

Tony needed and regularly indulged his taste and gifts for physical pursuits, the element of danger adding to their attractions. Sailing, windsurfing at which he was an expert, sub-aqua diving to extreme depths, skiing, riding powerful motor cycles between Lyons and Paris against the stop watch: life always required some drama.

One cannot be surprised that Kurt Hahn's philosophy found as ready an echo with the son as it had done with father and mother.

Tony Besse and Kurt Hahn

From his father's death onwards Tony had maintained an intermittent and respectful correspondence with Kurt Hahn and made the occasional visit to Gordonstoun. Already in 1952 he had assured Hahn that he should not hesitate *'to appeal to me if ever there is a scheme of yours for which you would like to have a special sum of money'*. He was rapidly persuaded during an evening walk on the Gordonstoun estate that, as Tony later expressed it, it was *'my privilege to endow the school with a proper lookout tower for the Coastguard Unit. The stroll up the hill marked a turning point in my life.'* But by the autumn of that same year Hahn was no longer Headmaster of Gordonstoun and was struggling to regain his health. Within a few months he was however to enter on arguably the most fruitful period of his life. His schemes became abundant in both number and scope. His foremost ambition from 1955 onwards was the Atlantic College.

Tony was now intensely preoccupied by his business and family affairs, and there can be no doubt that the critical personality in these years was Hilda Besse. Her loyalties to her husband, the man and the ideas, were now transferred to Kurt Hahn. She was distressed beyond expression by what she regarded as his shabby treatment by the Gordonstoun Governing Body over his departure. Her letters give passionate expression to her feelings. Her inner turmoil was made the more acute by the divisions that had opened up within her own family, and by her longing that Tony should succeed in following in his father's daunting footsteps. How disinterested was Kurt Hahn's skilfully attentive support in these years? He must have found welcome encouragement in her unquestioning confidence in his life's mission, and his immediately warm responses to her requests for counsel in her family affairs were a

natural response to such openly expressed admiration. Cynicism in such matters can always creep in by the back door but if, as noted above, Hahn was a skilful angler of men, his fish was in this as in so many other instances a very willing victim, as is clear from Tony's letter of 21st June 1959 to Eric Warburg:

> *'I made the acquaintance of Atlantic Colleges nearly three years ago when I had the privilege of accompanying Kurt Hahn on his German tour of Outward Bound Schools … our recent fumblings within the Atlantic Alliance have been lamentable indeed … against this fragmented tableau, common and purposeful action in the field of European education assumes greater urgency and, like you, I feel strongly that at least a 'pilot' college should be endowed with the peculiar vigour of Kurt Hahn's faith and sincerity … For the purpose of wider prospection … you may fairly assume that, at worst, response from this quarter will not be disappointing.'*

It was entirely sensible and in line with common donor practice that Tony Besse should eventually have offered one half of the St. Donat's purchase price on condition that British sources confirmed their commitment by finding the other half: hence the tense meeting in Kurt Hahn's habitual London den, Brown's Hotel in Dover Street, in October 1960, just 72 hours before the option to purchase expired. It was also entirely in line with the lead-up to the fateful meeting that a part of the Besse donation had been promised by his mother. The fact that, in the end, the entire donation came from him has ensured him his pre-eminent place in the UWC story. In excitement and drama it had been a saga worthy of the Castle's previous owner, William Randolph Hearst. The purchase completed, Tony Besse flew in a small private plane from London to Cardiff with Kurt Hahn sitting alongside the pilot and has never forgotten how Kurt, in his fanatical pursuit of fresh air, pulled open the window as they were taxiing for take-off (and how the pilot quietly lent across and closed it again as they left the runway). When I heard this story, I was reminded of the occasion in 1947 when Hahn had insisted on joining Malcolm Douglas-Hamilton, a crucial ally of his in the very early days of Outward Bound, in his open Tiger Moth for a flight from Aberdeen to Kinloss. Hahn borrowed a scarf from another lady guest whom he had successfully supplanted for this flight. Those who knew his ability to lose almost every object that was entrusted to him were not surprised to learn that he lost the scarf too, the pilot Douglas Hamilton having dived twice in efforts to recover it in mid-air.

Tony Besse and the United World Colleges

The Besse family had now launched two major enterprises that were finding their feet: St. Antony's College in Oxford, and Atlantic College. The reputation that Atlantic College rapidly established under Desmond Hoare's leadership would have thrilled the father, who had once written that *'The development and strengthening of character can only achieved by methods applied in certain schools – by tests of physical endurance (sea, mountains), by increasing responsibility – by intellectual tasks that the pupil must prepare as if he were attending a conference, and in the course of these tasks the teacher will pose even paradoxical questions to judge the level of interest and the knowledge acquired in order to confirm in the pupil his mastery of the subject and to give him full confidence in it.'* [●]

But Tony took a back seat in Atlantic College affairs, more than fully occupied in extracting himself and his business from the turmoil of the Middle East, until Mountbatten came along and insisted on his personal involvement. Under Mountbatten's International Presidency Tony took on the first Chairmanship of the International Board. It was a somewhat thankless task. The early colleges to join Atlantic College, now The United World College of the Atlantic, were set up by strong-minded and strong-willed individuals who had little time for centralised financial accountability and a common scholarship fund. Colleges and National Committees responded to Mountbatten's relentless energy and inspirational leadership (they had little choice); but submission to administrative control was another matter.

Tony's renown in UWC affairs does not however rest alone on his donation of St. Donat's Castle, decisive, courageous and farsighted as that was; and he happily remembers those experiences that have given him life-long satisfaction. They have been his travels with Mountbatten, his decisive achievements as a co-founder of the United World College of the Adriatic, his similar role in setting up the College in Bosnia and Herzegovina, his membership of the Council of Foundation of the International Baccalaureate in a critical phase of its development, and his single-handed achievement (and again generosity) in ensuring that Yemen also began to send students to the United World Colleges.

The UWC of the Adriatic

The story of Tony Besse's patient determination to bring the Adriatic College project, initially launched by Mountbatten and Gianfranco Facco Bonetti, to fruition is reflected in the chapter on Corrado Belci. What survives in his own memories is the straightforward enjoyment of working with warm-hearted Mediterranean colleagues whose response to every new problem requiring yet another Italian miracle for its solution was *'siamo in Italia'.* [●] His friendship with Gianfranco, with Bartolomeo Migone, with Gaspare Pacia the lawyer, his deep respect for the wisdom, integrity and utter dependability of the Region's President Avvocato Comelli and his governmental colleagues, was mirrored in <u>their</u> confidence that he was 'their man', that he would bring the United World Colleges, despite all the scepticism and anxiety, to the table. He was moved by their trust in him and responded accordingly. In the endless negotiations over the purchase of a major property in the centre of the village of Duino, the Hotel Ples (finally achieved years later) with a resistant lady owner in Ljubljana, he was told on the eve of yet another mission into Slovenia by Comelli that *'my car will be waiting for you at the hotel tomorrow*

[●] *'Le développement et l'affermissement du caractère ne peuvent être obtenus que par les méthodes appliquées dans certaines écoles – par des épreuves d'endurance physique (mer, montagne), par une responsabilité grandissante – par des travaux intellectuels que l'élève devra préparer comme un conférencier et du cours de cette épreuve, un professeur poserait des questions même paradoxales pour juger de l'intérêt pris, des connaissances acquises afin de confirmer l'étudiant dans la certitude qu'il est de même de posséder un sujet, et de lui donner confiance en lui.'*

A frequent chore – the signing of legal documents. In the background the regional lawyer Gaspare Pacia, a key founding personality

[●] *'We are in Italy'*

The Adriatic College's Founding Ceremony October 1982. From the left: Corrado Belci, Tony Besse, Governmental Commissioner in the Region Friuli-Venezia Giulia Prefetto Marroso, the Minister of Public Instruction Guido Bodrato, President of the Constitutional Court Leopold Elia, Rector of the University of Trieste Paolo Fusaroli (speaking), the Mayor of Trieste Manlio Cecovini, Professor Denis Mack Smith (hidden by the microphone), David Sutcliffe

Tony Besse is presented to President of the Italian Republic Sandro Pertini in February 1982. On the right: Senator Valitutti, a former Minister of Public Instruction, then Chairman of the Italian UWC National Committee

morning at 08.00, and whatever agreement you reach with the lady, we in the Region will back you'.

Nor can he forget the arrival at a meeting of the Italian National Committee of Andreatta, the Italian Minister of Finance, who on being told that they needed money, replied dryly *'then let us make some'*; and explained that the Italian mint owned a large supply of silver that had been purchased cheaply long ago, that the College could purchase it at a rock-bottom price and, with the minting of a new commemorative coin, stood to make a large contribution to the College's finances. The outcome was a silver coin that won prizes for its design, outsold almost all other commemorative coins in the history of the Italian mint, and raised more than 820,000 Euros for the College's budget. Indeed, *'siamo in Italia!'*

Bosnia and Herzegovina

When Tony learned that a former student of the Adriatic College who had specialized in Balkan languages and affairs, Pilvi Torsti, and I were travelling to Bosnia in January 2001, he simply said that he was coming along too. He had not been there before! This was the beginning of a six-year struggle to set up the movement's first college in a post-conflict country. Pilvi and I found we could always count on two things: his absolute refusal to lose heart, and his unfailing generosity in covering all those minor expenses, usually hospitality for those whose good will and help were important, that individually amount to little but collectively represent a major sum. We could not have done it without him. And then came the day when Pilvi had to decide whether, with her husband and then one child, she could move from Finland to Sarajevo to set up an office and to see the plans through to actual implementation. She wisely and firmly refused to do so unless she could be guaranteed a minimum budget to carry out the essential preparatory programmes in the City of Mostar. It was Tony who came forward with legally binding underwriting. *'Pilvi can make plans in the secure knowledge that she will not be running aground. I do not feel particularly happy or comfortable taking on this commitment but I am prepared to do it, against the odds, for the sake of not turning back. I believe in the project and it is not in my temperament to give up or give in.'* Again, a College (his third) could not have started without him.

Other Experiences

Tony was invited on to the International Baccalaureate Council of Foundation by its Founder President, John Goormaghtigh. He completed his IB tenure as Vice-President. Once again it is the friendships he remembers most warmly: John Goormaghtigh of course, Alec Peterson, Jacqueline Roubinet of the Ecole Bilingue in Paris, Piet Gathier from Holland, Monique Seefried, Greg Crafter, George Walker, Robert Blackburn. As always, he covered all his own expenses. Little known is the fact that, at a moment of special financial insecurity, he also covered anonymously a major part of the salary of the IB Deputy Director General, Robert Blackburn.

There were mixed memories and mixed feelings too. The money-raising recital he arranged for the UWC, given by his friend Kiri te Kanawa in Monte Carlo, with Sir John Pritchard conducting, attended by some 1,000 guests including the Monaco royalty and the UWC President the Prince of Wales, was an immense organisational task. It raised ten scholarships but achieved, in his eyes, little echo and little support in UWC circles.

France too has been a disappointment. His home country was first invited to join the UWC in 1962 when the philosopher Raymond Aron, a friend of Lawrance Darvall, attempted unsuccessfully after meeting Desmond Hoare to interest the Ministry of Education. Repeated efforts have been made to set French involvement on a more secure and ambitious path. No one was more enthusiastic than Mountbatten, who even pressed for a French college in Fontainebleau. Tony has never been an advocate for a French college, but the constantly renewed efforts of the French National Committee have reminded him of his father's disheartening experience: *'France has all the institutions it needs.'*

Continuing Besse Generosity

The Besse reputation and Besse wealth have generated many pressures on Tony's life. He has enjoyed the benefits – the sailing and the yachts, the sub-aqua diving, the skiing, the beautiful homes, art works and comfortable hotels – but he has never done anything other than try to share these things with as many friends as possible. *'Beiti Beitak: My House is Your House.'* His mother left her entire estate to St. Antony's, Oxford; hence the Lady Besse building. Tony was the executor of her will and contrasted ruefully the dons' anxiety to 'encash' the will with the university's long hesitations when his father first proposed his initial donation. He takes his wheelchair-bound sister, for 40 years a recluse in Monte Carlo, there as often as she feels up to it. She too has made major donations.

His father made gifts of Ethiopian art to the British Museum, where they are exhibited over his name. When

Tony and Christiane were leaving Aden, they were asked to purchase a large collection of Arab artefacts that had been assembled over many years by a rather remarkable, formally uneducated Indian. They refused them but successfully launched the idea of a Department of Antiquities, whose prospects were also much improved when Tony persuaded the British to insist on export licences for national treasures in order to prevent indiscriminate and large scale selling to foreign buyers.

Some of his quietest charitable work, which he mentions only with shy embarrassment, has been done on behalf of sick people. He discovered that he had a bookkeeper in Ethiopia suffering from glandular fever that had become cancerous. He sent him to England to combine medical treatment with a course in accounting. Thus qualified, this man soon became the chief accountant of the new national bank. He repaid his debts. The bank created unending trouble for the Besse Company. His accountant remained his faithful warning friend, telephoning him one day to tell him it was time for him to leave. 'When?' 'Soon.' The government humiliated him, refusing him an exit visa three times when he was already at the airport. He left Aden for the last time on 10th June 1969, the French consul carrying his bag to provide a touch of diplomatic protection and immunity.

He found another invalid after insisting on entering a local home, discovering a young girl, hidden by her parents, crawling on all-fours because polio had robbed her of the ability to walk upright. One leg was a matchstick. He brought her to Paris, where the surgeons insisted on immediate operations to rebuild the missing limb before calcification set in. Tony paid for 18 years of operations and treatment. She has spent half her life in bed. The psychological problems have been daunting. She was two and a half when Tony discovered her. She is now 37 and *'hops around like a gazelle'*. Her brother had colon cancer. The father paid the immediate costs but Tony has covered *'everything else'*. Medical treatment of this range and ambition runs, Tony says, counter to all local superstition, especially among women and mothers.

Reflections

Looking back, Tony describes his life as an inverted pyramid.

Nothing in his story made family life easy. Family life would not have been possible without Christiane. Her loyalty to Tony bears admirable comparison with the loyalty of Hilda to Anton. Starting on married life with 14 servants, a house the envy of the country and beyond, a role as hostess especially in both Aden and Beirut that rivalled

that of old Anton Besse in Aden, she never complained when the screw turned. When Tony found himself in jail in Yemen because a Yemeni, having bought shares, thought he now owned the company and had Tony imprisoned, she brought him his coffee every morning. Now, generally agreed to be the finest literary translator in France from English into French – James Baldwin, William Boyd, William Shawcross and Amitav Ghosh have been or are among her authors and close personal friends – she has her own publishing company in Paris, the Editions Philippe Rey.

Tony Besse is not everyone's man. The explanation lies in his background. He came into inherited wealth and inherited duties and assumed along with them an inherited right to the top table. He is impatient. *'Andre (his brother) and Tony have one characteristic in common – rapid and impulsive outbursts of anger'*, Hilda wrote to Kurt Hahn on 15th November 1951. And he has a disdain for authority and for constraints on his freedom of action.

His access, first through his parents and then on his own account, to the founding figures of the Atlantic College – Hahn, Darvall, Hoare, Schuster – was succeeded by his leading role in the setting up of two further Colleges. For him, intermediaries are either subordinates or obstacles. But Shell's documented judgement on his father rings true for Tony too: *'Besse's motives must always be assumed to be noble, whatever the actual sins of commission may be … if he feels he is with friends he will give of his utmost.'*

The Middle East has left its mark on him. He feels the injustices of the Arab-Israeli confrontation daily and personally. Among his closest friends are Crown Prince Hassan and his wife Princess Sarvarth, she a former IB Council colleague and founder and patron of the outstanding IB school in Amman.

Life in the region was a constant struggle for survival, always against the background of lawlessness. But he also remembers that Letters of Credit, or IOUs, were widely used in lieu of banks, which meant that everything was dependent on personal trust. *'Shiploads were disposed of in this way'*, and he could not recall a single instance of default. His most important contribution to this practice of personal trust has been his decision, after he had rescued his firm's Provident Fund from the Yemeni confiscation and transferred it to London, to honour all the distributions to members. This was considered miraculous, and he received tributes for years afterwards. *'Not even BP (British Petroleum) did this.'*

And it explains his stubborn determination to ensure that Yemeni students enter our United World Colleges, the scholarships offered by College Heads but the selection carried out by him each year on personal visits, the incidental costs such as travel and insurance very often carried by him too. His motto for this commitment could serve as a motto for all our efforts to identify and sponsor students from the world's poorest and most conflict-ridden areas: *'From nowhere to somewhere.'*

Tony's daughter Joy, an Atlantic College graduate, describes her father as the Don Quixote of Arabia. Like his great Italian friend Bartolomeo Migone, he has never failed to tilt hard against the windmills. His unusual personal engagement gives for me meaning to the phrase *'If education is understanding the rules, experience is understanding the exceptions.'*

Tony has lived his life against the grain. He has talked movingly of an acute sense of inadequacy and failure in the Middle East – *'We did not return to Aden or to Yemen … Yemen, the environment, my own temperament … I was not made for a primitive and lawless society'* but *'by then UWC had caught up with me: Mecklenburgh Square, Blackburn, Gourlay, the IB, George Schuster, the Mountbatten years, the setting up of the International Board, the establishment of new colleges under the Mountbatten impulse and thrust. I was no longer idle. I was busy. I was happy.'* We should also recognise that our Arab world advocates and interpreters have been few. Tony has held this fort often alone. Its importance is now becoming clearer by the day.

In 1968 Tony sent the Schusters a magnum of champagne for their Diamond Wedding. In 1970 George Schuster wrote him a letter. *'We had often looked at this splendid bottle without, hitherto, finding a worthy occasion for drinking it … I have just come back from two days at St. Donat's … on Saturday evening, at the closing ceremony, we had a large dinner party … the duty to make a closing speech on this occasion fell to me … I decided to take the line that, after we had been spending two days reviewing the present state and achievements at St. Donat's and in discussing the aims and tasks for future international development, I would like to ask them to look back over the past … I said that there was one man, a Frenchman, M. Anton Besse, who made that beginning possible … I said that I wanted them to drink your health and to send you a special message of appreciation and gratitude …'*

It has all been our gain.

Paweł Czartoryski

'The best teacher lodges an intent not in the mind but in the heart'[●]

The Cold War

It is crystal-clear that the Atlantic College was launched in 1962 as a contribution to the solidarity of the Atlantic Community – Western Europe and North America uniting to safeguard their values and common interests against the Soviet threat. Kurt Hahn made no bones about this. For Hahn and his early Atlantic College allies, the preservation of freedom in the 1960s was a western, an Atlantic matter, an issue of the spirit, a contest for the loyalty of the young. *'Ever since Khrushchev admitted in 1956 that murder and massacre were essential elements in the Stalin regime, many young people in Poland and in Russia today look towards the West, full of distrust and also full of hope, asking a question which makes us blush: "are you in earnest about the ideals you profess?"' Who shall give the answer?'* When challenged by a letter in *The Observer* newspaper to *'place himself outside the world struggle and to appeal to character-builders the world over, irrespective of race, colour or creed, or political persuasion … (to avoid being judged as) interested in winning rather than ending the Cold War',* Hahn replied with a characteristic aphorism*: 'I am all for loving our enemies, but I recommend as a preparatory exercise that we do not hate our friends.'* For the time being, it was challenge enough to bring young Germans to South Wales where, not so many years earlier, there had been German prisoner-of-war camps in nearby Bridgend.

In the early 1970s, under the passionate advocacy of the College's founding Headmaster Desmond Hoare, now devoting himself to expansion beyond Britain, it was in the Western Pacific and the developing world that the

[●] Anna Michaels *Fugitive Pieces* Bloomsbury Publishing Plc. 1998 page 121

United World Colleges began to see their future. Were the historical, intellectual and cultural legacies of Central and Eastern Europe to remain ignored, lost in the monolithic anonymity of Soviet hegemony?

Noteworthy nonetheless Hahn's specific reference to Poland in his hopes of an eventual response from behind the Iron Curtain! This was prescient, not unconnected with his own family history.

For me, a five-year-old when the Second World War broke out, the scale and brutality of events on the continent of Europe between 1939 and 1945, and after, remain beyond comprehension. And in the post-war years, the richly complex history, even the geography, of Eastern Europe, remained for me a grey blanket of threatening, inhuman uniformity. An attempt to see the celebrated Helene Weigel in a play by Berthold Brecht in East Berlin, thwarted by the obstructive, aggressive, ill-mannered behaviour of the communist border guards at the Friedrichstrasse crossing point, gave little encouragement to seek a human face on the other side of the infamous Curtain.

It takes outstanding individuals to break though such barriers. When I reflect now on the reciprocal commitment between Central and Eastern Europe and the United World Colleges, I think of Irena Veisaitė in Lithuania, Halyna Freeland in Ukraine, Olga Fadina in Russia, Vladimir Kolas in Belorussia, above all of Paweł Czartoryski in Poland.

The Czartoryski Family

The name Czartoryski has resonated throughout Polish history, for centuries standing for one of the country's leading noble families. Paweł Czartoryski's best known forebear was probably Adam Jerzy Czartoryski (1770–1861), perhaps the only man to have been at different times the head of government of two mutually hostile states. He was the Russian Imperial Minister of Foreign Affairs, *de facto* Chairman of the Russian Council of Ministers (1804–1806), later President of the Polish National Government during the November 1830 uprising against Imperial Russia. After losing favour and influence in Russia, he became the principal drafter of the 1818 Constitution of Poland, regarded as the most liberal in Europe at the time, although Poland remained under the control of Russia with the Tsar formally the King of Poland. As the President of the Provisional Government, Adam Jerzy Czartoryski summoned the Sejm (Parliament) of 1831 and was elected Chief of the Supreme National Council. The uprising that followed almost immediately afterwards saw crushing defeat by Russia and the death sentence for Czartoryski, commuted to exile. For his last 30 years he led the Lambert Circle, a group of Polish exiles named after the palais in Paris that he purchased and made his home. His *Essai sur la Diplomatie* includes comment of more recent relevance as he sought to win friends for his *'stateless nation'* that, he argued, was nonetheless an essential component of Europe. On Russia, for example: *'Having extended her sway south and west, and being by the nature of things unreachable from the east and north, Russia becomes a source of constant threat to Europe …'*; it would, he writes, have been in Russia's interest to have surrounded herself with *'friends rather than slaves'*. He also foresaw the future threat from Prussia and urged the incorporation of Eastern Prussia into a resurrected Poland. And in the same document he developed the concept of diplomacy based on moral principles, a follow-up to ideas he had expressed earlier on a Society of States, a forerunner of a League of Nations or United Nations.

It was Adam Jerzy's mother Izabela Czartoryska who, in 1796, had founded the Czartoryski Museum in Puławy – it is now in Krakow. Its aim was to preserve the Polish heritage in the conviction that the past gives inspiration for the future. Her son Adam Jerzy was her most active collector, acquiring in Italy Leonardo da Vinci's incomparable *The Lady with an Ermine* and Raphael's *Portrait of a Young Man,* together with other chiefly Roman treasures. In 1914 most of the contents were taken to Dresden for safe-keeping. Ironically, they returned to Dresden in 1940 as Nazi war booty, intended for Hitler's private collection at Linz. By a miracle, they survived both the war and the post-1945 communist regime and are now in the museum in Krakow, which is administered by the Prince Czartoryski Foundation, established in 1991 thanks in large measure to Paweł Czartoryski's determination and leadership.

If I had been left with any doubts about Paweł Czartoryski's lineage, they would have been scattered to the winds as, on our first visit to Poland in 1974, he walked my wife and me through his family's former castle in Krakow, gesturing with comfortable familiarity toward his ancestors' portraits as we tried to take it all in.

Paweł's Youth and War

As islanders, we Britons have always been rather relaxed over definitions of our nationality and constitution. Nature has set our boundaries – *'this precious stone set in the silver sea'* – and the constitution has remained unwritten, an oral understanding between us as citizens. The ever-shifting borders over centuries in Europe have imposed a dramatically different history 'over there', with remorseless consequences. After we moved to the Adriatic College in 1982, Eastern Europe became a greater reality for us. This College had the aspiration of becoming the UWC bridge between Western and Eastern Europe. We were fortunate in our timing. As we recruited students from an increasing number of the socialist countries, and were able at the same time to secure the generous support of other Colleges for the same purpose, I began slowly to understand more clearly how much was being done for us by this self-effacing university professor in Warsaw. He it was who found allies in Lithuania and Estonia and Latvia and Belorussia and Kaliningrad; he who took Polish UWC graduates with him on journeys to these countries to provide knowledge and support over committee building and student selection; he who provided the cultural cement that helped to convince these countries that they had a common interest in bringing some of their best young people into the international experience of the United World Colleges.

Paweł Czartoryski was 15 when Germany invaded Poland in September 1939. He had been brought up in the traditions of the Polish landed aristocracy which, as the memoirs of Countess Marion Dönhoff, Hans Graf von Lehndorff and many others tell us, were strikingly similar to those of their Prussian neighbours – Spartan living, an intense involvement in the natural environment, physically healthy pursuits, respect inculcated by parental education and family heritage for neighbours and especially those of more humble social status and, in this instance, a high regard for intellectual engagement and religious observance, with hymns and prayers every morning. His mother Zofia had a life-long influence on him. She was the eldest of four children, orphaned at a young age and brought up by another remarkable lady, Rose Raczyńska. Their foster mother Rose was the mother of Edward Raczyński, who was later the President of the Polish Republic in Exile in London during the Second World War. She spoke fluent

Three Czartoryski generations: grandfather Prince Witold, father Prince Włodzimierz and Paweł in the old traditional kontusz

English and French and had been compelled to earn small sums of money during and after the war in Poland by giving clandestine English lessons to help maintain her family.

Paweł was, in the words of a childhood friend, a *'wonderful boy'*, always the leader of the group. Taught hunting and shooting by his father, he was allowed to hunt wolves on his own. He was a fine horseman. He was always working with his hands, making presents from alabaster and wood, and a boat in which they went on fishing expeditions. He went skating and skiing. And not only the outdoors: when in September 1939 his grandfather celebrated his 50th wedding anniversary Paweł, one of 25 grandchildren, wrote a play *The Wawelian Dragon – A Tale of the Vistula River*. This re-tells the story of a Krakow shoemaker who wed the princess as a reward for saving his country. In Paweł's version the shoemaker, fully understanding and supporting the social hierarchy, prefers to remain a shoemaker rather than engage in ruling over his fellow-citizens. The rivers that join the Vistula, emulating the choirs of

classical tragedy, sing their comments in verses of varying rhythms taken from well-known folk songs. But he had a childish sense of mischief as well. When archaeologists were excavating a site nearby, he crept out in the night and buried a toothbrush in the soil still to be uncovered to give them a morning surprise.

But with the German invasion from the west in September 1939 the golden childhood was over. The Russian invasion from the east followed two weeks later. The Czartoryski estate lay in a central position between the German and the Russian fronts on the San River, thus becoming a natural refuge for relatives and friends fleeing from both the west and the east. The German occupiers moved into the house. After the German invasion of the Soviet Union a camp was set up in the grounds for Russian prisoners-of-war. Notwithstanding the dangers, the family provided refuge for intellectuals, disguised as labourers, who were being hunted down by the Nazis. One of these was the priest Kazimierz Kowalski, another reputedly the later Cardinal Wyszyński; yet another Professor Władysław Tatarkiewicz, to become one of the leading historians of philosophy and aesthetics in Poland. It was above all from these priests that Paweł, in secret, continued his education, the excellent family library an indispensable asset. Under Kowalski's guidance was born his life-long interest in theology, and he was reading St. Thomas Aquinas in Latin from the age of 15. Despite all the circumstances it was a happy home. Paweł found himself driving a tractor and working with the Russian prisoners. He was also the house electrician.

This account may suggest an isolated rural retreat from reality. We should be clear about the background. *'On 1st September some 1.8 million German troops invaded from three sides … they were supported by 2,600 tanks, of which the Polish army boasted barely 180, and over 2,000 aircraft … on 17th September Russian armies invaded from the east … the Germans lost over 50,000 men, 697 planes and 993 tanks and armoured cars. But the dogged resistance cost the Poles nearly 200,000 in dead and wounded … Priests, landowners, teachers, mayors, lawyers and persons of influence were summarily shot or sent to a concentration camp that was started at Oswiecim (Auschwitz) … .'* And roughly as many Poles had died in the bombing of Warsaw in 1939 as were later to die in Dresden in 1945. [•] Poland was now divided between the Germans and the Russians. The rump territory left under German control after the annexation

[•] Timothy Snyder: *Bloodlands* The Bodley Head London 2010 page 405 of extensive areas directly into the Reich was named the General Government and placed under the infamous Hans Frank. The straightforward intention was to erase the name and nation of Poland. This was a shorter-lived but even more savage reprise of the Third Partition of Poland in 1795, when the country was divided between Russia, Prussia and the Habsburg Empire and the name of Poland passed out of existence for 123 years. Now, under the Nazi regime, *'over the next five years 750,000 Germans were imported into the areas that had been attached to the Reich; 860,000 Poles from the same areas were resettled in the General Gouvernement … while a further 330,000 were shot … in all some 2,000,000 Poles were moved out of the Reich … while another 1,300,000 Poles were taken and shipped to the Reich as slave labour … over the next four years 2,700,000 Polish citizens of Jewish origin were taken from the ghettos and murdered …* [●]'

In 1942 Paweł took his Matura or high school certificate, having followed lessons at underground classes. The examining commission had also been set up in secret. He then immediately matriculated in the Law Department of the equally secret Jagiellonian University, teaching at this time being a mortally dangerous activity. [○] In 1945 he was able to legalise his academic status and, with a shortened academic year, to gain his Master of Law in 1946 at the University of Poznan. Thus qualified, he moved to Warsaw to work, first for the Ministry of Finance, then for the National Bank of Poland, where he edited their publications. His future was not however to be in banking but in the academic world.

[●] These details and other historical references in this essay are taken from the admirable, transparently loyal account of Polish history, *The Polish Way*, by Adam Zamoyski, himself the descendant of a family that has played a central role in the country's story, and a cousin of Paweł Czartoryski. *The Polish Way* Hippocrene Books New York 1994

[○] The Poles were practised in such matters. Clandestine classes under Russian domination in the 1880s had provided for the teaching in secret of the Polish language, history and religion which, with the addition of a 'flying university', eventually involved some one-third of the entire population. During the 20 years of its existence its courses were attended by some 5,000 women and thousands of men. Among the most famous of the women was the future Nobel Prize winner, Maria Skłodowska-Curie.

His Academic Career

The range of Paweł Czartoryski's subsequent intellectual activities is daunting. Indeed, the people responsible for the Warsaw University Library alphabetic catalogue, incapable of believing that a single person could be the author, editor and translator of so many books on such strikingly different subjects, created four distinct author's records under the heading *Czartoryski Paweł* for him. Already solidly grounded in Latin and Greek, and near fluent in French, English and German, he submitted and successfully defended a doctoral thesis in 1948 in the law faculty on markets for the sale of Polish coal. Whilst working on his PhD he was an assistant in the Department of Legal Economics at Warsaw University. From 1948 and until 1960 he was on the staff of the Catholic University of Lublin, first in the Faculty of Law, then of Philosophy. In October 1954 he was made an associate professor. In 1956–1957 he added public lectures on behalf of the Maria Curie-Skłodowska University to his commitments. In the same year he received a research position in the Centre (later Institute) of the History of Science at the Polish Academy of Sciences (PAN) where he worked until 1994. In 1957 he was made Chair of the Department of Econometrics at the same MCSU, a position he held until 1979. A scholarship from the Ford Foundation took him to the United States in 1957, where he took an MA in economics at Yale, followed by an autumn research project on cross-branch outflows at Harvard that made him a Polish pioneer in econometrics. His academic experience was further enriched by a six-month scholarship at the Ecole Pratique des Hautes Etudes in Paris. From 1960 he was cooperating with the National Committee of Spatial Development, part of the Polish Academy of Sciences, leading two teams in cross-branch outflows and in transport issues in Warsaw. In 1966/1967 he carried out investigations into cross-branch structures in the chemical industry. These were, however, all subsidiary interests.

Always drawn to philosophy, Paweł had seized the opportunity in the early 1950s of joining the new school initiated by Stefan Swieżawski, formed to study the old Polish sciences in the Jagiellonian University, in preparation for his *habilitation*, the essential prerequisite for a full professorship. And in 1956 he was enthusiastically welcomed *'as one of the most serious and best prepared historians of the social sciences'* by Professor Henryk Barycz, the leader of a team working on the history of science at the University of Krakow.

His first monograph on the way towards his *habilitation* was completed in 1956 on Sebastian Petrycy of Plzen. [•] It was noteworthy, and recognised as such by his intimate academic colleagues, for its skilful avoidance of Marxist cliché in both language and thought, a courageous accomplishment given the nature of the ruling regime; for its clearly stated, closely reasoned implication that the major previous work on this figure was nothing more than a compilation of well-known facts; and above all for its defence of the bourgeoisie and the peasantry against the demands of the nobility and the ruling classes, whilst making clear that wise politicians and *'landed conservatives'* alike must strive for an ever-increasing extension of civil rights to an ever-better educated population as the sole avenue for the avoidance of civil strife and public disobedience. Its translation into the contemporary political scene was clear for every discriminating reader.

In 1963 came his thesis *The Early Reception of Aristotle's 'Politics' in the Jagiellonian University of Krakow.*

Paweł had taken advantage of his autumn at Harvard to explore the almost complete collection of catalogues of medieval manuscripts available in the Harvard library. The result was a list of some 500 mss. and over 50 authors, with many additional anonymous texts. The library of the University of Krakow (1364) was found to hold more than 42 codices containing commentaries on the work of Aristotle, one of the largest collections in the world and evidence of intense preoccupation with these matters in Poland in the past. By comparison, all Oxford libraries together have 32 and the Vatican Library 30. Supporting these codices were numerous additional commentaries, many of them anonymous, and a complete list of lectures delivered in the university from 1487 onwards.

Paweł Czartoryski's research underlined the influence of the social theories of Aristotle on Krakow University teachers and, through them, on Polish public life in earlier times. And the Polish codices were, he wrote, essential elements in the preparation of students for public life and public service. *'Considering moral philosophy from the point of view of power, the Krakow masters maintained that ethics teaches one how to rule oneself, economics how to rule the home, and politics how to rule society. In the last of these, power and wisdom are united; however, to hold power does not merely involve wisdom, but it also teaches it. The essence of this science is to prepare men for public duties and to show how society should be organised. It teaches how to distinguish good and bad political systems and how to rule the best type of state in the best possible way. In tackling the problem of political power, the Krakow masters made it clear that its basis is freedom and natural equality among men … Philosophical utilitarianism – which penetrates so powerfully into this view – finds full expression in the problems of relations between the contemplative life and the life of action: contemplation is presented as absolute activity in conditions in which a man, left by himself, has full power over himself. Thus the active life, and hence the holding of power, is only a limited activity …'*

His thesis was declared outstanding. He received the degree of Associate Professor.

It was Paweł's knowledge of Latin and Greek that had enabled him to enter with such depth and precision into the messages of these ancient manuscripts. It was his family upbringing that made the subject matter so congenial, so immediate to him. It was his patriotism that illuminated his emphasis on the Polish nature of this contribution to European learning and to the evolution of society in the Middle Ages. It was an intellectual and a human posture that challenged and transcended contemporary political thought and action in his native land.

Paweł's fascination with previously unknown texts led him next to Copernicus. After his *habilitation* he began editing and publishing the writings of the great Polish scientist. In 1966 he was appointed Head of the Copernican Research Workshop at the Faculty of History of Science and Technology at the Polish Academy of Sciences. In 1969 he became a member of the Board of the History of Science and Technology of the Polish Research Council. By now he was supervising many doctoral theses. His students benefited from the methods that he had been able to bring from his experiences in France and the United States, and from the contacts he had made there. He is remembered to this day for his calmness and precision, for his insistence that international colleagues should always be fully acknowledged, for his perfectionism in the completion of texts, for his mastery of so many areas

[•] Sebastian Petrycy (d. 1626) was the first Polish translator of Aristotle's *Politics* and *Ethics*. He accompanied his translation with personal comments on conditions in Poland at the time. The 'natural' way of making one's living lay in agriculture, all the remaining forms of employment being associated with urban living. But the landowners, or nobility, were not only oppressing the serfs; they were also taking to commerce as a means of making large profits, with a consequent decay in town life. Nor were they taking proper care of their country estates, leading to national impoverishment and decline. He supported his case for a return to an uncorrupted form of government based on the three estates (the gentry, the burghers and the serfs) with references to Aristotelian principles: all one's actions must be based on virtue, the only foundation of true nobility.

of knowledge and languages, for the monthly seminars at which the scientific work of colleagues and students was meticulously reviewed, for the priority he gave to teamwork. In many respects he was to become a manager of science, the creator of teams with a visionary approach in the service of his country. It is felt now by many that he sacrificed his own efforts for the sake of inspiring the efforts of others. In the words of one, he was a monarch of Polish science, triggering movement over generations. The outcome speaks for itself. By the time of his death in 1999, he had edited and published 37 volumes of the *Studia Copernicana*. The series has now been completed with 43 volumes.

Science and Technology in the National Life

In 1970 Paweł published a monograph on the history of Polish science in the Middle Ages. His previous academic work having alerted him to the significance of the documents in the Jagiellonian Library, his mind was now opened to new horizons. He intensified his efforts to relate Polish social and scientific achievements to the new challenges of technology and political thought.

Noting in passing that Paweł also applied the word science to the study of moral philosophy, we learn from his writing at this time the following:

'There is an important difference between the concepts of the advance of pure technology and the advance of technology within its social context. The economic factors are almost always ignored. The most effective choice of technology is not always the most modern and up-to-date. Example: the inappropriateness of a fully automated factory in a country such as India with its enormous problems of unemployment.

Contemporary understanding of the history of science continues to assume the omnipotent, absolute and benevolent impact of technology on the human race. But there are innumerable problems and situations that escape the embrace of the exact sciences, notably the survival and flourishing of the human personality, that require the intervention of philosophy. All this despite the fact that philosophy may appear to have lost touch with the exact sciences! Not to be overlooked are the important contributions of epistemology and logic to the development of the exact sciences.

Given that science is only one of the intellectual or cultural activities of man, it is clear that the history of science may consequently be focused on this one dimension. But

our researches and our teaching in the history of science will be far richer if our teaching has deep roots, not only in general culture but also in the challenges of creating a harmonious relationship between the two for the future. Furthermore, the exploration of the culture of science will have an enormous impact on the cultural development of a given country and on its political, social and economic growth.

Finally, an understanding of the speed of the spread of scientific and technological advances, in both time and physically (or geographically), is essential for an appreciation of the impact of the great currents of human thought on our intellectual culture.'

Writing a few years later, Paweł Czartoryski emphasised his belief that the social framework within which science develops and is applied is usually national. Much the same, he claimed, applied also to the social sciences, especially perhaps history and literature. In a happy phrase the *'social radiation of science',* he underlines the impact of science on the life of the country. Of course, the greatest work in all areas will have international significance, but if one takes a comprehensive view that embraces the social, the economic and the political, the national elements remain fundamental. Referring to those science graduates who do not choose a scientific career, engaging instead in teaching and public service, he writes that their work *'is an additional link between science and social life, demonstrating also, at the basic level of the community, the interactions of science and religion, philosophy, literature and art.'*

If one seeks evidence of courageous independence of thought, remembering the crushing dominance of the Marxist-Leninist thinking that governed all activities in Poland at this time, allied with proof of his respect for colleagues and loyalty to teamwork, one finds it in the same piece of writing: *'The historian of science should have deep belief in the creative powers of the human mind, in its freedom of choice and autonomy. Each author or school in the development of science, even the least important, should be given the credit of independent thought. This is the only way of saving human values in the history of science … Let us examine closer the scope of such independence. It is obvious that not everyone is a genius, that the great discoveries and new basic ideas are the lot of a chosen few. Their followers however were also intelligent, thinking and living creatures, directed in their intellectual work by their own motivations; they had the freedom of choice within existing conditions, and above all they had definite aims and definite ideas concerning the sense of their intellectual work. If history of science is approached in this way, every* intellectual activity in the past becomes interesting and important ...'

He then draws on the age of the Enlightenment in Polish history, a period of political disintegration owing to the partition of the country between Germany, Austria and Russia. '... the Polish scientific activities of the period cannot be judged exclusively by intellectual standards, but they should be strictly connected with much broader motivation. Such men as Stanisław Konarski, King Stanisław Leszczyński, Hugo Kołłątaj or Stanisław Staszic were all engaged in the fight for the renewal of their country, treating science as one of the basic tools leading to this aim. Thus, they should not be judged exclusively by intellectual standards, since it is only the understanding of very complex political, social and cultural motivations that explains the autonomy of their choice and the real aims of their work.' [●]

In truth he was also writing about himself and his own time.

Extra-Curricular Activities!

We might reasonably conclude that Paweł Czartoryski's academic engagements were more than enough to fill his days. But he is remembered also for his general love of life – music, parties, and good food on the rare occasions it became available (and for his efforts to discipline his sweet tooth); for his practical jokes; for his expert dancing; perhaps above all for his continuing love of the mountains and wild country. He made frequent excursions to the Tatra, abandoning climbing by agreement with his wife Weronika when the first of their three children was born. Some of these outings included illegal cross-border entries into the Slovak Tatra. At least one long winter expedition on skis was devoted to tracking down remaining elements of ethnic identity in the former Polish-governed region of Ruthenia. Following this traverse of the Bieszczady Mountains he wrote a small book which suffered censorship on account of its references to burnt-out villages and other elements of ethnic suppression. In 1948 he took part in three mountain rescues, saving the life of a young girl in one of these. In the United States in 1957–1958 he undertook winter expeditions in the Appalachian and the Rocky Mountains. He founded the Lublin High Mountain Club and ran camps and courses for new members. In time the mountains became for him an aesthetical experience rather than a physical challenge – his closest mountaineering

[●] *Some Remarks on National History of Science – Organon 3 – 1966*

companion recalls however that he was never competitive, challenging only himself, and one is reminded of the comment by the Headmaster of Eton, Claude Elliott, much quoted by Kurt Hahn: *'mountaineering is the triumph of victory without the humiliation of the conquered'.* But his most significant contribution to Polish mountaineering was probably his membership of the Board of the Polish Alpine Club, of which he was for several years the Vice-President. The government of the People's Republic of Poland, especially in the 1960s under Władysław Gomułka, was anxious to gain international prestige. The Czartoryski name, Paweł's academic activities abroad including British Council-sponsored visits to British universities, and his command of foreign languages, which were suppressed severely by the communists and thus rare in those days, led to precious contacts with the mountaineering world in other countries and to the prizing from the government of funds for Polish expeditions with colleagues in other countries. And it was he who in the 1960s brought Sir John Hunt, the leader of the first successful Everest expedition, to Poland, to the evident satisfaction of the Party leadership. Until his withdrawal in 1967, Paweł always carried the responsibility for the allocation of the scarce funds placed at the disposal of the Polish Alpine Club.

The Sufferings of the Polish People

But even this picture is incomplete without recognition of the dominating influence in his life – his Catholic faith. Here too his family history played its part. On 25th April 2004 Pope John Paul beatified Prince August Czartoryski who, in April 1887, had defied his father and abandoned all the worldly rewards that awaited him to enter the novitiate and become, in 1893, a Salesian priest, having to overcome many *'habits'* and adjust to community life, frugal meals and other sacrifices, which he did *'with great serenity and abandonment to God'.* After the Second World War, as the process towards beatification, initiated already in 1927, was accelerating, the communist regime began to make trouble about his grave. Paweł Czartoryski ensured the safe-keeping of his ancestor's remains by having them moved from Sieniawa to their present resting place in Przemysl in a simple farmer's cart, concealed under sacks of potatoes. And in the August 1944 Warsaw uprising his uncle Prince Jan Franciszek Czartoryski, known as Father Michał, a Dominican priest and activist in the youth organisation *Odrodzenie* (Renaissance), refused to desert the wounded he was caring for, and together with them was shot by the German troops. He too was beatified on

13th June 1998, named as one of the 108 Martyrs of the Second World War.

Paweł Czartoryski's spiritual life, and that of his fellow Polish Catholics, must be seen against the background of national events.

Back on 5th October 1939, barely a month after the invasion, Hitler would have been blown to pieces whilst taking the salute at his Victory Parade in Warsaw, had last minute rearrangements not resulted in the man charged with detonating the explosives under the podium being moved beyond effective reach. By 1944 the Polish AK, the *Armia Krajowa* (Home Army) numbered over 400,000, the largest resistance group in Europe. The Delegatura, the political masters of the AK in liaison with the exiled National Government in London, controlled everything – underground law courts, universities, schools. The life of the nation, in Adam Zamoyski's words, was *'lived in hiding'.* Again to quote Zamoyski: *'The Poles are the nation who really lost the Second World War. They fought continuously from the first day to the bitter end and beyond. They put more effort into the struggle than any other society; they lost over half a million fighting men and women, and six million civilians; they were left with one million war orphans and over half a million invalids. According to the Bureau of War Reparations, the country had lost 38% of its national assets, compared to the 1.5% and 0.8% lost by France and Britain respectively … Although they were faithful members of the victorious alliance, they were treated as a vanquished enemy".'* [●] In the morbid scrum of comparative statistics, one notes that more Poles were killed in the 1944 Warsaw Uprising alone than in the combined atomic bombings of Hiroshima and Nagasaki. [○] And we must recall with shame that, under pressure from Stalin, the British Government forbade their participation in the 1946 London Victory Parade. Churchill's words in the House of Commons became bitter irony: *'His Majesty's Government will never forget the debt they owe to the Polish troops who have served them so valiantly and to all those who have fought under our command. I earnestly hope it may be possible to offer them citizenship and freedom of the British Empire, if they so desire … but as far as we are concerned we should think it an honour to have such faithful*

and valiant warriors dwelling among us as if they were men of our own blood …'

In the post-1945 chaos and the imposition of Soviet rule, up to 16,000 former AK members are believed to have been interrogated, tortured and – usually – murdered. In the 1947 elections, one million people were disqualified from voting by bureaucratic trickery, thousands were arrested or beaten up on election day, 128 activists of the largest party, the Polish People's Party (PSL) were murdered, 149 of their candidates were disqualified, 28 were elected of whom 14 were subsequently also disqualified. After further turmoil, including the setting up of two new concentration camps with some 30,000 prisoners, a Soviet constitution was imposed in 1952 and the country became the People's Republic of Poland.

Against this backdrop of limitless repression, indoctrination and physical hardship, the Catholic Church was the one indomitable opponent. All Church possessions had been 'nationalised' in 1949, religious instruction forbidden in schools, chaplains banned from prisons and hospitals. In 1952 three bishops and several priests were charged with spying for the United States and punished with imprisonment or death sentences, and in 1953 Cardinal Wyszyński was himself imprisoned. But Khrushchev's speech to the 20th Party Congress in Moscow brought a measure of change. The Polish President Bolesław Bierut who heard him speak died with doubtlessly unintentional symbolism of a sudden heart attack. Gomułka, previously disgraced, returned to power promising socialism *'with a human face and a Polish costume'.* Cardinal Wyszyński was released.

In the vicious ebb and flow of events in Poland between 1945 and 1990, three elements gradually and courageously emerged that frustrated and finally defeated the socialist tyranny. They were the Catholic Church, the alliance that was forged between the intellectuals and the workers, and the sense of national identity and patriotism that had already sustained the country throughout the war, indeed for many preceding decades. And on 16th October 1978 the Cardinal Archbishop of Krakow became the Pope, his election *'not only a solace in their misery, as well as a great national honour; it was also the final breach in the wall behind which they had been kept since 1945 … the Polish question once more hovered over the international stage'.* [●]

[●] Timothy Garton Ash echoes this judgement: *'… the end of Yalta also began in Poland. No country did more for the cause of liberty in Europe in the 1980s, and no country paid a higher price.' History of the Present*, Allen Lane, Penguin Press 1999 page 91

[○] Timothy Snyder. *Bloodlands* page 405

[●] Adam Zamoyski page 389

His Personal Beliefs

The Czartoryskis and the future Pope were close neighbours in Lublin for several years in the 1950s. They had often shared simple meals together, dominated, it seems, by blood sausage and tea; engaged in endless discussion; gone on pilgrimages together. A constant theme had been their determination to avoid compromising themselves with the so-called *'regime Catholics'*. The problems affecting the entire country in the 1970s and 1980s brought them ever closer together. It was an almost natural development that Paweł should have subsequently provided ideas and texts for some of the Pope's speeches on his return visits to his homeland. But what was Paweł doing as the crowds assembled to hear their Pope for the first time in Warsaw in June 1979? His wife's cousin, Elżbieta Cielecka, remembers the euphoria, the white and red flags, *'the heat of a June day that seemed to have no effect on the people'*, *'the sudden peace that engulfed the city'*, when she heard a familiar voice behind her. It was Paweł shepherding a group of small boys to a place from where they could see and hear what was going on properly! On later visits to Rome, Paweł was a key advisor to John Paul II on internal Polish affairs. His daughter Irena says that the Pope was always *'at his disposal'*.

Catholicism, one may reasonably argue, was given to Paweł Czartoryski with his mother's milk. He brought to his adult faith his family's respect for tradition as well as spiritual convictions that rested on rigorous intellectual scrutiny. Whilst he favoured church reform in response to changing social conditions, he was not a liberal. His love for the Latin of the old traditional liturgy and the language of the *Wujek* translation of the Bible that had accompanied generations of his family in their devotions undoubtedly led to sadness when they were abandoned, but he was glad of the greater accessibility to the people of holy texts that resulted. His beliefs lay in civilisation, culture, ideals, openness to all for the common good, no truck with Masonry, no compromise with the communists, daily attendance at Mass, private prayer, and a reserved attitude towards Cardinal Wyszyński who, somewhat distrustful of the surviving urban intellectuals, invested his confidence and his pastoral strivings in the simpler, more intuitive Catholic communities in the countryside and in their less sophisticated priests, but to whom he did not hesitate to express the people's concerns. But when a 'black sheep' member of the family in Krakow, seeking a divorce, was boycotted and disowned by all her fellow Catholics, Paweł went immediately to see her to understand the circumstances. Their disapproval may have been aristocratic rather than Catholic, but Paweł did not hesitate to provide the money for the lawyer's fees.

It is a little-known fact that the first step in the reconciliation between Germany and Poland, the ultimate fruit of which was Willy Brandt's *Ostpolitik*, was an open letter addressed by the Polish bishops to their German colleagues in 1965 calling for mutual forgiveness and reconciliation: *'Wir vergeben und wir bitten um Vergebung'.* [●] This remarkable gesture is fully and generously acknowledged by the former German President Richard Weizsäcker in his memoirs *Vier Zeiten*.

The Dominicans, the Poles and the Jews

The Dominican Order was the natural spiritual home and inspiration for Paweł Czartoryski. His boyhood reading of Thomas Aquinas had led on to intensive discussions with fellow-students, mostly at breakfast meetings, [○] in the immediate post-war years, when he was bemused to discover that there were rivalries between the Dominicans and the Jesuits over youth issues. This was a period of deep religious commitment on the part of students, who defied efforts of the secret police to invade their meetings and debates. On one still celebrated occasion, university and high school students, Paweł among them, were sitting together after prayers when their meeting room was invaded by brutal police agents who suspected a gathering of armed partisans. Police shouts: *'Have you got arms?'* The students spontaneously and as one drew forth their rosaries, furthering angering the police who assumed mockery. But of course nothing suspicious was found, and the event became a small symbol of the victory of the church over the police state.

The English Catholic writer G. K. Chesterton's allusive, in part elusive monograph on St. Thomas Aquinas makes clear what an attractive figure St. Thomas must have been for Paweł Czartoryski, for St. Thomas had rehabilitated Aristotle in contemporary theology. In Chesterton's reflections on

[●] *'We forgive and we ask for forgiveness'*

[○] These breakfast meetings would have further endeared him to Kurt Hahn, whose breakfast occasions in Brown's Hotel in London were legendary, not least because he was in the habit of conducting two or three simultaneously in different rooms. When Pope John XXIII was elected in 1958, Kurt Hahn declared (over breakfast) without the slightest hesitation or delay that he was destined to be a great Pope uniquely on the grounds that he invited guests to breakfast.

the saint '… *the intellect is at home in the topmost heavens; … the appetite for truth may outlast and even devour all the duller appetites of man* [●] … *There never would have been any quarrel between Science and Religion …he (St. Thomas) did his very best to map out the two provinces for them, and to trace a just frontier between them* [○] … *He was in a double sense an intellectual aristocrat but he was never an intellectual snob …'* [■] and even '*if he had traces of true Christian mysticism, he took jolly good care that they should not occur at other people's dinner tables …'* [□]

The loyalties of St. Thomas Aquinas to the teachings of Aristotle fed Paweł's need for intellectual conviction – a harmonious balance between reason and belief in a God-determined social and hierarchical structure of the world and the Church, set apart from the political manoeuvrings of the contemporary world, disciplined, civilised ideas formulated by a member of the aristocracy who became a saint. He shared with St. Thomas the confidence '*that all men will ultimately listen to reason … that men can be convinced by argument, when they reach the end of the argument. Only his common sense also told him that the argument never ends.'* [◆]

G. K. Chesterton, writing in 1933, conceded that '*St. Dominic is still conceived as an Inquisitor devising thumbscrews (whilst Francis of Assisi is already accepted as a humanitarian deploring mousetraps …)'.* [◇] The implication is the leading role played by the Dominicans, the Cani Domini, the Hounds of God, in prosecuting heresy under the Inquisition, causing the deaths of thousands of Jews in Spain under Queen Isabella and their eventual expulsion in 1492, many of them fleeing to Poland for safety. No reflection on the tragedies suffered by the Poles is separable from their shared destiny with the Jewish people, nor is either divisible from their common struggle of both doctrine and blood with communism.

The Poles have given many hostages to fortune, been burdened with relentlessly evoked commentaries on their alleged anti-Semitism. The historian Lewis Namier, himself of Central European origin, tells us that all the fighting on the Eastern Front in the First World War took place in the Polish Pale, that its Jewish population in 1921 was over six millions, that almost 3 millions (but probably more) were in Poland itself: '*these suffered from the all-pervading anti-Semitism of an intensely nationalistic regime and people, in an overcrowded and impoverished country'.* [●]

It is a deeply complex subject.

Who can match the heroism of the young Polish and Catholic woman Irena Sendler who, dressed in a nurse's uniform and wearing the Star of David to identify herself with the Jewish population, smuggled 2,500 babies and infants out of the Ghetto, placing them with sympathetic Polish families, orphanages, hospitals and convents, who taught them Christian prayers and how to make the sign of the Cross so that their Jewish ancestry might not be suspected; who after capture and torture during which both her legs and her feet were broken, refused to betray either the children or her helpers?

The penalty for assisting the Jews under the German occupation was death. None could have survived without Polish help. And according to one historian, it is almost certain that more Jews fought in the 1944 uprising alongside the Polish combatants than in the Jewish uprising in 1943. [○]

The commitment of countless young Jewish men and women to the supra-national egalitarian idealism of the new communist world, [■] the subsequent identification of the Jews with Bolshevism, the conflation of these two worlds with anti-Semitism, created the conditions under which all the peoples across the entire vast region of Eastern Europe were to pay a formidable price in both blood and conscience in the second half of the 20th century.

These matters bore heavily on Polish society in the three decades after the Second World War, for the Jews had long been seen as the main propagators of communism and therefore as agents of Soviet domination. It was communist Soviet Russia after all that had liberated the country from the Nazis, and several leading members of post-war Polish governments were Jews. But the resurgence of Polish self-respect and patriotism was to turn

---

[●] G. K. Chesterton *St. Thomas Aquinas* Dover Publications Inc. New York page 40

[○] Ibidem page 51

[■] Ibidem page 79

[□] Ibidem page 78

[◆] Ibidem page 14

[◇] Ibidem page 18–19

[●] Lewis Namier: *Conflicts* Macmillan and Co Ltd. 1942 page 141

[○] Timothy Snyder *Bloodlands* page 302

[■] *'The motivation of youthful converts to Communism in this period was selfless and altruistic, and their own life prospects – notwithstanding the promise of a bright, happy future for generations to come – were virtually certain to include imprisonment, material want, and living on the run.' Jan Gross. Fear: Anti-Semitism in Poland after Auschwitz* Princeton University Press 2006 page 193

with growing force and confidence against communism, against Soviet Russia, against the country that (as was now well known) had been responsible for the Katyn massacre of Polish officers. The manipulative encouragement of anti-Semitism, fostered by the Kremlin after Stalin had turned against the Jews in 1948, became a particularly unattractive feature of the Polish political scene; and explicit Polish condemnation of the Holocaust was lost in the confusion of conflicting loyalties as Catholic Poland sought to reassert its national pride.

Politics

Paweł had won early insights into the lives of the miners in Silesia with his doctoral thesis of 1948. In the 1970s he began to work closely with the mining communities. He respected the miners. They trusted him. Paweł Czartoryski the nobleman, the Prince, stayed with miners in their homes; miners came to his. He also arranged the visits of children to the mines, officially forbidden but for him a way of strengthening social understanding.

It has been calculated that 5,000 million dollars worth of Polish coal was given away free to the Soviet Union between 1946 and 1955 at a time when coal was virtually the only means of acquiring foreign currency. In 1957 1,500 miners were sacked in the interests of discipline. It was now that not only students but members of the adult and professional intelligentsia made common cause with this oppressed, suffering part of the national community. The involvement of the intelligentsia helped to make the situation better known abroad through the skilful and carefully focused passing on of names and events. International attention was alerted. Paweł Czartoryski was one of the focal points around whom all these developments coalesced.

But international attention did not solve their financial problems. In June 1980, the struggling Premier Edward Gierek suddenly raised food prices. Lech Wałęsa and his fellow-workers occupied and closed the shipyards of Danzig, protesting against the illegal dismissal of a colleague, and Solidarity was born. Within two months the government had signed a far-reaching agreement with a movement whose members totalled over ten million, in effect almost the entire working population. Perhaps the most remarkable feature of this explosion of democracy was its programme of education: writers, artists, priests, all suddenly sensed the freedom to express and communicate their ideas. It was not to last. The economic crisis persisted; all public services but notably health and education were in acute crisis; many members of Solidarity wanted the organisation to move towards direct political

Paweł with workers in Śląsk (Silesia) in 1992

action; and the Soviet Union intervened in December 1981. The consequence was the sudden imposition of martial law, nominally by the Polish government under General Wojciech Jaruzelski. Its brutality is difficult now to recall. '… *virtually the entire leadership of Solidarity was arrested … thousands of people were dragged from their beds and ferried through the freezing night to prisons and concentration camps … the Wujek mine in Silesia was the scene of a spectacular underground occupation, which ended in tragedy as the enraged ZOMO (Citizens Militia) opened fire on the surrendering miners … their colleagues in the Piast mine held out longer, but the last 900 came to the surface on 28th December … in all, some 10,000 of its members were detained, while another 150,000 were hauled in for "preventive and cautionary talks" …' [●]*

Whilst General Jaruzelski, the Soviet-imposed leader, moved within 15 months to release the detainees, including Lech Wałęsa, the persecution continued. In 1985 some 100 senior academic figures were arrested. It is especially astonishing that the Pope was able to visit again in 1983, for many Catholic priests were being beaten up and several were murdered. Pope John Paul II visited yet

[●] Adam Zamoyski *The Polish Way* page 393

again in 1987, speaking with both General Jaruzelski and Lech Wałęsa, without however succeeding in bringing the two together; and that summer ZOMO units once again stormed mines in Silesia. A threatened general strike led to agreement that round table talks should take place, and the justly celebrated Round Table was born, with the talks beginning in February 1989. On 5th April an accord was reached that seems almost as astonishing in retrospect as it must have been at the time. Freedom of speech and the independence of the judiciary were established and democratic elections were decided on for June. Solidarity candidates won all of the open seats for the lower house whilst 33 of the party's candidates for seats reserved for Party members failed to achieve the minimum number of votes (including General Czesław Kiszczak, the Minister of the Interior, and the Prime Minister Mieczysław Rakowski). Solidarity took 99 seats of 100 in the Senate. Solidarity refused to join a coalition government with the Party and, after horse trading, the Catholic intellectual Tadeusz Mazowiecki [●] was nominated head of the new government. Lech Wałęsa now became effectively the Head of State and addressed the American Congress in November. In the same year, from June until November, the Hungarians conducted their so-called *'triangle table'* talks, which led to an agreement on free elections that were held in March 1990. By then the Czechs had elbowed aside party rule and the East Germans torn down the Berlin Wall. Yalta had been overturned. [○]

Paweł Czartoryski's links with the miners gave his role in the Solidarity movement a natural authority based on close familiarity with the mentality and living conditions of these hard-pressed and vital workers.

[●] Special UN emissary to Bosnia and Herzegovina in 1992 and author of a report on human rights violations in the former Yugoslavia, Mazowiecki resigned in 1995 in protest against the world powers' lack of response to the atrocities committed during the Bosnian war, especially in Srebrenica. He and Paweł Czartoryski were close colleagues in setting up the Catholic Intellectuals Club in Warsaw in 1956. Paweł drafted for him his Stettin speech to an audience of young people in 1990 that was picked up by the international press and achieved much prominence in the ongoing international debate over events in Poland: '… *I know very well that you sometimes feel marginalized, that you believe social involvement, politics, public activities – may seem unattainable as they belong to an older generation, whose debates are irrelevant to you. Nonetheless, it is YOU who make future … without you all our plans would be futile…'*

[○] These paragraphs are a simple summary of pages 390–398 of Adam Zamoyski's *The Polish Way*

In the early days of Solidarity, Paweł Czartoryski was active in the Centre of Socio-Professional Activities (*Ośrodek Prac Społeczno-Zawodowych*), which was an integral part of the National Coordinating Committee (*Krajowa Komisja Koordynacyjna 'Solidarności'*). Later, he was a member of Lech Wałęsa's Civic Committee (*Komitet Obywatelski przy Lechu Wałęsie*), a 'Shadow Cabinet', in which he was responsible for the areas of youth and education. In the official Round Table discussions he was the spokesman for educational reform and joined Lech Wałęsa's Citizens' Club that prepared the first elections of 1990. Thus he was throughout the tense 1980s an active, trusted member of the opposition, an advisor to the leaders of both the miners and of Solidarity, maintaining close contact with the miners during martial law when things had to be done in secret, *'a quiet talker but with a really important role in creating new initiatives'*; described by another observer as *'the main mover in the spiritual dimension of the work with the miners and with Solidarity',* although when a more secular group emerged he continued unhesitatingly to work with them as well. He is remembered for his lectures in the mid-1980s to Solidarity members, for the days of culture in the regions, for the concerts, the lectures, the discussions and debates, the prayer sessions, the theatre performances.

Striking achievements in the 1990s included the 'train conference' that crossed the country by rail on its educational mission; another the setting up of the Youth Agency that, among its other accomplishments, paved the way towards the creation of the National Committee for the United World Colleges.

The remarkable election of 1989, however, confronted Paweł Czartoryski with new dilemmas. These had already emerged during the Round Table discussions, for the Sub-Table in which he took part, on education and youth, took so uncompromising a line with the communist participants that it threatened the success of the Round Table as a whole. For now politics and the need to compromise became dominant, and 'Paweł *was unable to play political games. He wanted to do something useful for society. He had no personal ambitions, and the shallowness and unfairness and meanness of the politicians disgusted him. His were different aims and different manners.'* Matters were all the more unbearable for him because these compromises were being made with former communists who were anxious, not only to retain power, but also to ensure that their own past was not opened to public scrutiny. It is at this point that post-communist history in Germany and Poland were to take different paths, for it was the prior existence of two German states that made possible the

A session of the Forum of Educational Initiatives in Warsaw in 1999

opening of the Stasi archives whose length, stacked side by side, was 158 kilometres. No such cleansing has yet become possible for Poland.

Invited to stand as a Member of Parliament, Paweł refused. Aristocratic disdain? Distaste for the inescapable compromises of politics? I have found myself drawn at this point to the horrifying war memoirs of his relative Karolina Lanckorońska, who survived several German prisons, solitary confinement, a death sentence and the Ravensbrück concentration camp before dying in Rome at the age of 104. *'We firmly believed that the Germans would beat the Muscovites, after which the Germans, already weakened, would be finished off by the Allies. Then, both our enemies having fallen, Poland would rise between them, morally powerful in the unity and collective harmony imparted to us by this terrible strife. We knew that the ransom – the price to be paid in blood – would be immeasurable, but we felt that we possessed today something that many nations (Poland among them) had never possessed in their history, for we were creating a national unity in the face of which class or party political differences would be seen as mere childhood illnesses outgrown, never to return ... Amid the general great misfortune, there was a period of the most intense happiness, when nobody bothered about anybody else's class origins or party affiliation. There was only that collective moral strength, which was Polishness'.* [●] For all too long, as Adam Zamoyski concedes, all virtue had lain in opposition. The future imposed different challenges. This future was not,

in the words of Timothy Garton Ash, to escape *'images of endless discord and noble anarchy'.* [●]

Personal Principles

One must ask oneself: How did Paweł Czartoryski engage in all these activities and survive? His ability to be creatively active in so many related yet distinctive academic spheres was paralleled by his capacity to live his social and political life in different compartments, a pattern also dictated by considerations of security. It was said that he had a taste for working in secret, that he loved the whiff of a benevolent conspiracy. But he also had stamina in these matters. His contacts with the silent, hidden opposition had begun in the early 1970s. From then on, every year of survival seemed a miracle. It was not a matter of charisma – public speaking was stressful for him – but of trust. The miners trusted him and Solidarity trusted him. He was always measured and careful in his contacts with the authorities but ruthlessly faithful to a few crucial principles. He refused to sign Party documents, even in order to secure travel visas, and rejected all contacts with the secret police. With meticulous skill he sidestepped the normally obligatory references to Marxism in his writings and yet managed to get them published. Those who knew him well knew also that he suffered greatly under the communist regime, both spiritually and materially, but no one heard him complain. When communists were present at meetings he would seek neither to stand out nor to initiate dispute. Whilst he was determined to show that very few Poles were Stalinist, he nevertheless always sought harmony in human relations. His actions were substantially governed by two principles: – *lustracja* (investigate and make peace) and *gruba kreska* (resolve problems without trials and condemnation). Years earlier, a friend had commented: *'You can trust Paweł completely. He is amenable, but no one will ever turn him into an opportunist.'* His spiritual strength and calmness gave Solidarity power.

He must have been protected too by the traditional Polish respect for intellectuals, communism notwithstanding, and by the regime's constant need for international acceptability. The communist rulers had learned a lesson from their disastrous attempt to mount an intellectual offensive against the West with a conference in Wroclaw in 1948. A Soviet assault on Jean Paul Sartre, the left-wing

[●] Countess Karolina Lanckoronska: *Those Who Trespass Against Us – One Woman's War against the Nazis* Pimlico page 205

[●] Timothy Garton Ash *History of the Present* Allen Lane, Penguin Press 1999 page 88

idol, backfired and led the otherwise Russian-friendly historian A. J. P. Taylor to declare, in comments broadcast not only in the conference hall but in the streets of Wroclaw and Warsaw, that it was the duty of intellectuals to fight all authoritarian influence, whether from Wall Street or the Kremlin. The conditions under which Poles were allowed foreign travel were well known and applied to all: a formal invitation from hosts abroad with full financial guarantees, and one family member only at a time. Thus Paweł was able to travel with relative freedom between 1956 and 1981 and again after 1990, but his wife was never able to accompany him as long as the Communists were in power.

Paweł married Weronika Ponińska on 26th December 1952 in Kraków. The oldest of eight children, her father was killed at the outset of the war in September 1939. Her mother was again pregnant and suffering from severe depression. Weronika took responsibility at the age of 19 for the entire family, fleeing first from the Germans, then from the Russians, by horse and cart, surviving the war by staying with relatives. A little later she became an active member of the AK, the Polish resistance. Some say she gave up her life to her husband's life. Others talk with great sensitivity and warmth of their *'interlocking faiths'*, their equal intellectual gifts, of Paweł's consistent practice of awaiting her views before expressing his own, of the calm home atmosphere that was especially welcoming to *'lost'* people, of her *'radiation of kindness and love'*. It is probable that neither of them expressed personal feelings easily. In principle Paweł qualified as a full professor in 1964. Party reasons postponed his formal nomination until 1992 with severe implications for his salary. The need for money to maintain his family of three children is at least a partial explanation of his exhausting schedule of lectures and other academic work at three different research institutions – in Warsaw, Krakow and Lublin. And there was a shadow too across their lives. In 1948 Weronika had been arrested by the secret police and imprisoned for nearly a year. In those days most of those in prison were tortured; many died. Weronika has never described what she experienced. Her children do not know. This direct exposure to regime brutality must have remained a permanent reminder within the family of the perils of independent thought. No explanation for her imprisonment is known. The archives have remained closed or even been partially destroyed. Weronika died on 22nd October 2010.

His Educational Ideals

Paweł Czartoryski's ideas on education follow in a straight line from his family background and religious beliefs, and we have already seen how they were strengthened and confirmed for him by his study of early Polish manuscripts whose lessons were at such grave odds with the practices imposed by communism. [•]

> He was convinced of the importance of an educated elite.
> This elite must have deep roots, must not think of itself as better than the rest, must belong *'to the world'*, must not be provincial.

[•] Once again Paweł had family history to encourage him. Adam Kazimierz Czartoryski, the father of Prince Adam Jerzy Czartoryski, already mentioned, was a member of the Polish National Commission for Education of 1773, the first 'Ministry of Education' of its kind in Europe. Its aspiration was the social and political regeneration of the state. It was in control of every school in Poland, state and private, thus in effect an all-powerful if temporary Ministry of Education. Its inspiration was the saying of Helvetius: *L'education peut tout.*

Paweł with his wife Weronika in Laski in 1995

A UWC regional conference in Warsaw in 1995

Passion in intellectual discovery is fundamental, but
there must always be the social involvement.

The highest social duty is to help the less fortunate,
but he was not a socialist and he instinctively
distrusted the reactions of the majority.

A healthy society will respect merit and accept the
hierarchical consequences but will be based on
an equal start in education that is wholly free of
financial elitism.

There must be elements in society that nurture
virtue to counteract the state monopoly. These
elements must be spiritual and intellectual. The
social tissue of society must be built from the
bottom and based on complete emancipation.

The educator's role must be focused, not on
solutions but on methodologies.

But it was his relationships with his students that bring
him to life for us.

His instinctive sympathy for people who were timid,
frightened or felt left out led naturally to his concern to
draw out the best in his pupils and their minds, to open
them up. He always helped with his own knowledge and
his personal connections. He was constantly concerned for

the financial situation of junior colleagues. *'Conversations
with him were a privilege.' 'He helped me when first my
parents and then my husband were dying.'* Tutorials begun
in Warsaw were continued on skiing trips. He *'caught'* the
differences in children. He much preferred oral examinations and never tried to *'break'* candidates, always seeking
to ask them what they knew. One special memory concerns
his support for the camps arranged for the children of
intellectuals who had been imprisoned under martial law.

These, too, are the memories of United World College
students. He kept eye contact with all of them as they faced
the interviewing panel. Whenever possible, he would sit
with them and their parents during the lunch interval to
learn more about them. Always on the lookout for potential, he searched for unusual features in their personalities.
He followed their later careers and always remembered
them. Interviewing applicants in Lithuania, he uncovered
one boy's interest in a Lithuanian writer, Oscar Miłosz,
whose poetry was about his religious enlightenment
and the relationship between faith and philosophy. He
told this boy he would better understand this poet if he
learned Polish, indeed that this alone was reason enough
to learn Polish. Sitting with this boy and three others over
coffee, he discovered that another was an orphan who

had been left to run his parents' small farm on his own and yet managed to succeed in school. When some of this same group came to Poland to attend a UNESCO summer school, Paweł met them at the central railway station and saw them off again on their departure. The orphaned boy later completed his doctorate in the field of optics; the literary enthusiast learned his Polish and in 2000 published his first article about the correspondence of Czesław Miłosz with Lithuanian authors. On opening the journal that contained his essay he trembled, for there was an obituary and *'the face of Professor Paweł Czartoryski looking at me – alongside an article about his love for the mountains, and about mountaineering. It seemed that he was checking whether I had really fulfilled my promise … I had the feeling that he was still watching over me.'*

Paweł Czartoryski and the United World Colleges

It is not clear when and how Paweł made his first contact with the United World Colleges. One strong possibility is through the British Council. Another version has it that he

Paweł Czartoryski in a characteristic conference posture

met the former British ambassador to Poland, Eric Berthoud, who was an early member of the Atlantic College Council, in the mountains on a walking expedition. Paweł's son Witold became the first Polish student, selected by the British Council, to win a two-year scholarship (and become in his second year the Chairman of the Students' Council). His daughter Irena, together with a student friend, the daughter of the then Minister of Education Jerzy Kuberski, spent some summer weeks at Atlantic College as trainee teachers. It was Kuberski, Minister of Education in the communist regime who had both his children baptised, who provided, uniquely for a communist regime, three governmental scholarships for Atlantic College in 1974. The funds rapidly dried up, and it was Paweł's extraordinary achievement nonetheless to ensure that the Polish scholarship entry to Atlantic College continued without a break during the period of martial law, mostly funded by Polish expatriate friends of his who were living in London. After Pope John Paul's election to the Holy See, Kuberski was sent to the Vatican as the Polish Ambassador there, another intriguing link in the chain of human relationships. It is in retrospect of remarkable interest that he as Minister, together with Paweł Czartoryski, was already in the 1970s, however briefly, examining the possibilities of setting up a United World College in Poland. Paweł pursued this idea with determination and later had the Castle of Kazimierz Dolny on the Vistula in his sights. It was not to be. But his other UWC work bore impressive fruit. [●]

[●] Paweł's cousin Zygmunt Tyszkiewicz tells the following anecdote: *'I was reminded of my visit to Poland in 1968, the year of the Prague Spring and a year in which Poland also experienced political unrest and severe reprisals from the authorities. It was a tense time. I was in Warsaw and Paweł invited me to join him and all the family on an outing to the country. We were joined by another family, whom I did not know but assumed were intimate friends of Paweł, so I took little care of what we talked about or of the comments I made. Inevitably, because of the troubles in Poland and in Prague, the conversation was highly political. Next day I asked Paweł to tell me more about the family which had accompanied us on the previous day's outing. Who were they exactly? I was astonished to learn that the Dad was Minister of Education in the Communist Government. I said to Paweł "Why on earth didn't you warn me? I would have been more careful about what I said!" Paweł replied "I deliberately did not warn you, because I wanted you to discover for yourself what sort of 'Communists' we have here in Poland". He then went on to say that very many (but not all) the political bigwigs were no more communist than me, but needed to keep up the pretence for reasons of job security and income. They had their children baptised in secret.' 'Dad' must have been Minister Kuberski.*

In the early 1990s the International Baccalaureate was beginning to interest Polish schools, but their progress was severely impeded by the persistent refusal of the Ministry of Education to recognise the Diploma for university entry. I then became a direct witness of Paweł's influence and ability to achieve results. Having successfully persuaded the Minister to visit a UWC conference in Kazimierz, he cornered his unsuspecting target in a small room with only two others present and insisted with quiet but forceful words on the urgent need for action. Just 14 days later recognition for the IB in Poland was confirmed.

In the 1990s, with a democratically elected government in power, Paweł became determined to *'change everything'*, to bring Polish education up to European standards, to reintroduce the concept of *Erziehung* – education, not simply instruction – the formation of personality and character, to complement purely academic training, to give physical activities and challenges a legitimate role, to teach pupils how to handle issues of aggression, to bring social issues and a commitment to help for the needy into the school curriculum, to emphasise living languages, to promote information technology, to give Polish education a more European, even a world dimension. In 1989 he had prepared the papers on education and youth for the Round Table. Now he started seminars on education, attended by parliamentarians and professors, intended to influence educational reform. In 1992 he set up an Institute for Research on Youth in Warsaw University, to be followed in 1997 by the Forum for Educational Initiatives. Under his presidency this body was registered as a legal entity in order to provide stronger support for the Ministry of Education, which was facing enormous financial problems, in its attempts to press ahead with reforms. He wanted to bring in Poland's eastern neighbours, to have Poland provide educational leadership in Eastern Europe. His inspiration arose directly from his experiences with the United World Colleges. It was thanks to him that the UWC movement now had national committees in Belarus, Estonia, Latvia, Lithuania, Kaliningrad and Ukraine. He was a cautious admirer of the Polish hero Józef Piłsudski, who with the 1921 Treaty of Riga had attempted to set up a vast Polish Commonwealth embracing Ukraine, Lithuania and Belarus. But this was Polish leadership of a different nature. Vladimir Kolas in Belarus remembers the significance for him of having a professor with a record going back over generations of public and cultural service; this relationship with a truly spiritual aristocrat was, he said, fundamental for his UWC work in profoundly difficult, hostile circumstances. And Irena Veisaitė from Lithuania recalls meeting Paweł for the first time in 1993 at the UWC gathering in Kazimierz. She had heard about him from a friend. Her immediate reaction: *'Lithuania must also catch this virus'* (thus unknowingly echoing Hahn's phrase: *'our spiritual defences need strengthening. There are not only infectious diseases; there is such a thing as infectious health'*) [●] *'He was,'* she said, *'full of love, pity and deep faith, always ready to help.'*

On 11th November 2008 the Paweł Czartoryski United World Colleges Association was awarded a prize in the annual Pro Publico Bono competition for the best contributions to citizenship and service. The most prestigious contest of its kind in Poland, and presided over by the former Prime Minister Jerzy Buzek and the former Ombudsman and President of the Constitutional Court Professor Andrzej Zoll, it had drawn more than 300 contestants.

Some Concluding Personal Impressions

For all his outstanding achievements, and the calm courage and beliefs that made them possible, Paweł Czartoryski remains a strangely elusive figure. His daughter Irena cannot conceal some sadness in remembering that her father did not have the time both to act and to share his experiences – we can, he always said, discuss these matters when you have more time after bringing up your eight children, but we can talk now about gardening and pruning fruit trees, on which he regarded himself as something of an expert. Of course this reticence also marks the secret and dangerous nature of much of what he was engaged in. It remains clear that no single professional colleague, no single student, no family relative or friend had an all-embracing picture, but the impact of his personality lies beyond any debate.

A Hungarian friend has given us some personal insights. On his first ever visit abroad in 1962, the late Professor András Nagy was in Warsaw attending a conference on economics and met there *'the most prominent specialist in the theory of input-output in Poland … I realized at once that I could trust him'*. Paweł's immediate questions (*'he always asked more questions than he gave answers'*) on the 1956 uprising in Budapest were: how did it happen that neither the army nor the police defended the system, indeed even gave their weapons into the hands of the insurgents; and what led to the spontaneous forming of rebel committees and workers' councils all over the country? Visiting

[●] From Hahn's first memorandum in 1956 setting out the case for the Atlantic College

Paweł's parents later in Krakow, still unaware of his family backqround, he was puzzled by the combination of the tiny apartment and the valuable china. He recalls Paweł's condemnation of the Russian invasion of Czechoslovakia, of the anti-Semitism that drove many Poles abroad, and his judgement that Poland had been fortunate in the 1980s to escape Soviet invasion and massacres. He had never met *a wiser, more balanced person'.

Paweł's natural identification with history, historical figures and family defined his role in society. His example helped to ensure that communism failed to kill aristocracy, not to be sure the aristocracy of the landed gentry, but the aristocracy of the spirit. In him was the meeting place between aristocracy and democracy. His commitment to social justice, personal merit and the freedom of the individual carried the message that civil society and non-governmental organisations and initiatives must become responsible for the standards of virtue in public life. Patriotic but wary of nationalism, he feared above all the abuse of privatisation and corruption. At a time of a general lack of trust, he demonstrated that the most powerful influence on human relationships is trust itself. Whilst never seeking to step forward as a leader, he was clear that he must act in such a way that his ideas were never misused – the key element here is personal integrity. It was certainly not by chance that most of the leaders of the silent opposition met in his local parish, or that the Catholic University of Lublin, where his presence and influence were strong, was the one free seat of learning throughout the communist rule, or that it was this university that brought together priests and laymen to found the influential Club of the Catholic Intelligentsia. Bronisław Geremek, a close friend of Paweł Czartoryski, speaks in interviews published in *The Year 1989* of *'the mission of the Polish intelligentsia, which has always served Poland above all, not selfish ambition or advantage'. 'A romantic self-image, no doubt'*, comments Ash, *'but hardly an ignoble one'.* [●]

His last months were months of illness, almost completely concealed from others. In the past, one relative said, he had had his moments of pessimism but had always kept them to himself. *'I felt in later visits he made to England that he had become far more serious and remote.'* One former examination candidate and later colleague remembers how, at their last meeting, he placed a cross on her forehead – she failed to realise its significance. At a final meeting with his fellow-editor of the Studia Copernicana,

he could do no more than point in silence at Volume 37 with his finger. Always a self-effacing man, he slipped away quietly on 11th August 1999 when everybody's attention was on the solar eclipse. One who first met him on a 1984 pilgrimage to Czestochowa summarises her memories of him in the eloquent language that played so large a part in his life: *'le travail méticuleux de la perfection si nécessaire dans celui de l'édition – la lutte clandestine, de dénuement, de confrontation avec un pouvoir hostile inquisiteur mais curieusement avide de ces personnalités dont les familles ont marqué le cours de l'histoire du pays – l'enracinement dans une foi vive et profonde qui se manifestait par un parfait détachement – les nouvelles générations ont pu se sentir chez elles dans la maison européenne … '.*

His UWC students – the word 'his' merits special emphasis – were utterly devoted to him. In my UWC experience, only Bartolomeo Migone from Italy comes close to him in this regard. With both, this relationship was born in the scholarship interviews, in the manner in which the two men, in examining their candidates for the colleges, embodied a respect for the personalities and aspirations of the young people in front of them which was then never forgotten. And I have no doubt at all that the Polish students were as moved and as impressed as I was by the readiness of Paweł Czartoryski to travel all the way from Warsaw to Venice by bus to enable him to visit them and to represent his country at the meeting of the UWC International Council at Duino in 1990. No other delegate, of whatever age, accepted so modest, tiring and economical a form of travel. And for him it was a given that all Polish students in Duino would, whatever the difficulties, find their way at least once to Rome and the Vatican City during their two years in the College.

The historian Norman Davies writes tellingly of *'the cultural imperative'* that *'constituted the nation's chief treasure and its last line of defence, to be preserved at all costs'*, and how *'the creation of the National Education Committee in 1773 was the price which the Sejm of the Old Polish Republic exacted for consent to the Treaties of Partition'. 'In the end, where the generals and military planners failed, the educators triumphed … The way in which this was achieved can best be likened to a relay of Olympic runners, where each man carries the torch of learning for a stage before passing it on, exhausted, to the next runner.'* [●]

With its changing borders and centuries of struggle for survival, its often desperate fights to keep the language

[●] Quoted on page 80 of Timothy Garton Ash: *History of the Present*, Allen Lane, Penguin Press 1999

[●] Norman Davies: *Heart of Europe* Oxford University Press 2001 pages 229–230

alive against the aggressive impositions of Russian and German, there have been three threads of consistency in the Polish story: the nobility, Catholicism and the intelligentsia. The backcloth is national loneliness, isolation and humiliation, perhaps most bitterly so in the latter part of the 20th century. Poland had after all driven back the Bolshevik armies in 1920 – *Lenin's Failed Conquest of Europe* [•] is the sub-title of Adam Zamoyski's account of the Polish achievement under Piłsudski – and had tasted some 20 years of reasonably democratic cooperation with the West before being abandoned to Hitler, Stalin and their successors.

In her *The Three Weeks' War in Poland*, an account of the German and then the Soviet invasions in September 1939, the adventurous, distinguished *Daily Telegraph* correspondent Clare Hollingworth describes how she goes to meet Mademoiselle Kazimiera Iłłakowiczówna, the former secretary of Marshal Piłsudski and now friend and supporter of Colonel Beck. She and Beck have escaped to Romania, but *'I can't stay here. I must go back to Poland. For me it is impossible to remain permanently away.'* But *'you wouldn't wish to be under Russian rule'. 'I don't care what rule I'm under. It's all the same to me if it is communist or not. I have nothing to lose. And it is Poland.'* Clare Hollingworth concludes: *'Polish patriotism has a special meaning. It is not the preservation of free institutions and personal liberty, as it is to an Englishman, a Frenchman or an American. It is not the power of the state, as it is to a German, or perhaps an Italian. It is not a social system and an ideology, as it is to a Russian. It is simply the Existence of Poland.'* [o]

In his epilogue to Aileen Orr's intriguing account of Wojtek, the bear that accompanied Polish troops during the war from Bandar Pahlavi on the Caspian Sea through Palestine, Alexandria, Monte Cassino and the rest of the Italian campaign into exile in Scotland, Neal Ascherson describes the disastrous Polish uprising of 1863, the one year's resistance, the subsequent police terror, public hangings and files of men and women chained together and marched off to Siberia. The lesson, he writes, was that the time for romantic sacrificial rebellions was over, that *'patient positivist campaigns'* now became necessary to build up the nation's strength. The Second World War was a tragic replay, and the aftermath required the same response. This was the critical insight that inspired Paweł Czartoryski's life.

We in the United World Colleges, especially if we are not from Poland or Eastern Europe and belong to larger nations that have not faced the constant historical fear of extinction, must try to understand the exceptional quality and achievement of this man. For, in the end, what passed as communism under the Soviet regime was ultimately defeated, not by NATO solidarity, important though that was, but by the *'cultural imperative'*. The Communist rulers and their malpractices were brought down by men and women who were probably more intelligent, quite certainly more cultured and who, having greater faith, were ready to debate and to wait. In the brief speech in which he accepted his Nobel Prize for Literature Yosif Brodsky, no stranger to persecution, tells us *'I am quite sure that a man who reads poetry is harder to prevail upon than one who does not.'* The Welsh author Jan Morris gives a moving account of *'the magnificent outpouring of ritual and ceremony which surrounded the Catholic Church in Poland in the days when it stood alone against the dingy autocracy of Communism … on a weekday evening in the 1950s one often saw citizens slipping into church, out of the cold and snowy city, rather as commuters elsewhere popped into a bar before catching the train home, entering hurriedly, crossing themselves as one might sign in at a club, and emerging a few moments later buttoning up their coats, pulling on their thick gloves, and hurrying away to the trolley bus – stocked up, as it were, with some reviving stimulant.'* [•] This was spiritual, not political engagement. It proved more powerful.

The English historian Macaulay has this to say about the British aristocracy: *'… our democracy was, from an early period, the most aristocratic, and our aristocracy the most democratic, in the world.'* [o] Can one imagine a sentiment more appropriate to the Pole Paweł Czartoryski? His family history endowed him with standards and obligations to which he gave added nobility by his life. An English author, Peregrine Worsthorne, a colourful and combative believer in the principles of the nobility, wrote: *'Character is what redeems the dirty work of politics, and character is what the aristocracy produced.'* [■] Recalling Paweł, it is difficult to conceive an outwardly less aristocratic, an inwardly more noble character than his.

We should be clear. Paweł Czartoryski could have turned his back on his native land. He had friends and professional colleagues who would have welcomed him in Britain and in

[•] Adam Zamoyski: *Warsaw 1920 – Lenin's Failed Conquest of Europe*. Harper Press 2008

[o] Clare Hollingworth *The Three Weeks' War in Poland* Duckworth London 1940 pages 162–163

[•] Jan Morris: *Europe – An Intimate Journey*. Faber and Faber Paperback Edition 2006 pages 37–38

[o] Quoted in Peregrine Worsthorne: *Democracy Needs Aristocracy* – Harper Perennial paperback edition 2005

[■] Ibidem page 78

the United States. His academic and social standing would have cleared all obstacles. But he had other values and other priorities. Neither a priest nor a monk, he was nonetheless, to quote the words of Patrick Leigh Fermor, engaged in *'the scaling of heavenly mountains and the exploration of inner mansions'*, committed to reducing *'the moral overdraft of mankind.'* [●] His life outgrew his circumstances. Like his country, and on behalf of his country, he looked above all to the West for friendship and collaboration. His faith in the outcome was enduring. I wish he could have encountered Kurt Hahn. He would have been enchanted by Kurt's stories of his legendary Polish grandmother. His devotion to the United World Colleges remains enrichment for us all. Is it too fanciful to liken him to the trumpeter of St. Mary in the great square of Krakow, with his warning salute, the *hejnał Mariacki*, the bugle call that also rang out over Monte Cassino after the final successful assault by the Polish troops, his call broken off in mid-phrase but the message clear? [●]

[●] Patrick Leigh Fermor: *Time to Keep Silence* Penguin Books page 34

[●] This image is taken from Jan Morris *Europe – An Intimate Journey* Faber and Faber Paperback Edition 2006 page 174 *'Every hour, night and day, a trumpeter appears in a high window of the Church of St. Mary to blow a slow, sad call north, east, south and west, the most plaintive of tocsins, breaking off always in the middle of a phrase, as tradition demands (a thirteenth century predecessor having been shot dead by a Mongol arrow before he could finish his warning).'*

Lawrance Darvall

If, with no spark of originality, we may contemplate human relations as a series of links in an unending chain, we shall be helped to understand why Lawrance Darvall, little known to either staff or students even in the earliest days, was so decisive a personality in the Atlantic College story. One can never be sure about these things, especially with as unpredictable an educational entrepreneur as Kurt Hahn in the frame, but I doubt whether even the magician Hahn could have translated his NATO Defense College lecture experience of 1955 into the Atlantic College of 1962, had the Defense College Commandant, Lawrance Darvall, not been the man he was.

Senior military command in war-time must impose strains on the human spirit that are beyond my comprehension, but I can well remember, in my brief four months in 1960 when I was a stand-in secretary for Kurt Hahn and Atlantic College business was his top priority, constantly meeting those impressive military figures Air Marshal Sir Lawrance Darvall, Admiral Sir Michael Denny, Rear-Admiral Desmond Hoare, whose truly passionate concern was to accomplish something in what remained of their active lives that would help to diminish the chances of renewed warfare. I can recall also a sense of unease that idealism was supposed to be the prerogative of youth, and that I was not matching up.

Character was not short in the Darvall family. Lawrance was the second of five sons and one daughter. His elder brother got a First in Engineering in Cambridge. The third brother never achieved much in life despite apparently being able to read a page out of a book, then repeat it immediately afterwards from memory. Brother number 4 bought a dying preparatory school with 20 boys and no applicants and transformed it into two schools with 100 boys each and waiting lists as long as your arm. Son number 5 went into the diplomatic service, married an American, became President of the English Speaking Union, but gave it all up when they lost their only son. The daughter became the head and owner of a secretarial college in Hampstead, took up mountaineering at 40, was a member of the first

The Air Marshal

women's Everest expedition, and eventually President of the Ladies Alpine Club. Neither she nor the preparatory school headmaster married. The Darvall children were, to put matters modestly, not spoiled by their parents, and the boys, who all attended Dover College, were known for being without pocket money for extras.

I think it is recognised and accepted that military men are generally reluctant to recount their wartime experiences until very late in life. At first they want to put their memories behind them, or are unable to achieve communication with others who have not shared their intense battle emotions. Later, usually much later, they sense the need to leave their mark, however small and personal, on posterity, at least within the family. Lawrance Darvall died young, at 69, an important reason why he remained almost unknown to the Atlantic College community; and his family, I have found, know little about his military career. What we do know is this.

At the outbreak of the First World War he was a cadet at Sandhurst. By being evasive about his birth date he enrolled, under-age, with the Green Howards Regiment and received his officer's commission on 16th August 1916. Attached in November to the 14th King's Regiment, he fought in the trenches at Saloniki, where he won the Military Cross for gallantry on 3rd June 1917. Attracted by the new adventure of flying, he transferred to the Royal Flying Corps in November 1917. Returning officially to the Green Howards in March 1918, he remained seconded to the RFC and was subsequently re-seconded to the RFC, now Royal Air Force, for two years (1919–1921). He was granted a permanent commission with the RAF on 17th November 1921 with the rank of Flying Officer.

From 1923 to 1927 Lawrance Darvall, known to all as Johnny, was posted to India, where his chief task was acting as the liaison officer between the troops on the ground and the flying groups that were engaged in frequent punitive expeditions against insurgent forces. In 1932 he was posted

to the RAF Staff College and from there to Iraq, where for three years he ran the staff division at the headquarters of the RAF Commander-in-Chief. In 1935 he was promoted Squadron Leader and in 1937 Wing Commander. After Iraq he was appointed to the Air Ministry in London.

The outbreak of the Second World War saw him commanding the RAF station Hawkindge. He was however rapidly moved, in January 1940, to become Deputy Director of the War Planning Department at the Air Ministry, and dispatched to join the Allied Military Committee in Paris. It was now, a month after Hitler had launched his Blitzkrieg through Holland, Belgium and France, that Lawrance Darvall was invited to lunch at the Dorchester Hotel by Sir Louis Greig, the Personal Assistant to the Secretary of State for Air, to meet the best-selling novelist Dennis Wheatley.

Dennis Wheatley, whose writing of thrillers and in particular of a series of books on the adventures of a secret agent in Germany between 1939 and 1941 had given him some useful background, had written a paper *Resistance to Invasion* that had attracted the attention and interest of the War Office.

Lawrance Darvall was very quick to recognise the value of exploiting Dennis Wheatley's imagination and capacity for rapid writing – the paper *Resistance to Invasion* of 7,000

With General Douglas MacArthur (Lawrance Darvall on the right)

words was written, typed and corrected in about 16 hours. Wheatley went on, mostly at Darvall's instigation, to write some 13 papers in the first year of the war which went to the Joint Planning Staff, of which Wheatley was the only civilian commissioned to become a member, and to the King. All these papers were eventually published in 1959 with an introduction by Lawrance Darvall.

Darvall wrote: *'I saw the possibilities of using his genius; so suggested subjects to him with which we were ourselves wrestling, thus encouraging him to burn the midnight oil and to summon to his aid all his imagination, background knowledge and enthusiasm.'*

Dennis Wheatley was unhesitatingly grateful. *'That he should have born with my ignorance, stupidities, and sometimes absurd suggestions … shows the breadth of his own inquiring, vigorous and imaginative mind.'* And he goes on to relate a telling incident.

'As an illustration of the mental attitude of such officers as Lawrance Darvall, I may mention the matter of sub-machine guns. At the outbreak of the war, we had not got one in this country. We had to buy half a dozen from the Italians to find out what they were like. By May 1940 they were in the process of manufacture here, but few, if any, had actually been delivered to the Forces. [...] mentioned that he had a business associate in Chicago who, on receipt of a cable, would at once dispatch 5,000 to us, but he could get no satisfaction from the War Office who were still arguing whether or not to buy them. Darvall, although then only a wing-commander, told him over the lunch table to cable for them right away, and that he would take responsibility for this quarter of a million pound order.'

In 1941 Lawrance Darvall became ADC to the Commander-in-Chief of South East Asia, Air Chief Marshal Sir Robert Brooke-Popham, with whom, in the words of his daughter, he *'retreated from every known bit of the British colonies in the face of the advancing Japanese'* until he found himself a member of General Wavell's planning staff in India until 1943, at which point he was sent back

Escorting King George VI and Queen Elizabeth

to the Air Ministry in London as Director of Air Transport Policy and Operations. From 1944–1946 he commanded No. 46 and 216 Groups in Transport Command and in 1946 became Air Commodore and Air Officer commanding Air HQ in Italy, an operational area that covered Egypt, Cyprus, Malta and the entire Middle East. From 1947–1948 he commanded No. 3 Group Bomber Command (Austria and all Italy) and was promoted to the rank of Air Vice-Marshal. From 1951–1953 he was Commandant of the British Joint Services Staff College and from 1953–1955 of the NATO Defense College in Paris. He retired in 1955 with the rank of Air Marshal and having been made a Knight Commander of the Bath (KCB).

This may all sound a shade conventional and office-bound, however impressively successful: unbroken promotion with rapid moves to ever more senior ranks and more demanding responsibilities, but essentially administrative. But this account omits the excitements and stresses of the early flying, the Indian sorties, the complexities and dangers of constant withdrawals from Japanese advances. There we catch glimpses of unusual qualities. In June 1933, whilst stationed in Iraq, he passed examinations in spoken Arabic. He was a tall, imposing figure, very good-looking, with prematurely whitening hair. When he was serving as ADC to Brooke-Popham, who had a small, unremarkable physique, the bands struck up for Darvall, not the C-in-C, before they learned to hide Darvall until all danger of embarrassment was gone. During Operation Overlord, the Allied invasion of Normandy in 1944, Darvall flew as second pilot in one of the lead aircraft during the initial aerial attacks. When Montgomery's Arnhem operation was running into bad trouble, he flew into the battle area and landed to see the conditions on the ground for himself, the only senior RAF officer to do so, returning with a dead German's helmet as a souvenir for his son. And in 1945, no doubt wanting to see some of the victory action for himself, he took an aircraft without any prior consultation and with a small handful of companions into Oslo, a day and a half before the war ended, where he was confronted by German soldiers. *'They were a bit hostile at the airfield at first, but I told them "the war is over anyway and you might as well surrender now".'* He drove on into the city where he single-handedly accepted the surrender of the astonished German commanding officer who, already taken aback by Darvall's unannounced appearance, found his handshake after the signature of documents refused, a scene that was captured on film and made Darvall into an immediate national hero for the now liberated Norwegian nation (and has remained an episode that appears again and again in film summaries of the Second World War). One of his first

With General Montgomery

post-war tasks was to recommend a site for a new London airport. Londoners living near Heathrow will not bless his name, but he foresaw from the outset the size of the area that would be needed.

Lawrance Darvall's tall, striking, indisputably military appearance was, very soon after his retirement, to generate comment and some mystification in Hahn's various schools, Salem, Gordonstoun and Outward Bound, for it was Hahn's unfailing practice to ensure that all important new allies ('brothers-in arms') should visit his schools, where they acted, none more so than Darvall, as both ambassadors for the Hahn mission and reporters on morale to the ever-anxious founder. Thus Lawrance Darvall spent one period of six weeks in Salem at a problematic period in the school's history, joining the governing body and imprinting the concept of NATO perhaps rather too firmly on the next stage in Hahn's school-founding journey. He also joined the governing body of Gordonstoun, likewise that of his former school Dover College and of Sevenoaks School near his home where the Headmaster, L. C. Taylor, with Darvall's warm encouragement, was taking the first steps towards giving the school an international character.

As a fellow-Englishman living in the enormous castle, formerly monastery, of Salem (I was still teaching at the school), I saw something of Lawrance Darvall in those weeks. Without his wife, he seemed rather lonely and under-occupied, but I discovered that he spoke near-fluent French, painted with enthusiasm, was a considerable expert

With Baron 'Pug' Ismay, the first Secretary General of NATO, as Commandant of the NATO Defense College in Paris

on the French impressionists, and a Fellow of the Royal Society of Arts. In the summer of 1960, I found myself a silent guest at lunch whilst Lawrance Darvall and a lively lady producer from the BBC exchanged almost two hours of occasionally shared memories of working with the alcoholic Dylan Thomas and his wife Caitlin, their desperate efforts to get writing out of him, to get him to the microphone to record war-time broadcasts.

Whilst working as a part-time office boy for Desmond Hoare and Robert Blackburn in the spring of 1962 I was detailed off to accompany Lawrance Darvall on a visit to The Hague where he hoped to pick up some scholarships. As we approached the reception desk of the hotel he startled me by ordering two single rooms and four Dutch gins (which were immediately produced without the slightest gesture of surprise). After he had swallowed his second he turned to me and said: *'Well, hurry up! We have work to do. Come to my room in ten minutes.'* I stumbled there in a very dazed frame of mind to find him busy leafing through the telephone book, after which he made a number of calls; and the next morning we/he did indeed secure promises of two scholarships. In the afternoon he explained to me that it was not proper to come to The Hague without visiting the Mauritzhaus, and he then led me through the gallery room by room, commenting on many of the pictures in great detail, with Shakespearean quotes thrown in by way of illustration, and often alerting me before we entered a new room to what we were going to see there. And then he turned to me and said: *'Well, I must go home now. You had better stay on for two days and do the follow-up.'* And so

it was that I spent two rather miserable, guilt-ridden days in The Hague on my own, trying to persuade myself that I was in the vanguard of a major, new and really important international undertaking that was going to save the world, in reality having no idea what to do with myself until with relief I was able to catch my flight back to London.

Leadership of the NATO Defense College in Paris in the Cold War days of the 1950s placed one at the heart of the military and diplomatic world of the Western Alliance. For a few years after retirement, there was hardly a door not open to Darvall. A three-month visit to South Africa enabled him to address the Institute of International Affairs and the Parliamentary Association in Cape Town. A typewritten note dated 6th December 1957 lists his appointments over a one-week period in the United States on Atlantic College business: President Johnson (with the Carnegie Endowment Fund), Ellen McCloy (wife of the former US High Commissioner in Germany), Lewis Douglas (former US Ambassador in Britain), David Rockefeller, Dean Rusk (to become John Kennedy's Secretary of State for Foreign Affairs), Thomas Finletter (former Secretary of the US Force and in charge of the Marshall Plan for Britain), Senator Adlai Stevenson, and Eleanor Roosevelt. The second page of this programme is unfortunately missing.

A note to Kurt Hahn in his illegible handwriting summarises his feelings after this visit and what kept him going: *'I leave tomorrow after a very tiring, interesting and not entirely unsuccessful voyage of adventure, sustained by your admirable ideals and by your thoughts and by my firm belief in the ideals and affectionate admiration for yourself.'*

On a later visit to the United States the Atlantic College message seems to have gone *'off-line'*, judging by the introductory paragraph of *The New York Journal* of 31st January 1959: *'a proposal by an outstanding British war hero to combat juvenile delinquency on an international basis has won wide approval in Washington government circles'*. Not surprising in the light of his quoted remarks: *'our youth of today has no feeling for leadership because it has not been trained for it. Young men the world over are making little or no contribution to their communities. As a result, the trend to lawlessness and listlessness is getting out of hand. The spread of juvenile delinquency has left us wide open to the infiltration of communism and the return of fascism. It will facilitate the moral degeneration of the Western world.'* The plan, the report adds, was *'well received'* by Under-Secretary of State Christian Herter, Arthur Flemming, Secretary of Health, Education and Welfare, Senator James Fulbright and General Alfred Gruenther, former NATO Commander.

Much of this, we must recognise, was undigested and confused Hahnian rhetoric, although Darvall was on surer ground when he ended *'the greatest unifying force among the free nations today is the common fear of communism. This must be supplanted by a code of morality and cooperation which will give us a limitless future.'*

We are back to the theme that constantly animated Hahn's endeavours: the freedom, integrity and morale of the western world, of the Atlantic Alliance.

What then were Darvall's own ideas? I find them most convincingly and winningly expressed in a small number of essays published in the year after his retirement, notably in a long article in *The Times* of 29th June 1956 that was subsequently adapted for *The Times Educational Supplement* of 2nd November of the same year.

In these two articles Darvall places the Atlantic College idea firmly within the context of the human lessons emerging from the NATO experience: *'one feature of the alliance's strength is the constantly increasing number of political, civil and military officials from the NATO countries who have experienced NATO cooperation and built up a firm basis of friendship … if we do not wish to throw away all the advantages built up with so much effort over the last seven years, what should we do? … we must examine how to breathe into Article II of the Treaty that dynamic impulse which in the military field has so surely and so relatively quickly established the existing measure of security … a change in priority and emphasis from overriding military priority to action in the non-military fields could take place without any major alteration … I believe therefore that our first requirement is to define a long-term political concept within which progress can steadily be made until the time is ripe for the satellites, and even Russia*

herself, slowly but surely, perhaps even unconsciously in the beginning, to join in a congeries of States, united in a belief in the relative freedom of the individual, the advantage of continuous consultation and cooperation, the superiority of discussion over argument, and the conviction that resort to physical force is childish, useless and unworthy. We need, in fact, to find a political concept offering eventual security and the chance of development for all …'

In just one sentence he draws attention to the Atlantic College idea. *'The idea has been mooted by that great educationalist, Dr Kurt Hahn, that the time is ripe to establish a NATO Public School.'* He goes on: *'Universities throughout the Alliance could set up NATO colleges or organizations on the lines of the Rhodes Scholarship scheme, the Commonwealth Fund, International House, Columbia University New York, etc. The NATO college itself could be developed and extended to cover not only one category of NATO officials as at present, but also include shorter courses for parliamentarians, trade unionists, business executives, and other people who would benefit enormously from the opportunity of discovering that the other animals in the alliance are also human, sensible, and attractive when seen at close quarters, engaged in a common task, and with a firm belief in the practical and spiritual task at hand.'*

The text for *The Times Educational Supplement* included this brief statement: *'The teaching syllabus would be so designed as to qualify the successful students for a university entrance examination to be recognised by all the NATO nations.'*

The importance of these articles, at least for me, is that the most obviously 'NATO' member of the Atlantic College founding team was a man whose ideas and hopes went far beyond the military. The Report of the Atlantic Community Conference in Bruges of November 1957 (Commission on Institutional Framework) stated: *'We are most interested in the establishment of Atlantic Schools and commend this idea for study and sympathetic consideration'*. Further sound evidence that NATO was moving in his direction is found, for example, in the record of the Eleventh Annual Session in 1965 of the NATO Parliamentarians' Conference. We read here of the existence of the Atlantic College in St. Donat's (*'similar institutions might well be established in other countries'*); that the Alliance's essentially military character *'tends at first to rebuff inquirers … NATO can only answer the challenge presented by the monolithic culture of the Communist world by fostering an alliance between different cultures and encouraging their inter-penetration, in other words, by means of the cultural freedom of its member States'*; and that *'several organizations – notably the International Schools Examinations Syndicate and the Atlantic College*

Lawrance Darvall and Ismay

– have begun in concert to create an international university entrance examination'.

The early anti-NATO critics of the College had no grasp of this breadth of vision. Later statements and articles carrying Darvall's signature were far more strongly influenced by Hahn's aspirations and language. Already by 1957 the annex to his letter to the Ford Foundation, with proposals for six Atlantic Colleges in Canada, France, Great Britain, Greece, Germany and the USA, referred to *'training designed to build up that vital health about which the totalitarian governments feel such a deep concern and which is treated with such indifference within the established educational systems of the Western world … a brotherhood which is even stronger than the comradeship of the battlefield … compassion which is the negation of the totalitarian creed with its contempt for human life and dignity …'* and to a mass movement to be inspired by *'the Atlantic boys'* which would be created by

'Introducing into schools those vitalizing activities in which we believe

Offering to the young in industry increased opportunities of a training holiday lasting one month

Presenting both to boys at school and at work a challenge likely to be accepted. It will be similar to that presented by the Duke of Edinburgh's Award Scheme.'

In a word (at the close): the founding of *The Atlantic Trust for the Free!*

It was left to those who created a reality from the core ideals, Desmond Hoare, George Schuster and their colleagues, to restore a sense of focus – and to enable women to join this great endeavour.

Lawrance Darvall had married Aileen Mahoney from County Cork in 1923. She must have been a critical support for her husband above all in his later senior roles, but we met her rarely. We knew she had suffered the trauma of being out hunting when her father was thrown from his horse and died instantaneously from a broken neck in front of her. Now, in retirement, she saw her husband travelling constantly, if only up to Brown's Hotel in London, to breakfast or lunch yet again with the insistent Hahn who had, it almost seemed, taken her husband from her. She worried about him because she knew he was unwell, and that they could not easily afford the expenses that were inseparable from a commitment of this kind. Nor was she sure that the mythical college would ever emerge from all the documents and travel and talk. But by the time the College did open, in 1962, Lawrance Darvall was increasingly taking a back seat.

My episode with Lawrance Darvall in The Hague gave me an insight into why, from the purchase of St. Donat's in October 1960 onwards, he could no longer play a major role. *'You stay on for two days and do the follow-up.'* He had been a very senior staff officer and had staff to *'follow up'* once he had given the orders. Both Desmond Hoare and George Schuster became impatient over his inability, after the first successful 'strikes' in 1960, to buckle down to the nitty-gritty of governance and fundraising; nor was Lawrance Darvall entirely reassured by the less than strictly naval style adopted by Desmond Hoare as the College got underway. I myself hardly saw him again after the College had opened and in retrospect would have given a great deal to have had a really good discussion with him about the way our enterprise was developing. His *Times* obituary brings him very clearly to mind: *'truly international in outlook … a freshness of mind … a refusal to accept ready-made solutions … an insistence on bringing fresh thought to every problem … those piercing eyes looking down from a great height … his gaiety and charm'.* And Kurt Hahn knew very well what he and the Atlantic College in its incubatory period owed him, describing him in 1962 as *'an imaginative observer of human behaviour, as a peace maker … I owe him more than I can say …'*

Lawrance Darvall's daughter Rosemary Schlee, who attended the same school as Hahn's niece Benita Hahn during the war, told me that she and her mother felt regret over not having much believed in the project in the early stages, especially as her father was unwell and was wearing himself out going to meetings. She was sad when her own daughter Oriel initially failed to gain acceptance at the College, then when a place came up, extracted her with some difficulty from a convent school in Cambridge

Laying the foundation stone of the Atlantic College science laboratories: Desmond Hoare, Lawrance Darvall, George Schuster

where Oriel, having just been made a prefect, was enjoying her new privileges. A rushed train journey to Wales was spent hastily sewing on name tabs, and was followed by a telephone call from the College when she got home: detailed orders for outdoor camping equipment for *'some survival course'*, a request for notes for talking with Prince Charles, and an account of herding cattle, after which the line went dead. All seemed to be well.

Rosemary Schlee made as big a name for herself as a helmswoman of Wayfarer sailing dinghies as her aunt had enjoyed as President of the Ladies Alpine Club. She was still chartering larger boats at the age of 74. One such expedition found her and her husband and daughter crew off Peddar Bay in British Columbia. Shyly venturing up the inlet to the Pearson College jetty, they went ashore and introduced themselves. *'The cry went up: the Founder's daughter has come, and by boat.'*

At the end of her note to me, Rosemary writes:

'If anyone goes to see the Atlantic College, perhaps they will notice the barbecue area with some stonewalling and lawns. This was converted from waste ground with a donation from the money my parents left me, and includes a wall plaque … I wanted to be sure that his name was commemorated in some permanent way at the College. In a similar but much smaller way we had a bookcase fixed at the Singapore College with an inscription and a photograph on the wall above. Perhaps a Darvall will go there one day too. I tried hard for a similar thing at the Lester Pearson College on Vancouver Island, the one we visited by boat, but was unsuccessful.'

Her note left in me feelings of regret and remorse. Because we saw little of Lawrance Darvall after the College opened he has not been given his due. To adapt Kurt Hahn's tribute: we owe him more, far more, than we have expressed.

Desmond Hoare

The old saying *'success has many fathers'* has of course its relevance too for the United World Colleges. As the movement has become more complex and developed new strands, successive colleges and successive initiatives have had their own founders. Going back however right to the beginning, there were four key figures: Lawrance Darvall, Kurt Hahn, George Schuster and Desmond Hoare. For that early time, the metaphor of the chain may be appropriate. Each link had to hold, and each link had differing and generally very great strains to bear at different times. Had Darvall and Hahn not met and conspired so passionately and so effectively in the 1950s, there would have been no proposal. Had they not found in Desmond Hoare an idealist of extraordinary imagination, courage, leadership and executive ability, the proposal must have sunk. Had George Schuster not taken over the fundraising in 1964, there would now be no tale to tell.

One does not, I am quite sure, diminish in any way the roles of Lawrance Darvall, Kurt Hahn and George Schuster by identifying Desmond Hoare as the one truly irreplaceable figure in the pioneering narrative of the first, the founding college. It is a complex story, especially in the later stages, marred by personal conflicts for which all involved, including Desmond himself, must accept their share of responsibility; but there are compelling reasons why, a half-century after the Atlantic College accepted its first students, the United World Colleges should understand and acknowledge their debt to him. Of the four, he was the only one to suffer professionally, financially, emotionally and physically as a direct consequence of the absolute nature of his commitment; and he was the only one who continued relentlessly, until he died, to seek challenging, provocative new avenues through which the original ideals might, he believed, be made more relevant and more effective.

The purpose of this memoir is therefore to summarise the extraordinary achievement of Desmond Hoare in creating the Atlantic College, and to re-state, mostly in his own words, the ways in which, in his eyes, the United World Colleges (how he – typically – hated that title!) could move forward after the first College had been securely established.

His Early Life and the Royal Navy

If Desmond Hoare was at every stage of his life an unusual figure, this only reflects the rather unusual manner in which he was brought up. Born in Cork in 1910, he was taken to Australia at the age of three in the company of his father, mother, brother and nanny. He spent five years in a Roman

---

OPPOSITE: Deirdre, Michael Schweitzer's widow, is a gifted amateur painter. Naomi Hoare asked her to paint Desmond's portrait for the College from photographs, and I am very grateful to Deirdre for allowing me to include her work in this book. Here are some comments I sent her as she was engaged on the task.

His hands were very large, broad, with extremely strong fingers that were accustomed, I suppose, to tightening nuts and bolts and undoing them, getting filthy with oil and being scrubbed clean, real workman's hands. I found it hard to understand how they could generate such almost childish, small but remarkably legible handwriting. … and the breadth and strength of his shoulders and upper body which he seemed to want to disguise when seated, his shoulders hunched, almost as if he were ashamed of sitting idle instead of being up and about. Do not forget the handkerchief in his cuff which he was always picking at, perhaps thinking it was a rag with which to clean his oily hands. The breadth and depth of his shoulders must be very difficult indeed to convey in the sitting position …

A formidable figure to face across the table!

Catholic convent in Sydney, followed by two in a similar institution in Melbourne, but his most vivid memories of Australia were witnessing the unsuccessful attempt to rescue a swimmer who had lost his leg to a shark, and the death of a man well-known to him who broke his neck when diving into an empty swimming pool. 'Rescue' and 'safety' were realities for him long before he met Kurt Hahn.

The family returned to England in 1919. Desmond was sent first to Wimbledon College, then King's School in Rochester, before joining the Navy as a cadet in 1929. The manner of his acceptance into the Navy must have influenced his later scepticism about formal qualifications. He was colour-blind, but there was a helpful uncle on the examining board who pointed out the dials: 'Come on, Desmond. Surely you know that red dials are on the left, green on the right.' Later, I remember the crew members of the Atlantic College life boats being briefed by Desmond before their medical examination if they were short-sighted. 'Learn the number of the doctor's car by heart – that's all you are asked to look at.'

His first ambition had been to become a surgeon. This did not work out, so he embarked on six years of engineering training at the Royal Naval Engineering College Keyham and the Royal Naval College in Greenwich. He spent his first years afloat in the Mediterranean and the waters of Latin America.

From 1936 to 1939 Desmond Hoare served on the battleship *HMS Exeter*. When she was sunk by Japanese aircraft off Malaysia in 1942 he lost many friends. From 1942 to 1944 he was Commander (Chief Engineer) of *HMS King George V*, the flag ship of the Home Fleet, escorting the notorious Arctic convoys that ran between Scotland and Murmansk. Memories of those days found their way into the extensive training notes he wrote for the Inshore Life Boat crews at the College: 'During the war, on the run to North Cape, waves which could not be spanned from trough to crest … by a 40,000 ton battleship were quite often seen in winter'. And he would describe how, in following seas, the battleship would surge forward like a small dinghy.

From 1949 to 1955 he was aboard *HMS Vanguard* and in charge of all the machinery of this newest, post-war battleship. His engineering skills were then transferred to aircraft matters: as Director of Aircraft Maintenance and Repair in the Admiralty from 1958 to 1960 he oversaw the introduction of the Buccaneer fighter plane into the Fleet Air Arm. In 1960 he was promoted to Rear-Admiral and became Chief of Staff and Command Engineer on the staff of the Commander-in-Chief in Plymouth. He was on the threshold of the rank of full Admiral and of becoming the senior engineer in the Royal Navy – his life-long professional ambition. It was all not to be.

A closer look at his naval career tells us why.

He has written about his time spent in the pre-war years in South America. His accounts illustrate two qualities: his human leadership, and his curiosity about unknown or little-known parts of the world and especially the natural world. Here is their flavour:

'There is a strange fascination in untrodden grounds which one can experience most strongly in remote places like the offshore islands of the Chilean archipelago. The wild Araucanian Indians are tamed but not quite all gone and one is never sure what strange things may not step out of the brushwood or round the next cliff …'

'In these (naval) sailing craft, in use every day summer and winter, youngsters can leave their moorings and harbour, get caught on the falling tide, try to make further harbours and fail to do so, get in the way of more important vessels and get cursed out of it. They can mistake one light for another, round the wrong buoy, crash into one another, and capsize; they can encounter rocks and eddies, overfalls and those awful tidal races where the sea comes up on all sides and glowers at the poor mariner in evil-looking pyramids. They can meet horrible mists and fogs; and false ground where the anchor does not hold and false ground where it won't come up. There is nothing in all these worlds which is not also reflected in life itself. In a small boat at sea, as in life, nothing ever quite happens as planned; which is a good reason why the one is such excellent value for the other …'

The war over, his concern with leadership and the training of the young men entrusted to him became at least as important to him as his engineering work. He was to write eloquent papers on the subject. Here are some extracts:

'What do we want to do with our stokers? In short we want … (to make) whole men out of them, mind, body and soul. We want to give them morale, the quality which makes men endure and show courage in time of fatigue and danger, and to achieve this we must give them leadership, discipline, affection, and self-respect. We want to give them opportunity to discover and develop their strength and overcome weakness; to allow them to draw self-confidence from physical and moral achievement, to provide adventure and danger in company with men who have known it and to revive the spirit for it in those who have already resigned themselves to some imagined inadequacy. We must lessen their reaction time, equip them with willing bodies, foster capacity for feeling and moral judgment, and fortify them against temptation by the development of interests conducive to a healthy use of their own time.'

He was clear about the contribution to be made by our physical surroundings:

'The human race owes much of its strength to the necessity in earlier generations to battle with nature. Men who now work on the land, those who go fishing at sea in small boats and others who still contest with natural forces in various ways develop easily and naturally the qualities of watchfulness, integrity, endurance, and resource …'

'Not only danger but also peace is good for the soul. The peace of a mountain side rarely fails to move the young, likewise that of the sea seen from a small boat at anchor by night. Whenever it is possible therefore we can do no better than give the stokers their necessary body training in natural surroundings where they can not only develop their physical strength and resilience but also free their souls from some of the artificialities of modern life.'

He was no less clear in his distrust of academic education alone:

'No comprehensive satisfactory alternative to the examination system has yet been found but let us recognise its dangers: the influence of examinations is three-fold. It affects the treatment of examinable subjects themselves, tending always to exalt the written above the spoken, to magnify memory and mastery of fact at the expense of understanding and liveliness of mind. It depresses the status of the non-examinable so that the aesthetic and creative side of education with all its possibilities for human satisfaction and cultural enrichment remains largely undeveloped and poorly esteemed. And, lastly, the examination which begins as a means becomes for many the end itself.'

And he also wrote that *'most boys do not recognise their need for solitude …'* and if periods for reading could be insisted upon, most boys would acquire *'for the first time in their lives a reading habit … there is hardly any greater step which could be taken towards producing contented sailors at sea'.*

It cannot surprise anyone familiar with Kurt Hahn's ideas that their paths should cross, or that their first meeting of minds was over the distinction between happiness and morale. What was unusual, and became significant in the development of the Atlantic College project, was Desmond Hoare's decision to subject Hahn's ideas to some comparative analysis before adopting them. He has described how in 1949, having first received some written advice from *'the oracle'*, *'I was in control of the teaching situation in two ships, a battleship and an aircraft carrier. A common technical examination for the boys in both ships was held at the end of each six months' course. Using one ship's boys as the control group and applying Kurt's ideas to the other group, I was gratified to find that, after taking away 25% of the technical teaching time of the experimental group for Kurt Hahn type activities, they defeated the control group in the technical written exams by about 20%. This was, I believe, the result of higher morale.'* It was only two years later that he met *'the oracle'* for the first time.

In 1955, in another move that was to be influential in committing him to the Atlantic College Project, came his posting for three months to the Imperial Defence College on a course that brought together senior officers from all three of the Services for non-military training, experience and reflection. (This was the year in which Kurt Hahn addressed the officers at the NATO Defense College in Paris.) They visited the Palestinian refugee camps. His comment: *'As long as refugee camps exist on this scale and in such misery, there can be no peace in the Middle East.'*

As a naval officer he was clear that his loyalty was to the Queen and, in a curiously old-fashioned way, he believed that military officers should not have the vote, but there was nonetheless another strong side to his character: his concern with political issues and his readiness to risk and to rebel. During one of his pre-war leaves he had disappeared to Spain to witness the Civil War at first hand and to make his own personal contribution to the Republican cause. It is quite certain that, had he been found out, his naval career would have been over.

Youth Work, Kurt Hahn – and the Atlantic College comes over the Horizon

From 1955 onward, Desmond Hoare was no longer aboard ship. He was seeing more of Kurt Hahn, who arranged for him to join the Originating Committee of the Duke of Edinburgh's Award Scheme. This led him to recognise his ignorance of youth work in civilian life. He became a volunteer in the Harrow Boys' Club in Notting Hill Gate, then a very tough area indeed. He began to spend evenings and every weekend, Friday evening until Sunday, with the Club. When he came out after his first evening there, he found the tyres of his car slashed to pieces. After the second evening, the car was missing altogether. He called the police, who took him around the London streets in one of their own cars in search of the missing vehicle. When it was found it was being driven by members of the club. Only then did he 'remember' that of course he had lent them the keys earlier in the evening. It was no wonder that he became so popular and so respected. He introduced canoeing. The boys built their own high-performance slalom craft. Never had the London Federation of Boys' Clubs, or the River Thames, seen so many canoes. Kurt Hahn introduced him to Judge Adrian Curlewis, the President of the Australian Surf Life-Saving Association. The outcome was the launch of the Corps of Canoe Lifeguards, and the British Canoe Union came under his relentless pressure to create a wide-ranging series of Proficiency Tests.

As Hahn and Darvall developed the Atlantic College Project in the late 1950s, it became almost inescapable that Desmond Hoare should be urged to become the Founding Headmaster. It cannot have been an easy time. Efforts by Kurt Hahn and Antonin Besse to have him released from the Navy without loss of pension rights were unsuccessful. His earlier confidential letter to the Naval Secretary reveals the firmness of his concern now with human rather than engineering issues. '*I have absolutely no ambitions for high rank as such. It is the work that matters. I may over-rate my own abilities, but I am convinced that I could do something worthwhile for the Navy in the personnel field, and would then leave very content. I am sure you will appreciate that, with a strong sense of vocation, I can only press to stay as close as I can to the area in which I think there is most to do, and the most important things to do.*' But a later letter, written in 1960 to a potential sponsor when the creation of the College was in the balance, makes brutally clear the degree of the sacrifice involved for him and for his family: '*I am a normally poverty stricken naval officer with three children*

still to educate, another step in rank clearly in sight, with five more years' service, a large salary and, at this stage, a rapidly growing pension. I could not afford, for family reasons, to throw all away were I not certain of the alternative ... I just felt that I wanted to express to you, for the first time in writing, my complete conviction and determination over this matter.'

But a throw-away remark of his, made in casual conversation after the College had opened, is also illustrative of the depth of his determination to live the whole life – '*mind, body and soul*'. One reason he had taken on the College, he said, was that it was always important '*to be in a growing business, not a declining one*' – a formidable comment for a life-long naval officer of senior rank.

Desmond Hoare has described how, in 1958, when visiting the USA on naval business, he was given introductions by Kurt Hahn to Christian Herter, then Under-Secretary of State for Foreign Affairs, and to Allen Dulles, Head of the CIA, both of them friends of Kurt since the days of the First World War and the Treaty negotiations in Versailles. Indeed, such was Hahn's standing with Herter that Desmond was provided with an aircraft, two Area Directors of Education, a Washington Headmaster, and the freedom to fly wherever he liked in the country to study secondary education. But he remained his own man. When Hahn, whose affection for Scotland banished rational reflection, pressed him to accept Dunrobin Castle in Sutherland as the site for the College, he was quite clear that the following were vital needs: easy access from London, the proximity of a major city and preferably university, industry, and a genuine need for real rescue services. St. Donat's Castle on the foreshore of the Bristol Channel in South Wales, advertised in the magazine *Country Life* at the critical moment, provided the irresistible answer. Characteristically, Desmond set out in one of his many manuscript letters of the time a statistical comparison of weather conditions in Dunrobin, Gordonstoun and St. Donat's: average temperatures in January and July, average hours of sunshine daily throughout the year, total rainfall, the percentage figures during the year for offshore, onshore and along-the-shore winds, and, significantly, the comparative safety of wind and sea state conditions for small boat sailing – Dunrobin the best and St. Donat's the worst!

The Creation of the College

'*I have always found intelligent sailors to be about the most adaptable of all professional men; and to see this retired Rear Admiral – looking exactly like a Welsh Doctor Who in his skin diver's suit running the outdoor side by energetic participation and the indoor side by sympathetic delegation – is to realise*

The early years were rugged

that, had he not existed for Atlantic's purposes, he would have had to be invented …': Gordon Brook-Shepherd, writing in the *Daily Telegraph* after the College opened, captured the spirit and the achievement of the man in a single sentence.

An early worry (among many!) was that the Atlantic College was often seen as a junior college of NATO. Desmond Hoare's frequent references to it as a staff college for teenagers were unhelpful, although his explanation – that the College was offering carefully selected and promising young men an unusual challenge outside all their previous experience – made very sound sense. The preponderance of military men among the founders did not help either, although their motivation – that they had experienced war and wanted no more of it for their grandchildren – was unassailable. It is worth recalling that, at the critical meeting in London in October 1960, when the option on the purchase of St. Donat's Castle had to be exercised or abandoned for ever, it was the offer of their pensions by three military men – Air Marshall Sir Lawrance Darvall, Admiral Sir Michael Denny and Rear-Admiral Desmond Hoare – that moved the businessmen present to leave the room and to return shortly afterwards with the necessary financial guarantees.

Another worry, highlighted by unsympathetic visitors and observers and even quietly shared by some academic colleagues, was the emphasis given to the sea and the activities of coast rescue. But Desmond Hoare had nailed his colours to the mast long before in one of his papers on naval training and morale: '… the sea … for the development of the qualities we need, meets every requirement that has been

stated: natural surroundings, some danger, some peace, bodily exercise, development of resources and capacity to endure, conquest over adversity, informal contact with officers, and a ready graduation to a position of personal responsibility'.

I think the simple truth of the matter is that the task of creating the College was beyond the grasp of the traditional or even the heterodox schoolmaster. Fifty years on, it is easy to forget that Atlantic College was Britain's first Sixth Form College and that the business of motivating and disciplining residential school pupils without team games, prefects and supportive, fee-paying parents had not been attempted before. Desmond's service training, his studies of human leadership, his intimate familiarity with the mentality of the late teenager in both the disciplined environment of the Navy and the untamed world of the inner-city youth clubs, combined with his sharply analytical mind, gave him incomparable advantages. It was not always easy for academic teachers to work for such a man, but their eyes were opened to a new vision of education. Their horizons would have been further enlarged had he achieved the ambition he announced publicly in 1963 at a local school prize-giving: his hopes within a couple of years of introducing a one-year industrial apprentice entry to the Atlantic College. A senior colleague, the Head of History John Lello, described him as *'controversial as a Head but a stunning catalyst for action, cohesion and hard work'*.

And behind it all lay both the idealism and the ability to express it. He wrote the first prospectus in one evening at home in Hampstead. It contained phrases which have not been bettered in later UWC literature and are a standing

Naomi Hoare at the wheel of Tony Besse's Ocean Joy *– but ashore in an Italian marina*

rebuke to the prolix mission statements which now afflict us all in international education. Here are some of them: *'We need to show in a convincing manner that the educational needs of modern society do not have to be met at the expense of more important human characteristics. The heart of the matter is the need to demonstrate that self-discipline, devotion, imagination, courage and response to challenge can be developed in materially prosperous societies … the instinct to helpfulness is present in every youth; it can either be fostered and flourish or it can be neglected and fade away. It is not enough to preach the virtue … we need … an education adapted to meet the needs of our time …'* He wrote, and often spoke, with direct, distinctive eloquence. It is not a surprise to learn that, in his year of entry into the Navy, he achieved the top mark in the examination in Latin.

Desmond, and with him the College, was more fortunate than even he can have known at the time. His wife Naomi, deeply attached to her family home in Hampstead, and with a huge circle of friends and an extremely active social life, viewed *'this mad venture in Wales'* with agony and despair. The personal sacrifice she made rivalled in every degree the professional sacrifice made by Desmond, and it all came out years later when she wrote to one of the first female students: *'I remember being furious as all those dinner parties were jolly expensive – I, of course, did all the shopping, cooking, washing up, and laid the breakfast table before I finally got to bed … I also began designing skin suits and helping the baffled students to glue them up – obviously for no pay, and we paid for all the scissors and chalk and glue etc. Oddly this is not a complaint …'*

Her role in setting up their new home in the attractive but wildly impractical four floors of the Lady Anne Tower, her entertainment first of the students and then of the unending stream of VIP visitors, all of them so crucial to the College's survival and success, made her a partner in the whole enterprise without whom Desmond could never have managed. She was also to make a very special contribution to the sea-going story as an expert helm of Fireball dinghies and fully-qualified Royal Yachting Association Instructor, skills she acquired alongside the students after the College opened.

The Sea and the Rescue Services

In the early years of the College, sailing was the most popular activity, with typically half the students taking part. The College maintained a fleet of some 12 two-man Fireball dinghies and half as many one-man dinghies. Additionally, there was surf-canoeing and surf-board riding. Sea-going took place on every afternoon in the week including Sundays, with only Saturdays excepted.

In a letter to the Chairman of Outward Bound in February 1966, Desmond Hoare summarised the challenges of the Bristol Channel. *'Our sailing is conducted in the most dangerous waters in which I have operated small boats. Before we opened the school, all the local experts said we would never sail dinghies off our beach. The Deputy Chief Inspector, RNLI, has said that we probably have the most difficult operating conditions of any of their 50 or so other Inshore Rescue Boat stations around the coast of Britain … we have a tidal race a mile to the East and another a mile to the West … the spring tides run at five knots off our foreshore …'*

How, on a coast which records the second highest tidal rise and fall in the world (after the Bay of Fundy) was this all achieved in safety?

The first answer was the neoprene skin suit, now commonplace all over the world. Desmond had astonished the naval apprentices in Plymouth by appearing on the beach in a strange rubber suit with TARZAN across his chest in large yellow letters. The estate staff at the castle was not less bewildered in the winter of 1960 to see him floating on his back in the Bristol Channel, wearing this same suit and smoking a large pipe, testing the strength of the local currents. All sea-going students learned to make and maintain their own rubber suits. Naomi Hoare took on the formidable task of measuring each individual to ensure the close fit that alone guarantees the suit's effectiveness in protecting from the cold. It was she who designed the first-ever one piece suits (jacket and trouser combined) one Christmas holiday which thereafter became the standard

[1] *The RIB patent taken out by Desmond Hoare*

[2] *The letter of thanks from the Royal National Lifeboat Institution*

[3] *… and the cheque for £1.00, never cashed*

RNLI

1824 1974

ONE HUNDRED AND FIFTIETH ANNIVERSARY CELEBRATIONS

WEST QUAY ROAD
POOLE
DORSET BH15 1HZ

Telephone: Poole 71133
(STD code 020-13)

The RNLI is supported entirely
by voluntary contributions

Patrons:
Her Majesty The Queen
Her Majesty Queen Elizabeth,
The Queen Mother
President:
HRH The Duke of Kent
Treasurer:
The Duke of Northumberland, KG, DCL

Chairman:
Commander F R H Swann,
CBE, RNVR
Deputy Chairmen:
The Duke of Atholl
Major General R H Farrant, CB
Director:
Captain Nigel Dixon, RN

D/SB

23rd July, 1974

Rear Admiral D.J. Hoare, C.B., M.I., Mech.E.,
MRINA.,
Bally Island House,
Skibbereen,
Co. Cork,
Irish Republic.

Dear Desmond,

I have much pleasure in enclosing a cheque for
£1.00 as a token payment for the patent for
the Atlantic 21' life-boat which you so generously
handed to the R.N.L.I.

I am sure that you are aware of the gratitude
of the Institution, but I would like to take
this opportunity of expressing, once again, my
appreciation and sincere thanks for this magnificent
gesture.

Yours ever,
Nigel
DIRECTOR.

THE YEAR OF THE LIFE-BOAT

[1]

Patent No. 1290864

Provisional Specification
18 August 1969

Date of Patent...24 June 1970
Date of Sealing ...24 January 1973

Elizabeth the Second by the Grace of God of the United Kingdom of
Great Britain and Northern Ireland and of Her other Realms and Territories, Queen, Head of the
Commonwealth, Defender of the Faith: To all to whom these presents shall come greeting:

WHEREAS a request for the grant of a patent has been made by

Desmond John Hoare a British subject of St. Donat's Castle, Llantwit Major,
Glamorgan, Wales,

for the sole use and advantage of an invention for

Boats:

AND WHEREAS We, being willing to encourage all inventions which may be for the public good, are graciously pleased
to condescend to the request:

KNOW YE, THEREFORE, that We, of our especial grace, certain knowledge, and mere motion do by these presents,
for Us, our heirs and successors, give and grant unto the person(s) above named and any successor(s), executor(s),
administrator(s) and assign(s) (each and any of whom are hereinafter referred to as the patentee) our especial licence, full
power, sole privilege, and authority, that the patentee or any agent or licensee of the patentee and no others, may subject
to the conditions and provisions prescribed by any statute or order for the time being in force at all times hereafter during the
term of years herein mentioned, make, use, exercise and vend the said invention within our United Kingdom of Great Britain
and Northern Ireland, and the Isle of Man, and that the patentee shall have and enjoy the whole profit and advantage from
time to time accruing by reason of the said invention during the term of sixteen years from the date hereunder written of
these presents : AND to the end that the patentee may have and enjoy the sole use and exercise and the full benefit of
the said invention, We do by these presents for Us, our heirs and successors, strictly command all our subjects whatsoever
within our United Kingdom of Great Britain and Northern Ireland, and the Isle of Man, that they do not at any time during
the continuance of the said term either directly or indirectly make use of or put in practice the said invention, nor in anywise
imitate the same, without the written consent, licence or agreement of the patentee, on pain of incurring such penalties as
may be justly inflicted on such offenders for their contempt of this our Royal Command, and of being answerable to this patentee
according to law for damages thereby occasioned :

PROVIDED ALWAYS that these letters patent shall be revocable on any of the grounds from time to time by law
prescribed as grounds for revoking letters patent granted by Us, and the same may be revoked and made void accordingly :

PROVIDED ALSO that nothing herein contained shall prevent the granting of licences in such manner and for such
considerations as they may by law be granted : AND lastly, We do by these presents
for Us, our heirs and successors, grant unto the patentee that these our letters patent
shall be construed in the most beneficial sense for the advantage of the patentee.

IN WITNESS whereof We have caused these our letters to be made patent
as of the   twenty-fourth   day of   June
one thousand nine hundred and seventy   and to be sealed.

Comptroller-General of Patents
Designs, and Trade Marks.

[2]

Royal National Life-boat Institution **RNLI**   18-00-0 2

Supported entirely by voluntary contributions

Life-boat House, 42, Grosvenor Gardens, London, SW1W 0EF

Messrs. Coutts & Co., 440, Strand, London, WC2R 0QS

| DATE | Pay | | | or order | £ | 1.00 |
| JUL 18'74 | the sum of Pounds   REAR-ADMIRAL.D.J.HOARE.   ONE XX | | | | | |

Amount other than Pounds as in figures

C. & CO. LONDON, S.W.R.

For and on behalf of the Institution

072780   18 0002   36273659

[3]

pattern. So well known did the College suits become that Naomi was invited to create a skin suit for Sean Connery to wear for the James Bond film *Thunderball*'s premiere in London (she declined). None of the early students will forget the all-pervasive odour of rubber, glue and talcum powder, not just in the workshops, but in the dormitories, the classrooms, the dining hall as well.

The second answer was the rigid-hulled inflatable lifeboat.

Desmond had observed the use in the navy of high-speed inflatable boats, driven by outboard engines, light and easily handled ashore. He soon found however that the ordinary commercial inflatable boat would not stand up to hard work six days a week off a rough beach and usually in rough water. Improvements to inflatable boat design were therefore started in the College's first year. In the College's second year, the Royal National Lifeboat Institution decided to develop a fleet of inshore rescue boats around the coast of Britain to supplement its main fleet and turned for the same reasons to the inflatable. Hearing of the College's activities, the Chief Inspector and some of his Management Committee came to take a look. In October 1963 the RNLI and the College entered into an association that led directly to the Atlantic Class 21 Lifeboat, named after the College. The concept of the hollow rigid floor high-speed boat was entirely a College achievement. Like the skin suit, it is now known worldwide. Desmond submitted an application for the patent in August 1969. It was granted in September 1972. He handed the patent rights to the RNLI for which he received a cheque for £1 in

Desmond Hoare in his element – teenagers and engines!

token payment. How many have speculated on the funds that would have accrued to the College scholarship funds had it been possible to exploit the patent commercially!

It was a remarkable technological project for a school to have undertaken and brought to outstanding success. Desmond himself was dismissive of personal achievement. The boats were, he said, *'designed by the Bristol Channel with the midwives of trial and error and 500 students as development officers'*. In a letter to a former student some years later he wrote more bluntly: *'Did you never realise that the main purpose of the boats was to instil respect for skill of hand in the academically besotted students?'*

The publicity breakthrough for these boats occurred after an almost casual telephone call to the College. A young man, John Caulcutt, wanted to take part in the first Round Britain Power Boat race of 1969, which was sponsored by British Petroleum and *The Daily Telegraph*. His builders had let him down. Could the College help? Desmond designed the hull that night; two Dutch students, Willem de Vogel and Otto van Voorst tot Voorst, and the College carpenter, began work the next morning. Three weeks later, christened *Psychedelic Surfer*, she was in the water, undergoing trials. In a race with over 70 starters she was the smallest, cheapest, lowest powered, most quickly built, and nineteenth to finish. The organisers of the race had, they admitted in a subsequent book, been inclined to bet against her completing the first two legs: *'We put her among the outsiders at 200–1'*. But at the finishing line *'the crush barriers folded and the crowd surrounded the platform to give an ovation for what was perhaps the greatest performance of all the finishers'*.

The RNLI B Atlantic Class boat was developed directly from *Psychedelic Surfer*. By August 1993 the RNLI was able to report that the Atlantic 21, since its introduction to the fleet in 1972, had launched on service 15,601 times, saving 4,717 lives and giving assistance to a further 2,802 persons. There were at that time 49 Atlantic 21s on station with a further 26 available for relief, emergency relief and training duties. A total of 95 craft had been built.

There were other comparable excitements and achievements, all stemming from Desmond Hoare's enthusiasm and leadership. The *'workshop experience'* became a central feature of College life for dozens of students each year. *'If it looks right it is right'* and *'you are no good until you can smell the difference between copper and brass in the dark'*, he told them, and the design and construction work on the lifeboats was matched by the simultaneous development of open-ended trolleys which very greatly eased the launch and recovery of these craft in the surf rolling on to the foreshore. A four-man canoe was built, intended

Tutorials in mathematics were a short-lived 'extra' in the early months

Wet, cold but enjoyable!

to surf the green waves rolling in to the Bristol Channel from the Atlantic, an ambitious attempt to achieve perpetual motion (it failed); and another group of students spent one summer holiday building an enlarged Fireball dinghy which, with three trapezes and a flotation cube at its masthead, generated some admiring and astonished comment in the highly experienced local Barry yacht club.

His influence above all on the 'seafront students' was profound. *'Inside his Lady Anne Tower Headmaster's office Admiral Hoare was serious and grim'*, one student from Latin America remembers. *'In the boat shed and in his wetsuit, discussing wind speed and tides while preparing to slide down the ramp into the sea, he was a cheerful and grinning man, a 16-year-old boy just like the rest of us.'* 'He had', says another, *'a lot of patience born from knowledge of the sea.'* And whilst there was sometimes disagreement, there was always respect. *'As is often the case in boarding schools, in the absence of a father against whom I could rebel, Admiral Hoare provided a superb surrogate. We had a few stormy moments, but I have come to cherish the fact that he maintained very high expectations of me.'*

College Leadership in the Development of Coordinated Coast Rescue Services

'It is not too much to say that Inshore Rescue had much to do with the choice of site for the first Atlantic College; first because it is one of the firmest of College rules that students

are to stay alive, and secondly because the rescue of others is both worthwhile and good fun' – but the background to all this adventurous activity and innovation was serious and idealistic purpose. In a memorandum he prepared in June 1964, Desmond, drawing attention to the emergence of new ideas for young people such as Voluntary Service Overseas in Britain and the Peace Corps in the United States, called for rescue groups in schools to have equal status with cadet corps and pre-Service training for the Armed Forces. There was, he claimed, a need for an *alma mater* of coast rescue training in a place which is concerned with the education of youth and where comprehensive facilities exist for the training of instructors. The competence of the College students was accepted by the RNLI, by HM Coastguards, by the Surf Life Saving Association of Great Britain, by the British Canoe Union and by the Royal Life Saving Society; and it was the only place in Britain operating a fully coordinated coast rescue service manned entirely by teenagers and safeguarding 20 miles of coast. It was, he wrote to the Minister at the Department of Education and Science, the high academic intent of the College that was exactly the reason *'why we should seek not just a part but a leading part in a development affecting the human attitudes of youth at large'*.

A year later, in 1965, the number of drownings off British beaches reached 167, with a single organisation, the SLSA, recording 124 rescues. Yet the pattern of organisations with some role in the rescue of people who endanger their own lives in coastal waters was bewildering. A conference at the College in April 1964 had concluded that upwards of 1,000 youngsters – boys and girls – could be engaged in coast rescue in Glamorgan alone. The figure for Britain as a whole could engage some 25,000, each of whom, as a result of training, would have skills in first aid and life-saving which would be invaluable in homes, on the roads, and in countless other situations as well.

The College had begun the training of local youth in rescue skills in its first summer of 1963. By 1967, Desmond Hoare was able to record in his autumn Progress Report that, between April and September that year, 1,326 young people had received swimming and life-saving instruction at the College, an achievement which had nonetheless failed to meet the growing demand. Three new Welsh Lifeguard Clubs had been formed and had already registered their first life-saving rescues. 800 children from local schools had attended the College for swimming and life-saving instruction; cadets from eight Police Forces had attended fortnightly residential courses and had been joined by Fire Service cadets and a small number of apprentices from industry. The City of London Police Cadet Team had, after their training at the College, taken first place in the Royal Life Saving Society Lifeguard Championships. The Glamorgan County Council set up a steering committee, and discussions with the Home Office were leading to consideration of further developments throughout the country. The principal sponsor of all this College extra-mural activity was the Grant Foundation of New York. It was however becoming clear that additional residential accommodation was needed if the College's efforts were not to seem *'too localised and small to fit our human aims'*.

This was the background to the establishment of the National Coastal Rescue Training Centre a few months later at Aberavon, some 15 miles from St. Donat's, under the leadership of Charles Thomson, the Director of Activities at the College. By this time the College had been responsible for creating eight new life-saving clubs in South Wales. Twenty-nine lives had been saved by them and no fatalities reported on the beaches under their supervision.

Desmond Hoare was now becoming a national authority, and his views on safety matters were increasingly sought. In 1966 he had responded to the Chairman of Outward Bound with a lengthy and comprehensive review and critique of accident investigation for sports casualties and 'near misses', drawing on his naval experience and embracing the RNLI, HM Coastguard, the Royal Yachting Association, the Royal Life Saving Society, the British Canoe Union and the Surf Life Saving Association in his comments. The principles of independent investigation and adherence to national standards, exemplified by College practice, formed the core of his recommendations. He became a member of the RNLI Management Committee in 1969, serving until 1978, and was for the same period also a member of the Boat and Search and Rescue Committees.

The Beginnings of Overseas Development of the Atlantic College Project and of Alternative Interpretations of the Original Concept

It was always fundamental to Desmond Hoare's idea of Atlantic College that it should be outward-looking and should express this philosophy through external projects. The one closest to his heart was clearly coastal rescue. Another, which he delegated fully to academic colleagues and about which he was later to have the most serious misgivings, was the International Baccalaureate. The third, implicit in all the College literature, was the development and expansion of the Atlantic College project itself. Impatient for progress, he withdrew from the Headship in 1969 and, with the curious title of Provost, a clumsy and unfortunate imitation of Eton College, embarked on proselytising activities overseas. For a person of his temperament, it was a fateful decision. However, by 1969 the financial position of the College, thanks above all to Sir George Schuster's inspired work, had become relatively stable. Desmond's earlier hope of adding an apprentice entry had not come to fruition, but he had successfully responded to a fundamental criticism voiced by a visiting journalist in 1967: Why are you excluding half the human race from the College? As early as 1960 he had prepared a memorandum for the College architects laying down that one quarter of the accommodation should be suitable for female students, but it was not until September of 1967, after a fierce tussle with his Governing Body, that the first girl students were officially admitted (his daughter Stephanie and the daughter of the first Bursar having slipped in unnoticed at the start). Now he was ready for new challenges.

The Atlantic College had started out as a European-North American venture. The key concept was the Atlantic Alliance. Yes, there had been a nod towards Eastern Europe, and the Russians would of course be welcome at a later stage, but the concept was essentially regional. Towards the end of his Headship, Desmond had been persuaded by students that it was time for 'the world' to enter; and this wider vision was given almost irresistible impetus by Mountbatten's insistence on the change of name to

United World Colleges. So Desmond and Naomi set out on the first of their many journeys to Asia. In 1971–1972 they were to cover more than 100,000 miles and spend over 300 days outside the UK on these travels. It was of course not long before detailed and lively reports were finding their way into the hands of the growing numbers of UWC grandees, committee members and executives. New scholarships were generated, notably in Hong Kong, Japan and Malaysia, but the important development was the change in Desmond's thinking.

By January 1971 he was addressing himself to the audience that lay closest to his heart. It was the audience over which he believed himself to have the greatest influence, and he wanted that audience to take the lead now in influencing the movement as a whole: the former students. He wrote to them:

'The success of the first college, now at full size, must however not lead us to believe that the "practical demonstration" at St. Donat's is the only kind which will serve the philosophy … Our original philosophy may be, and, I believe, still is sound and rewarding but it must remain relevant … intelligent journalists who have visited in recent years have remarked to me that no one could quarrel with our philosophy or intentions but that in the event we had placed one "World" College in cosy safe Britain and planned two more in the almost equally cosy safe corners of Germany and Canada. What had this to do with the real "World" problems of poverty, repression and strife? What had this to do with the student revolution and their hesitant rejection of long accepted values, the defeat in Vietnam of the most sophisticated technology, the still growing disparity between the very rich and the very poor, the shift in thinking on how and why and in what to educate, the development of human instruments controlling human change social and personal … In the particular case of the founding College at St. Donat's we have exhausted our first projects (coastal rescue and the International Baccalaureate) and must seek afresh …'.

'If it works, improve it. If it does not, throw it out.' His engineering principles dictated constant revision and change. He had now got to know another world. In his report to the International Board of Directors in January 1973, he wrote: *'When we decided to put our first school, Atlantic College, in Britain, it seemed a rational choice. Western Europe was disunited, a source of worry to statesmen on both sides of the Atlantic, and an Iron Curtain existed. China was quiet and Japan had not re-emerged. It was reasonable to think of the North Atlantic as the centre of the world. The situation is now different and the main cockpit of the world is the Pacific basin in which the four super powers USA, Russia, China and Japan confront each other with India not far away.'*

It was not just politics. There was also the practical issue of costs and the idealistic issue of social justice.

'In encouraging a particular country to develop a UWC, it is rational to look at building costs which are, for example in Malaysia, one quarter of those in Europe. It is even more important to look at student scholarship costs. A European teacher is paid nearly ten times the salary of an Indonesian teacher and a North American teacher twice as much again.' It was necessary, he said, returning to the principle he had included in the first Atlantic College papers, to promote education suited not only to the needs of our time but also to place. Some years earlier, he had stated his position to George Schuster: *'You believe … that this project can most usefully progress within the Western World for some years more, and I believe that it should not be limited in this way from now onwards … A confrontation (sic) to undesirable human attitudes is not a western matter but a world matter …'* And in a collection of memoirs commemorating Kurt Hahn's life, he wrote: *'If his (Hahn's) strength had lasted another ten years, he would, I am sure, be pushing the Atlantic College project into the problems of the 1980s, especially the problem of world hunger in the Third World. His passion for rescue as an educational force could not have led him elsewhere.'*

And the title United World Colleges he thought arrogant and conceited. *'It is quite beyond our powers financially and in other ways to attempt to put the world to rights. We are just one of many do-good organisations seeking peace instead of strife … we should be more closely associated with other organisations … I think that we may have fallen into some danger of emphasising "international understanding" when what we are actually doing is achieving understanding between individuals regardless of race, etc. … the aim of the project is to give practical international demonstrations by young people that the challenge (of confronting attitudes which are an affront to civilisation) is being accepted … practical demonstrations which will carry conviction…'*

Insisting, correctly, that the first college had always been intended to be experimental, and that the project should learn and develop as it went along, he wrote a paper *A Third Experimental Shape*, that summarised his thinking and had the former students, who were slowly growing in influence in the governance, again as his principal audience. The planning for Pearson College was crystallising rapidly, and a college in Germany was also under active preparation. These two, and Atlantic College, he said, have four things in common:

> They are (or will be) extremely expensive.
> They are for an academic elite only.
> All are in prosperous parts of the world.

> *Three quarters of humanity are (or will be) virtually unrepresented.*

It was thus impossible to maintain that the UWC was providing or planning an education *'suited to the needs of our time'. 'There is a widespread feeling expressed by people such as Bishop Camara that the approach of the western world to the developing countries is somewhat disorientated to the latters' needs. If this is true, the United World Colleges should bring some of the younger generation to a more first-hand understanding of what the real needs are. This understanding cannot be created in colleges of the kind we have, up to the present, envisaged. In other words we must design a new form of educational community placed in developing countries in which young people from the prosperous world can learn for themselves the problems that will face them as WORLD citizens in later life. In all our interests, young people from the developing world must also understand, whether they agree or not, with the ways of the prosperous world, since they too must become WORLD citizens, if conflict is to be avoided.'*

Of course he then went on to design this community. The overriding emphasis was to be on land management and cultivation, in a physical context that reflected the conditions under which most of the population of the world would be living for decades to come. Some students would attend for two to three years, others for one year or less. The short courses would embrace the study of land development, agriculture, forestry, banking, engineering or business, with a focus on good managerial ability and with no qualifying examination at the end of the course. *'By choosing a slightly older age group and working with students between school and university, I have escaped the restrictions and international complications of an examination-bound curriculum.'* A bewildering combination of aims, one might say, but he was setting out to provoke and to challenge.

This concept was the third shape because the second shape had already come into being with the UWC of South East Asia. In his early days as Provost, Desmond had envisaged another Atlantic College in Singapore. Lee Kwan Yew made it very clear that he was not interested, far less persuaded. Given the hostility between Singapore, Malaysia and Indonesia, Desmond also developed the highly idealistic and, as it proved, impractical concept of *The Tripod*, a college with bases in the three antagonistic countries in each of which the College students would spend one third of their UWC time. The final outcome was a combined operation with an existing international school. Desmond immediately recognised and then advocated the merits of this seriously different approach – an all-age school in a key city in the rapidly developing Asian world and a far wider range of academic ability, the latter a theme to which Peter Jolley, of the Atlantic College founding staff, was to give eloquent expression soon after he became Headmaster in Singapore: *'Certainly there is an urgent need for all young people to share their views and feelings in an international context and there are good reasons to suggest that the urgency is greatest among the socially and intellectually disadvantaged . . . academic achievement is fine, but it has not saved mankind, and modern man needs a quality of caring and concern built into his life style which mercifully is not the sole preserve of an intellectual elite . . .'*

Thinking being valueless unless followed by action, Desmond did not hesitate to give practical expression to his ideas. Once the link with the Singapore International School was firm, he planned an associated residential 'Developing World Study Centre' in neighbouring Johor in cooperation with the Malaysian Government. Intended as a prototype for similar UWC centres in other countries, it was to provide developing world study courses of one year for students between school and university, a base for outdoor adventure and exposure to jungle conditions for senior students from the urban-bound school in Singapore, and a centre for sea rescue facilities once the tourist area planned by the Malaysian government came into being. At the same time, he allied himself with a headmaster in Thailand who, an early visitor to Atlantic College, was preparing a venture similar to Atlantic College but to be constructed by the students themselves working under the supervision of local skilled craftsmen, the latter giving their time free in return for the promise of the education later of their own children. Although eventually most students might be aiming at university entry, self-help and a productive school farm would remain central features. *'The large site will be intensively farmed and students will be encouraged to earn by their own labour in order to pay their own fees.'*

The Johor Centre was set up and functioned very effectively for a number of years, albeit not as a Developing World Study Centre. The Thailand venture disappeared from the UWC orbit. The Simon Bolivar College in Venezuela, established several years later thanks to the personal interest of the Prince of Wales and owing much to the leadership of Dr. Luis Marcano, was an unmistakable reflection of Desmond Hoare's thinking.

What happened in the meantime to Desmond Hoare?

Internal Conflicts Emerge

The answer is, I think, two-fold. Desmond the engineer was indeed improving what was working – creating new interpretations of the founding aspirations of the Atlantic College, dreaming up as a result of his travels new contexts for the confrontation of undesirable attitudes deriving from race, politics, religion and economic circumstances. But he was throwing out with some vigour too.

Is it not the case that the founders of any venture are more able to adapt and modify the interpretations and instruments of their ideas than are the second generation adherents? They have more confidence in questioning the original assumptions and indeed more right to do so. But their questioning creates a challenging environment for their successors who must add security and sustainability to the original vision. And where should the loyalties lie?

Desmond had insisted when becoming Provost that residence at St. Donat's was vital to his new role since personal knowledge of events and personalities at the College, first and foremost the students, was fundamental if he was to represent the project convincingly to others. But he was creating a situation that would require much self-control.

It was not long before he began to feel unhappy with the evolution of the College and perhaps especially the more extensive academic demands of the International Baccalaureate. But if it was human nature to succumb to frustration when walking the decks of a ship no longer under his command, his continuing presence at St. Donat's alongside his far younger successor eventually gave his committee colleagues in London a plausible stick with which to beat him. It was however not just that he grew unbearably impatient with the failure of London-based colleagues to move at his pace in the exploration of new ideas; not just that he found his earlier almost absolute powers (and responsibilities) now constrained by committee procedures; not just that he was no longer the undisputed philosopher king of the Atlantic College project; he was, and perhaps his naval background and the clear naval chains of command offer a partial explanation, seriously unqualified as a committee man. He was suspicious of agreement and instinctively distrusted the majority view. He had little time for consistency of argument as a virtue. Courtesy in discussion was rather less important than sincerity and forcefulness.

The outcome, to reduce an intensely complex and intensely emotional succession of events to a single sentence, was that he and Naomi were compelled to leave their beloved St. Donat's in 1974, whence they retired, seriously impoverished owing to Desmond's idealistic – or foolhardy – use of much of his naval gratuity for covering expenses in the exercise of his headmasterly duties, to a small, almost primitive cottage in western Ireland. Here

they set up a new home, sustained materially and spiritually by the support of numerous former students, for the majority of whom the Bristol Channel continued to be their mostly lively bond and subject of conversation.

Desmond maintained an impressive correspondence, all by hand and, in accordance with his life-long practice, all letters being answered on the day they were received, until a stroke struck down this physically powerful, unassailably fit man – or so one had thought. His last years were hard and painful, but he never complained. He could not abide self-pity, and left me unnerved with his last letter: *'We must be sensible about this sort of thing and nothing has changed except the date which remains …? I can't do anything more useful here.'*

Some Final Provocations

In 1983, somewhat recovered from his stroke but still heavily marked by it, Desmond with Naomi attended the formal opening of the RNLI Lifeboat Station at the College, named for him and for Naomi. After his visit his frustrations boiled over in a letter to Tony Besse.

> *Atlantic College has too many students. They do not know each other even after two years.*
> *The site is over-developed with increased running costs.*
> *A good school project (coast rescue but not only) demands more student hours than the IB permits.*
> *Skimping on time for projects and rescue services involves risk to life and limb.*
> *The school is taking on too many ancillary activities appropriate to other social organisations (he was referring to the Extra Mural Centre which had succeeded the College's extra-mural work in coastal rescue).*
> *Scholarship funding practice is becoming too expensive to sustain or to permit desirable spreading of the whole plan.*
> *The nil proportion of bamboo colleges (shorthand for projects in the developing world) is outrageous on human grounds and discredits our whole activity.*
> *Young people of great character and promise are excluded from entry on academic grounds. This is contrary to our original policy.*
> *Please let us forget and abolish that arrogant and untrue title United World Colleges … it is quite beyond our powers financially and in other ways to put the world to rights … we are just one of many do-good organisations seeking peace instead of strife. We should be much more closely associated with other organisations regionally.*

> *If we want some black faces in the school why do they not come more from troublesome areas closer to home? Why are we importing the son of a black African tribal chief instead of boys or girls from Notting Hill Gate, Brixton or Toxteth?*

> *Why are we still seeking to unify Europe? The job of unifying Western Europe has been done in these 20 years by the EEC and especially by tourism. The young of Europe integrate themselves with their rucksacks and student fares …*

> *Why do we not tackle more energetically the problems on our own doorstep? I refer especially to Ireland … Atlantic College is not doing much for the Irish problem. There should be a dozen students from each of North and South. The Welsh are great catalysts.*

> *Pearson College is doing the same as us … they should be dealing more with their own Red Indians, Eskimos and with the appalling chaos and prejudices of Central and Southern America … our Colleges are falling into the trap of playing the numbers game, more nations meaning more success. This is not so.*

> *My only criticism of the modern students is that they do not protest enough … the pressure of our academic education is largely responsible for the present apathy and irresolution …*

> *In the Western world there are two fundamentally different approaches to school education … the European systems … all put the same emphasis on written and, of course, creative abilities … the Americans are hard-headed and practical and the American nation is founded and built with rebellious young immigrants from a multitude of civilisations … at age 18 the average American youngster is two years behind the average European youngster in terms of knowledge and what we loosely call education, not surprisingly so because he has spent most of his young life in the classroom talking … at the end of the second degree course … the American young man or woman is years ahead of the European, hence their pre-eminence in sciences of all kinds, mathematics, etc. … we started this College using British examinations and we never failed to get a really bright young thing into a good university – no credit to us. The plain fact is that every university in the world is competitive for customers, meaning the brightest children, and provided one can produce the brightest children they will take them from any educational system … in the US, 3–4 million reach the age of 18 every year and 50% go on to third level education. Only the computerised College Board system could handle the task of selection … Atlantic College should*

> *have broken new ground in Europe, in accordance with our traditions … instead we have committed a crime against our aims and ends by introducing the demanding International Baccalaureate.*

> *We have had only one significant project since this school opened … this school invented and tested daily for seven years in the Bristol Channel a new type of boat which culminated ten years ago in the hollow rigid floor inflatable family of boats. We made a better prototype than could the Royal National Lifeboat Institution, and we handed it over to them for their further professional development. The educational value of this project to about 500 students was immense. It gave the intellectual youth pride in his hands and in his courage and skill in mastering the Bristol Channel, one of the most dangerous waters in the world … it would however have been completely impossible to pursue our project with the burden of the International Baccalaureate on the shoulders of every student. We must forget the IB or forget the project …*

> *The Atlantic College is just one peace-seeking unit. The Pearson College is one more … each is not a United World College but just a little isolated worker for humanity, a provider of education suited to time and place. The basic components of a peace seeking unit are two or more disputants and one or more catalysts, e.g. Northern or Southern Ireland in dispute, Wales as catalyst, Arabia and Israel in dispute, USA as catalyst, Central America in dispute, Canada as catalyst. This was the original plan of the project – area groupings … there is no need for a London Office behaving in a coordinating or even controlling role …*

And, under the heading 'Development by, say, 1990':

> *Each unit to be totally independent, adopting own fee, scholarship and educational structure.*

> *National Committees to continue and strengthen. National committees feed units with students by mutual arrangements.*

> *Course length not to be mandatory.*

> *Developed world units to have non-academic projects and simplified education to USA standards.*

> *The whole to be guided by 3–6 wise men, unpaid, called inspectors …*

> *Each unit to have a director and a provost.*

> *No International Council to exist and no President, Vice-President or other high-sounding titles.*

> *Some bright young thing to think up a better phrase than 'peace-seeking unit' and an abbreviation.*

He was especially vehement on the International Baccalaureate and came back to it frequently in manuscript correspondence: *'I think there is some danger that we are now using the UWC as a vehicle for the IB, which is certainly putting the cart before the horse. The IB is not, and never has been to me, an essential element in the development of human understanding …'* and *'It is contrary to our aim of 'understanding' to inflict the ethos worldwide. Schools should be entirely free to adopt whatever school-leaving examination suits their situation … we should look ahead and not put our head in a noose.'*

He was not reticent either on the matter of scholarships. *'There should be no insistence on a scholarship entry, only on a merit entry. Even a merit entry is impracticable at all-age schools … scholarships should of course be aimed for as school situations permit, aided by the International Office. All good schools and universities worldwide do so. But don't let us make a phobia of it.'* [●]

Contemporary UWC readers may be shocked by many of these sentiments. Those who knew Desmond will be reminded sharply of the man. But none can or will be surprised that his relationships with the emerging governance of the organisation had by now become irretrievably conflictual. He and Naomi paid a heavy personal price.

How does one judge all these matters fairly?

Desmond Hoare's Hinterland

Desmond's hero in naval history was Nelson. He referred to him often when addressing naval audiences on leadership, revealing the qualities he himself admired and aspired to.

'He (Nelson) never lacked the roots of this quality (courage), but what a wonderful forcing ground was given him when, for two years as a boy of 14 and 15, he took charge of a clumsy cutter crewed by tough seamen sailing from the Nore, in all weathers, the Thames Estuary …'

'It is fundamental, most of all in a disciplined service, that loyalty to the Establishment should never take precedence over justice to a man. Nelson saw this and his men saw that he saw; the boys of today see things in a similar light …'

'Nelson was a selfless man who always placed honour before riches, who was more concerned with the failure of the country to bestow honours on his subordinates than with what he got himself. For the prize money of yesterday we have what is called today "fruits of office" which offer equal incentives for self-service and greed; and which few ignore today as Nelson did yesterday …'

[●] He must have intended *'fetish'*

His youth club work made him knowledgeable and sensitive about social change and its implications for naval recruitment and training, but was the Navy ready to draw the necessary conclusions? *'The Navy is ready to go far and wide outside its own body for technical and scientific advice on material; it shows less enthusiasm for outside advice on personnel.'*

On personal leadership: *'There should be less emphasis on the leader influencing his men and more on his receptivity to influence by his men. A circular response which must go on all the time is required and, if the flow gets dammed up, effective leaderships stops … efficiency is always reduced whenever a long distance order is substituted for a face-to-face suggestion …'*

And on the importance of friendship between officers and men: *'The full use of leisure … provides the best meeting ground for officer and man to achieve real knowledge one of another … in leisure activities formality disappears and real knowledge grows more rapidly. In general, the harder and longer the physical demands of a leisure activity and the greater the element of danger, the more rapidly will true comradeship be achieved.'* And he clearly took pride in the relationship he achieved with the tough boys of Notting Hill Gate: *'I have been known only by my Christian name since the beginning of the year. The boys have shown little interest in my background and have taken me just as they found me, a rather antique simpleton who helped with odd jobs but was of no importance.'*

His experiences in Notting Hill Gate have much significance for his interpretation of the role of the Atlantic College. *'The middle and upper class families in Britain have for a long time abdicated a large part of their family duties to masters at boarding schools and no undue harm seems to have resulted; but the poorer classes have no access to such satisfactory foster parents.'* Boys must come to Atlantic College from state schools and on scholarship.

On teachers: *'I have very rarely heard a club boy speak with respect or affection of his school teacher as he will of a club leader or of some adult he knows in the outside world. The teaching profession is suffering from inbreeding. The teachers go from school themselves to university or to training college and then straight back to schools as teachers. It is a closed circuit unfreshened by the leavening of men who have lived part of their lives in the outside world … the boys are quick to see the limitations of their teachers outside the field of knowledge, and many of the teachers are themselves on the defensive …'*

And on co-education: *'Where we can and should help our boys is by sheltering them from undesirable girls and pushing them into the company of the better girls in controllable* situations; better the mess hall than the hedge … there are those who think that girls soften boys but on the whole the Mixed Clubs do just as well as the Boys' Clubs at tough outdoor pursuits. And we must not forget that many of the boys need softening; the affection of a girl may be for many the first true affection he has known …'

The Navy, engineering, the war, and youth club work were the influences on Desmond Hoare and, through his Headship, determined the tone of the early years of the Atlantic College. But there was one more element, perhaps the most important. *'One person should not give orders to another person but both should agree to take orders from the situation …'* He was, I suspect unconsciously, echoing Rousseau: *'Mettre l'enfant en présence de la nécessité, jamais du devoir.'* The Atlantic College – the self-discipline required to study hard for university entry in unfamiliar circumstances, the discipline imposed by cooperative effort in hazardous circumstances on the waters and cliffs of the Bristol Channel, the exposure to class and room mates of hitherto unimagined diversity – created an evolving chain of expectations that set its own demands for all, teacher and student alike. Commenting on attitudes to religion in the boy's clubs, Desmond had written: *'… (the boy) is influenced far more by what is taken for granted, and by whom it is taken for granted, than by what is taught in words.'* It was what was taken for granted at the College that imposed the discipline and generated the morale.

Desmond Hoare Looking Back

Desmond Hoare's proposal in January 1969 to withdraw from the Headship in order to develop the Atlantic College project overseas was 'a bombshell'. But it was seized upon by Kurt Hahn, who had no doubts: *'… Desmond … has two qualities which I consider invaluable … deep concern about the individual destiny and the gift of inspiration, not only in personal contacts but when talking to a community. When he feels strongly, he can express himself in beautiful words which are not forgotten … a new outlet must be found for his creative powers. He combines vision with meticulous attention to detail … we need a master plan to carry conviction. Desmond is the man to design it. We need him as a consultant, campaigner and inspector …'*

Desmond Hoare's great quality was the ability to transform thought into action through rapid decision and command. The abandonment of executive responsibilities was in the event to cripple his creative potential. Nor did he have that caution possessed by all successful diplomats whose world he now entered – he was careless in his choice of enemies.

Idealists and volunteers are necessarily persons of strong convictions. Absent the disciplines and obligations imposed by professional organisations, individual personalities play a more dominant and, it may happen, a destructive role. The one person within the UWC whom Desmond Hoare respected without reserve, George Schuster, for most of his Headship his Chairman of Governors, once wrote of Desmond that he was *'an exceptional mount but needs a loose rein'.* But then George Schuster had been an exceptional horseman, and the metaphor and its implications came naturally to him. They came less naturally to others.

But let us recognise, however far in retrospect, the three strains that dominated Desmond's life from the moment he put off his naval uniform for the last time: the really serious financial sacrifices he had made through forfeiting the final years of his pension credits, the months of not knowing whether the College could survive the remorseless funding crises, and the deep, emotionally taxing disagreements over educational policy with Kurt Hahn, detailed in another chapter, when failure to have taken his own line would have handed victory to the College's sceptics and critics.

Ruthlessly honest and hard with himself, Desmond Hoare drew his strength from the company of the young, from aloneness and wild country (his holidays on Lundy Island, later in his simple cottage in County Cork, were his annual lifeblood), and from limited but intensely concentrated reading.

He was a complex, private man who needed a cause if he was to express himself and be at peace with himself. For him to be at peace with others, they had to share his dedication and his cause. He used to say of himself that he suffered from arrested development. Perhaps this is not so bad an analysis. He fought with most adults sooner or later as if he felt he were not justifying himself unless he were challenging them to their roots. With his total – I have to say, ruthless – involvement in the task in hand, he all too often showed a sharp, even shocking, disregard for consistency of argument, or personal feelings. He needed opposition as a filter for his ideas because there was so little space in his make-up for the dividing line between an idea and a conviction, and 'a conviction required action'.

He was fascinated too by the role of imagination in the exercise of power. I imagine him fired by the graffiti of the Parisian students in 1968: *'L'imagination au pouvoir'.* But he gave away his own executive powers without foreseeing the consequences, and found himself disarmed in his determination that the project should not lose itself in the comfortable paths of orthodoxy and establishment approval.

Desmond saw that Kurt Hahn's dream was profoundly realistic because he knew and respected the strength of will of idealistic and motivated adolescents. Is it not extraordinary that Britain's first ever fully co-ordinated cliff, beach and inshore lifeboat service should have been provided by a school of international teenagers whose period of training was compressed into nine months from September to May; that this service should have been in the forefront of training methods and equipment for both the National Coastguard Service and the Royal National Lifeboat Institution; that the world's first one-piece neoprene rubber suits should have been designed and created at the College; that the Atlantic Class Inshore Lifeboat, now in service world-wide, should have taken its name from the College because it was there that the first 18 prototypes were designed, built and tested? Desmond once speculated on paper about the talk that went on into the night in the cuddy and wardroom of *HMS Beagle*, and the capacity of Charles Darwin to listen and to use the wisdom of simpler men in the unfolding of his great principles of evolution. How did Desmond design the phenomenally successful Atlantic Class boat? *'I didn't make any complicated drawings, just sent the boats to sea, then listened to the students' comments.'* Arrested development? It is more accurate to realise that he identified himself to an extraordinary degree with the late teenager, his concerns, emotionalism, ideals, naïvety, scepticism, and high spirits – not for Desmond the *'law-abiding because they are listless'*. Above all else, they are to be taken seriously, and given serious tasks, and proper training, and the best equipment, and they will never let you down.

But lest all of this conveys the impression of utter self-certainty, let us take note of a letter handwritten one summer in *'the tranquil paper-free climate of Kerry'* to Kurt Hahn. *'I continue unendingly to admire your persistence and your certainty; you have not shifted much ground since I first met you … as regards certainty I stick to my religion because I cannot perceive anything better as a guide to conduct, but I am not at all certain about it. Similarly with education! One cannot possibly be doing any harm by following our present methods, but I am far from certain that they are adequate to the situation … are we giving our energies to the right people – good students, good characters who go on to conform at universities … what about people like Joan Baez, Bob Dylan, the Beatles … are these not the people to whom we should be devoting our main effort? The survival of mankind depends on the intelligent selection of resources and on their effective deployment … is this a crackpot idea, the invention of the leprechauns in which these bogs abound? I lack certainty'*

Desmond and Naomi Hoare were followed – a great blessing this – to Ireland by their son Mark and his family. Grandchildren gave family comfort. Some sailing and an involvement with the local RNLI Station were reminders of

Desmond Hoare recalls the history of the rigid-hulled inflatable

The line-up at the formal opening of the College RNLI station, named after Desmond and Naomi Hoare. Present are Desmond and Naomi, the Principal Andrew Stuart (in glasses) with on his left the American Ambassador John J. Lewis, on his right the Bishop of Llandaff, John Poole Hughes, and James Whitaker. On Naomi's left, Deon Glover

the active life led at St. Donat's. Observing him in profile, I was sometimes struck by the thought that, in another age, he might have been the Abbot of a monastery. But not of a silent order – he could not have held his tongue. It was natural that he should have donated money neither he nor his family could afford to that courageous venture, the inter-denominational Logan College in Belfast. *"I am the only UWC person who gave it a few pounds when it was near bankrupt'*, he wrote to Lola Hahn in November 1984. He was angered and deeply disappointed that the UWC had refused to associate itself with the school.

Defending the Atlantic College against a sceptical, indeed critical leader article in *The Yorkshire Post* in 1962, Desmond Hoare had written: *'it is manifestly true that 20th century warfare has been lethal and too frequent. It is equally true that airy slogans about international cooperation are a common and dangerous form of intellectual tranquiliser … the (College) activities will, by their very nature, permit the boys to assemble unforgettable memories and may, we hope, plant a life-long obligation to help their fellow men …'*. This is not a bad epitaph.

When I reflect on his last, lonely years in Ireland, I am reminded of lines from that great poem, *The Seafarer*:

*'Wherefore he who is used to the comforts of life
And, proud, and flushed with wine, suffers
Little hardship living in the city,
Will scarcely believe how I, weary, have had to make the
   ocean paths my home.
The night-shadow grew long …' [●]*

I have recounted elsewhere in this book how, on 23rd November 1963, the morning after the assassination of President Kennedy, Desmond Hoare told the students of Atlantic College that *'for most ordinary people, life is a voyage from harbour to harbour, along a fairly safe coast. We run no great risks, nor do we work very hard to make our passages. A few men in this world are not of this kind.'*

Desmond was also one of these.

[●] *The Seafarer*, Anon, translated by Kevin Crossley-Holland, taken from the *Oxford Book of the Sea*, edited by Jonathan Raban

Desmond Hoare's address to the College Assembly on 23rd November 1963

At our morning assembly a week or so ago, a student quoted the lines of John Donne which open with the words: *'No man is an island'* and which close with *'seek not to know for whom the bells toll, it tolls for thee'.* Today it is tolling everywhere for President Kennedy.

For most ordinary people life is a voyage from harbour to harbour, along a fairly safe coast. We run no great risks, nor do we work very hard to make our passages. A few men in this world are not of this kind, President Kennedy among them, and his whole gifted life has been one of great endeavour.

He sought power to influence policy, and his policies were guided by the two great passions of his life, the love of his own country and the love of freedom. The wanton futility of his killing is the ultimate denial of freedom, the use of a bullet to silence a voice.

The two great issues of public policy on which was engaged just prior to his death were those of racial discrimination in his own country, and of his overseas aid programme which had been cut back by Congress. John Kennedy saw that freedom was indivisible, that there could not be freedom for the whites in the USA unless there was also freedom for the coloured; that there could not be freedom for white and coloured in the USA unless there was also freedom from want in Africa and Pakistan.

To me as to many other people, President Kennedy seemed a most fitting representative of his nation, young, and young for his years, vital, confident, powerful, but above all humane.

In this international school the sympathy of the rest of us goes out to the USA students, and because they are here, it is our sad privilege to fly their flag over this Castle at half mast. We have been told that John Kennedy came to St. Donat's with his father as a 16-year-old boy and swam in our pool. If this is true, and it seems very likely, I have no doubt that he also leant on the sea wall and dreamed his dreams. He must have looked out from our foreshore across the Atlantic to his own country; and not only to his own country, but also to Ireland whence his ancestors came. I have thought it appropriate therefore to read what an unknown early Irish poet had to say on the death of their Chieftain:

In his own ground by the wild western sea,
Where oft this true Knight led the galloping band,
Now his homecoming saddens all the land.

The land held high his generous renown,
From Beare to Diarra, from Lee to Liffey brown,
From Galway west to southernmost Cape Clear,
Kilkenny to Loch Ce – afar, anear.

Peace, to give peace where he may not return,
To heal our hurt, to light the eyes that mourn,
Shield of our hearts, strength to sorrow found,
Lord grant the peacemaker thy perfect peace.

Bartolomeo Migone

The Atlantic College was on its second Headmaster. Desmond Hoare as Provost had brought Asia into the UWC with new National Committees and scholarships and been the decisive figure in transforming the Singapore St. John's International School, initially the British Army School, into the United World College of South East Asia. The Canadians, seizing the opportunity of commemorating their former Prime Minister and Nobel Prize winner Lester Pearson with a College on Vancouver Island, had presented Lord Mountbatten and Sir George Schuster with inscribed safety helmets at an International Council meeting at St. Donat's as evidence that their campus was on the way. And now here were the Italians with detailed plans and architectural models, drawn up in only three weeks, wanting to join the procession!

The Italian College, it was clear from the start, was going to be different. *'So you give us the red light!'* said an excited Bartolomeo Migone, Secretary of the Italian National Committee, after Mountbatten had made encouraging noises. *'No, Ambassador, surely you mean the green light.'* *'No, no, red! In Italy, when we see the red light, we accelerate!'* It reminds you of the Italian taxi driver telling the policeman to fine his passenger in the back seat – when he went through it was still green.

Bartolomeo Migone with Hartmut Rahn, Secretary General of the German Studienstiftung des deutschen Volkes

Several more years were to pass before the Italian College actually opened, but who would deny that it was Bartolomeo Migone's passion and idealism that sustained the founders?

A move on to the European continent in the early 1970s made a great deal of sense for the UWC – after all, Kurt Hahn had wanted the first college to be in Germany, and there had briefly even been a proposal in 1969 for a Franco-German College – but Italy! And Bartolomeo Migone's upbringing and personality were an improbable background. They were however the maverick impulse we needed.

Bartolomeo Migone was born in 1901 into a once rich Catholic family in Genoa. They were 11 children. His father was an intimate of Pope Benedict XV; his mother, who died at 99, described by her grandson as *'very intelligent and very conservative (bigoted – sic)'* in religious matters; his 'crazy' uncle a close friend of Mazzini. Over generations, the Migones had been associated with great social initiatives in Genoa and Turin. Patricians, they looked down on freemasons and the lay world in general.

Bartolomeo did not attend school, receiving private tuition at home. The law required him to take a validation examination each year. He passed it only once. Rich Catholics, the family assumed, were tested more rigorously. Bartolomeo does not study, someone said. *'He is too intelligent to bother with what teachers impose on him.'* He learned sympathy for those who failed – the *bocciati*. Later, he always gave them presents – those who had been successful already had their reward!

By the 1920s even a Migone had to earn his living, and the father insisted on education and a profession. Left alone, Bartolomeo would have allowed music to dominate. He eventually chose political sciences at the University of Florence. Still a student, he became the music critic of a Florence newspaper. Later, he took lessons in pianoforte and composition and became friends with many celebrated musicians – Furtwangler, Benedetti Michelangeli, Claudio Arrau, Tito Gobbi, the Quartetto Italiano and many others.

The Trio of Trieste, one of the world's leading chamber music ensembles, as well as Benedetti Michelangeli, always went to him for guidance on which interpretation to record and to publish of their performances. Diplomacy was a fortuitous career choice.

Too young for service in the First World War, he could not escape the dilemmas posed by Fascism. His siblings split along age lines, he and the younger ones allying themselves with Don Sturzo and the Partito Popolare of the non-Marxist Catholic working classes, the older ones with the Catholic clerical fascists. When Bartolomeo entered the Italian Diplomatic Service, he was embarking on 43 years of service to the State. Private means were assumed and class was important. It was one of the merits of Fascism that this tradition was broken, but by the mid-thirties every member of the Civil Service had to be a member of the Party. For a time, the teachings of Thomas Aquinas provided a solution – obey your chiefs unless they compel you personally to do evil. The Concordat between the Pope and Mussolini in 1929 had reconciled Bartolomeo and his younger brothers with Fascism to a degree – the rights restored to the Pope were reassuring.

He was given posts in Washington, Santiago and Moscow. This last was decisive. It was the time of the 1930s' show trials. His Ambassador and professional father figure for life was Augusto Rosso. He became close to the British diplomat Fitzroy MacLean, later Churchill's emissary to Tito and the partisans in the Second World War and a good friend of the Adriatic College during the break-up of Yugoslavia in the 1990s; to the American diplomats George Kennan, later the author of the US policy of containment of the Soviet Union and the Truman Doctrine, and Charles (Chip) Bohlen, who became interpreter and advisor for Roosevelt at Teheran and Yalta and for Truman at Potsdam and later himself ambassador to Moscow; to the German Ambassador Schulenburg who was executed in 1944 by the Nazis for his role in the resistance to Hitler; and to the German diplomat Johnnie von Herwarth who, as Germany's first Ambassador in London after the war and subsequently as State Secretary to the President of the Federal Republic, played a major role in securing German governmental funding for Atlantic College (in retirement he became the Chairman of the German UWC National Committee).

On the evening of 16th August 1939 von Herwarth told both Bohlen and Migone that the secret treaty between Germany and the Soviet Union was so far advanced that Ribbentrop was expected shortly in Moscow for the signing. Migone had his Ambassador telegraph the news through to Rome at 1 a.m. It transpired after the war that Admiral Canaris, the Head of German counter-intelligence, had also been briefing the Italian military attaché in Berlin. The sources of this critical information remained hidden from Nazi investigation.

Gian Giacomo Migone, Bartolomeo's son, for many years President of the Italian Senate Committee on Foreign Affairs, believes that the NATO anti-totalitarian philosophy – anti-fascist and anti-communist – was to some extent created in those Embassies in Moscow during the purges and trials. This is a bold claim, but the subsequent commitment of many of the main personalities throws an unmistakable light on the motivations that led to the founding of the Atlantic College. For Bartolomeo Migone, the Soviet experience was confirmation of the totalitarian evils of his own government. On the fall of Mussolini in 1943, aged 42, he was immediately made Head of the Press Office of the Ministry of Foreign Affairs in Rome. In 1945 he was dispatched to London to open the Italian Mission, for one year acting as *chargé d'affaires*, remaining there until 1948 and developing a keen admiration for the Labour Foreign Secretary Ernest Bevin and a close relationship with him. From 1948–1951 he was Minister to Sweden, from 1951–1954 Head of Cultural Affairs at the Ministry in Rome. From 1955–1957 he was chief of staff *(capo di cabinetto)* at the Ministry, and from 1957–1964 Ambassador to the Holy See, where he experienced three Popes, Pius XII, John XXIII and Paul VI. There could be no more fitting climax for a man of his family background. His career path sounds elegant and smooth. It was not. He was never made Secretary General of the Ministry of Foreign Affairs, the position his talent would have deserved. Looking back, he was sometimes regretful, but his daughter, Denyse, told him that he had after all achieved a high measure of success despite his personality and behaviour. His personality and behaviour are in the end, however, among the chief reasons why we should treasure his memory.

He liked nothing better than to provoke the conformists. A short temper banished caution and made him fearless. Apprehension within the family was ever-present. They knew he had a temperament and a vocabulary that only he could control – if he cared to. He deplored the fascist manipulation of First World War mythology – *'I will spit on those veterans who exploit their mutilation.'* He detested the misuse of these things. When a German corporal appeared to want to arrest him on the streets of Rome in 1943, he shouted at him in such a loud voice, in front of many passers-by, that the astonished man let him go. It was all part of the family's uninhibited linguistic impetuosity. Somebody told his sister Anna's daughter: *'We should all kiss our mother's ass for what she did during the war.'* A

Bartolomeo Migone (in spectacles), enlivening the dark officialdom of a NATO meeting with his Foreign Minister, Gaetano Martino, and his life-long friend Alberto Rossi-Longhi, Italy's permanent representative

German soldier had been killed and ten hostages were to be shot. The mother told an officer: *'I thought German officers were supposed to be gentlemen, but I see you are just a butcher.'* The hostages' lives were spared. On his retirement after seven years in the Vatican Embassy, where he had developed an enthusiastic relationship with Pope John, his deputy asked him for the traditional portrait. *'You can take my backside. There should not be too much of a difference between me and my predecessors.'* More diplomatically serious, more politically significant, and more damaging to his professional prospects, was the telegram he sent his Foreign Minister from London when he was being criticized for failing to defend Italy's right to colonies: *'It is difficult as a losing government to defend colonies to a victorious government which is busily engaged in liquidating its own.'*

At the heart of it all was his conviction that the State and institutions must exist for the benefit of individuals and serve them, not the reverse. In reality, commented one speaker at his funeral, he used to say that he had worked for something that did not really exist, or was a superfluous invention of the lawyers, or an institution that was imposing itself on the citizens and ought to be totally transformed. No-one more than him, and in words that cannot be repeated in public, could rail more strongly against the delays and injustices of a State whose very existence he questioned. And, to transform the realities he was facing, he was ready for every possible sacrifice. Nothing upset him more than to see persons close to him retreat into resignation or, worse, cynicism. He once said to his son: *'You may think that I am tilting against windmills, but one fine day they must be brought down.'* The sober Protestant realism and organisational talent of his Swedish

wife Quettan threw his impulsive, idealistic personality into high relief. He worshipped her.

In the first decade of the Atlantic College, a small and uncertain trickle of Italian students had found their way to St. Donat's. Donna Marella Agnelli, the wife of the Avvocato Gianni Agnelli, the Head of FIAT, was taking an interest. Her father and the father of Bartolomeo Migone had been fellow officers in the Italian cavalry. Gianni and Marella Agnelli tried to persuade Migone's son Gian Giacomo to take on the UWC commitment on behalf of Italy. Gian Giacomo felt himself too left wing to support an elitist school and suggested his father. But his father did not really like schools at all – education only began at university. He did not like academic selection – personality and preferably rebellious personality was more important. And the British public schools with their discipline and their corporal punishment! But it was the scholarship principle that won him over, as long as it was understood that academic merit was incidental and that the real objective was to identify mavericks like him.

In October 1969 the UWC International President Mountbatten asked the Italian President Saragat to become the Patron of the newly-founded Italian National Committee, a tradition which has been accepted by every subsequent President. Migone became the first Honorary Secretary. Seven Italians had attended the Atlantic College so far. By the time of his death in May 1983, the number had risen to 152 and the Adriatic College had opened. One of his earliest actions was to remove the knowledge of English as an entry requirement – he knew well that English was then a social distinction in Italy. In the Adriatic College we soon followed his precedent for all applicants. It had a dramatic impact, above all on the social backgrounds and personal qualities of our students from Latin America.

His years as Secretary of the Committee gain their lustre through personal memories. I remember his visits to Atlantic College, usually announced at the last minute (*'I am just catching the train from Paddington'*). His suitcase was always full of Italian pasta. Within minutes of my alerting the first Italian student I encountered, all knew. The kitchen in the Lady Anne Tower was made ready, and Italian celebrations went on late into the night (deliberately, it seemed, until after they were all supposed to be back in the residences). I remember being called to Trieste at the usual short notice to give some advice on possible locations for the planned Italian College. After a hair-raising drive from Venice Airport in a regional government car, I found myself in a primary school in Sistiana, entirely unsuitable for its suggested use as the future academic building. There was Bartolomeo Migone sitting on the floor, surrounded by

On the terrace of the Migone home in Genoa, a few days before his death

But it was nonetheless the individuals who mattered, not the institutions.

One Italian girl left Atlantic College after only a few months, thus wasting a scholarship. *'After I returned to Italy I was asked to visit Ambassador Migone. I was afraid of this meeting because I expected to be taken to task for having forfeited this opportunity. Imagine my astonishment when he said: "I am so grateful that you came to see me. We work hard to support the Colleges but, of course, we do not know what does not work or could be done better at Atlantic College. So you, having left it, presumably because you were unhappy there, are the best person to tell us!" I answered that it was a failure of my own doing, not of the College.'* It was typical of Bartolomeo Migone – the College, or the institution, was for the people, not the people for the institution.

Senator Valitutti, a former Italian Minister of Education and the second Chairman of the Italian National Committee, paid this tribute: *'I who had far more experience with the young was sometimes hesitant where he was enthusiastic. But I had to recognise that I was not wiser but only more tired, and that he was not more innocent but more trusting and more far-sighted.'*

It is true that others, notably Corrado Belci, Gaspare Pacia and the senior political personalities in Friuli-Venezia Giulia, with Antonin Besse monitoring affairs closely on behalf of the International Board, took over the practical responsibilities in the months leading up to the opening of the College in September 1982; but Bartolomeo had laid a sound groundwork and had been extraordinarily tenacious in assembling the best left wing representatives of the Christian Democrats, the party in power since the end of the Second World War, and of other centrist parties – Paolo Rossi, Sandro Valitutti, Cesidio Guazzaroni, Beniamino Andreatta, Leopoldo Elia.

His final months were cruel, but he was determined to witness the College in being. He arrived for the Opening Ceremonies in a wheel chair but abandoned it as the students rushed towards him at the airport. That evening he could no longer rise to his feet and was in tears as he was taken to the departing aircraft. In November 1984 the Prince of Wales, with his widow Quettan at his side, dedicated the College library to his memory.

dozens of enthralled primary school pupils who refused to let him leave! Tony Besse, with whom he worked closely in the years leading up to the opening of the College, recalls lunch in a restaurant in Rome. *'The padrone of the restaurant, as is usual in Italy, did his Cicerone act, and then told us what we were going to eat. Migone turned to him and said in a loud voice: "I have been eating here for over 30 years and I have still not been allowed to eat what I want!"'* And on another occasion, after the College had opened: *'Did you warn David Sutcliffe against the Italians and against accepting the Headship of the College?'* But to me he said: *'If we had six Adriatic Colleges, we could change Italy.'* He was expressing a sentiment shared by many of the early founders: They wanted a college above all for the future health and development of their own national societies.

John Nichol

Education – a Weapon for Peace

Lord Mountbatten had become the first International President of the United World Colleges in 1967. Desmond Hoare had stepped aside from the headship of Atlantic College in 1969. Both these extremely active and single-minded personalities were determined to expand the project, and both were impatient. Mountbatten with his personal prestige and access to leaders across the world made his first impact on the project's national committees, animating many to increased activity and creating

The Senator John Nichol

new ones. Desmond Hoare pushed in the same direction, above all in South East Asia, but gave his mind and his energies with increasing conviction to new interpretations of the Atlantic College model. The United World College of South East Asia came into being in somewhat fitful stages; but Atlantic College itself, the two-year scholarship entry school, remained alone. Could it be replicated? Attempts were made in Germany, the United States, and also in Canada with a fairly detailed proposal for Banff in Alberta. All lacked the leadership in local and national public life that was an absolute requirement for so ambitious an undertaking.

Lester Pearson had visited Atlantic College twice. He had heard all about the early plans from Lawrance Darvall in the 1950s. On his death in 1972, it seemed natural to commemorate him with a Canadian college. His family gave their warm and grateful blessing. But who could bring it off?

To listen to John describing it all, the setting up of the College was just another enjoyable adventure.

'Well, you know, the things that are fun generally work out financially.

When I got into it, Jack Matthews had got quite a long way down the road … I said, I'll start putting together a team to build the College … I wanted one man committees. Because they were not committees but individual executives, it was all very smooth …

We made two mistakes … the primary mistake was architectural … we built the buildings too close to the ground, dumped them into the rocks, so they were dark on the back. The other one may have been the location ... it was very isolated, and the cold side of the Victoria Peninsula, but by this time it was too late … I would have paid a little more attention to climate. Then we had to negotiate with the Department of National Defense to secure the property … The government said: Yes, you can have the land, but you have to put an 8 foot fence, steel poles with barbed wire on the top, round the whole property … to make sure the students do not get mixed up with the training of the soldiers. Anyway, we had a good Minister, and we negotiated a fence which you can't even see.

We built the College as cheaply as we could … we didn't have any money … in the full knowledge that those buildings were going to need a lot of maintenance in later years.

One of the main architectural ideas was that we were not going to build an institution; we were not going to build a physical plant that intimidated the students who came from simpler cultures. I had a sense at Atlantic College that the castle was a fairly formidable piece of architecture…for people from Papua New Guinea, for instance … I wanted to set up buildings that gave the message of a village that wasn't threatening to people who came from less sophisticated cultures.

At this point, the question was whether the government and the Pearson family would want this College built as a memorial. Trudeau struck a committee … there were lots of other applications right across the country – the question was, would we be the principal memorial to the late Prime Minister? One way or another, the politics of it were that we ended up being named a principal memorial. We took the point of view that that was fine – nobody else was going to build one … the "a" would turn into "the" with time. The principal memorial to him has been this College. We started to build the college in 1973 and finished in 1974 … a real breakneck construction … the students came and unpacked the beds and then built the docks.'

No Pearson College student can be warmer about his college than John about his own school – the Thacher School in California. It had started out as a support school for Yale in the days of tuberculosis, when people were sent to the desert. 'My aunt put up the money for me. The teachers were so good … it was a fabulous institution.' He talks about the camping out in the sands, the rattlesnakes, the horseback riding. The school journal records his winning the Essay Prize, the Poetry Prize, the 'Notes' Prize, the Prize in Public Speaking and Debate, his editorship of the journal, the loudness of his whistling, and the colour of his socks. He graduated in 1941. After one year at the University of British Columbia he had a year at the Royal Canadian Naval College. After graduation he served in the North Atlantic, the English Channel and the Bay of Biscay in the HMCS Saskatchewan and later the HMCS Victoriaville, finishing the war as a Lieutenant.

The official histories of the Canadian Navy are factual and cool. In Operation Neptune at the end of May 1944, Escort Group 12 was on anti-submarine patrol south and east of Land's End. Later, in July, following the Normandy landings, Brest and all the strong naval bases along the French Biscay coast were still held by the Germans. U-boats were arriving and departing in considerable numbers.

Escort Group 12 (HMCS Qu'Appelle, Saskatchewan, Skeene and Restiguche) embarked on Operation Dredger south of Ushant. In the early morning of 6th July they encountered three armed minesweepers and two U-boats. The first minesweeper was destroyed. HMCS Saskatchewan missed the second with its torpedo but destroyed its bridge with a direct hit. HMCS Qu'Appelle was riddled by enemy fire, with a depth charge set on fire, havoc on the bridge, its steering gear out of action, the commanding officer and several men seriously wounded.

John's Captain, Alan Easton, wrote a book, 50 North, in which he described the Saskatchewan's activities in the closing months of the war:

On their way south from Scotland in preparation for the Normandy landings, 'heavy masts with fighting tops came up over the horizon and soon developed into bulky battleships and heavy cruisers, accompanied by the inevitable fleet of destroyers. The battle squadron bore down, the sun glinting on the damp armour-plated sides, a picture of towering strength … But now, as this great squadron drew abeam of us, we suddenly realised that another was following very close behind. It was instantly apparent from the very shape of the ships that they were American. They too were beautiful; a little higher freeboard but massive. And their destroyers, spread out in their protective fashion, were larger than the British and our own. Here were the lions of the great armada and the flags of the two nations bent together. I had never seen them quite that way before. As they ploughed on past, up the north Cornish coast into the head breeze, I lost any feeling of doubt I might have had for the success of the invasion, at least as far as the sea-borne operations were concerned …

… our job was to prevent U-boats from attacking the con-voys as they rounded Lands End and to stop any from getting into the Channel … (John) sounded rather disconsolate. But there was plenty of optimism in him really. He was young, the junior among the officers; humour normally hovered around his eyes and mouth …

… the next night we sailed for our usual haunt, the coast of Brittany … as far as I knew, we were the first Allied ships to enter the approaches to the famous U-boat base since the fall of France …

(After Operation Dredger): On our way back we saw one ship only, the burning third, and although we passed close to her I could not bring myself to fire on her. She was silent. A feeling of pity ran through me. I felt for a moment desperately sorry for the crew and for the men of the other two ships which I thought were either sunk or sinking … was it weakness on my part to hold such feelings for an enemy who had been guilty of bringing such devastation on the world? No. These

Germans were sailors; they were men of my own cloth, my own profession.

The battle itself had lasted 25 minutes. Our ship had expended 280 high explosive shells and 2,400 rounds of smaller ammunition …

… the doctor had found it necessary to cut off an arm of one of the wounded. He was a fine big fellow of Polish descent from a farm in Manitoba, and he looked at me as he lay on the table as though there were almost nothing the matter. I said something futile in an effort to cheer him, then watched him go under as John, under the guidance of the surgeon, applied the anaesthetic… (John: "I had no idea how to apply anaesthetic – I just poured the ether on a washcloth and kitchen strainer.")'

Demobilisation, the University of British Columbia and a degree in commerce, and then life moved forward in ten-year cycles. First, ten years in the lumber business working for some Jewish families who had been chased out of Poland by the Nazis. They also employed other people who had escaped the Holocaust. John says he greatly admired them and learned a lot from them.

Following that, ten years in politics!

There are interesting parallels between John Nichol of Canada and Corrado Belci, the Founder President of our Adriatic College in Italy. Both experienced the war as young men, if in very different ways. Both achieved political influence at the most senior levels without themselves holding high political office. Both experienced the same conflict between single-minded political ambition and family life. Both were journalists with national reputations and a magical mastery of words. Both were public speakers whose style was neither declamatory nor exhortatory but which achieved a human rapport with their audiences that 'spoke more than words'. Both took their obligations with utter seriousness, themselves with a disclaiming smile and the immediate turning aside of compliments and tributes. For both, much of life was taken up by tasks assumed voluntarily. Both put the founding, survival and welfare of their respective colleges at the very top of their daily agendas. Both were, quite simply, inspiring personalities.

In 1964 John Nichol was elected President of the Liberal Federation of Canada and appointed to the Senate in 1966 by the Party Leader, the Hon. Lester B. Pearson. That same year, there was unrest in the Party about Pearson's leadership, and the Conservatives were about to change theirs. *'As President of the Party, I had to deal with it, so I had conversations with Mr. Pearson. Conventional wisdom was that whoever got the new leader first would have a big electoral advantage. I had a different intuition'*, John said. 1967 was the year of the World Expo in Canada. Lester

Pearson spent the year entertaining the world's leaders. Nobody could attack him – he was invulnerable. Then he announced his retirement. John wrote a Party President's letter to Pearson, drafted the reply, and chaired the leadership convention. It was attended by 10,000 people. He would *'never be frightened of anything again'*. He then ran Trudeau's election campaign. Trudeau won by 158 seats, the biggest margin in 15 years. John never sought office, never aspired to membership of the cabinet, was diffident about his ability and his motivation to run a department, found the broad brush of work in the party more appealing, was content to have been in politics long enough to have been Party President and Campaign Chairman.

Mike Pearson died at Christmas in 1972. In the spring of 1973 John resigned from the Senate and began the job of building the Lester B. Pearson College of the Pacific. The next ten years were taken up in working for the College as well as attending to matters arising from corporate directorships of some major corporations – Canadian Pacific, Alcan, Crown Zellerbach, Time Canada and others. He also served on the Advisory Board of the Capital Research Group: *'fascinating, one of the biggest money management businesses in the world'.*

There were also almost ten years of journalism.

John wrote a weekly newspaper column from 1967 to 1975, syndicated in 14 newspapers. He set out, he said, to offer *'an irreverent look at life, politics, economics and international affairs and anything else that came to mind'.* He once praised a fellow contributor: *'You had the wisdom to write with simplicity.'* This was his own benchmark – he knew the power of words used well. He also had something to say. Some examples!

On television: *'The healthy cynicism which says, "I never believe what I read in the newspapers" is transposed in to the chillingly naïve "It must be true – I saw it on television". So we grab the image and run. The facts and practical arguments are left to catch up as best they can.'*

On sportsmanship: *'The whole psychological atmosphere of professional sports fits like a glove the acquisitive society. The hockey player who spears his opponent when the referee isn't looking is soul brother to the income-tax evader.'*

On smoking: *'… and then the doctors found out what cigarettes really do to people. It was shocking news, like finding that a trusted friend is really the agent of a foreign power … And so farewell!'*

On pomposity: *'Although we have catalogued our inventory of oil, gas, coal, uranium and hydro power, and we talk about harnessing the tides of the Bay of Fundy, we have another source of energy of great potential. I refer of course to Hot Air (or Verbal Gas, as it is sometimes called), which* rises in unmeasured quantities all over our country, 24 hours a day, 365 days a year … there is the output of 10 provincial legislatures, innumerable municipal councils, parks boards, school boards, Royal and other commissions, leagues, committees, conventions, associations, unions, meetings, think-ins and freak-outs; all of which sound off non-stop on every conceivable subject … save your pennies for the day when the energy of this hot air is harnessed for man's use and (if you get a chance) buy the stock – you will make a fortune.'

On government: 'The Anti-Ballistic Missile system is the beginning of a new major escalation in the arms race – no one knows if it will work and no one knows what it will cost. In short – the perfect government project!'

On the Law of Difficult Exits: 'Next time you thump a ketchup bottle with your fist, think! If the ketchup manufacturer had as much trouble getting the ketchup into the bottle as you have getting it out, he would be broke in a week … the classic example in our time is Vietnam. Each step into the morass seemed logical to someone. The various governments in the US completely ignored the Law of Difficult Exits and now the country is faced with the most difficult exit of all … the old saw "look before you leap" was an early expression of the Law of Difficult Exits. It did not suggest that one should not leap. It suggested that one should examine the purpose of the leap, from whence, and, most particularly, into what.'

There was more than irreverence.

'President Nixon's evocation of "the silent majority" in support of his policies should bring us all up short, because in doing so he is calling up the uneasy ghosts of all the millions and millions of faceless human beings who, down through the ages, have tolerated evil in the name of apathy … Leadership involves the stimulation of people's minds so that they can see problems and search for solutions, and a leader who simply mirrors public lack of interest is not a leader in any sense of the word … Jesus defied the establishment of his day, and his words have defied every establishment since. He said: "He that is not with me is against me" and thus he forbade his followers membership in the silent majority. On Christmas Eve, although there will be warmth and the singing of carols in churches around the world, there will also be marchers out in the dark streets protesting against war and the brutality of man to man. It is hard to believe that, if Jesus were here in 1969, he would not be out with the marchers.'

His references to Watergate led some to accuse him of anti-Americanism. His reply was robust. 'Watergate … may well be the greatest conglomeration of illegal acts and immoral behaviour ever to be exposed in a modern free society … the pack of grand juries, prosecuting authorities, civil and criminal suits, and senate hearings is sniffing under every rock. The President is like a bear in his den, listening to the hounds grow closer, occasionally growling with anger, getting ready for the big fight … When the smoke all clears, the American people will have seen their government and their system with a clear and probably unforgiving eye … perhaps it's naïve to hope that a major or moral reform will result from Watergate, but at least in a democracy, a chance exists. No other system can make that statement.' Misplaced confidence? His more recent views suggest so. 'I despair for America. My family were American. I loved America – Woodrow Wilson and FDR and the Marshall Plan and the whole generous spirit of that country which Churchill admired so much. But it has all changed – I am sure it has all changed deeply … the fundamentalist Christian movement, which is a bizarre aberration of everything Jesus ever said, wouldn't exist without television, which is a huge fundraising engine of those fundamentalist preachers. 53% of American people believe the bible to be literally true, and at the same time, there are 150 people at this time waiting to be executed in Texas alone.'

In 1970 he wrote:

'… out of the rubble of economic disaster came Hitler … nationalism, both political and economic, was the kindling for the fire of World War Two. The world took a blood oath that these things would not happen again. There was a burst of internationalism … the winners helped the losers … in the world outside the Iron Curtain, international co-operation was the order of the day … internationalism is still a powerful force because the memory of war and depression is still alive, but the memories are dimming. Even though the international structure is not crumbling, if you listen carefully you can hear the termites gnawing in the joists. Those who are so sure that nationalism is the cure for all things should tell us what new ingredient they have which will make nationalism work this time – when it has never worked before.'

And in 1974, only days before Pearson College opened: '… and isolationism is pure poison … The floods in India, the drought in the Sahara, the bad crop in the US, the Arab oil prices, inflation in Brazil, the collapse of a German Bank, the British trade deficit, the war on Cyprus, to name a few recent unhappy events, all have a direct effect on every Canadian. An individual may not be able to trace the cause, but the cause is there just the same.'

Admirable and appropriate reflections, one might think, for the creator of a United World College, but John Nichol is quite clear where the decisive motivation lay. And anyone who has ever encountered the College founding team gets the same answer: Lester Pearson and the intense personal loyalty he inspired. This was what had taken John Nichol, Jim Coutts and many others of their generation into politics at the outset of the 1960s. John Kennedy had just become President of the United States. He represented something *'really charismatic about politics, made it look like a good thing to do'.* Canada at the time had a Nobel Peace Prize Winner who was available to become the country's Prime Minister – Lester Pearson. *'And so it became a great cause among young people to get into politics, to get Lester Pearson elected. Mike Pearson had a high streak of idealism – he gathered many around him who produced some of the great changes in the Canadian social system – Medicare, the pension plan, the Canadian flag, "all that stuff". The big feeling at the time was that politics was an honourable avocation. There was this deep feeling that the country was in need of someone like Pearson.'*

You get the feeling with John that the things that are fun generally work out politically as well. *'They knew instinctively how to make politics fun. They loved the game and they loved their leader'* – one political historian's comment. They practised, John in the lead, *'psychic patronage – the art of keeping the supporters happy and involved by personal contact (and by the judicious exploitation of Ottawa rumours to make them feel like insiders)'.* He was not in politics to wear a hair shirt. There were the Thursday evening parties when they lay on the floor and sang Irish songs. One senior party leader sternly refused to offer alcohol to his guests. Enough was enough! Asked one night whether he would like a drink, and not waiting to find out whether he would be offered coffee, coke or lemonade, John snapped open his briefcase with a flourish and brought out a bottle of expensive Scotch and two glasses, one for himself and one for his wife. But he also understood the realities of politics. Later, in 1973, he was to comment: *'Politics is like a circus. In the first act, the star rides in on an elephant while the people cheer. From then on, he walks the high wire, watched intently by the silent crowd.'*

John married Elizabeth Kenyon Fellowes, 'Liz', in Vancouver in 1951. They had three daughters – Marjorie, Barbara and Sarah. But *'people who go into politics pay a terrible price. It is very hard on family relationships, very hard on the children. It is very easy to become seduced by power, to the point where you sacrifice things that you should not in order to retain it … There were times when I had to choose between a birthday and a big meeting – I don't think I always answered that the right way, but I got out in time.'* In 1990, Liz fell ill with Parkinson's disease. It is humbling to hear him talk about her. Accompanying her to the hospital for treatment, he had asked whether there was anything he might do to help the research efforts. In 1992 he founded the Pacific Parkinson's Research Institute of Vancouver to raise funds for the work being undertaken into Parkinson's disease and related movement disorders

at the University of British Columbia and the Vancouver Hospital and Health Sciences Centre. He was, to quote the consultant who led the research, a *'dynamo in furthering the interests of Parkinson's patients through research … He was crucial in enabling Canada to accept an offer from the World Federation of Neurology to host the XIII International Congress on Parkinson's disease in 1999 in Vancouver. No other institution in Canada would take the financial risk. The Congress was larger that any previous Congress, with over 2000 delegates.'* Liz Nichol died on 2nd December 2000. She had, John said, fought like a lion. There followed the nights when he awoke in his chair in the early hours of the morning, cold, the dog asleep, the glass empty, alone. In 2002 he married again – Rosanne Cashin, a family friend of many years. They both talk about Liz a great deal. It is not possible that he could have married someone Liz had not known, who had not been a good friend, who would not have had her blessing.

The creation of Pearson College may to all of us appear to have been a natural challenge for such a man. But no one – no one – takes on the founding of a United World College without a level of personal motivation that goes well beyond the ordinary expectations of public service and public reward. His first reactions to Atlantic College had been cautious, even critical. He had found it too formal, Germanic, with a touch of the *Jugendbewegung*, its buildings forbidding. He was frank, then and later, about the UWC meetings in London: he liked the people and the hospitality, but he resented the pressures to take rushed decisions on questionable grounds. He could not, he said, have been recruited for a College without Pearson. There were plenty of schools for rich kids; hence the Pearson College scholarship policy which declined all family contributions to the costs. Everyone thought it was too idealistic and unrealistic. Few outside the Pearson Board thought it could work. And here, a characteristic tribute to a colleague: *'Jim Coutts went out and raised the first 96 scholarships. I don't mean he headed a committee. I mean he raised them himself.'* 1974 was a time when the Atlantic College was struggling to adapt to the changes of the late 1960s. A cynic might have said that it was losing its way between the ethos of the British Navy and the English public school. John and Jack Matthews brought life-saving fresh air into the United World Colleges. They brought the political and the business world of Canada behind their project, a reminder of the early days of the Atlantic College. But it was the informality of the village campus, the teachers and students on first name terms, the genuinely democratic 'village' meetings that made redundant all the earlier experimentation with student councils, the scholars recruited from Latin America and Asia in numbers that broke dramatically with the European-North American context of existing UWC National Committees, that made the great impact. It was a new vision in international education, and those early PC scholars have no doubt that they were transformed by the experience.

Is that the end of the story? Have all the hopes been fulfilled? Have the results justified the investment? Can more be done?

John Nichol is in no doubt, and here one senses discouragement. The numbers are so small. The task must be to construct something that is *'way bigger'*.

In 1994 he wrote a paper: *Education as a Weapon for Peace.*

'Education in its broadest sense, and in all its forms, is the ultimate weapon in the battle against ignorance, bigotry and prejudice, and their offspring, conflict, violence and war.

Education is the ultimate weapon in the battle of humanity against the dark.

Education is the ultimate weapon for peace within nations, between nations, and between conflicting ideologies.

The really critical part of any strategy must be to disseminate and promote these ideals to the widest possible international audience … the model to follow is that of the environmental movement … we should use the world's news and public relations engines in a more sophisticated way to mobilize public interest and support … we should cast as wide a net as possible and not be too fussy at the first cut.'

And as to the possible difficulties he quoted Lester Pearson: *'I do not intend to fall off that bridge before I get to it'.*

And what would be the role of the UWC?

'Take the Colleges as a nucleus of energy. Discover how to use that nucleus. Look after the hundreds, thousands of applicants who so narrowly fail the College selection. For every one who wins a place, there are ten, twenty, more, who are qualified. Give them something to belong to. Demand more from the graduates. It is all a matter of communication.'

When he was setting up the College, the really important thing was to make sure that everyone knew that it was a good idea. *'How did the Ayatollah Khomeini, in exile in Paris, prepare his revolution? By clandestinely sending the cheapest, smallest tape-recorders in to every village in Iran, then following them up with regular recordings, inciting revolution! The pen is far, far mightier than the sword. The problems of the Middle East will never be solved on the*

John Nichol with Rosanne in company he treasures, canine and human (students of Pearson College)

battlefield. *The only thing that will stop the conflict is that, at some time in the future, people will think differently. And they will only think differently if in some way they are taught differently.'* But he is not imprisoned by the one idea. He reminds me of Desmond Hoare who, at a dark moment in the fortunes of Atlantic College, said: *'Well, if this thing falls apart, there are plenty of other good tasks to tackle in life.'* The world, says John, is full of vacuums. He has spent his life *'being drawn into vacuums – vacuums in which action was required but no one was doing anything about it'.* What is the point in having all the structures in place – systems, committees, trustees, task forces, constitutions – if nothing is happening? *'Set up some simple human machinery and then put pressure, real pressure, into the pipeline, from the bottom end.'*

Perhaps, at the end of it all, the decisive thing that drives John Nichol is that strongly Canadian and strongly Pearson concept of complete harmony between pride in country and the pursuit of peace. In part it is literally the love of country and of the country's creatures: *'The sea is blue, the grass is green … there is a feeling that the world is good, the air is clean, and tomorrow is someone else's problem – Canada's Pacific coast in the summer! That's a sight to make a strong man cry.'* John is a long-standing patron of the Vancouver Public Aquarium, a past trustee of the North America Wildlife Foundation and the Delta Waterfowl Foundation of Manitoba, of the Waterfowl Research Foundation of New York, and director of the Pacific Salmon Foundation. In part, it is a clear perception of Canada's role: *'for 30 years, Canada (has been) an intellectual leader in the internationalist movement. We have made a contribution far beyond our size in the fields of freer trade, mutual security, aid to developing countries and, through the UN, to the cause of international law.'* And

in part it is his concept of society: *'The producers … are the workers at all levels of society … they build buildings, drive trucks, dig ditches, run banks … are doctors, lawyers, dentists, bricklayers, farmers, housewives, secretaries … they generate the energy of our system, they produce the money to make it survive and the aesthetics to make it tolerable. Civilisation was built by the producers. On the other hand there are the controllers … mostly found in government … alert to the dangers of uncontrolled democracy … their job is to draw up rules, regulations and laws … and to direct the producers' efforts into channels of which the controllers approve.'* John is a producer.

Lester Pearson recalls in his memoirs how, after World War One, the Treaty of Versailles created a problem for the Canadian navy with its requirement that all navies reduce their fleets by one half: *'We had three ships!'* John Nichol after World War Two had another view: the Canadian navy can no longer exercise any military power or influence. Better therefore to transform all its vessels into well-equipped hospital ships, to stand offshore whenever a humanitarian disaster strikes, and to set a new example of international Samaritan service. That idea, he says, did not get far.

In 1980 John Nichol became an Officer and in 1997 a Companion of the Order of Canada. The citation stated: *'His devotion to his community and his lifelong experience have contributed to his reputation as a most exceptional Canadian.'* But the mirror we should hold up to him is best described in the words he himself wrote about his hero, Lester Pearson:

'He reached across the dark gulfs of race, colour, creed, age and background and built bridges of understanding. He could do this because he really liked people – and they knew it. He liked to talk to them, to shake their hands, to laugh with them. He had his arm around the shoulder of mankind.'

David Sutcliffe and Desmond Hoare

Alec Peterson

To record a life is not necessarily to measure it. The life of an educator has in any event more judges than most, and their judgements are likely to vary in ways without number, for the judgements of pupils are emphatically personal and subjective. For better and for worse, the educator is remembered.

What remains striking, however, about Alec's life is the sense of unity and harmony between his personality and his style of living – his versatility, the volatile range of his mind and his interests, his refusal to be confined to one place or one job for too long – and the nature of his accomplishments. His influence during his working life on war-time and university colleagues, school pupils and teachers must, one assumes with confidence, have been contagious, extensive, memorable, almost certainly long lasting, but the principal educational battles he fought were lost causes until he reached retirement. Then, fully armed by argument and experience, his powers of persuasion compellingly enhanced by his enjoyment and understanding of other cultures, he led the creation of his life's memorial – not his creation alone, for sure, but without his sophisticated, intelligent leadership, it is hard to imagine the International Baccalaureate emerging into reality from the disparate strivings of a handful of idealistic teachers.

Alec was born on 13th September 1908. His parents lived in India, his father a member of the Indian Civil Service. He attended a boarding prep school in Britain from a very early age. He recalls worrying intensely that he might not recognise his mother when she came to visit. He was right. He confused her with the wife of the Headmaster. He was looked after in the holidays by aunts. One, Aunt Minnie, he later described as a *'puritan, an ascetic and an idealist … with a strong sense of duty, a Burnsian contempt for rank or ceremony, a taste for poetry, and a high regard for academic learning',* but her large house was always freezing cold, and there were no hugs or kisses. Powerful influences! His decline as a scholar set in, he was to claim, when at the age of ten Greek was added to Latin. But, as he also said,

Alec Peterson

people nowadays are surprised to learn that at 12 he was reading and translating Sophocles and Euripedes. In his final year at school, a tutor from Oxford attended a class on Virgil and, after hearing him perform and make a slip, said: *'That's a very idle boy. Put him in for Balliol and we'll give him a scholarship.'* In the same year, when top of the Classical Sixth Form and Editor of *The Radleian*, the school magazine, he was, he recalled, beaten by the Captain of Boats for leaving an oar in the wrong place in the Boat House. In his family memoirs, he wrote that the horror of school had not really been the bullying or the caning or the persecution, but the *'deadly deadly boredom'.* Small wonder that he treasured above all others the comment of an old boy of the Adams Grammar School in Shropshire, where he held his first Headship: *'We had such fun'.*

University was another life.

'What,' I asked his widow Corinna, *'should others remember him by?'* *'He was so energetic, loved new challenges, travel, writing, he was so versatile, too versatile, switched around, he*

had such stamina, he was a wonderful father, and … gosh, he was so good-looking.'

He was. His IB image is all wrong. There is this photograph of him with a beard, and a thin, drawn face. Late one night, preparing to move house the next day from Oxford to London, he fell from a ladder. The next morning his furniture went to London, he to hospital to wait for three months to know whether he would walk again. He grew the beard to conceal an ugly face injury.

Oxford! Friends. The Classics. History. Philosophy. Acting. The Union. Counting himself something of an anarchist, he found himself cast as the Unjust Argument in Aristophanes' *The Clouds*. Early sympathies for lost causes made him a life-long Liberal. He founded a new university weekly which was suspended after two issues for obscenity. Undeterred, he went on to write simultaneously for *Isis*, the *Oxford Magazine* and *Cherwell* under three different *noms-de-plume*, editing the last for two terms. One of many close friends, half English, half French, introduced him to French literature – poetry, Proust, Gide. He made his first proposal of marriage. *'Oh Alec! I'd marry you tomorrow if I thought you would be faithful.'* And this without their having even held hands, let alone exchanged a kiss! His description of another friend reveals the qualities he admired and no doubt wished for himself: *'He had an extraordinary capacity for the enjoyment of life, a wit which sparkled on the surface of things and, very deeply concealed, a real commitment to people and to causes.'* Looking back, he described Oxford as *'a world of love and friendship – I envied anyone whose family came from and lived in one place and had connections – to find myself accepted by people who liked books and politics and travel and yet were funny and frivolous and light-hearted, and yet were romantic and felt or thought they felt deeply about each other and about social causes, was like entering an enchanted garden.'*

Having convinced his oral examiners in Philosophy that he was worth a First, he was unexpectedly called back for a second *'viva'* in History and, in what he pithily called *'a model of the exposure of a fraud by oral examination'*, ended with a Second. And with no idea of how he wished to spend his life! Captains of Industry were however to be the men of the future, the more so if they had no scientific training – strange how this illusion persisted, unweakened, into the 1960s! He applied, and was accepted in 1930 by Unilever, with whom he spent three *'wasted years'*, living initially in the East of London, supposedly learning from invoice clerks and soap-boilers, working in the packing room, canvassing the local shopkeepers in Peckam to stock the latest promotional offer. He had an insight into poverty and social distress through some involvement in the activities of Toynbee Hall. (*'I remember asking Quintin Hogg to dinner in a Chinese restaurant in the East India Dock Road. "This isn't really a poor neighbourhood, Alec", he said. "I can see into some of the houses and there are still banisters on the stairs. When they are really poor they break up the banisters for firewood"'*). In the second year he was sent to Zurich, for the first time living on his own, learning some German, becoming attracted by the peaceful, domestic Swiss countryside, and meeting C. G. Jung. *'An impressive man'*, and *'the impression he gave was that of a peasant craftsman, just like Thomas Hardy'*, whom he had met just before he died. But the decisive consequence of his years in industry was the recognition, which was to accompany him throughout his life, of what makes life worth living and work worth doing well. In his words:

'I had long believed in the truth of Aristotle's remark that happiness is a by-product of unfrustrated activity. One reason why I was such a failure and so unhappy at Unilever was that I was condemned to years of passive observation … Of course, the conviction that the job is worth doing in itself is an important element … The one motivator which I have never personally experienced in relation to a job is the one by which contemporary society is commonly supposed to be powered: money … Certainly, I have never changed a job, and I have changed it often enough, because a different one offered a higher salary. Nor when I have been offered a new job have I ever asked what the salary was. Indeed, some of the most engaging and fascinating work I have done has been in voluntary projects in which no money was involved at all. … And all around there is an economic doctrine that it is only the forces of the market which will call out the commitment and the talents of the human race.'

In 1932 he went back to the Oxford University Appointments Board to ask for a job *'working with people'*. The Headmaster of Eton was in the next room urgently looking for a temporary master. Thus casually Alec entered education.

Three weeks at Eton were followed by another short-term appointment at Shrewsbury. The pleasure of working as part of a group of like-minded contemporaries convinced him that he now knew what he wanted to do. He sought and was offered a permanent post. His younger brother was a senior prefect there. Alec had no illusions about the realities of public school life. Whenever he had disciplinary problems, he told the offenders he would report them to his brother. He began to experiment in the classroom. In studying the *Aeneid*, he gave each boy 30 different lines to prepare for homework. The principle was that they helped one another. They completed the first four books in one term. They wrote a Shakespearean play, *The Tragedy of Dido and Aeneas* – some boys wrote the tragic speeches, others the comic. *'Today, neither you nor I know any American history. We shall learn it together.'* He was later proud of a geography book he published – *The Social Geography of the Far East* – which went into three editions, was translated into French, and used by Australian universities; he had studied no geography after the age of 14. He remained passionately opposed throughout his life to one-subject teaching. I recall his comment when he was Director of the Department of Education at Oxford about researchers *'crawling along the frontiers of knowledge with a magnifying glass'*. Perhaps he had been influenced by the example of his Uncle Fred, who devoted the last 20 years of his intellectual life to the study of snails' teeth (he was much in demand at the London Natural History Museum).

Absorbing work, the company of like-minded friends, theatricals both in the school and locally, with a 1935 tour in Nazi Germany, the lovely Shropshire countryside – these interests were now supplemented by a growing fascination with schools and education in general. He began to attend the conferences organised by T. F. Coade at Bryanston, and made his first visit to the United States on a one-year teaching exchange sponsored by the English Speaking Union. One summer holiday, probably in 1937, he and a colleague set off *'to see how the anarchists were getting on in Barcelona'*. They crossed the Pyrenees by bicycle. Four hundred Gauloises cigarettes stood in for passports on a minor road crossing – they had already seen, on the main roads at least, that passports did not work. On the way out, Alec still without papers, police boarded the train to check documents. Alec avoided the controls by the simple method of stepping out on to the platform to smoke until they had gone, a strategy much admired by his fellow travellers. At the frontier, he was stopped. *'Where is your exit permit?' 'I speak little Spanish. Here is my English passport.' 'You cannot leave without an exit permit.' 'This is intolerable. I am due to address a meeting in Trafalgar Square London tomorrow in aid of the Spanish Red Cross and you prevent my leaving.'* He left. Back in Shrewsbury, he was a declared pacifist until Abyssinia and respected his Headmaster for making no attempt to prevent him inviting Bertrand Russell to lecture in the school. He fell in love – not for the first time, it must be said – but this time it was serious. He proposed and was accepted. He married Pauline on 28th December 1939, and they set up house and home in Shrewsbury, Pauline leaving from time to time to complete her medical training and examinations. He was not however to be left undisturbed during the war to teach.

Alec's experiences during the Second World War were typically special. He was seconded to the Propaganda Branch of the Special Operations Executive. The great initial difficulty was to find anything to do which could help win the war. The main task was to concoct rumours with a sufficient substratum of truth to keep them in circulation. One, later taken up by Evelyn Waugh in *Men at Arms*, was the pre-invasion claim that Britain could set the sea on fire. Then an agent of Alec's, a waiter in a hotel in Poole from which VIP travellers left for Portugal by flying boat, was arrested because he had sent his white waistcoat to the laundry with the rumours he was supposed to be spreading copied out on a note in the pocket. Alec gained his first, invaluable experience in inter-departmental feuding, more time-consuming (and more intellectually demanding) than combating the enemy. But then there arrived a request from the Special Operations Executive in India, asking for someone experienced in the creation of rumour. So Alec travelled for the first time to the country where his father had made his career and had been on speaking terms with Jinnah (and his grandfather with Motilal Nehru). It was to be for three or four months. He returned after four years. The outward journey, by Sunderland flying boat for most of the way, took four weeks – Lisbon, Bathurst, Lagos, across Africa via Kano and Maidi-Guri, down the Nile to Cairo, Baghdad, Basra, Sharjah, Bahrain, Karachi, Gwalior, Delhi. IB colleagues later wondered at Alec's capacity for long-distance travel, his freshness and alertness on arrival. They will have fond memories too in reading Alec's recollections of that time: *'It was a marvellous experience for a young man of my age. I have always loved, and looked back with nostalgia to, the beginnings of enterprises. It is the time when everyone knows everyone else and decisions are taken quickly, but in a huddle that goes on for 24 hours a day; it is the time when no one is quite sure where the enterprise is trying to go or whether it will get there, but everybody is utterly committed to the cause and there are no internal jealousies or jockeying for power … Later, as the enterprise grows, even perhaps the more successful it becomes, bureaucracy and fissions seem to become inevitable.'*

His task was to have been to generate rumours to reassure the population against the background of an expected Japanese invasion. But events had been moving too fast, and now he was to set up cells of resistance to operate against the Japanese occupiers. He writes with acute appreciation of the instruction from the Viceroy that, whatever steps were taken against the Japanese, nothing whatsoever was to be done which would exacerbate communal tensions in the country. *'Pathetic'*, he thought his resistance cells would have been, and when the danger had passed, they had to race round Calcutta removing the secret demolition charges which were now exploding in the hot weather. His responsibilities grew. He became head of the Propaganda and Political Warfare Unit. This led in turn to the setting up of the Indian Field Broadcasting Units (IFBUs) which, with the help of Japanese speakers, operated independently on a small scale and provided early intelligence of Japanese movements and infiltration. On one occasion, a section of the Royal Welsh (Welch) Fusiliers had become trapped behind Japanese lines. How to convey instructions to them without alerting the Japanese? The company commander took over the IFBU loud speaker and gave his orders in Welsh. It was at this time that Alec made the significant educational discovery that, despite all the horrors of the time, he could not find any individuals who, having learned Japanese as a foreign language, were able to harbour feelings of hatred towards the Japanese people and military. He was also engaged, briefly, in seeking to make contact with the Burmese nationalist leader, Aung San.

It was also the time when he received *'the worst shock that I have ever experienced',* a letter from Pauline asking for divorce. Kind colleagues, his new Supreme Commander Mountbatten the most active of all, found urgent war business requiring his immediate return to London. Close to home, the aircraft over the sea, the navigator drew their attention to Lundy Island in the Bristol Channel. *'Where are we',* they asked when they landed. *'Port Reath in Cornwall',* said the navigator. *'North Wales',* said the ground staff. The marriage lasted a few more months, but the whole business was all the more distressing because *'we both took marriage, and even such things as marriage vows, a great deal more seriously than people do now'.*

On his return, Alec was seconded to Mountbatten's headquarters staff as Deputy Director of Psychological Warfare. It was the beginning of the close relationship which later achieved so much for both the International Baccalaureate and the United World Colleges. It placed him very close to the post-war issues of decolonisation. *'One thing I was quite certain of was that the European empires of the nineteenth century could not and should not survive after the war, and since this was also Mountbatten's conviction we spoke freely on these informal occasions.'* His paper for Mountbatten supporting recognition of Aung San had, it is generally accepted, a real influence on the final decision.

The end of the war in Asia saw Alec attending the Japanese surrender in Singapore, where he was the 'conducting officer' for the Communist leader Chin Peng, and the victory celebrations in Bangkok, where the local victors had been on the other side until a few weeks earlier! His final post was as Head of Propaganda and Information in Java. Independence had been agreed by the USA and Great Britain for the Philippines, India and Burma. France and Holland wanted to stay. The nationalists in Indonesia were in control, but hundreds of thousands of Allied prisoners, including many Dutch, were held in the interior. The only available troops were Indian, but how could they be employed against a nationalist movement? Semarang was saved by arming and deploying the Japanese prisoners in its defence. They, having learned the lesson of surrender once, obligingly surrendered once more to the British after they had completed the job. It was Alec's task to promote law and order and to secure the release of prisoners, negotiating at the same time with the nationalists and the Dutch. Perhaps the latter were being more realistic on the spot than in their political statements at home when they nominated their representative – Dr. Posthumus. Shortly after, Alec was dismissed. He had taken it on himself on the radio to interpret an ambiguous speech by the British Foreign Secretary as not intended to imply British support for continuing Dutch colonial rule. Mountbatten sent him to Saigon for three weeks, and then demobilisation.

Alec returned without hesitation to schoolmastering. He wanted to run a school in a quiet part of the English countryside, remarry and raise a family. *'Fate was very kind in the end.'* He met again Corinna Cochrane, whose family he already knew well. They married in late August of 1946 and moved to Shropshire in September, where he took up the Headship of Adams Grammar School. One can almost inhale his happiness from the pages of his family memoirs. Married couples are often said to grow more alike as they age. How often is it that their handwriting becomes so similar that, at first sight, it is not clear which one has written?

The years at Adams were the years of establishing the family, building up this rural 'Voluntary Aided' grammar school into a reputable academic institution with competent sports teams, entering the school's first ever candidates for Oxford scholarships, teaching Italian by keeping a few lessons ahead of the boy who needed it for the scholarship examinations, and writing his *The Far East: A Social Geography* and *A Hundred Years of Education*. Some broadcasting and journalism completed the picture, but it was not long before he was back in Asia.

General Templer, High Commissioner and Commander-in-Chief in Malaya, appointed by Churchill to master the insurgency after the assassination of General Gurney, had asked for a list of all those who had done strange jobs for Mountbatten in the South East Asia Command. Alec was needed for two months to give advice. The summer holidays were at hand. It was too exciting to miss, but it was the end of life in Shropshire. Alec was told by Templer that his report would be accepted in full only if he came out for two years to implement it. He came. His family followed. Alec became quite sympathetic to the integrity and even ideals of the Chinese guerrillas. Once again, he put his faith in seeking to reach the hearts and minds of the local population, now using mobile film units rather than the IFBUs of India. Every major rural community got a visit once a month. Eight years later, under the independent government, 99 of the 103 he had set up were still in operation. Important visitors passed through, among them Adlai Stevenson and Richard Nixon. Corrie, his wife, wrote an analysis of communist propaganda, later referred to publicly as *a major work in the field*. Alec himself was described by Templer in a dispatch to the British Government as *an absolutely first class man*. He left most of his work when he departed in the hands of local people. Full independence followed three years later, in 1957.

It was in his next post, as Head of Dover College, that Alec began his serious involvement in international education. Early vigorous action was necessary to keep the school within the prestigious Headmasters' Conference (HMC), and to secure funding for new science laboratories from the Industrial Fund which was supporting the Public Schools, but the school began to develop its public profile and reputation with its innovative international sixth form, taking pupils from other countries, especially the nearby European mainland, for the last two years before university. Never short of striking ideas or, it seemed, 'names' for his causes, Alec launched an appeal in *The Times* over the signatures of Lord Ismay, Rene Pleven and Adlai Stevenson. These initiatives brought him an invitation to a NATO conference in 1957 on international education in Bruges. There he met Kurt Hahn. He was also coming to grips, for the first time seriously, with his other and overriding passion, curriculum renewal for the British Sixth Form. [●] A broadcast in 1956, subsequently printed in *The Listener*, which attracted much attention and support, including that of Lord Mott, the Nobel Prize physicist, and the Estlin Carpenter Lectures he delivered in Oxford, published in 1957, had been evidence of his continuing concern with

[●] This was precisely the time when Kurt Hahn, with the support of Lord Mott among others, was setting up his Trevelyan Scholarships for entry to Oxford and Cambridge. This scheme was intended, through the inclusion of individual projects in the qualifications for admission, to loosen the grip of the narrow, specialised curriculum of the English sixth form in preparation for university studies.

wider educational issues. In January 1958, rather to his surprise, he found himself Director of the Oxford University Department of Education.

It cannot have been easy. Maurice Bowra of Wadham College told Alec he could count on him as a *'malevolent neutral'*. His opposite number at Cambridge was a medievalist. When asked by the selection board what he proposed to research into, this man had replied: *'Well, I couldn't research into education, could I? That would be ridiculous. I shall continue my researches into medieval sermons.'* The appointment was confirmed, together with a Fellowship to Trinity.

Alec's educational activities mirrored faithfully his devotion to 'generalism'. He was already the Chairman of the Royal Commonwealth Society's Education Committee, and became a member of a government working party on youth activities in the Commonwealth (under Templer's Chairmanship). He was *'of some help'* in the setting up of Voluntary Service Overseas (VSO) and a great admirer of the founder, Alec Dickson. He was a member of the Annan Committee on the Teaching of Russian and Chairman of the Army Education Advisory Board. He persuaded an American idealist, Gene Rietzke, to fund an Anglo-American Conference at Ditchley Park on *Correspondence Education* which was to become a seminal influence in the creation of the British Open University. Having met David Wills who sponsored the Anglo-American Conference Centre at Ditchley Park, he developed his American connections and interests and chaired three conferences at the Centre. One was on *The Relevance of the American Liberal Arts College to Higher Education in Britain*. Its title reflected Alec's belief that university education in Britain had gone too far towards specialisation and research in ever more limited fields. Nothing came of the subsequent proposal to attach a Liberal Arts College to one of the British Universities, with Alec as the first Principal, but Alec, accompanied by the family, had teaching spells in Philadelphia and Berkeley. Nor did another of his proposals, for a two-year Diploma in Higher Education, prosper. Faithful to one political party throughout his life, he was for a time the educational spokesman of the Liberal Party. On one occasion he stood for Parliament. *'Peace. Progress. Prosperity.'* Can those who knew Alec imagine him standing, as he did, at the entry turnstiles of the Oxford Football Club on a Saturday afternoon, haranguing the soccer fans through a megaphone with his election message? But it was another Oxonian lost cause.

But the cause to which he was now really devoting himself was the reform of the curriculum in the British Sixth Form.

Alec's broadcast and *Listener* article in 1956 was his first really clear, focused statement on the issues, but the key document is *Arts and Science Sides in the Sixth Form: A Report to the Gulbenkian Foundation*, published by the Oxford Department of Education in 1960. Its findings have the beguiling distinction of having never been either refuted or implemented. Consensus is and has remained limited to agreement on the existence of the problem.

The defining strength of the Gulbenkian Report lies in the assurance with which Alec draws on European and North American practices to refute British assumptions. The apparently uniquely British phenomenon (but one must except the Scots whose practices have always been different), used to justify the intensive specialisation imposed on British youth between 16 and 18, is that *'able boys and girls are ready and eager by the time they are 16 – the ablest by 15 – to get down to the serious study of some one aspect of human knowledge which, with the one-sided enthusiasm of the young, they allow for a time to obscure all other fields of endeavour. "Subject-mindedness" … is there whether we use it or not. It is sensible to direct this great emotional impetus towards intellectual effort … given the right teaching, a boy will by the end of his schooldays begin to come out on the far side of "subject-mindedness"… as he sees how the facts in his own subject knit together, he begins to wonder how his subject fits into the whole field of knowledge. He reaches out for himself towards a wider synthesis.'* [●]

Alec Peterson made no bones about asking why this phenomenon should be unique to Britain, or about the price that was paid: *'a curriculum which deprives one third of the nation's ablest pupils of any advanced mathematics and the other two thirds of any serious contact with foreign languages or with the literature of their own country'*. But he was equally clear-minded about the prevalent weaknesses in other countries – that education means the *'acquisition of a body of knowledge rather than the development of the power to think'* (*'so hackneyed a cliché that such a criticism is bound to seem either trite or false'*).

Why the problems in Britain? There is no Ministry of Education, argued Alec, with the powers to insist on a national curriculum. Teaching in the final two secondary years is driven by competition for university entry and the grades in the school leaving examinations. Schools, teachers, universities and the Ministry do not share a common interest in reform. Alec was not uncritical of the European Ministries or of standards in American High Schools, but he looked with some envy and admiration at the role of the College Board in the United States. Remarks made at the 25th anniversary of the Board, in 1925, make it clear why: *'The important thing is the close and intimate association of the secondary schools and colleges in dealing with a common interest and a common task. What this Board has done is to break down the isolation of the schools and the isolation of the colleges and to bring them into close and constant contact for the solution of their common problems.'* [●]

The Gulbenkian Report has these important passages:

'We shall not solve the problem of combining general education with the requisite skill or understanding in a specialist field until we cease to think of general education in terms of general knowledge. It is not a sign that a man lacks general education if he does not know the date of the Treaty of Utrecht, the latitude of Singapore, the formula for nitro-glycerine or the author of The Four Quartets. *It does denote a lack of general education if he cares nothing for any of the Arts, confuses a moral with an aesthetic judgement, interprets the actions of Asian political leaders in terms of nineteenth century English parliamentarians, or believes that the existence of God has been scientifically disproved.'*

And

'If Sixth Formers are to begin to get a conception of the true unity of knowledge … then the differences in the different modes of mental activity must be made explicit to them … (the fifth block) should therefore include a course, similar to the best and not the worst of the Classe de Philosophie, on the methodology of the subjects. It may be suggested that this is beyond the capacity of the average Sixth Former. I do not think so. It is certainly not beyond their interest … it is not the factual knowledge but the "learning to learn"' which is the real purpose of these programmes …. It does not matter if the pupil has never heard of Leibniz, Marx or Leonardo, provided that he has begun to understand how scientists reach their conclusions, how a mathematical truth differs from a moral one, and what is meant by poetic imagination?'

And finally:

'May it not be that we are all feeling for the same thing, and that in France and Germany by reducing the number of subjects, England by increasing it and America by rationalising it, may arrive at very similar conclusions?'

These lines of thought will be very familiar to the many thousands who teach the IB programmes. The reason for including them here is that these comments had been conceived, formulated and published by 1960.

[●] Central Advisory Council for Education, 15 to 18: A Report, London 1959 (*The Crowther Report*)

[●] Nicholas Murray Butler on the twenty-fifth anniversary of the College Board, 6th November 1925

One of life's great blessings must be to enter retirement with physical and mental capacities unimpaired and the sense that, for a few more years, one may still have a contribution to make. True, Alec took early retirement in order to concentrate *'single-mindedly'* on the IB, but his single mind now embraced such breadth and richness of experience that all his qualities were able to be fused in the realisation, internationally, of the pedagogical *credo* which had proved impossible within national borders. Strength and authority were conferred on the early work quite simply because there was a group of senior educational figures, all of whom had been unsuccessfully proposing reform within their own countries: Recteur Jean Capelle of the University of Nancy and former Director of Pedagogy in the French Ministry of Education, Madame Hatinguais, Directrice of the Centre for Research and Experiment at Sevres, Hellmut Becker, Director of the Max Planck Institute for Education and later President of the Bildungsrat, Georges Panchaud, Professor of Education at the University of Lausanne. Add the *'chalk face'* enthusiasm of the early teacher pioneers, and the shared awareness that this was an experiment *'for real'*, not just theory and doctoral theses, and the impetus may have seemed unstoppable. But the drawing together of the threads, the maintenance of a sense of direction which called for fast, empirical but sensitive decision-making, required Alec's masterly touch. Let one example stand for many. The example has been quoted by Gerard Renaud, a French teacher at the International School of Geneva, a true co-founder of the IB and, for a time after Alec, its Director General. It is important because it concerns the Theory of Knowledge.

As recounted in Alec's book *Schools across Frontiers*, Gerard had initially pressed for philosophy as a compulsory subject, but had been persuaded to accept it as one choice in the humanities group. His later talk with a senior French Inspecteur led to the proposal to add to philosophy as an optional course another compulsory course of reflection on the nature of knowledge and of personal experience. The term Theory of Knowledge was born in this very conversation. Recounting all this later to Alec, Gerard recalls how his face lit up. How could it have been otherwise when one recalls what he had already written in his Gulbenkian Report? In Gerard's words, Alec responded: *'Dans les comités ... on parle surtout des disciplines et des examens ... mais nous sommes en train de passer à côté de l'essentiel ... un tel cours est de nature à modifier complètement la nature du curriculum dans le sens que je souhaite.'* Given the scepticism of all except French teachers towards anything resembling compulsory philosophy in the secondary school curriculum, it was Gerard's role to

insist that only Alec as an Anglo-Saxon, not he Gerard as a Frenchman, could carry colleagues with him on this issue. Alec's reply: *'Laisse-moi faire.'* In Gerard's considered judgement years later: *'sans Alec, la Théorie de la Connaissance ne serait peut-être jamais née'.*

And a second example, this time related to Germany. In a similar endeavour to rescue German education from the burden of encyclopaedic knowledge in favour of learning how to learn, Hellmut Becker had promoted optional courses, paradigmatic learning (*'exemplarisches Lernen'*), and *'the courage to leave gaps'.*

Alec's alertness to the value of ideas coming from differing national traditions and differing national problems enabled him swiftly and readily to incorporate this thinking too in the preparations for the IB curriculum. [•]

Alec's decisive leadership of the early IB is beyond question. What of his other retirement cause, the United World Colleges? Atlantic College, on its foundation in 1962, had no choice but to offer the British G.C.E. Advanced Levels. Equally, with students from many European countries, it had no choice but to offer a wider curriculum. Alec, as a member of the Founding Committee, had the opportunity of initiating experimentation with a range of subsidiary courses. These proved to be acceptable for the time being to the relevant European Ministries and universities, but they suffered the usual fate of General Studies and the like in British schools – they were sharply reduced or dropped when the real examinations came near. But it was a start. The students of the Atlantic College were not the first to sit the Diploma examinations, nor were the teachers among the original pioneers. The College's decision, however, with the 1971 entry to abandon the national examination system in favour of the International Baccalaureate for all its students, made it the first school in the world to take so radical a step, conferring credibility and strength

[•] He was not above subterfuge either when there seemed to be no other way forward. One Atlantic College colleague recalls attending an early workshop in the 1960s intended to produce, within 48 hours, a new syllabus for Psychology. So strong were the disagreements between the Anglophones and the Francophones that Alec, as Chairman, resorted to writing two sets of minutes which recorded different conclusions in the two languages. I personally remember the IB Executive Committee Meeting in Sienna at which Alec was determined to secure agreement on the introduction of a second examination session in November. He knew the majority of committee members were against. He also knew that enough of them had to leave early to enable a favourable majority to emerge. He simply delayed the relevant agenda item until he knew he was safe on the IB at a most critical moment. This decision would have been unthinkable had Alec not patiently encouraged the participation of College teachers in frequent workshops in Geneva, ensured that important meetings were also held at the College, and nurtured the concept of the College as a real field laboratory for international academic education. It might have been equally unthinkable had the parents not been 'absent' (all the students being boarders), and for the most part incompetent in English. What for them was the difference between GCE and IB? Thus was educational innovation accomplished! The tradition and the expectations were maintained as successive Colleges were opened.

Later, in 1978, Alec became Chairman of the UWC International Board. Typically, this took him by surprise. Under Lord Mountbatten as International President from 1968 to 1978, and with only one College in existence at the outset of this period, the UWC International Office was a powerful source of energy and action in founding new National Committees and in the vigorous pursuit of opportunities for opening new Colleges. But the Colleges were and are legally and financially independent, substantially responsible for their own public relations, fundraising and financial survival. It was Alec's achievement, quite certainly not limited to his two-year chairmanship, to keep before the eyes of all the concept, not of individual Colleges, but of a movement linked by common values and aspirations. He was never afraid to make the case for élitism in the UWC context, or to question ideas and policies which wandered too far from empirical common sense. For the UWC teachers he was a true point of reference and authority. In the vast majority of cases, their sense of pride and professionalism in their IB work was extraordinary, their desire to implement and initiate untiring. Increasingly, but especially in the 1980s, the IB became a leading reason for seeking appointment to a United World College. But if the Colleges, their example and energy and the quality of their students – and their influential ten-year President Lord Mountbatten – were sound reasons for Alec's loyalty and support, they were not the only ones.

Alec's intensive cooperation with the powerful personalities of Mountbatten and Templer had given him an acute sense of the importance of combining thought with action. He rarely tired of quoting Plato: *'He who wishes to help his people must combine the power to think with the will to act.'* Kurt Hahn's vision, which he had first encountered in Bruges, fired his enthusiasm. What was international education about if not to affect attitudes and to stimulate a sense of practical obligation and service to one's fellow human beings? Was there perhaps a touch of romanticism,

a lingering attachment to lost causes? Was it the remarkable group of people who united to create these Colleges (described by one College Chairman as *'comparable with the characters in a Shakespearean play'*)? Was it simply the challenge? Another favourite quote of his is from Lester Pearson: *'We've got a great idea, we've got a great bunch of people; what are we making all this fuss about a little money for?'* Without a doubt, he was fascinated by the ethics and practicalities of the UWC scholarship policies. He was attracted by the concept of selecting students on scholarship, on merit, who were voluntarily and for idealistic reasons ready to change school, language, teachers, and to leave home, for the sake of the international experience. It was an evolution on a larger, more ambitious scale of what he had pioneered at Dover College. But I am also reminded of his reflections written as part of the final chapter in the 1957 edition of his *The Far East.*

'What the people of the Far East require are food, order, justice and peace. Unless the food is produced, tens of thousands will starve, but unless order is maintained, the food will neither be produced nor distributed. Order is threatened by two forces – conscious destruction and the revolt against injustice. Therefore, if the forces of order are to conquer those of destruction, they must also remedy injustice. Finally, not even a regime of food, order and justice could survive another war.'

Ever conscious of wider issues, and open to new ways of tackling them, he energetically supported the proposal for a radical departure for UWC – the creation in Venezuela of an international post-secondary Training College in Agricultural Management. The signing of the agreement for the setting up of the College was his last act as Chairman. The College has had to struggle unceasingly for survival. It is at least arguable that its struggles might have been eased had Alec remained a little longer in the chair.

International education is nothing if it is not concerned with human attitudes. The point is obvious. Alec was understandably concerned to show that the IB inculcated the qualities of humanity and citizenship. He believed in *'the call of the hero'* and in the impact of models taken from literature. For eight years he was the Chairman of the rather quixotic Farmington Trust in Oxford which was founded to promote moral education. True to form, he assembled able colleagues and commissioned a series of inter-disciplinary papers and seminars. He wrote a paper *Results obtained by Schools affiliated to the International Baccalaureate Office in the Domain of Moral Education.* Some of his conclusions cannot be without interest to us today as we seek to review and refine our understanding of international education for the 21st century.

Alec saw special opportunities for schools which were international, which educated young people between the ages of 16 and 19, and which subscribed to rational and humanistic values. A non-believer, he was convinced that IB graduates were more likely to *'judge more justly and act more effectively in the moral domain'* as a result of their educational experience. IB students, he thought, should be aiming to

> *Recognise all other persons as of equal value*
> *Develop the skills to empathise*
> *Acquire the knowledge to understand the emotions and motivations of oneself and others*
> *Gain awareness of the seriousness of moral situations*
> *Form a commitment to generate an autonomously accepted set of moral principles and to act upon them*

In the Theory of Knowledge he saw the opportunity to include an intellectual attempt to refine the understanding of what it is to take moral decisions. Physical and aesthetic activities and community service, all of them obligatory elements in the IB, were to contribute to the formation of the essential link between the intellectual and imaginative development of moral awareness and practical moral action.

Was this, he himself worried, too rational and 'cold' an approach? He also drew specific attention to *'one of the moral blind spots which the IB is seeking to illuminate (and which) arises from the fact that students in international schools often come themselves from the relatively rich countries and find themselves living and going to school in the relatively poor ones'.* I believe he would attach even greater significance to this last point were he still alive today.

In prodigiously active retirement, Alec Peterson achieved full self-realisation. The instruments he helped to create, shaped and used, were the International Baccalaureate and the United World Colleges. In the critical early days, they complemented each another. The presence and the influence of the IB in particular are now worldwide. An obituary on his death described him as *'one of the most pervasively influential educationalists in Europe'.* But his last publication, written in the year of his death, *Three Decades of Non-Reform*, tells another story. In a thorough review of

Alec is awarded an honorary degree by Rector Paolo Fusaroli of the University of Trieste on 29th October 1985

Alec addresses the award audience

university entry "left as they are now to operate freely" continue to produce "a state of affairs which is widely deplored", as a Committee of Vice-Chancellors and Principals recognised in 1962.' So that other obituary was also right which described him as 'among the best known – if not especially influential – educationalists of the 1960s and 1970s'. It is noteworthy that the only university to recognise him with an Honorary Degree was foreign, not British, the Italian University of Trieste in 1985. This seems curiously appropriate.

Yes, a versatile and varied life, by talent, circumstance and express personal desire, but a harmonious life with clear inner direction and purpose. 'One of the great advantages', Alec told *The Times Educational Supplement* in 1961, 'of varying one's experience is that one learns more what can and what can't be done in forming the world. Also, some teachers suffer a lurking doubt as to their own capacity to have done anything other than teach. It is most satisfying for a man to have done some work, knowing he could have done something else instead.'

One of my most distinct memories of Alec is watching him write – fast, legibly, with no prior draft or notes, making scarcely a correction in his manuscript. One had the feeling that the distance between his brain and the paper was short, direct and unhesitating, the communication instantaneous. Another is of his ability to work immediately, without preamble, in any circumstances or surroundings. It was noble of him, having retired from the Directorship of the Department of Education to become the first full-time Director General of the IB, to take a part-time teaching post at the Hammersmith and West London College for which his payment was a very part-time secretary and 'a largish cupboard' which served as his office in the UK; but it was entirely typical and will not have impaired his performance one iota. It was also typical that he was writing his private memoirs for his children and grandchildren (of which much of this document is essentially a summary) until within one month of his sudden death at the age of 80 years; and that, on the day he died, Robert Blackburn, the Deputy Director General of the IB, received from him two handwritten letters and the draft of a speech.

the debate from 1959 onwards, he lists the almost unending series of commissions and enquiries and investigations into alternatives to the traditional specialisation in English and Welsh schools, including the decision of the Schools Council not to back a limited, carefully monitored pilot experiment with the IB in volunteer state schools. His penultimate paragraph contains the forlorn challenge: *'But will they (the Ministry, the universities, the schools) take such risks? Or will the pressures caused by competition for*

George Schuster

That Lively Youngster George Schuster 1881–1983

We were all of us in awe of George Schuster. The immediate reason was his age. He was 83 when, following up a suggestion by the Director of the Industrial Society, John Marsh, he went to Brown's Hotel in London to introduce himself to Kurt Hahn. He had been told that the Atlantic College, launched a few weeks earlier, needed help, and he was looking for something to occupy him in his later years. I remember that gathering in London in 1978 to mark the publication of his memoirs on which he embarked (with, it must be said, the really critical assistance of the College's Head of History, Colin Reid) at the age of 95. His son was coming to represent him. *'What does his son do?'* I was asked. *'Well, he retired many years ago.' 'Of course'*, and a long pause!

I remember too the last time I saw him. My wife Elisabeth and our youngest son Edward and I had called on him in the summer of 1982 on our way to Italy to open the Italian College. He had recently turned 100. Our 14-year-old Edward could scarcely grasp that he was meeting a man over 100 years old and did not take his eyes off him – wide open eyes – throughout our visit. On the mantelpiece was the traditional birthday telegram from the Queen. It was written out in pencil, presumably by the local postmaster, with spelling mistakes. I was angered at first by this: could a royal message to so distinguished a centenarian not arrive in more correct, more dignified, more respectful form? On reflection, I felt sure he would have much preferred the local and rural nature of this congratulation to a colder, more regal, more impersonal missive. He was deeply attached to the English countryside, the Oxfordshire countryside above all other. He and his wife Gwen had bought their fine manor house in Nether Worton in 1919. It had been their home ever since.

The Family

George and Gwen Schuster, she the acutely sharp-witted daughter of a Lord Chief Justice, the 1st Lord Parker of Waddington, and the sister of a Lord Chief Justice too, the 2nd Lord Parker of Waddington, seemed to personify the English county aristocracy. Both loved horses, both hunted, and Sir George was admired locally for having ridden his last point-to-point on his 70th birthday. They were once described as *'the handsomest couple in England'*; and the two full length portraits hanging in their sitting room were convincing testimony. But his respect and affection for English life were also inspired by foreign insights.

His forebears were German. His grandfather had brought the family across to Britain in 1808 to escape Napoleon but

George Schuster on his 100th birthday

had retained his merchant banking business in Frankfurt until 1866, when it too was transferred to England to escape the Prussian occupation. Originally of the Jewish faith, his grandmother had led the family into Christianity after her own conversion. The Schusters had encouraging predecessors, as George Schuster himself suggested in his contribution to a collection of essays on *The Character of England* in 1947: *'The English story of the Baring family begins in 1717 when John Baring came from Bremen and, "liking of the soyle", married in England and set up as a wool merchant in Exeter. His three sons established the London house in 1763 … and Alexander Baring became the outstanding figure in the post-Napoleonic years … the rise of the Rothschilds equally illustrates how the "City" of international repute grew up, how it was ready to treat business objectively, and foreigners on their merits …'*

This was nonetheless a difficult background for George Schuster as he entered the British Public School Charterhouse where, as he recalls, his happiest memories were of the holidays. Not until Oxford did he become *'intellectually and socially alive'*, and he has described the defining moment in his Oxford time which set the compass for the rest of his life. *' … I still see a picture of Hadow, then a very young man, striding up and down the lecture room with his gown flying behind him. In this lecture he was dealing with Aristotle's conception of happiness (eudaimonia) in human life which he saw as active work … (energeia) done with a quality of excellence (arête), and if a man has a capacity for "excellence" in more than one form of work, then in that kind of work for which he has the best capacity … later I came to realise that Aristotle's ideas were too cold, self-centred and intellectual and that to give true meaning to my life my conduct must be founded on a religious and, for me Christian, faith … in particular His interpretation of the second of the two great Commandments.'* One biographer of his nephew, the writer and poet Stephen Spender, has suggested that George Schuster was for years deeply scarred by his schizophrenic pedigree. If so, he kept it in good English style to himself. More to the point was perhaps another comment – that he grew up in a world of servants, silver-service dinner parties in the evenings and starched linen on the dining-table.

One must regret that George, perhaps because they were written so late in his life, reveals so little about his family in his memoirs. Not for nothing were they entitled *Private Work and Public Causes*. His mother Hilda, daughter of the renowned physician and pioneer in the treatment of tuberculosis Sir Hermann Weber, emerges from Stephen Spender's memories of her as a truly remarkable woman: *'the spiritual territory she inhabited was a democracy of the*

emotions, where she understood everything which was an appeal from person to person … she grieved over the lack of love as a guiding spirit in the world'. He gives extraordinary accounts of her self-discipline, her Spartan living throughout her many years as a widow, her public service during the Second World War. In the First World War she had lost her favourite son Alfred, George's younger brother. She and her family had been under attack by the viciously anti-German Northcliffe Press and others, including the writers Hilaire Belloc and G. K. Chesterton, who viewed the war, in Spender's words, as a defence of universal Catholicism against wicked Germany and German Jewry. *'My grandmother told a story of how a man, incited by universal Christian love of the Chesterton-Belloc variety, walked into my grandfather's rooms in Chancery Lane and, finding him there, asked my grandfather how, with such a name, he could have the impertinence to allow his son to fight in the British Army. My grandfather simply handed him the telegram he had just received to announce that Alfred Schuster had been killed on the Western Front, and told his visitor he need disturb himself no longer.'* This same grandfather was a little later to be a member of the British delegation in Versailles.

After University, the First World War

After a First Class Honours Degree in 'Greats' (philosophy) at Oxford, training at the Bar and a number of successful legal cases, George Schuster accepted a substantial business appointment with responsibilities in mining and metallurgy covering South Wales, Cornwall, Spain and France, but remained dissatisfied. He turned to politics and became a parliamentary candidate for the Liberal Party, fighting one election in vain before standing on the threshold of success in another at the outbreak of the First World War. The business he belonged to was German; his name was German; political activities were now impossible; and he secured an officer's commission in the Oxford Yeomanry at the age of 33. Like so many on both sides of the divide, he felt *'matched … with His hour'*, but by November of 1914 he had lost his younger brother at Ypres.

George Schuster's war saw little direct fighting but revealed his life-long gift for encountering really notable personalities. One was Winston Churchill, who arrived after political resignation following Gallipoli to join the same regiment. Schuster recalls his relief when he moved: *'If he had stayed on with us he would certainly have tried to win the war with the Oxford Yeomanry, which would have meant the end of us.'* Another was Alan Brooke, later Field

Marshal Lord Alanbrooke, Chief of the Imperial General Staff and Chairman of the Chiefs of Staff Committee in the Second World War. *'His thoughts were concentrated on getting effective action based on an accurate appreciation of available resources.'* Schuster was left with a lasting belief in the qualities of the really first class soldier, a conviction he shared with Kurt Hahn (and with Goethe).

George Schuster's memoirs suggest his unease over his distance from the fighting and danger, and his more significant military experience came after the Armistice, when he was posted to the Headquarters of the British Forces at Murmansk in Northern Russia. An early excitement was meeting Ernest Shackleton there, the Antarctic explorer, who was full of tales of his adventures. The post-Armistice task of the British mission was to support the White Russians in their efforts to combat the Bolsheviks. But in a letter to his wife on 12th April 1919 George Schuster expressed his own view of the sentiments of the local population: *'… although they hate the rule of Lenin and Trotsky they are nevertheless more strongly influenced by their dislike of foreign intervention … the picture that one likes to conjure up of all the patriotic Russians flocking to us and welcoming us as deliverers is unfortunately not a correct one and one cannot say that in general the British are at all popular with any class of Russians …'*; and later: *' … the fact of foreign intervention has all along been a great unifying force on the Bolshevik side'.* He might have been writing from Iraq in our own time. He was also ready to acknowledge that at least some of the Bolsheviks were fighting for an ideal and not for personal aims. *'I should feel so much happier if on our side there were more such spirits.'* He left as one of just three passengers on the last transport out of Murmansk on 9th October 1919.

The next three years were the confirmation of his destiny as a public servant.

The Immediate Post-War Years

Recruited by a London City group of merchant bankers who were keen to revive the economic life of the so-called Succession States (Austria, Hungary and Czechoslovakia), George Schuster was sent out to report on the prospects. His direct insights into some of the consequences of the Versailles Treaty arrangements left him with the overriding impression that, the frontiers having been drawn without adequate consideration of local conditions, trouble in the future was inescapable. He was deeply disturbed by the snobbish aristocratic ideas of the Hungarian educated classes and the virulent anti-Semitism of the Head of the Government Admiral Horthy, whom he met in

circumstances of extreme pomp and ceremony; and by the bitter hostility of the Czechoslovaks towards the large minority of Germans now within their new borders. These impressions were to create problems of conscience for him as Hitler consolidated his power and his policies in the 1930s. Only Masaryk made a favourable personal impact on him as the one far-sighted statesman in the region.

Alongside his banking activities, George Schuster was cultivating close contacts with leading members of the Labour Party with which he felt instinctive sympathy. His work in Central Europe resulted in an invitation to attend meetings of the Finance Committee of the League of Nations. This in turn led to his appointment as Secretary to the Head of the Organiser of International Credits and his departure from private banking. He formed friendships with prominent League of Nations personalities such as Nansen and Philip Noel Baker, the latter a close friend and ally of Kurt Hahn, and became a member of the Economic Research Organisation of the Labour Party. All these developments were a preliminary to his most important post so far. He was invited in 1922 to serve as the Financial Secretary to the Sudan.

The Sudan

George Schuster does not mince words in his memoirs on the Egyptian record in administering the Sudan, an area of one million square miles, between 1820 and 1884 – *'one of the blackest stories of maladministration in human history'.* Now, the country having been re-conquered in 1898 by the British, it was being governed as a condominium jointly by Egypt and Britain. The reason for Schuster's appointment will not surprise those who welcomed his intervention in the affairs of the Atlantic College in the 1960s – the Sudan Government had got into financial difficulties. Schuster for his part rejoiced that the Sudan was under the Foreign and not the Colonial Office. *'The Foreign Office had no machinery for controlling overseas territories and this left me completely free to do my job.'*

This is not the place to give a detailed account. It is enough to record the elements that characterised his beliefs, accomplishments and methods of work.

> *The replacement of the Egyptian officers and units and the setting up of a Sudan Defence Force owing allegiance to the Sudan Government.*
> *Making the case back in London with the Labour Party for continuing British control, the Party being naturally inclined to side with the anti-Imperialist Egyptians. Egyptian agitators were a major problem.*

The young George Schuster

> *Intimate discussions with senior Foreign Office officials and then with the Prime Minister Ramsay MacDonald in his private study in Downing Street.*
> *The insistence that 'finance' is not a mystery but a requirement to set priorities in which every member of the government must play an active part.*
> *Technical and administrative efficiency.*
> *The imperative need to recognise that the interests of the local population were paramount.*

It is worthwhile however to dwell for a moment on the Gezira Project. This was a massive irrigation scheme covering some one million acres, with a later extension of another 800,000. The local inhabitants were assured of ownership of their plots of land, received in addition a rental for them, benefited from the governmentally organised irrigation improvements, and received 40% of the profit from all cotton sold and the entire profits of all other crops. This was indeed an investment in partnership with the people, who were not simple wage-earners but members of a joint venture, nor were its effects only short term. Arthur Gaitskell, writing in 1959, reported that it was the Gezira Scheme that kept native trade solvent during the years 1925–1928 of drought and misfortune by providing employment and putting money into the home market.

'Looking back to 20 years before, when Financial Secretary Schuster had taken such a big risk in pushing up the Scheme's area to break even at a net divisible return of £E12 million per feddan, the last four seasons of the partnership, when seen in summarised form, gave a heartening finale, and the liquid assets of the country had gone up from their highest yet figure of £E12 million in 1945 to over £E30 million in 1950.' It has been claimed that this enterprise served as a model for subsequent agricultural developments in the Third World.

The personal impact made by George Schuster in the Sudan has also been recalled by Sir Geoffrey Archer, Governor General of the Sudan: *'With Sir George Schuster my relations were of the happiest. He was a strikingly handsome man – his sobriquet locally was "Handsome George" – with a brilliant financial brain which gave him a complete grasp of every subject with which he was concerned. He dominated our Council meetings when any question of finance arose, and no one was prepared to question his opinion …'* This judgement is the more noteworthy in that it had fallen to George Schuster to reproach Sir Geoffrey for a serious error of political judgement in his dealings with an emerging political and religious leader, a matter that led shortly afterwards to Sir Geoffrey's not entirely voluntary resignation.

In 1914 George Schuster had been moved by Rupert Brooke's sonnet:

> *'Now, God be thanked who has matched us with His hour,*
> *And caught our youth, and wakened us from sleeping,*
> *With hand made sure, clear eye, and sharpened power,*
> *To turn, as swimmers into cleanness leaping,*
> *Glad from a world grown old and cold and weary …'*

In 1927, saying farewell to the Sudan, he quoted the well-known words of George Santayana: *'The Englishman carries his English weather in his heart wherever he goes, and it becomes a cool spot in the desert, a steady and sane oracle among all the deliriums of mankind. Never since the heroic days of Greece has the world had such a sweet, just, boyish master.'*

As with Rupert Brooke, so too perhaps with George Santayana: subsequent events and the spirit of our age have tainted their words. But they were the context in which George Schuster worked, and it is not surprising to find him quoting with approval Lord Cromer's criteria for the selection of candidates for the Sudan Political Service: its members should be chosen *'by selection (rather than by examination) … from the English Universities … young men endowed with good health, high character and fair abilities'.* It is the order of these criteria which is significant.

There was to be no respite.

Africa and India

In October 1927 he was asked to become the Finance Member of the Viceroy's Council in India. As he records, this once again represented a great strain on his family life with two school-aged sons and another five years abroad. He accepted the new challenge but with a year's delay, for he had two other tasks to complete: to serve as a member of the Hilton Young Commission on proposals for closer union between the East and Central African colonies and, in his capacity as Financial and Economic Advisor to the Colonial Office, to make recommendations on a number of African development projects.

The Hilton Young Commission has rarely if ever been associated with the Versailles Peace Treaty of 1919, but the issues had something in common in the context of nationhood for mixed ethnic groups in the 20th century. Thousands of white settlers had moved above all to Kenya. Their presence was increasingly resented by both the native Africans and the large Indian community, also immigrant. Of the four members of the Commission, Schuster was the only one with personal experience of Africa (another, J. H. Oldham of the International Missionary Council, was to become an intimate and firm ally of Kurt Hahn in the 1930s). The Commission's recommendations had the potential to set the direction for the whole of British policy on the continent.

Given the three different population groups, whose interests were paramount? What form of government would give best expression to them? How was even enlightened trusteeship to be reconciled with democratic self-government in the longer term as the African peoples came into contact with modern methods of transport and trade? Could lingering paternalistic oversight combine forces creatively with tribal custom that was by tradition aristocratic? Was it not clear that the moment the white settler community demanded and secured political control, the Africans would demand the same – and on what grounds should this be refused – and then *'the sudden jump towards politics, political agitation and demagogy'*? The proposed move towards federalism between Uganda, Kenya and Tanganyika could only mean an increase in the white domination of government. George Schuster left Kenya in particular with a consciousness of lost opportunities, the failure to embrace a truly progressive approach to race relations throughout Africa. Moving on to the other African territories Nyasaland and Northern and Southern Rhodesia, he was impressed by the calibre of the white leaders in Southern Rhodesia, but *'how can a member of parliament who owes his seat to the votes of the*

white settlers really be trusted to be not merely – negatively – not unfair to the native, but, positively, keen to push forward his interests? I am very doubtful about this.' His overriding conclusion was the need for all to recognise their common interests which furthermore *'extended beyond the limits of the British Empire to all other European Powers who are responsible for the administration of African territories'.* He mentions, almost as a footnote, Jan Smuts' vision in 1928: *'Africa from the Equator downwards … to take a high place with Canada and Australia among the great dominions of the Empire'.* He contrasts this with the views expressed to him by Smuts in many of their later meetings: *'… (Smuts) could not see a satisfactory final solution for the basic problem of how to establish satisfactory relations between the white population and the vastly greater black population in Southern Africa … he gave me the impression that he felt that the political structure, in the establishment of which he had played the greatest part, would survive for his lifetime and he could not look beyond that …'*

The Hilton Young Commission was unusual in that it was the Chairman who submitted minority reports on all the main issues. This was partly a matter of substance, but it had much to do with a form of Chairmanship that Schuster found an unhelpful burden throughout the Commission's work – a lack of consultation, private and individual drafting, no meeting of minds. It was the antithesis of his own style. He was not alone in his judgement. *'Sir Hilton Young is back from East Africa where he has been Chairman of an East African Commission on Closer Union. He is a man of many parts, with a brain that is far above the ordinary. He has brilliance combined with a well-developed intolerance which finds expression in an icily cutting manner.'* [•]

It was time to leave for India, but some African commitments remained. The Colonial Office was awaiting his recommendations on development schemes in East Africa. In a letter to his wife: *'It is a great thing how it has fallen to my fate to decide important points about building railways all over Africa – the Sudan – Kenya – Uganda – Tanganyika – and now this bridge (the Zambezi bridge in Nyasaland) … and on this question I really have no one whose judgment is worth anything to help me …'* He won the support of the Colonial Secretary, Leo Amery. Amery wrote a strong letter to the Chancellor of the Exchequer, Winston Churchill: *'Nyasaland's special services … are at*

[•] Private letter 28th June 1928 to his Prime Minister from R. G. Casey, then political liaison officer in the Australian High Commission in London, later (1965–1969) Governor General of Australia

a scandalously low ebb … the death rate is disgraceful … in a total revenue of less than £400,000 you charge over £50,000 interest and sinking funds for past loans … in the present circumstances this African Cinderella cannot pay for necessities let alone raise money for bridges and railways …'. There was no immediate response, although the two-mile long bridge that Sir George had argued for was built and opened in January 1935. This episode too was to play a role in George Schuster's judgements in the late 1930s.

With his arrival in India in 1928, George Schuster stepped on to a much larger stage but his principles remained the same. It was to be a testing time, but he felt and acted throughout *'as a responsible member of the Government of India and not in any sense as a Whitehall civil servant'.* He was in effect both Chancellor of the Exchequer and Head of the Currency Authority. As in his previous posts, he was soon to make really meaningful friendships, one of the first with a leading member of the Opposition, Motilal Nehru, father of Jawaharlal. He relieved the long and wearying hours of the Budget debates by making sketches of the Indian personalities facing him (the walls of his home in Nether Worton had many pencil and water colour sketches of his journeys and holiday destinations), but on one occasion he was fortunate to survive when a would-be assassin dropped two substantial bombs from the balcony on to the steps beside his seat. The heavy wooden benches protected him from serious injury.

A critical moment occurred in October 1929 when the Viceroy, Lord Irwin, made his statement, the outcome of much detailed deliberation beforehand with London, announcing the intention of preparing India for self-governing status alongside Canada and Australia as dominions within the British Commonwealth. Irwin was grateful to Schuster for his help with the drafting. Its impact on leading Indian opinion was initially strong and positive. It was Schuster's retrospective judgement that the bitter criticism it generated in Conservative circles back at home was responsible for driving influential personalities such as Motilal Nehru and Gandhi into the campaign of Civil Disobedience – *'one of the great tragedies of my time in India'.* His pragmatic approach was well illustrated by his comments in 1929 to Lord Simon, who had been charged by the British Government with reviewing the 1919 Act that had brought greater Indian participation in government. The Simon Commission had no Indian members, an omission that had directly strengthened nationalist feeling and general antagonism. *'He (Simon) told me he left India with his mind in greater confusion that when he had started. I told him it was no use his thinking of wonderful constitutions;*

what he had got to do was to stage the whole business so that for the next five years the British Government in India could work together with Jinnah and Malaviya – taking them as representing the moderates.' Noteworthy, given later events leading to partition and the creation of the Muslim state of Pakistan, with appalling bloodshed, was his identification of Jinnah as a moderate, a judgement that has received interesting support in a recent, admittedly controversial biography that maintains that, had certain safeguards been put in place for the Muslim community in a federal nation, partition need not have taken place. [●]

In September 1930, barely one year later, George Schuster returned to London to advise the British delegation attending the first Round Table Conference on the future of the sub-continent. Utterly dismayed by the ignorance and amateurishness of the Lord Chancellor, who had been entrusted by the Labour Government with making the preparations, he took it on himself to telephone the Prime Minister Ramsay MacDonald directly. The following day, Sunday, he spent four hours alone with him at his weekend home Chequers and was then asked to attend two meetings in the House of Commons attended also by members of the Cabinet. He was deeply impressed by MacDonald's grasp and by his conduct of the subsequent conference proceedings. Indeed, he remained convinced that, had MacDonald retained his full political authority and intellectual powers, the All-India Federation under discussion might have become a reality. This too would have been a powerful influence against partition.

1931 was a year of political peace but financial turmoil. Without any prior warning, sterling was *'taken off gold'.* The news reached Simla in India at 08.00 a.m. on a Monday morning. It was essential to prevent the opening of the governmental currency offices in Calcutta and Bombay at 09.00 a.m. This required an ordinance from the Viceroy. This was all achieved within the space of a few minutes and for a period of three days. The resulting devaluation of sterling eased the situation of the rupee, but an emergency budget became imperative. He successfully imposed both a surcharge on all existing taxes (becoming thereby *'Sur-Charge Schuster'* in the Indian press), and a 10% cut in all salaries. He records in his memoirs his admiration and gratitude towards all members of the Indian Civil Service in India and his shock and anger that the Secretary of State in London attempted to block this salary cut for British, not Indian members of the Service, on the grounds that the measure required London parliamentary approval.

[●] Jaswant Singh *Jinnah: India-Partition-Independence*

He was backed fully by the Viceroy. The following year no changes in taxation were necessary.

In 1932 he travelled to the Imperial Economic Conference in Ottawa where he was pleased to observe the Indian delegates being regarded as the equals of representatives of the Dominions. *'If the whole series of discussions about the constitutional development of India had been conducted in this kind of atmosphere and spirit the final result might have been very different.'* On the same occasion he was impressed by Neville Chamberlain, another factor which influenced his conduct in the late 1930s. His optimism about the future prospects for independence was undoubtedly influenced by his personal friendships with the Nehru family and with Mahatma Gandhi, an occasional visitor to his home.

One major task remained: the implementation of the recommendation of the Royal Commission on Currency for India of 1926, conducted under the same Hilton Young, for the establishment of a Reserve Bank for India, independent of government. His predecessor had failed to secure the necessary Indian parliamentary approval. This task required an extension of his mandate for another six months and, with it, the preparation of a sixth annual budget. The legislation for the bank was achieved in December 1933. The budget for 1934–1935 provided a remarkable benchmark of his achievements. On his arrival in 1928, the military expenditure had for example been £41.25 million annually. By 1932–1933 this had fallen to £34.25 million, further reduced by £1.5 million as the result of a decision by a tribunal, set up at George Schuster's insistence, which had decided in 1932 that the Indian contribution to this expenditure, rather than being increased as was proposed by London, should be reduced. The London *Times* was complimentary. *'The people of India have every reason to view with satisfaction the stringent reductions which have been effected in Government expenditure which has fallen since 1930 from 93 crores of rupees to 76 crores … (Sir George Schuster's) record during his six years of office is one of which he may justly be proud.'*

Sir George was ready to describe his methods as the *'bows and arrows'* of economic policy, whilst also emphasising that he was in constant consultation throughout his Indian period with Maynard Keynes. They probably owed much of their success to his refusal to allow his colleagues to have their *'heads in the air whereas they ought to have their noses to the ground'*.

Writing later, in 1941, George Schuster felt that the world war now being fought might offer a new atmosphere and new opportunities for tackling India's problems. Carrying over into these reflections his more recent experiences of the commercial and industrial scene in Britain, he was convinced that the system of private enterprise in India would have *'no justification for survival unless those directing it recognise themselves as carrying a prior responsibility for the public interest and the welfare of the workers'.* As in the Sudan, so too in India: it was the rural scene and agriculture that held the key, even to subsequent industrial development, but here again it was the calibre <u>and the health</u> of the rural peoples that mattered most – better nutrition and better education. He suggested (unconscious anticipation of Mao Tse-tung!) that every university graduate should be encouraged to spend two or three years teaching in village communities, living simply and achieving their satisfaction through giving service. This would also help to combat one of India's greatest problems – *'educated unemployment'.* But in noting that the war would assuredly lead to new international alliances, he expressed his hopes for a strengthened Commonwealth in which India would be the bridge between East and West. *'Indian opinion',* he wrote, *'should realise that a deep impression has been made on the liberal-minded friends of India in England by what has appeared to them as a failure to give the Act (of 1935) a fair trial.'* But it must be an equal partnership: *'making full allowance for the comradeship which has existed between many individuals and classes, it remains a true charge that the British in India have failed to build up for the people as a whole any warmly felt idea of common citizenship. British administration, though just, has been cold and frigid. Too little has been done to make India understand the true spirit of the people in England. If there is to be understanding between the two nations, the British must do more than in the past to make themselves understood … a more serious cause of friction lies in the treatment as unwelcome immigrants of Indians who seek to settle in the Dominions or Colonies. The reasons for such treatment lie not so much in racial or colour prejudice as in the fear of a possible threat to economic standards laboriously built up … it may be that distinctions between races have to be recognised; but, if so, the position must be frankly faced; there must be complete reciprocity, and the distinctions must be distinctions as between equals. An impartial statement of the facts covering the United Kingdom, the Dominions and the Colonies, an intensive campaign for public education, the widest possible discussion are long overdue.'*

Industrial Relations in England and the Second World War

On his return to England in 1934 Schuster was 53. He found his appointments to the boards of several banks to be not fully satisfying. After a few months he took on the Chairmanship of Allied Suppliers, the largest retailing group in Britain which had the irresistible bait to secure his interest – financial difficulties. His most effective contribution to pulling the business round was to establish a close and respectful relationship with the leader of the Shop Assistants Union, who remained a life-long friend. But the urge to play a public role remained strong. He was developing two lines of thought to guide his future conduct: *'Britain now had a special role to play in the world, not as an Imperial Power but as a Trustee for the peoples of the territories of the British Empire …'*; and Britain faced the need *'to work out social and economic solutions to provide for the true welfare of her own people'*. How could Britain and other developed countries organize the processes of economic production in such a way as to provide not only a basis for a proper standard of living for the whole country but also an opportunity for the working population to find a satisfying form of activity in salaried or wage-earning employment? This was a challenge not for government alone and required the voluntary, cooperative effort also of the private sector. On journeys to the United States he addressed several large meetings and met President Roosevelt. On his return home he made a practice of calling on Neville Chamberlain to report his impressions. In other meetings such as those at Chatham House he developed distinctions between the *'Welfare States'* and the *'Power States'*.

Events were not on his side. His all-encompassing approach made him a natural candidate for the Liberal Party, of all parties the one with *'the least distinctive party colour'*, in whose interest he contested and won a parliamentary by-election in November 1938 in support of the government in the immediate aftermath of the Munich agreement. It must have weighed with him that his former chief, Lord Irwin, now Lord Halifax, the embodiment of integrity and enlightened patriotism, was the Foreign Secretary. [●] But he lacked the bite, and probably also the ambition, to make a political career. In any event he was compromised. Convinced even at this stage that the country was not yet ready to respond *'to an heroic appeal on Churchill's lines'*, he was a Chamberlain, not a Churchill man. His judgement of Churchill was already formed: Churchill had mistakenly and fatefully returned Britain to the Gold Standard as Chancellor; he had vehemently opposed political advancement in India; he had been

[●] The post-war British Prime Minister Clement Attlee, well known for his economy with words, thought Halifax a 'queer bird … very humorous, all hunting and Holy Communion'. Some common ground here too with George Schuster!

wrong on the Abdication issue; and his vigorous support of the White Russian campaign in 1919 had been a decisive factor in uniting the Russian people behind the Bolshevik Party. When it came to the all-important 1940 vote in the House of Commons, Schuster sided with the government and with Chamberlain. In his later self-defence he explained that he had come under pressure to vote against the government on the grounds that this was the only way of securing an important post in the new administration. This pressure, he felt, compromised his personal integrity. He was to devote himself to vital if unglamorous committee work, above all as a member of the *Parliamentary Committee on National Expenditure* and as Chairman of its *Sub-Committee on Weapons of War*, and alongside Sir Stafford Cripps the Minister of Aircraft Production, but the letter he treasured from this time was a reply from Neville Chamberlain in answer to one of his: *'… you have put into words what happily for me I believe to be true, namely that though peace could not be maintained, the three things that were gained – a united country and Empire, the moral support of a decent part of the world, and time for preparation – constitute a sufficient sum of achievement to satisfy one's mind … I am proud to think that I may have been instrumental in bringing you into political life.'*

The war did not leave him untouched. In 1941 he sent his friend Jawaharlal Nehru a copy of a book he had co-authored: *India and Democracy*. Nehru replied from the district jail in Dehra Dun where he was held by the British authorities: *'… I was happy to meet your wife and sons … I was distressed to learn that one of them is no more. What an infinity of human misery has descended upon this world …'* This is the only reference in Schuster's memoirs to his loss. His brother's death in the First World War passed unmentioned.

In the 1945 election he lost his parliamentary seat. His commitment to public service remained. *'I see it as a matter of the highest public importance that people with practical experience, when they come to the age of relinquishing daily executive responsibilities, should not pass into private retirement but be ready to give their services for public purposes.'*

There followed more committee work, notably concerned with the cotton industry and with the *Henry Tizard Committee on Industrial Production*. His warm sympathies with the aspirations of the Labour leaders with whom he worked – Stafford Cripps, Ernest Bevin, Herbert Morrison, and those of the Trade Unions, contrasted with his growing unhappiness with what he described as *'the negative and uncooperative attitude of the leaders of British industry'*. He treasured the words of one of the most left-wing Labour commentators in *The Tribune* of August 1951, Ian Mikardo:

'… the Chairmanship of that lively youngster George Schuster … his panel initiated a number of important studies … that are must-reading for every industrial manager and every trade union leader in the country …' But he remained above, or outside, the party political conflict: '… all the problems which I have discussed, and all the measures which I have advocated, will be required, whether the industries are owned by the State or by private citizens … it is these things which really matter when one is considering the application of Christian principles to human relations in industry'. [●]

During the war-time Parliament, George Schuster had become a friend of Aneurin Bevan, the Labour founder of the British National Health Service. Bevan now asked him to take on the Chairmanship of the Oxford Regional Health Board. In his 12 years in this role he found himself working with eight successive Ministers of Health. He firmly resisted the membership of his management committees being determined on party lines and cited with pride the social range – 'from the Duchess of Marlborough … to a railway guard at Aylesbury'. A close colleague and friend, Dr. Ludwig Guttmann, the Head of the Paraplegic Unit of Stoke Mandeville Hospital, was to become a founding figure of the Paraplegic Olympic Games. [○] But he deplored the increasing bureaucracy and cost – in 1963, the headquarters in three small houses in Oxford and a staff of 140; in 1975 headquarters an enormous range of buildings and a staff of 362. Looking back years later, he was saddened by the handing over of so many public tasks to civil servants, with the National Health Service as a leading example: 'the work has been de-humanised and made less efficient and more costly … great numbers of public-spirited men and women … have been deprived of the opportunity to give voluntary personal service …'

Other public service for him in these years included advising the government on the economic development of Malta and possible governmental grants (his principal task

---

[●] George Schuster *Christianity and Human Relations in Industry* The Epworth Press 1951

[○] The historian Fritz Stern recalls Ludwig Guttmann in his memoirs *Five Germanys I Have Known*. An outstanding young Jewish surgeon, Guttmann left Germany in March 1939 and was knighted in 1966 for his work on behalf of the British war-wounded and the paraplegic. Stern, whose own father was a doctor, also Jewish, describes the occasion when a senior Nazi officer consulted his father privately (wearing civilian clothes) on whether there was any alternative to having his mother, suffering from a brain tumour, operated on by '*the Jew Guttmann*'. '*Not really!*' The operation went ahead and was successful.

---

to persuade the Maltese Prime Minister Dom Mintoff to be reasonable in his demands and the Colonial Secretary to appreciate Mintoff's creative qualities – this characteristic human bridging operation was to have its echoes in the Atlantic College story a few years ahead), and to advise the Indian Chambers of Commerce on future policy, a task in which he was conscious of failure. A personal memory was of lunches in the home of Jawaharlal Nehru and of meeting '*a very young girl … with no picture of the Indira Gandhi of recent years attempting to exercise a dictatorship which her father would never have contemplated*'. He was also for 22 years a member of the Oxfordshire County Council.

The Atlantic College: Rescue and Survival

Back in 1939 George Schuster had become the Deputy Chairman of his old Public School Charterhouse. By formal statute the Chairman was always the Archbishop of Canterbury, which brought him into close working relationships with Cosmo Lang, William Temple (another close friend and ally of Kurt Hahn), and Geoffrey Fisher. He was influential in establishing the *Governing Bodies Association* for the independent public schools and the *Public Schools Appointments Bureau*. Of perhaps greater significance, and closer to his life-long interests, was the part he played in first saving and then setting on a firm footing *Voluntary Service Overseas* (VSO). The inspirational Alec Dickson, who had cut his educational teeth as the founder Warden of Hahn's first Outward Bound School in Africa, Man o'War Bay in Nigeria, was plausibly said to keep all the files under his kitchen table. As a result, his magnificent initiative in the creation of the now well-known gap year, in his original concept exclusively a year of service in developing countries by young people between school and university, was in danger of foundering. George Schuster was persuaded to become the Honorary Treasurer in 1961. *Christian Aid* was providing £50,000 a year. It was by far not enough. George Schuster almost immediately secured a governmental grant of £17,000. Within two years this had grown to an annual figure of £500,000. The time had come for his journey to Brown's Hotel and to Kurt Hahn.

There is no one of the time who disputes that, without George Schuster, the Atlantic College would have folded in 1964. No United World Colleges: The baby would have died in infancy.

Was the whole enterprise practicable? The Chairman of the first College Founding Committee before the purchase of St. Donat's, Sir Alexander Fleck, was the Chairman of ICI, but his own Appeals Committee initially turned the College down with a letter about the project, *'the implementation of which seemed to them less likely to prove successful than the high ideals which lie behind it envisage'.* And when, in 1964, the College was competing to become a major beneficiary of the British John F. Kennedy Memorial Fund, Sir George put his sharp finger on an issue which may never go away: *'… what Lord Franks will wish to know is whether Atlantic College is a well-founded institution on the permanence of which, as the beneficiary of a scholarship endowment fund, he can absolutely rely. Rhodes could rely on the permanence of Oxford University as the home for his scholars. Our position at the Atlantic College is very different today …'*

But ahead of the funding problems there were some of governance.

Desmond Hoare, aided by his Deputy Robert Blackburn, had begun work on 1st January 1962 out of a small office in London. By September they had assembled staff, students, accommodation and programmes. The pace was brisk and they took their decisions swiftly and with minimal consultation with a Council that was, perhaps understandably, ill-equipped to keep up. This could not last. Kurt Hahn had asked Schuster to join the Council and both the Executive and the Finance Committees. Sir George had immediately recognised the scale of the financial problems. On 28th September he wrote to the Chairman of the Council, Sir Lawrance Darvall: *'The determining factor in my attitude is my faith in Dr. Kurt Hahn. His belief that we must go forward in confidence that we shall raise the necessary money and his undertaking to devote his own energies entirely to this matter during the next three months entirely altered my attitude … My confidence in Dr. Kurt Hahn, however, does not justify me in evading my own responsibilities … I have therefore decided to let you know that I will take up to four of the proposed guarantee units provided that you can get the equivalent of 24 others to do the same thing … I hope therefore that my undertaking may prove a stimulus to others to do something.'* He was to be profoundly disappointed. Already by October, Desmond Hoare had taken the initiative in writing to him: *'I hope you will excuse (my exasperation at the Council meeting). It was only that I felt that we were spending far too much time discussing how best to spend the money we have not got, a matter which I think we have reasonably in hand, and far too little time discussing how to raise some more money, a matter which we have not got adequately in hand.'* In December George Schuster addressed himself directly to Kurt Hahn in a private manuscript letter: *'I am deeply disappointed that my gesture … has produced no more effective response … what is much more serious is my criticism of the way in which the Atlantic College office (in London) performs its function … there is no vision of what is required, no drive, no enthusiasm … no one can be surprised that as a result the whole effort to provide the essential financial support has been totally inadequate … I am so disgusted that in spite of my enthusiasm for the purposes of Atlantic College I would now resign … were it not for my faith in you …'*

The next few months were no better. The increasingly active, self-confident college community in Wales was being critically endangered by the absence of effective governance and of a businesslike approach to the formidable challenge of raising funds to follow up the well-publicised launch in September 1962. For Schuster, this was inadmissible human failure, and he wrote to the President of the Council, Lawrance Darvall, in October 1963: *'I as you know think it important to get all people who allowed their name to appear as members of Council to recognize that by doing so they have accepted a definite responsibility …'*

The crisis broke in early 1964. The annual deficit was running at £50,000. A break-even figure was not in sight until the student numbers reached at least 300. At St. Donat's the Bursar told the Headmaster that funds were insufficient to pay the salaries at the end of the month (news that was mercifully and wisely withheld from the staff). But this was the year too in which George Schuster took charge and in which the foundations were laid for survival. The College bankers, Glynn Mills and Co., had given formal notice that they could no longer maintain the overdraft facilities and asked for a formal meeting which Schuster was invited to join. He took over, swiftly commissioning an auditors' report. This pronounced the death sentence and recommended immediate closure. Kurt Hahn reacted with a characteristic comment: *'my brother (Rudo, a successful businessman) … felt from the first deeply disturbed about Peat Marwick being let loose without proper guidance … he said accountants on their own have a bias towards funerals …'*

Schuster had few doubts about the way ahead. Already on 27th February he had prepared a memorandum, a plan of action. First, the government – a direct financial grant was unlikely, but their moral support was essential if the City were to respond; contacts must be taken up with the Prime Minister, the Minister of Education and the Foreign Secretary. Secondly: the Bank of England – a meeting with the Governor was vital. Thirdly: the City of London – the Merchant and other Banks might respond generously but only if the first two steps were taken successfully. Fourthly: the City Livery Companies. Fifthly: Industry across the country. Sixthly: Renegotiations with the College's bankers on the basis of a carefully revised assessment of the longer-term needs which would aim to place the *'menacingly formidable task'* in a less menacing light.

Schuster entered into personal consultation with the Chairman of Barclays Bank, who responded on 30th April: *'We have … every sympathy with the aims and ideals, but we are as you would expect very depressed at the financial situation and outlook … on the existing basis there seems to be a cash shortage of about £1,000,000, assuming that the break-even figure of 360 boys is reached by 1968, and that rising costs can be met by increasing fees, which will already at £550 be high in comparison even with our more expensive Public Schools.'* George Schuster did not falter. Replying on 4th May, he expressed the view that *'looking to the future, the success of the Atlantic College as a British initiative might have an effect of national importance, and that on the other hand the failure of the Atlantic College would have disastrous effects on a scale which was difficult to calculate …'* He was, he said, hoping to put up a proposal to be considered by the Clearing Banks Committee meeting on 7th May and to make a direct approach also to Lord Cromer, Governor of the Bank of England. From St. Donat's Desmond Hoare had informed the Council that it would be necessary to take a definite decision in the first week of June on whether to cancel the entry for the following September. Schuster wrote nonetheless to the President of the Council, Lawrance Darvall on 21st May: *'My own feeling is strong that we ought not to agree to cancellation …'*

George Schuster had suggested to the bankers Glynn Mills that adequate security was provided for the overdraft by the seven-year covenants from existing donors. Their reaction was that, if the College closed, these covenants would immediately become ineffective. George Schuster then persuaded almost every donor to make an interest-free loan against the security of their own covenants. He secured underwriting from Antonin Besse of £40,000 and contributed £10,000 of his own money in the same way.

Of enormous symbolic as well as material value was the decision of the National Union of General and Municipal Workers at this point to make an interest-free loan of £50,000. Jack, later Baron Cooper of Stockton Heath, the Union's General Secretary, was already a member of the College's Governing Council. From this same year onwards until 1975, the Union also sponsored one student each year, the son or daughter of a Union member, at the College. And in 1970 the Union created an annual scholarship at the College for French students, investing the money derived from the sale of a gold bar which had been entrusted to it in 1940 by a French trade union that could no longer be reliably identified in the post-war period. This Union support, and the subsequent membership of the College Council by Jack Cooper's successor David Basnett and by the General President of the Electrical Trades Union Leslie Cannon, was a remarkable tribute to the respect in which George Schuster was held across British society.

The recruitment of the students for September went ahead.

Atlantic College: Consolidation and Build-Up

It was not all defensive action.

From 1945 onwards, Kurt Hahn had been intensively engaged in securing American funding for the re-education of German youth – indeed, so intensively that the strain led to a major breakdown of his health in late 1952 and his enforced retirement from the Headship of Gordonstoun in 1953. He had made a friend and ally of the American High Commissioner in Germany, John McCloy, and of his influential wife Ellen, who was German by birth. On McCloy's staff was Shepherd Stone who later moved to an important position in the Ford Foundation. All these contacts, carefully nurtured within the United States by Eric Warburg, the brother of Kurt's sister-in-law Lola Hahn-Warburg, opened the door to the Foundation's support. Following an eventful visit to the College in January 1963 by a Foundation representative and much internal debate, the Foundation broke its own rules by making its first ever grant (£50,000) to education below university level outside the US.

Kurt Hahn had been keen that Germany should host the first college. This did not happen, but he had secured the support of the Federal Government in principle as early as 1961 for the Atlantic College. Now, at the end of 1963, Adenauer's Cabinet approved a capital grant of £45,000 which was to be followed up in 1965 with a second grant of £27,000, a total of £72,000.

These two successes had encouraged George Schuster to intensify his efforts in Britain. In January 1964 he wrote to his friend Sir John Masterman, Warden of Worcester College, Oxford, who was already a member of the Atlantic College Council. John Masterman had also known Kurt Hahn since the time he had been interned in Germany in the First World War – Hahn had taken an interest in a number of Englishmen in this situation. Masterman was due to see the Prime Minister shortly. Schuster was well aware that the College was looked on in *'the highest circles'* as *'something rather cranky and controversial'*. Aided by Robert Cecil, the Head of Cultural Relations in the Foreign Office, Schuster engaged in intensive lobbying through Mountbatten with

George Schuster entering 10 Downing Street with the Prince of Wales for a UWC reception

the Foreign Secretary and the Chancellor of the Exchequer, finally gaining an audience at the Foreign Office at which he made the case. Following inter-departmental meetings between the Foreign Office, the British Council, the Treasury and the Department of Education, he received a letter on 17th August which announced, against assurances that the government was not entering into an open-ended commitment, a grant of £50,000. The remarkable feature of this grant was its follow-up the next year of a supplementary sum of £30,000, the first having been approved by a Conservative, the second by a Labour administration. A second supplementary grant raised the total to £100,000.

All this success, so decisive for the College, was satisfying proof of George Schuster's firm faith in *'the capacity for interaction between statesmen and business leaders when national needs demand it'*. He had not hesitated to see the survival of the Atlantic College as a national need. *'Businessmen are also citizens.'*

In this same year the Drapers Livery Company in the City of London made a donation of £35,000 for a new dormitory; the five major clearing banks responded to Schuster's personal appeal by making available £35,000; and the Dulverton Trust now entered the picture in a very significant manner with the first of a series of donations which in the

coming years reached a total of £365,000. The key figure, David Wills, was an Oxfordshire neighbour whose major interest had hitherto been the Anglo-American relationship. Once the Atlantic College was on a firm footing he was to press very strongly, albeit unsuccessfully despite continuing generosity, for a college in Germany.

As in his earlier work, so too at Atlantic College: finance was not allowed to be a mystery. In correspondence with a successor as Chairman of Atlantic College, George Schuster laid out his own simple principles. *'In discussing the whole question of fundraising, I have always taken the line that there are two issues involved: (a) The nature of the practical tasks that have to be done and (b) the allocation of responsibilities for doing them. I think it futile to discuss (a) without reference to (b).'* But, in a rare display of frustration and disagreement, he also felt compelled to add, *'I put to you the simple question whether the kind of fund raising wizard whom you have in mind could have secured a three-hour interview with Artur Rubinstein; could have spent six hours in gaining the friendship and arousing the interest of Maresi; could have been listened to with interest by the leading personalities in IBM, Unilever or Shell; or have made personal contact with the Polish Ambassador ...'* and, in a different letter: *'reliance has been and must be placed on the work of individuals of high standards and ability who believe in the project and are ready to give their help without remuneration'*.

The winning over of the Dulverton Trust offers a useful insight into George Schuster's qualities as a fundraiser. He learned that Lord Dulverton, after a successful visit to the College, had one overriding doubt: the funding task was so great that it might all end in failure. George Schuster asked for a personal interview: *'I was sure that I could dispel this fear.'* After the first donation came in, Dulverton wrote to him: *'We have gained the impression, from various sources, that had it not been for your own personal efforts there would have been a very real danger of complete financial disaster, spelling the end of an experiment which is not only immensely important for itself, but in which the international standing of our own country is involved.'* George Schuster to Desmond Hoare: *'... I have written to Dulverton that his letter made me feel as if I could see daylight coming, or, to take another simile, as though the fog were clearing and hounds could move off and start hunting ...'*

The implications were clear. It was left to Kurt Hahn to draw the conclusion, which he did in a letter to Schuster at the end of the year: *'The quality of your contribution is irreplaceable but the quantity of the work involved could be reduced if you were in command not only through the strength of your personality but through your authoritative position in the hierarchy ...'*

On 16th March 1965 the governance arrangements were radically revised. A College Governing Body was set up under Schuster's Chairmanship, and the Council from this point on devoted itself to overseas development. His financial leadership continued to strengthen the financial position month by month, but his human leadership was now to become no less critical to the College's welfare. The first public test came in 1966.

Desmond Hoare told a visiting journalist, in response to the question as to why he excluded half of humanity from the College, that he would commission a dormitory building for girls the next day if someone would give him £40,000. This made the rounds of the national press, to the fury of many members of the newly constituted Governing Body, and Sir George had to call an emergency meeting. Desmond Hoare for his part was unaccustomed to having a Governing Body at all (it was soon to emerge that he did not have a contract either), and his impatience with the restraints now imposed on his freedom of action were well illustrated in the concluding sentences of the memorandum he was compelled to prepare for this meeting: '… in almost every aspect other than team games, the Atlantic College is at present a half-school … this paper is brief, but there is really nothing more to say on a decision which only in Britain could be regarded as very significant …'

By the time the meeting took place, a cheque had arrived from Sonny and Phebe Maresi, wealthy Italo-Americans who, one account has it, had read the newspapers whilst held up at Geneva Airport. Most Governors wanted it returned, but Sir George was having none of this. One resigned, others were strongly displeased, but Sir George's instincts proved trustworthy. In a letter to Desmond Hoare he wrote: 'My general feeling is that there is no need to force the pace in this matter, but rather that it is much better for us to let it drag on, because the longer it does so the less likely will Maresi be to say that he wants his money back because we cannot build a girls' dormitory block. As a matter of fact, I do not believe that he will ever do that and I also have a hope that if Kurt can inspire his enthusiasm he may allow us to use it for general purposes and possibly even give us more.' He arranged for Kurt Hahn to call personally on Sonny and Phebe Maresi. They were thrilled; the money was kept for other purposes; the Maresis subsequently became the most generous donors the College experienced in its first half-century; and their first letter after receiving full details of the College made clear that their gift had in fact been motivated by their admiration for 'the Hahn schools'. No word on co-education! But this was the spark that led to the entry of the first girls in 1967. Before contemporary readers marvel at this seemingly incomprehensible turn of events, it is worth recalling that the very few co-educational and residential schools that existed in England were, almost without exception, viewed indeed as 'cranky and controversial', and that none of the Colleges of Oxford and Cambridge had yet set out on this path. So once again the College was breaking new ground.

Developments Overseas

All along, the Atlantic College in Wales was George Schuster's first love and his first priority. He knew the value of personal commitment. As Chairman, he made a practice once a year of inviting a group of the teaching staff to dine at his London club, speaking himself before the dinner on a College matter, inviting a member of the staff to speak over coffee. The aim was to exchange opinions and the outcome was staff respect, indeed deep affection, for him and those fellow-Governors who were also present. Robert Birley, the former Headmaster of Charterhouse, Eton and a Governor, described these occasions as unique in his long educational experience.

But with the College Governing Body now under his direct leadership, George Schuster began to worry about the International Council. More international exposure could only help the Atlantic College, and the longer term aim was in any event the setting up of a chain of Colleges. He took the decisive move by addressing himself to Lord Brabourne on 22nd July 1965. 'I feel an urgent need now for really dynamic leadership of the Council. Is there the slightest chance that your father-in-law might consider this as something which would be worthy of his interest?' The father-in-law was Lord Mountbatten. He took it on with irrepressible energy and a flair for attracting public attention of a kind that had not been available before. His contribution during the ten years of his Presidency is another story, but a part of that story brought testing times for Sir George as well.

Desmond Hoare had borne the responsibility for St. Donat's in the early years practically alone. It is not easy to know which were the heavier – the financial worries, or those of ensuring that the College's uniquely adventurous activities on the waters and cliffs of the Bristol Channel did not end in disaster. A letter from him in 1965, at a time when he was being pressed to make an important fundraising visit to the United States, indicates the strain he was under: 'I have given further thought to this idea of my going to the USA in term time and have come down firmly against it. Our good luck up to the present must not blind us to the dangers of our coast rescue training … if it is really essential, which I very much doubt, I can go to the USA during the first

A conversation with Atlantic College students and Graham Loveluck, Head of Chemistry and a member of the founding staff in 1962

week of August or at any time in January ... I cannot leave for a fortnight after the end of term and I simply must have a decent break in July this coming year ... I have not had more than a two-week break since the school opened... I am sorry to disappoint you but it is not worth the risk.'

Thoughts and energies were indeed now turning increasingly to expansion overseas. Most of these thoughts and most of these energies stemmed from Desmond Hoare. In 1969 he stepped down on his own initiative from the Headship, determined to achieve abroad what he had already achieved in Wales. Kurt Hahn, basing himself on the Eton practice of having both a Headmaster and a Provost, had already experimented in Gordonstoun with a Headmaster and a Warden, so he welcomed the proposal that Desmond should now become Provost, resident at St. Donat's, and use his creative energies to give the Atlantic College Project, renamed the United World Colleges by Mountbatten, a truly world profile. Desmond now found himself in a nutcracker, constrained on the one hand by the need for loyalty to a successor on the same campus, on the other by the obligation to work closely with a very

senior figure indeed, the last Viceroy of India and former Chief of the British General Military Staff who, to express the matter very mildly, had a mind of his own. At its best this was a situation of creative tension, but it fell to Sir George to maintain the emphasis on the creativity. Again it was Kurt Hahn who, one year into this new arrangement, best recognised the nature of his extraordinary achievement: *'... you have worked wonders with Desmond, tuning his wayward genius to fruitfulness in a way no other man could have done ...'* But it was a great strain.

George Schuster brought this same almost disarming simplicity and clarity of analysis to the challenge of translating Desmond Hoare's powerful push for UWC engagement in the Third World into policy proposals. It is characteristic that his background paper of April 1973 for the International Council, *UWC Projects in the Developing World*, opened with the following observations:

'... it seems to me important to record that the "driving force" which led to the moving of the Resolution came from ... the living body of the UWC project – namely former students and staff, together with the present students and teaching

staff of the one fully developed United World College at St. Donat's ... I feel that the point is important because it is necessary to recognise that the effective influence of the project in the world will depend on the life-work of the human beings passing through its Colleges ...'

The scope of action was identified with equal simplicity and straightforwardness 'in three broadly different ways'.

1) 'By the provision of places and scholarship support for students from such countries at United World Colleges in the more fully developed countries
2) By the provision of opportunities for former students from United World Colleges to do work of various kinds in developing countries
3) By the establishment in developing countries of educational institutions fulfilling the UWC aims.'

And of the aims hitherto defined and accepted by the International Council – to make education a force uniting nations, and to provide a form of education suited to the needs of the times – 'the question of policy which the International Council must now decide is whether the form of education hitherto adopted must be regarded as fixed for all time and for all areas ... the view put forward in this paper ... is that such a decision would result in imposing too narrow a restriction on the possible development of the whole project'

In underlining the importance of the Western Pacific (this at a time when our College in Singapore was, at best, half-heartedly acknowledged as a member school), he was happy to quote Professor George Thompson: 'this area contains in microcosm the macrocosmic problems of the world in divergence both of cultures and standards of living. It contains in China and Japan two of the oldest cultures in the world. It contains in Australia and New Zealand forms of indigenised Western Culture; and in South East Asia it has nations struggling on the upward economic path.' And on Africa: 'The aim of making education a force for uniting nations would have great significance in Africa even if its effects were confined to "uniting nations of the different African States".' And in a paper in 1978: 'India is the ideal location for a College in the Third World ... this is a long-range project, but a well-qualified representative should be sent on a special mission to India to explore the position.' He wanted this representative to engage his old friend Morarji Desai, the Prime Minister.

In giving expression to these views, George Schuster was once again creating bridges between opposing parties, for Desmond Hoare's own pungently delivered papers on the need for the United World Colleges radically to alter their aims were generating precisely the degree of

sharp controversy that he regarded as essential to creative debate and progress.

A Full, Patriotic Life

There can be no doubt that George Schuster felt a quite special sense of loyalty to Britain, the loyalty born of the special appreciation, understanding and gratitude that can arise from an immigrant family background. He led innumerable UWC committee meetings in London, remaining the one truly authoritative personality apart from Mountbatten at sessions of the new International Council, ever conscious that the survival and success of the Atlantic College itself was the essential premise for the setting up of similar colleges in other countries. But his recognition that the Atlantic College was a British initiative, and reflected on Britain's name, was also allied with the profound nature of his personal relationship with Kurt Hahn. This was reciprocal. In mid-1964, after George Schuster had secured the British Government support, Kurt wrote: 'I do not think you realize that you brought into our negotiation something intangible which made all the difference ... people felt ... if George Schuster believes in this enterprise and devotes practically all his strength and time to securing its survival, we must look at it very carefully. Not one of us could have elicited this response.' Later that year, after Kurt Hahn had telephoned good news from Germany, George replied: 'I feel that we are climbing a new mountain together – you have just negotiated a most difficult traverse and it has brought us to a position from which one can just begin to see a possible route right to the top ...' In 1966, when he was struggling to maintain unity and harmony in the fall-out from the Maresi donation for a girls' dormitory: '...as I have told you many times, I cannot go on bearing the Atlantic College responsibility without your spiritual aid as well as your contribution to our practical tasks ...' Kurt to George in 1967: '... the fact that you write and the way you write makes the donors feel that there is a safe bridge from vision to reality ...' And in 1970, George to Kurt, when Kurt was no longer well: 'I long to hear news from you. I shall need your inspiration and support. If I have done anything to help this great project towards success, you can regard this activity as entirely due to _your_ influence. It has meant a lot of work and some anxiety for me but it has given me an inspiring purpose in my old age and I am immensely grateful to you.'

George Schuster, it is clear, led a full life. He was born into a gifted and prosperous family. He had an exceptional intellect and, whatever the unhappiness of his schooldays, an education of the finest quality which, at every stage, brought him into relationships with others of comparable talent. If he encountered problems and setbacks on the way, he kept them in English gentlemanly fashion to himself, and he was at every stage largely able to choose his own way forward. His ability to manage the financial affairs of others reflected his ability to manage his own with equal success, and his large, attractive manor house in Oxfordshire was partnered by his suite at the Savoy which, at least in his Atlantic College time, was his London base for a few days every week. *Private Work and Public Causes* is a well-chosen title for his memoirs since the distinction between the two was often hard to perceive, above all in his latter years. But the impressions he left behind run on different lines.

This *'lively youngster'* who took on the fortunes of the Atlantic College at their lowest ebb was 83 at the time and he relinquished these responsibilities as he was approaching his 94th birthday. Nor did his interest lessen one whit in his final years. But one missed his regular visits to St. Donat's, driven by his wife Gwen who chauffeured him fearlessly (on one occasion, in the wrong direction on a motorway) in their fine old Bentley – she was by the end so stricken by arthritis in her hands that it was necessary for someone else to switch on the ignition before they swept out of the gates. Why, I wondered, did he always refer to her, and in her presence, as *'My House of Lords'*? Was it because, if she felt one had outstayed one's welcome and George might be getting tired, she would enter the room and announce *'The horse and carriage are at the door'*? Was she the final court of appeal? She drove him every year to Scotland or to Norway, always for salmon fishing, and Sir George once wrote to Kurt Hahn when he was 85 and she was 82: *'I got a good salmon on Monday night and Gwen had a tremendous fight with one which eventually got off after 1¼ hours in pitch darkness …'.*

Stephen Spender recalls visits to Nether Worton in George's last years with the same slightly ironic yet warm appreciation he had shown for his grandmother Hilda. *'He is now 97 … in a reclining chair … very arthritic. His mind was active but imprisoned by his body. He was delighted to see us and asked me, as he has always done whenever I have met him over the past 30 years, "tell me what you think of the state of the world". I did what I have always done … passed the question back to him after I had mumbled a few commonplaces. He told me that it was very depressing …then he said, "here I am, scarcely able to move, my sight gone with the last year, unable to read. I'd hoped to spend the end of my life reading Gibbon and other great masterpieces …"'.* And after a later visit: *'If anything, George seemed better than last time, now that he is 100 … He said that a secretary of Prince*

The Schusters' Christmas card of 1970. 'I got a good salmon on Monday night and Gwen had a tremendous fight with one which eventually got off after 1¼ hours in pitch darkness …'

Charles had been to consult him about Atlantic College. "He agreed with every word I said."'

Stephen had attended the reception at the Athenaeum Club in London at which Sir George's memoirs were presented by the Governors of Atlantic College. *'The strange thing is that none of his cronies ever succeeded in making my uncle sound quite human.'* His final summing up of Uncle George has the freedom and authority of a member of the family: *'My uncle, like the best and most humane men, always made the impression of redeeming and wanting to be redeemed. He was always charitable, imaginative, liberal, liked by people with whom he worked, but of course he could not in middle age escape from having an air of self-importance … "Men improve with the years" … is a dubious generalisation, but it is probably true of certain people who have gone into public life for honourable reasons and then become enlarged beyond the scale of private personal relations – they return, the public importance drops away from them, they shrink back into human beings … they are lonely, they need love; physically they are their own husks. Something like this happened to my uncle. The last thing he said to me was: "you can't realise how much it means that a few people come and talk to me. This is all I have". There were tears in his eyes, but not of weakness or senility.'*

The 90th birthday surprise at St. Donat's: John Brabourne with his back to the camera, George Thompson from Singapore and Elisabeth Sutcliffe

Yes, one recognises, looking back, that Sir George was very dependent on being well thought of by those he was working with – that this, alongside an intensely high respect for the activity of work as such, gave him his drive and motivation. It is undeniable that his financial background and education gave him the security to work across class, nationality and race, but they do not alone create or explain his instinctive sense of identity with his human surroundings. Throughout his life, he gave examples time after time of his ability to manage small teams through intensive consultation, personal generosity, and the conferment of trust and 'nobility' on every aspect of human relations. His expressedly Christian instinct was to think well of others until the contrary evidence was utterly overwhelming, and the sooner working coopera- tion could be transformed into personal friendship, the better! Two days before his 90th birthday, at a dinner in St. Donat's Castle of the UWC International Council, the students, acting entirely on their own initiative, switched off all the lights and entered bearing candles and gifts. The tearful old man who made a wonderful spontaneous response to their greetings must have known what a rare gesture this was for students of a school for a Chairman of Governors, their Chairman of Governors. But then, without him, none of them, or their predecessors or successors, would have been there.

Adventurous marine activities off the Atlantic College foreshore five or six afternoons a week throughout the year

Michael Schweitzer

His Chance of a Life

The impact of conflict on the origins of the United World Colleges is clear. It is hardly a surprise that the strength, the unanimity of conviction shown by our founders, arose from experiences they wished to spare their grandchildren. It is acutely appropriate that the idea was born in the NATO Staff College in Paris, where Kurt Hahn lectured in 1955, invited there by an Italian admiral, and that the Commandant, Air Marshall Sir Lawrance Darvall, should have become his first ally.

The name Atlantic College was also right. It was right because, as Thor Heyerdahl has suggested to us, it is oceans,

Michael Schweitzer: Kurt Hahn amanuensis and Atlantic College Bursar

not lands, which have so often in the past been the link between far flung peoples and cultures. The Atlantic is the true meeting place between Europe and North America. The Atlantic College was born of the Atlantic Alliance, the partnership between Western Europe and North America.

If the Atlantic College project was an achievement of transatlantic cooperation, its birthplace was the conflict in Europe of the 20th century. The complexities are well expressed in Kurt Hahn's own life. A Jew, some of his forefathers from Poland, Kurt Hahn was brought up in Berlin. Studies in Oxford, friendships there and in Scotland and an early admiration for British education, bound him and all his future activities closely with Great Britain. But on the outbreak of war in 1914 he returned, not without difficulties, to Germany. Recruited into the Foreign Office, he demonstrated a passionate loyalty to his country of birth, language and culture. Expulsion from Southern Germany in 1933, following his public criticism of Hitler, flight to Britain, the acquisition of British nationality and entry into the Anglican Church, documented his membership of that multitude of outstanding German Jewish refugees, once unskilfully described as *Hitler's Gift* [•] to Britain and America.

The efforts from the 1970's onwards to 'universalise' our educational message – *the United World Colleges* rather than the *Atlantic College Project* – were necessary, understandable and probably inevitable, and in harmony with the speed of international developments generally. But it can do no harm to recall the birth of the enterprise in the experience of individual lives amid the bloodily confused years in Europe of the First and Second World Wars.

One such life was that of Michael Schweitzer.

[•] *Hitler's Gift: Scientists Who Fled Nazi Germany*, by Jean Medawar and David Pyke. The word *Gift* in German means poison

His Early Family History

In 1830 a poor itinerant Jewish peddler froze to death in the mountains of Upper Silesia. His elder son Isaac then worked as a scribe for the local peasants and as a musician at weddings and other occasions to keep his mother and younger siblings. One of his brothers was thus enabled to attend school and become a physician. Isaac himself went on to learn several languages, become a schoolmaster, marry and have nine children. His life is recorded in an autobiographical novel, the foreword by Thomas Mann, by his nephew Felix Hollaender, the cabaret artist and composer of film music whose best-known score was that written for *Der blaue Engel*. Twenty-five of his direct relatives and descendants were to die in the Holocaust.

Another young Jew, Moses Simon Pappenheim, born a generation earlier in 1780 in Upper Silesia, had moved to Berlin at the age of 20, where he benefited from the government's growing toleration under the influence of Moses Mendelssohn, who was urging the education of Jews to promote their participation in Europe's cultural and intellectual life. Returning to Breslau, he too became a teacher, exploited his knowledge of French in negotiating with the authorities during Napoleon's occupation of the city, was also a successful stockbroker and city councillor, and was remembered for his patriotism and his work on behalf of the poor. It was his daughter Rosalie, *'the beautiful rose of Breslau'*, whom Isaac married around 1840. In turn, their daughter Algunde married Eugen Schweitzer in 1884. They had first met in London where her sister, Alma, was a well-known pianist.

Eugen was a tea and coffee taster and broker in Hamburg and London. After he moved to Berlin, his success in the import/export business led to a large fortune. He established a notable collection of paintings, antiques, first editions and rugs. He became sufficiently knowledgeable to lecture and to publish on the Italian masters. He had a summer home on the Wannsee Lake. He venerated and supported Brahms. He died in 1911. He is buried in the cemetery at the Wannsee, his tombstone engraved with the line from Heine: *'Tod ist die kühle Nacht'*. [●] His wife, now widow Algunde, had played the piano, attended philosophical and theological lectures, served on the Board of a Berlin hospital, but lost her daughter Maria just one year after her husband. In 1912 she sold the family's art treasures. When war broke out she converted five million

[●] *'Death is the cool night'*

gold marks into war bonds that rapidly became worthless. Thus she ended her life in relative poverty. She died in 1930 and is buried with her husband and daughter in the Wannsee cemetery in Berlin.

His Father and Uncles

Algunde and Eugen had three sons, Kurt, Ernst and Carl-Gunther. All three were baptised into the Christian faith in 1892. All three learned only later of their Jewish background. All three fought, and valiantly, in the First World War. Carl-Gunther volunteered at the outset, bringing his own horse to join the Lancers' Guards; he was seriously wounded in the second month and was back in hospital again in 1916. Ernst served as a physician on the Eastern Front. Kurt was an officer in the famed Alexander Guards, serving as adjutant to the colonel. He was the only Jewish and non-aristocratic officer in the regiment. He survived the war including the entire Battle of the Somme with only one slight wound and was awarded the Iron Cross.

All three brothers, despite their war service, were later to experience Nazi prisons from the inside.

Carl-Gunther, who had earlier made speeches on behalf of the conservative German National People's Party and was now a minister in the German Evangelical Church, was imprisoned in 1935 along with fellow churchmen who had protested against the introduction of the Aryan Paragraph into the Protestant Church. He was forced into hiding in 1938 under a false name after the pogrom of that year.

Ernst was arrested in 1938 after the Kristallnacht and sent to the concentration camp of Sachsenhausen, from where he was released after seven weeks, head shaved, physically weakened, coughing badly, never to talk to anyone about his experiences there.

Kurt found himself engaged in legal work on the reparations imposed by the Versailles Treaty, when details such as the royalties paid by the Germans for the use of British Vickers machine guns, and British payments for steel plates from Krupp for the construction of their battleships the Dreadnoughts, encouraged no little cynicism. Later cooperation on patent law with scientists including Heisenberg, Schrödinger and Niels Bohr failed to save him from being sent to Sachsenhausen at the same time as his brother Ernst. Again, like Ernst, he was released after some eight weeks, returning home much weakened and with his head shaven and, again like Ernst, remaining silent for the rest of his life about what he had witnessed there. And he kept until his death the letter he had received on his release in which, *'regretfully'*, he was expelled from his old regiment. (When his son Michael asked on a visit to Sachsenhausen in the 1980s for information about his father, he was shaken to be handed his camp reference card after a delay of less than two minutes, as if he had asked for an old driving licence.)

All three men had married women of non-Jewish background who remained unshakeably faithful to their husbands despite all the Nazi persecution. All three were compelled to emigrate, Carl-Gunther and Kurt to England, where they were much helped by the Church of England under the inspiration of George Bell, the Bishop of Chichester, with whom Kurt Hahn was to cooperate so closely during the Second World War in defence of *'the other Germany'*. Ernst fled to the United States.

After the war ended, Carl-Gunther again became active in the Protestant Church in Germany, completing many publications and receiving the Grosser Bundesverdienstkreuz First Class. Ernst dedicated himself to his psychiatric patients in New York and, a widower, wrote and published a collection of poetry reflecting his great learning, his isolation and loneliness, and his search for the answers to life's problems. Kurt, after British internment on the Isle of Man (again with his brother), and menial jobs as porter in a wine cellar and railway clerk, received restitution and a German pension from 1952 onwards. He turned to philosophy and science, learned Spanish to read the Spanish classics in the original, and wrote an autobiographical novel and an extensive diary relating his reading and his reflections on his past.

Nazi Persecution and the War

Michael was seven years old when, coming home one day from play, he found his father Kurt had been taken away to Sachsenhausen. His sister has described how their father, with his left leg resting on a stool, had been shaking so much that the stool rattled on the stone floor. After the Gestapo had left, the family turned on Michael. Had he said something? *'I can still see his desperate face, full of guilt.'* Their mother Jutta was the daughter of a long-serving, highly respected mayor of Berlin. An influential neighbour helped to secure release from Sachsenhausen, but her contacts were no longer a safeguard for the future. The elder sister and brother left for England, followed five months later by their father. Jutta, awaiting their fifth child, was unable to gain an entry visa into Britain and remained behind in Berlin with the 12-year-old daughter Sabine and with Michael. The baby was born 20 days after the outbreak of war.

After Sachsenhausen, it had been the mother who had travelled briefly to England to look for a home in exile for the family, and who had insisted on the timely departure of two of her children and her husband. Now she held the remaining family in Germany together. Summoned several times to the Gestapo headquarters in the Alexanderplatz, she firmly refused all pressures to divorce her husband.

Five years in war-time Berlin as a *'Mischling'*, a half-Jew! An interview in 1941 for the Hitlerjugend was memorable for the temptation of the black sheath knives carried by the party members, but of course he was not accepted, initial disappointment giving way to later relief. Weeks later, he took and passed the entry examinations for the prized French Lycée, only to learn the following day that he could not be accepted. A sense of rejection set in for the first time.

Michael watched old ladies wearing the Yellow Star, found himself being shouted at in the local swimming pool (*'Geh 'raus, du Judenjunge.' 'I left without a murmur'*), learned some French secretly from another half-Jewish lady, and listened in even greater secrecy to the BBC World Service. As the war neared its end, he learned how to interpret the flight paths of the Allied bomber squadrons that were broadcast in code. One evening, his younger brother walked out on to the terrace and saw a false dawn, a sky turning from pink to red near the horizon. In the morning they chased tiny fragments of ash as they floated down from the sky – the airborne debris from Dresden, 90 miles to the south. This was indeed an education for life without the *'quarantine of the classroom'*.

And then the Russians! The family takes refuge in the cellar. They are joined by neighbours – three couples, several girls and women and eight young children, 23 in all in a windowless storeroom underground. After two days, the Russians storm up the hill. They are all ordered out, then allowed to return to their basement. A soldier is even placed on guard at the door, and they have a peaceful night. The next day, after a period of silence, the fighting breaks out again. The German SS retake the hill. When the Russians finally return, having suffered heavy losses, they are ferocious. Three young men are dragged out; one is shot, the other two are never seen again. There is a knock on the cellar door. A soldier orders the mother and the daughter to come out. *'"Frau komm mit." There is no escape and nowhere to hide. Suddenly, my 13-year-old brother Michael rushes forward, flings his arms around the Russian's neck, kisses him on both cheeks, and pleads with him to spare us and leave us alone. I can still see the astonishment on that soldier's face. Then he smiles, ruffles Michael's hair, turns on his heel and leaves us.'* Michael's recollections: *'I can still smell the smell of his war-stained uniform and see the bright red enamelled Russian star deeply embedded in his furry hat. I can still feel his hand stroking my head. He indicated that we would not be disturbed, and all the women in the house remained unmolested.'*

They stayed in the cellar for several more days until the final fall of Berlin. Then came a strange noise. The house was on fire, engulfed by flame throwers. Alexander, his younger brother, aged five, remembered it all. *'Mother's hand pushed my face away with the words "Don't look there!" And then I really looked at the headless soldier still sitting at the tripod that supported his machine gun …'* And later Michael recalls: *'nothing was frightening at all, just interesting … I climbed on to a burnt-out tank with my brother and looked inside at what seemed like mummified black bodies … I crouched in the road and felt with my fingers the beautiful fins of mortar bombs sticking out of the asphalt … I found big lumps of molten glass that had been the windows …'*

Escaping from the cellar, they had walked for several hours though ruins and bodies, taken refuge in a hospital in Dahlem, returned home to devastation and more bodies, then found accommodation in a flat formerly owned by the Nazi leader Martin Bormann. Michael, a 13-year-old, was to earn the family's living by looting food from warehouses, carrying sacks of potatoes for the local greengrocer and, for his own amusement, *'quite happily'* stealing boats, outboard engines and petrol from the American officers' mess, surviving the pot shots of Russians from across the water at Gatow, playing with abandoned ammunition, on one occasion dismantling an anti-tank missile and disconnecting the warhead. He entered secondary school for the first time at the age of 14.

England after the War

After another year he, his mother, younger brother and sister travelled to England to rejoin their father, sister and brother in London. His father, now a poorly-paid railway clerk, had one small room. They all stayed with Carl Gunther in the country. No local school was interested in an uneducated boy with German nationality and no English. *'Who was I? Where was I? No home. No roots.'* Again, his mother, earning a precarious living by taking a catering job for some 40 people in a home, found the solution. She wrote to Kurt Hahn whom she had known in Berlin in her youth. After an interview he rapidly agreed to find the money and enrolled Michael in his Gordonstoun School in Scotland.

Michael with his brothers Reicke and Alex

Life – Professional and Personal

After three and a half years, Michael passed examinations that, following two years of military service back in Germany, took him into Oxford. The next task was to find employment. He answered an advertisement and found himself in Brown's Hotel in London, facing the man who had taken him into his school ten years earlier. Papers all over the floor, the filing cabinets a series of laundry boxes! *'Such' mal weiter' ('Go on looking')*, without saying what for! With these words, Hahn disappeared. Unfazed, Michael took the job thus cursorily offered him by implication, sorted the papers and, when Hahn returned an hour later, laid his hands unhesitatingly on the first memorandum ever written on Atlantic College. His life's work had begun. Michael claims that *'Such' mal weiter'* became in that moment his life's creed. It is an enviable one.

In his six years as Kurt Hahn's private secretary, Michael developed the dedication to the man, his principles and causes, with the mixture of idealism, affection, loyalty, common sense, ability to criticise with tact and sensitivity, irritability when confronted by rhetoric or affectation, which came to be so valued during his 32 years at Atlantic College. There, he was in succession Secretary of the College Appeal Fund, Deputy Bursar, and then Bursar. His ability to extract meaning from arcane figures, draw the necessary conclusions, then wrap them up again in mystery so that no one else could understand them, must have seen the College budget through many a crisis.

In 1960, on Christmas Eve, Michael had met Deirdre Bendit on the flight from Zurich to London and chatted her up. She too had a German-Jewish grandfather. She had worked as an occupational therapist in a hospital in Lower Saxony for the treatment and rehabilitation of soldiers and civilians who had been wounded in the war, many of them amputees and most of them either survivors of the Eastern Front or the victims of air raids. All were impressed that an English girl had come to work and to help in Germany. The following year Deirdre and Michael met again. Wisely ignoring his own motto in life, he looked no further and they married shortly after.

Michael with Deirdre, who painted the portrait of Desmond Hoare

The Cousins

Of the three sons and 12 grandchildren of Eugen and Algunde Schweitzer, all but two survived the war and Nazism. One of these, Friedel, died in England at the age of 23 from epilepsy after a tortured period of schizophrenia provoked by earlier experiences of Nazism. The other, Eike, motivated by comradeship, love of horses, courage, and the wish for personal and active involvement, had enlisted in 1939 and earned the Iron Cross in 1940. Discharged because he was of mixed blood, a *Mischling*, he was able to re-enlist in 1942. Briefly on leave in Berlin in January 1945, he ignored the opportunity of disappearing and returned to the Eastern Front, convinced that his duty lay in rejoining his fellow officers and defending his country against the Russians. Wounded in the head, chest and stomach on 5th February, he could not be brought back to safety. His final time and place of death are unknown, but he is commemorated on the family grave in Wannsee. He was also remembered warmly by a school friend, Richard von Weizsäcker, later President of the German Federal Republic.

Other cousins too had demonstrated their moral values and courage.

Wolfgang had attended a protest in 1923 against the French and Belgian occupation of the western industrial zone in Germany; with his classmates he had joined *The Society for the Support of Germans Living Abroad* (i.e. in territories Germany had lost in 1919 after the Treaty of Versailles); active in church matters, he played the harmonica at religious services in the drawing room of his father's vicarage during his father's suspension by the Nazis from his religious functions. Thus both father and son were members in the earliest stages of the Confessing Church (*die Bekennende Kirche*, of which Dietrich Bonhoeffer was to become the foremost symbol and leader). When like his cousin Eike he was dismissed from the army in 1940 as a *Mischling*, the officers of his unit at first did not want to let him go, but on his comment that he did not see why he should attack the country that had taken in his family, they rapidly concluded that their government knew best. Entrusted by the church with pastoral work in the Swabian Alps, he was betrayed in 1944 to the Nazis and went into hiding, to escape in September 1944 by cycling across the front lines westwards towards the Americans. A few days after 8th May, the day of the German capitulation, he heard once again the voice of his father in a German language religious broadcast from the BBC.

Gabriele, 'the typical German girl with blond, curly hair' and unaware until the age of 17 of her Jewish antecedents, developed political interests tending towards socialism and communism and was therefore a natural opponent of Hitler, irrespective of her racial 'taint'. Her efforts and those of her comrades to 'stop the wheels of history', with leaflets and small, amateurish acts of sabotage, led to the imprisonment, torture, double suicide attempt and escape to England of the group leader. Another young member of their political group, anxious to prove his Jewish courage, set off a bomb on the assembly field of the National Socialist Party in Nurnberg. He was arrested on Christmas Day 1936, tried before the People's Tribunal and executed in Berlin. Some months later, Gabriele too was arrested, faced weeks of interrogation, and was then consigned to the concentration camp of Lichtenburg. Her brave non-Jewish mother did not hesitate to visit her. Released in 1938, she found employment at Birklehof, the boarding school in southern Germany that Kurt Hahn had founded as an outpost of Salem. Her father and sister Marianne had emigrated already; her mother and brother Christoph were to follow in 1941. Once again she was interrogated repeatedly in the Prinz Albrechtstrasse headquarters of the Gestapo – she had taken part in the distribution of Bishop von Galen of Munster's letters protesting against the killing of the mentally ill. The end of the war found her safe with her two children. She had survived, 'unable to develop any patriotic sentiments', yet equally unable to live without the German language or the culture that surrounded her.

Marianne, like her brothers and sister, was prepared for Christian confirmation, entering a class taught by Martin Niemöller, the First World War U-Boat captain and fervent anti-Nazi pastor. She confessed openly that her instinctive dislike of the Nazis was based in part on snobbishness – 'the educated classes looked down on the common people who followed Hitler'. A member of the Freischar, one of the youth organisations that tried to maintain its independence, she was betrayed by her best friend in school whose reconnaissance visit to her home had led to a Gestapo search. Mother and sister were taken away, the mother held in isolation, the daughter released after weeks. Ignorant of her friend's role, which was revealed to her only after the war, she asked her father to warn her friend that she figured prominently in the diaries that were now in the hands of the secret police. In 1939, urged by friends, she left for London and was in mid-Atlantic on her way to the United States when Hitler invaded Poland and Britain, with France, declared war on Germany.

His sister Sabine remembers her grandmother coming over for Christmas Day in 1938, two weeks after her son-in-law had been released from Sachsenhausen, and saying 'I have just listened to a wonderful speech by Goebbels. I do *think Kurt (her son-in-law) should adopt a more positive attitude to Hitler. My father leaves the room; my mother picks up my new descant recorder and hurls it at her feet. "How dare you, how dare you, get out of my house and don't ever come back again"!'*

'It is school sports day … My vest is plain and I am spoiling the order … My friend Ute quickly finds a spare vest with the swastika. I am wearing it, happy to be like everyone one else. My mother in the audience is horrified.'

'After Christmas (1944), cousin Eike comes to see us, radiating confidence in his smart officer's uniform. He shows us his jauntily curved peak cap. He is about to return to the Russian Front …'

After all this, the family reunions after the war must have echoed the Austrian poet Hofmannsthal:

'Ist ein Traum, kann nicht wirklich sein,
daß wir beieinander sein'. [●]

In all three families, it had been the courage of the non-Jewish mothers that had secured their survival because it was they who had recognised and accepted the need to emigrate, to flee from their fellow Germans. It was the Jewish husbands who had clung to illusions of safety, founded on notions of patriotic identity – was it not they who had risked their lives for Germany from 1914 to 1918? *'Was die überwiegende Mehrheit der Juden jahrelang davon abhielt auszuwandern, lässt sich kurz sagen: Es war nichts anderes als der Glaube an Deutschland'* [○].

In 1937, Carl-Gunther had narrowly escaped the notorious pogrom. His son had urged emigration on him whilst there was still time. He had replied: *'I do not have a calling to another country.'* And the children? Maria felt herself to be Prussian as well as Christian. *'After all, my grandfather had*

been mayor of Berlin … and many people still remembered him.' Gabriele was unable to live without the German language or the culture that surrounded her. *'Your language is your country.'* [●]

The Schweitzers and their forebears, with their roots in Central Europe, had once moved easily across borders. *'Our people wandered before they were driven.'* [○] The war years had scattered most of them from Germany to Britain, the United States, Cuba and Spain.

Michael's Life – Symbol and Commitment

In Britain Michael, first as Kurt Hahn's private secretary, then briefly at Salem, finally at the Atlantic College, became intimately associated with the achievements of the great Anglo-German, Jewish-born Anglican educator. In his brief six years as Hahn's secretary, there were founded the Duke of Edinburgh's Award Scheme, the Oxford and Cambridge Trevelyan Scholarships, the Medical Commission on Accident Prevention and the Atlantic College, all alongside steady expansion of existing enterprises, notably the Outward Bound movement across the world. Hahn was in his seventies, yet this was perhaps his most creative, most productive period. Desmond Hoare wrote: *'No tribute to Kurt's wealth of activity in his post-Gordonstoun years would be complete without a mention of his secretary, Michael Schweitzer, whose steady care permitted the great mind to work without too many worldly worries.'*

The founders of the Atlantic College Project and many that came thereafter drew their idealism and their determination from what they had faced in one and, in some cases, two world wars. Michael Schweitzer understood them perfectly.

[●] 'It is a dream, it cannot be true, that we are all together'

[○] 'What held the overwhelming majority of the Jews back from emigrating can be stated very briefly: It was nothing other than their belief in Germany.' Marcel Reich-Ranicki: *Mein Leben*

[●] The French writer Leautaud
[○] Mordecai in George Eliot's *Daniel Deronda*

The Dutch JF rigid-inflatable The Jan van Engelenburg, directly derived from the Atlantic College rigid-inflatable boats

Irena Veisaitė

'Complicity is not sudden, although it occurs in an instant. To be proved true, violence need occur only once. But good is proved by repetition.' [•]

Some years ago, in 2004, I was a guest at a reunion of my wife Elisabeth's classmates in Tübingen, in southern Germany. Outside the mainstream of conversation, I began to question my neighbour at table, the wife of a classmate. It turned out that she was a refugee from Silesia. As a young girl she had fled first the Russians and then the Poles in 1944 and 1945. She was on the point of publishing her memoirs. I was already familiar with such memoirs. I also remembered Kurt Hahn's description of his visit to Berlin in 1945: *'I was driving … through scenes of misery that will haunt me all my life … starving refugees had recently arrived, many of them lying helpless on the pavement. My driver was a friendly young American; he listened to jazz on the wireless all the time. The poor man had a dispersed soul which he could not assemble before the majesty of death'.*

Her book arrived a few weeks later. I wrote to her that the events she had described were *'unbelievable'.* [o] I was taken aback when, at our next meeting, she reproached me for suggesting that she had written fiction. A justified rebuke, and not only for loose use of language; but the brutality of the events on the continent of Europe between 1939 and 1945 lies to this day outside my ability to comprehend and to absorb!

The Spanish philosopher George Santayana provided us Englishmen long ago with our comforting alibi: *'Never since the heroic days of Greece has the world had such a sweet, just, boyish master.'* When George Schuster brought these words to the attention of Kurt Hahn, Hahn was thrilled – *'it is a wonderful definition of the virtues which were characteristic of the best of the old Empire builders'.*

[•] Anne Michaels: *Fugitive Pieces* Bloomsbury 1998 page 162

[o] Katharina Elliger: *Und tief in der Seele das Ferne* Rowohlt Taschenbuch Verlag 2004

'Irena … showed us forbidden books in her apartment which were hidden behind others in the front row … she was for us a new kind of intellectual. She maintained her integrity even when questioned about Solzhenitsyn, and we students adored her'

Naïvety and simplicity of purpose are great strengths, especially in an idealistic endeavour. Keynes called it that *'exuberant inexperience which is necessary, it seems, for success'.* These qualities were there in abundance when the Atlantic College was launched. What was our purpose? Hahn writing in 1961: *'Today the discords in the free world are a menace to peace. They encourage the would-be aggressor. I have often been asked: Why call these colleges Atlantic Colleges? Could you not have found a name such as would not reflect existing international dissensions (of the Cold War)? My answer is: I am all for loving your enemy, but I recommend as a preliminary exercise not hating your friends.'* And a few days later: *'… This (Britain's) country's mission (is) to strengthen the faith of Western nations in the common cause of freedom …'* He was intensely attracted by the Churchill quote (from 1938) which he also inserted into the early Atlantic College papers: *'Ought we not to produce in defence of Right, champions as resolute and missionaries as eager … as are at the disposal of the leaders of totalitarian states …?'*

So we set out in 1962 as missionaries of the free world, our purpose clear-cut, our confidence strong. It is easy now to mock the rhetoric. Yes, we were to be both a fortress and a bridge – a fortress for the spiritual defence of freedom, a bridge to a better Russia. It was to be only a matter of time before the United World Colleges became engaged with the satellite states of the eastern bloc. The debt we owe in this regard to personalities such as Paul Czartoryski from Poland and Irena Veisaitė from Lithuania is immeasurable and all the greater for having been for so long little known within the UWC movement.

George Soros was intensively engaged in the late 1980s in setting up his Open Society Foundations in the emerging post-communist world. At the beginning of 1990 he sent a representative to Lithuania to find leaders. This representative set out with a long list. It included Irena's name. Irena was in pain with a bad back and did not want to see him. He insisted, and ended up spending three hours at her home. Two days later he invited her to Dubrovnik to meet Soros. She travelled there with a university colleague who spoke only Lithuanian, Russian and Polish, so Irena was the main speaker. She told Soros he should have set up his Foundation the day before yesterday. *'You can overthrow a government in one night, but if you do not change mentalities, you will not succeed. It must be an educational foundation.'* Soros was worried that Lithuanian policies and impatient pressures for independence were endangering Gorbachev perestroika. He refused the use of his name but gave them US $100,000 for a 'Dubrovnik Committee' to see what they could achieve.

The Foundation *Open Society Fund-Lithuania* was registered in 1990. Irena was the Vice-Chair of the Board from 1990 until 1993 and the Chair from 1993 until 2000. By 1998, the annual budget was more than $5 million, and some $25 million had been distributed in the first eight years. Over 50 programmes were being run by a staff of 70. More than 500 books had been published; over 1,000 participants were being sponsored for conferences, seminars and study trips abroad; access to the internet had been set up for almost 700 organisations; a performing arts programme was developing modern theatre, dance, cinema and music; the education programme was sponsoring the *Step by Step* movement for teachers, the Egmont Kindergarten and many High School teaching programmes, field trips, the integration of children from ethnic communities with a particular emphasis on Romany children, child-centred classrooms, and the democratisation of pre-school education; and curriculum development was being carried out

through the *Transformation for Education* programme. In addition there were the Health Education, the Library, and the Social Care Programmes for street children and for the mentally and physically handicapped; the Lithuanian Journalism Centre was established; new law clinics promoted the legal education of citizens; amendments were drafted and put forward with the support of the United Nations Development Programme to the laws on charity and relief; and there was too the part-sponsorship of students to the United World Colleges and the funding and running of ten UWC Short Courses in Lithuania. All these and other projects and programmes were developed under Irena's leadership. George Soros was once asked what he remembers when thinking about Lithuania. His answer: *'I see in front of me Irena's face.'*

So who is Irena Veisaitė?

'I was born of a Jewish family. My grandparents from my mother's side were observing Jews, my grandfather a milkman. They had ten children, of whom five died in infancy. They and their other five children perished in the Holocaust. My own parents left the provincial world of their parents but retained great respect for them. My father and mother were both educated in Germany. Although they were non-observing Jews, my mother and I always went to my grandparents' home on Friday evenings. I attended a Jewish school, also somewhat left-wing, where I was a good pupil, with excellent teachers. I learned Yiddish. In 1938 my parents divorced. My father left for Belgium and, after the war, for the US. He was a great influence on me – I still appreciate his rather severe methods of education. He encouraged me to be responsible and independent. I did not see him again until 1968. I consider that I was born into a very stable world of 19th century values.

My father had been left-wing and sympathised with the Soviet Union – he was an idealist and believed in Russian communism, although he never lived in Russia. His father had been a rich man whose other sons all became revolutionaries before the First World War. One, the head of a big publishing house, a party member, was arrested by Stalin in 1937 and shot in the Gulag in 1942. Another, a professor of coloured metal who had even known Lenin's wife, refused to join the Party after witnessing the civil war in the Crimea in 1919–1922. He survived arrest by the Bolsheviks as a German spy in 1930 but remained silent on all these matters until Khrushchev spoke at the 20th Party Congress in 1956.

In 1938 I was on holiday with my father and we visited Berlin briefly together. We saw the white and yellow benches in the Kurfurstendamm. My father told me not to worry – "they are not meant for you, you are not a German citizen, but you should remember them as an act of discrimination". The years 1938 and 1939 were ones of growing fear. We heard of the Kristallnacht. Everyone was talking about the approach of a world war. In the autumn of 1939 Polish refugees appeared in Kaunas. I had nightmares that I was in a camp; Hitler was also there; I was summoned to his tent and made to sit on his knee. On 1st September 1939 my mother was in Stockholm. I was sent to join her, flying via Helsinki. I went through customs but the plane from Warsaw never arrived. It was the first day of the Second World War. My mother returned to Kaunas because of me. She was ill when the war with the Soviet Union started. She had undergone rather severe surgery which had however been successful. The operation was on 16th June 1941. The Germans invaded on 22nd June. On 24th June they arrived in Kaunas. On 23rd June the Lithuanian Activist Front (LAF) rose up because they were hoping to ally themselves with the Germans in order to secure their national independence from the Russians. On 26th June one of the so-called LAF'ists came to arrest my mother in the hospital, mainly because she was Jewish, and in those times Jew and Communist were used as synonyms. I was sent home to fetch some spare clothes for my mother. On Friday, 27th June I had my last conversation with her. I remember to this day the three guiding principles she gave me for my life:

Be independent and never a burden on others.

Live with the truth. Lies have short legs.

Never take revenge.

My mother also told me where to seek help. I went to a family friend whom my mother had saved from deportation to the Soviet Union. He turned me away. Another family friend, an army colonel, told me to bring valuable things from the family home for use as bribery. Once, when I visited him bringing some of them, he tried to abuse me sexually. I ran away a long distance to my grandparents. My mother was already in prison. When I tried to bring her food for the second time, it was the middle of July. I was told she was no longer there. I learned much later that she had been interrogated by the Gestapo who had not wanted to believe that she was a Jew. She spoke German very well "I am a Jew", she told them. She made no request for mercy. She was heard singing in the prison – had she lost her mind? I think she was killed in July. She was 35. I can never come to terms with those events. I was 13'.

On 15th July Irena was ordered into the ghetto. On 15th August the ghetto was closed. Irena was looked after by her aunt. Her good looks and fluent Lithuanian enabled her to enter non-Jewish shops – after removing her star. But she felt terrible. *'One by one, when you met people you knew, they averted their eyes. I tried to understand what was happening. Are they ashamed that they treat you as if you did not exist, or just as a dirty Jew. It was very painful. Everybody seemed to have become an enemy. You were frightened of your own shadow. The Nazi propaganda was taken over by the local nationalists. "All Jews are communists." You could kill a Jew like a fly. To be in the ghetto was in many ways some kind of relief.'* But immediately after the closing of the ghetto the so-called Aktions started. The main purpose was to take over Jewish property and to select Jewish people to be killed at the Ninth Fort. *'I remember the so-called big "Aktion" on 28th October 1941 when almost 10,000 people were taken to the Ninth Fort. The whole ghetto population was made to stand on the Demokratu square from the very early morning. I was there with my grandparents. It was in the late afternoon, and getting dark. The guards were Lithuanian partisans working with the Nazis. We were standing in columns, as far as I remember, four people in a line, waiting for the selection. I had dressed up as an adult. When we finally arrived in front of the Nazis who were carrying out the selection I managed almost to hypnotize the Nazi officer Rauca. He suddenly said "This girl has beautiful eyes" and he sent me to the "good" side. He probably didn't notice my grandparents and I ran with them over to the so-called "good" side. This time I was able to save them from the fate of most elderly people.'*

Irena was registered for work and sent out to do night shifts on a nearby aerodrome, digging pits. The reward was a slightly more generous ration of bread. After six weeks she collapsed and was nursed by her aunt and grandparents. On recovering she got another job, making toys from the clothes of fellow Jews who had been killed – the dolls were sent to the families of German soldiers. Many people in the ghetto were ill and severely deprived. Her grandmother died. She witnessed the torching of the hospital in the small ghetto, which was burned down with all the doctors, nurses and patients imprisoned inside behind nailed-up windows and doors. The spirit in the ghetto was marked by the constant fear of hunger and death, although some escaped hunger – the members of the ghetto establishment exploited by the Nazis and the police brigade. There were also the speculators, a minority of Jews who worked for the Gestapo and who were allowed out every day into the town. But there was also the determination to survive, to outlive Hitler, and to tell the world what had happened. It was vital to bear witness; the world must be told; it must never happen again. It was also the time of the growth in her of a fierce hunger for learning. There was an illegal school in the ghetto. Irena was taught the ballads of Schiller and *'learned from them high standards of behaviour'*. She had her first romance – *'we are still friends'*. At this point in her filmed account for the

'The following day 60 Jews, among them Irena's favourite uncle, were herded into a garage for forced labour. Many were killed in a public square with crowbars and spades, the others taken away and shot ... 2,000 Jews were killed in the same week in Kaunas alone.'

Holocaust Museum in Washington, Irena pauses and hesitates: 'Now, one can have no more illusions – human nature will never change – look at what happened in Yugoslavia.'

Lithuanian friends came from Belgium and traced Irena in the ghetto. All of them knew in 1943 that the Jews were destined to die, that they must try and save themselves one by one. The headmaster of the Marijampole gymnasium gave Irena his own daughter's documents. It was decided that she should leave the ghetto after the Aktion of 26th November, when 3,000 Jews were deported to extermination camps in Estonia. She left the ghetto at six o'clock in the evening with the work brigade. One of the Jewish police had been informed and did not count her. Her yellow star was pinned, not sewn, on her back, and removed once outside the ghetto by a friend. 'The most terrible thing was to force oneself to step out from the column and to walk slowly on the pavement. This was a shooting offence for a Jew ... There was no one on the bridge waiting for me as had been arranged – I was two hours late. So I went to the house, uncertain of the number, and rang the bell. The caretaker came to the door. I was terrified, because most of

the caretakers were serving the secret police. The next day in the early morning I was taken to Vilnius, to the sister of my rescuer. The poor woman I was taken to was so worried that she could not eat or sleep for three days. Then I was moved to the brother-in-law of my rescuer and stayed with him as a relative from the countryside. He was a surgeon. I met many artists in his home. I was found a job washing and looking after small children in an orphanage'. One day the orphanage was surrounded by the Gestapo. 'I was sure they had come for me. I decided not to run. Three Gestapo men came into the room. I remember seeing only their boots. They thought the director was hiding Jewish children, which was actually true. My not running away saved me, and I worked in the orphanage until the end of the Nazi occupation.' Her fluency in Lithuanian, in pre-war times unusual for a Jew, helped to save her.

One day the Gestapo also searched the house where Irena was living. She was not found because she used to sleep in the storage area, but she had to leave the flat immediately. Within 24 hours she had a new home. Stefanija Ladigiene had six children. Irena was brought into the family. *'Stefanija knew about the suffering of the Jews in Lithuania and wanted to help.'* Her husband had been a colonel and later a general in the Lithuanian army, fighting for the independence of Lithuania in 1919 and 1920, and had become well-known for helping to throw the Bolsheviks out of the country. But he later quarrelled with the country's leader, President Antanas Smetona, arguing that the army should be de-politicised. He was dismissed. In 1940, when the Soviet Union occupied Lithuania, the Lithuanian President offered no resistance and ran away to the West, whilst General Ladiga stayed in the country, was arrested, and later executed in the Gulag in 1942. His widow Stefanija Ladigiene also remained in the country even when the Soviet Army re-occupied Lithuania in 1944–1945. She was a Christian Democrat and had served in the Lithuanian Parliament and in leading women's organisations. From a religious family, she had attended school in Saint Petersburg. Her father, a peripatetic bookseller, had brought books secretly into Lithuania from Prussia in the period 1864 to 1904 when the Latin alphabet was forbidden.

'I remember my uncontrollable crying when she kissed me goodnight after I arrived. How could she kiss a Jewish girl? I had thought that there was something wrong with us. She became my second mother. We talked until four in the morning.'

Later, in 1946, Stefanija was arrested. Irena made desperate efforts to see her and to help her. She went to the prison at five every morning to bring her food. Hundreds stood in line. Stefanija was finally sentenced to ten years in prison and five further years of banishment from Lithuania. *'Those were the Troika courts which announced their verdicts behind closed doors. I and two of my adopted sisters were standing outside the court building almost the whole day. I managed to send our mother a small note with the help of a guard, and I received from her a short note with a peace of her plait which I have kept ever since. The moment she was driven off in the black car, I ran screaming down the street after her. This was Soviet power and cruelty. She was sent to the gulags. Only in Siberia did she learn of her husband's execution in 1942. After Stalin's death she was released and returned. She never complained, and always talked about the wonderful people she met in the gulags.'*

Studies in Moscow and Return to Lithuania

After the war, Irena wanted to study. She finished school and attended the University of Vilnius. The KGB ran a file on her because she had a bourgeois father who lived abroad

and because she was living with *'enemies of the people'*, the Ladigiene family. In 1948 she was detained and placed under pressure by the KGB to become an informer. She felt a strange strength and was not intimidated. She was advised by friends that it would be better for her to leave Lithuania, so she went to Moscow, where many relatives from her father's side were living, to study, at first part time, then full time with a grant. Now free of KGB pressure, she excelled as a student and won a Stalin Award. Then, again compelled to reveal that her father lived abroad, she was stripped of both the award and the grant. She had married a Russian fellow Jew in Moscow. She was determined to return to Lithuania but needed an invitation to be able to do so. A senior party official at home refused to help, stating that he was unable to compromise his loyalties to the State. Stalin died. Snieckus, the communist leader of Lithuania, came to Moscow for the funeral. He too had known her family. She was persuaded to approach him. Had it been a problem for her to seek him out? It had not been easy – a friend had pressed her. Snieckus received her. He telephoned Vilnius and she was given the necessary authorisation after 40 minutes. She got a teaching position at the Pedagogical Institute in Vilnius and immersed herself in teaching, lecturing and theatre criticism. It was here that she established herself as a moral authority in Lithuania, in the words of one of her former students as *'one of the leading five women in Lithuania's history'.*

Who was this person who, it was known, also had a daughter married to a Russian dissident in London? The students were proud of their professor who had contacts with dissidents in Russia, wore the Lithuanian freedom jacket, and had attended performances of the British theatre director Peter Brook. She was cosmopolitan, not nationalistic. She took her students on theatre visits to Riga, Moscow, Minsk and other places. She was one of the best known theatre critics in the country. *'We all noted her speaking talent and recognised her voice in her theatre articles. Through literature we talked about ourselves. The old classics became contemporary. Love and honour returned to our lives.'* Where did her power come from? *'From the ghetto, from the imminence of death, from her gratitude to those who had saved her! All this had taught her to love life. It was known that the KGB had been after her, that she had resisted, that she had kissed the earth on her return to Lithuania, that she came from a family loyal to Lithuania and had had a wonderful mother. The Iron Curtain was also mental. Every prominent person was under scrutiny and it was a risk to be open-minded. Irena had the ability to be frank without ceding points of attack. We read Dante, Shakespeare, Hegel, Goethe,*

Cervantes, Arendt, Schopenhauer. All our texts had political sub plots. She made us understand why it was important to study literature. She could perhaps have gone to London to live with her daughter, but she was dedicated to achieving our transition into Europe at the level of other nations. She showed us forbidden books in her apartment which were hidden behind others in the front row. Her priorities were people, then books. She was for us a new kind of intellectual. She maintained her integrity even when questioned about Solzhenitsyn, and we students adored her. She showed an instinctive support for small places and poor families. She was the envy of her pedagogical colleagues, but her informal relations with her students were not approved of. Other professors serving the regime and themselves made efforts to expel her from the university in 1987. The students organised a meeting in her defence.'

Lithuania's Past

From time to time history bequeaths us extraordinary individuals who stand out like beacons on rocky outcrops against the swirling, all-powerful tides of events. The radiance of Irena's life acquires its brilliance against the dark shadows of her country's recent past.

Lithuania has for centuries lain on the boundary between Catholicism and Russian Orthodoxy. The Polish-Lithuanian Commonwealth was partitioned three times in the 18th century by Russia, Prussia and Austria. The third and final partition in 1795 completed the destruction of the state and Lithuania fell under Russian domination for 120 years. In June 1812 Napoleon marched through with 60,000 soldiers and 1,400 guns – the Lithuanian attempts to make peace with him are described in Tolstoy's *War and Peace* – and Lithuanians hoped briefly for the regaining, with his help, of independence from Russia. By December Napoleon had returned in defeat, and thousands of French soldiers are buried in Vilnius. In 1863, 37 leaders of an unsuccessful uprising were hanged and countless others deported to Siberia. The name of Lithuania was removed, the Latin script was banned, and the Polish and Lithuanian languages disappeared. This long era of suppression saw the greatest flourishing of the Jewish community. Vilnius was the centre of Jewishness in the Russian Empire and, in the years after 1750, the largest Jewish community worldwide. Vilnius became the cradle of the Jewish Labour Movement. The Bund, the Yiddish Socialist Party, was founded in Vilnius in 1897. The Lithuanian dialect of Yiddish became the language of Yiddish literature.

The Russian grip had begun to loosen in the early years of the 20th century, but the Lithuanian Jews were suspected by the Russians of cooperation with Germany. Thousands were deported to Russia. Early in the First World War, German troops under Ludendorff overran the western parts of the Russian empire. The German victory over the Russians at Tannenberg in 1914 and the Treaty of Brest-Litovsk of early 1918 appeared to confirm Lithuania's fate as a German satellite state, but the Lithuanian Council proclaimed independence on 16th February 1918. Polish aggression after the war led to the Polish occupation of Vilnius and much of the surrounding countryside. 'An international scandal', said Lord Cecil in Britain, but war-weary peoples and complicit statesmen acquiesced and Lithuania did not have the strength to resist. The result was a complete break in diplomatic relations between Poland and Lithuania from 1920 until 1938.

For a few years democracy and civil rights prospered and the Jews were given parliamentary representation alongside other minority groups. Vilnius itself became the centre of modern Jewry and Lithuania had the largest Jewish population in the Baltic States. 1925 saw the foundation in Vilnius of *The Institute for Jewish Research*, a scholarly institute with Freud and Einstein as members of the honorary presidium; 1927 of the writers' association, the World Jewish PEN. A nationalist and military coup in 1926 abolished the multi-party system and discriminatory laws curtailed the rights of Jews, but the President Smetona was not anti-Semitic and, despite these restrictions, it was possible for Paul Johnson to comment in his *History of the Jews* that *'in Lithuania, the minority guarantees worked very well, and the large Jewish community there was perhaps the most contented in Eastern Europe between the wars'.* It was a brief interlude. The ideologies of Fascism and Bolshevism were rampant in the west and the east, and once again Lithuania, with her fellow Baltic States, was to be the nut in the nutcracker of Germany and Russia.

The 19th and early 20th-century Russian fears that the Jews were cooperating with the Germans were now mirrored in the suspicions of nationalist Lithuanians that their descendants were in league with the Bolsheviks in Moscow – the prominent role of Jews in the Russian revolutions made these suspicions all too plausible. Irena Veisaitė's own father, well-to-do, had dreamt of equality and given money for political prisoners – Irena called him a *salon* communist; and her mother was openly left-wing with communist friends and associates. It was a time when many were captured by the idealistic motivation of early communism. Was it not true that, in the ideal communist world of the future, ethnic identification would be a thing of the past; wider principles would prevail? [●] Irena says it was clear that *'the Jews preferred Stalin to Hitler, but who understood then the real nature of Soviet communism – only Andre Gide had recognised the reality.'* Mark Mazower has written of the Balkans at roughly the same time: *'The era of religion was over; that of ideology lay ahead.'*

Then came the Ribbentrop-Molotov Pact of August 1939!

Two Invasions, the Holocaust and Deportations

The Soviet invasion of Eastern Poland which followed the German invasion from the west in September 1939 was rapidly extended to include occupation of all three Baltic States. Vilnius was restored to Lithuania, leading to short-lived gratitude. 'Elections' were held on 14th and 15th July 1940. The new Labour Alliance received 99% of the votes, a London newspaper publishing the results as prematurely announced by an official Russian agency 24 hours before the polls closed. Three weeks later, the assemblies in all three Baltic States approved the entry of their countries into the Union of the Soviet Socialist Republics.

At first the Jews did well. They represented 16% of the communist membership. One even became a Minister. A Department of Yiddish language and literature was created in the University of Vilnius. Jewish theatres opened. But by June 1941 general purges had started. The secret police arrested 30,000 and deported them to Russia – capitalists of all backgrounds, religious leaders, intellectuals, Jewish

[●] *'Much in human life results from contingency … but human beings try to instil some rationality into their lives … the Universalist and egalitarian impetus of Marxism could be very appealing to anyone confronted by the social inequalities of early twentieth-century Europe. No-one was immune to this appeal – neither German workers nor French intellectuals nor East European Jews … the motivation of youthful converts to Communism in this period was selfless and altruistic, and their own life prospects … were virtually certain to include imprisonment, material want, and living on the run …'* Jan Gross; *Fear – Anti-Semitism in Poland after Auschwitz.*

'The collective impulse of the Jews leads them toward revolution; their critical powers (and I use the word in their highest sense) drive them to destroy every idea, every traditional form which does not agree with the facts or cannot be justified by reason … the idea of inevitable justice had sustained them, the belief that the world would one day be ordered according to reason, one rule prevail over all men, so that everyone gets their due. Is that not the spirit of socialism? It is the ancient spirit of the race …' Paul Johnson in his *History of the Jews*, quoting the words of Leon Blum in 1901

Zionists and members of the Lithuanian Nationalist Party alike. Once again, as in the First World War, the scene was set for a Lithuanian welcome for German soldiers.

By the time the Nazis invaded on 22nd June, greeted as liberators with flowers, most leading Bolsheviks had fled. The Jewish role in the small, now illegal communist party left them as the scapegoats – the fact that so many Jews had also been deported to Russia was ignored. The government, in the vain belief that it would thereby secure national independence, sacrificed the Jews in the name of patriotism. The accounts of Lithuanian brutality are revolting. On 25th June uniformed volunteers massacred 1,000 Jews – rabbinical students, their teachers and families, ironically and unforgivably the most implacable enemies of the communists! The following day 60 Jews, among them Irena's favourite uncle, were herded into a garage for forced labour. Many were killed in a public square with crowbars and spades, the others taken away and shot. A photograph of the slaughter remains one of the indelible illustrations of Second World War anti-Semitic brutality. 2,000 Jews were killed in the same week in Kaunas alone. The Catholic bishop of Kaunas, under pressure to intervene, made a public statement that *'it was not in his power to intervene against a spontaneous expression of the people's wrath'.*

The Holocaust in Lithuania and throughout the East was visible to all. There were ghettos and execution sites but no concealed and fenced-off concentration camps. The planning and the supervision were German, but 80% of the killing was done by Estonians, Latvians, Lithuanians, Croats, Hungarians, Romanians, Ukrainians and Poles. Under the Nazi administration, over 90% of the remaining Jewish population of Lithuania was murdered between 1941 and 1944. The notorious Jaeger Report covers the period from 4th July to 25th November 1940. The number of those killed in these weeks alone was precisely 137,346, the horror only intensified by the absolute precision with which these figures were recorded in the daily reports. Some 34,500 were left alive to carry out essential work on behalf of the Nazi war effort. These massacres were effectively a technical dress rehearsal for the implementation of the Final Solution, agreed by the Wannsee Conference in 1942. The mass of the local population did not object, for brutality towards the Jews had become an area of common interest with their Nazi occupiers. Nazi propaganda took every opportunity to demonstrate that it was the communities they had liberated that were acting against the Jews – the more the guilt was shared, the less would fall on them.

Massive deportations of non-Jewish Lithuanians to Germany as the war progressed began to reveal to their fellow citizens the realities of their position. With the defeat at Stalingrad, Lithuanians were now also being sent to fight the Russians on the Eastern Front. There followed the extraordinary phenomenon of Lithuanian men climbing secretly into the remaining ghettos to seek concealment and help from the Jewish inmates. The Lithuanian tragedy was however far from complete. In July 1944 the Soviet armies returned.

Once again, the change of regime brought some initial hope – the Jewish Museum for example was re-opened – but for the country as a whole it was short-lived. It was now the nationalists who suffered. Stalin told Djilas in 1945: *'whoever occupies a territory also imposes his own social system ... it cannot be otherwise'.* Between 1945 and 1953, 118,000 Lithuanians were deported to camps in the USSR [•] Partisans took to the woods and were brutally hunted down, their executed corpses displayed in villages and towns to drive the message home. 21,500 were killed. Nor did the lot of the Jews improve. Many returned, destitute, from their own earlier deportation to the Soviet Union in 1941 (a greater proportion had survived Stalin's camps than had outlived the Nazi occupation), but their homes and properties were either destroyed or in the hands of others who were not ready to give them up. *'What, you are still in this world!'* Thousands left for Israel. The Great Synagogue in Vilnius, for centuries the main spiritual centre of the Jewish community in Lithuania and a focus for Jewry throughout Europe, was utterly destroyed. Nothing of it remains. This persecution reflected not just Stalin's increasingly obsessive mistrust of the Jews. The Russian war against the Nazis, the sufferings and the millions of fallen, both military and civilian, was now transformed into The Great Patriotic War. Stalingrad had re-taught the Soviets the values and power of nationalism; for them, the Holocaust, the fate of the Jews, was not unique, and must take its place against their own suffering. It was, Irena told me, a great and lasting shock after the war to realise that there was no interest, or at least no humanitarian interest, in their fate, only interest for political reasons; *'there was no interest in our testimony'.* In Soviet times, the Holocaust was never mentioned. Jewish life did not exist.

Rebirth

We have seen how, in the early years of the 20th century, the Tsarist hold over Lithuania had weakened. Now, in the 1970s and 1980s, faltering communism was slowly to give way to renewed national pride. The Lithuanian author Tomas Venclova writes that, within the USSR, Vilnius was always a special city. *'Through Vilnius, the influences of modern Western thought and art, moods and fashions found their way into the Soviet Empire ... the best jazz, an original school of painting and graphic art ... non-standard films. As in Tsarist times, Vilnius was "the third city of the empire".'*

In 1987, demonstrations began. On 11th March 1990 the Supreme Council of Lithuania, the future *Seimas*, or Parliament, proclaimed independence. Soviet soldiers attacked the television tower and the parliament building on 13th January 1991, killing 14 but not daring to molest the deputies. In August 1991 the newly re-born state of Lithuania was given international recognition. In 2004 Lithuania joined NATO and the European Union.

With the revival of Lithuania in the 1990s there began the revival of Jewishness, and all the old questions arose again. It was bitterly difficult to acknowledge the role of Lithuanians in the deaths of so many thousands of their Jewish compatriots. The government, Irena assured me, took the appropriate and necessary steps: genocide was condemned, the participants were condemned, the day of the liquidation of the Vilnius ghetto on 23rd September became the Day of Genocide; the Jews were given equal civil rights, a House of Memory was opened, and the truth began to be confronted. But anti-Semitism was always present. There was the infamous press article on the Jews and the Gays. Soros himself was attacked for seeking to take over the state – was not he also a Jew? And the Genocide Museum in Vilnius records, not the genocide of the Jews, but the Soviet persecution of the Lithuanians and the post-war strife between the Lithuanian partisans and the Soviet communist authorities.

Irena's Convictions

'Did you never consider emigration to Israel? How can you live in a country soaked in Jewish blood?'

[•] Deportations were a tragically recurrent feature of life over centuries in the lands between Eastern Germany and Russia. It is almost impossible for westerners to visualise the logistics, let alone their brutality. In his *Bloodlands*, Timothy Snyder cites innumerable examples. *'On a single day, 19th November 1943, the Soviets deported the entire Karachai population, some 69,267* (questionable precision of numbers, one must admit) *to Soviet Kazakhstan and Kyrgyzstan ... over the course of two days, 28th–29th December 1943, the Soviets dispatched 91,919 Kalmyks to Siberia ... in April 1944, right after the Red Army reached the Crimea, Beria proposed and Stalin agreed that the entire Crimean Tatar population be resettled. Over the course of three days, 18th–20th March 1944, 180,014 people were deported, most of them to Uzbekistan ...' Bloodlands* pages 330–331.

Irena's answer was immediate. *'What a strange question! My homeland is Lithuania. You cannot choose the place where you are born, just as you cannot choose your parents. I am bound to Lithuania through language (I can find my full expression only in the Lithuanian language), through culture, and even through all the graves. I experienced the tragedies as both a Lithuanian and a Jew. Have patience with Lithuania!* [●] *We all need time to reflect on our past. You cannot blame a whole nation. The Nazis initiated everything. Some Lithuanians were auxiliaries of the Nazis, but Lithuanians were also victims of the Ribbentrop–Molotov pact and its consequences. It is easy to manipulate people's minds. Goebbels exploited the Soviet deportations by saying that they were initiated and executed by Jews. It was a lie, but many Lithuanians*

[●] Jan Gross writes: *'… Max Weinrich of the YIVO Institute for Jewish Research … organised three contests for autobiographical youth in the 1930s. More than 600 submissions were received … one may find therein numerous confessions, often in a highly cultured literary style, of unrequited love by young Jews for their native country.'*

believed it. Jews have suffered so much from nationalism, and they should therefore be tolerant and understand others, never accusing a whole nation of committing crimes which were done by a small minority. This is the only true meaning of suffering. You cannot think only about your own sufferings. I will always remember the Holocaust, but I will not impose my memories on others.'

So is religion her inspiration?

'I have deep feelings that do not fit into a religious doctrine. I recognise that our human experience cannot be limited and defined by the empirical world, but Christianity has not penetrated the hearts of men. God is, in my opinion, wrongly imagined in human terms – the King, the hierarchy, you have blindly to obey … Religion, which is often wrongly understood, divides people and creates enemies, not unity and love … I have no anger or hatred inside me. Perhaps that is God's gift, but it also comes from my family – the lessons from my mother, the great tolerance of my grandfather. I have encountered so much kindness in my life.' In Vilnius, we attended two concerts together in the old Franciscan Church of St. Bernardine. It is still practically in ruins. *'This does not matter. The building is safe, and the priest hopes it*

will never be fully restored. In this condition it reminds us of our past and of the state that the church and people are now in … It has a lesson for us. The religious services are carried out with simple ceramic vessels – this is so much better than silver and gold. I hope it will always remain like that.'

To walk with Irena through the streets of Vilnius is to meet the people – every other passer-by stops to greet her and speak with her. 'That was a remarkable woman', Irena explains. 'Her daughter died a few months ago of AIDS. She has just published her daughter's poems. This took great courage, but I told her she must do it … And that was another remarkable person. She was on the train for deportation to the Soviet Union with her parents. The President's daughter was in the same school class and he intervened at the last minute to save her. She had no other relatives. She never saw her parents again.' Irena showed us the orphanage where she had worked during the Nazi occupation. Every morning and every evening she had walked through the town alone. Not far from the orphanage was the Nazi soldiers' bordello, where the queues had stretched along the street.

Our Debt

It is of course not possible to place a figure on Irena's contribution to the moral economy of post-war Lithuania. When I asked a senior colleague from the Soros Foundation about this, and about Lithuania's progress towards democracy and Europe, she quoted Durkheim's concept of the three clocks all moving at different speeds – the clocks of the law, of economics and of mental attitudes. It will, she said, take several decades, and perhaps something different is needed now. 'There are still huge gaps. We do not share the same values as other democratic countries. Post-communist countries have double standards. Or do we have too many illusions about the West?'

Irena's contribution has not been as a university teacher and as Chair of the Soros Foundation alone, formidable though this has been. She has responded to the historic and continuing multi-ethnic nature of Lithuanian Society by helping to create the Centre for Stateless Cultures at Vilnius University. Soros has established a permanent Fellowship there in her name. She has collaborated with the Borderlands Foundation in Sejny in Poland, which is led by 'a wonderful man, an artist, who when communism was finished had no more reason to be a dissident. So he went to a small provincial town where all the Jews had been killed to build a dialogue of cultures; educational work, publishing, a fine library, art workshops for children, concerts, above all reconciliation between Poles and Lithuanians'. Irena cares

about modern culture. 'It is a high priority, and must be taken out of the zone of isolation, because it has been a forbidden fruit for so long.' With the support of the Open Society Foundation a Centre for Contemporary Art has been created. 'During the long years of Soviet occupation there was an acute lack of information, not only from the West but also from our closest neighbours. Our answers and our actions must be prompted by life itself, by our history, and by the necessity to contemplate a time of deep change and our own position within its flow.'

And then there are the United World Colleges, on whose International Board she also sat for six years.

What does she now think of them, looking back?

It was Paweł Czartoryski from Poland who introduced her to them. She says his friendship was a consuming inspiration.

Why people are so hostile to each other and unable to find a common language is a very painful question, so she was struck by this idea of bringing such diverse students together to fight stereotypes. It had enormous importance for Lithuania. 'But Lithuania does not have much time, and we need to work faster. The UWC Short Courses were a way forward. Soros helped. The results were tangible and attitudes changed. Many members from abroad of past courses return to Lithuania. Lithuanian college graduates are succeeding in life, but they have not yet contributed much to their own country. The new capitalist society creates great pressures for personal survival, and altruism is not yet common in Lithuania.' It had been a dream of hers, shared with Czartoryski, to create an influential UWC community in the Baltic States, but the funding is difficult, people are needed to dedicate themselves to the task, more publicity is essential. 'There is an urgent need to work faster, lest other pressures take over'. The first two Lithuanian students nominated for the United World Colleges had been a Pole and a half Jew. It was a source of great pride that her country was to be represented by young people from minorities.

The Atlantic College and the United World Colleges were created by idealists from among the western victors of the Second World War. For me, Irena represents those who suffered on the other side. Have we lived up to her ideals or fulfilled her hopes of us? I do not think so, and this is our loss and our failure, but this should only be a spur to more imaginative and more knowledgeable commitment in the future.

Mark Mazower, again discussing the Balkans, but he could as easily have been describing the Baltic States, writes: 'The long struggle to create a nation state – of which the Yugoslav wars could be seen as the final phase – had taken the entire 20th century. The irony was that, just as this struggle *ended, economic and political changes at the international level threw the very idea of the nation-state into question.'*

This is, I believe, the arena for the United World Colleges.

Jan Gross quotes Tacitus: *'It is indeed human nature to hate the man whom you have injured'* and comments: *'… people could not bear the Jewish presence (in Poland) after the war because it called forth their own feelings of shame and of contempt in which they were held by their victims'.* Perhaps this is too immediate an interpretation that takes too little account of historic anti-Semitism over the ages. But Irena's life-long commitment to the memory and words of her mother, the qualities imbued in her by Stefanija Ladigiene's love and example, her unwavering refusal to abandon the language, culture and nation of her birth despite all the hard truths of its recent history, give expression to perhaps the only way to remove the burden of guilt and hatred. And her refusal to pass judgement on or against her fellow Lithuanians leads to another important insight. It is natural for us, distant in place and time, to identify ourselves with the victims, not the perpetrators. Timothy Snyder asks us however whether *'this identification with victims brings much knowledge, or whether this kind of alienation from the murderer is an ethical stance … the moral danger, after all, is never that one might become a victim but that one might be* *a perpetrator or a bystander';* and *'to deny a human being his human character is to render ethics impossible'.* [●] Irena gives us powerful inspiration in her response to this challenge.

Irena has been awarded the Lithuanian Order of Gediminas, the Medal of the Lithuanian Queen Barbora Radvilaite, and in 2002 was named The Person of Tolerance by the Japanese Sugihara Foundation in Lithuania. She has been awarded the Goethe Medal in 2012 by the Goethe Institute for her services to cultural exchange and the promotion of German language and literature.

Of special, deep significance to her was the invitation to speak at the Brandenburg Gate in Berlin on behalf of Lithuania at the ceremonies marking the acceptance of the ten new States into the European Union on 1st May 2004. She felt proud and good to be speaking as a Lithuanian of Jewish origin in the capital of the state which had desired her death. She personifies the truly open society. The United World Colleges have been profoundly privileged and enriched by her involvement.

[●] Timothy Snyder. *Bloodlands* pages 309–400

A Haitian boy watches as rigid-hulled inflatable boats arrive ashore in one of the many relief projects undertaken by the US Coastguard after the earthquake disaster of 12th January 2010

The Warburgs: Max, Eric and Lola

The Invitation to Lecture at the NATO Defense College in 1955

The concept of the Atlantic College was born with Kurt Hahn's visit to the NATO Defense College in Paris in 1955. It was not by chance that his invitation to lecture to the assembled NATO officers was brought about by members of the Warburg family.

Kurt's younger brother Rudo and his wife Lola were visiting their daughter Benita, whose husband Egidio Cioppa, an Italian naval officer, later an admiral and Head of Naval Armaments for NATO, was attending a course there. Egidio arranged a lunch for them with the Commandant, Lawrance Darvall. At Benita's prompting, Rudo invited Darvall to some salmon fishing in Scotland. At the Hahns' home Burnside, a mile or so from Gordonstoun School, Lawrance Darvall met Kurt Hahn. No sparks were generated by this first encounter. By Lola's account they did not even talk to one another, but Benita, Rudo and Lola insisted nonetheless that Kurt visit the College in Paris. Egidio Cioppa negotiated the invitation. Hahn was captured by the vision of achieving even more with idealistic adolescents than Darvall was already accomplishing with middle-aged military officers. Darvall was enthralled by Hahn's rhetoric and record. Their intensive partnership from 1955 onwards, Darvall firing the big guns with Hahn supplying the ammunition, led directly to the creation of the Atlantic College in 1962.

The Warburg Family

Kurt Hahn's life and achievements – political, educational, personal, even financial – are inseparable from the Warburgs. This was not just a matter of his brother Rudo having married Lola Warburg in 1921. The relationship began in the cooperation between Max Warburg and Kurt Hahn in the First World War

The American writer Ron Chernow, in his all-embracing account of the Warburgs, [●] introduces the German Jews as *'a people shipwrecked by history'*, their identity ultimately defined for them by Adolf Hitler. But one can also see them, with their talents and accomplishments, their courage and their despair, their struggle between their religious roots and their secularism, their problems with the concept of patriotism, their triumphs and their disasters, as emblematic combatants in the issues of our age.

The family took its name from the Westphalian town of Warburg. Their family home, still lived in, dates back to 1537. Around 1640 they moved to Altona, then in Denmark – a 1668 grave in the old Jewish cemetery in Altona bears clearly the Warburg name – and to Hamburg. For our present story, the landmark date is 1798, when Moses Marcus Warburg and his brother Gerson founded the banking firm M. M. Warburg in Hamburg. Still in business in the 21st century under the same name, it had never been more important, more influential, in the end more expressive of historical turmoil and the Jewish fate, than in the years from 1900 to 1950.

From 1856 onwards this growing bank was managed by the two brothers Siegmund and Moritz under the fierce control exercised daily by their formidable widowed mother Sara. After their mother's death in 1884 it was Moritz who brought the bank up to the forefront, increasing its annual takeover six-fold between 1891 and 1910. He and his wife Charlotte, née Oppenheimer, were strictly Orthodox – Jews first, Germans second. It was their seven children who found themselves exposed to the challenges, opportunities, conflicts and physical dangers of the new century. In loosening, probably in reaction against the discipline imposed on them by their parents, their observance of the family religion they, like many of their generation, became more German than Jew. This transformation had its importance even for those of them who moved to the United States.

They were by any measure a remarkable group.

[●] *The Warburgs: A Family Saga* Chatto and Windus London 1993. My account relies very heavily on this fine book.

The Brothers Aby, Max, Paul, Felix and Fritz

Aby, the eldest, was the first to mark out his own path, and this at the age of 13. In a legendary family episode, already a bookworm, he offered his next brother Max the future leadership of the Warburg bank in return for an open-ended book token for the rest of his life. They shook hands solemnly on the deal. The outcome was a pioneering career in art history research, interrupted by tormenting periods of mental instability and confinement to a sanatorium in Switzerland, and the assembly of the Warburg Library in Hamburg which was miraculously saved from the Nazi regime and transferred to England, where it now contains over 350,000 volumes and as the Warburg Institute is a part of the University of London, housed in Woburn Square. Aby Warburg died in 1929.

We shall return later to Max, the second brother.

Paul, the third, married the American heiress Nina Loeb of the Kuhn Loeb banking dynasty but remained active full-time in the Hamburg bank for seven years before moving to the United States in 1902, where he became a naturalised citizen in 1911. Trained in European banking methods, he was shocked by the free-wheeling, unco-ordinated operations, all in the name of free enterprise, of the 20,000 national, state and private banks he found there. In 1907, the year when he finally withdrew from the family bank in Hamburg, he both foresaw the market panic of that year in the States and drafted a proposal for a central reserve bank, an adaptation of European practice to American conditions. By 1913 the Federal Reserve Bill became law. In 1914 he was nominated Vice-Chairman of the Federal Reserve Board, his own creation, by President Wilson. His appointment preceded the start of the First World War by six weeks. It was of course also the onset of his conflict of loyalties. He supported American policies with *'the bitter soul-searing neutrality of the man whose reason tells him one thing while his emotions cry out the other'*. In 1918, all too conscious of his German background, he refused re-nomination to the Reserve Board. In 1919 he began planning and in 1921 successfully launched the International Acceptance Bank, an effort to inject funds and cooperation into the heavily war-damaged transatlantic trade. It was owned jointly by banks in the United States, Sweden, Britain, The Netherlands and Germany. By the late 1920s he was warning all who would listen that the Wall Street crash was on the way. He was not heeded, not even by his brother Max in Germany. He was to give much of his personal money to Max to tide him over. He funded the Loeb Classical Library which had been set up by his

brother-in-law James Loeb. He was a co-founder of the Council of Foreign Relations. He died in 1932, one of the great citizens of America in the first half of the 20th century.

Felix, the fourth brother, also married a wealthy American, Frieda Schiff, daughter of, it was said, the best-known Jew in New York. For him it was immediately clear that he would spend his life in the United States. In both his marriage and his move he was ahead of Paul, and he was to make his mark in a decisively different way. But if he abandoned his German roots, he was to remain intensely loyal to his Jewish obligations. It was not a straight road. Outstandingly generous with his own money, he became an almost mythically successful fundraiser, charity organiser and conciliator, bringing together into the Federation of Jewish Charities by 1916 the 75 organisations that were said to be engaged in Jewish relief work in New York alone. This was the more outstanding an achievement, given the different strands in Jewish life that were already threatening unity – the sophisticated American Jews, usually wealthy, often of German origin, the orthodox Jews of the shetlachs of Eastern Europe, the ideological socialists, and the growingly influential Zionists. Was Palestine, following the British Balfour declaration of 1917, to be the National Home or the National State of the Jewish people? Were the Jews now to become nationalists, or were they to remain citizens of the world? Chaim Weizmann exerted his charismatic influence, and Felix visited Palestine for the first time in 1924, donating half a million dollars for the School of Jewish Studies, later to become the Hebrew University of Jerusalem. The same issue arose: a Centre for Jewish Studies and Culture, or an academic agent of Zionism? Despite his reservations, Felix accepted the Chairmanship of the Administrative Committee of the Jewish Agency in Palestine in 1929, but he was not then, or later, of Weizmann's way of thinking. *'I am for action'*, he wrote that year to a fellow Board member, *'which shows we want to reach agreement with the Arabs, and for action which expresses our reduced ambitions plainly.'* The final break between him and Weizmann came after the conference of the Jewish Agency in Zurich in 1937 at which the Agency accepted by a large majority the recommendation, prepared by a British Royal Commission, that Palestine be partitioned into separate Jewish and Arab states. His dismay, his fury, his passionate efforts to have this decision reversed, must have hastened his death just three months later.

Fritz, the last son, may have lived his life in the shadow of his elder brothers, but he respected family traditions in his own manner. Little motivated by the business life despite a senior position in the family bank, he devoted himself to charitable causes. He ran a hostel for the poor in the red light district of Hamburg. He was the President of the city's Jewish Hospitals Committee. His wife, a trained teacher, earned herself an international reputation for her work in youth organisations in the 1930s until the Nazis made this impossible. Together they provided shelter and accommodation in their Hamburg home and estate for more than a thousand Jewish families who were anxiously awaiting emigration papers. And, despite already having left in 1938 for the safety of Sweden, he did not hesitate to return in October that year for an important meeting of the Hospitals Committee, whereupon the Nazi threw him into prison. He was released in May 1939 following negotiations carried out on his behalf with the infamous Reinhard Heydrich, an agreement also being made whereby some one hundred Jewish children and impoverished adults were ransomed into the safety of Sweden. The Nazis were still anxious to rid themselves of as many Jews as possible into other lands – against substantial sums of money. Fritz and his wife were the only Warburgs of their generation eventually to move to Israel, where they died in the 1960s.

Against this powerful sibling backcloth it is nonetheless Max who remains for us the key figure. Once described before the First World War as *'the uncrowned king of Hamburg'*, in 1938 he could still be referred to as *'arguably the most powerful man in German Jewry'*. His daughter Lola and his son Eric are essential figures in the Kurt Hahn and Atlantic College story. His life merits our attention, but the historical is as important as the family background. Paul Johnson and others have called it *'the German-Jewish love affair'*.

The German-Jewish Background

The Enlightenment had been a fateful flame for the Jewish world, above all in the societies that were later to be welded by Bismarck into the German or, as many prefer to remember it, the Prussian nation. For it stimulated intellectual debate over spiritual assumptions. It confronted dogma and tradition. It invited the individual to assess and re-assess his own position. It was a charter for individual choice for those prepared to grapple with the challenges. Above all in Germany it was, again in Johnson's words, *'serious, sincere and creative'*. The pivotal Jewish figure had been Moses Mendelssohn (1729–1786), whose first concession to the Gentile world was to write in German rather than Hebrew or Yiddish. Seeking to protect the Jews from the stark alternatives of persecution or conversion, he emphasised the voluntary nature of all churches, the obligations of belonging actively to society whose claims

were legitimate, and the conviction that discrimination would ultimately give way to reason. *'This'*, comments Johnson, *'was a formula for securing civilised treatment of the Jews, but it was not Judaism.'*

Germany was a latecomer on the national scene. This delay enabled its early prophets, notably Fichte and Herder, to dream of an as yet unrealised ideal – *Die Menschheitsnation* – a nation defined by culture and serving universal mankind. This was the great challenge, the noble aspiration, the elusive dream. And as the German Jews increasingly demonstrated their remarkable gifts in literature, scholarship and research, they felt that they too were becoming part of a high-minded endeavour. Was it not possible for the *'love affair'* to lead to the fusion of two great cultures, to create a yet higher achievement? Legitimate dream or fateful illusion, it was to seduce personalities as distinguished and as cultured as Aby Warburg and Thomas Mann into vigorous defence of Germany against *'the Anglo-Saxon barbarians'* in the First World War. Of course, and especially in retrospect, the sceptics and the critics have a powerful case. For Gershon Scholem (1897–1982), the Jewish scholar born into an assimilated family in Berlin but who joined the Zionist movement as a young student and moved to Palestine in 1923, as the points of contact multiplied between the two communities, so too became stronger and more numerous the areas of conflict! With the acceleration of the process of Jewish assimilation, the German themselves felt increasingly threatened. *'Gratitude the Jews were to find quite often; the love which they sought – never!'*

Max and the First World War

German society, which so deeply respected intellectual and cultural accomplishment, gave gifted Jews all possible individual satisfaction, but with their growing success their need to prove themselves as citizens became ever stronger. When war was declared in 1914, all the leading Jewish intellectuals with the one notable exception of Einstein signed a petition in support of Germany's aims. That one of the enemies was Tsarist Russia only strengthened their faith in the homeland – had not thousands of Jews fled to Germany from the Tsar's pogroms? And who did not soon learn of the Cossacks sacking Jewish villages in the East in the early days of the war, and of the wonderful treatment and help these villagers received from the advancing German armies? Although Jews were not able to gain officer commissions, almost one in five of the total Jewish population served in the army, winning 31,500 Iron Crosses for gallantry.

Max Warburg

The pre-war years of the 20th century had seen the high point of the Warburg Bank. Max the banker was now also one of Hamburg's most distinguished social hosts at the family estate Kösterberg, from 1902 an elected member of the Hamburg Chamber of Commerce and from 1903 of the Hamburg State Parliament. But if the German-Jew dilemma appeared to be receding, it was being rapidly replaced by the accelerating quarrels between Germany and Great Britain. Hamburg was the most *'English'* of German cities. Max had become the Treasurer of the King Edward VI Fund, set up against the threatening background in 1912 to safeguard Anglo-German friendship. His efforts to support and fund German colonial adventures, notably in Morocco and Nyasaland, went adrift but had given him political status. He was in London three times in 1914, negotiating on the diplomatic margins for peace. In May 1914 he was consulted by the German Chancellor Bethmann-Hollweg, in June by the Kaiser. Once war broke out, he saw his patriotic duty clearly, resented what he saw as British arrogance, and was the main mover in establishing war credits to finance the war effort after having warned strongly and vainly in 1908 against Germany's financial

unpreparedness. His two influential brothers in the States were not yet his nation's enemies.

Max Warburg was a conservative and a royalist, but here too he faced inner conflict. He foresaw clearly the consequences of the German declaration of unrestricted submarine warfare in January 1917 – the entry of the United States into the war – and had advised forcefully against it when consulted in 1915. He recognised that the Kaiser was in the hands of ambitious, dictatorial military leaders, above all Ludendorff, who had neither political understanding nor integrity. He travelled abroad – to Belgium, Bulgaria, Romania, Sweden and, most significantly, Holland in March 1918 – in loosely approved efforts to negotiate peace settlements. But his faith in German civilisation was being sorely tested. Of his visit to Belgium in 1915 he wrote: *'the Belgians … tell many stories of murder, theft and looting … that one simply cannot refute'.* This Belgian experience led him to admire the American Herbert Hoover who, after German refusal to feed the Belgians, launched a relief effort, and also brought him together for the first time with Hjalmar Schacht, who was likewise dismayed at the German record in Belgium and who was to become a major, controversial figure (*'Hitler's banker'*) in the 1930s. It also brought him together with a young member of the German Foreign Office, Kurt Hahn.

Max Warburg and Kurt Hahn

Kurt Hahn had been appointed to the Ministry of Foreign Affairs in 1914 to analyse British morale and policies through study of the British press. He rapidly achieved an astonishing reputation for the precision of his commentaries. He too, sometimes with Max, travelled abroad on discreet, partially independent peace negotiations. He never relaxed his criticism of the German occupation of Belgium, and opposed the declaration of unrestricted submarine warfare with such vehemence that he was transferred in February 1917 to the Foreign Affairs Department of the Military High Command. By 1916 he had become convinced that the only figure in Germany who could negotiate a dignified settlement with the Entente powers, soon to be reinforced by America, was Prince Max of Baden. In a remarkable sequence of private moves, and with Max Warburg as one of his allies, Hahn manoeuvred and conspired to such effect that, in October 1918, Max of Baden was finally appointed Chancellor by the Kaiser with the task of seeking a dignified ceasefire on the Western Front. It was too late. Although no foreign troops crossed German borders, German morale folded both in the army and at home. The Entente governments of Britain, France and the United States were subjected to all the emotions generated by the war in their elector-ates. President Wilson's early idealism was compromised by the fierce passions of his European allies and the lack of support from Congress at home. The Versailles Treaty imposed humiliating conditions.

The fall-out from the Treaty, manipulated by the defeated military leaders and exploited by the right wing parties, was unhesitatingly ascribed to the Jews, prominent among them Max Warburg and Kurt Hahn. Both had attended the Peace Conference. No matter that they had both fought relent-lessly against the terms, above all the level of reparations and the war guilt clause!

Golo Mann, a son of Thomas Mann and an early Salem pupil under Kurt Hahn, gave his judgement when lecturing at the World Congress of Jews in 1966: '… The American Jews are Americans … the French Jews … are Frenchmen … the German Jews were Germans …' but '… I would venture the judgment: never were the anti-Semitic passions in Germany stronger than in the years 1919 to 1923. They were far stronger then than between 1930 and 1933 or between 1933 and 1945 …'[1]

Max Warburg was nonetheless to rebuild his bank and his personal position in the 1920s despite all the pressures. By 1928 he and his partners held directorships in 86 firms across Czechoslovakia, Holland, Austria and the United States in addition to Germany. He dared to join the Deutsche Volkspartei and the Central Committee of the Reichsbank in spite of the anti-Semitic elements in both.

Later events make it difficult for us to recall that the Weimar Republic gave German Jews full rights in all respects for the first time. Its very constitution had been drafted by Hugo Preuss, a Jew. The 1920s saw, again to quote Chernow, 'an explosion of Jewish cultural, political, and economic achieve-ment. Jews would advance in the arts, universities, upper civil service, business, and mass media.' Why then should these highly educated, prominently successful Jews be afraid of those coarse, uneducated anti-Semites? They had after all faced problems before; they would face them again. In embracing the Enlightenment they had embraced German culture, which was now an integral part of their lives. The attacks on the Jews were an attack on the Republic itself; therefore they would stand by the Republic and defend it. [●]

[●] And anyway: 'How servilely Hitler bows before the ramrod old field marshal. How disdainfully that old soldier looks down on that little man – the Bohemian lance-corporal, he calls him privately … even Hitler would have to mellow in the end. Political realities, last but not least the great powers, would see to it.' George Clare: Last Waltz in Vienna, also quoted by Peter Pulzer in his essay The Beginning of the End

The deepening relationship between Max Warburg and Kurt Hahn in the 1920s, proven in the furnace of dramatic events in the final months of the First World War, now gave Hahn his most important ally in the German Jewish com-munity, confirmed his sense of political mission, enabled his school Salem to survive its early financial crises, and brought him warm, new family ties and affections. Two Max Warburg children, Eric and Lola, were later to become his most faithful personal disciples, above all in the found-ing of the Atlantic College. Another, Anita, was to attend Salem as a pupil, together with a cousin Ingrid Warburg, the daughter of Fritz. And, most important of all, Lola was to marry his brother Rudo in 1921.

Max Warburg and his Beliefs

There were four threads in Max Warburg that governed his conduct.

The first, the most closely related to his professional life, was his inherited concept of banking. He defined it with precision on 30th May 1938 at the moment when, under Nazi coercion, he was handing his bank over to Aryan management: 'The banker must experience the worries of his client as his own … in order that the smallest client feels bound to us … it is not the largest clients who create the strength of a bank; the variety of the small clients provides the foundation, the undergrowth, in which the large trees can prosper … a bank does not have blast furnaces; good service by all employees replaces the machines of the factory …'[2]

The second concerned personal integrity and conduct: 'I thought (in 1922) of an academy for good manners, for in Germany everything has to be discovered anew … nature ennobled … this academy would act against corruption, loud-mouthed heroics, unprovoked and frivolous attacks, anti-Semitism, attacks on social class … attacks on our past, on the activities of all dukes and kings who in their time have given of their best …'[3]

The third was his honourable patriotism, made the more poignant by his Jewish heritage. It was for the sake of Germany's name that anti-Semitism must be abhorred: 'He who is left untouched by the wrongs against individual Jews should at least take fright at the harm being inflicted on the German soul …'[4]

The fourth – civic obligation: 'The division between politicians and economic experts is nonsensical. Only if they work together can we expect improvement …'[5]

In truth, there was a fifth – the precious gift of self-mockery that protected him from pomposity and helped him to retain his optimism and personal serenity through-out the 1930s.

Max Warburg was one of the many leading Germans who held with increasing desperation and increasing bitterness post-Versailles to the fateful belief that Wilson's Fourteen Points had offered a binding commitment to 'a just peace'. After the Versailles terms were handed down, he had advised the government firmly against accepting them and resigned from all further negotiations. In December 1919 he had written with bitter realism to Kurt Hahn: *'The whole world is an economic unity, and however repulsive we may be to one another, we must tolerate each other … a world order in both the political and the economic senses is only possible if Germany regains her stability …'* [6]

In February 1918, when the German army had seemed to have the upper hand, he had been expressing more positive, forward-looking thoughts, again in exchange with Hahn. It was necessary to develop the concept of the state in opposition to the concept of the nation. Neighbouring states must be assured of their absolute freedom in internal affairs subject to clear understandings on neighbourly relations, as in society between individuals. An international court must be empowered to resolve disputes. He pressed for an immediate start on these matters with Germany's neighbours and wartime allies. *'… this idea of the settlement of disputes could be immediately worked out between us and our allies and brought into effect. The concept of adjudicators will in any event be placed in front of us at the end of the war by our opponents, and we shall never be able to set ourselves against this idea.'* [7] With notable foresight he was critical of the pressures for the creation of small states based on self-determination and ethnic groups. *'In a large state minorities can come together, achieving their fulfilment in their sense of belonging, … whereas in a small state the balance and a peaceful association of the like-minded is far more difficult … in any event Germany is in the future going to have to take a far more tolerant attitude towards minorities …'* [8]

Max Warburg's voice was raised in influential circles. *'The Reichskanzler has expressed a longing to see me, and I am going to Berlin on Tuesday to present my non-existent pearls of wisdom.'* (May 1921) [9]

In late 1922 he spent four months in the United States, seeking to combat the impressions left by a recent visit of the French leader Clemenceau. *'Be tactless over the Fourteen Points'*, Max von Baden had urged him before he left. Max continued to insist that the economic recovery of Germany was essential for European recovery and prosperity. *'A nation of beggars is more dangerous than one that still has something to lose.'* And yet he maintained his sense of humour: *'The bad thing is that, not only did I always*

say the same things, but I always got the same things to eat. The Americans are in this respect wholly without taste.' [10]

But the pressures of politics in Britain, France and the United States, driven by war-begotten passions, were, in his words, stronger than conscience and reason.

All this was not without personal cost or personal danger. On 24th June 1922 the Jewish Foreign Minister Rathenau was assassinated. Max was warned to withdraw from public life and spent several weeks with a personal bodyguard, then moved to Amsterdam. In explanation he wrote to Hahn: *'in times of excitement (one must) take account of the emotions that happen to exist'.* [11]

Historians are in general not overly sympathetic to the German attempts in the 1920s to mount a moral offensive against the terms of the Versailles Treaty in spite of the trump cards they gave Hitler for his climb to power. For Max Warburg, Prince Max von Baden and Kurt Hahn it was the only honourable course of action.

The Birth of Kurt Hahn's First School Salem

The opposition to Versailles shared by Max Warburg, Kurt Hahn and Max von Baden was a powerful motivation in the opening of the school Salem in the Baden castle and estate in South Germany in 1920. Max Warburg's role was never prominent, but it is unlikely that the school could have survived without his faithful, self-deprecating, loyal support in the background.

Kurt Hahn was no accountant. *'Since all statutes of such foundations are drawn up in rather an idiotic way, I fear that these statutes which require a totally safe investment will prevent me from operating in the inspired manner that would match your frivolity,'* Max wrote to him on 21st November 1921. [12] [●] And on 10th August 1922: *'A budget consists of figures for income and expenditure set against one another from 31st December of one year until 31st December of the following year – the four figures dashed down here in such haste by you are not enough …'* [13] He had his gifted, authoritative hand in all the important financial decisions, and was always ready to enter into impressive detail. From the background he stage-managed fundraising visits to the USA, securing annual donations that came largely from personal friends there and from his two brothers and their families. He did his best to temper Hahn's idealism

[●] The German text makes reference to those investments which by law must be used by guardians on behalf of young persons, wards, entrusted to their care.

with realism: *'In the meantime I beg you, without turning the school into one for plutocrats, to accept new pupils who do not, as a condition of entry, have to be penniless.'* [14] He was teasingly patient with administrative practices that he would not tolerate from banking colleagues: *'I wrote to you on 15th inst. May I ask you, as you are after all an educator, to instruct me on the reasons why my letters are not answered promptly?'* [15]

In truth he admired and was profoundly grateful for Hahn's absolute dedication to German youth without ceding one millimetre in his good-humoured mockery of his frenetic life style. *'I assume that you have an aeroplane permanently in your (Berlin) garden, equipped with a rubber band, so that it can whip you back very quickly to Salem.'* [16] And once, when he felt the urgent need for some political consultation, he sought *'for once a peaceful (foreign word for you?) quarter of an hour to discuss the matter in hand'.* [17]

It was a profoundly human relationship, movingly expressed by Hahn when he was thanking Max already in 1921 for a decisively timely donation for Salem: *'But, happy as we are over every material improvement, I rejoice and am grateful for the blessing with which you endow my life's work. I have hitherto missed this blessing bitterly and, since we have got to know each other more closely, have become accustomed, in all enterprises of pith and moment to which I devote myself, to seek and to receive your fatherly blessing.'* [18] It was not just politics however, or Salem and education. Since 1918 Aby Warburg, his mental health finally undermined and destroyed by the war, had been confined in the renowned Binswanger psychiatric clinic in nearby Constance, his son Max Adolph a fellow patient in another room. Hahn was a faithful, trusted visitor, comforter and rapporteur for the Warburg family in Hamburg, not reticent either in putting forward suggestions for treatment and for doctors that were gratefully received by Max and the family. And then there was the newly-married couple Rudo and Lola.

The 1930s

If Max Warburg remained influential in banking and political circles throughout the 1920s, the financial crash of 1929 and the relentless rise of National Socialism confronted him with new dilemmas whose dangers he was slow to recognise but finally met with great personal courage. He may have been foolish to describe his bank as *'more than a building … it is our fortress',* and he certainly gave a hostage to fortune when, along with Hitler, he signed the document that nominated Schacht as President of the Reichsbank in 1933. But the patriotism of the German Jews

was very deeply felt – to what other country could they now turn? And we must therefore understand why their hard-won sense of German identity made it so difficult for them to recognise the realities of the Third Reich and to accept its dark implications.

One group was able to adjust more easily: the Zionists. Zionism had always drawn its strength from the East. Those Eastern orthodox Jews held little attraction for the assimilated German Jews who had immersed themselves in the 'higher' culture of their fellow-citizens. But Nazism was to drive the Jews of Germany remorselessly towards emigration. This made it easier for Zionists to cooperate with the Nazis whose early intentions were to rid Germany of Jews by expelling them abroad. It was Max Warburg's dilemma that he believed first, that Jews should stand firm in Germany, and secondly, that Zionism and a Jewish national state which displaced Arabs would lead to an unending cycle of conflict.

Ultimately, compelled by events, he made his choices. In 1933 his influence was critical in creating the Reichsvertretung, a central organisation to represent the interests of all Jews in Germany, although he refused the Presidency, leaving this to the saintly Rabbi Leo Baeck. He immediately set in train methods of transferring Jewish funds abroad, sent a personal representative, Wilfrid Israel, to London the same year to negotiate with British Jewry, and remained discreetly but decisively involved in the transfer of funds and fellow-Jews to Palestine, with the knowledge and indeed the cooperation of Nazi officials, right through until the outbreak of war in 1939. In 1936, as the Nazis stepped up their activities after the Berlin Olympic Games, he persuaded his brother Felix in New York to send to Germany an American who might liaise between Jews seeking emigration and Nazi party officials. There followed the extraordinary achievements over two years of David Glick who, courageously confronting the highest party members from the outset, notably Himmler and Heydrich, arranged for Jews to deposit funds in Germany and receive compensation for them from Jewish agencies abroad after emigration. In October 1937 he achieved the release of 120 Jews from Dachau. In response to his work, a German émigré millionaire in Argentina sponsored the entry of 3,000 refugees to Bolivia. There is an unconfirmed suggestion that as many as 90,000 escaped to South America thanks to these efforts. So secret were Glick's endeavours that they were not revealed until written up in the *Harvard Law Bulletin* in 1960, a short while before he died. Max, despite losing positions, influence and money, and recognising after the Kristallnacht of November 1938 that he could no longer live safely in Germany (he was on a visit to the US at the time), maintained his involvement, as is illustrated by the long letter he received in 1943 from Wilfrid Israel, who was bravely endeavouring in Lisbon to save the lives of Jews there, in Spain, and in Poland, Hungary and elsewhere. Wilfrid Israel lost his life almost immediately afterwards in the plane that was shot down by German fighters *en route* from Lisbon to London in the mistaken belief that Churchill was aboard. Max himself died peacefully in the United States in 1946.

Max Warburg is important in the pre-history of the Atlantic College for the close identity of thought and action between him and Kurt Hahn in the First World War, at Versailles and in its aftermath, in the early days of Hahn's first school Salem, and in the intimate family relationship that was established. His son Eric carried this relationship forward as the Atlantic College came over the horizon.

Eric Warburg and the Passing of the Torch

Eric's memoirs *Time and Tides: A Log Book* are a personal document. They were privately printed and individually numbered. When he gave me my copy, he insisted that, if and when I no longer had space for it, I was to return it to the family – under no circumstances was it to be found 'remaindered' on the shelves of a second-hand bookshop.

This, I realised later, and with the help of comment from a distinguished historian who had known him well, was a revealing gesture. Eric was the one son in the family, accompanied through life by sisters of formidable charm, determination, talent and courageous accomplishment. *'Der Herr Sohn'*, as he was known to banking colleagues, had to make his way and his name against the utterly dominating background of his father and uncles. Could he live up to the family reputation? Could he in his generation become their equal? This was a nigh-impossible task, but the challenge determined his life's choices.

As assimilated Jews the Warburgs were distant from the practices of Judaism. Eric was driven nonetheless by a consciousness of family background. Influence, achievement and the exploitation of opportunities were the keynotes. Of course he had a privileged start. But he kept his ears and eyes open and was a keen observer of the current scene. He recalls hearing one of Hitler's early speeches in Munich and Einstein being heckled by students during a university lecture. In his banking apprenticeship in the inter-war years in the United States, he met the McCloy family (John McCloy was to become the American High Commissioner in Germany after the Second World War, when he and his German-born wife Ellen were to assist

Eric Warburg

Kurt Hahn greatly); and both Dulles brothers (John Foster Dulles the US Secretary of State for Foreign Affairs under Eisenhower, Allen Dulles the American link in Switzerland with the German resistance from 1942 onwards, later Head of the CIA).

In the first winter of the war Eric was consulted in New York by his friend Adam von Trott, later executed by the Nazis for his leading role in the 1944 assassination plot against Hitler. Eric, joining the US army after Pearl Harbour, was posted to intelligence and found himself one day called to the Pentagon, where he became involved in a heated discussion on the future zones of occupation after the expected German defeat. The principal issue was the line to be drawn between the Western and the Soviet zones, and Eric claims indirect credit for the cancellation of plans to allow the Soviets to advance as far as the river Elbe. It is curiously typical of his opportunistic life that he met his American friend Shepherd Stone on the beaches of Normandy on the day after the Allied invasion – Shepherd Stone was later to be the key figure in the Ford Foundation when it made its critically important grant to the Atlantic College in 1963. After the war's end, it was Eric with others who interrogated leading Nazi leaders including Goering and several of the generals – von Rundstedt, von Falkenhausen and Franz Halder among them. One close friend of the 1920s and 30s, Albrecht Graf Bernstorff, had like von Trott been executed by the Nazis. Another, Fabian von Schlabrendorff, had by a wonder escaped execution and was to write the first personal account of the German Resistance. Kurt Hahn secured an early copy of the manuscript and insisted on its immediate translation into English and publication.

It was Eric who, in the chaotic aftermath of the surrender in May 1945, dispatched a driver to the concentration camp in Theresienstadt in Czechoslovakia, where his father's friend and ally Rabbi Leo Baeck had miraculously survived. A second visit, also arranged by Eric, led to the evacuation to Bavaria of the last 600 survivors who had not yet found refuge elsewhere. It was Eric who, manipulating official procedures, enabled Kurt Hahn to enter the French zone of occupation a few weeks after the war's end to revisit Salem and to set in motion the necessary steps for the re-opening of the school, the first of which, again with Eric's participation and rapidly achieved, was the evacuation of some 600 French troops from the school premises. In Hamburg, Eric found the family home Kösterberg in a shambles, but he nonetheless organised almost immediate accommodation there for orphans of concentration camp victims, numbering from 100 to 150 at a time. This programme continued until 1949, when the estate was turned over in part to long-term charitable purposes. The Swedish Elsa Branstrom, called The Angel of Siberia for her work in Siberia in 1914–1918 for prisoners of war, had spent her last days at Kösterberg before fleeing Hitler's Germany for America in 1939. A home dedicated to her memory was opened on the Kösterberg estate in 1950 for social workers, refugees and nurses under training. Another fulfilled family obligation was his successful revival of his Uncle Fritz' Jewish Hospital.

At the political level, Eric Warburg was able to exercise personal influence when his old acquaintance John McCloy was appointed US High Commissioner in occupied Germany in 1949. Eric intervened directly with McCloy in favour of the controversial revocation of many capital punishment sentences on certain German generals, the so-called Landsberg judgements, for which Kurt Hahn had also campaigned in the cause of combating *'victors' justice'*. He also opposed the wholesale dismantling of German heavy industry as foreshadowed under the Morgenthau Plan. He was less successful in seeking the renewal of the award of Rhodes Scholarships to Germans, receiving nonetheless a courteous response: *'I do not know the position of German Rhodes Scholarships at present but at your suggestion I will enquire into the matter. I agree that the time would appear to have come for them to be re-instituted. With good wishes! Sir William Morgan, KCB, DSO, MC, British Joint Services Commission, Office of the Combined Chiefs of Staff, Washington. 1 November 1948.'*

Eric Warburg is especially remembered in Germany for his decision in 1956 to leave the United States and to re-settle in Hamburg, rejoining the family bank, a decision called by Kurt Hahn *'truly a proof of great-hearted confidence'*. [19] In doing so, he overrode the fears and distress of his Austrian wife Dorothea, whose memories of the Nazis had made her fearful of ever returning to German or Austrian soil. But the inner call to 'become the father' once more determined Eric's life. Delicate but tenacious negotiations in which Kurt Hahn and Siegmund Warburg played notable parts led eventually to the restoration of the Warburg name to the bank in 1970.

Eric Warburg's Unrecognised Contributions

There are two threads in Eric's life that emerge with clarity: his determination to respect the moral legacy entrusted him by his father's memory, and his rapt support for the enterprises of his father's colleague and friend, now his relative by marriage, Kurt Hahn. This latter relationship has remained somewhat buried in files of spasmodic but at times intensive personal correspondence. Already in 1924 Kurt was seeking his assistance over fundraising for Salem in the US. He had another more personal request in the same year. A group of early Nazi thugs had planned to assault and probably murder him. The plot had been betrayed by a participant, a young mechanic called Schuholz, who was committed to German nationalism and anti-Semitism but not to violence. The resulting court case publicity had placed him too in danger. *'Could Eric find him employment in the US?'* asked Kurt Hahn. He could and did.

As Kurt Hahn sought in the 1940s and early 1950s to revive and restore not only Salem but also other residential schools in Germany, and to carry the success of his British Outward Bound Movement into the occupied zones, he turned to Eric for help in the United States. When the banker Tom McKittrick learned in 1949 of the imminent departure of Shepherd Stone to join McCloy in Germany *'to take charge of education, cultural relations, press, radio and other related matters'*, he and Eric got hold of him and *'I think, sold him on your (Hahn's) proposals …'* Intensive campaigning in support of Hahn's ventures in both Britain and Germany had led in 1948 to the setting up of the

American-British Foundation for European Education, later to become The Atlantic Trust for the Education of the Free. Trustees included Tom McKittrick (Senior Vice-President of Chase National Bank), Allen Dulles (Ex-President of Johns Hopkins University, soon to become Director of the CIA), Abraham Flexner (Director Emeritus of the Institute of Advanced Study at Princeton), Congressman Christian Herter (soon to become Governor of Massachusetts, later Secretary of State for Foreign Affairs), Henry Pitney Van Dusen (President of the Union Theological Seminary), and of course Eric himself. Their aims were scholarships for Salem and fellow German boarding schools, three German Outward Bound Schools (two were successfully opened, a third in Berlin *'within sight of the sector border with the Soviet zone'*, was not), and a German Department at Gordonstoun for 30 German boys a year. By 1954 the restoration of the old sail training vessels *Pamir* and *Passat* had joined the programme, again with success. But the most significant initiative taken by Eric was to suggest, already in 1955, that the 'NATO Schools Project' should be brought to the attention of the Ford Foundation.

On 9th December 1955, Eric wrote to Kurt Hahn, alerting him with three days' confidential notice that the Ford Foundation was about to announce new grants totaling $500 million with a stronger emphasis than hitherto on education, albeit solely in the United States. Eric persisted. In August 1957 he learned that the Foundation was making informal enquiries about these NATO schools with the authorities at the well-known Andover prep school. These enquiries no doubt arose from his lunch that spring with Shepherd Stone, who was now working in the Foundation. In early 1958 he learned at a casual airport meeting with Shepherd Stone that the rules of the Foundation were likely to be changed within the coming 12–18 months to open up the possibility of grants at the secondary level. It was not long before the Headmaster Designate for the Atlantic College, Desmond Hoare, entered the scene with his visit soon after to the US. Eric's letter of 23rd December 1959 to Shepherd Stone indicates the turning point: *'… I fully realize that it is a very open question whether the Ford Foundation will underwrite this project. But your personal feeling that this is the moment to strike boldly in the field of international education is such a very important factor and may tip the scales in favour of victory instead of defeat'*. His concluding contribution was to marry together in April 1962, with the benefit of much personal awareness of the personalities involved, the lines of argument submitted separately by Kurt Hahn and Desmond Hoare in a final paper that went forward to the Foundation Board. The outcome was the life-saving grant of $140,000 to the College in

1963, the first-ever Foundation grant to secondary education outside the United States. And it cannot have been entirely coincidental that the Foundation was to make a similar life-saving grant of $300,000 to the International Baccalaureate in 1966.

Meanwhile, Eric Warburg had become private banker to the family of Antonin Besse. In June 1959 he first raised with Besse, in a long and skilful letter, the prospect of a donation, building carefully on the warm relationship of personality and ideas that already existed between the Besse family and Kurt Hahn. By February 1960, within weeks, indeed almost days, of the discovery of St. Donat's Castle and its availability for sale at the scarcely credible price of £65,000, he had secured from Antonin Besse a pledge, on conditions, of £60,000.

One may wonder a little at this distance in time at the access and influence that Eric clearly enjoyed in senior American circles. The historian whose assessment of Eric I referred to earlier, Jonathan Steinberg, attributes it to his charm and the *'European polish'* of his manners of the kind that Americans typically find attractive. Eric also offers the characteristic, almost perfect example of the discreet, backstage nature of fundraising success in the years following the Second World War, his achievements rooted in personal contacts and a strong, determined sense of direction and purpose. The modern professional fundraiser, understandably obsessed with networking, has, one might suggest, something to learn from him of the greater value of dialogue and personal consultation over colourful documentation. His friendship with the German banker Hermann Abs added some critical leverage to the Atlantic College's success in securing its first governmental grant in 1964 from the German Federal Republic. In loosely related efforts to strengthen Anglo-German cooperation and understanding, he joined Kurt Hahn in renewed efforts to revive the former Rhodes Scholarships for German graduates at Oxford and Cambridge, to be told in 1961 that the Trust's priorities, despite the distinguished record of former German scholars in the Resistance movement, were now Commonwealth students (the acceptance once again of German students, two a year, was to be announced by the Trust in March 1969); and he tried too with some despair to keep alive the King Edward Foundation of which his father had been a founding member and first Treasurer back in 1912. Nor was Salem forgotten. His enthusiasm for a United World College in Germany was however not rewarded by success.

The correspondence leaves no doubt that Eric's spiritual mentor was Kurt Hahn, or that Kurt saw himself as the mentor, for Kurt the schoolmaster was always ready to give friendly tutorials. *'If you had become a burglar, you would have entered the records as one of the finest opportunistic thieves in the history of crime. As a professional burglar you would not have made your way. The reason is that the impressions of the moment make such an impact on you that patient, painstaking attention to detail does not play its proper role'*, he writes on one occasion. [20] But the pupil never lacked energy or persistence. Thus we find Eric's secretary addressing a desperate note to Kurt's secretary in 1959 when trying to complete some unclearly defined business on Hahn's behalf: *'Herr Warburg is firing questions all through me – how, why, what for …'* [21]

Germany and Hamburg had good reason to be grateful to Eric Warburg. Celebrating his father's centenary with a gathering of all the bank's employees on 5th June 1967, Eric said of him: *'if he had been younger, he would have found his way back here after the war – among us all – as a pioneer of the rebuilding …'* [22] Eric had made his father's beliefs fully his own. His return to his birthplace explicitly, courageously to overcome the legacies of Hitler and the National Socialists, generated widespread admiration and gratitude. The Federal Chancellor Helmut Schmidt became one of his great friends and admirers. In a final rather characteristic twist, he became the first recipient of the prize sponsored by the 'Atlantik Brücke' Foundation and already named after him. *'Eric Warburg is in his person the bridge across the Atlantic'*, [23] said the President of the Republic, Richard Weizsäcker, as he presented the prize to a now sick and bedridden Eric in January 1988.

It is worth remembering that it was precisely this bridge that made possible the creation of the Atlantic College.

Unforgettable Lola

If Eric was in the background, his sister Lola was in the foreground – always! To start with, however, she had to fight her way there.

'Dumme Lola' – stupid Lola. This was her mother's phrase for her, and Lola was kept at home whilst her brother and two sisters attended school and secured their Abitur. But none of them were allowed to use the front door, dine with their parents until they were 16, or discuss the food (a fine was levied if they did), and they were compelled to record every cent they spent in a notebook for presentation to their father on Sunday morning for approval.

All this, and early poor health, led Lola to develop a remarkable strength of character. Nor was she backward in exploiting that most unfair feminine advantage – great physical beauty. Almost all her later close friendships were with men – never did she conceal her enjoyment

Lola with Benita and Oscar

of flirting, nor deny its influence; and she was quick to comment that other women in the immediate or even the more distant family were cautious in their welcome and her presence. But the men who attracted her were those who engaged her mind and her longing for causes in which to immerse and to prove herself – compensation for her early frustrations – and she repaid their attentions with passionate loyalty.

Soon after the First World War and after a spell as a British prisoner-of-war, Rudo Hahn, Kurt's younger brother, joined the Warburg bank for training. In 1921 he married Lola, the marriage held at home because there was rioting on the streets following the assassination of the Catholic finance minister Matthias Erzberger. In 1927 she met Chaim Weizmann and, overwhelmed by his personality and charm (he was a noted lady-killer) entered the Zionist debate. This intense personal relationship was to cause the Warburg family much anxiety. Years later, on Weizmann's death in 1952, Kurt recognised the strength of the relationship in his handwritten letter to her: *'Israel sorrows for a great man. Few people know how tender and easily wounded Chaim was. I have experienced how he would be near despair and how he drew strength from your loving faith which never faltered in him and in the cause. Without you he would not have rallied again and again till the miracle of victory was won …'*

Lola's Zionism may have been less powerful (and possibly less principled, at least at the outset) than that of her younger sister Gisela, but it contributed to some conflict in the family. Weizmann's dismissive comment on the Warburgs is well-known and often quoted: *'… The usual type of Kaiser-Juden, like Albert Ballin or Max Warburg, more German than the Germans, obsequious, super-patriotic,*

Lola Hahn: '… my beautiful horse … reacted to each of my movements … I, tall and slim, dressed in white …'

eagerly anticipating the wishes and plans of the masters of Germany …' But her sympathies were now clearly focused on the Zionist cause. She made her first visit to Palestine, where she helped to set up Ben Shemen, the first children's village there, the start of her life-long involvement with Youth Aliyah, and she attended the important Zionist conference in Zurich in 1929. Albert Einstein's guest book at his home in the United States contains entries on the same page by Lola and Chaim Weizmann dated 13th September 1932. But in the midst of all these developments there was a curious episode in Egypt.

Spending several months near Aswan, she was in the habit of riding out into the desert in the cool early morning hours. Her written account reveals her full consciousness of her own beauty and romantic nature: '… *my beautiful, full-bred Arab horse … reacted to each of my movements … I, tall and slim, dressed in white …*' She discovered a village inhabited by '*tall, slim and regal*' Berbers and a young cripple lying helpless under a Tamarisk tree. She persuaded a doctor staying in the same hotel to visit this man. The doctor, discovering the cripple seemingly to be under hypnosis, broke all his limbs, arms and legs, and straightened them, '*leaving my friend lying under the Tamarisk tree, his face serene and peaceful*'. Confusing events followed – an army delegation visited the village ('*the colonel of that command had asked me to give him English lessons because he felt attracted to me. I went to the army base quite often to give him lessons. He also had a band which sometimes played Beethoven for me …*'). The local consul (who was he?) initiated a court case because of unrest in the village. '*The wonder happened when we left Aswan: there stood on the platform ten elders of the village, together with the chief. He made a speech: "I speak for all the villagers. We have only one wish – that you should come back to the village at the*

hour of death. We can only go to Allah with straight limbs and that is what you have done for our friend. He was made whole again by you …"'

This Aswan adventure remained a key memory for the rest of her life. Of course it illustrates her self-awareness, her love of the romantic, her individuality, her courage, her growing need to feel important in the lives of others. It must also have encouraged in her a sense of invulnerability to danger. She was now to need all these qualities.

The 1930s

In 1933 her 10-year-old son Oscar caught infantile paralysis. The shock brought her back with dramatic abruptness from her infatuation with Chaim Weizmann to family concerns. There are moving accounts of her relentless, single-minded care for him and of the rejoicing when the entire family, against medical advice, spent the following Christmas in their small forest hut in bitter cold and snow, even the toilet outside, but with Oscar, wrapped in a fur-lined bag and with hot water bottles, once again installed in the quiet look-out with his father, on the watch for wild boar.

And there were the political concerns.

'*In Germany the fires were being lit that would later burn the whole world …*'

In Lola's approach to Zionism '*the discovery of our Jewish roots and identity through our encounter with the Ostjuden in Berlin's East End was the strongest link in this relationship. It gave us the opportunity for social and educational work*' [●] Now, in 1933, the year of Oscar's illness, her father

[●] Quotes from George Clare's *Last Waltz in Vienna* are again relevant: '… *I was already second-generation Viennese, and Viennese-born Jews felt resentment towards the less assimilated Jews from the East. We were, or thought we were, quite different from that bearded caftaned lot …*' and '*perhaps we … subconsciously envied those strange alien creatures from the East for they possessed something that we, the coffee-house elegants steeped in German culture, had lost: a strong religious conviction with its belief in a divinely ordained future. This enabled them to bear lowly social status and prejudice with equanimity, while we trembled at the slightest sign of discrimination …*'

Joseph Roth has left us, in his essay *Juden auf Wanderschaft*, an evocative memorial to these Eastern Jews, the Ostjuden, at this time – their immigration into Europe's major cities Berlin, Vienna and Paris, and to the USA and Soviet Russia (albeit culminating in optimistically trustful assumptions about their status and prospects there after the Bolshevik revolution): '*Die Ostjuden haben nirgends eine Heimat, aber Gräbe auf jedem Friedhof – the Eastern Jews are without a homeland but have graves in every cemetery.*'

with others set up the Reichsvertretung, the umbrella organisation for all Jewish statutory organisations in Germany, and soon the only body with which the Nazi authorities would negotiate. She became one of the leading members. She worked closely with Rabbi Leo Baeck. Another friend and ally for her as for her father was Wilfrid Israel, like her of a wealthy Berlin family, who increasingly gave his time, his money and finally his life in the service of Jewish victims of the Nazi persecution. She became the bridge between the Zionists and the Reichsvertretung; she argued the Zionist case with leading German Jews who were not ready to accept Zionism, and the Jewish case with non-Jewish Germans. The overriding aim was to enable Jews to leave Germany, with the absolute priority given to children.

It was not without a price. A mutual friend wrote to Kurt, now in Scotland, in Germanic English in October 1935: *'the day before yesterday I saw both your sister-in-law and your brother, and was frightened by their state of mind. Especially L – due to her overwork and daily mental suffering – was dangerously exhausted. I cannot imagine she will be able to stand any longer. She is rather clear about things coming but too weak and discouraged for decision.'*

It had all become increasingly dangerous. In early 1938 a close colleague was summoned by Adolf Eichmann with accusations of making propaganda abroad against Germany. Lola did not hesitate to call a conference of leading Zionists at her home in Wannsee (how ironical that Eichmann should have called his own far more fateful Wannsee conference four years later to decide on the final elimination of the Jewish race!) to plan the next steps. Another guest in her home was Adam von Trott, her brother's friend and later conspirator against Hitler.

Within the family Lola had been showing the same outspoken courage. Many years later she recalled: *'Two years after I married my husband I realised that Kurt became a close brother … our family became the testing ground whenever he gave birth to a new idea or foundation …'* The giving of courage was from the beginning a matter of reciprocity between them. In 1925 she had fallen seriously ill in Switzerland. One surgeon refused to operate – *'it would be a matter of life and death'*. The second said: *'if you want to survive, I must operate immediately'*. She was given a night nurse (*'more a nightmare than a night nurse'*) who read to her from the Bible, *'always choosing passages that prepared me for death'*. But it was Kurt who had found the second surgeon; Kurt who gave her the courage to undergo the operation. *'Kurt has enough imagination to sense fear in another person but also the rare gift to develop courage in a creature. It was he, and he alone, who gave me the strength when I had to face the operation in Davos. His belief put victory into my soul …'* Ulcers, kidney stones, sinusitis – were all maladies that accompanied her throughout her adult life. They gave her unusual strength. When Kurt's brother was killed in January 1933 in a skiing accident, Lola was commissioned to bring the news to Rudo, who was lying ill in bed. When Kurt was arrested by the Nazis three months later, it was again Lola who was sent to break the news to Kurt's mother. When she was warned by a loyal servant that she must expect the Nazis to search her Berlin home that afternoon, she sent everyone away bar this one man whom she instructed to hide all Kurt's compromising papers in the bee hives, where they remained undiscovered.

The events in National Socialist Germany finally exacted their toll. By now, Rudo, that *'passionate creature and force of nature …'* had become a significant businessman. In June 1936, Robin Barrington Ward, the Deputy Editor of *The Times* and a contemporary and friend of Kurt Hahn from Oxford days, was in Berlin. After a meeting with Hitler's Deputy Rudolf Hess, he went to lunch with Rudo at his Wannsee home. Here is his account:

'Hahn had been taken from his office by the Gestapo, without charge or warning, and kept a night in a detention cell. Wife not allowed to be informed. She did not know where he was. Three Gestapo men visited her and ransacked his books and papers, threatening her at the time.

In the prison Rudo was made to undress and lie on a dirty bed. At intervals during the night a warden flashed a torch in his eyes and called him a Schweinehund, etc. About 11 a.m. he was let go.

Rudo's wife's morale is quite unbroken, through the nerve strain is terrible … she could leave but she stays to help her compatriots … Hundreds of Jews in the arts and the professions have lost everything. The plan is to keep one of their houses going there and to provide a good midday meal and a meeting place to keep body and soul together. Otherwise men of education would sink, isolated and destitute, into sheer despair and annihilation …'

We must react to this account with caution. It is taken verbatim from his diary, but when it was shown to Lola in 1968 by Donald McLachlan, Barrington Ward's biographer, who had quoted it, Lola responded that *'in its present form, it is rather incorrect.'* Ronald Chernow reports, without citing his source, that after Kurt's earlier arrest in 1933 she had consulted a Berlin analyst who had treated Rudolf Hess in the hope of discovering ways of securing his release. Lola, many years later, gave a tape-recorded account of how she went to Hess' home to plead the cause of Salem. In her account she described the high fence, the walls, the security guards – Hitler was due that night. What is certain is that Hess took a protective interest in Salem and also that he was directly helpful over enabling a half-Jewish Salem boy to take up a university place – as it happens, a nephew of Kurt. Lola was also summoned later to Gestapo headquarters for interrogation following an anti-Nazi speech given in Sweden by Ingrid, the daughter of Fritz Warburg.

But in 1938 the inevitable finally took place. Rudo was now the prosperous, successful part-owner, with the Warburg Bank, of the Lubeck Blast Furnace Company. The notorious industrialist Friedrich Flick, supported by Goering, bought the Hahn and Warburg shares at a 50% discount, payment made in foreign currency, thus enabling Rudo and Lola to move to Britain. At the Nuremberg trials, Rudo made it clear in the witness stand that threats of arrest and dispatch to a concentration camp had played their part in the deal. It can give no satisfaction to anyone that Flick was one of those whose seven-year prison sentence was reduced by John McCloy, and that he was publicly thanked and congratulated by Adenauer on his 75th birthday, in the name of the Federal Republic, for his life's work.

Emigration to England and the *Kindertransport*

On 1st September 1938, after *'watering all the flowers in my garden with all my tears',* Lola and her family became the last of the Warburgs to go. The Flick lawyer was on the same plane – on business. Arriving in England, Rudo was told by the immigration officer: *'Your wife's heart isn't too good. It will not be long before she is a public liability.'* She was to outlive Rudo, her son Oscar and all her siblings with the one exception of her sister Anita who died in the United States at the age of 100. Once in Britain, she immediately joined the Committee of the Refugee Children's Movement and was a member of the delegation that went to the Home Office to plead for special provision for juvenile refugees from Germany after the Kristallnacht on 9th November. This was the launch of the *Kindertransport*. As a direct result, the United Kingdom took in nearly 10,000 Jewish children from Nazi Germany and from the occupied territories of Austria, Czechoslovakia, Poland and the Free City of Danzig. The children were placed in British foster homes, hostels, and farms, the Jewish community providing financial guarantees. *'I was a recent witness of the suffering … my relief at pouring out my heart … at last I felt I could be useful …'* Gerard Friedenfeld describes in *The Jewish Chronicle* of March 2010 arriving at Liverpool Street Station in London from Nazi-occupied Prague at the age of 14 with 124 other Jewish children who had become instant orphans and were now heading into the unknown, among strangers. *'As I stepped off the train, walking laboriously with the aid of two canes, I spotted the first truly beautiful and elegant woman I saw in my then short life. … The beautiful lady introduced herself as Lola Hahn-Warburg.'*

The end of the Second World War brought renewed needs as the crimes of the concentration camps were revealed, but first Lola was to confront Kurt over his decision, so difficult in its timing for her, to enter the Anglican Church. It was a moment of deep emotional stress, even imbalance, in his life, and in the event he sidestepped open discussion by simply leaving a note for her in which he reported his baptism by Bishop Bell of Chichester. Her Jewish obligations continued. The historian Martin Gilbert, and many others, have told the story of the 1,000 concentration camp children survivors who were authorised by the government to enter Britain in 1946. 732 arrived, only 105 of them girls because girls had been especially earmarked for the gas chambers. A committee of three, one of them Lola, made all the arrangements. It was not just a matter of physical recovery. These children *'had been in contact with every kind of vice and wickedness that the human mind can conceive … for them, during the whole of their childhood, honesty was the very worst policy; it led immediately to destruction. How then can they be expected to learn in a short while to reverse the maxim taught them by bitter experience?'* [●]

Let two accounts illustrate Lola's special contribution in creating conditions in which faith in humanity might be restored.

'A boy of 18 came to see me. Nobody else … wanted him in the building … he was aggressive and undisciplined … when he was behind my chair he jumped up suddenly, took out a knife and cut the telephone wire. Then he opened the window and started climbing out on the ledge … I said to him "I am very unwell. I have bad kidney trouble. It is so cold here with the window open. Will you please come back into the office" … we talked for a long time … eventually I persuaded him to go with me to the hospital … he let me drive him in my car and gave no further trouble.'

Lola used regularly to visit a girl in a mental home. Each time she brought a bunch of flowers which the girl took and held close for an hour or more but without speaking a single word. Years later the girl, now a young woman, came to see Lola. Her first words were: *'I shall never forget your visits.'*

[●] Leonard G. Montefiore, one of the three members of the committee

Lola and Kurt

In 1945, Gordonstoun School was able to return to Scotland from its Welsh war-time exile. Rudo and Lola had bought a house, Burnside, just outside the grounds. If for Lola the attractions were Kurt and his continuing schemes and projects, for Rudo they were the Scottish salmon rivers. Their son Oscar had meanwhile become an almost legendary Hahnian and Gordonstoun personality. First, there was his physical courage. With one leg amputated, the other paralysed, he had forced himself to engage in physical pursuits. As a university student at Oxford he had arranged and won a wheelchair race from Oxford to London. He became as passionate a sailor as his father was an angler and hunter and went on to own and skipper two yachts. As a schoolboy at Gordonstoun before the war he had learned to imitate his uncle Kurt to the extent that, over the telephone, no teacher could be sure who was at the other end of the line, and Oscar exploited his uncle's unpredictable working habits by mischievously summoning masters, on occasion several at a time and at most uncomfortable hours, to the Head's study, where they found either an empty room or a rather surprised occupant. He is even rumoured to have dismissed one unpopular teacher over the telephone. '*Being with Oscar'*, wrote his friend the journalist Peregrine Worsthorne, '*is to be privileged to watch the spectacle of nature's arbitrary malice being thwarted by human fortitude.'*

Gordonstoun had had barely six years of existence before being forced to move to mid-Wales. Now it had to start all over again. Peregrine Worsthorne remembers Burnside: '*The setting, overlooking the Moray Firth, was superb*

Lola Hahn with the former British Prime Minister Ramsey MacDonald whose letter in 1933 to the Nazi government sought Kurt Hahn's release from prison. Ramsay MacDonald, here visiting Gordonstoun's activities, was from nearby Lossiemouth. On his death Lord Allen of Hurtwood wrote: 'He has died at sea – what more fitting place to witness the death of a great man whose early boyhood was spent in a humble cottage among the fisher folk of Lossiemouth? He was to become one of the greatest figures of our time, and yet he never lost his love for that sea-coast where he was born …'

and the hostess took after the setting.' He attributes much of Gordonstoun's '*astonishing success'* to her '*persuasive advocacy and social gifts'.* The surviving correspondence between her and Kurt, his almost always in his distinctive handwriting (handwritten letters from him are none too frequent), hers few and far between and generally type-written because her hands shook too much for her to be able to write, illustrate an extraordinary intimacy of outlook and mutual trust. One does not need to develop suspicious thoughts – Rudo was an equally intimate member of this remarkable trio – and it was in any event Rudo's renewed business success in the metal industry in Birmingham that made much of it possible. For there is no doubt that Kurt benefited from the old Jewish custom that brothers and sons engaged in spiritual matters had a claim on the income of other members of the family. Kurt had been well-to-do in his youth, but he had earned little money as the Headmaster of a school that was for years on the threshold of financial disaster. Reputed by 1950 to be the man with the biggest telephone bill in Scotland, for ever on the move between Morayshire, London, Germany and the United States, surely one of the most regular patrons of Brown's Hotel in Dover Street in London, his disregard for the boring trivialities of making ends meet was accepted for years by the patient, supportive, loyal Lola and Rudo. After all, had Max Warburg done less for his brother Aby?

The autumn of 1952 brought another crisis. Kurt Hahn's pace of work, especially since the end of the war, had

The writer Peregrine Worsthorne attributes much of Gordonstoun's 'astonishing success' to Lola's 'persuasive advocacy and social gifts'

Oscar Hahn shows his schoolmate, the Duke of Edinburgh, over his place of work at BKL Alloys, Birmingham

been quite phenomenal. Every venture he was engaged in required money. His susceptibility to heat, his inability to go out into bright daylight, his utter dependence on the impact of his personality rather than rational delegation in running Gordonstoun School, his increasingly frenetic absences and even more frenetic action on return, and his collapse in the heat of New York in the late autumn, led to a breakdown. He was by now 68 years old. The school, bitterly divided within itself at every level, decided that he must go and failed even to accept the face-saving formula he himself suggested that would have allowed him to remain in post until the end of the school year. It was Lola who, to her never-ending regret, signed the papers that committed him for a period to a mental home in Northampton for treatment. His handwritten notes on scraps of paper pleading for release make deeply sad reading, but he understood nonetheless that she had acted for him. By February of 1953 he was able to write to her: '*…a blessing went forth from your loving care and forethought. And your companionship was a breath of health for me.*' It was now a double blessing that Burnside existed. It was his only home in Scotland. Visits to the school and meetings with former colleagues brought almost only pain, but *'you have given me a great feeling of home in Burnside* (Kurt to Lola on 29th September 1954). *I owe it to you that I could co-exist with Gordonstoun and that a wound ever breaking out was closed again and again.'* And during his Headship she had been his official hostess, guests including the Duke of Edinburgh, Richard von Weizsäcker the future President of Germany, and of course Anton and Hilda Besse, before whose visit he had implored her to be *'on her best behaviour'*.

Looking back, it is quite clear that Kurt's enforced abandonment of the daily worries of Gordonstoun's Headship

was the best that could have happened. After a brief period of recovery, physical and mental, he was liberated to set out on the consolidation and expansion of the Outward Bound Movement, the development of his Moray Badge Scheme into what became the Duke of Edinburgh's Award, the sadly short-lived Trevelyan Scholarships for Oxford and Cambridge, the Atlantic College and the Medical Commission on Accident Prevention. In all these ventures the support of Rudo and Lola remained as important as it had been in the re-establishment of Gordonstoun after the war. Indeed, without them in the background, it must be doubted whether any of these things could have come to pass. It was no small debt.

The Final Years

On two occasions Kurt was hit by a passing car. He recovered well from the first accident in December 1950, although he was taken unconscious to a London hospital calling, it was said, for Lola as he came to. The second accident, in 1968 on the road outside Burnside, led to more serious ill-health and the recurrence of earlier symptoms of unmistakable manic depression. He spent many weeks in her flat in London, isolating himself in his room, refusing visitors with the single and very occasional exception of Lancelot Fleming and, on one occasion only, Michael Schweitzer. Lancelot Fleming had been a long-standing ally when Bishop first of Portsmouth and then of Norwich, later Dean of Windsor. Kurt had lost all confidence in himself and in his life's work. There came a period of recovery. He returned to his old home Hermannsberg, near Salem in South Germany. Lola telephoned him daily and visited often. *'When my brother-in-law, Kurt Hahn, folded up his life and had no more strength, I flew to him in South Germany*

Lola in later years

many, many times. Words did not come easily to him – one morning, he came into my room, sat on my bed and said, 'the difference between you and me is you always have faith and hope, I wish I had the same'.

Lola had by now been a widow for a number of years, but Kurt's death in December 1974 was followed by an even crueller, more intimate, truly devastating blow, the sudden death from a heart attack of her beloved son Oscar. The only consolation was that he had been in the cockpit of his boat, living life as always to the full. Despite all his physical infirmities, he had become Managing Director of the steel firm BKL Alloys Ltd., a Council Member of the Birmingham Chamber of Commerce, a member of the Council of Birmingham University, a Director of the Birmingham Repertory Company and a governor of the Atlantic College. It was one of Hahn's firmest beliefs that 'the handicapped often develop a remarkable power to overcome through the very challenge they have accepted in their daily lives: the challenge of their disability'. He surely drew this lesson from his nephew.

Burnside and the family home Lexten House in Banbury were now sold, and Lola had for some time been living in 'my golden cage', her flat in Eaton Square in London. With her old imperious, irresistible charm she dictated letters, telephoned, summoned visitors, worried actively about the pensions of the early members of staff at Gordonstoun for whom little provision had been made, followed the fluctuating fortunes and legal battles that were taking place over the future of Kurt's first school in Salem, questioned the Principal of Atlantic College relentlessly about events there, intervened (some would say interfered) unhesitatingly in

matters concerning the membership and leadership of the College's Governing Body. 'I hope you will realise that I am full of conspiracy.' 'Keeping Kurt's spirit alive is killing me', she would say. When Arthur Rubinstein revealed in his memoirs that as a boy he had been a member of the reading group in Berlin that was led by Kurt Hahn, she got him to give recitals for Atlantic College in London's Albert Hall and at St. Donat's. She summoned up the energy to protest vigorously against the suggestion, rapidly abandoned, that Kurt Waldheim should be asked to take the Presidency of the United World Colleges. When she learned that the Roman Catholic bishop in Cardiff had forbidden the Catholic students to attend mass in St. Donat's Church, she went to a service led by Cardinal Hume in London. Afterwards there was a reception for the Cardinal. Lola, by that time, was in good form. 'You won't get any whisky here', she told her friend Norbert Magnus, who was managing her wheelchair, 'but I must talk to the Cardinal.' Norbert felt shy about asking him to come to her wheelchair but she insisted, and he came. 'You don't know me, my name is Lola Hahn. I have written a letter to you, but I haven't had an answer yet.' Cardinal Hume knelt down next to her wheelchair, asking what she had written to him. On the way home, she drily remarked: 'as far as I know, this is the first time in history that a cardinal has knelt in front of a Jewish woman'. She had asked the Cardinal to intervene in Cardiff. The intervention was, of course, successful. And her friendship with her Oxfordshire neighbour George Schuster, almost a last flirtation, he in his late nineties, the financial saviour of the Atlantic College in the 1960s, gave them both the chance of reliving memories of the man they both so much admired, Kurt Hahn.

For a long time she had organised every second year an art auction in support of Youth Aliyah, ruthlessly returning to donors any items that she thought were not up to the mark. 'I am always amazed that people still talk to me because my so-called friendship certainly makes them poor …' But Israel gave her sleepless nights. She corresponded regularly with her friend Teddy Kollek, the liberal mayor of Jerusalem. One of her Jewish friends, commenting that she was never a mere observer of the Israeli scene, especially in the conflict with the Arabs, wondered whether she had missed the experience of real life by not becoming a full Israeli; but Lola herself was too aware of the dreams dreamt by Chaim Weizmann, Achad Ha'am, Shmarya Levin, Judah Magnus, Robert Weltsch and others – 'The outlook of Chaim Weizmann was for deep understanding between Arabs and Jews – these great personalities visualised Israel differently. I am of the opinion that due to the persecution of

Jews, many, many went to Israel because no other country would take them: they were not true Zionists.'

'I found myself, being the only so-called Hahn, carrying all the memories … my health is nothing to boast about. I have too much time to follow events and the whole world makes me sad, especially all the murder and suffering … I feel definitely that I have stayed long enough in this world. I cannot add anything more and am only a worry to family and friends … I have the feeling that I am travelling alone to the end of the road …'

These remarks, made at different times in her last years, suggest unhappiness as well as loneliness, but they do not reflect her courage and her consciousness of duty and obligation. Chernow called her *'Mona Lisa with a field marshal's soul'*. In a revealing misuse of English idiom, she had once declared, *'looking back on my life, I must be grateful that I had my <u>hand</u> in so many pies'*. *'We must drink the dream in.'* Once, a serious setback *'took the wings out of my flight'*. For all her love and admiration, she knew where she was with Kurt. Referring to an earlier supporter and ally, *'he ignored him as he did many people who had been instrumental to him, like a squeezed-out lemon'*. And on the money: *'I cannot help but feel that Kurt was not so naïve about money; there was shrewdness, and he certainly took with a smile advantage of Rudo and myself. It was all very well to say he was modest about himself, with it all the best shirts and suits, pullovers and silk dressing gowns were just good enough. Most of the things were just given away or left in the sleeper. But I did not begrudge him any of this …'* Her constant question was: *'Do you burn for the cause?'* Nothing less would do. Her optimistic view of human nature was shared with a deep concern for the world's future, and she accepted with courage and humour all the problems – no, not problems, challenges – that came her way. Her father had after all written to her from the Versailles Conference when she was just 18: *'the people on either side of the fence are by no means all that edifying. But, then, we are also given our eyes to overlook certain things, our ears not to hear everything. But the mouth – to eat whatever is served …'* For others, her friends, her allies, her co-conspirators, in the words of the old Salem pupil who had been an active member of the German Resistance, Eddy Waetjen, *'You are for me one of the few with whom the conversation is never interrupted – whether we hear from one another or not.'* [24]

After her death, David Astor of *The Observer* newspaper wrote of her family's tradition, with its complete fearlessness and largeness of outlook, but it was Peregrine Worsthorne who caught her essence: *'… a radiance of spirit which made men want to go out and slay dragons to win her favour …*

(hers was) an inspiring, haunting tune, and I cannot bear to think that it will be heard no more …'

It is for sure undeniable that Hitler and National Socialism forced the Jewish people into a renewed examination and ultimate strengthening of their identity. Lola's passionately Zionist younger sister Gisela even accepted that *'Hitler … also did something for the Jews. He forced them to recognize again what history had taught them, but that they had forgotten in Germany: Judaism doesn't mean only a community of faith, but also a community of struggle and a community of destiny.'* Wilfrid Israel, writing to Max Warburg in 1943, had similar thoughts: *'we have been stampeded into reacting as a separatist body all over the world since 1933 … it would be reckless pessimism to believe that the Jewish heritage can be wiped out in a generation. If we begin as Jews to think merely in secular terms, merely in terms of power politics and numbers, we shall certainly crumble to dust.'*

For Ortega y Gasset, before Hitler came on the scene, the Jew was *an itinerant cosmopolite, the yeast of many cultures'*.

Today, the fate of the Jews and of their national home remains at the heart of the world's anxieties. Israel is a fulcrum of all our destinies.

The students of the Atlantic and our other colleges are not united by a faith or dogma. Unlike the Jews, they are not carrying a centuries-old history on their backs, nor are they searching for a national home. For the most part they have not faced hardship or persecution. So any hint of a comparison is really nothing more than a frivolous impertinence. But they, as the statistics show us, are very mobile cosmopolitans. Can they also become the yeast for the dissemination of their beliefs? The strivings and the achievements of all those thousands of immensely gifted German Jews, in their often conflicting intellectual, cultural, civic, religious, national and international aspirations, hold messages for us all. It is important to recognise and to remember that the Atlantic College arose from all that turmoil.

German Language Quotations

[1] „Die amerikanischen Juden sind Amerikaner … Die französischen Juden … sind Franzosen … die deutschen Juden waren Deutsche" but „Ich würde die Behauptung wagen: Nie war die antisemitische Leidenschaft in Deutschland wütender als in den Jahren 1919 bis 1923. Sie war damals viel wütender als 1930 bis 1933 oder 1933 bis 1945 …'

[2] „… der Bankier muß die Sorgen des Kunden wie die eigenen miterleben … damit auch der kleinste Kunde sich uns verbunden fühlt … es sind nicht die großen Kunden, die die Stärke des Privatbankiers ausmachen, die Vielfalt der Kleinen gibt die Grundlage, das Buschwerk, zwischen dem die großen Bäume dann gedeihen … Hochöfen hat eine Bank nicht, Dienstbereitschaft aller ersetzt die Maschinen der Fabrik …'

[3] „… ich dachte (1922) an eine Akademie der guten Sitten, denn in Deutschland muß alles erst neu entdeckt werden … das veredelte

Natürliche … eine Akademie gegen Bestechung, Maulheldentum, Angriffe leichtfertiger Art ohne Begründung, Antisemitismus, Verhetzung ganzer Stände … Verhetzung unserer Vergangenheit, der Tätigkeit aller Fürsten und Könige, die in ihrer Zeit das Beste geleistet haben …'

[4] ,Wen die Ungerechtigkeit gegen den einzelnen Juden … kalt läßt, der erschrecke wenigstens über den Schaden, den die deutsche Seele zu nehmen droht …'

[5] ,Die Trennung von Politikern und wirtschaftlichen Sachverständigen ist widersinnig. Nur wenn sie zusammenarbeiten, kann man eine Besserung erwarten …'

[6] ,Die ganze Welt ist eine wirtschaftliche Einheit und wenn wir uns noch so widerlich sind, wir müssen uns ertragen … die Weltordnung auch in wirtschaftlicher und finanzieller Beziehung (ist) nur möglich, wenn Deutschland zur Ruhe kommt …'

[7] ,… diese Idee der Schlichtung von Streitigkeiten wäre auch zwischen uns und den uns verbündeten Mächten jetzt sofort auszuarbeiten und einzuführen … Die Schiedsgerichtsidee wird uns am Schluß des Krieges doch von unseren Gegnern gebracht werden und wir werden uns diesem Gedanken nie widersetzen können.'

[8] ,In einem großen Staate können die Minoritäten sich gruppieren, ihre Befriedigung in der Zusammengehörigkeit finden, …, während in einem kleinen Staate ein Ausgleich und ein friedlicher Zusammenschluß der Gleichartigen viel schwieriger ist … allerdings wird Deutschland in der Zukunft den Minoritäten gegenüber eine viel tolerantere Haltung einnehmen müssen … .'

[9] ,Der Reichskanzler hat Sehnsucht nach mir, und ich reise am Dienstag nach Berlin, um ihm meine nicht vorhandene Weisheit zu präsentieren.'

[10] ,Das Schlimme war, daß ich nicht nur immer das gleiche redete, sondern auch leider immer das gleiche zu essen bekam. In der Beziehung sind die Amerikaner von einer unglaublichen Geschmacklosigkeit.'

[11] ,In Zeiten der Aufregung (muß man) den nun einmal vorhandenen Stimmungen Rechnung tragen.'

[12] ,Ich befürchte fast, da alle Statuten derartiger Stiftungen ziemlich irrsinnig gemacht werden, daß die Statuten, die eine mündelsichere Anlage verlangen, mich daran hindern, so genial zu operieren, wie es Ihrem Leichtsinn entsprechen würde.'

[13] ,… ein Budget besteht darin, daß man Einnahmen und Ausgaben einander gegenüberstellt, vom 31. Dezember eines Jahres bis 31. Dezember des nächsten Jahres … die von Ihnen in großer Geschwindigkeit hier niedergeschriebenen vier Zahlen genügen nicht … .'

[14] ,In der Zwischenzeit bitte ich Sie aber, ohne zu verplutokratizieren, neue Schüler, die ja nicht unbedingt mittellos sein müssen, noch aufzunehmen.'

[15] ,Ich schrieb Ihnen am 15. Mts. Darf ich Sie, da Sie doch Pädagoge sind, um Belehrung darüber bitten, warum meine Briefe nicht prompt beantwortet werden?'

[16] ,Ich nehme an, daß Sie ein Flugzeug unentwegt in Ihrem Garten stehen haben, mit einer Gummilitze daran, sodaß Sie sehr rasch wieder nach Salem … zurückgezogen werden können.'

[17] ,einmal eine ruhige (Fremdwort für Sie?) Viertelstunde über die Angelegenheit zu sprechen.'

[18] ,Aber eben so glücklich wie über jene materielle Erleichterung bin ich froh und dankbar über den Segen, den Sie damit meinem Lebenswerk geben. Ich habe diesen Segen bisher schmerzlich vermißt und ich bin, seitdem wir uns näher kennenlernten, gewohnt, in allen Unternehmungen von Mark und Nachdruck, denen ich mich widme, Ihren väterlichen Segen zu erbitten und zu erhalten.'

[19] ,wahrlich ein Beweis großherzigen Vertrauens'

[20] ,Wenn Du Verbrecher geworden wärest, würdest Du als einer der besten Gelegenheitsdiebe in die Geschichte der Kriminalistik eingegangen sein. Als Einbrecher hättest Du Dich nicht bewährt. Das liegt daran, daß die Eindrücke des Augenblickes oft auf Dich zu überwältigend wirken und dazu führen, daß die geduldige, mühselige Kleinarbeit nicht zu ihrem Recht kommt …"

[21] ,Nun löchert Herr Warburg mich mit Fragen wieso, wodurch, inwiefern …'

[22] ,Wäre er jünger gewesen, er hätte sich nach dem Kriege hier eingefunden – unter uns allen – als Pionier beim Wiederaufbau …'

[23] ,Eric Warburg ist in seiner Person die Brücke über den Atlantik.'

[24] ,Du gehörst mir zu den wenigen, mit denen das Gespräch nie abreißt, – ob wir von einander hören oder nicht.'

[1] *Naomi Hoare measuring, students gluing their neoprene skin suits*

[2] *A typical if quiet afternoon*

[3] *Unusual skills*

[4] *Early sea-going was rigorous …*

[5] *The cliff rescue unit operates the hinged crane equipment designed by the College's head of biology and director of studies, Peter Jolley*

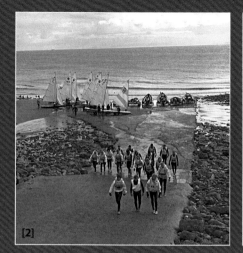

Afterword

UWC: Mission Accomplished?

I am writing these words 51 years after Tony Besse put up the funds for the purchase of St. Donat's Castle in 1960, 49 years after the Atlantic College opened in 1962. It is a good moment for reflection, both backwards and forwards.

Of course the world has changed in these five decades, so one loosely assumes that the United World Colleges must change too. But how?

Globalisation is now driving international education at all levels.

In 2006 it was estimated that well over 100 international schools were educating close to half a million pupils. This estimate excluded national schools with international programmes and/or international pupils.

At a conference in China in 2006, a Chinese delegate is reported as remarking quite casually that his country urgently needed another 3,000 international schools.

In May 2010 the International Baccalaureate organisation had over 3,000 member schools in 139 countries educating 824,000 pupils, admittedly of all grades from early primary through to senior secondary levels. Their estimate for the year 2020 is 10,000 programmes in 147 countries with two million pupils.

The IB is currently training 60,000 teachers every year.

How many schools, international or other, still exist that do not have community service somewhere in their programme?

So what are the challenges that the United World Colleges remain competent to confront that will enable them to justify into the future the moral and the financial investment that has sustained them thus far?

The Underlying Issue

This is the classical dilemma that faces all progressive schools. They are founded to advocate and to demonstrate educational reform as a matter of principle. If unsuccessful, they disappear and are forgotten. If successful, their ideas are absorbed into the mainstream. Furthermore, their funding becomes increasingly dependent, not on sponsors interested in principles but on families who seek their benefits for their children and grandchildren (or find their benefits more readily and more cheaply in other schools that have adopted these ideas).

We pride ourselves on the distinctive quality of our performance, but quality is an elusive element, difficult to measure except perhaps in examination grades – and would we readily accept examination grades as a legitimate criterion for UWC achievement?

Those responsible for UWC policies have devoted hours, reams of paper and gigabytes of electronic communication to the task of path-finding into the future. The starting point has to be an agreement on what remain the unique features.

I believe that simplicity of concept and language is vital.

Unique Assets

After these five decades, I see two UWC things only as unique in education. They are the two-year, residential international colleges and the scholarship programme [•] Some will add the framework of the 130 or so national and selection committees, but these committees are direct appendices of these first two elements and could scarcely exist without them, although the relationship is of course reciprocal.

The Magical Age

It is good to recall that the Atlantic College was the first and ground-breaking two-year college for 16–19-year-old students in Britain, a sixth form college in English terminology. Good too to recall some of the thinking indirectly

[•] This firm statement is not intended to question the validity of the several current variations on the two-year scholarship colleges, but they are not unique in international education

behind it as expressed by the Director of Education for the County of Surrey who had much wanted a similar institution for his own area: *'In the English educational pattern, round about 16 is the point of change and decision ... a successful transition to a new environment is a stimulating experience for a spirited and growing personality ... If you cannot perceive that the youth of 17 is nearer to the young man who is four years his elder than he is to the child who is four years his junior; that at bottom he no longer wants to be in the environment where he spent his twelfth birthday, and that this is a part of his search for adult dignity; that the watershed comes at about sixteen, some little time after puberty; then I can only classify you among the great majority of adults ... who just do not understand young people.'*

This national assessment had even more intensity of relevance for the international and residential Atlantic College. The College has validated the claim that 16–19 is the magical age of curiosity, idealism, readiness to explore challenge, a time that young people are indeed old enough to start taking real responsibility for their own lives without having yet committed themselves to careers or even to particular courses of study. And, as a severely practical matter, they are able to leave home, family, school, teachers and language for the international experience that awaits them in our two-year colleges.

The Scholarship Programme

The scholarship programme is as vital to the United World Colleges as are the sea dykes to the survival of The Netherlands. Without the programme, the movement will be swept away. How badly is it leaking? Is it going to be possible to mount not only a sound maintenance programme for the preservation of the existing dykes but to secure also the resources for a more ambitious network in the future?

Presentation and Content

The United World Colleges, in common with many other organisations, have in the recent past dedicated serious resources to the matter of branding. This is a pre-eminently business decision taken in the context of fundraising. It may be necessary. It will be superfluous if it outruns more important issues of educational substance, and my instinct is that the United World Colleges, with help, need to make a careful study of where and how their formidable energies and resources can best be directed in the coming decade.

A former Hahn pupil from Salem School in South Germany, Hans Christof von Sponeck, is a lecturer in conflict studies at the German University of Marburg. Outspokenly loyal to the core principles of Kurt Hahn's teaching – the ones that stand out in his case are a sense of justice and (an extract from the original Salem Final Report sent to parents) *'the ability to follow what he believes to be the right course in the face of discomforts, hardships, dangers, mockery, scepticism ...'* – Hans Christof, at great personal cost, resigned his post in 2000 as UN Assistant Secretary General and UN Humanitarian Coordinator for Iraq in protest against the sanctions imposed by the UN Security Council. They were, he said, aimed at the wrong targets, punishing innocent civilians and especially children.

In his university work von Sponeck analyses with his students the reasons why the multilateralism of the UN Charter, accepted by all 192 UN member states, is consistently side-stepped by governments when they face choices between immediate national and longer-term international interests. The political focus on symptoms rather than causes, on criminality rather than poverty, on terrorism rather than ethno-centrism, has given rise to more and more confrontation among nations, regions, groups and individuals. Conflicts, he adds, have been further intensified by the glaring double standards in international justice and the widening gap between the haves and the have-nots.

Schools across frontiers, we sometimes say. *'Médecins sans Frontières'*, too! But we must add: *'Crises across frontiers'*. No crisis, says von Sponeck, exists today in isolation. All are inter-connected, involving politics, financial and human resources, trafficking in drugs and human beings, and terrorism. Are we, he asks, sufficiently aware of emerging conflicts such as the one between the 28 NATO states and the ten SCO (Shanghai Cooperation Organization) states? Are we familiar and happy with the spread of military bases that are in place worldwide to ensure hegemonic viability?

Can human security, the freedom from fear and the freedom from need, be achieved across the world unless the global community, through the United Nations, accepts that political accountability is mandatory for all leaders, the most and the least powerful?

The 21st Century: Formidable Challenges

The former German Chancellor Helmut Schmidt was arguing already in the mid-1980s that the 21st century was set to be the most dangerous century in the history of mankind.

There was, many now recognise, a paradoxical degree of stability in the days of the East-West nuclear confrontation, high though the stakes were. [●] Von Sponeck's work underlines the instability of our present condition. A major problem facing the democratic nations today is the relationship between conflict, regime change and state failure. Add to this the knowledge that the 51 sovereign states of 1945 have grown (or fragmented) into over 200 today, and there is no remotely conceivable shortage of scope for international education. Global cohesion and the dismantling of confrontation are essential for survival.

There is no organisation in the world more suited to taking up these formidable challenges than the United World Colleges, with their political-educational ideals, their proven success, their commitment to scholarship and merit selection, and their independence from the roles and activities of expatriate communities.

We face, not one but an entire series of challenges that are ultimately political in nature.

This is no reason for hesitation.

Education: The Keystone of Statesmanship and the True Political Spirit

Hartmut von Hentig, a consistent, indeed outspoken critic of Kurt Hahn in Germany, had this to say about him in the 1990s: '… with Hahn … the former, politics … not only leads to and contributes to the latter, education; the latter not only has "political rank"; it is itself the beginning of politics. It is from this reflection that Hahn develops his schools, his secular "Order" for our time, his experience-based educational principles, his themes of response to challenge and responsibility, his international Atlantic College. This reflection enabled him as a matter of course to raise educational matters with the most senior statesmen, to stimulate them to the foundation of schools … We understand once again what education is and how integral it is to politics.'

We are naturally talking here not of party politics, but of the politics that the great 19th-century British Prime Minister Gladstone spoke of: 'the true political spirit … the faculty of nation-making', and that the Oxford Shorter English Dictionary defines as 'that branch of moral philosophy dealing with the state or social organism as a whole.'

[●] Giorgi Arbatov, one of the Soviet leadership's most senior and trusted advisors during the Cold War and after, is recorded in his obituary in the Daily Telegraph newspaper of 15th November 2010 as having told the Americans that they would soon miss the comfortable status quo of the superpower standoff: 'We are going to do something terrible to you. You will no longer have an enemy.'

Some years after his withdrawal from Atlantic College to Southern Ireland in the 1970s, Desmond Hoare became intensely irritated by the slogan adopted by the UWC for a while: A Pathway to Peace. We were, he wrote, just one of many 'do-good organisations' making our own small contribution. It is difficult to get the balance right. Do we have a unique contribution to make? Unless we believe so, it is difficult to justify the ambitions of our continual campaigns for support.

On what shall we focus our energies?

The Environment

Are we right to commit ourselves publicly to an education for a sustainable future? It would be almost courageous now not to express and to advocate environmental stewardship, but are we well-placed to beat this particular drum, given the number of air miles we are responsible for each year with our movement of students, of our teachers engaged on international errands, our international meetings?

Inequality

We made an effort to respond to the inequitable distribution of natural resources, the Third World issue, in our third decade with the setting up of the post-secondary agricultural and vocational college in Venezuela. It has faced huge problems whilst notching up notable, little-known achievements, especially in its extra-mural, rural development programme. It is neither sensible nor just to make glib simplifications about its recent closure or replicating its message elsewhere, but might there not be a renewed effort to examine our obligations as an international educational organisation to the developing world?

Immigrant and Minority Communities

The past five decades have seen vast movements of populations worldwide from the countryside to the towns and cities. Immigrant communities gather in urban environments, almost always to the discomfort of the local people. Similar discomfort, often of an ever sharper nature, is the consequence of the parallel movements across borders and continents, discomfort that makes national communities acutely fearful of the loss of their national identity and culture. Numerous governments are struggling with the cultural and economic clashes that arise. At the same time, despite all the problems, there are outstanding inner-city schools and outstanding inner-city teachers whose accomplishments are remarkable. It is true: we have colleges in the cities of Hong Kong and Singapore, more recently in Maastricht. But are we failing in our international task and, of equal (perhaps greater) importance, losing the benefits of priceless additional experience, by having remained isolated from the worldwide challenges of the education of immigrants and minorities?

Modern Technology

Are we keeping pace with others in the exploitation of modern communications systems? Have we examined carefully the possibilities of creating an entirely new type of college, embracing perhaps hundreds of different schools including those in impoverished parts of the Third World that, with the aid of modern technology, could be enabled to share something of our philosophy and activities? At a conference in Milan in April 2011 the internet was described as the planet's nervous system. The statistic was also quoted that, once there is 20% internet penetration in a country, democracy begins to emerge, however difficult the political conditions.

Personal Relationships across the Divisions of Conflict

'The world is a hospital' – another phrase and theme from the Milan conference!

Visitors to our colleges continue to be deeply impressed when they encounter students who have become friends across the frontiers of hostility back at home. I remember a young Israeli of stubborn views who found that he was to spend his second year sharing a room with a German. He fought this situation bitterly until I told him that he must either accept it or leave the College. Eighteen months after he had completed his examinations he wrote to me: *'in Atlantic College I lived among folk of 51 different countries and there I found that I felt closer to the Arabs than to the people of any other nation. Now I can point to myself as one of the few Israelis who understands the Palestinians and Arabs – we Israeli ex-students, people in conflict with other nations, have strong national feelings alongside a longing for peace and an end to our suffering.'* But, in a vibrant community of motivated, idealistic adolescents, who are distant both physically and emotionally from the scene of conflict at home, these issues become relative – relative to the comparable problems of others, relative to the many powerful motivations that sweep the community life along on its way. The Atlantic College in the peaceful Welsh countryside becomes the healing influence in part because it creates this distance. To an important degree reality is diminished.

A word now much in vogue in UWC circles is *'transformational'*. We have no lack of former students ready to acknowledge the transformational nature of their college experience. We ask ourselves anxiously whether they then will become transformers, for this is surely the litmus test.

The Colleges are small. Are they too small for the big challenges? Can the UWC be transformational in the key areas of conflict and peace? If yes, then through the lives of individuals or also in a wider, more institutional sense?

The years lived in a United World College are marked by intensity and focus, but our numbers and our resources are limited. We do things on a small scale. The implication is that the aspirations of our organisation require similar intensity and similar focus.

Going to where the Trouble is (1)

John Nichol, the founding Chairman of Pearson College, expresses the matter with his usual pith and precision. *'We must concentrate on young people from countries and regions recently at war, from countries and regions now at war, and from countries and regions at risk of going to war.'*

This approach, with the help of analyses such as that offered by von Sponeck and others too, can guide us towards the countries from which we might take students in increased numbers into our established colleges. It is likely at a stroke to resolve the issue of principle over parental contributions to the costs and will provide a compelling case for continuing financial support for our scholarship programmes.

The presence of large numbers of young people from such countries, ideally a majority, will by itself transform our colleges. It will transform the lives of the students chosen. It will transform our mission. Impossible to achieve? But it would be a 'line of advance' – *'… to say that an ideal has never been fully achieved is merely to say that it is an ideal'.* [●]

Is it therefore enough, in seeking out the world's tectonic plates of conflict, to assemble promising individuals from these areas for our existing colleges? I believe we can do much more. It is relevant that the UWC Short Courses in their original form were sited in countries that were felt to have a special need for international education but, for economic and other reasons, could not contemplate colleges of their own: Malta, Cyprus, Turkey, Jordan, Chile, Montenegro, Lithuania.

Going to where the Trouble is (2)

I think we can add now another strand: bringing our future colleges to those countries, communities and people who are truly in most urgent need of them. I refer to post-conflict societies. It is a matter of transferring expertise, idealism

[●] Timothy Garton Ash of St. Antony's College, Oxford

and resources to where they are most lacking. The project in Bosnia has offered just such a route. But let me quote from an early document on this initiative.

> 'What we propose must be convincing and rewarding, with recognizable practical consequences, for the local people. It must be tailored to the local situation, taking advantage of national traditions and accomplishments. If it is elitist, it must nevertheless be reasonably accessible to those who want it. It must be capable of further local development to ensure relevance. It must be value for money by standards and figures that we are not accustomed to. To ensure sustainability, it must be dovetailed into existing structures and have strong local participation. To secure funding it must be convincing to international agencies and therefore politically alive. It will indicate clearly a path towards local takeover. To gain credibility and create confidence, it will almost certainly be programmed in incremental stages. Idealism and practical necessity will move hand in hand.'

Expressed differently, projects in post-conflict countries must demonstrate beyond dispute that their purpose is to serve their host country and region. Ancillary activities such as teacher training and curriculum development must ensure that the College itself is a practical laboratory for national educational reform. And there must too be direct cooperation with the national system. The Mostar United World College has the advantage, unique within our organisation, of being sited within a national school. No capital building or maintenance costs, heating or cleaning! It offers among other things admirable opportunities for the secondment of teachers from other more established state school systems to experience teaching directly in a post-conflict situation, with important benefits for their subsequent work and career back at home.

Nor should the business side be overlooked. For the cost of educating one student in a 'western' economy, the Mostar College can educate three.

A Possible Lesson for the Future

The Bosnian College, eminently capable of replication in other similar environments of which there is an abundance, is just one example of the way in which the United World Colleges might build their future whilst remaining unhesitatingly faithful to their underlying principles: quality holistic education for an idealistic community of 16–19-year-old students, all selected on merit, but with the local background of recent strife being more expressive of the reasons for their attendance than any quantity of propaganda or branding.

It is in the context of such reflections that the current move towards additional colleges in expensive, non-conflictual countries in Western Europe must be measured. For whilst it is true that no College has been started without almost spontaneous local leadership, any world organisation with a sense of its own relevance will also have ideas of geographical and political areas in which it seeks a role. It will make its wishes known and, with appropriate solicitation, look forward with confidence to the offer of fertile soil.

Inside the Box or outside it: the Perils of Excessive Governance and the Acceptance of Risk

In today's complicated and bureaucratic world it is frustratingly difficult to be active and to conceive and to execute significant concrete projects without them being maimed or killed in some kind of 'machinery'. UWC must cherish the need to maintain character, to welcome new ideas, to be a risk taker, to think 'out of the box', to trust its own partners, to allow free hands for eager people, to avoid seeking excessive control in the name of collective benefit. Finding and retaining strong-willed, imaginative individuals whilst safeguarding institutional accountability is of course a challenge, but there is a vital distinction between unity of the highest and the lowest common denominator. The fatal price of the latter is the stifling of initiative and true diversity. Nor must we underestimate the importance of momentum and thrust in our development. If we are not in a hurry, then what we are doing is not important. If the world can wait for our solutions, why bother to invest in them?

Let me close with a metaphor drawn from a conversation with a concerned former student of the Atlantic College.

Every organisation, as time goes by, and this is a natural development, acquires members – many of them very active members – who may be compared with passengers in a train. They are moving forwards, they enjoy one another's company, they know the destination they have booked their tickets for, and they are paying their way. My point is simple: we should be out in front, planning and laying the track. Or are these simply the nostalgic longings of an early participant, captive to the words of George Steiner: 'You cannot be a prophetic voice in a comfortable consensual position in the heartlands. Return to the margins.'

David Sutcliffe

Is it already over?

Do you remember, my dearest friends, do you remember that hot day in August, when we came to this beautiful city of Mostar with our pockets full of hope and dreams? Do you remember, my friends, the first tears we shed here; our first romances, our first friendships … Doesn't it sound like a fairytale?

There was once a generation at the United World College in Mostar. It was the fifth generation … and in that generation 51 young souls … 51 different worlds. But one desire. Desire for change in this big world of ours …

This is my house, this is my home, this is the place of my most beautiful memories. I don't know what any of us will become, how society or our own ambitions are going to form us, whether we are going to become good or bad people, but in my memory, in the golden department of my memories, you will always be my friends.

Because all of us have been to the Old Bridge numerous times and you have witnessed how it still stands tall even after five centuries, defying the green time that relentlessly runs through it. And what will become of the bridges that we've built? Bridges that know no nationality, religion, skin colour, eye colour, good or bad people, bridges that can't be seen with an eye but are felt with the heart. …

But we're parting now.

We're as close as birds from the same nest. As the leaves of one tree. As the petals of a single flower. We're family. Yet, we have to part. …

So many things have happened during these two years and so much has changed within us. … Even now, as I stand before you, the Neretva continues to flow indifferently, caring not for some 50 boys and girls who are going through the greatest moments of their lives. But the Neretvas in our hearts cannot be more sensitive to every heart beat and familiar smile …

Because, we're parting now.

I wonder, how much have we actually learned? Is there a true knowledge hidden somewhere under the piles of papers and books? How much did we learn about the world, life and the people that we are supposed to change …

We know that life in this world is not a game.

We know that people can often be unjust.

But we also learned that the power of true honesty, love and friendship should never be underestimated. There is no river that newly built bridges cannot bridge and there are no coasts that bridges cannot connect. We dare to embrace with open eyes and arms the life we have been preparing for these last 18 or 19 years …

Once, there were 51 young people who loved each other and one city of Mostar. That is how our story begins and it is up to us, my dearest friends, to finish it happily. And I've told a lie during this speech.

It's not true that we're parting. Our physical selves are parting, but our hearts will always remain united.

Thank you all. Goodbye, my friends, and peace be with you. Never stop dreaming, for I'll search for you in my dreams, whenever I think of you.

Farewell remarks from his speech at the 2012 graduation ceremony in Mostar by the Bosnian student Nermin Sehic

Index